The Abiding Word

The ABIDING WORD

AN ANTHOLOGY OF DOCTRINAL ESSAYS FOR THE YEAR 1945

Volume One

Edited by THEODORE LAETSCH, D. D.

Concordia Theological Seminary
St. Louis, Mo.

CONCORDIA PUBLISHING HOUSE

Saint Louis, 1946

Preface

THE title of this book, *The Abiding Word,* indicates the reason for its publication. Our Missouri Synod, in 1947, looks back on a century of its existence. The fourth generation is taking up the work in our part of the Lord's kingdom on earth; and they are inheriting, undiminished and undiluted, the chief treasure which the fathers came to these shores to save: The Word of our God. For that we give thanks to Him in our centennial year.

Time has brought many changes. The world has changed. Our fathers spent many weeks at sea crossing the Atlantic; today we fly from coast to coast in a few hours. Life has changed; the hardships encountered by the pioneers of our Synod are unknown to their children. Their language has changed, and the number of those in our ranks who still speak the tongue of the early immigrants is waning. But the confession of the men of 1847 is still the confession of 1947. They left their country "because they saw no possibility of retaining in their present home that faith undefiled and transmitting it to their children." They looked for shores friendly to those who wished to serve their God according to the dictates of their conscience. They found them here in America. And we, a hundred years later, present to the reader "the fathers' faith in the children's language"—essays containing the gist of doctrinal treasures laid down in the reports of early synodical conventions, now discussed and adopted by the conventions of 1945.

By instruction of the General Convention of 1941 the venerable President of Synod, Dr. J. W. Behnken, appointed a committee to prepare for a suitable observance of the centennial: Dr. Theo. Hoyer, chairman; Rev. H. W. Romoser, secretary; Dr. L. Fuerbringer; Dr. H. B. Hemmeter; Dr. E. T. Lams; Teacher A. H. Kramer; Mr. G. A. Fleischer. Under the auspices of this committee this volume is presented to our people as evidence that the Lord has been good to us; He has preserved unto us His saving Word.

Contents

Foreword

SOLOMON says: "A word fitly spoken is like apples of gold in pictures of silver" (Prov. 25:11). Golden fruits presented in plates of chaste silver, skillfully wrought in openwork pattern, are indeed, as Martin Geier comments, both helpful and delightful, pleasing the eye by their glorious beauty, the smell by their delicious fragrance, the palate by their rich lusciousness, and helpful in satisfying the hunger and quenching the thirst of the guest to whom they are offered. So, says Solomon, is a word fitly spoken, a word spoken in the right manner, at the proper time, suitable and appropriate to the circumstances under which it is spoken.

In the early literature of our Missouri Synod there is presented in silver receptacles to all that will read a rich selection of choice golden apples worth more than their weight in gold or diamonds. These golden apples were gathered from the Tree of Life, from God's Holy Word, that Word of which Christ says: "Thy Word is Truth" (John 17:17); that Word which Peter calls the incorruptible seed, the Word of God, which liveth and abideth forever (I Pet. 1:23); that Word of the Holy Scriptures which is able to make us wise unto salvation through faith which is in Christ Jesus and which is profitable for doctrine, for reproof, for correction, for instruction in righteousness, and for comfort. (II Tim. 3:15-16; Rom. 15:4.)

These golden apples of God's own truth were presented by the fathers of our Synod to their audiences and readers on silver platters, in choice language, whose beauty often equalled the best products of German literature. For that reason they make not only profitable but delightful reading, particularly since their words, being the abiding Word of God, are so eminently suitable for our time and circumstances also.

In this volume, the first of a series of two, entitled *The Abiding Word*, Synod's Centennial Committee offers to the readers the essays based on the writings of our fathers which were read at the District conventions in 1945. If the beauty of the silver platter could not always be reproduced or has sometimes suffered in translation, that does not affect the profitableness, the value of the golden fruit. In preparing the essays for publication, the Editor again realized what a glorious heritage our fathers have bequeathed to the generations after them. May we value and cherish this heritage in ever-increasing measure and remain faithful also in the second century of our Synod's history to the Abiding Word.

THE EDITOR

The Abiding Word

The Doctrine of Creation

1. THE SOURCE OF THE DOCTRINE OF CREATION

No man was present at the creation; therefore we are entirely dependent on the authentic record of creation which God Himself published in Scripture. Also the account of creation belongs to the Scripture which is given by inspiration (II Tim. 3:16) and cannot be broken (John 10:35). From the things created by God we men can and ought to draw the conclusion that there is an almighty and wise Creator (Rom. 1:20). But for the details of creation we are altogether dependent on God's revelation in Scripture. If we men presume to correct God's account of creation through inferences from the present condition of the world, we are indulging in unscientific conceit and pretense which does not become a Christian or any man for that matter. The disagreement among geologists concerning the age of the earth and man is so great that they can speak of the assured results of geology only if they completely give up the use of that small amount of reason which we still have after the Fall. Some are satisfied with a few hundred thousand years, others demand millions of years. Among these gentlemen a million of years is a mere trifle. They are very generous; a million more or less does not matter, but is that scientific? (F. Pieper, *Christliche Dogmatik,* pp. 570, 571.)

"The account of creation in Genesis is very simple, but the things revealed there are great, deep, yea unfathomable. No man's mind can penetrate them, no reason can comprehend them. . . Among the Jews it was forbidden to read and expound Genesis before the thirtieth year (Jerome quoted by Luther). . . . The greatest scientists and keenest minds have tried to penetrate the great mystery of the origin of the world, to explain it by natural means, but what childish and foolish theories have they concocted! God is marvelous and incomprehensible in his essence and works. . . . In this essay we shall not try to give a plausible explanation of creation, but simply follow and understand, as far as possible, God's own account of creation" (R. Pieper, "Die Schoepfung," Southern District, 1910, pp. 7, 8).

One of the so-called scientific theories concerning the origin of the world is the nebular hypothesis. "According to this theory (which was advanced by Kant in 1755 and especially by La Place in 1796, but which, in a modified form, was held by Greek philosophers) the origin of the planetary system of the universe, in which our earth is viewed as an incidental part, is traced to a vast primeval nebula (a fiery, cloudlike, self-luminous mass of attenuate matter), which filled all the space at present embodied by the planets. In this nebulous mass, according to La Place, motion originated, and as a result of this rotation there was a gradual cooling and contracting of the nebula. In consequence of this rotation about the sun, the original nebula separated into a series of rings; these rings continued to rotate and likewise to cool and to contract until they had changed from gasses to solids and later to the various planets, satellites, and other bodies of the solar system, including the earth." This theory, which many scientists have adopted is, of course, not in agreement with the Bible, but neither is it scientific (W. A. Maier, Notes on Genesis, p. 5). For a detailed refutation of this theory read the same author. Dr. Maier concludes his refutation with the following remarks: "There are many other scientific objections against this theory. Cf. Theo. Graebner: *Evolution; an Investigation and a Criticism,* pp. 31-34. Chamberlain and Moulton have shown the fallacies of this theory. In his *New Geology,* p. 31, Price writes: "We may safely say that it is no longer in standing among men of science, though it still survives in some belated textbooks and is still quite popular among people who have a slight acquaintance with scientific facts" (W. A. Maier, Notes on Genesis, pp. 5-7).

"Where the statements of great scientists and those of the Scriptures are at variance, those of the Scriptures must prevail, not although, but because, the Bible is not a scientific textbook, because it is more, it is the Word of God. All due honor to the wisdom of Solomon, but a greater than Solomon is here" (Matt. 12:42; A. L. Graebner, *Theological Quarterly,* Vol. III, pp. 1, 2). Moses did not write a history of the world, but rather a history of God's kingdom here on earth; he did not write fiction, but facts; "Moses hat nicht gedichtet, sondern berichtet" (R. Pieper, South. Distr. 1910, pp. 9, 10). There is a great difference between the simple, unaffected account of Moses and the weird, fantastic cosmogonies of heathen writers, *e. g.,* Hesiod (8th century B. C.), Gilgamesh Epic, etc.

2. THE DEFINITION OF CREATION

Pagan pantheism regards the universe as an emanation from, or a manifestation of, God, so that God and the universe are identical. Pagan dualism assumes the eternal existence of matter fashioned by a deity into this world. The Bible teaches that the Triune God created all things that exist outside of Himself, *i. e.,* the universe, out of nothing. From Gen. 1:1, Heb. 11:3, and Rom. 4:17 we learn that before the creation of the world nothing existed but God Himself. God did not have to create the world, as though He needed the services of creatures. Creation is not a necessity, but an act of His free divine will (J. T. Mueller, *Christ. Dogm.,* p. 179; F. Pieper, *Christl. Dogm.,* p. 571).

3. THE ORDER OF CREATION

According to the Bible, God did not create all things at once, but gradually, observing an admirable order. He proceeded from the lower to the higher, until He made man, the crown of His creation. We may distinguish three steps in the work of creation: a) the production of crude material on the first day; b) the separation and disposition of simple creatures during the first three days (light on the first day; the firmament on the second; the separation of the earth from the waters on the third); c) the furnishing and completion of the world, which was brought to perfection in three more days (the celestial bodies on the fourth day; the fish and fowl on the fifth; the creation of land animals and of man on the sixth).

This order of creation must not be looked upon as an evolutionary process; for, according to Scripture, the world was not developed by forces that were in matter itself, but by the creative power of God. Experimental science cannot disprove this fact, since it can prove neither a development of organic things from inorganic nor a development of higher forms from the lower (J. T. Mueller, *Christ. Dogm.,* pp. 179, 180).

Luthardt claims that two factors were active in the process of formations: the activity of natural forces and the creative influence of God. That is wrong. According to Scripture, grass and animals do not come into existence partly through God's work and partly through their own activity, but entirely through God's work. Luthardt proposes a regulation of boundaries between Scripture and natural science. Nothing wrong about that. But he is seriously mistaken when he claims: "Religion tells us that God gives us our daily bread; natural science teaches us how grain is growing in the field." He corrects himself when he writes later on: "Even now the origin of life is, as yet, an impenetrable mystery. No man can tell how something comes into being, and we never shall find out." Dr. Walther used to say: "Scientists can have lice, but they cannot make any" (F. Pieper, *Christl. Dogm.*, p. 573).

Evolution must be rejected as untenable even on rational grounds, since it does not account for the existence of primeval matter and since it rests upon a principle disproved by nature, namely, on the supposed transmutation of species. Scripture agrees with reason in the following points: the creation of all things by an omnipotent God; the orderly procedure in the work of creation; the propagation of creatures after their kind (Gen. 1:21). As all creatures came into existence through the creative command of God, so they are preserved and propagated through the divine omnipotent will (Acts 17:28). The existence of the universe with all its manifold creatures is due to the blessing which God pronounced upon the whole creation after the completion of His creative work (Gen. 1:22; Col. 1:17; (J. T. Mueller, *Christ. Dogm.*, p. 180; F. Bente, "Evolutionismus und die Wissenschaften," *Lehre und Wehre*, 1904, pp. 215-223; 1900, pp. 8-15, 39-47, 135-141, 164-170, 217-239; J. Hoeness, "Die Evolution und die Bibel," *Lehre und Wehre*, 1909, pp. 289-299, 351-359, 454-464, 499-510, 546-550; Theo. Graebner, *God and the Cosmos*, "Evolutionism," pp. 173-350).

4. THE SIX DAYS OF CREATION

The Bible teaches distinctly that the world was created within six days of twenty-four hours each. To change the six days into a mere moment (Athanasius, Augustine, Hilary of Poitiers) or to expand them into periods of millions of years is equally contrary to Scripture (Gen. 1:31; 2:2). Ex. 20:9, 11: "Six days shalt thou labor . . . for in six days the Lord made heaven and earth." The above-mentioned Church Fathers contracted the six days of creation into a mere moment for pious reasons; they wanted to enhance and glorify God's omnipotence. Modern theologians who expand the six days of creation into millions of years do this for impious reasons. They wish to reconcile Scripture with the alleged "assured results" of science. The days of creation cannot be changed into indefinite periods because they are limited by morning and evening. This fact compels us to accept them as days of twenty-four hours (F. Pieper, *Christl. Dogm.*, Vol. I, p. 572; J. T. Mueller, *Christ. Dogm.*, pp. 180, 181).

The First Day: The expression "In the beginning" means "when this world began to be." There was no material out of which things were created. Only since things outside God have begun to exist is there a beginning. Before that there was no beginning, because God has no beginning (Ps. 90:1, 2). Outside Him there is nothing. Time and space are the creatures of the infinite God.

The expression "heaven and earth" designates the universe (Col. 1: 16, 17, Acts 17:24). Since the divine record in Genesis describes in detail the creation of the various creatures out of the original substance, we rightly understand the expression to denote the crude material. Together with the earth, God created the water, since this surrounded the earth (Gen. 1:2). Catholic and Reformed theologians think that by heaven the supposed region of pure fire is meant, in which God dwells with the angels and the saints. Quenstedt calls this supposed heaven of fire a mere figment. The text in Genesis furnishes no basis for such an assumption. In this connection Dr. F. Pieper reminds us that the heaven of angels and perfected saints is not a created space, but the beatific vision of God *(der Zustand des beseligenden Schauens Gottes)*. During their ministry on earth the angels are at the same time in heaven, because, while serving, they always see the face of God.

The light which God created on the first day is the "elemental light," which later (on the fourth day) was connected with luminous bodies. According to the clear testimony of Scripture, light existed before sun, moon, and stars. To this we cannot object as long as we believe in an almighty God (F. Pieper, *Christl. Dogm.* I, pp. 574, 575; J. T. Mueller, *Christ. Dogm.*, pp. 181, 182). Various theories have been advanced by scientists to explain the mysterious nature of light. "The earliest scientific view of the nature of light was that it was a material emanation radiating from the luminous body in straight lines so long as the medium through which it passed remained the same. Now, however, it is recognized that light is a particular kind of motion in a medium believed to fill all space and permeate all matter. The motion is a wave motion, and is propagated through free space with a speed of 186,000 miles a second" (Nelson's *Encyclopaedia,* Vol. XIV, p. 319). Friedrich Bettex has written a very beautiful essay on light (*Handbuch der deutschen National-literatur,* O. Hattstaedt, pp. 490-92).

"The fact that Moses records the creation of light before the creation of the sun has been called unscientific, *e. g.,* by Celsus (2d century A. D.) and Francois Marie Arouet Voltaire (1694-1778). However it is now universally recognized that light may be independent of the sun and that it may be produced by chemical or electrical action. Any solid body can be rendered incandescent by being heated up to 700 and 800 degrees Fahrenheit. Liquids likewise will emit light when heated to a sufficient degree" (W. A. Maier, Notes on Genesis, p. 14).

The Second Day: On the second day, God created the "expanse or the firmament," by which is not meant the stratum of atmosphere about the earth (Baier and others), but rather the visible vault of the sky (Luther and others). According to Gen. 1:6-8 the "firmament" divides the waters above and those below it, so that we must conceive of waters beyond the visible vault of the sky. "Is that not dangerous?" asks F. Pieper. Then he answers: "The water beyond the firmament is not more dangerous than the waters of the sea, which are likewise kept in their place only by God's omnipotence." The creation report everywhere exhibits God's omnipotent power and majesty, but does not answer all questions which the ever-curious mind of man is inclined to ask (F. Pieper, *Christl. Dogm.* I, p. 575; J. T. Mueller, *Christ. Dogm.,* p. 182).

R. Pieper, South. Distr., 1910, pp. 26, 27, claims that the waters beyond the firmament are nothing but the clouds, the waters below the firmament are found in the sea, the rivers, etc. These are in a continuous circuit, drawn up by the sun, gathered in clouds, coming down again in the form of rain, dew, and snow. Millions of tons of water are drawn up by the sun every day and come down again. Silently, inconspicuously, such immense amounts of water are drawn up by the sun every day, we hardly pay any attention to this astounding miracle. Bettex says that if the Lord would have set up gigantic steam engines all over the world which would pump the water out of the ocean with deafening noise and squirt it all over the earth, we might pay more attention to it. Now, when He does it so silently and so much more efficiently, we pay no attention to it. Some of the delegates of the Southern District did not agree with R. Pieper's views on the firmament. They did not think that the firmament was the atmosphere surrounding the earth, but the star-spangled vault of the sky, that the clouds were not the waters beyond, but rather under the firmament. The waters beyond the firmament were, in their opinion, not fog or vapor, but water whose nature is unknown to us.

The Third Day: On this day God gathered the waters under the heavens unto one place, so that the dry land appeared. In chaos, solids and liquids had been mixed; now they were separated. The dry land God adorned "with grass and herb yielding seed after his kind and the tree yielding fruit, whose seed was in itself, after his kind" (Gen. 1:12). The plants existed before the seed, since God created mature plants "yielding seed" (F. Pieper, *Christl. Dogm.* I, p. 576; J. T. Mueller, *Christ. Dogm.,* pp. 182, 183).

Ever since plants have been created by God, they have unfolded a miraculous activity. Silently, in rain and sunshine, they produce immense amounts of grain, oil, wine, luscious fruits, spices, medicines, coffee, tea, cotton, hemp, linen, etc., to feed and to clothe millions of men every year. The plants have a life of their own, they are produced, grow, and die; they absorb light and heat, drink water, and breathe air. There are thousands of different varieties, gigantic trees several hundred feet high, seaweeds that have their roots at the bottom of the ocean and grow, at times, more than a thousand feet through the water till they see sunlight, rock their branches on the waves and form immense submarine forests, swarming with marine animals. In the hot sands of the desert grows the date palm under the scorching rays of the sun if its roots can find subterranean springs. Therefore, the Arabs say, it likes to have its foot in the water and its head in the fire. Even in the icy wastes of the polar regions there are some plants which appear as soon as the sun shines, delicate moss with pretty tiny flowers, diminutive trees a few inches high, their trunks as thick as a pencil. Some plants, like

Edelweiss and *Alpenveilchen,* are found on high mountains; bushes and tall trees grow from clefts of sheer rock. Plants are so strong that they can split rocks.

The Lord has given to plants the power to reproduce themselves; there are male and female blossoms, some produce pollen, others receive it through wind and insects. The fertility of some plants is amazing (R. Pieper, South. Distr., 1910, p. 32-34). Adam Clarke in his commentary claims that the elm tree produces one thousand five hundred and eighty-four million of seeds. . . . In the fourth generation these would amount to six sextillions, two hundred ninety-five thousand three hundred and sixty-two quintillions, eleven thousand one hundred and thirty-six quadrillions. Sums too immense for the human mind to conceive (W. A. Maier, Notes on Genesis, p. 20).

Repeatedly the statement is made in the Sacred Record that plants are to propagate after their kind. This rules out the evolutionary idea that present plants are descended from simpler and lower forms. Burbank and other botanists are not creating new species of plants, they are only changing and improving existing species. These hybrids cannot reproduce themselves, and if left to themselves, they will soon revert to type (W. A. Maier, Notes on Genesis, p. 21).

The Fourth Day: On this day, God created the sun, the moon, and the stars (Gen. 1:14ff.). The matter out of which God made the celestial bodies is not stated; but their purpose and the recipients of their blessings are stated (Gen. 1:14-18). The Bible does not teach an astronomical system, but it teaches the following truths: The earth was before the sun. The earth does not serve the sun, but the sun serves the earth; both sun and earth serve man, who has been created for the purpose of serving God. All astronomical systems set up by men rest upon hypotheses, which are beyond positive proof (F. Pieper, J. T. Mueller). As far as I am informed, some claims of astronomers are not based on mere hypotheses, but on scientific experiments. Over against all astronomical systems we must maintain: Scripture never errs, not even in matters of science (John 10:35; II Tim. 3:16). Scripture accommodates itself to human conceptions, but never to human mistakes, since it is always the truth (John 17:17). We know so little about astronomical data that it is unscientific to correct Scripture on the basis of human speculation. It is unworthy of a Christian to discard the infallible Word of God in favor of science falsely so called (F. Pieper, *Christl. Dogm*

I, pp. 576, 577; see also the Lisco-Knak controversy mentioned in note 1,454; J. T. Mueller, *Christ. Dogm.*, p. 183).

The two main astronomical systems are the Ptolemaic and the Copernican. Ptolemy, geographer and astronomer, flourished at Alexandria in the second century after Christ. He maintained that the earth is the fixed center of the universe, about which the sun, moon, and stars revolve. Copernicus, 1473-1543, asserted that the earth not only revolved about its own axis every twenty-four hours, but that, with the other planets, it also revolves about the sun in a circular orbit every year.

Our Church has never officially taken any position on these theories. While individuals within the Church have advocated the Ptolemaic system in the face of "scientific" ridicule, insisting that the statements of the Bible, especially in Josh. 10: 12-14, are to be taken literally, others have adopted the Copernican system, believing that this theory is not out of harmony with the Bible. The last word has not been spoken in the scientific study of the universe, and some recent developments (Einstein) urge caution in stressing the Copernican system (W. A. Maier, Notes on Genesis, pp. 22).

In the first number of *The Lutheran Scholar,* March, 1943, appeared an interesting article, "Some Thoughts on the Ptolemaic and Copernican Systems," by Oswald B. Overn, Concordia College, St. Paul, Minn. According to Professor Overn there seems to be much confusion about these two systems in the minds of some theologians and scientists. He cites some instances of such confusion. He stresses the fact that all motion is relative, that there is no absolute motion or absolute rest known to man. Concerning the Ptolemaic system he writes that it is a true description of the apparent motion of the heavenly bodies viewed from the earth. It is no hypothesis, but, as long as these motions are considered relative, it is truth. If, however, we add the idea that the earth is stationary and that the motions are absolute, it becomes a hypothesis which no one has a right to accept as truth. He thinks that Galileo's observation of Venus in the gibbous phase (less than full, but more than half full) may be regarded as the first deathblow to the Ptolemaic system.

After describing the Copernican system, he states that the corrected Ptolemaic system will satisfactorily answer all the facts kinematically. Einstein has shown that it will also work dynamically. Nothing more can be claimed for the Copernican system. Both systems are true and equivalent. Yet he prefers the Copernican system because it can be expressed with far simpler and less tedious mathematics. Then he gives several proofs for the motion of the earth. After these proofs Professor Overn continues: "These lines of evidence are perhaps sufficient to convince the most skeptical that the idea of an earth at absolute rest is untenable. The most careful observations show that also the sun is in constant motion just like the earth and the planets. Anyone can observe with a small telescope and a smoked glass that the sun is rotating on its axis, since the sunspots are seen moving across the face of the disk. The varying gravitational forces exerted by the planets cause the center of the sun to trace an irregular curve. In addition to these motions there is a steady shift in the parallax (the apparent shifting of an object caused by change in the position of the observer) of the stars, which indicates that the whole solar system is drifting through the universe at the rate of something like twelve miles per second. Many of the so-called fixed stars have proper motions of their own, and the spectroscope indicates that some of the distant galaxies are moving with tremendous speeds relative to the earth. Absolute rest? Where is it to be found? Only God knows.

"All motion is relative. If this statement is accepted, it is immaterial whether we describe the solar system according to the Ptolemaic or the Copernican view. These two systems are equivalent descriptions from two points of view, and both are equally true. They cannot properly be called theories because they involve no assumption beyond those involved in every observation or measurement" (*The Lutheran Scholar*, Vol. I, No. 1, March, 1943, pp. 3-11).

On the fourth day God did not create light, but luminaries, light bearers, to divide the day from the night, to be for signs and seasons, for days and years, to give light on the earth. Sun, moon, and stars became the bearers of the light which existed before. Day and night existed and followed each other in regular rotation before without sun and moon; from now on the dividing of day and night is specifically tied up with these luminaries.

Furthermore, they should be for signs and seasons, for days and years. They are signs from various points of view. They are signs to devout faith, declaring the glory of their Creator (Psalms 8 and 19). They are signs by which men get their bearings. They may convey signs in reference to future events (Matt. 2:2; Luke 21:25).

They furnish quite reliable signs for determining weather in advance (Matt. 16:2, 3). They may be signs of divine judgments (Joel 2:30; Matt. 24:29).

Besides, the luminaries are for seasons, appointed times. These may be agricultural or festive seasons (Hos. 2:9, 11; 9:5), seasons for beasts and birds (Jer. 8:7), times that are fixed and come with stated regularity. They are for days and years, the shortest and longest measures of time fixed by the movement of the heavenly bodies.

God made the greater luminary to rule the day, and the lesser to rule the night, and also the stars. They are the two great luminaries in reference to the earth and also in view of how they appear to man. Finally, the purposes of these luminaries are stated once more lest anyone attribute any other further purpose to them (Leupold, *Genesis*, pp. 70-77).

All the heavenly luminaries, the sun, the moon, the planets, and all the thousands of stars are miraculous creatures. For thousands of years men have gazed at them with awe and admiration, have studied them with powerful telescopes, have photographed them. While there are many things which we do not know about the heavenly bodies, it is amazing what men have discovered about them. Their dimensions and their distances are, according to astronomers, almost inconceivable.

What a tremendous ocean of fire is the sun, sufficient to illumine and warm the earth and many other planets. Throughout the centuries the sun has furnished light and heat, and yet his brilliance and strength seem to be undiminished; every morning he rises in all his splendor as if he just had come forth from the hand of the Creator. Throughout the years the sun has remained at just the proper distance from the earth. If the sun should get too close, the earth would go up in smoke; if he should wander off too far, everything on earth would freeze. For thousands of years the heavenly bodies have been moving through space with incredible velocity and exactness, never colliding, never one split second too late, so exactly that all the clocks on earth are regulated by these movements.

The Fifth Day: On this day, God created "the moving creature that hath life" in the water and the "fowl that may fly above the earth" (Gen. 1:20, 21). J. T. Mueller in his *Christ. Dogm.*, p. 183, states that the fish were created out of water, but that the material out of which the birds were created is not stated directly. F. Pieper in his *Christ. Dogm.* I, pp. 578-579, writes that there is a difference in viewpoint among Lutheran theologians concerning the material out of which the birds were created. All agree that the matter out of which these and other creatures were made was in no wise self-creative. Luther and Calov think birds were created out of water, Baier and Hollaz believe they were created out of the earth. Walther quotes both, but does not decide which is right and which is wrong. We may leave the matter undecided and admire God's creative work both in fish and fowl. H. C. Leupold translates Gen. 1:20: "And God said: 'Let the waters swarm with swarms of living souls, and let the birds fly above the ground across the face of the firmament of the heavens'." His comment in part is: "The situation is not analogous to the work of the third day, where 'the earth brought forth.' Here it is not the waters that bring forth. The Authorized Version is in error when it translates: 'Let the waters bring forth abundantly.' Luther did not make this mistake. . . . We simply do not know from what source fish and birds sprang. They are simply bidden to people their respective domains" (Leupold, *Gen.*, p. 78). R. Pieper, South. Distr., 1912, p. 7, has the same exegesis as Leupold and corrects Luther's exegesis, not his translation.

The Hebrew word which Luther and A. V. translate in v. 21 with whales really means great sea monsters, which includes not only whales, but all larger marine animals. Some of these inhabitants of the sea are of immense size, others so small that we can see them only with the help of a powerful microscope. These animals God blessed and said: "Be fruitful and multiply," etc. The fertility of the fish is amazing. In a single herring 68,000 eggs have been found, in one carp 200,000 to 300,000, in a sturgeon 3,000,000, in a codfish four to nine millions. On the banks of Newfoundland millions of fish have been caught for many years. During certain seasons Norwegian fishermen used to catch 300 millions of herring in a few weeks (R. Pieper, South. Distr., pp. 8-10).

The birds are also wonderful creatures. Their meat serves as an excellent food, their feathers are used for pillows and covers; many of them are valuable assistants of farmers in their fight against insects. When birds are destroyed, insects increase. With their gorgeous plumage they delight the eye of man, and by their sweet song his ear. R. Pieper mentions especially the meadowlark and the nightingale. If a man has an ear for these voices, they sing into his heart the wisdom and goodness of his Creator, and admonish him to join them in the praises of the Creator, forgetting useless, heathenish cares and worries. The Savior himself directs our attention to the birds, makes them models to be imitated by us when He says: "Behold the fowls of the air, for they sow not, neither do they reap, nor gather into barns; yet your heavenly Father feedeth them. Are ye not much better than they?" (Matt. 6:26.) Dr. Luther writes: "There fly the little birds before our eyes and above us, putting us to shame *(uns zu kleinen Ehren)*, that we might take our hats off before them and say: My dear Doctor, I must confess, that I cannot do *(die Kunst nicht kann)* what you can. You sleep during the night in your little nest without all worry. In the morning you get up, are cheerful *(froehlich und guter Dinge)*, sit down on a tree, praise and thank God; then you look for your food and find it. For shame, what did I old fool learn, that I don't do it also, I who have so much reason to be grateful" (R. Pieper, South. Distr., pp. 11, 12).

God also blessed the birds, gave them the power to propagate, but not in the same degree as the fish. He said to the fish: "Be fruitful and multiply and fill the waters in the seas." To the birds he said only: "Let the birds multiply." For the fish a threefold, for the birds only one blessing. Accordingly the fertility of the birds is much less than that of the fish. Some birds lay only two eggs, others more, but what is that compared with the thousands of fisheggs. Again a proof of God's wisdom. If the birds should increase in the same ratio as the fish, the sun would be darkened by their multitude. Some birds, like the pigeons, produce always a pair of young, a male and a female (R. Pieper, South Distr., pp. 12, 13).

The Sixth Day: On the last day God created both the beasts of the earth and, as the crown of His creative work, man (Gen. 1:24, 27). Animals and plants which after the Fall have become injurious to man were also created within the six days, but their functions were beneficial, not harmful, to man. Before the Fall, nature was not yet under the curse and corruption of sin; therefore even these creatures yielded to man their willing service.

The supreme glory of man, as the crown of creation, appears from the following facts: Man's creation was preceded by a divine consultation in which all three persons of the Trinity concurred (Gen. 1:26). While all creatures came into existence through the almighty divine word, God formed the body of man out of the dust of the ground (Gen. 2:7) and breathed into his nostrils the breath of life, so that he became a living soul (Gen. 2:7). God made man an intelligent and rational being to rule in His stead over the world, which was created for him by God (Gen. 2:7; 1:28). God made man in His own image, so that he was like God in holiness, righteousness, and wisdom (Eph. 4:24; Col. 3:10). God supplied Adam with a helpmeet, who was made in the divine image and endowed with intelligence and an immortal soul (Gen. 2:22-24; J. T. Mueller, *Christ. Dogm.,* pp. 184, 185).

All of God's creatures are wonderful, especially man. What an amazing creation is our eye! It dilates and contracts according to the needs of vision. It is a world of tender nerves and muscles, which receive millions of light rays and pictures and tell our soul how the outside world looks. The ear is a musical instrument such as no human art can produce. In it are 4,300 delicate rods, which vibrate with every sound as the strings of a harp, through which our mind perceives the wonders of sound and, above all, hears the greatest wonder, the Word of God. In a short time the stomach changes food so that it can be assimilated by the body. The blood is pumped by the heart into the remotest parts of the body. In a normal adult the heart contracts and expands about 70 times a minute, 100,800 times a day, 36,792,000 times in a year. The lungs work just as unceasingly: through thousands of cells they inhale and exhale. What marvelous instruments are the organs of speech, mouth, throat, tongue, teeth! Thought and speech are an incomprehensible miracle; so are understanding, knowledge, memory, consciousness.

All plants, animals, and men are made up of millions of little cells, which may be seen and studied under powerful microscopes. Each tiny, little cell is a marvelous creation of God, endowed with unbelievable properties and powers. Let me read to you a few lines from Theo. Graebner, *God and the Cosmos,* p. 65: "All the wonders revealed to us in the atom, molecule, and compounds that are found in protoplasm appear commonplace beside the wonders revealed in the cell.

"Consider the structure of the cell. Imagine for the sake of comparison a balloon filled with the unboiled white of an egg, in the center of which there floated a smaller balloon filled also with the raw white of an egg. In the latter (the nucleus) imagine a string of beads twisted into a network. When fertilization takes place, this network disentangles itself until it becomes one long, continuous string, or coil. This string then breaks into a number of segments, or rods, called chromosomes. The number of such chromosomes is always the same for all members of a given species or group of plants or animals. Thus, for instance, in all cells of the frog this number is 20; in the cells of the grasshopper it is 24; in the cells of the onion 16; in the cells of the human body 48. In some species the number is a small as 2, in others as large as 200.

"Many widely different species have of necessity the same number of chromosomes. Thus 16 chromosomes are found in the cells of the onion, wheat, snail, and many other animals and plants. From this it is apparent that the number as such is not the essential feature in the cell division; it is the make-up, or constitution, of the individual chromosomes. This cell division is inaugurated by a series of processes going on within the nucleus, which are so enormously complex, and withal so beautifully ordered, that to my mind they constitute the most wonderful—if not also the most suggestive—which have ever been revealed by microscopical research. As soon as the chromosomes have formed, they arrange themselves in groups, then each splits lengthwise, so that we now have double the number. Half of these move toward one end or pole of the cell, while the other half move toward the opposite end or pole. Meanwhile the whole cell has become somewhat elongated, a constriction appears along the midline of the cell wall, and finally this constriction becomes complete, and we have two cells from the one, each of the two having again the same number and the same kind of chromosomes. This is the marvelous process of cell multiplication.

"However, the amazement of the student increases when he considers that these chromosomes are the carriers or determiners of all hereditary traits or characters. Small as they are, they consist of still smaller bodies, called genes, these again built up out of molecules, and the molecules out of atoms. The genes of the egg (female) and sperm (male) cells combine into new patterns, and upon the composition of these patterns depends every character, whether physiological or mental. From the manner in which in the moment of conception these genes become distributed everything which distinguishes each of us individually from every other human being had its origin. Not only our racial characters, which make us members of the human species, but the individual characters, the color of the hair and the eyes, the length and shape of our fingernails, acuteness of sight or hearing, our ability to hold a musical note or to remember dates and names, our emotional natures, our intellectual preferences, our likes and dislikes, have been established through this organization of the inscrutable specks of protoplasm which were organized in the original cell, or ovum, from which each of us had his beginning, in a mass so small (1/125 of an inch) that it can be represented by a dot which you make upon the margin of this page with a well-sharpened pencil. Need we wonder that physiologists are constrained to look beyond a mechanical explanation of these wonders and begin to postulate the existence of a Supreme Mind that has poured these life-giving forces into the cell protoplasm?" (Ps. 139:14.)

The Fixity of Species: When God created plants and animals, he created them in their kind. A certain amount of cross-breeding is possible, but there are definite limits beyond which it cannot go. There is no scientific, historical evidence that, *e. g.*, a potato changed into a strawberry, a cat into a dog, a cow into a horse, or an ape into a man. Even where cross-breeding is possible, the plants and animals always revert to type if left to themselves. To preserve the original species, God in His wisdom has set up certain barriers to prevent endless cross-breeding. In *God and the Cosmos*, pp. 203-224, Theo. Graebner discusses three of these barriers of heredity: Mendel's Law, the germplasm, and the chromosomes. These germplasms and chromosomes are very tiny creatures, and yet what a powerful influence do they wield, what definite laws do they follow. They are infinitesimal in size, yet extremely stubborn little things in carrying out the functions which the Creator has assigned to them; all the power and ingenuity of men cannot change them.

5. THE ULTIMATE END OF CREATION

According to Scripture the ultimate end of creation is the glory of God; the world was created for God's own sake (Prov. 16:4) or for His glory (Ps. 104:1ff). Therefore not only men, but all creatures are exhorted to praise God (Ps. 148). By His creation God showed His goodness (Ps. 136); His power (Ps. 115); His wisdom (Ps. 19; 104; 24; 136:5). The objection that it is unworthy of God to regard Him as having made all things for His own glory is against Scripture, since Scripture teaches this very truth (Rom. 11:36); it is unreasonable, since it measures God by human standards; it is atheistic, since it dethrones God and puts man in His place. The ultimate end of creation is God, the intermediate end is the benefit of man (Ps. 115:15, 16; J. T. Mueller, *Christ. Dogm.*, p. 188). "For of Him and through Him and to Him are all things, to whom be glory forever. Amen" (Rom. 11:36).

II

The Person of Christ

JOHANN BRENZ, the Reformer of Swabia, writes: "There are many in our day who say: 'Why so much preaching about Christ, since we are neither Jews nor heathen?' They think it much more necessary to preach against gluttony, drunkenness, theft, fraud, usury, adultery and other vices than always to shout about Christ, since no man is against Him. Now it is true, one must needs testify against social evils, but such preaching is not the principal message; in addition, nothing much is accomplished by it. All depends upon preaching Christ. Where Christ is not proclaimed, little is achieved by ethical discourses, or people are made hypocrites who seek salvation in the merit of good works" (Michigan District, 1886, pp. 13-14).

There is then no need for an explanation as to why at this convention of the Atlantic District we devote some time to a study of the person of Christ, the Redeemer of the world. There is much preaching today which does not conform to the principle of St. Paul: "We preach Christ crucified" (I Cor. 1:23). Our topic is timely also because of the violent onslaughts that have been and are being made by false apostles against the revelation of the Bible as to the subject of Christology. What a pity that the Church must constantly draw the sword of the Spirit against heretics who do not weary of mutilating, falsifying, corrupting, and destroying the central truth of the Scriptures, as set forth in the ancient Creed: "I believe in Jesus Christ, His only Son, our Lord!" Luther complained in his day: "O Lord God, in this blessed, comforting article (the person of Christ) one should always rejoice in true faith without doubt and quarreling, and sing and praise and thank God, the Father, for such unspeakable mercy that He gave us His dear Son as man and our brother, like unto us. But through high-minded, vainglorious people the wicked Satan creates such displeasure that our happy, blessed joy is hindered and ruined. God have mercy!" (XVI:2231.)

Thesis I

Jesus Christ is true God, begotten of the Father from eternity, and also true Man, conceived by the Holy Ghost and born of the Virgin Mary.

1. THE DEITY OF JESUS CHRIST

So completely is the doctrine of Jesus' deity the foundation of the Christian religion that Jesus recognizes only that faith which acknowledges Him as the Son of God. According to Matt. 16, Jesus questioned His disciples on the trend of public opinion regarding His person. The disciples responded that the people thought He was a mere man, such as John the Baptist, Elias, Jeremiah, or one of the Prophets. The answer to the next question: "But whom say ye that I am?" was given by Peter: "Thou art the Christ, the Son of the living God." Thereupon Jesus assured Peter that upon this confession, revealed to him from heaven, the salvation of all men depends, saying: "Thou art Peter; and upon this rock I will build My Church; and the gates of hell shall not prevail against it."

Names of the Son of God. His names are not mere titles, but accurate descriptions of His person. The name "Jesus" is Hebrew and signifies "Savior," as the angel said: "He shall save His people from their sins" (Matt. 1:21). How vital it is that we know this name is stated by Peter (Acts 4:12): "Neither is there salvation in any other: for there is none other name under heaven given among men, whereby we must be saved." To a Christian ear there is no music to thrill the soul as this most blessed name, in which the whole Gospel is contained as in a nutshell. The other name, "Christ" (Christos), is Greek, which means "Anointed." Jesus was anointed with the Holy Spirit at His Baptism. Prophets, priests, and kings were anointed with oil, a symbol of the Spirit of God, but Christ, with the Spirit Himself. The Holy Ghost moved the former occasionally, but He *rested* or *remained* upon Christ, as the Evangelist John testified: "I saw the Spirit descending from heaven like a dove, and it *abode* upon Him" (John 1:32-33; Is. 11:2). A third name is "Messiah." That is the designation the Jews used after the Babylonian captivity when they referred to the Savior who was to come. The Samaritan woman at Jacob's well knew of the Messianic hope of Israel, saying: "I know that Messias cometh, which is called Christ" (John 4:25; see also 1:41).

Jesus Christ Is True God

A: In the *Old Testament*.

Jesus appears as God on the pages of the Old Testament. He reveals Himself under such titles as "the Angel of the Lord," "Jehovah," "Lord," etc. Whenever in the Old Testament the name "Lord" occurs, it is pre-eminently not the Father, nor the Holy Spirit, but the Son of God. Ex. 13:21 Moses writes of the Israelites in the wilderness: "And the Lord went before them by day in a pillar of a cloud, to lead them the way; and by night in a pillar of fire, to give them light." Who is this "Lord"? Ch. 14:19 He is called "the Angel of God," which is a well-known appellation of Jesus in the Old Testament. Here the Angel of God is directly termed "Lord." All doubt is removed by Paul (I Cor. 10:3-4): "Our fathers did all eat the same spiritual meat; and did all drink the same spiritual drink; for they drank of that spiritual Rock that followed them; *and that Rock was Christ.*"

The Prophet Isaiah describes a vision he saw in the Temple (ch. 6:1-5), which is the subject of the hymn: "Isaiah, Mighty Seer, in Days of Old." He saw the Lord sitting upon a throne and, above it, two seraphim, each having six wings. Then the Prophet exclaims: "Woe is me! . . . Mine eyes have seen the King, the Lord of Hosts" (v. 5). Who was "the King, the Lord of Hosts?" The Holy Spirit replies through John (12:41): "These things said Isaiah, when he saw His glory, and spake of Him." In the verses preceding and following, John plainly states that he is referring to Jesus, and that therefore it was the Son of God whose glory Isaiah saw.

Which person of the Godhead summoned Moses to the summit of Mount Sinai and gave him the two tables of the Law? Again it was the Son of God. The evidence is presented in the Ascension Psalm, 68; vv. 7-8, and 17-18. And all doubt is excluded by Heb. 12:18-26, especially v. 24. (Central District, 1883, pp. 61, 66.)

Luther writes: "The God who led Israel out of Egypt and through the Red Sea; who went before them in a pillar of a cloud and of fire; who nourished them with bread from heaven and did all the miracles which Moses relates in his books; again, who brought them into the land of Canaan and gave them kings and the priesthood and everything, is this God and none other than Jesus of Nazareth, Mary's, the Virgin's, Son, whom we Christians call our God and Lord, whom the Jews have crucified and still today blaspheme and curse, as Isaiah says, 8:21: 'They shall fret themselves, and curse their King and their God.' Again, He it is who on Mount Sinai gives Moses the Ten Commandments. . . . Yes, Jesus of Nazareth, who died for us on the cross is the God who says in the First Commandment: 'I, the Lord, am thy God.' If the Jews and Mohammed should hear this, how would they rage!" (Walch III, 2853 f.)

So then, the same God on Sinai and Calvary. What comfort for the believers! Now the flames of Sinai can no longer fill us with terror. Indeed, we daily transgress the holy Law of Sinai, but we break through its condemnation and flee to the Redeemer on Calvary, who Himself fulfilled the Law for us and paid its penalty.

B. In the *New Testament.*

Naturally *the New Testament* provides clearer evidence of the deity of our Lord. We refer to the prooftexts given in the Catechism and to the Gospel according to St. John, the purpose of which is stated by the author, chap. 20:31: "These are written, that ye might believe that Jesus is the Christ, the Son of God; and that, believing, ye might have life through His name." Other prooftexts from the New Testament follow as we present the chief support for our confession of the divine sonship of our Lord.

C. The Eternal Sonship.

Christ is begotten, or born, of the Father from eternity. The eternal generation of Christ by the Father is the outstanding proof of His deity, as Johann Gerhard writes: "Therefore and therefrom the Son is true God, because the Father through the eternal generation imparts His divine essence to the Son." This truth is stated in all passages of the New Testament in which Jesus is called "the only-begotten Son of the Father," as in John 1:14 and 18; "His Son," "His own Son," as Rom. 1:3; ch. 8:32; I John 1:7; also in the many texts in which God is called "the Father of our Lord Jesus Christ," as in I Pet. 1:3; I Thess. 1:1 etc.; Heb. 1:5 we have the plain words: "Thou art My Son; this day have I begotten Thee." According to the Athanasian Creed: "The Son is of the Father alone: not made, not created, but begotten. . . . God of the substance of the Father, begotten before the worlds." We know less of this eternal generation than of other Scripture truths and acknowledge with the Fathers: "What it is to be born, what it is to proceed, I confess not to know."

Luther writes: "I customarily use a homely, simple comparison as an aid to understanding somewhat this generation of God's Son by the eternal Father, namely thus: As a human son has flesh and blood and his essence from his father, so also the Son of God, born of the Father, has His divine essence and nature from the Father from eternity. However, we cannot reach it with this or any other simile. It cannot be as perfect as in the divine majesty, in which the Father gives the entire divine essence to the Son, whilst the human father cannot give the son his whole essence, but only a part. . . . But in the Godhead the entire divine essence and nature goes over into the Son, and yet the Son remains in the same Godhead with the Father, and is one God with Him. This one must believe. Reason may be ever so wise, sharp and pointed, yet no one can grasp and comprehend it." Ambrose exclaims: "It is impossible to know the mystery of this eternal generation. The mind is too weak. Language, not only mine but also that of the angels, is hushed. If the peace of Christ passes all understanding, how much more this high generation. . . . You may know that He was born; but you dare not search as to how He was born." (Mich. Dist., 1886, pp. 23-24.)

We confess in our Creed: "Begotten of the Father *from eternity.*" This accords with Scripture. Micah foretells of the Messiah: "Whose goings forth have been from of old, from everlasting" (5:2). In the Second Psalm the Father says to Christ: "Thou art my Son; this day have I begotten Thee." "This day" is the eternal day of the Father, before whom a thousand years are as a day and a day as a thousand years. In His eternal life the Father has generated the Son. In this the birth of Jesus differs from that of a creature. A human son is younger than his father, but the Son of God is as old, as eternal, as the Father. As heat is as old as fire; as light is as old as the sun, so the Son of God, "being the Brightness of the Father's glory," is co-equal with Him in eternity. "From eternity" also implies that this generation continues on, world without end. It is a process which never reaches an end. Certainly, it is beyond our understanding that this generation of God's Son is always complete, yet it continues forever. Quenstedt writes: "We distinguish between an earlier and a later birth of Christ. The earlier is without beginning, the later without parallel. The earlier is without a mother, the later without a father. The earlier inconceivable, the later unspeakable." (Mich. Dist., 1886, p. 27.)

We give only passing notice to the men who have become infamous in history by denying the deity of our Lord, such as Cerinth, Arius, etc. The offspring of these ancient heretics today are the Socinians, the Unitarians, the Universalists, the Christian Scientists, many leaders in the Federal Council of the Churches of Christ in America, Fosdick, and many more. St. John pronounces the verdict of God upon all who would rob our exalted Lord of the glory due His name, saying: "Every spirit that confesseth not that Jesus Christ is come into the flesh," *i. e.*, is true God and man, "is not of God." That which is not of God is of the devil. It is one of the "doctrines of devils" to reject this foundation truth of the Christian religion.

2. THE HUMANITY OF JESUS CHRIST

We confess in the Apostles' Creed: "Conceived by the Holy Ghost. born of the Virgin Mary"; and in the Athanasian Creed: "Man of the substance of His mother, born in the world."

His Conception. The Holy Spirit describes the conception of Jesus in clear language. The angel said to Mary: "The Holy Ghost shall come upon thee, and the power of the Highest shall overshadow thee" (Luke 1:35). "As the children are partakers of flesh and blood, He also Himself likewise took part of the same" (Heb. 2:14). The flesh and blood of the Virgin Mary is the matter from which the human nature of Christ originated. This is stated (Matt. 1:16): "Of whom (*i. e.* Mary) was born Jesus." The Greek word for "of" is "ek," which means "out of," out of the flesh and blood of Mary. Christ is the "Woman's Seed" (Gen. 3:15); "made of a woman" (Gal. 4:4). By a miracle—for with God nothing shall be impossible (Luke 1:37)—the Holy Spirit caused that the Virgin became the mother of Christ according to the human nature. The patriarch Isaac and John the Baptist were also conceived contrary to some laws of nature, yet both of them received flesh and blood from their respective parents, God having revived their generative powers. However, the human nature of Jesus originated not from a human father and mother, but solely from the substance of His mother, the Holy Spirit acting as the creative cause.

A Sinless Conception. The angel had announced to the Virgin: "Therefore also that holy thing which shall be born of thee shall be called the Son of God" (Luke 1:35). We ask how a sinless human nature could originate out of the sinful blood of Mary. Several theories have been advanced. The Church of Rome replies with the doctrine of the Immaculate Conception of Mary, for which she cannot offer any evidence. Mary was afflicted with the original sin and the hereditary guilt of all men (John 3:6; Rom. 5:18). Others have said that God has preserved a sinless flesh through all generations since Adam, of which, however, Scripture knows nothing. Others hold the view that the Holy Spirit created a sinless flesh and blood in the womb of the Virgin, from which the body of Jesus was then formed. We accept the opinion of Luther, Chemnitz, and other theologians, who hold that the Holy Spirit cleansed and sanctified the "massa corrupta" in the Virgin and out of this cleansed flesh and blood created "that holy thing." The words of the Holy Spirit (Luke 1:35): "The Holy Ghost shall come upon thee and the power of the Highest shall overshadow thee" lend support to this view. Luther writes: "Flesh and blood was corrupted by original sin, yet so that it could be healed. . . . For sin and death are such afflictions as may be removed and from which we may be redeemed. Therefore, in the moment of conception by the Virgin the Holy Spirit cleansed and sanctified the sinful flesh and wiped off the poison of the devil and death, which is sin." (II:1171f.) Chemnitz states: "In the article of redemption the Scriptures testify mightily that the Son of God assumed our human nature, which in conception was cleansed of sin." (Cen. Dist., 1918, pp. 25-26.)

Born of the Virgin Mary. The Virgin Birth (Parthenogenesis). Isaiah had prophesied: "A virgin shall conceive and bear a son" (7:14). The Lutheran Church confesses in the Solida Declaratio: "Who (Christ) showed His divine majesty even in His mother's womb, inasmuch as He was born of a virgin, with her virginity inviolate. Therefore, she is truly the mother of God, and nevertheless remained a virgin." (*Triglot.*, p. 1024.) The Bible calls Mary a virgin before the conception (Is. 7:14): "A virgin shall conceive"; while she was pregnant (Matt. 1:23): "A virgin shall be with child"; as she gave birth (Is. 7:14): "A virgin . . . shall bear a son." Whether Mary remained a virgin, bearing no other children, is a question that cannot be answered.

By His birth Jesus became man in the full sense of the word. He took part of the flesh and blood of the children of men (Heb. 2:14). "Of the fathers, as concerning the flesh, Christ came" (Rom. 9:5). And John says (1:14): "The Word was made flesh." His name was entered upon the official records of the Roman Empire as a member of the human family. He had a real body and soul and a human will, as the Scriptures abundantly testify. He was subject to the laws of human living on earth. He ate, drank, slept, grew weary, and died a real death. Of His death Luther writes: "Here we have an unusual dead body. . . . It is flesh and blood as our bodies and dies. But since His flesh and blood is without sin, He dies in such a manner that also in death there remains an evidence of life. While otherwise the blood becomes cold and coagulates, it remains warm and alive in the Lord Christ's body, so that as soon as His side is opened, it springs forth, just as it does when you open the artery of a well person. St. John wants us to note this diligently and learn to know the real nature of our dear Lord Christ's blood, namely, that it flows, lives, and has its effect also after death. . . . and all who are sprinkled with it have forgiveness of sin and are children of eternal life." (XIII:490f.)

We cannot identify Christ too closely with our humanity. As we are creatures, so His human nature is a creature, as stated by John: "The Word was made flesh" (1:14). Only in one respect does He differ from His brethren: He was without sin. His sinlessness is due to the immaculate conception. Because He is separate from sinners, there are several features of the Man Christ which are peculiar to Him. His body was not subject to death. Death results from sin. "The wages of sin is death" (Rom. 6:23). His body was free of the germ of death. He died because He gave His life into death. "No man taketh My life from Me, but I lay it down of Myself" (John 10:18). Because of the sinlessness of His human nature, His mental powers were not weakened, but were superior to those of any other human being. The Bible extols His wisdom (Luke 2:52) and His understanding (v. 47). It is true that on the body of our Redeemer there appeared the marks and consequences of sin. Paul writes: "God, sending His own Son in the likeness of sinful flesh" (Rom. 8:3). His appearance, His form was that of man, not before the Fall, but after the Fall. We see in Him the general frailties of mankind: He became hungry, thirsty, weary; He sorrowed and wept. However, the Scriptures do not report that He suffered from any individual ailments or diseases, such as fever, lameness, etc. By reason of His holy birth, our Savior was free from original sin, for He "was separate from sinners" (Heb. 7:26). Neither was He tainted with Adam's guilt, as all mankind is (Rom. 5:18-19). Yes, He calls others to repentance; He Himself has nothing to repent of. He instructs others to plead for forgiveness, not only publicans and sinners, but also the self-righteous Pharisees, yet He does not ask the Father for personal forgiveness. When He confesses in the 69th Psalm: "O God, My sins are not hid from Thee," then He is speaking of a foreign sin and guilt which was imputed to Him, for "God made Him to be sin for us who knew no sin" (II Cor. 5:21); (Mich. Dist., 1904, p. 37).

The humanity of Christ is essential for our salvation. "God sent forth His Son, made of a woman, made under the Law" (Gal. 4:4). The Redeemer of the world had to assume the guilt and the penalty of the Law which was binding on all men, and this was possible only if He became like us in all things, in a perfect human nature. Cyril of Jerusalem: "If the incarnation is a fantasy, salvation is also a fantasy." Kromayer: "What the Son of God has not assumed, that He did not redeem."

Whilst otherwise a human nature is also a person, it is peculiar to the human nature of Christ that it does not constitute a separate being (enhypostasia). Jesus' human nature never existed by itself. It is an impersonal nature. In the moment of conception Christ received it into His person in this manner that the divine nature took the initiative. The human nature did not receive the divine, but the divine assumed the human nature. He took part of flesh and blood. He took on Him the seed of Abraham. The human nature also will remain an integral part of the person of our Redeemer into all eternity.

Thesis II

Jesus Christ is true God and true Man in one Person, in which the human nature and the divine nature are united in intimate Communion.

Jesus Christ is true God and true man. The question arises: Are there two Christs? Nestorius answered, Yes! He separated the two natures in Christ and held that there is a divine Christ and a human

Christ. The Bible, however, answers, No! We have only one Lord, one Mediator, one Redeemer. For prooftexts we quote: "The Word was made flesh" (John 1:14). Here John says not: Christ assumed a human person, but *flesh*, a human nature, humanity, and received it into His person. "There is one God and one Mediator between God and men, the man Christ Jesus" (I Tim. 2:5). The uniting of God and man in one being is called the Personal Union, *unio personalis*. In this unique union the divine nature is in the human nature, and vice versa. Luther writes: "Do not let the two natures in Christ, God and man, be separated, but let them remain together, as the text clearly states: 'The Word became flesh'; which does not say: the Deity became one person, and the humanity another person. So God's and Mary's Son is one son, not two. . . . God is man, man is God, undivided in one person. God's child and man's child is one child, and all depends on this article; for if this person is divided, we are lost." (Erl. 46, p. 41.)

These two natures are united in the divine-human Christ in the most intimate communion. "Great is the mystery of godliness: God was manifest in the flesh" (I Tim. 3:16). "Jesus Christ, our Lord, which was made of the seed of David according to the flesh; and declared to be the Son of God" (Rom. 1:3-4). God and man are united in Christ, not as our body is with a suit of clothes which it wears, or as a letter is enclosed in an envelope, but as soul and body in one person, or as fire and iron are one in glowing iron. Luther explains in this manner: He who touches the man Christ touches also the Son of God. Here is an example. The woman with an issue of blood touched the hem of His garment and was healed at once. Whom did she touch? Not only the man, but also the Son of God. She might have touched the hem of an ordinary person without benefit. But when she touched the hem of this man, she was made whole, because in the Son of Man she touched the Son of God. (Nebraska District, 1901, p. 59.) This truth is expressed in the axiom: Neither is the flesh without the Word, nor the Word without the flesh.

However, despite the intimacy of the union of the two natures in Christ, each nature remains intact, just as soul and body remain what they are, though united in one person. There is no commingling of the natures. By the union of God and man in Christ there did not originate a third nature, the divine-human nature. Eutyches advanced the theory that the divine nature absorbed the human. In that case Jesus is no longer the God-Man, nor, consequently, the Redeemer of the world. Since the divine and the human nature form one person in Christ, this union is called the Personal Union. It is as intimate as that of soul and body in man. Likewise, as the soul is the active part of man, permeating the body, so the divine is the active nature in Christ, while the human nature is passive and receptive. "In Him dwelleth all the fullness of the Godhead bodily" (Col. 2:9). Luther writes: "If you could show me a place where God is and not the man, then the person is divided already, because I could then say, Here is God, who is not man and never became man. None of that God for me! For from this would follow that place and space separated the two natures and divided the person, which in fact death and all the devils cannot divide or tear apart. . . . No, friend, where you place God, there you must also place the humanity; they may not be severed and detached from each other; it is become one person which does not put off the humanity as Master Hans does when he takes off his coat and lays it away at bedtime." (Erl. 30, p. 211ff; Neb. Dist., 1901, p. 69.)

Because the two natures are so closely conjoined in Christ, the dogmaticians speak of *propositiones personales,* personal statements. Such a statement is given Luke 1:31-32, where Mary's Son is called the Son of the Highest; in other words, the Son of Mary is the Son of God. On the basis of Scripture we can say: this man is God; and: this God is man. We have illustrated the Personal Union of the divine and human natures in Christ by comparing it to the union of soul and body and to glowing iron. However, these illustrations are imperfect. We cannot say: the soul is the body, or: the body is the soul. Yet of Christ we may say: this God is man, and this man is God. God and man are essentially exclusive concepts. Still we are in full accord with Scripture when we say: The Son of God is the Son of man, because the divine Christ received the human nature into His person. That this union is beyond understanding should not disturb us, because the Holy Spirit has said: "Great is the mystery of godliness: God was manifest in the flesh" (I Tim. 3:16). It behooves us to say: "Alleluia! Salvation, and glory, and honor, and power, unto the Lord, our God!" (Rev. 19:1.) (F. Pieper, *Christliche Dogmatik,* II, 93ff.)

Now we should be done with this essay. If things were as they should be; if all teachers in the Christian Church had followed the direction of the Apostle Peter: "If any man speak, let him speak as the oracles of God" (I Pet. 4:11), then our work would be finished. For nineteen centuries, however, there have been bishops, pastors, and reformers in the Church who have rebelled against the Word of the living God and against its teachings. Therefore, we must add another thesis, which deals with the Communication of Attributes, in order to ward off the sinister attacks on the doctrine of Christ's person and to preserve for ourselves the vital truths of our redemption. The Book of Concord devotes many pages to the Communication of Attributes. Luther and other Lutheran theologians have written volumes on this subject. Our Catechism deals with it. Yet, strictly speaking, the Communication of Attributes is not another doctrine. That which will be said in the third thesis is in its entirety contained in the first two theses. The Communication of Attributes does not go one iota beyond the Personal Union in Christ. It is merely viewed from a different angle. Then why another thesis? Why does Dr. Pieper write 163 pages in his *Dogmatik* on the Communication of Attributes? The answer is: "An enemy hath done this!" Or, as Dr. Pieper has it: Because three strange things have happened in the Christian Church: 1. Men have admitted that the Son of God became man; in other words, they accept the Personal Union of the two natures in Christ, yet they separate the Son of God from the attributes of His human nature, *e. g.,* being born of the Virgin, saying that it is blasphemous to ascribe such a human attribute to Him. Nestorius and Zwingli are guilty of this inconsistency which dissolves the union of the natures in Christ. Therefore, it became necessary to draw up the first group of the Communication of Attributes. 2. Reformed and Catholic theologians granted that the Son of Man is the Son of God, again accepting the union of the two natures, but they separated from the Son of Man the divine attributes, such as omnipotence, omniscience, etc., saying that the finite is not capable of the infinite. Therefore, the second class of the Communication of Attributes became necessary. 3. Men have denied that Christ performed the deeds of redemption according to both natures in one divine-human action; they say, for example, that Christ wrought His miracles just as the Prophets and Apostles did. Therefore the third group. (F. Pieper, *Christl. Dogm.* II, pp. 148-149.)

Thesis III

The Communication of Attributes

What is the Communication of Attributes? A short answer is: In Christ each of the two natures partakes of the properties of the other nature, as: "The blood of Jesus Christ, His Son, cleanseth us from all sin" (I John 1:7); or: "The Father hath given Him authority to execute judgment also, because He is the Son of Man" (John 5:27). Another short definition is: The Scriptures ascribe to the person of the God-Man all divine as well as human attributes, whether He is designated according to the divine nature, or the human, or both natures. There are three groups of such communication.

1. GENUS IDIOMATICUM

Dr. F. Pieper writes: "Since the divine and the human nature in Christ form one person, the attributes which essentially belong only to one nature are always ascribed to the whole person; however, the divine attributes according to the divine nature, the human attributes according to the human nature" (*Christl. Dogm.* II, p. 160). "Sometimes the Bible expressly states to which nature a certain quality is attributed, as Rom. 1:3: "Jesus Christ . . . was made of the seed of David *according to the flesh*" (see also 9:5); see also I Pet. 3:18; "Christ . . . being put to death *in the flesh*" (4:1). The two natures are united in one person; however, they are not transfused into each other, but each retains its own essential characteristics. We cannot say that the human nature is eternal, or that the Godhead died. But the qualities are ascribed to the whole person. We have an analogy in the union of soul and body in a human being. The body has the property of size and expansion. The soul has not. The soul is not limited to space. Yet a property of the body, space, is communicated to the soul, for the soul fills man when he is a child and when he is full-grown. Thus a quality of the body is lent to the soul, though space never will become an essential property of the soul. Likewise, the body obtains certain attributes from the soul, for example, life, the power to think, etc. However, these communicated attributes never become essential properties of the body, for it loses them immediately when the soul leaves the body at death. (Mich. Dist , 1886, p. 64.) So the Scripture ascribes to the person of Christ both divine and human attributes. It assigns to Him eternity: "Before Abraham was, I am" (John 8:58)—and an age of thirty years: "And Jesus Himself began to be about thirty years of age" (Luke 3:23); omniscience: "Lord, Thou knowest all things" (John 21:17)—and limited knowledge: "And Jesus increased in wisdom" (Luke 2:52); omnipotence: "By Him [Christ] were all things created" (Col. 1:16) —and limited power: "The officers of the Jews took Jesus and bound Him" (John 18:12). Because of the Communication of Attributes the Bible asserts that God died, and the Church sings: "O sorrow dread! Our God is dead!" That seems impossible; yet the mystery is no greater than the fact that God became man. Zwingli endeavored to solve the difficulty by his *alloeosis,* which means substitution. We shall let him explain it: "You must know that the figure which is called *alloeosis* is used innumerable times by Christ Himself. And the figure is a trading or exchanging of two natures which are in one person, when one designates the one and means the other, or designates what both are, but means only one of them." (F. Pieper, *Christl. Dogm.,* II, 153.) As an illustration he quotes Luke 24: "Ought not Christ to have suffered these things?" Here he substitutes "human nature" for "Christ," because the divine nature cannot suffer. Luther's judgment of Zwingli's *alloeosis* is a classic. He writes: "Zwingli calls that an *alloeosis* when something is said of the deity of Christ which really belongs to the humanity, or vice versa. As Luke 24:26: 'Ought not Christ to have suffered these things, and to enter into His glory?' Here Zwingli juggles, asserting that for "Christ" one must substitute "human nature." Beware, beware, I say, of the *alloeosis!* It is the devil's mask, for at last it manufactures such a Christ after whom I certainly would not be a Christian; namely, that henceforth Christ should be no more and do no more with His sufferings and life than any other mere saint. For if I believe this, that only the human nature has suffered for me, then Christ is to me a poor Savior, then He Himself needs a savior. In a word, it is unspeakable what the devil seeks by the *alloeosis.* . . . If the old weatherwitch, Dame Reason, the grandmother of the *alloeosis,* would say, Yes, but God cannot suffer or die; you shall reply, That is true; yet, because in Christ deity and humanity are one person, Scripture, on account of the Personal Union, ascribes also to the deity everything which the humanity experiences, and vice versa. For this you must say, that the person (Christ) suffers and dies.

Now the person is true God; therefore it is rightly said: The Son of God suffers. For although one part (so to say), the deity, does not suffer, yet the person, which is God, suffers in the other part, namely, in His humanity; for in truth God's Son has been crucified for us, that is, the person which is God. As when one says: Solomon is wise, although only his soul is wise; Peter is gray, though only his head is gray. . . . This is the mode of speaking in all the world, not only in the Scriptures, and it is also the truth." (*Triglot,* 1029.)

In short, if Nestorius and Zwingli are right in tearing the human attributes from the divine nature of Christ, then our faith is vain, then we are yet in our sins, then also they which are fallen asleep in Christ are perished. That which renders the suffering and death of our Redeemer meritorious before God is the fact that we are reconciled to God by the *death of His Son.* To preserve this priceless truth of our redemption, the first group of the Communication of Attributes is necessary.

2. GENUS MAJESTATICUM

The second class of Communication of Attributes may be designated as the communication of majesty, because the full divine glory and majesty was bestowed upon the human nature in the incarnation. In a human being the communication of the soul to the body has the effect that the body partakes of the properties of the soul (life, reason, etc.), and through the communication of the divine nature to the human in Christ, the human nature received all the divine attributes. The difference between the first and the second group is this: In the first, divine and human properties are predicated of Christ, the divine according to the divine nature, the human according to the human nature; in the second group, however, *divine* attributes are given to *the human nature.* It should be noted that this bestowal is not mutual, but, so to say, one-sided. No human attributes are communicated to the divine nature, because God is unchangeable (Ps. 102:28). By reason of the Personal Union, the human nature in Christ has received, not excellent, unusual, finite gifts and qualities, but infinite, uncreated, divine attributes; or, as the Formula of Concord expresses it, "supernatural, inscrutable, ineffable, heavenly prerogatives and excellencies in majesty, glory, power, and might above everything that can be named." (*Triglot,* p. 1003.) This truth is set forth in two classes of Scripture texts;

first in those which say that the Son of God entered into the human nature with the full glory of the Deity, as Col. 2:9: "In Him [Christ] dwelleth all the fullness of the Godhead bodily." The human body of Christ is the temple of the sublime majesty of God. "The Word was made flesh and dwelt among us, and we beheld His glory, the glory as of the Only-Begotten of the Father, full of grace and truth" (John 1:14). The disciples beheld the divine glory and majesty in the flesh of Christ. The second group of Bible passages are those in which specific divine attributes are ascribed to the human nature; for example, *omnipotence*: "All power is given unto Me in heaven and in earth" (Matt. 28:18). For the comfort of His disciples and the Church, the risen Lord here asserts that He has power which is not restricted to one land, or to the whole earth, but all power in heaven and in earth. And since this power is "given" Him, He is here speaking as the Son of Man. "The Father hath given Him authority to execute judgment also, because He is the Son of Man" (John 5:27). To judge the world on the last day presupposes omnipotence, and that is given Him, "because He is the Son of Man." *Omniscience:* "Jesus . . . knew all men and needed not that any should testify of man; for He knew what was in man" (John 2:24-25). In His prophetic ministry Jesus revealed that He "knew the hearts of all men" (Acts 1:24), a divine prerogative of the omniscient God. "In Christ are hid all the treasures of wisdom and knowledge" (Col. 2:3). When Christ taught on earth, He did not speak by inspiration as Prophets and Apostles did, but as He who "was in the bosom of the Father" (John 1:18); as He to whom the Father had given "the Spirit not by measure" (John 3:34). *Omnipresence:* "No man hath ascended up to heaven, but He that came down from heaven, even the Son of Man, which is in heaven" (John 3:13). While the Son of Man was speaking to Nicodemus on earth, He was at the same time in heaven. "Lo, I am with you alway, even unto the end of the world" (Matt. 28:20). This gracious promise of the Savior's presence with His Church unto the end of days must be understood of His human nature, in view of the words immediately preceding: "All power is given unto Me." *Divine Honor. (Cultus vere divinus.)* "All men should honor the Son, even as they honor the Father" (John 5:23). That such adoration is due Christ according to His human nature is apparent from the words going before: "The Father judgeth no man, but hath committed all judgment unto the Son." "That whosoever believeth in Him" (John 3:16), in Him who was lifted up on the cross. Yes, we adore the human nature of Christ, though many theologians seek to ridicule such worship and denounce it as idolatry. If we believe in Him as our Redeemer, He is worthy of divine honor. "In whom we believe, Him we piously adore; we believe, however, in Christ, the man" (Scherzer). Paul Gerhardt's seven hymns addressed to the members of Christ's body—"Passionssalven." (F. Pieper, *Christl. Dogm.*, II, p. 237ff.)

All divine attributes are bestowed upon the human nature; not only the active, as just set forth, but also the inactive, or quiescent, as, eternity, infinity (or boundlessness), to be a spirit. However, the former in a direct manner, the latter indirectly. For example, the human nature can never be eternal, yet Jesus said: "Before Abraham was, I am" (John 8:58). Here Jesus ascribes eternity to His human nature by reason of the Personal Union. Indirectly eternity was communicated to His humanity. In the same sense we can say: the human nature of Christ has an eternal wisdom, an everlasting omnipotence, etc. Luther writes: "Thus the human nature in Christ receives the honor that it carries *all* the attributes which otherwise belong to God alone." (Erl. 47, p. 178.)

Certainly, the divine attributes are not, and never can become, essential qualities of the human nature; however, they were communicated to it in the moment when the two natures were joined in the Personal Union. The moon has no light, yet it shines at night. To send forth rays of light is a property of the sun. The moon shines with a borrowed light which never becomes her own, as we observe in the waxing and waning moon. So the brightness of divine glory is reflected in the humanity of our Redeemer.

Through the incarnation the human nature in Christ was enriched, magnified, exalted, and glorified, but the divine nature did not correspondingly lose any of its majesty. There is no subtraction or addition in the divine nature: "With whom (God) there is no variableness, neither shadow of turning" (James 1:17).

Our fathers confessed in the Formula of Concord: "We regard it as a pernicious error when such majesty is denied to Christ according to His humanity. For thereby the very great consolation is taken from Christians which they have in the aforecited promise concerning the presence and dwelling with them of their Head,

King, and High Priest, who has promised them that not only His mere deity would be with them, which to us poor sinners is as a consuming fire to dry stubble, but that He, He, the man who has spoken with them, who has tried all tribulations in His assumed human nature, and who can therefore have sympathy with us, as with men and His brethren. . . . He will be with us in all our troubles also in the nature according to which He is our brother and we are flesh of His flesh." (*Triglot*, p. 1048.)

The objection of Zwingli: "Finitum non est capax infiniti" (the finite is not capable of the infinite) proceeds from rationalism and destroys the highest comfort of believers, which is that Christ is present with them, not as God only, but as man, as their brother, saying: "Lo, I am with you alway, even unto the end of the world" (Matt. 28:20).

3. GENUS APOTELESMATICUM

All official acts which Christ wrought and still works for the salvation of mankind as our Prophet, Priest, and King, He performs according to both natures, each nature doing that which is peculiar to it, not separately from the other, but in constant communion with the other nature in one undivided, divine-human action. (F. Pieper, *Christl. Dogm.*, II, p. 272.) The Formula of Concord defines the third group of the Communication of Attributes in this manner: "As to the execution of the office of Christ, the person does not act in, with, through, or according to only one nature, but in, according to, with, and through both natures, or, as the Council of Chalcedon expresses it, one nature operates in communion with the other what is a property of each (quod sibi proprium est). Therefore Christ is our Mediator, Redeemer, King, High Priest, Shepherd, Head, etc., not according to one nature only, whether it be the divine or the human, but according to both natures." (*Triglot*, p. 1031.) The third division of the Communication of Attributes has been called the practical division. The first two prepare the way for the third. In the first class of the Communication of Attributes we emphasize, in opposition to Nestorius and Zwingli, that not a human being, but the Son of God was born of Mary and died on the cross. In the second class we uphold against the same opponents that to the human nature of Christ there was communicated omnipotence, omniscience, and omnipresence, in order to maintain in the third

group that all the deeds of redemption wrought by the Redeemer
are divine-human actions and are therefore effective for our salvation and comfort. (F. Pieper, *Christl. Dogm.*, II, pp. 277-278.)

Also the *genus apotelesmaticum* is definitely implied in the Personal Union of the two natures in Christ. As by the incarnation the
human nature was elevated into the sphere of divine being, so also
into the sphere of divine activities. We have an analogy in the co-
operation of the human soul with the members of the body. The
soul sees, but through the eye; it hears, but through the ear; the soul
thinks, but through the brain. Still we say: the eye sees and the ear
hears. It is a united action of both soul and body. Thus Christ
could die only according to the human nature; however, by reason
of the Personal Union this dying received from the divine nature the
infinite power to cleanse the whole world from sin. St. Augustine
wrote: "The Mediator is not the man without the deity, nor is the
Mediator God without the man. But between the deity alone and
the humanity alone the Mediator is the divine humanity and the
human deity." (*Lehre und Wehre*, 25, p. 315.)

The Reformed theology rejects the third class of Communication
of Attributes, which is consistent with its denial of the second class.
According to its *proton pseudos:* the finite is not capable of the
infinite, Hodge asserts: "Omnipresence and omniscience are not
attributes of which a creature can be made the organ"; and: "The
human nature of Christ is no more omniscient or almighty than the
worker of a miracle is omnipotent." The Reformed theologians thus
separate the human nature of Christ from His miracles. Because
Jesus predicated an omnipotent work of His human nature, saying
(John 6): "My flesh is meat indeed," Zwingli applied his *alloeosis:*
"The divine nature is meat indeed." Again, the Calvinists separate
the divine nature from suffering and dying. However, if the two
natures do not co-operate, then Christ's life and death have no more
value than that of an ordinary saint, and, consequently, there is no
redemption of the world.

As *Prophet,* Jesus did not teach as Isaiah and Paul did, who were
merely mouthpieces of God. Jesus taught in the plenitude of His
own authority and knowledge. "No man hath seen God at any time;
the only-begotten Son, which is in the bosom of the Father, He hath
declared Him" (John 1:18). He taught through the medium of His
human nature, but in a divine-human action. The unique character

of Christ's prophetic ministry consisted in this that in Him God taught on earth, as it is announced: "God, who . . . spake in time past unto the fathers by the Prophets, hath in these last days spoken unto us by His Son" (Heb. 1:1-2).

The divine-human action of the Redeemer must be emphasized in His office as *Priest*. Certainly, He did not suffer and die according to the divine nature. Cyril of Jerusalem expressed it in this way: "The Son of God suffered without suffering (apathos epathen)." However, since the human nature is united with the divine in one person, therefore by the co-operation of the two natures a passion resulted which accomplished the reconciliation of the world with God. Because, in Luther's language: "Although the one part—to speak thus—namely, the deity, does not suffer, yet the person, which is God, suffers in the other part, namely, in His humanity; for in truth God's Son has been crucified for us, that is, the person which is God." (*Triglot,* p. 1029.) What this means for our salvation the Reformer expresses in these words: "We Christians must know that if God is not also in the balance and gives the weight, we sink to the bottom with our scale. By this I mean: If it were not to be said, God has died for us, but only a man, we would be lost. But if 'God's death' and 'God died' lie in the scale of the balance, then He sinks down, and we rise up as a light, empty scale." (*Triglot,* p. 1031.)

Concerning the ministrations of Christ as our *King*, as King of the Church, the Scriptures teach that He fills and rules the universe and protects His Church as the Lord God over all, and also as our human brother. "He that descended is the same also that ascended up far above all heavens, that He might fill all things" (Eph. 4:10). "Lo, I am with you alway, even unto the end of the world" (Matt. 28:20). As King of the Church, which is His body, Christ does not rule over Christendom in absentia (in absence), as earthly kings and sovereigns must do, but as our Brother who is ever present according to His human nature also. (*Triglot,* p. 1044.)

The fact that Calvinistic theologians separate the human nature of Christ from His ministrations as King of the Church leads Krauth to say in his *Conservative Reformation*: "Cold speculation has taken our Lord out of the world He redeemed, and has made heaven, not His throne, but a great sepulcher, with a stone rolled against its portals" (p. 357). Finally, Luther writes: "I have no other God either in heaven or in earth; I know of no God separate from the flesh which lies in the lap of the virgin Mary. God without flesh is of no benefit." (F. Pieper, *Christl. Dogm.*, II, p. 284.)

We close with another quotation from Luther: "The order is to believe, not to see, not to measure, not to grasp. And what Jesus said to unbelieving Thomas applies also here: 'Blessed are they that do not see,' see into, comprehend, know, 'and yet believe'." (John 20:29.) (Mich. Dist., 1886, p. 75.)

III

The Person of the Holy Ghost

T HERE never was a time when Christians did not confess their faith in the Holy Spirit. And there never was a time in which Christians did not speak of the Holy Spirit and His work. Nor was there ever a time when the Christian Church did not occupy herself with the investigation of the mystery of the Person and work of the Holy Spirit, specially since the days of the Reformation, when the work of the Holy Spirit, in the application of the redemption wrought by Christ to the needs of sinful man, gave impetus to an intensification of the study of this part of our faith.

Though clearly taught in Holy Scripture, the exact confessional definition of the doctrine of the Holy Spirit, like that of other teachings of the Bible, came as the result of certain theological controversies which arose in the Church. At first the Church was content to confess her faith in the Holy Trinity, for this was accepted as the distinctive character of Christianity. At the command of our Lord the Apostles went into all the world and preached this Gospel. They faced a pagan, hostile world, whose whole attitude and thinking was diametrically opposed to the doctrine of the Apostles. When they emphasized that there was but one true God and that the risen Jesus Christ is the Savior of a sinful world, they roused the infuriated enmity of all worshipers of heathen idols, the ignorant rabble as well as the learned philosophers. Undaunted, the Apostles continued to emphasize the Christian conception of God over against the vanity of the pagan conception. In the post-Apostolic age numerous Christian writers were occupied with the defense of Christianity and its worship of the Triune God, since Christians were being charged with introducing new gods.

However, as more and more Christian young men during the great expansion of the Church attended prominent schools of the time, such as Athens and Alexandria, through contact with the pagan philosophies of these schools dangerous infiltration of the ranks of the Church occurred. Philosophical speculations entered into the thinking of these men. Soon heretical tendencies appeared which gave rise to the first great controversies within the Church. While the earlier of these controversies concerned themselves largely with the Person of Jesus Christ (Nicene Creed, 325), they also involved the Person of the Holy Spirit. Soon after the Council of Nicaea the doctrine of the Holy Spirit—His personality, His deity, and His work—came under scrutiny and definition. This continued down to the sixth century, culminating in the Niceno-Constantinopolitan Creed of 381 and the Athanasian Creed of unknown origin. The initial cause was Arianism and then Sabellianism, or Unitarianism.

Thereafter, with the disintegration of the old Roman Empire and the rise of the Papacy as a political power, we have the more or less barren period of the Middle Ages whose scholasticism, dominated by the principles of Aristotle, produced little of note. The philosophical speculations of scholasticism were tolerated by the Papacy, which rigidly enforced the acceptance of the established formulas.

This rigid crust which overlaid the thinking of the Church, as the Papacy extended its political power over Europe, was broken, so to speak, by the volcanic eruption of the Reformation in the 16th century. The restoration of the doctrine of the Holy Spirit, His Person and function, is largely the gift of the Reformation, growing out of the great Scriptural principle that a man is saved by faith alone and not by works. The dominant emphasis on the doctrine of justification by faith inevitably had to involve the doctrine of the Holy Spirit, not merely the personality and the deity of the Holy Spirit, but on a much broader scale his work, the application of the merits procured by Christ to sinful, helpless man.

On the basis of Scripture Luther again taught the total depravity and helplessness of man and therefore stressed the work of the Holy Spirit, that of applying to man the treasures of God's grace in Christ. Luther's writings are full of references to the Holy Spirit in all directions; for in expounding the personality, the deity, and the function of the Holy Spirit, Luther had to face in three directions, had to oppose with Scripture weapons the assaults of Romanism, Calvinism, and Socinianism.

In our time, or since the last century, when Higher Criticism cast its baneful shadow and influence over the thinking of the Christian world, a so-called philosophical or scientific theology brought on a return of Sabellianism and Socinianism, which today is known as Unitarianism, both in its gross and fine form. Today the doctrine of the Holy Spirit does not play a large role in modern religious thinking. A "social gospel," with its implications of a this-world tendency as opposed to an other-world tendency, can have little use for the doctrine of the Holy Spirit. However, in view of the infiltration of Unitarianism in Protestantism today, there is need for an emphasis not only on the doctrine of the Trinity as such, but on the doctrine of the Holy Spirit as well.

1. THE PERSONALITY OF THE HOLY SPIRIT

The Scriptures teach that the Holy Spirit is a person.

What is a person? It was Augustine who introduced the term "person" (*persona*), to define the personality of the Holy Spirit. The Eastern Church used the Greek term "hypostasis," having the same significance. We have a simple definition of the term in the Augsburg Confession, Article I: "The term 'person' they [our churches] use as the Fathers have used it, to signify, not a part or quality in another, but that which subsists of itself." A person thus is a self-conscious, self-subsisting being, which speaks, hears, thinks, wills, acts.

Admittedly the word "spirit" is used in a great variety of ways in the Scriptures. A concordance of the Bible under the word "spirit" will give you columns of references where the word is used throughout the Bible. Unquestionably it is frequently used in the sense of an attitude or state of mind, as a tendency, an influence, a power, and the like. The question then arises whether it is possible to determine when the word "spirit" is used in a special sense for a divine personality. Some claim that it is impossible to make any distinction. But there is a rule or axiom which can be applied, namely, the axiom that in Scripture as well as in all literature actions are always predicated of persons, never of abstract ideas. Hence the term "spirit" is always a personal subject whenever it is placed on the same level or co-ordinated with other personal subjects whose personality is unquestioned. Again, whenever in such a relationship of personal subjects the same predicate or similar predicates are used, then accord-

ing to the rules of logic and good grammar we may safely conclude
that we are dealing with a personal subject. According to this fair
rule we can collect a considerable number of passages in the Scriptures where the word "spirit" is used in a personal sense, with verbs
of action which can be applied to a person only.

In the New Testament we are exhorted by the Apostle "not to
grieve the Spirit of God" (Eph. 4:30). Grief is certainly a personal
affection or emotion, of which a quality or attribute or power is not
capable. We are assured that "the Spirit maketh intercession for us
with groanings that cannot be uttered" (Rom. 8:26). We can understand what are interceding persons, but we have no apprehension
of interceding or groaning qualities. The Apostle tells us that "God
hath revealed them to us by His Spirit, for the Spirit searcheth all
things, yea, the deep things of God" (I Cor. 2:10). He tells us
further that "the things of God knoweth no man, but the Spirit of
God" (I Cor. 2:11, 13). This cannot be the description of a power
of God, for personal predicates are used. Speaking of the diversity
of spiritual gifts in the Church, the Apostle states that "all these
worketh that one and the selfsame Spirit, dividing to every man
severally as He will" (I Cor. 12:4-11). Here discretion is exercised
in the distribution of spiritual gifts, and discretion is the determination of the will of a person. Besides, the gifts themselves are clearly
distinguished from the Spirit, who is the Author and the Giver of
these spiritual gifts. In verse three of that same chapter the Spirit
is distinguished from Jesus Christ. "No man speaking by the Spirit
of God calleth Jesus accursed."

The Spirit speaks to the sons of men in the nature and after the
manner of a person. "For the Spirit said unto Peter, Behold, three
men seek thee. Arise, therefore, and get thee down and go with
them, doubting nothing, for I have sent them" (Acts 10:19). Again,
"Then the Spirit said unto Philip, Go near and join thyself to this
chariot. . . . And when they were come up out of the water, the
Spirit of the Lord caught away Philip, that the eunuch saw him no
more" (Acts 8:29-39). Again, "The Spirit said, Separate Me Barnabas
and Saul for the work whereunto I have called them" (Acts 13:2, 4).
It is reported that "when they [Paul and his associates] had gone
throughout Phrygia and the region of Galatia and were forbidden
by the Holy Spirit to preach the Word in Asia . . . they assayed to

go into Bithynia, but the Spirit suffered them not" (Acts 16:6-7). When St. Paul landed in Italy, he met with a number of Jews and expounded to them the Gospel of Christ. But the Jews were reluctant to believe what he said. "They departed, after that Paul had spoken one word, Well spake the Holy Spirit by Isaiah the Prophet unto our fathers" (Acts 28:25; 20:28). In all these Scripture passages the Holy Spirit, the Spirit of God, the Spirit of the Lord, appears as a personal being.

Christ speaks of the Holy Spirit. He makes such statements as these respecting the Holy Spirit. "The Comforter, which is the Holy Ghost, whom the Father will send in My name, He shall teach you all things." "He shall testify of Me, and ye also shall bear witness." "If I go not away, the Comforter will not come unto you; but if I depart, I will send Him unto you. And when He is come, He will reprove the world." "He will guide you into all truth; for He shall not speak of Himself [that is, not in His own right], but whatsoever He shall hear, that shall He speak, and He will show you things to come. He shall glorify Me, for He shall receive of Mine and shall show it unto you." (John 14:26; 15:26-27; 16:7-8, 13, 14.) In these words of our Lord we have the description of a person—a person hearing, a person receiving, a person testifying, a person speaking, a person reproving, a person teaching.

In the Old Testament the term "spirit" is also used for a person. Here we, first of all, have Jesus Himself as Interpreter. He proved to the Pharisees, for instance, that in Psalm 110 the Messiah is not only David's Son, but also David's Lord, that is, God. In that same connection Jesus speaks of the Spirit as a person. He states that David by the Spirit calls the Messiah his Lord (Matt. 22:42-45). Jesus here, however, merely repeats what David himself said: "The Spirit of the Lord spake by me, and His word was in my tongue" (II Sam. 23:2).

In the Prophet Isaiah's writings there are noteworthy passages which indicate that the Spirit of the Lord is a person. Such a passage is Is. 63:8-10: "For He [Jehovah] said, Surely they are My people, children that will not lie. So He was their Savior. In all their affliction He was afflicted, and the Angel of His Presence [the uncreated Angel, the Son of God, in the Hebrew original] saved them. In His love and in His pity He redeemed them. And He bare them and carried them all the days of old. But they rebelled and vexed His

Holy Spirit." In this passage there are three persons—Jehovah, the Messiah [the Angel of His Presence], and the Holy Spirit. Another passage: "Hearken unto Me, O Jacob and Israel, My called: I am He, I am the First; I also am the Last. Mine hand also hath laid the foundations of the earth, and My right hand hath spanned the heavens; when I call them, they stand up together. . . . Come ye near unto Me, hear ye this: I have not spoken in secret from the beginning, from the time that it was, there am I. And now the Lord God, and His Spirit, hath sent Me" Is. 48:12-13, 16). In this passage the Speaker is God, the Creator of the world, the First and the Last, the only true God. But God, the Speaker, also speaks of God, saying, "And now the Lord God, and His Spirit, hath sent Me." Here again there are three persons, one of them the Holy Spirit.

In Psalm 33:6 we read: "By the Word of the Lord were the heavens made and all the host of them by the breath of His Mouth." Here we have a reference to the Spirit of God at creation, moving on the face of the waters (Gen. 1:2). In the original Hebrew in that Psalm the phrase "breath of His mouth" is "Spirit of His mouth." Job speaks of the Spirit as the Creator of man: "The Spirit of God hath made me, and the breath of the Almighty hath given me life" (Job. 33:4). Noting that in the Hebrew the thought of the first clause is repeated in the second, the phrase "the breath of the Almighty" is the same as the expression "the Spirit of God." In general we may say that when the Old Testament says that the Spirit of God was present at creation (Gen. 1:2), that the Spirit passed judgment on the wickedness of man, that His patience was limited (Gen. 6:3), that He spoke through David (II Sam. 23:2), was vexed, provoked, grieved by the rebellion of Israel (Is. 63:10; Acts 7:51), the actions and emotions are those of a person.

So both from the Old Testament and the New Testament we have gathered a sufficient number of passages which clearly indicate that the word "spirit" is frequently used in a special sense to signify a distinct personality who is known as the Holy Spirit, the Spirit, the Spirit of the Lord, the Spirit of God. And we have the authority of Christ Himself for this interpretation. In the Greek the name used is *pneuma to hagion;* in the Hebrew it is *ruach Jehovah.*

From the very early days of the Church the distinct personality of the Holy Spirit has been denied. The first positive denial seems to have been made by Arius in the fourth century. Although he contended that Christ was not equal to God, but a man, and the controversy then revolved chiefly around the person of Jesus Christ, Arius also, although cautiously, claimed that the Holy Spirit was only the first of beings brought into existence by Christ as the creating agent of God. But when the doctrine of the person of Christ was defined in the Nicene Creed of 325, the subject of the Holy Spirit gradually came to the fore. Sabellius contended that the Holy Spirit meant simply the operation of the divine mind, an attribute of the divine activity. According to his view the eternal divine unity appeared in three modes or phases of development. The Father, the Son, and the Holy Spirit are not three persons, but merely phases of various appearances or manifestations of the one God. The one God reveals Himself as the Father in creating the world; as the Son in the redemption; as the Holy Ghost in the application of salvation. This error was known as modalistic monarchianism. Another form of monarchianism was taught by Paul of Samosata (deposed 272), who held that the Holy Spirit was not a person, but merely a power or influence of God (dynamistic monarchianism). This is really the beginning of the philosophical treatment of the doctrine of God, in accord with the philosophy of the time. However, although these ideas were condemned by church councils, they were revived time and again during the centuries.

In the sixteenth century occurred that revival of Sabellianism, known as Socinianism, so named for Faustus Socinus, a Pole, who had quite a following in southeastern Europe. He is really the progenitor of full-blown Unitarianism, which insists that the Holy Spirit is not a person, but an exerted energy of God, a personification of the influence or power of God. The Jews, the Mormons, the Universalists, the Anabaptists, and some other sects, are all anti-Trinitarian. They all take the view that there are no persons in God at all; consequently the Holy Spirit cannot be a person.

For the sake of demonstrating the futility of their argument let us apply their views to some of the Scripture passages. One may say from the outset that if the Holy Spirit is not allowed to be a person, then the majority of these Scripture passages become unintelligible. By making the Holy Spirit to be a personification of some attribute of God, an energy or power of God, they reduce these passages to meaninglessness.

"God anointed Jesus of Nazareth with the Holy Ghost and with power." According to Socinianism this means that God anointed Jesus with the power of God and with power. St. Paul uses the phrase "in demonstration of the Spirit and of power." This Socinians suppose to mean a demonstration of the power of God with power. Again, St. Paul prays "that ye may abound in hope through the power of the Holy Spirit." This, they say, means to abound in hope through the power of the power of God.

Manifestly that is no longer interpreting the words of St. Paul, *i. e.,* giving the meaning of the text. That is reading into the words one's own opinion and preferring to attribute to St. Paul an absurdity rather than to accept the personality of the Holy Spirit so clearly expressed here.

An offshoot of Socinianism is modern Unitarianism, which during the last hundred years has rapidly spread in America. Its tenets are finding fertile soil in many of the Reformed church bodies, and there are, no doubt, many more Unitarians outside of the Unitarian Church than within. Unitarianism denies the doctrine of the Trinity and rejects not only the deity, but the personality of the Holy Spirit. William E. Channing, d. 1842, whose works are still being distributed by the American Unitarian Association, in his "Discourse on Unitarian Christianity," defines the Holy Spirit as "a moral, illuminating, and persuasive influence, not physical, not compulsory, not involving a necessity of virtue" (*Works,* p. 380).

Another proof for the personality of the Holy Spirit is the ascription to Him of works such as only a person can perform. The Old Testament states that the Spirit of God was present at creation, moving on the face of the waters (Gen. 1:2). Here the work of creation is ascribed to the Holy Spirit. That the work of creation is said to have been effected by all three persons in the Godhead, although acting in different aspects, so that each person is the Creator, can be explained by the unity of the divine essence. But if the Holy Spirit is merely an influence or the personification of the power of God, then He is not the Creator, because He is then not a person.

As the three persons were active in the work of creation, so there is a co-ordination of divine persons in the work of conservation. "These wait all upon Thee that Thou mayest give them their meat in due season. . . . . Thou hidest Thy face, they are troubled; Thou takest away their breath, they die and return to dust. Thou sendest forth Thy Spirit, they are created; and Thou renewest the face of the earth" (Ps. 104:27-30). This surely does not mean that the Spirit by which all things are preserved and kept alive is the wind! And if the Spirit of God is called an attribute, such as wisdom or power, where do we find that such attributes are being sent, sent forth from God, or sent to renew the face of the earth?

Another co-ordination of persons is to be found in the inspiration of the Prophets, as stated in the New Testament. "God spake in time past unto the fathers by the Prophets" (Heb. 1:1). "Holy men of God spake as they were moved by the Holy Ghost" (II Pet. 1:21). "The Spirit of Christ, which was in them (the Prophets)" (I Pet. 1:11). On the basis of these three passages we defy those who deny the personality of the Holy Spirit to make Him an influence or attribute of God or to reduce Him to a figure of speech. God in the first passage is unquestionably God the Father. The holy men of God are unquestionably the Prophets. These, then, would be moved by the influence of the Father. But according to the third passage this influence, which is the source of inspiration, was the influence of Christ. By the Unitarian interpretation these passages are made to contradict one another. Correct interpretation avoids any contradiction. Allow each agent here to stand for a person, and there is no difficulty in designating the Spirit, on the one hand, as the Spirit of the Father and, on the other hand, as the Spirit of Christ. Make the Spirit merely the personification of the influence of God, then that influence cannot be the influence of two persons or agents, of which one is a God and the other, according to Unitarian interpretation, a creature. Here, as elsewhere, they resort to a subterfuge by making the term "Spirit of Christ" to mean the spirit that prophesied of Christ. This is gratuitous and needs no refutation.

The Holy Spirit can be the object of blasphemy. Jesus said: "The blasphemy against the Holy Ghost shall not be forgiven unto men" (Matt. 12:31). The blasphemy consisted in ascribing the deeds of Christ to Satan's power. That the Holy Spirit is capable of being blasphemed proves that He is a person, otherwise he could not be blasphemed.

We may add here the co-ordination of persons in the great commission of Christ and in the Apostolic benediction (Matt. 28:19; II Cor. 13:14; see also Rev. 1:4-6; 22:1).

The Scriptures teach that the Holy Spirit is a distinct personality, distinguished from the Father and the Son.

The Holy Spirit is not the Father. The Scriptures teach that He "proceeds from the Father" (John 15:26). Again, the Scriptures teach: "But the Comforter, which is the Holy Ghost, whom the Father will send in My name" (John 14:26). He who proceeds from the Father is not the Father Himself, because a person cannot proceed from himself. He who is sent by the Father is not the Father, because a person is not sent by himself. The Holy Spirit is therefore not the Father.

The Holy Spirit is not the Son. The Scriptures teach: "But when the Comforter is come, whom I will send unto you from the Father" (John 15:26). "If I go not away, the Comforter will not come unto you. But if I depart, I will send Him unto you" (John 16:7). He who is sent by the Son cannot be the Son Himself. Therefore the Holy Spirit is not the Son.

The Scriptures teach: "Howbeit, when the Spirit of truth is come. . . . He shall glorify Me, for He shall receive of Mine" (John 16:13-14). He who receives that which is the Son's and by receiving it glorifies the Son cannot be the Son, for no person can be said to receive from Himself that which is his own and to glorify himself in so receiving. Therefore the Holy Spirit is not the Son.

The Scriptures teach that the coming of the Holy Spirit was dependent on the departure of the Son. "If I go not away, the Comforter will not come unto you" (John 16:7). He whose coming is dependent on the departure of the Son cannot be the Son.

The Holy Spirit, then, is neither the Father nor the Son, because the Scriptures represent Him as distinguished from the Father and the Son. This is also plainly exhibited in the Baptism of Jesus. There the Holy Spirit descended as a dove and lighted on Jesus, while the voice from heaven spoke approval of Jesus as the Son of God (Matt. 3:16). The distinction of persons is very clear.

The Apostle states: "God sent forth His Son . . . that we might receive the adoption of sons"; and "because ye are sons, God hath sent forth the Spirit of His Son into your hearts, crying, Abba, Father" (Gal. 4:4-6). Once more He writes that "through Him [the Son] we have access by one Spirit unto the Father" (Eph. 2:18). It is plain that the Holy Spirit by whom we come to the Father is not the Father to whom, nor the Son through whom, we have the privilege of access. Other passages: John 14:26; 15:26; Matt. 28:19.

We therefore conclude that the Holy Spirit in the Scriptures is a personality, distinct from the Father and the Son. We maintain this in opposition to every form of Socinianism and Unitarianism, which pretends to merge the identity of the Holy Spirit in the Father or the Son.

2. THE DEITY OF THE HOLY SPIRIT

That Socinians have always made a determined effort to prove by every sophistry at their command that the Holy Spirit is not a person, is natural. For if it is conceded that the Holy Spirit, who is named side by side with the Father and the Son, is a person, then it is natural to believe that like the Father and the Son also the Holy Spirit is God. And the Scriptures clearly teach that He is God.

a. In the Scriptures He is expressly called God. In the incident of Ananias and Sapphira Peter says: "Ananias, why hath Satan filled thine heart to lie to the Holy Ghost? . . . Why hast thou conceived this thing in thine heart? Thou hast not lied unto men, but unto God." (Acts 5:3-4). Here it is plainly stated that to lie to the Holy Spirit is to lie, not to men, but to God. The Holy Spirit is not an angel nor a man nor any creature nor a personification of a quality of God, but God Himself.

Socinians seek to argue this away by saying that Ananias here was accused of counterfeiting the Holy Spirit. But that cannot be the sense of the term "lied" (v. 4). For Sapphira was guilty of the same sin that Ananias had committed. Peter said to her: "How is it that ye have agreed together to tempt the Spirit of the Lord?" (Acts 5:9.) To tempt the Spirit of the Lord and to counterfeit Him are two separate things. In this case tempting the Holy Spirit is nothing but lying to Him. Wherein did this tempting consist? It consisted in the hypocrisy of Ananias and Sapphira, and hypocrisy is a lie. It is most certain that both lied, and it is just as plain that they lied to the Holy Spirit. And when they lied to the Holy Spirit, says the Apostle, they lied to the eternal, living God.

In the Old Testament the Holy Spirit is called God. "The sweet Psalmist of Israel (David) said, "The Spirit of the Lord spake by me, and His Word was in my tongue. The God of Israel said, the Rock of Israel spake to me" (II Sam. 23:1-2). Here the Spirit of the Lord, who spoke by David is called the God of Israel, the Rock of Israel, terms which are properly used only of the eternal God,

Jehovah. We may add here that the name Jehovah in the Old Testament is the special and distinctive name given to the divine majesty. This name denotes the immutable and indivisible divine essence, the absolute Being, the personality of the eternal, holy One. God Himself interpreted this name as "I am that I am" (Ex. 3:14). To the Jews this name was always inexpressibly holy. The other name that is used for God in the Old Testament is *Elohim* in the Hebrew. This name is not always used in that distinctive sense for the true God as is the name Jehovah. For example, it is also applied to magistrates (Ps. 82:6) because of the august function which they perform in administering justice. *Elohim* is also used to designate idols. Moses prophesied that if Israel was not faithful to the true God, as punishment the people would be dispersed among the nations and serve gods (Elohim) (Deut. 4:28). The name Jehovah, however, is always applied to God in the special sense to designate the majesty of Him whom we worship above all things. So David speaks of the Spirit of the Lord, that is, the Spirit of Jehovah (cf. I Pet. 1:12).

Take another example in which the Holy Spirit is regarded as God by the Scriptures. The Apostle writes: "Know ye not that ye are the temple of God and that the Spirit of God dwelleth in you?" I Cor. 3:16). He repeats that same thought: "Know ye not that your body is the temple of the Holy Ghost, which is in you, which ye have of God, and ye are not your own?" (I Cor. 6:19.) The only person who can make a place holy is God. Where He dwells, there is His holy habitation, His temple. The habitation by a creature or a created person does not make a place holy or a temple. Believers are the dwelling place of the Holy Spirit, the temple of God. This can be taken in no other sense than that the Holy Spirit is God.

Speaking of spiritual gifts, such as are only within the power of God to bestow, the Apostle writes: "Now there are diversities of gifts, but the same Spirit" (I Cor. 12:4). Throughout this entire passage there is an interchange of terms, Spirit, Lord, God, the selfsame Spirit. There is here no distinction made by the Apostle between the Holy Spirit and God. To him they are the same Lord, the Giver of all good and perfect gifts.

In Ps. 95:6-9 we read: "Oh, come, let us worship and bow down; let us kneel before the Lord, our Maker. For He is our God, and we are the people of His pasture and the sheep of His hand. Today if ye will hear His voice, harden not your heart, as in the provocation and as in the day of temptation in the wilderness, when your fathers tempted Me, proved Me, and saw My work." This passage is quoted in the New Testament as follows: "Wherefore as the Holy Spirit saith, Today if ye will hear His voice, harden not your hearts, as in the provocation, in the day of temptation in the wilderness, when your fathers tempted Me, proved Me, and saw My works forty years" (Heb. 3:7-9). Here the Lord, our Maker, is interpreted to be the Holy Spirit, who spoke. He is God.

We have a parallel case in Isaiah 6:9. The voice of the Lord said to Isaiah, "Go, and tell this people, Hear ye, indeed, but understand not; and see ye indeed, but perceive not." St. Paul quoted these words when he met with those Jews on his arrival in Italy. He says: "Well spake the Holy Ghost by Esaias, the Prophet, unto our fathers, saying, Go unto this people, and say, Hearing ye shall hear and shall not understand; and seeing ye shall see and not perceive" (Acts 28:25-26). To the Apostle the Holy Spirit was the Lord God, Jehovah, the Lord sitting upon a throne, high and lifted up. He identified the Holy Spirit with the Lord of Hosts.

b. The Scriptures not only call the Holy Spirit God, but they also ascribe to Him such attributes as properly belong to God only.

"Whither shall I go from Thy Spirit, or whither shall I flee from Thy presence?" (Ps. 139:7-10.) In this passage the divine attributes of infinity and omnipresence are ascribed to the Holy Spirit.

"Now there are diversities of gifts, but the same Spirit. And there are differences of administrations, but the same Lord. And there are diversities of operations, but it is the same God, which worketh all in all" (I. Cor. 12:4-11). In this entire passage the divine attribute of almighty power is ascribed to the Holy Spirit, for none but God possesses the power to bestow these spiritual gifts.

"But God hath revealed them [the things prepared for believers] unto us by His Spirit, for the Spirit searcheth all things, yea, the deep things of God. For what man knoweth the things of a man, save the spirit of man which is in him? Even so the things of God knoweth no man, but the Spirit of God" (I Cor. 2:10-11). In this passage the divine attribute of omniscience is ascribed to the Holy Spirit, knowing even the deep mysteries of God's being. Such wisdom and knowledge is not within the possession of a creature. See also Is. 40:13.

"But when the Comforter is come, whom I will send unto you

from the Father, even the Spirit of Truth." "And I will pray the Father, and He shall send you another Comforter that He may abide with you forever, even the Spirit of Truth" (John 15:26; 14:16-17). The Holy Spirit is the Truth, even as God is the Truth. See also Psalm 33:4; 143:10 (cf. Matt. 19:17).

c. The Scriptures ascribe to the Holy Spirit such works as properly belong to God only.

He is described as the Creator. "And the Spirit of God moved upon the face of the waters" (Gen. 1:2). He is the Giver of life: "The Spirit of God hath made me, and the breath of the Almighty hath given me life" (Job 33:4). "By the Word of the Lord were the heavens made and all the host of them by the breath of His mouth" (Ps. 33:6). In Him all creatures live and move and have their being. "Thou sendest forth Thy Spirit, they are created; Thou renewest the face of the earth." Ps. 104:30. To the Holy Spirit is ascribed the work of regenerating man. "Verily, verily, I say unto thee, Except a man be born of water and of the Spirit, he cannot enter into the Kingdom of God" (John 3:5-6, 8). He is the Dispenser of spiritual gifts in the Church (I Cor. 12:4-11). The incarnation of the Son of God is ascribed to His operation (Luke 1:35). The Holy Spirit was with Jesus in the exercise of divine power. "How God anointed Jesus of Nazareth with the Holy Ghost and with power" (Acts 10:38). Jesus says: "But if I with the finger of God cast out devils, no doubt the Kingdom of God is come upon you" (Luke 11:20). Since Jesus uses the expression "finger of God," we may attribute the writing of the Law to the Holy Spirit, for it is said that God gave to Moses "two tables of testimony, tables of stone, written with the finger of God" (Ex. 31:18).

d. Finally, the Scriptures accord to the Holy Spirit such honor as properly belongs to God only.

In Christ's great commission the Holy Spirit shares equal honor and worship with the Father and the Son. In being baptized in the name of Father, Son, and Holy Spirit, we dedicate ourselves to the worship of this distinctly Christian God and none other. In the Apostolic benediction the Holy Spirit is invoked equally with the Father and the Son. This is a prayer, a form of worship. All the angels worship Him: "Holy, holy, holy, is the Lord of hosts. The whole earth is full of His glory" (Is. 6:3). Whenever we call upon God the Father, as we do in the Lord's Prayer, we at the same time

call upon God and the Son of God the Holy Spirit. God is our Father only through the vicarious atonement of Jesus Christ, and we know God the Father and the Son only through the revelation and illumination of the Holy Spirit. Whoever worships the Son, worships the Father, who sent Him (John 5:23). And at the same time he worships the Holy Spirit, who glorifies the Son in the heart of the worshiper of the true God (John 16:14). Whoever worships the Holy Spirit at the same time worships the Father and the Son, for the Holy Spirit is the Spirit of the Father (Matt. 10:20), as well as the Spirit of Christ or the Spirit of the Son (Gal. 4:6). When Christians, therefore, pray the Lord's Prayer, they worship the Triune God.

3. THE PROCESSION

As the Son stands in a peculiar relationship to the Father in that He is begotten of the Father (John 1:14), so also there is a peculiar relationship of the Holy Spirit to the Father and the Son, according to the Scriptures.

As we have seen, the Holy Spirit is a distinct personality, and He is God. Jesus, however, says: "It is not ye that speak, but the Spirit of your Father, who speaks in you" (Matt. 10:20). The Apostle writes: "The things of God knoweth no man, but the Spirit of God." (I Cor. 2:11-12.) He is called the Spirit of the Father and the Spirit of God.

But He is also called the Spirit of Christ, the Spirit of the Son. "Because ye are sons," writes the Apostle, "God hath sent forth the Spirit of His Son into your hearts" (Gal. 4:6). Again, "Now, if any man have not the Spirit of Christ, he is none of His" (Rom. 8:9). Writes Peter: "The Spirit of Christ, which was in them [the Prophets]" (I Peter 1:11). St. Paul makes the statement: "I know that this shall turn to my salvation through your prayer and the supply of the Spirit of Jesus Christ" (Phil. 1:19).

The explanation for these expressions respecting the Holy Spirit is to be found in the special and peculiar relationship of the Holy Spirit to the Father and the Son. This Scripture describes as a procession or spiration. The procession is stated by Jesus: "When the Comforter is come, whom I will send unto you from the Father, even the Spirit of Truth, which proceedeth from the Father, He shall testify of Me" (John 15:26). "It is expedient for you that I go away; for if I go not away, the Comforter will not come unto you;

but if I depart, I will send Him unto you" (John 16:7). "Because ye
are sons, God hath sent forth the Spirit of his Son into your hearts"
(Gal. 4:6). The spiration is reported thus: "He [Jesus] breathed on
them [His disciples] and saith unto them, Receive ye the Holy
Ghost" (John 20:22). This procession is a divine act within the
divine essence, or being, of the majesty of God, and very clearly
distinguishes the three persons in the one indivisible essence. The
Quicunque, or Athanasian Creed, expresses it thus: "The Father is
made of none, neither created, nor begotten. The Son is of the
Father alone, not made, not created, but begotten. The Holy Spirit
is of the Father and the Son, neither made, nor created, nor begotten,
but proceeding." This procession, however, must not be conceived
as a physical process; just as the eternal generation of the Son by
the Father is not a physical process. It is an ineffable, unexplainable
process which occurs within the majesty of God Himself, of which
the Scriptures tell us no further details.

The construction of the clauses in Jesus' statement in John 15:26
is worthy of particular attention. Jesus first says of the Comforter:
"whom I shall send unto you." The verb in this clause is in the
future tense. The reference is to a temporal act, one which will occur
on His departure (John 16:7). In the third clause Jesus also makes
a reference to the future: "He shall testify of Me." Here the verb
again is in the future tense, referring to an act that will occur when
the Holy Spirit is come after His departure. But between these two
clauses, both in the future tense, Jesus says, "the Spirit of Truth, who
proceeds from the Father." Here we have a definite change in the
form of speech. The verb is in the present tense; evidently inten-
tionally. The procession from the Father is therefore not an act
which occurs in time, but is an eternal act, ceaselessly going on,
ever-continuing, in a manner which will ever remain a mystery to
the human mind.

There are two matters that must be referred to in this connection.
The one is the attitude of the Eastern Church. The Greek Church
has insisted during the centuries that the Holy Spirit proceeds only
from the Father. Originally the Nicene Creed of 325 contained the
simple statement that the Holy Spirit proceeds from the Father.
Later Augustine called attention to the fact that the Scriptures
teach the procession of the Holy Spirit from the Son as well. Reference was made to such passages as, "But the Comforter, which is

the Holy Ghost, whom the Father will send in My name" (John 14:26); or, "God hath sent forth the Spirit of His Son into your hearts" (Gal. 4:6). "But when the Comforter is come, whom I will send unto you" (John 15:26). "I will send Him unto you" (John 16:7). Later the Western Church, in opposition to Arianism and semi-Arianism, which was spreading in Europe, in the "Filioque" Creed, adopted at Toledo, Spain, in 589, amended the statement of the earlier Nicene and Niceno-Constantinopolitan Creed to read, "who proceeds from the Father and the Son." This brought on the so-called "Filioque" ("and from the Son") controversy between the Eastern and the Western Church, the former charging the latter with unauthorized addition to the Creed, because the Eastern Church was not represented at the Council of Toledo. This caused the schism which still remains.

The other matter to be mentioned in this connection refers to philosophical speculations which have occupied theologians of the last and this century. Here one cannot avoid touching upon the doctrine of the Trinity, because that is involved.

When the Scriptures teach that the Holy Spirit is God, this cannot mean that He is a third of God or a third God or a third nature in God. The divine essence is one and indivisible. There are neither three Gods nor three natures in God. Referring to the sacrifice of idols, the Apostle states that the idol is nothing. "There is none other God but One" (I Cor. 8:4). This truth is emphasized throughout the Bible.

However, the Scriptures also teach that there are three distinct persons in God and all three are God. Each person possesses the eternal divine essence without division or multiplication. The Holy Spirit is therefore not a third of the divine essence. He is God in the totality of the divine substance. Just as the Scriptures teach that in Christ "dwelleth all the fullness of the Godhead bodily" (Col. 2:9), so they also teach that the Holy Spirit is very God of very God.

Just as there can be no division or multiplication, so there can be no gradation in the divine essence. Each person is the One, indivisible, very God. There is no subordination of one person to the other, since the Scriptures ascribe to the individual persons divine attributes, works, and honors. All three persons possess simultaneously the whole divine essence and all the attributes, works, and honors. They belong to them equally. The Scriptures never divide or dis tribute the attributes of omnipotence, omniscience, and omnipresence in such a manner as to give a third to the Father and a third to the Son and a third to the Holy Spirit. On the contrary, the Scriptures ascribe all divine attributes indiscriminately, without any limitation or modification, to the Holy Spirit as well as to the Father and to the Son (Ps. 33:6; I Cor. 2:10; Ps. 139:7). The same is true of the divine works and honors.

It is argued that the fact that the Son is of the Father and the Holy Spirit is of the Father and the Son, indicates that the Son is lower or lesser than the Father, and the Holy Spirit, in turn, is lower and lesser than the Father and the Son. But as God has revealed Himself in the Scriptures, it is erroneous to say that the Holy Spirit is subordinate to the Father and the Son because He proceeds from the other two persons. This is a philosophical notion which reason has read into the act of procession, but of which human reason has no knowledge or experience at all. We must bear in mind that each of the three persons in the Trinity is equally God, possessed of the divine essence totally and without measure and simultaneously. To speak of a subordination of the Holy Spirit to the Father and the Son is, in the last analysis, equivalent to the abandonment of the Scriptural concept of God as One.

Neither can it be said that the Holy Spirit is more recent than the Father and the Son. In this case the element of time is carried over into eternity. In doing that we deny the eternity of God, which repudiates any idea of time. This is even contrary to the natural knowledge of God, for St. Paul states that the eternal power and Godhead may be clearly seen in the works of nature (Rom. 1:19).

We use such expressions as the first, the second, and the third person. This is Scriptural; for the Father is of none, the Son is of the Father, and the Holy Spirit proceeds of the Father and the Son. But when we speak of the third person in the Godhead, we are merely using the order of natural enumeration, not implying any kind of subordination either in dignity or rank. The Father and the Son did not exist before the Holy Spirit, for then the Holy Spirit would not be the eternal God. There can be no subordination in any sense, for inevitably this leads to polytheism. This so-called subordination theory is really a revival of Sabellianism and stems from philosophical speculation, not from the Scriptures.

This, then, is the doctrine of the Holy Ghost which the Lutheran

Church on the basis of Holy Scriptures has always believed and confessed. The Holy Ghost is the third person in the one undivided Trinity; eternally proceeding from the Father and the Son; true God with them, of equal majesty and glory; like them eternal, omnipotent, omnipresent, omniscient, holy, just, merciful, gracious; together with the Father and the Son the Holy, Holy, Holy, the Lord of Hosts. As such He can perform the work that He, according to the counsel of God, is to do—the sanctification of sinful mankind by bringing sinners to faith in their Savior, by preserving and strengthening them in this faith, by enabling them to prove their faith by good works, and finally by gathering them into the heavenly garners. Since our sanctification and all it includes is the work of the Holy Ghost, it is no less a work of God than the creative work of the Father and the redemptive work of the Son. As sure as we can be of man's creation as human beings because of the almighty fiat of the Father, as sure as we can be of our redemption because the Son of God died for us, because Jehovah is our Righteousness, so sure can we who in true faith call Jesus our Lord and Savior be of our sanctification, for no one calls Jesus Christ the Lord but by the Holy Ghost; and so sure can we be that He will keep us until the end, for He, the Holy Ghost, that has begun in us that good work is God and therefore is able and willing to perform it until the Day of Jesus Christ. To Him, our Comforter, together with the Father and the Son, be honor and glory forever and ever. Amen.

The Clearness and Sufficiency of Scripture

THE CLEARNESS OF SCRIPTURE

I

SCRIPTURE is God's revelation to man, who has the ability to understand the thoughts of others when expressed in intelligible words of human speech. Therefore God both in the Old and in the New Testament has caused His revelation to be recorded not in a language which no man could understand, but in a human language which those to whom this revelation was primarily given could readily understand and which to this day may be understood by anyone who takes the time and trouble to study these languages. "The Law speaks in the tongue of the sons of men," says an ancient rabbinical maxim.

II

In order that all men, young and old, learned and unlearned, may be able to understand His revelation, God has not spoken in terms unintelligible to a vast majority of people. He did not use scientific parlance, difficult or even impossible to understand for the average man. In plain, simple, lucid language the all-wise God speaks to the children of men. "Clearness, distinctness, perspicuity, is one of the prominent features of the Book of Books. Intended to make wise the simple as well as the intellectual giants, it employs plain, simple, familiar language. The Author of this Book, who is by far the greatest Master of a clear style, said to Israel, 'This commandment which I command thee this day, it is not hidden from thee, neither is it far off. It is not in heaven, that thou shouldest say, Who shall go up

58

for us to heaven and bring it unto us that we may hear it and do it? Neither is it beyond the sea, that thou shouldest say, Who shall go over the sea for us and bring it unto us that we may hear it and do it? But the word is very nigh unto thee, in thy mouth and in thy heart, that thou mayest do it'" (Deut. 30:11-14). (C. F. Drewes, *Theological Quarterly*, Vol. XII, p. 97.)

Because of its simplicity the language of the Bible can be translated into plain and simple words of any human language and thus become available to all that dwell on earth, to every nation, and kindred, and tongue, and people.

III

Originally the Scriptures of the Old Testament were written in Hebrew (and Aramaic), the New Testament in Greek. In the interpretation of Scriptures, Hebrew and Greek grammar and syntax must be and remain the decisive factors. Therefore the knowledge of these two languages is an indispensable necessity for correct understanding and interpretation. "As intensely as we love the Gospel," says Luther, "so intensely let us study the languages."

This does not mean that in order to understand God's message correctly, everyone must acquire a reading knowledge of Greek and Hebrew. The translations made by reliable men are sufficient to acquaint men with the contents of God's revelation and make them wise unto salvation. Even from a Roman Catholic version the way to eternal life may be found if one accepts the plain words of the text and is not mislead by the added comments changing the Bible truth to Romanistic error.

Yet wherever a dissension arises as to the exact meaning of a Scripture passage, only the original text can decide the question. The text as it was originally written by the holy men of God by inspiration of the Holy Ghost is the highest court of appeal, whose word is final.

IV

Speaking of the clarity of Scripture, we mean, above all, to say that, as God's revelation to man, it clearly sets forth all that a person must know to have everlasting life. The two chief doctrines of Scripture are sin and grace. Sin man knows by his own experience, from the Natural Law still written in his heart, and from the voice of conscience warning him against what it regards as wrong and rebuking him when he has done wrong. Yet no man by nature knows the true character of sin, its insidious power, the total depravity of man's heart, the damnability of every sin in thought, word, and deed. Of grace, the grace of God in Jesus Christ, man knows absolutely nothing by nature. That remains a mystery to natural man, and even if he hears of it, it remains to the unregenerate, folly and foolishness (I Cor. 1:23; 2:14). Yet in God's revelation in the Bible He clearly, in language unmistakable, presents to us a true picture of sin as it appears to the eyes of the Holy One. He does this in His holy Law. And in His Gospel, the tidings of great joy, He presents in equally clear language His plan of eternal salvation, that He so loved the world that He gave His only-begotten Son, that whosoever believeth in Him should not perish, but have everlasting life (John 3:16). His whole counsel regarding our salvation from its first conception in eternity to its fulfillment in Bethlehem and on Calvary, in Joseph's Garden, and on the Mount of Olives, and in its final consummation in eternal life is revealed to us in Holy Scriptures in so detailed a manner and in such clear language that nothing essential to obtain everlasting salvation is omitted or remains unintelligible to us. Therefore Jesus tells the Jews: "Search the Scriptures, for in them ye think ye have eternal life; and they are they which testify of Me" (John 5:39); and Paul could give to the elders of Ephesus that wonderful assurance: "Wherefore I take you to record this day, that I am pure from the blood of all men. For I have not shunned to declare unto you all the counsel of God." And again: "And now, brethren, I commend you to God, and to the word of his grace, which is able to build you up and to give you an inheritance among all them which are sanctified" (Acts 20:26, 27, 32).

Yes indeed, "We have also a more sure word of prophecy, whereunto ye do well that ye take heed, as unto a light that shineth in a dark place, until the day dawn, and the Day Star arise in your hearts" (II Pet. 1:19). Holy Scripture can make even a child wise unto salvation through faith which is in Christ Jesus (II Tim. 3:15). And throughout the life of the Christian "All scripture is given by inspiration of God and is profitable for doctrine, for reproof, for correction, for instruction in righteousness; that the man of God may be perfect, throughly furnished unto all good works" (II Tim. 3:16, 17).

V

When we speak of the clearness of Scriptures, we do not mean to say that our intellect can fully understand, our reason can fully fathom, all doctrines revealed to us in the Bible. St. Paul very definitely states that such intellectual comprehension is impossible. "We speak the wisdom of God in a mystery, even the hidden wisdom, which God ordained before the world unto our glory; which none of the princes of this world knew; for had they known it, they would not have crucified the Lord of glory. But as it is written, Eye hath not seen, nor ear heard, neither have entered into the heart of man, the things which God hath prepared for them that love him. But God hath revealed them unto us by his Spirit; for the Spirit searcheth all things, yea, the deep things of God. For what man knoweth the things of a man save the spirit of man, which is in him? Even so the things of God knoweth no man, but the Spirit of God" (I Cor. 2:7-11). But these deep mysteries, which will ever remain unsearchable and past finding out for the human mind, are revealed in language so clear that a child may understand what God means to say and by this divine message may be saved. Who can fully grasp the mystery of the simple words: Christ, the Son of God, has shed His blood for me, and His blood cleanses me from all sin? Yet is there anyone that understands the English language that will not understand the meaning of these words? Therefore Christ says: "I thank thee, O Father, Lord of heaven and earth, because Thou hast hid these things from the wise and prudent and hast revealed them unto babes. Even so, Father; for so it seemed good in Thy sight. All things are delivered unto Me of My Father; and no man knoweth the Son but the Father; neither knoweth any man the Father save the Son and he to whomsoever the Son will reveal Him" (Matt. 11:25-27).

VI

The clarity of Scripture does not imply that there are no passages which appear dark to us or which we are unable to explain to our own satisfaction. The reason for this darkness lies not in our Bible or in the supposition that God failed to express Himself with sufficient clarity. It lies in the human reader. Let us take, for example, the word rendered "Bow the knee" in our English Bible, which Luther has translated, "This is the father of the land" (Gen. 41:43). The word in the Hebrew Bible, "abrek," occurs only in this passage, and while it was perfectly clear to the people who heard this word and most likely to the first readers of Genesis, it defies to this day the efforts of interpreters to establish its exact meaning. The darkness is in our mind, not in the original word, which was clear to Moses and his contemporaries.

In other instances a passage may seem dark to us because we do not know all the circumstances. We find great difficulty in piecing together the various accounts of Peter's denial, of the events of Good Friday and Easter Sunday. But we know that everything recounted in the four narratives occurred exactly as it is related. Being the Word of the omniscient God, we know that every detail is correctly, even if not fully, presented. And what has been told, and the manner in which it has been told, is deemed by our all-wise and gracious Father as sufficient for our knowledge of these important events, sufficient, above all, for our salvation in time and eternity.

The dark passages very frequently become clear to us by further study of the Bible. There are enough clear passages in the Bible to cast a light on many passages we did not understand at the first reading. Never must our interpretation of dark passages, of symbolic prophecies, of figurative language, conflict with clearly revealed truths. All truths necessary for us to know are clearly revealed to us, and if a passage remains dark to us after prolonged study, we must not put our own interpretation on its language and boast of having discovered a new and important truth. That would not be interpreting God's Word, but forcing one's own opinion and fancy and error upon the sacred Word of the Holy God. The dark passages are placed into the Bible to keep us humble, to make us realize our own ignorance and helplessness in matters divine, to test our willingness to confess that God is wiser than we, and learn to wait for full understanding in the realms above.

VII

The clearness of Holy Scripture is not disproved by the many different interpretations found among the various denominations and even among orthodox interpreters. Many of these differences of interpretation may be due to imperfect knowledge of the language or circumstances on the part of the interpreters; or the exegete may have been guilty of negligent reading, of flighty work; or the cause may lie in some doctrinal error or prejudice held by the interpreter, which makes it difficult or impossible for him to see the clear sense of the passage.

There can be only one true and divinely intended sense. To assume any other possibility would be charging God with deceiving us when He calls His Word a light unto salvation. It must be clear. It must have only one sense, one meaning; else it could not show the way to life to travelers groping in darkness.

Aside from these facts, it is illogical to use the varying interpretations of the Bible as an argument against its clarity. By the same argument no law passed by any legislature would be clear, for there is no law which has not been variantly interpreted. And yet we maintain the clarity of many human laws though there are different interpretations. Why charge the Word of the God of truth with lack of clarity merely because human minds differ in the interpretation of this Word? Rather let God be true and every man a liar (Rom. 3:4) than deny the clarity of Scripture which God Himself asserts time and again in no uncertain terms.

VIII

"This clearness and plainness of the Bible is the same for *all* readers, alike for the regenerate and the unregenerate. As the true and intended meaning is but one—*sensus literalis unus est*—so also the external clearness is but one. The Holy Spirit has not shed a light on the sacred page for the believer which is not there also for the unbeliever. Neither does the Spirit's action by which man is led to the saving knowledge of the Bible consist in casting an additional light on the Scriptures, but in shining in the heart of man. The action is not upon the Book, but wholly on the reader. This Book *is* luminous. It is a 'lamp,' a 'light,' 'a light that shineth in a dark place'." (*Theological Quarterly,* Vol. XII, No. 2, p. 98.)

THE SUFFICIENCY OF SCRIPTURE

I

Scriptures are no encyclopedia giving exact information on everything that it is possible to know. Scriptures do not even reveal all the thoughts and counsels of God. There are many questions which are not answered in the Bible. Even Paul, the great Apostle, who had been caught up into Paradise and heard unspeakable words, did not know whether at that time he was in the body or out of the body. He informs us that it was not lawful for a man to utter the words he had heard. On another occasion he exclaims, "Oh, the depth of the riches both of the wisdom and knowledge of God! How unsearchable are His judgments and His ways past finding out! For who hath known the mind of the Lord? Or who hath been His counselor? Or who hath first given to Him, and it shall be recompensed unto him again? For of Him, and through Him, and to Him, are all things; to whom be glory forever" (Rom. 11:33-36).

Yet Scripture is all-sufficient for the accomplishment of its purpose for which it was given to man as a precious gift by the God of grace. It is, as Paul says, able to make man wise to salvation. It is profitable for doctrine, for reproof, for correction, for instruction in righteousness, thoroughly furnishing, completely equipping, the man of God (II Tim. 3:15-17). And the God of comfort, who comforteth us in all our tribulation (II Cor. 1:4), does that through Scripture, for whatever things were written aforetime were written for our learning, that we through patience and comfort of the Scriptures might have hope (Rom. 15:4). What more do we need for our salvation?

Therefore God time and again repeats the warning, Ye shall not add unto the Word which I command you, neither shall ye diminish it (Deut. 4:2; cp. Deut. 12:32; Prov. 30:6; Rev. 22:18, 19). There is no need of the testimony of one rising from the dead (Luke 16:27-31). While not all the signs that Jesus did in the presence of His disciples are written in the Bible, yet what is written is sufficient to accomplish its purpose, that, believing, we might have life through His name (John 20:30, 31). Very bluntly the Apostle states: "If any man teach otherwise and consent not to wholesome words, even the words of our Lord Jesus Christ, and to the doctrine which is according to godliness, he is proud, knowing nothing, but doting about questions and strifes of words, whereof cometh envy, strife, railings, evil surmisings, perverse disputings of men of corrupt minds, and destitute of the truth, supposing that gain is godliness; from such withdraw thyself" (I Tim. 6:3-5).

The Scriptures are all-sufficient to salvation!

II

No traditions of men, of whatever kind they may be; no new

revelations claimed to be of divine origin; no systems of theology; no confessions of any church; no writings of any man may be placed on the same level with Scriptures, nor do the Scriptures stand in need of them. What could man produce that could be placed side by side with the Word of God? The very idea is preposterous. And still the Church of Rome included the Apocrypha of the Old Testament in the list of canonical books of the Bible and pronounced the anathema upon everyone who would not regard these man-made books as sacred and part of Holy Scripture. Moreover, the Church of Rome has placed tradition, that is, the interpretation of Scripture as held by the Holy Mother Church, which is infallible, side by side with the Bible, in fact above the Bible. "The Fathers of the Church plainly expressed their belief that the written Word of God by itself, without the help of tradition, would always leave disputes unsettled, points of beliefs and morals undetermined, and true religion a problem unsolved" (*Catholic Belief*, J. Fan Di Bruno, Benziger Bros., p. 29). The Word of God is not sufficient, the word of man must make it so! Blasphemous!

Zwingli laid down a principle fully as vicious as that of Rome when he said that God did not ask us to believe impossible things, such as the real presence of Christ's body and blood in the Lord's Supper. And to this day Reformed Churches make their reason the criterion of accepting or rejecting doctrines clearly taught in Holy Writ, while others overemphasize human ordinances, such as ordination, and make them church-divisive. There is Ellen G. White, who claimed divine revelation and inspiration of the Holy Ghost for her messages to her followers; and Mrs. Mary Baker Eddy, who claims that her fantastic folly is the Key to Scriptures.

Over against these and all other efforts to place human opinion, human reason, human folly, human blasphemy, on the same or even a higher level, our Lutheran Church confesses in the Formula of Concord: "We believe, teach, and confess that the sole rule and standard according to which all dogmas together with (all) teachers should be estimated and judged are the prophetic and apostolic Scriptures of the Old and of the New Testament alone, as it is written Ps. 119:105: 'Thy Word is a Lamp unto my feet and a Light unto my path.' And St. Paul: 'Though an angel from heaven preach any other Gospel unto you, let him be accursed! (Gal. 1:8.) Other writings, however, of ancient or modern teachers, whatever name they bear, must not be regarded as equal to the Holy Scriptures, but all of them together be subjected to them, and should not be received otherwise or further than as witnesses (which are to show) in what manner after the time of the Apostles, and at what places, this (pure) doctrine of the Prophets and Apostles was preserved. . . . In this way the distinction between the Holy Scriptures of the Old and of the New Testament and all other writings is preserved, and the Holy Scriptures alone remain the only judge, rule, and standard, according to which, as the only teststone, all dogmas shall and must be discerned and judged, as to whether they are good or evil, right or wrong. But the other symbols and writings cited are not judges, as are the Holy Scriptures, but only a testimony and declaration of the faith, as to how at any time the Holy Scriptures have been understood and explained in the articles in controversy in the Church of God by those then living, and how the opposite dogma was rejected and condemned (by what arguments the dogmas conflicting with the Holy Scripture were rejected and condemned)." (*Triglot*, 777, 778.)

V

The Proper Use of the Bible

DURING the 100 years of the existence of our Synod many thousands have been confirmed at the altars of its constituent congregations. We were among those who made vows of confirmation at such an altar. As a fundamental requisite for these vows we confessed that we held all the books of the Bible to be the inspired Word of God and that we intended faithfully to conform all our lives to the rule of the divine Word, to walk as it becometh the Gospel of Christ. In short, our membership in our congregation and in the Church of God is based upon the faith that the Bible is the true and only Word of God, that this Bible, for time and eternity, gives us the necessary revelation of God and His will concerning us. The faith that the Bible is the inerrant, eternally true, unchanging message from God as to our origin and final fate, of our creation by the almighty Creator and our salvation by Christ Jesus, is the basis upon which every other part of our Christian faith rests. Nothing in all of life is more important and more blessed than that belief.

This is true of pastors, not only as Christians, but also because of their office. A pastor's joy in the exercise of his office, the authority he has for holding it, the whole purpose and goal of his ministry, are essentially dependent upon his acceptance of the Bible as God's eternal truth.

Every congregation of Synod has included in its constitution, as its most important article, the confession of faith in the Bible as the divinely revealed Word of God. By so doing our congregations bear witness before friend and foe of the foundation of their faith and of what they demand of everyone who would hold membership in the congregation.

Our Synod demands that congregations hold to this fundamental article in confession and practice before being admitted to synodical membership.

As Christians, as pastors, as delegates of our congregations, as congregations, as synod we must regard it as a matter of highest importance that this foundation of our faith be preserved in its purity and certainty.

I

Only then do we use the Bible properly when we use it as the inspired Word of God, the perfect, complete, infallible, and final revelation of those truths which God would have us to know and believe.

In order to use an object properly, one must be acquainted with its nature and purpose. You can crack nuts with a watch, but you are not using the watch properly. You may know what radium looks like, but what untold suffering will be yours if you do not know how to use it properly. Only that may be properly used which is properly known and understood. We apply this truism to the Bible: No one can properly use the Bible unless he knows the nature of the Bible: that it is the living Word of the living God, and its purpose: to make men wise unto salvation through faith which is in Christ Jesus. The knowledge of the nature and purpose, moreover, must be more than a mere intellectual process, a mere mental perception. The Bible states that the natural man receiveth not the things of the Spirit of God, for they are foolishness unto him; neither can he know them, for they are spiritually discerned (I Cor. 2:14). Since the Bible was spoken not in words which man's wisdom teacheth, but which the Holy Ghost teacheth (I Cor. 2:13), only the Holy Ghost can teach the proper understanding of the Bible. "The Holy Ghost will guide you into all truth," says Jesus to His disciples (John 16:13), "will teach you all things" (John 14:26). Without the Holy Ghost no one can call Jesus the Lord (I Cor. 12:3), and without this knowledge of Jesus there is no understanding of the Bible.

This knowledge of the nature and purpose of the Bible is wrought by the Holy Spirit by means of this very book. "Search the Scriptures, for in them ye think ye have eternal life, and they are they which testify of Me," says Christ (John 5:39). "The words that I speak, they are spirit, and they are life," says the same Christ (John

6:63). And Peter writes, "Being born again, not of corruptible seed, but of incorruptible, by the Word of God, which liveth and abideth forever" (I Pet. 1:23).

Hence through reading, hearing, studying the Bible the Holy Ghost works in man that faith whereby he accepts Christ as his personal Savior and whereby he is assured of everlasting life. With this faith and assurance is kindled at the same time the faith and conviction that this Bible, which has regenerated him, changed his very nature, cannot be a human book, that it must be what it claims to be in all its parts: the infallible Word of the infallible God of grace, that all Scripture is indeed, as it claims to be, given by inspiration of God. God Himself creates the knowledge of the nature and purpose of the Bible in the heart of man by means of that Bible. And only he who has this saving knowledge of the Bible can use the Bible properly, as God wants it to be used.

While saving faith is possible only after God's Holy Spirit has given witness to our heart and brought us to faith by His Gospel, it is possible for man, by the use of his human reason and intellect, to acquire certain facts about and from the Bible and believe them without having come to saving faith. A man may reject Christ as his Savior and still believe in the superhuman origin of the Bible, basing his belief on purely reasonable arguments.

One of these lines of argument is based on the thought of the necessity of a divine revelation. The Creation, of which he is part, his own conscience, will convince man that there is a God. Says Paul: "Because that which may be known of God is manifest in them, for God hath showed it unto them. For the invisible things of Him from the creation of the world are clearly seen, being understood by the things that are made, even His eternal power and Godhead; so that they are without excuse" (Rom. 1:19, 20). When we find such as deny this, we need not be greatly disturbed. The ancient Psalmist has properly identified such people for us. "The fool hath said in his heart, There is no God. They are corrupt, they have done abominable works, there is none that doeth good" (Ps. 14:1).

If, however, sane reason has convinced me: There is a God, then an equal sanity of reason demands that I say: I cannot know that God by my own reason or strength. To be convinced of this fact one need only to study the religions of the heathen. The orderly unity of the universe testifies to one God. Yet the reason of man, unguided by revelation, has produced thousands of gods. Even in the ancient home of Greek wisdom and philosophy, Athens, Paul found a multitude of idols faithfully worshiped by the Athenians. And beside these statues he found an altar dedicated to the Unknown God, testifying to their inability to find out God by searching for Him. When, moreover, we recall that thousands of keen intellects have tried to present to man a system of religion based upon the perceptions of pure reason, and then read the refutation of these systems by other intellects equally keen; when we remember how these very systems of religion, acclaimed by awed contemporaries as the final word, became the laughingstock of the next generation; when we find that all of these systems, whether from darkest Africa or from the seats of highest culture, involve inevitable self-contradictions; then, on the basis of common reason we must say: Man cannot by his reason arrive at principles and tenets which he can accept as unalterable, divine truth.

Yet conscience and Creation tell me that there is a God with whom I must be intimately related. Who is He? What does He want of men? What are His plans for men? Will death lead me to Him or away from Him? Man's inability to answer such questions is evident. What is more reasonable than that God would and did supply the answers? Can the God who rules the universe have put me on earth and left me totally ignorant regarding these matters? Could He have provided for me with such a lavish hand for body and life and given me nothing for the spirit, nothing for the soul? Common sense ought to convince us that a revelation from God was a necessity.

Merely granting that a revelation was necessary would not demand, however, that the Bible be accepted as that revelation. Yet there are a number of rational arguments for the divine origin and nature of Holy Scripture.

"In consideration of the perfection of the Bible, the demand that the Holy Scriptures of the Old and New Testaments be accepted as the very Word of God, is not an unreasonable demand. It is a book unique in the literature of the world. Nowhere else do we find the teachings regarding the Trinity, the incarnation, the atonement, justification by faith, sanctification through the Divine Spirit, the resurrection of the body, and eternal life enjoyed by the reunited body and soul. And in these teachings the Old and New Testaments wonderfully, yes, amazingly agree. Divine authorship alone can account for the unity of the Old and New Testaments.

"Only consider: Here is a collection of books; in their style and character there is a great variety and diversity; some are historical, others poetical; some contain laws, others lyrics; some are prophetic, some symbolic; in the Old Testament we have historical, poetical, and prophetical sections; and in the New Testament we have five historic narratives, then twenty-one epistles, then a symbolic apocalyptic poem in Oriental imagery. The contributors to the Old Testament were men differing widely in ability, education, and social life. Moses was learned in all the wisdom of the Egyptians; David and Solomon were kings; Daniel was a minister of state; Ezra, Jeremiah, and Ezekiel were priests; Amos was a herdsman. David wrote some four hundred years after Moses, Isaiah about two hundred and fifty years after David, Daniel about one hundred and fifty years after Isaiah, Ezekiel about one hundred years after Daniel, and Malachi about two hundred years after Ezekiel. Between Moses and John there was an interval of more than fifteen hundred years during which the whole of revelation was made.

"In such a book, then, it is not likely that there would be unity; for all the conditions were unfavorable to a harmonious moral testimony and teaching. Yet there is an evident unity of design pervading the whole, which proves a unity of origin from some source not within the minds of the authors, but without, and so controlling each writer as to crystallize his thoughts around the same thread extended through all these centuries and especially with regard to Messiah, the Hope of Israel. Compare the Fall in Genesis—one link —with the resurrection in the Apocalypse—the other. Compare the old creation in the first chapters of the Old Testament with the new creation in the last chapters of the New. 'We open the first pages of the Bible,' says Vallotton, 'and we find there the recital of the creation of the world by the Word of God—of the fall of man, of his exile far from God, far from Paradise, and far from the Tree of Life. We open the last pages of the last of the sixty-six books, dating 4,000 years later. The same God is still speaking. He is still creating. He creates a new heaven and a new earth. Man is found there. He is restored to full communion with God. He dwells again in Paradise, beneath the shadow of the Tree of Life. Who is not struck by the strange correspondence of such a conclusion with such a beginning? Is not the one the prolog, the other the epilog, of a drama as vast as it is unique?' How is all this to be explained? Shall we say it may be accounted for by the infidel's suggestion that the Old Testament was forged to give credibility to the New? This is not only absurd in itself, but plainly impossible by the fact that the Old Testament was a book well known to the Jews, the bitter enemies of the Christians, for centuries before the New Testament was written, and by the further fact that the Old Testament was translated into Greek nearly three hundred years before the birth of Christ. In this translation all the promises of the Messiah are again recorded, which, when brought together, make an anticipated biography of Him wonderfully minute and distinct. The supposition of forgery is therefore a monstrosity of foolishness. This question then obtrudes itself: How could such a variety of events be predicted by such a variety of men living at such different times and places, and not one of the predictions fail as proved by correspondent events? There can be but one answer.

"In view, then, of these inner perfections of the Bible, these attestations to its divine origin, it is not unreasonable that reason submit to all its statements and teachings. It is not an unreasonable demand that men must read this volume as they read no other book —with unhesitating assent to all that it contains. And when we reject all other so-called revelations which men may claim to have received from God, we act in strict accordance with the testimonies, implicit and explicit, of the Bible to its uniqueness as the final revelation of religious truth to fallen mankind" (Southern District, 1919).

Although we might well carry out a similar procedure along other lines, *e. g.*, the evidence of its own claims, the certification of its writers by word and power, the complete fulfillment of its prophecies, the universality of its message, the clarity of its language, the indestructibility of its doctrine, its inherent powers to convert and change men, and many others, this one example, its unity, must this time suffice.

Yet we must never forget that these rational proofs cannot produce saving faith. At best they can produce a *fides humana,* an intellectual conviction. And as a rule they do not even produce this. "Whatsoever proceeds from reason can be refuted by reason" (Synodical Conference, 1884, p. 49). "If you give the impression that the truth of Scripture depends in the least degree on the validity of your rational arguments, you are making a concession to rationalism. We shall have to agree with the judgment of a writer in the *Journal of the American Lutheran Conference*, May, 1939, 16: 'So long as you imagine that you can formulate irrefutable proofs by means of reason, you are a rationalist, whether your brainchild is dressed in the garb of orthodoxy or of Modernism.' . . . There must be time given to apologetics, but give it sparingly. The one thing that counts is Scripture" (Engelder, *Reason or Revelation?* pp. 155, 157).

We repeat our thesis: *Only then do we use the Bible properly if we use it as the inspired Word of God, the perfect, complete, infallible, and final revelation of those blessed truths which God would have us know and believe.*

II

Many fail to use the Bible properly because they fail to recognize or refuse to accept the main design and the ultimate purpose for the giving of the Scriptures.

The purpose of Scripture is threefold:

1. It is a revelation of the counsel of God unto our eternal salvation (Luke 16:27-29, 31; II Tim. 3:15).

2. It is the means of God to create and preserve in us a saving faith (Luke 16:31).

3. It is the agency of God in instructing us in a God-pleasing way of life (Ps. 119:9; 105; II Tim. 3:16).

To use God's Word without remembering why God gave it would be as foolish as to plow the ocean and seed it to wheat. The ocean was given for another purpose. God gave the Bible for His own specific purposes, and with these purposes in mind we must use it. Sad to say, many a sermon has been preached, many a Bible Hour conducted, many a chapter from the Bible read in family and private devotions without this threefold purpose ever being considered.

The chief purpose for which the Bible was given to us is to make us wise unto salvation. Being God's Word, it is fully sufficient for this purpose, as we learn from Christ's own words in the Parable of the Rich Man and Lazarus. When the rich man was in hell, he said to Abraham: "I pray thee therefore, Father, that thou wouldest send him to my father's house, for I have five brethren, that he may testify unto them, lest they also come into this place of torment."

Abraham saith unto him: "They have Moses and the Prophets; let them hear them" (Luke 16:27-29). Moses and the Prophets, through whom God has revealed the way to heaven, are sufficient for man to escape eternal damnation and obtain everlasting salvation. No more revelation is needed, no traditions of the Fathers, as the Papists teach, no Swedenborgian illumination, no "making of the Scriptures" by the so-called living oracles of the Latter-Day Saints, no addition and extension of Scriptures by Mrs. White of the Seventh-Day Adventists or Mrs. Eddy for the Christian Scientists, no "new revelation" from the spirits of the departed for the Spiritists, no gradual gathering of the entire truth from the sentences of Brahma, Confucius, Christ, and others, as the Freemasons hold—only the Holy Scriptures are able to make us wise unto salvation. They alone contain the full and complete counsels of God for our salvation.

The Bible, therefore, is the only efficacious means of creating and preserving the true faith in us. It converts the unregenerate. "The Law of the Lord is perfect, converting the soul; the Testimony of the Lord is sure, making wise the simple" (Ps. 19:7). "They have Moses and the Prophets; let them hear them. . . . If they hear not Moses and the Prophets, neither will they be persuaded though one rose from the dead" (Luke 16:29-31). It preserves and strengthens the faith of the regenerate: "Then He said unto them, O fools and slow of heart to believe all that the Prophets have spoken. Ought not Christ to have suffered these things and to enter into His glory? And beginning at Moses and all the Prophets, He expounded unto them in all the Scriptures the things concerning Himself" (Luke 24:25-27). "But these are written, that ye might believe that Jesus is the Christ, the Son of God, and that believing ye might have life through His name" (John 20:31). It is the means employed by God's Holy Spirit in presenting to us the faith which saves, in operating on and in the hearts and minds of those who hear and read it. "The statutes of the Lord are right, rejoicing the heart; the commandment of the Lord is pure, enlightening the eyes" (Ps. 19:8). "We have also a more sure word of prophecy; whereunto ye do well that ye take heed, as unto a light that shineth in a dark place, until the day dawn and the Day Star arise in your hearts" (II Pet. 1:19). "If any man will do His will, he shall know of the doctrine whether it be of God or whether I speak of Myself" (John 7:17).

When a man becomes convinced from Holy Scripture that God

has given him the eternal promises for eternity, the assurance of a resurrection and life everlasting, then his perspective of the why and wherefore of his existence will be completely changed. He will realize that while he is still *in* the world, he is not *of* the world, that in his relations to God, to his fellow man, and to himself, his first obligation must be to make Holy Scriptures the norm of his faith and life. In Psalm 119 the writer asks: "Wherewithal shall a young man cleanse his way?" A very effective way of asking, How shall a believer live? Comes the answer: "By taking heed thereto according to Thy Word" (Ps. 119:9). God's Word, the Bible, is the only proper and correct instruction in righteousness, the only unfailing light on the way of life. "Thy Word is a Lamp unto my feet, and a Light unto my path" (Ps. 119:105). "All Scripture is given by inspiration of God and is profitable for doctrine, for reproof, for correction, for instruction in righteousness" (II Tim. 3:16).

In order to use the Bible properly, we must use it with the knowledge that it is the source of all knowledge of what God has done for our salvation, that by it God's Holy Spirit works faith in the hearts of men, and that through it we will be instructed how to live so that our life may be a testimony of our faith.

Scripture clearly teaches that Jesus Christ, God's own Son, true Man and true God, the divinely appointed Savior of all mankind, is the center of the Christian religion. All other religions are work religions, religious systems built up around some teachings and precepts telling their adherents what to do in order to lead a moral life and to gain the favor of their god or gods. The organizers of these religions had to say: Here are certain things we believe to be truth, and we shall attempt to lead you into them. Christ says: "I am the Truth." The founders of all other religions must say: We shall show you a way. Jesus says: "I am the Way." All others had to say and will always have to say: We hope to point you to someone or something that can help you. Jesus says: "Come unto Me!" The entire Bible presents the fact that Jesus' person is the center, the Alpha and Omega, of the Christian faith. He who takes Jesus out of the Bible destroys the Bible.

Every sermon preached from the Bible, every hour spent in its study, every minute devoted to its searching, will fail to bestow the full blessing intended by God unless such preaching, searching, and devotion are directed to finding the true Jesus in the Bible.

"Search the Scriptures, for in them ye think ye have eternal life; and they are they which testify of Me" (John 5:39). Luther says: "There you have the answer as to what you are to seek and find in the Scriptures: 'Me,' says the Lord, 'you shall learn to know there.' Commandments, histories, material promises, all ultimately point to Christ. For one may do nothing, ask nothing, have nothing, except through Christ, who has been accepted by faith."

Not all who give lip service to the glories of the Scripture have learned to use it properly. In many instances these people would be highly incensed if you accused them of misusing the Bible. Yet their use of Scriptures is wholly improper, since they do not know or do not bear in mind the origin and purpose of the Word.

There are many who use the Bible merely as a textbook for morals. A preacher of this stripe will find suitable texts throughout the Bible, on the basis of which he can thunder against the vices of man and orate about his virtues. But since he uses the Bible merely as a textbook for morals, he never touches the real center of Scripture nor the real need of mankind, the forgiveness of sin through the atoning sacrifice of Christ. To him any chapter of Proverbs is greatly to be preferred to the Easter Gospel. He indeed uses the Scriptures. To the unwary it may even seem that he uses it in a God-pleasing manner. But God knows that His Book and its message are being slighted. Luther: "See well to it that you do not make a Moses out of Christ nor a statute book or textbook out of the Gospel."

Others use the Scriptures only to enrich their own knowledge. The Pharisees and scribes of the Savior's day had acquired, through searching of the Scriptures, a thorough knowledge of its contents. When Herod asked them where the Promised One of God was to be born, they immediately answered and quoted the pertinent passage from Micah. But they never thought of making use of their knowledge for their soul's salvation. The Bible contains a great fund of instruction in many fields of human endeavor. He who really searches his Bible will obtain that fund of wisdom. But he who searches it only to enrich his mind, his intellect, is misusing his Bible. One of the most insidious temptations of Satan is his constant effort to turn even the Christian's use of the Bible into a mere mental exercise or a mere means of enriching his personal knowledge, while forgetting the very center of Scripture: Christ.

Then there are those who search the Scriptures only to attack it.

to find contradictions, chronological, historical, scientific errors, and on the basis of their findings seek to undermine the authority of God's Word, men like Thomas Paine, Robert Ingersoll, Clarence Darrow, and others, who spend their energies in trying to reduce the Bible to a book of fables. Closely allied to them are the modern unbelieving Bible critics, who profess great respect for the Word of God and then prove to their own satisfaction that the books of the Bible are not units penned by the same writer, but that each book is a compilation of materials gathered from various sources written by various authors at various times, often carelessly put together, containing contradictions and presenting religious views quite at variance with one another. That again is neglecting or deliberately setting aside what the Bible has to say of its origin and purpose.

Finally, there are in increasing numbers, as the end of all things comes closer, such as seek Scriptural proof and warrant for their own erroneous and ofttimes fantastic, foolish, and even blasphemous views. In order to gain adherents, they do not shrink from garbling Scripture texts, twisting the words, perverting their sense, for the sole purpose of winning disciples for their soul-destroying errors. Dr. Luther says: "That is the custom of all heretics. First they adopt some conceit which pleases them and which seems good and fitting to them. When they have adopted it, they go to the Scriptures, pick and search around in it to find some text that might seem to support their conceit. That is a terribly dangerous thing. Of this I shall give an example: When the heretic Arius wished to attack the person of Christ, his first thought was: Christ was born of the Virgin Mary; hence He is only a natural man." Likewise it would be a shameful abuse of Holy Scripture to use the sins of the saints as recorded in the Bible as an excuse for, or mitigation of, mortal sins. To use Noah's drunkenness as an excuse for overindulgence, or even riotous festivities, or Lot's incest and David's adultery as a cloak for licentiousness and marital unfaithfulness, or Paul's disagreement with Barnabas as an apology for one's quarrelsomeness and intolerance, would be a manifest abuse of Holy Scripture closely approaching blasphemy.

III

Proper use of the Bible is possible only if we correctly understand its message, if in reading we properly interpret the words used by the Lord so that we arrive at the meaning God intended to convey to us.

The Bible itself gives us the rules which must be used in its interpretation. According to II Pet. 1:19, the Bible is a sure word of prophecy. It could not be that if passages of Scripture could be proved to have more than one intended sense. Then God's Spirit would have given a revelation which would not serve as a light that shineth in a dark place (II Pet. 1:19) nor could make us wise unto salvation (II Tim. 3:15), but which would serve only to confuse the minds and souls of men and leave them groping in the darkness of doubt and error.

Since God speaks to us in the Bible in human language, the same laws of language and grammatical analysis must be applied to the Bible that are applied to any other book written in human language. Paul proves the Messiahship of Jesus by stressing the fact that God used the singular instead of the plural in His promise (Gal. 3:16; Gen. 22:18).

Numerous words and passages of Scripture are at once interpreted by the Holy Spirit, *e. g.,* Emmanuel, God with us (Matt. 1:23); Abba, Father (Gal. 4:6); "this temple" (John 2:19) is interpreted as referring to His body (v. 21).

In interpreting the Bible the following points must always be taken into consideration: 1) The context; 2) The purpose of the passage; 3) Parallel passages; 4) The purpose of the entire Scripture.

To discuss each of these points in detail would demand far more time than we have available. But it is essential that we look briefly at these fundamental requisites to a proper method of interpretation.

Taking words of the Bible out of the context, out of their proper connection, is a prime source of religious error. Worst offenders against this self-evident rule of Bible interpretation have been the Romanists and the Chiliasts. Let two examples suffice: In the year 1073 the doctrine of the Roman Catholic Church was promulgated that the Pope is the divinely appointed ruler over all governments of the earth. The Bible quotation adduced to prove this is Gen. 1. The Romanist's interpretation follows: "The apostolic power is that of the sun, and the royal power that of the moon. Even as the moon receives light from the sun, so the kings receive their power from the Popes." Who, in reading the story of Creation, can gain such an interpretation from it? Chiliasts teach that Christ will visibly reign on earth, with His saints, for exactly 1,000 years before the Day of Judgment. They attempt to prove this claim from the twentieth chapter of Revelation. Here from a chapter whose whole content is strictly figurative they insist that the 1,000 years be taken literally. One word is torn out of a figurative context and given a literal meaning.

Closely related to this requisite is the necessity of ascertaining the purpose of a passage under study: Why and under what circumstances it was spoken. St. Luke tells us that Paul circumcised Timothy (Acts 16:3). Paul tells us that he positively refused to circumcise Titus (Gal. 2:3). Here the circumstances must be known in order to understand Paul's actions. In Timothy's case Paul acted as he did in order not to offend those who were weak in the faith. In the case of Titus he objected to circumcision because it was a case of maintaining the New Testament freedom of the Christian against false teachers. By establishing the real purpose of a passage and considering the accompanying circumstances, most of the so-called contradictions of Scripture will vanish. In the use of this simple, common-sense, and fair method of finding the intent of a passage there lies also one of the best possible means of avoiding false doctrine and refuting the arguments of errorists.

In order to use the Bible properly, we must remember that parallel passages often do not merely repeat a statement, but will give added information or explain more clearly the meaning of the passage we are studying. Two examples will have to suffice.

From Matt. 8:5ff. it might appear that the centurion approached Jesus personally, while the parallel passage, Luke 7:2, states clearly that he approached Jesus through a delegation. Luke also adds other details characterizing the centurion as not only a humble, but devout, God-fearing person. Only by making full use of the parallel will we understand the situation briefly described by Matthew.

From Jesus' promise: "Again I say unto you that if two of you shall agree on earth as touching any thing that they shall ask, it shall be done for them of My Father which is in heaven" (Matt. 18:19) one might gather that every petition of Christians would be answered in the exact manner they wished. The parallel passages, such as John 14:13, 14; 15:16; I John 5:14, 15 teach us the important lesson that a Christian must and will pray in the name of Jesus, and in complete submission to His will, while Matt. 7:9ff.; Luke 11:11-13;

Rom. 8:26 tell us that our heavenly Father knows better than we what will serve our temporal and eternal welfare, and will answer our prayers accordingly.

Hence the use of parallel passages will often help to gain a correct or fuller understanding of Scripture, and in reading the Bible we ought to make constant use of the references added in the margin.

The chief purpose for which the Bible is given to us is to show us the way of salvation. Proper interpretation of passages in the Bible must take this chief aim of the Bible into consideration. Unless we constantly bear in mind that God had one great, all-encompassing, and all-permeating theme which He presents in Scripture, namely, the salvation of sinful man, we cannot properly evaluate the individual passages. In a beautiful mosaic we can inspect an individual piece and speak of its texture, composition, coloring, etc. But we do not properly evaluate its use unless we also view it as a component part of the whole work of art in which it appears. So also with passages from Holy Writ. Each passage forms a part of that great revelation which God gave to make man wise unto salvation and must be viewed in its relationship to the whole. Since all the doctrines revealed in Scripture are revealed by the God of truth, all the articles of the Christian faith stand in perfect and complete agreement and harmony. Luther uses the example of a golden chain. The different articles of Christian faith are the links of that chain. Break or destroy one of these links, and the whole chain is broken. If only one article of faith is attacked or destroyed by the interpretation of a passage of Scripture, then such an interpretation is no longer Biblical and must be rejected.

IV

The Bible must be used with absolute reliance upon its divine authorship, with unquestioning acceptance of all of its statements, with unreserved assent to all its teachings. But it must be used! Used by the individual, used for the instruction of children in the nurture and admonition of the Lord and by and for the adult in the ministry of the soul. For home, school, and church it must be the basis of all that is to be imparted as knowledge of and from God.

The right, proper, and saving use of the Word of God is, above all, a personal one. Even as one cannot believe for another, so also the agent of faith, instituted by God to give and maintain faith, the use of the Word, must be a personal one. No one will claim that because a wife received Holy Communion her husband would automatically receive the blessings of Communion also, even though he did not come to the Lord's altar at all. Likewise, there can be no learning, experiencing, exercising, and enjoying of the essentials of salvation for the individual unless the individual takes these out of the Word of God himself. Hence it is essential that the individual, at home, use his Bible and use it properly. (Cp. the essay on "The Use of the Bible in the Christian Home," p. 85.)

God's command and God's promise, our personal needs and our personal joys, demand that every Christian be a Bible student in his own right. This is something we cannot do for another and something another cannot do for us. There will and can be, of course, an exchange of ideas, a mutual helping to find the right word of God for the right occasion, the joint finding of the solution of problems of faith and living, but in the last analysis the use of the Scriptures must be a personal one.

From the personal proper use of the Scriptures, which is basic, derives the use of the Bible in the Church, both the local congregation and the church at large. The convictions gained personally from the Scriptures will make it imperative that a Christian life cannot be egocentric. Some argue: "I can be a good Christian by studying my Bible at home, attaining a full knowledge of God's revelation by my personal application to the Word, and therefore do not need membership in a congregation. For the same reason my congregation need not be a member of a synod." No! He who has properly studied the Bible and accepted the God-intended results of such studies knows from those studies that he cannot sever himself from association with fellow believers. He will have learned that his life of faith, gained from the Scriptures, will demand of him a joyous, happy, glad, and willing working together with those of like faith for the very purposes for which his personal Bible study was necessary. In joining with others, greater light and blessing will again flow from the Scriptures to the members of the Church individually and collectively.

Not externals, such as a pleasing order of service, proper appointments in the house of worship, active voting membership, and flourishing affiliates and organizations, a long membership list, full-blossomed educational facilities, overflowing treasuries—not these will guarantee a truly God-pleasing and successful congregational life and activity. These will be results when the essential of God's Word and its proper knowledge and application to the lives of the individual members are prime. The first thing must still be: To teach and know the Word of God, from which all blessings in the Church flow.

It is therefore a matter of the gravest concern to a congregation that its pastor, who leads in the study of God's Word in sermons and addresses, be given an opportunity of properly presenting God's Word and properly using that opportunity. It must be a matter of grave concern to a congregation whether its day school teachers and Sunday school teachers, as a part of the work originally assigned to the pastor, really are teaching the Bible to the children of the church. It should be a far greater concern of synodical officers to know whether a congregation is being truly indoctrinated than to know whether it has raised its quota. During the early years of our Synod some of the time at the conventions was used to make a survey on the texts used by the pastor in his sermons, the books of the Bible that had been studied in Bible classes in each congregation, the means used to lead the children of the church to a personal use of the Scriptures. That took time and effort. But I firmly believe that the great blessings which our Church is reaping today are directly traceable to just such and similar practices. Are we today still as insistent that our churches, pastors, teachers, really be devoted to a real study of the Bible for the good of all?

One of the matters which today seems to be agitating the entire Christian Church is the unifying of all Protestant churches, or at least sections of it, into an organic whole. Since the Bible is the foundation of all Christian faith and doctrine, it must also be the foundation of all Christian unity. Luther says: "My dear man, I will have no peace and unity by which the Word of God is lost. With it eternal life and all would be lost. The Word and its doctrines must establish Christian unity and fellowship. Where these are in harmony and at one, the other will follow."

That which divides Christianity is false doctrine. False doctrine cannot be discovered and corrected except by the proper use of the Word of God. Whether we be wrong or right cannot be established on any other basis than the wisdom of God as revealed in the Sacred

Scriptures. Such discovery and correction of error must not be delegated to seminary professors and professional theologians. Here, again, pastor and people, pulpit and pew, must personally know and understand what divides, in order that upon the basis of God's Word we may establish what will unify. This demands personal knowledge, personal faith, personal use of the Bible.

The entire work of the Church, of saving souls, of extending it by missionary endeavor, of internal unification, of presenting a fighting front against error and Satan, of doing God's work upon earth, is based on the Word of God and its use. Personal Christianity of the individual, the joining of these individuals into the Christian community of a congregation, the union of such congregations into larger groups for the prosecution of the Lord's work, is right, blessed, and eternally successful only in the measure in which the Bible is properly used. This must be to him who calls himself a Christian a potent incentive to constantly use this precious revelation of our God earnestly, zealously, and properly. This simply means that at home, at school, at church, as an individual, as congregations, as synod, the less we use the Scriptures properly, the less will the work of the Lord flourish. The more we use that Word, the more will those things that God wants and which He can and will bless, manifest themselves in our thinking, speaking, and living. To bring about a more universal use of the Scriptures, many and varied plans and devices have been suggested and recommended. We do not deny that many of these are of value, that they may serve to lead men to the Scriptures and into them. But we must never overlook the fact that the love for God's Word must essentially flow out of the love for God Himself. All of our plans for an increase in the proper use of the Scriptures will fail, and fail miserably, unless we lay the foundation upon the relationship which exists between man and God in Christ Jesus. Pastors, teachers, congregations, synod, can and must be everlastingly concerned in bringing to the hearts of men the knowledge that God loved the world, that God loved the sinner. From this love of God to men flows and grows man's love to God. Where that relationship of love is warm and intimate, there will also be found a willingness, yes, a zealous eagerness to know what that loving God has to say to sinners, there the Bible will be used in church, school, and home, and used as the loving God would have it used.

May the next century of our dear Synod's existence find that warmth of love to God ever on the increase among and in us. Then, and then only, shall we also be worthy of the blessings of the past and of the promises of the future. Then we shall indeed be and remain the Bible Church.

VI

The Use of God's Word in the Home

God's Word may be used in the home by the individuals privately or by all of the members or by any number of them collectively. The former is called private devotion, or worship, while the latter is designated as family worship, or devotion. We shall for convenience' sake combine the two forms in our presentation.

THESIS I

Definition

By "family devotion" and "private devotion" we understand the reverent contemplation of God's Word and the offering of true prayer in the family circle or by individual Christians, apart from public worship.

This thesis deals with the essence of private and family devotion or worship. The term "devotion" has reference to the attitude of heart of the participants, while "worship" points chiefly to the purpose for which God's Word is being used. Usually, however, this difference is not observed.

The first essential part of family and private devotion mentioned by our thesis is "the reverent contemplation of God's Word." As in the public church service, so also in family devotion the Word of God is the heart and core of the service, differing only in the mode of presentation. In church it is usually spoken, while at home it is mostly read.

To the essence of family devotion belongs, secondly, "the offering of true prayer." A divine service without prayer, whether it be in church or at home, is incomplete. True, the important thing is that

God speaks to us in His Word, but, as children of God, we will want to speak to Him also.

The adjectives "reverent" and "true" indicate the necessity of faith, if such acts of worship are to be pleasing and acceptable to God (Rom. 14:23). If performed by unbelievers or hypocrites, they are a mere lip-service and as such an abomination unto the Lord (Matt. 15:8).

To distinguish family devotion from public worship our thesis adds the words "in the family circle or by individual Christians, apart from public worship." The public service is attended by Christian families in the same locality; family devotion is confined to the members of one household. In charge of the public service is a duly called minister, while the family worship is usually conducted by the father of the family. The public service is usually a Sunday service, while family devotion takes place daily. Finally, in the public service the Sacraments are administered, which is not the purpose of the worship in the home.

Family devotion is as old as Christianity. In all ages God-fearing men have gathered their households about them for joint meditation in God's Word and for prayer. The patriarch Abraham, by his outstanding example in this respect, receives special commendation from the Lord (Gen. 18:19). David and Daniel, as the Scriptures testify, had regular hours for the contemplation of the Word and for prayer. In Timothy's home, family devotion was faithfully conducted, for he knew the Bible from his youth (II Tim. 3:15), having been taught by his mother and grandmother "from a child" (cf. II Tim. 1:5; Acts 16:1, 2). The outstanding Bible students of the New Testament are, no doubt, the Bereans who searched the Scriptures daily (Acts 17:11). May we be encouraged by the example of these men of God.

THESIS II

The Neglect of Family Devotion

In many Christian homes family and private devotion is sadly neglected.

In the Golden Age of the Christian Church, the days of the first love, the Christians continued daily with one accord in the Temple, breaking bread from house to house, praising God (Acts 2:46), continuing steadfastly in the Apostles' doctrine and fellowship and in breaking of bread and in prayers (Acts 2:42). The very fact that the Christians assembled for public services in private homes besides their attendance at the Temple, proves their love of God's Word and their eagerness to make use of every opportunity to hear and read and study the Word of God.

When the first love grew cold and the spirit of the world made inroads into the congregations, this was evidenced by their neglect to study the Bible, and the Apostles felt it their duty to admonish the Christians to let the Word of Christ dwell among them richly in all wisdom, teaching and admonishing one another in psalms and hymns and spiritual songs (Col. 3:16); and to warn them against neglecting the Word of God by pointing out the danger of such neglect (Heb. 2:1-3; 5:12-14; Rev. 2 and 3).

Neglect of family and private devotion is a sin recurring throughout the history of the Church. Gregory the Great, bishop of Rome, died 604, in whose congregation the Bible seems to have been widely disseminated, rebukes his members for their neglect in reading the Sacred Word and earnestly exhorts them to read the Bible diligently in their homes. Had all his successors in office been of the same mind, the Church of the Middle Ages would never have sunk so deeply. The Waldensians correctly ascribed the deterioration and corruption of the Church to the prevailing neglect of the Scriptures. In point of Bible reading they shine as a bright light in an otherwise dark age. Among them the Bible was widely distributed, diligently read, and whole books were committed to memory.

The invention of the printing press increased the number of Bibles, but there was no great increase in Bible reading. The learned were almost exclusively absorbed in the study of the Church Fathers and the scholastics, while the common people were encouraged neither by their priests nor by the existing miserable, almost unintelligible translations to read the divine Word. Luther's masterly and classical translation was welcomed as a refreshing rain after a severe and long drought. So eager was the demand that first editions were quickly exhausted and reprints had to be made. In the homes, in the workshops, in the taverns, by day and by night, the Bible was read. Family devotion flourished. Now the Romanists complained that the people were too well read in the Scriptures, and measures were taken for its suppression. But already before Luther's death a gradual weariness and satiety became evident, and Luther warned that the Word of God would again become a widely unknown book. A prophet, indeed! Under Jesuitism and Rationalism, his prophecy was fulfilled.

Shall history repeat itself in the life of our Church? Our fathers came to America with the love of truth enshrined in their hearts and the beloved Bible in their hands. Faced with the tremendous and consuming task of building a Church of the pure Word and of wresting a living from the wilderness, they yet found time to transform their mean dwellings into veritable houses of God with daily Bible reading and prayer. Does the same love for God and for His precious Word still move us Christians to diligent observance of family devotion? Are we worthy successors of our fathers? Let each one answer this question for himself.

Thesis III

Reasons for the Neglect of Family Devotion

In Roman Catholic homes the main cause for the neglect of family devotion is the prohibition of Bible reading and the suppression of the Bible.

It is the teaching of the Roman Church that the laity need not, in fact, should not read the Bible. Catholics, of course, deny the existence of any such Bible-reading prohibition, at least of any formal prohibition. Indeed, many of the pious Church Fathers of the first six centuries urged Bible reading upon the laity. Gregory I recommended it without limitation. Augustine earnestly pressed for translations of the Bible for the propagation of the Gospel. But as the Roman Catholic Church departed more and more from Scriptural doctrine and practice, it began to regard the unrestricted use of the Bible as dangerous. As time went on, the Bible was increasingly relegated to the background in favor of tradition. Beginning with Gregory VII (1073-1085), we find a definite antipathy toward Bible reading on the part of the people. Gregory himself feared that, if the Bible came into the hands of the masses, it might be held in contempt or be misunderstood and thus become misleading. When the Waldenses appealed to the Bible against the errors of Rome, Innocent III in 1199 prohibited the private possession and reading

of the Bible in the vernacular and ordered that such copies as could
be seized be burned. The Council of Toulouse in 1229 and of Ter-
racona in 1234 added their amen. To offset the influence of Wycliffe's
translation of the Bible, the Council of Oxford in 1408 declared its
opposition to the translation of a single Bible text without the consent and approval of the bishop or the provincial synod. Archbishop
Berthold of Mainz in 1468 forbade by decree the translation of any
religious book, in particular the Bible, into German, because the
people had no capacity for the understanding of such things.

Then came the Reformation. The Lord Himself opened the way
for the Bible through Luther's superlative translation. Immediately
a storm of opposition broke. Duke George of Saxony rigorously
forbade its distribution in the duchy, demanding that all copies in
the hands of the people be delivered up on pain of punishment.
Grandduke Ferdinand of Austria, the Duke of Bavaria, and the
Margrave and Elector of Brandenburg followed suit. Despite its
suppression Luther's translation spread as if borne on angels' wings.
As a countermeasure Duke George of Saxony authorized Luther's
bitter enemy, Hieronymus Emser, to prepare a Roman translation
of the New Testament. Emser paid the highest compliment to the
excellence of Luther's translation by retaining it almost intact, substituting, however, his own preface, title page, and comments.

But no matter how powerful the stream, Rome tried to stem it.
The Council of Trent (1545-1563) authorized the Pope to draw up
a list of books deemed unsound and heretical. In the resultant
famous Index Librorum Prohibitorum all of Luther's writings, including his Bible translation, were placed under the ban. In the
encyclical of Leo XIII, 1897, the rule is laid down that "all versions
in the vernacular, even by Catholics, are altogether prohibited,
unless approved by the Holy See, or published under the vigilant
care of the bishops, with annotations from the Fathers of the Church
and learned Catholic writers." Even with these safeguards, Rome is
far from enthusiastic about Bible reading on the part of the laity.

Rome took a similar attitude over against Bible societies. At the
beginning of the nineteenth century there was a movement among
certain Catholic scholars, who had experienced the blessings of Bible
reading, to circulate the Scriptures more freely among their own
faith. Consequently several translations were issued, notably those
of Wittmann, Bishop Seiler, Leander van Ess, and John Gossner. A

Catholic Bible society was organized in 1805 with the approval and active co-operation of the bishop and in twelve years of its existence disseminated half a million copies of the New Testament. A papal bull of 1817 brought its blessed work to a speedy end. The popes view the Bible societies with extreme displeasure. Their attitude is summed up by Leo XII, who called them "a pest."

In many Lutheran homes family devotion and the Bible are neglected for various reasons. Chief among these are: 1. There is no time; 2. parents are not habituated to Bible reading; 3. unfamiliarity with the content and divine power of the Bible; 4. antipathy, loathing, repugnance, and satiety. The real reason is indifference.

There are many Lutheran homes in which family devotion is regularly conducted. On the other hand, however, we must confess that in many of our Christian homes the Bible is indeed the forgotten book. What are the reasons?

1. Many people plead lack of time. Such an excuse is convenient, comfortable, but it is neither valid nor truthful. Time is taken for eating and drinking and sleeping. If one objects that these things must be done, else one cannot live, Christ's answer is, "Search the Scriptures, for . . . they are they which testify of Me" (John 5:39); and there is no hope of eternal life except through Christ (Acts 4:12); and Scripture is the only book which reveals to us this Christ as Our Savior. Moreover, our Lord said of the soul, not of the body, that it is more precious than the combined riches of the world. Where there is the will, a way will usually be found for conducting family devotion even in the busiest households. And if not all members can be present, then the individual members will be the more anxious to read the Bible for themselves.

2. Another reason for the neglect of family devotion is the fact that parents themselves have never become habituated to it. Habit and example are, admittedly, powerful educational means (Prov. 22:6). Now, when we consider that Christian children are flesh born of the flesh, and that the flesh of the Christian child dislikes God's Word and regards daily study of the Bible as a wearisome, disagreeable task, we see how vitally important it is that parents, by example and precept, train their children to this godly habit. Much more can be accomplished in the home than in the church or the Christian school, where time and opportunity for Bible reading are necessarily limited. Nor is it true that a child must be six, eight, or even ten

years of age before it can derive benefit from the reading or hearing of God's Word. Such a claim is not only an unwarranted limitation of the power of the Holy Spirit, who works in the heart through the means of the Word, but it is also contrary to experience and observation. The mere habit of reading the Bible, of course, does not save anyone, but the quickening Word can become a great blessing if it is used. Let us fix the Bible-reading habit in our children by instituting family worship and urging them to read and study their Bibles.

In some cases the blame must also be shared by the pastor and the teacher, when they offer little encouragement to parents in the establishment of family devotion, or fail to awaken in the children a sincere love of the Word and to provide opportunities to read it. Through sermons, public and private instruction, and evangelical admonitions the faithful pastor can exert a blessed influence toward the establishment and maintenance of this God-pleasing house service.

3. Unfamiliarity with the content and the divine power of the Bible is another reason why the Bible is not used in so many homes. The failure to form the Bible-reading habit in youth usually results in a defective knowledge of the Bible in later life, in spite of regular attendance at the Sunday services. Where such a meager knowledge is found, there is also little desire for the reading of the Scriptures. If such people would really apply themselves to Bible reading, they would, like Luther, find a wonderland of heavenly truth and comfort that would increasingly whet the spiritual appetite.

4. Our thesis mentions as a further reason for the neglect of Bible reading antipathy, aversion, loathing, satiety. When family devotions are extended beyond all reason and children are overfed with the Word, or when children are punished by being forced to read a psalm of repentance or even to memorize the 119th Psalm, then parents are well on the way to making Bible reading and devotion a loathsome business to their children. Coercion and force in any form will not produce love and respect for the Word, but will only strengthen the natural antipathy to the reading of the Scriptures. Here is the reason why children of respectable Christian families at times develop into prize rascals.

Loathing of God's Word may be caused also by spiritual pride. There may be Christians who formerly were diligent Bible readers but whom Satan has seduced to believe that they have absorbed all that the Bible teaches. Why then read the Scriptures further? Consequently, the appetite disappears. Satiety sets in, and the Bible collects dust.

Other excuses for the neglect of family devotion may be that some parents feel that they are not capable of leading the family in devotions; others regard it as an adiaphoron, or matter indifferent; still others consider it unnecessary in view of regular church and Christian day school attendance and private prayer. That would be too much of a good thing. Finally, there are those who frankly admit that family worship should be conducted in their homes, but simply do nothing about it. So go the excuses.

Underlying all these excuses is indifference—the same indifference and coldness that makes men neglectful of the public services, of Holy Communion, of active participation in the work of the Church at home and abroad. A combination of lukewarmness, weak faith, and the forces of evil within us will soon cause family devotion to be neglected. Even if the spirit is still willing, flesh and blood are weak and constantly exposed to the influence of sin that dwells in us. It is that old antithesis of which Paul writes: "For I know that in me (that is, in my flesh) dwelleth no good thing: for to will is present with me; but how to perform that which is good I find not. For the good that I would I do not; but the evil which I would not, that I do. Now, if I do that I would not, it is no more I that do it, but sin that dwelleth in me" (Rom. 7:18-20).

We are living in the last times, pressed hard by the world and unceasingly assaulted by the devil. Must we not, therefore, the more zealously conduct family devotion in our homes and arm ourselves with the invincible Word?

Thesis IV

Motivation for Diligent Observance of Family Devotion

A. IT IS A DIVINE SERVICE

The conviction that family devotion is truly a divine service, rendered unto God, should move and encourage us to diligent observance of the same.

Does our use of God's Word and prayer in family worship really constitute a service rendered unto God? Strictly speaking, God serves us, for we are the recipients of the benefits and blessings connected with the Word and prayer. Yet, when we, in obedience to the numerous Scriptural injunctions, devoutly and in childlike faith, read and consider the Bible, pray, and sing hymns, God truly looks upon these acts as a service rendered unto Him, acceptable and well-pleasing unto Him.

Furthermore, our Lord says in Matt. 25:40: "Inasmuch as ye have done it unto one of the least of these My brethren, ye have done it unto Me." Through our joint contemplation of God's Word and prayer we serve one another, strengthen one another's faith and love. When we serve Christ's brethren, we serve God. We have, therefore, the fullest right to call family devotion our divine service.

Here, under the parental roof, a real congregation daily assembles to worship God, a house congregation, consisting of souls purchased with the precious blood of the Savior and pledged to Him in Holy Baptism. The Lord's gracious promise pertains to them also: "Where two or three are gathered in My name, there am I in the midst of them" (Matt. 18:20).

Nor is this house-congregation without its priest. The Bible offers ample evidence for the glorious doctrine of the spiritual priesthood of all New Testament believers (Is. 61:6; I Pet. 2:5, 9; Rev. 1:5, 6; Rev. 5:9, 10). In contrast to the faithful of the Old Testament, God has vested in all Christians of the New Dispensation all the rights and privileges, as well as the duties and responsibilities of the priestly office. And, since all believers are priests before God, it is self-evident that just he who presides over the household by God's ordinance should exercise this office. Let the fathers, then, teach the Word and tell their households what great things the Lord hath done for them (Mark 5:19; Luke 6:45; Gen. 18:19), pray for and with them, sing His praises; in short, conscientiously hold family devotion. As the head of the house, that is the father's foremost priestly privilege and duty.

Finally, family devotion is a divine service, because the Word of God and prayer are used in connection and constitute its essence. (Cf. Thesis I.)

For these reasons we arrive at this inescapable truth: Family devotion is truly a divine service, rendered unto God, acceptable and well-pleasing to Him, and richly blessed by Him.

What a powerful incentive! Our hearts should leap for joy that we can serve the mighty Lord of heaven in our homes. Hindrances, which at times make our presence at the public worship impossible, such as impassable roads, sickness in the family, necessary bodily preparation, are here all removed. Quickly the family can assemble, just as they are, the old man and the child in the cradle, the strong and the sick—to serve God! He makes it exceedingly easy for us to serve Him. Should that not make us willing and eager for such service?

B. IT IS DIVINELY COMMANDED

A second motive for regular and diligent use of God's Word and prayer in family devotion is God's express command.

When we consider that the relation of the believer to his God is that of a child to a father, a command to read God's Word and to speak to Him in prayer would seem altogether superfluous and unnecessary. Would we need a command to read a letter received from an earthly king or a famous man? With what eagerness and pride would we read and reread it, treasure it, display it at every opportunity! The Bible is the autographed letter of the Lord of Lords and King of Kings. What bride would have to be asked to read a letter from her bridegroom? The Bible is the epistle of Christ, the heavenly Bridegroom, addressed to His bride, the Church, and every individual member of that Church, assuring them of His eternal love.

Because of our weak and sinful nature God has added the express command. Such a command to read the Sacred Record is found in Deut. 6:6-9: "And these words which I command thee this day, shall be in thine heart: and thou shalt teach them diligently unto thy children, and shalt talk of them when thou sittest in thine house and when thou walkest by the way, and when thou liest down, and when thou risest up. And thou shalt bind them for a sign upon thine hand, and they shall be as frontlets between thine eyes. And thou shalt write them upon the post of the house, and on the gates." A parallel passage, Deut. 11:18, expresses the command in this way: "Lay up these My words in your heart and in your soul." The heart and soul are the true ark of the covenant in which the Law of God is to be preserved. If the Law is to be preserved in the heart, then the children must be instructed in this word as often as there is time and opportunity.

God told Joshua: "This book of the law shall not depart from thy mouth: but thou shalt meditate therein day and night, that thou mayest observe to do according to all that is written therein" (Josh. 1:8). The expression "book of the law" is explained in the previous verse as "all the laws, which Moses, My servant, commanded thee," not merely the Ten Commandments, but the Pentateuch, the entire Bible as it then existed. According to God's command, Joshua is to proclaim this book of the law and meditate in it day and night, something which could not be done without reading it.

Let us particularly note God's exhortation Is. 34:16: "Seek ye out of the Book of the Lord and read: no one of these shall fail, none shall want her mate; for My mouth it hath commanded, and His Spirit it hath gathered them." A plain and definite command for Bible reading. To whom is it addressed? The first verse of this chapter tells us: "Come near, ye nations, and hear."

Now for some New Testament texts in which Bible reading is commanded. "Let the Word of Christ dwell in you richly in all wisdom; teaching and admonishing one another in psalms and hymns and spiritual songs, singing with grace in your hearts to the Lord" (Col. 3:16). It is apparent from the use of the words "richly" and "dwell" in this text that God has not a mere Sunday use of His Word in mind. Such weekly association with the Word for one hour could hardly be called a rich dwelling of the Word among us. Clearly, this is an express command for family devotion, in which the Word is not an infrequent guest, but a member of the family, a daily associate, an intimate confidant, a blessed companion.

Our Lord commands Bible reading when He says: "Search the Scriptures; for in them ye think ye have eternal life: and they are they which testify of Me" (John 5:39). The Scriptures referred to in this text are the writings of the Old Testament. Again, attendance upon the Word in the Sunday service can certainly not be termed a searching of the Scriptures. The expression implies, rather, an assiduous, diligent delving for the pure gold of the Bible with the untiring zeal and unwearied application characteristic of the gold miner. How can this command be fulfilled without private and family devotion?

"Ye fathers, provoke not your children to wrath; but bring them up in the nurture and admonition of the Lord" (Eph. 6:4) is God's brief but comprehensive course in pedagogy. The parental duty is given first negatively as avoidance of all harsh, cruel, arbitrary, inconsistent treatment tending to irritate or exasperate the children. On the positive side, fathers are instructed to bring them up, to nourish them to maturity, by giving them the spiritual food they need to become ever more useful members of the Christian Church. This should be done "in the nurture," or discipline, "and admonition of the Lord," by applying the pedagogical methods and correctives prescribed by the Lord in His Word. That presupposes a thorough knowledge of the Bible and a constant use of it.

Paul wrote his letters to congregations and individuals for the purpose that they be read and studied, as becomes evident from the opening verses of almost all his letters. (Rom. 1:7; I Cor. 1:2; II Cor. 1:1; Gal. 1:2; Eph. 1:1; Phil. 1:1; I Thess. 1:1; II Thess. 1:1; compare also I Pet. 1:1; I John 1:1-4; Luke 1:3; Acts 1:1; John 20:31; Col. 4:15, 16; I Thess. 5:27.)

God also commands the offering of true prayer in the family circle. In explaining the Second Commandment Luther mentions as the proper and God-pleasing use of the Lord's name that we "call upon it in every trouble, pray, praise, and give thanks." This is also commanded in I Thess. 5:17, 18: "Pray without ceasing. In every thing give thanks; for this is the will of God in Christ Jesus concerning you." The fulfillment of this command demands family prayers. The wording of the Fourth Petition: "Give us *this day* our daily bread," implies that we should jointly pray for God's gifts every day.

Wherever devout children of God are assembled, there is the spiritual temple of the Lord (I Cor. 3:16; Eph. 2:19-22); there prayers with and for one another should ascend to the throne of grace, and there is the promise of the abiding presence of Christ (Matt. 18:19, 20). In accordance with the will of his heavenly Father, the head of the house should together with the members of his house daily come to the mercy seat of heaven and offer his prayers, intercessions, and thanksgiving.

Do we need further encouragement?

Let us look at the examples of godly men. Although not anointed to the official priestly office, Abraham faithfully performed the functions of a priest in his house, proclaiming the blessed words and promises of God. David's love for the Law of God is attested to in numerous psalms (*e. g.*, Ps. 26:6-8; Ps. 27:4), while the same psalms afford an excellent view of the rich prayer life of this shepherd-king, prophet, and sweet singer of Israel. Joshua pledged himself and his household to the service of the Lord. Daniel, president of the great kingdom of Darius, daily and openly performed his prayers, even in the face of loss of position and life. Would that Christians everywhere would as zealously read the Bible on trips as did the treasurer of Ethiopia, and at home daily search the Scriptures with the readiness of those Berean Bible students!

Would God so constantly and earnestly command, exhort, and encourage us, by word and example, to daily contemplation of His Word and prayer, if the Word were not really necessary for us and for the members of the family individually and collectively? Far more than we need the three daily meals for the sustenance of the body, do we need the daily nourishment for our souls provided in family devotion.

C. IT BESTOWS DIVINE BLESSINGS

The inexpressible blessings connected with Bible reading and prayer are a further powerful inducement to faithfulness in family worship.

Joyfully will we carry out our Lord's command with respect to family devotion when we are fully aware that His Word is "the fount of heavenly grace, true manna from on high." But cannot the same blessing be received through the oral proclamation of the Word? The power of the Word is, of course, not dependent upon the medium through which it enters the heart, be it the eye or the ear. But who can deny the advantages of the more leisurely and deliberate reading of the Bible at home over against the swift and constant flow of thoughts in the sermon?

1. The first glorious blessing of Bible reading is, to use the words of St. Paul, that it is "able to make us wise unto salvation through faith which is in Christ Jesus" (II Tim. 3:15). In John 5:39 our Lord asserts that eternal life can be found in the Scriptures because they testify of Him. That glorious hymn of praise of God's Word, Ps. 119, declares that the testimony of the Lord gives life. St. Paul asserts that it was the Bible that imparted to Timothy the glorious wisdom of salvation. The Word is the vehicle of the Holy Spirit through which He makes of lost condemned slaves of the devil blessed children of God. David regards God's Word as more desirable than gold, yea, than much fine gold, sweeter than honey and the honeycomb (Ps. 19:10).

2. Faithful observance of family devotion increases Christian knowledge. Assiduous attention to the Bible at home is an excellent method of acquiring a greater familiarity with precious Scriptural truths and of treasuring them in the memory for use and application to situations as they arise. Bible reading makes the full Christian. Why the frequent complaint that many Christians who regularly attend the public services of the congregation are still as children in knowledge, unable to digest strong food? (Heb. 5:11-14.) The underlying cause is the neglect of Bible reading. And let us not forget the importance of prayer in the furtherance of spiritual knowledge. After all, Christian knowledge is a gift of the Holy Ghost, and God wants to be asked.

3. Family devotion not only produces an increase in knowledge, it also serves for the preservation and strengthening of faith, a great benefit indeed (Heb 13: 9), encompassed as we are by enemies of the faith from without and within. While all Christians possess the one and the same faith, there is a marked difference in the degree of faith among believers, a difference not pleasing to the Lord. He commends and praises great faith (Rom. 4:18-20; Matt. 8:10; 15:28); a weak faith merits his disapproval (Matt. 8:26). Just as it is God that begins the good work within us, so it is also He who preserves and strengthens our faith, and that He does—mark well—through the Gospel. If we thus search the Scriptures and daily and fervently pray, what an unfolding and development of faith would manifest itself in our midst, and what great things would be accomplished for the Lord!

4. A fourth blessing of family devotion is growth in sanctification. The daily association with God's Word in family devotion makes us realize more fully that there is still much lacking in our Christian make-up. We daily sin because of our weakness, ignorance, and heedlessness. Our best works are sullied by sin. Our love, the mainspring of all good works, is still imperfect. Simply to acknowledge this condition is not enough; we must grasp the only means for improvement. St. Paul declares that all Scripture is profitable also for correction, for instruction in righteousness, and able to make the man of God perfect, thoroughly furnished unto all good works (II Tim. 3:16, 17). The Law will show us the way we are to go, and the Gospel will provide the willingness to walk that narrow way, but

only if we use the Word. And our prayers will bring help and strength from on high.

Do we deplore the evil influence of the sinful flesh within us and in our children? The will to do what is good and right will be trained and strengthened through the Word. Is our love toward God and our neighbor like the flickering light of a candle? God's Word and prayer can kindle a bright flame. Do you find in your children a lack of reverence for all things holy? The Word will inculcate the fear of the Lord. Are you impatient under the cross? Through faithful use of the Word and prayer you will learn submissiveness to the will of your heavenly Father. Amidst the thousandfold distractions and allurements of this present world, the Scriptures daily sound the call to another and better world. When body and soul are fatigued, the divine Word holds before our eyes the eternal rest of the saints of God in heaven; when the battle rages fiercely, we have the promise of eternal victory and the crown of life.

What glorious things are accomplished through the Bible! Let us partake more fully of the offered blessings by a fuller use of the blessed custom of family devotion.

5. The reading of the Scriptures also strengthens the conviction that our Lutheran doctrine is founded on and agrees fully with the Bible. We Lutherans have always made the claim that our doctrine is true and pure. Rome makes the same claim, so do the sectarians. When you ask them, How do you know that yours is the true faith? the Catholic will answer with an appeal to tradition, and the sectarian, to reason. And the Lutheran? The Bible is the only source of my faith; all our doctrines are in agreement with the Scriptures, and therefore right and unadulterated. The Bible explicitly teaches that it is the sole source of faith. (Deut. 4:2; Josh. 23:6; Is. 8:20; Luke 16:29, 30.) Most severely it condemns the addition of man's word, tradition, and rationalism, for it is the complete and perfect and clear source of doctrine. And the more frequently we read the Bible and, like the Bereans of old, daily search the Scriptures whether those things are so that the Lutheran Church teaches, the more thoroughly will we be convinced that the doctrine of the Lutheran Church, like that of the Apostles, is not the word of men but in truth the Word of God. (Acts 17:11; I Thess. 2:13.)

6. Bible reading will also enable us to put to the test all the various doctrines advanced in our day and to reject and combat

error. God insists that we attain a man's stature in Christian knowledge in order that we may distinguish between truth and error (I John 4:1). Not only are such false prophets dangerous as are readily recognized as wolves, but in an even higher degree those who retain portions of the pure Word with an admixture of error—the wolves in sheep's clothing. Matt. 7:15 tells us to beware of them, and Rom. 16:17, 18; Eph. 4:14; I Thess. 5:21; Gal. 1:6, 7 to combat and overthrow their error and to shun them. But how can the common Christian judge doctrine? Do as the Bereans did. Apply the standard of the Word (Acts 17:11; John 8:31, 32). But in order to do this, you must know Sacred Writ with a thoroughness which only diligent personal and family worship can impart.

7. God's precious Word also gives us the spiritual wisdom needed for a correct understanding of the world and the signs of the times. In Luke 12:54f. and Matt. 16:1-3 the Pharisees are taken to task for their inability to discern the signs of the times. To avoid similar censure, we must be capable of a critical examination of the rapidly transpiring events in the world, and that in the light of the infallible Word, the true norm. Because our natural reason and judgment are faulty and untrustworthy, we need heavenly wisdom and sanctified understanding, which God will impart to us through regular use of His Book.

8. Family devotion will help to make the home a paradise. Where the Bible is reverently considered and joint prayers are offered, there, as a rule, you will find a God-pleasing and fine family life. Parents will love and honor one another, will earnestly endeavor to train their children in the fear of the Lord; and children will, in turn, serve and obey their parents in love. When the peace of the household is at times disrupted—for this paradise is not without sin —the sparks of discord will not be allowed to burst into bright flames and sear the lives of the family, but will be quenched at the beginning. Where Christian parents faithfully conduct devotions in their homes, apply the Word to themselves and their children, and take the welfare of their families to the Lord in prayer, there, in a measure, paradise on earth will be regained. But it must be remembered that even Adam had a Cain in his family.

9. Family devotion, finally, grants rich comfort amid the manifold sorrows and troubles of this present world. Our own experience and observation confirm the truth of Scripture that this world is a vale

of tears, that we must through much tribulation enter into the Kingdom of God (Acts 14:22). In one home it is extreme poverty with its attending anxieties; in another the grim reaper breaks the family circle; in a third serious and protracted illness casts a pall over the household. There is no Christian home without its cross. Where shall we find comfort? The Bible is an inexhaustible source of comfort in every need and trouble; it is the healing balm for every wound. In the hour of trial the blessing of family devotion reveals itself, for out of the treasury of divine comfort we can draw just those texts which offer particular healing for our peculiar need.

> O happy home, where Thou art loved most dearly,
>> Thou faithful Friend and Savior full of grace,
> And where among the guests there never cometh
>> One who can hold such high and honored place!
> O happy home where all, in heart united,
>> In holy faith and blessed hope are one,
> Whom bitter death a little while divideth,
>> Yet cannot end the union here begun.

Thesis V

The Manner and Mode of Family Devotion

All these blessings are assured if family devotion is conducted in the proper spirit and with due regard to its outward form and arrangement.

Family devotion must be conducted in the proper spirit if such glorious blessings are to be ours. Above all, it must be an expression of our sincere love of God, performed to the glory of our exalted Creator, Redeemer, and Sanctifier. With reverent and devout hearts and open and receptive minds we must assemble in our homes with the prayer on our lips: "Speak, O Lord, for Thy servant heareth." All distractions and frivolity should be cleared away and true composure sought on the part of the participants. Nor dare it degenerate into something mechanical, a mere routine, else much of the blessedness of this institution will be lost.

For a blessed observance of family devotion it is also necessary to give close attention to its outward form and arrangement, especially since the Bible offers no definite and detailed rules in this matter. However, the Apostle does enunciate a general principle when he says: "Let the Word of Christ dwell among you richly *in all wisdom.*" Christian wisdom is the ability to turn to good account the acquired knowledge for the benefit of self and others. It must decide how family devotion must be arranged in the individual case for the greatest edification.

Since the outward form of family devotion is a matter left to Christian liberty, we find almost every possible usage in the homes, in the matter of sitting or standing for devotions, in the use of the Bible and devotional books and hymns, etc. No prescribed form usually means a diversity of forms.

In our discussion of the outward form and arrangement of family worship, let us confine ourselves to the following points:

1. Who shall conduct the devotion in the home? As a rule, this is the duty of the divinely appointed head of the house, the father of the family. As the head of the family congregation, he is the representative of God, through whom God speaks to the family, and the representative of the family, through whom they speak to God. Of course, this does not exclude the joint recital of the Lord's Prayer, nor the confession of faith, nor the individual prayers of the children. Should the father be called by death or be absent from the home by reason of business, this duty of leading family devotion falls to the mother. Yet the parents may ask any member of the household to conduct all or part of the family devotion.

2. Who shall be present? If possible, all members of the family and also the servants, especially if they be of the household of faith; otherwise their presence is voluntary. Invite casual visitors and guests to take part as well. In no case, however, let any kind of company cause you to omit family devotion, for this could amount to denial of the Savior. (Matt. 10:32, 33; Luke 9:26.)

3. With regard to the time chosen for family worship, the exercise of Christian wisdom is doubly important, for every father will find it necessary, in the interest of regularity, to set a definite hour, most suitable to the members of the family. The most fitting and practical times are, without doubt, the regular mealtimes. There the best opportunity presents itself not merely to refresh the body with meat and drink, but also the soul with the Word of Life. Under our modern conditions it is extremely difficult and often impossible to

have the entire family united for worship. But Christian wisdom and determination will endeavor to find the best solution of this difficulty.

4. As to the length of devotions, Christian wisdom is indeed necessary to strike the happy medium. If it be too short and hurried, a reverent and blessed meditation in the Word is hardly possible; if immoderately protracted, a loathing for the Word may result, as the well-known example of Frederick the Great testifies.

What books are to be used in connection with family devotion? Since the consideration of the Word of God is an essential part of family worship, it necessarily follows that the Bible be the primary devotional book. At least once a day, in the morning or the evening, the Scriptures should be read. It would certainly not be in keeping with Christian wisdom if the divinely inspired Bible were neglected in favor of other devotional books. While good, orthodox devotional books have their proper place and their special blessings, yet they can never replace the inspired Scriptures. The Bible is and remains the devotional book of all devotional books.

In what sequence are the books of the Bible to be read? Even a little thought as to this matter will reveal that not all parts of the Bible are equally suited for the mixed group in family devotion, composed of mature and young Christians. Should one begin with Genesis and read, in order, all the books of the Bible? Those who have done this, find no particular merit in this plan. Far too much time is spent on the Old Testament. A much better and more profitable plan would be to alternate between the books of the Old Testament, reading such books, however, in their entirety. Very strongly Luther recommends that John's Gospel, the Epistles of Paul, especially Romans, and Peter's First Epistle be read first and most frequently. To this list one could add the other Gospels and books of the New Testament, Isaiah, and the Psalms. But do not despise the other books, for the goal must be to read the whole Bible. Even the pages of genealogies, usually skipped, are of value, for they testify in no uncertain terms that Jesus of Nazareth is the Messiah of promise.

6. Christian wisdom must likewise be employed in the choice and length of prayers. Avoid wearying the members of the household with excessively long prayers. Both printed and *ex corde* prayers

are permissible in family worship, the important thing being that such prayers proceed from the heart.

7. The singing of hymns in connection with family devotion seems to be falling into disuse in our circles. Yet how refreshing, vitalizing, and uplifting is the singing of the chorale! It is to be deplored that hymn singing in connection with devotion is becoming a thing of the past.

8. Excellent also is the common confession of faith and the recital of parts of the Catechism.

Thus, if family devotion is properly conducted, it proves to be a source of great blessings. How could it be otherwise? Wherever the Word is found, there God also is present, the bountiful, loving, heavenly Father, who has promised: "In all places where I record My name I will come unto thee and I will bless thee" (Ex. 20:24).

God grant that the old, God-pleasing, blessed institution of family devotion may be retained in our midst and be established in all Christian homes, and may all Christian parents declare with Joshua: "As for me and my house, we will serve the Lord" (Josh. 24:15).

VII

The Law and the Gospel

SOMEONE has said that the business of the ministry is "to comfort the afflicted and afflict the comfortable" (*Concordia Theological Monthly*, XV, p. 498). We do not know who said this first, but if it came from sectarian circles, it is an admission of that which Lutherans for years have taught, namely, that Law and Gospel are to be separated. The comfortable and secure are to be aroused to a realization of their sinful condition by the use of the Law. The afflicted are to be comforted with the promises of the Gospel. The thought that the minister is to "comfort the afflicted, but to afflict the comfortable" might well serve as a leitmotif for this essay.

We believe that the confusion which prevails in the preaching and teaching in sectarian circles is to a great extent due to the fact that the distinction between the Law and the Gospel is being ignored. For the right distinction between these two doctrines is the key to the Scriptures, without which a correct interpretation of the Scriptures is impossible (F. Pieper, *Christliche Dogmatik*, III, p. 290). It is this distinction which gives Lutheran preaching, the preaching of sin and grace, its characteristic nature. The Formula of Concord declares: "We believe, teach, and confess that the distinction between the Law and the Gospel is to be maintained in the Church with great diligence as an especially *brilliant light,* by which, according to the admonition of St. Paul, the Word of God is rightly divided" (*Triglot*, p. 801, 2; Eastern District, 1877, p. 47).

I. DEFINITION OF TERMS

A concise definition of the Law is given in Article V of the Formula of Concord: "Therefore we unanimously believe, teach, and confess that the Law is properly a divine doctrine, in which the

105

righteous, immutable will of God is revealed, what is to be the quality of man in his nature, thoughts, words, and works, in order that he may be pleasing and acceptable to God; and it threatens its transgressors with God's wrath and temporal and eternal punishments. For as Luther writes against the law stormers: 'Everything that reproves sin is and belongs to the Law, whose peculiar office it is to reprove sin and to lead to the knowledge of sins' (Rom. 3:20; 7:7); and as unbelief is the root and wellspring of all reprehensible sins, the Law reproves unbelief also" (*Triglot*, 957, 17).

What do we mean by the Gospel? The Formula of Concord says: "The Gospel is properly such a doctrine as teaches what man who has not observed the Law, and therefore is condemned by it, is to believe, namely, that Christ has expiated and made satisfaction for all sins, and has obtained and acquired for him, without merit of his, forgiveness of sins, righteousness that avails before God, and eternal life.

"But since the term 'Gospel' is not used in one and the same sense in Holy Scriptures, we believe, teach, and confess that if by the term 'Gospel' is understood the entire doctrine of Christ which He proposed in His ministry, as also did His Apostles (in which sense it is employed, Mark 1:15; Acts 20:21), it is correctly said and written that the Gospel is a preaching of repentance and of the forgiveness of sins" (*Triglot*, 801, p. 4f.).

We should note that there is a difference between Law and Gospel only in their narrow or proper sense, for in the broad sense Law may refer to all of divine revelation, including also the Gospel, as in Is. 2:3. Likewise, the word "Gospel" is used in a broad sense to refer to all of Christian doctrine including the Law; in other words, the whole of that which is taught in the Church is designated by the name of its choicest part. This is the use in Mark 1:1: "The beginning of the Gospel of Jesus Christ," which includes also the Law preaching of John, v. 4f. (F. Pieper, *Christl. Dogm.*, III, p. 262; Eastern, 1877, p. 35.)

II. LIKENESSES

Law and Gospel are alike in that both are God's Word and divine doctrines, and are therefore to be applied to all people everywhere. The Ten Commandments and other rules to be found in the Bible surely are God's Word and must be accepted and taught as God's holy will (Nebraska District, 1915, p. 53f.). All that tells us the good news of universal salvation through Christ by faith is a divine doctrine, a revelation of God's gracious will found nowhere but in the Bible (Nebraska, 1915, 46f.). And therefore both the Law and the Gospel must be taught side by side in the Church as the Word of the living God. It would be an error to say, as antinomians have done, that the Law belongs not in the pulpit, but only in the court-room and civil statutes.

The Law and the Gospel are both divine, unimpeachable doc-trines. Therefore they are alike also in that both are necessary (Nebraska, 1915, p. 55). Without the Law we cannot understand the Gospel. Without the Gospel the Law will be of no help, for the exclusive preaching of the Law will breed either hopeless despair or arrogant self-righteousness. (Eastern, 1877, p. 40). Both divine revelations must be preached in their proper order.

Law and Gospel are alike in that both are found in the Old as well as in the New Testament. It is wrong to say the Law is the doctrine of the Old and the Gospel the doctrine of the New Testa-ment. (Nebraska, 1915, p. 54). The Old Testament certainly contains Gospel (Gen. 3:15; Is. 53; etc.), and the New Testament preaches the Law. Jesus explained the Law in detail in the Sermon on the Mount and cleansed the Law of Jewish additions and misinterpreta-tions, and the Epistles of Paul and the other Apostles constantly apply the Law to the lives of the Christians (Iowa Dist., 1880, p. 25).

The Law and the Gospel do not contradict each other. Seeming contradictions vanish into thin air when the difference between Law and Gospel is kept in mind. The rich young ruler asked Jesus, "What good thing shall I do that I may have eternal life?" Jesus answered, "If thou wilt enter into life, keep the commandments" (Matt. 19:16). On the other hand, when the same question was directed to Paul and Silas by the jailer at Philippi, they answered, "Believe on the Lord Jesus Christ, and thou shalt be saved and thy house" (Acts 16:31). Jesus seems to contradict Paul. But the diffi-culty vanishes when we know how to divide Law and Gospel. The rich young ruler was still proud, self-righteous, secure; the mirror of the Law had to be held before him in order that he might learn that he was not yet perfect but a lost and condemned sinner. On the jailer, however, the Law had already done its work; he was on his knees, helpless and terrified, and would have committed suicide had not the Gospel been preached to him. The Law is right when it says, "This do, and thou shalt live." But since no man can fulfill the Law, the Gospel is also right which says, "Not through works, but through faith alone, heaven is yours" (Nebraska, 1915, p. 50).

Both Law and Gospel must be preached to the Christian. The Law is intended not only for the unbelievers, but for the Christians as well. As long as the Christians live in this world, their old Adam still is inclined toward all that is evil, and therefore the Formula of Concord correctly states: "Because of these lusts of the flesh the truly believing, elect, and regenerate children of God need in this life not only the daily instruction and admonition, warning, and threatening of the Law, but also frequently punishments, that they may be roused [the old man is driven out of them] and follow the Spirit of God, as it is written Ps. 119:71. And again, I Cor. 9:27. And again, Heb. 12:8; as Dr. Luther has fully explained this at greater length in the Summer Part of the Church Postil, on the Epistle for the Nineteenth Sunday after Trinity" (*Triglot*, p. 965). Furthermore, the Law serves the Christian as "a sure rule and standard of a godly life and walk, how to order it in accordance with the eternal and immutable will of God," and therefore "it is just the Holy Ghost who uses the written Law for instruction with them, by which the truly believing also learn to serve God, not according to their own thoughts but according to His written Law and Word." (Thorough Declaration, VI, 3; *Triglot*, p. 963.)

Antinomians, who hold that the Law no longer concerns the Christians, usually quote I Tim. 1:9: "The Law is not made for the righteous man but for the lawless and disobedient, for the ungodly and sinners." But it is an error to say that this passage denies the necessity of preaching the Law to the Christians. This passage "is not to be understood in the bare meaning that the justified are to live without law. For the Law of God has been written in their heart, and also to the first man immediately after his creation a law was given according to which he was to conduct himself. But the meaning of St. Paul is that the Law cannot burden with its curse those who have been reconciled to God through Christ; nor must it vex the regenerate with its coercion, because they have pleasure in God's Law after the inner man." (*Triglot*, p. 963, 5; Walther, *Gesetz und Evangelium*, p. 16.)

III. DIFFERENCES

In II Tim. 2:15 we find the expression "rightly dividing the Word of Truth." The term employed by the Apostle means to cut straight, to divide right (Barnes). The Word of Truth is obviously the Bible according to Jesus' own words "Thy Word is truth" (John 17:17). This must be properly divided, distributed, according to circumstances and the wants of hearers in order that each may receive what he needs at that particular time (Eastern, 1877, p. 49).

In his Letter to the Romans, Paul shows that there is a very definite line of demarcation between Law and Gospel. He writes: "Christ is the end of the Law for righteousness to every one that believeth" (Rom. 10:4). The Law is to remain in full force up to a certain point: Christ. So long as Christ is not there, the Law condemns, but with Him all threatening and punishment ends. For Christ has removed all cause for threats (Iowa, 1880, p. 40). Christ freed us from the Law inasmuch as He fulfilled it and took its curse away; we are no longer required to keep it in order to gain salvation (that would be impossible for sinners), for Christ now offers us His perfect righteousness, and he who receives Christ in faith is justified, God imputing to him the perfect righteousness of Christ and thus declaring him righteous.

Another passage which makes clear the distinction between the Law and the Gospel is Gal. 3:24: "Wherefore the Law was our schoolmaster to bring us unto Christ, that we might be justified by faith." The schoolmaster, the *paidagogos* was a stern supervisor of boys, usually a slave who conducted the boy to school. He was not the instructor. His duty was to lead the boy to school, and to watch over his behavior. The Law is likened to such a trainer because it arouses the consciousness of sin and is to conduct to Christ, the only Savior. It is here called a trainer "unto Christ" because only those who have learned from the Law their own sinful depravity and helplessness, will, by the grace of God, welcome and accept the hope of salvation offered them by the Gospel of Christ.

In interpreting this passage, we must be careful not to make a quasi Gospel out of the Law. The Law is not in itself a tutor unto Christ. It knows nothing of Christ; it works wrath, despair, and leads away from Christ. It shows sins and damnation, but does not explain how we can be rid of them. We are not to think that the terrors awakened by the Law are a part or the beginning of the movement toward Christ. We are in no part to be saved by the Law but only to be left empty, lost, bewildered, damned by it; thus the way is prepared for Christ and His Gospel. God at first concludes all under sin (Gal. 3:22) that He might in a manner different from the Law, by the promise and by faith, lead men to salvation. A priori it should not be said of people in general that the Law is a tutor unto Christ. But a posteriori it may be said of all Christians that the Law has become their schoolmaster unto Christ (*C. T. M.,* VI, pp. 192, 655; *Lehre und Wehre,* 33, p. 159).

An Old Testament passage which implies the distinction between Law and Gospel is Zech. 11:7: "I will feed the flock of the slaughter, even you, O poor of the flock. And I took unto me two staves; the one I called Beauty, and the other I called Bands; and I fed the flock." Every true shepherd has two staves: "Beauty," which is the Gospel, and "Bands," which is the Law. And he should know when to use the one and when to use the other, and not make the mistake of hurling the rod Bands among the sheep, the followers of Christ, and using the rod Beauty for wicked knaves (Walther, *G. u. E.,* p. 32).

Ezekiel uses similar language: "And will ye pollute Me among My people for handfuls of barley and for pieces of bread, to *slay* the souls that should *not die,* and to *save* the souls alive that should *not live,* by *your lying* to My people that hear your lies?" (Ezek. 13:9; Iowa, 1880, p. 29.) See also Matt. 13:52 and Luke 12:42.

This distinction between Law and Gospel was put to practical use in the Old and in the New Testament by the Prophets and Apostles. We think of Nathan's procedure with David (II Sam. 12:13); Christ and the adulterous woman who wept and washed His feet with her tears and hair (Luke 7:36-50); Peter in his sermon on the day of Pentecost (Acts 2:37-39); Paul and Silas in dealing with the jailer at Philippi (Acts 16:27-31); Paul with the man guilty of incest at Corinth (I Cor. 5:1-5 [Law] and II Cor. 2:6-8 [Gospel]).

Now we are ready to answer the question, What are the actual differences between Law and Gospel? One difference consists in the manner in which both were revealed to man. The Law was written into the heart of man at his creation (Rom. 2:14, 15). Through the fall of man this natural knowledge of the Law was partially erased, but not entirely wiped out. The remnant of the Law still known to natural man manifests itself in the activity of man's conscience; it also finds expression in some of the laws of civil government. This natural knowledge of the Law is true as far as it goes, but it is by no means perfect.

The Gospel, on the other hand, was given in an altogether different manner. No man knows of the Gospel by nature. It is not a product of human reason. The Gospel was revealed to man in a special way through Jesus and His Word of salvation. The idea of the Gospel, salvation without merit, but by grace, through faith in the Savior, is an idea foreign to the nature of man. That is the reason we call it Gospel—which term means good news—news, because it was not known before nor by nature. I Cor. 2:6-10 speaks of the "hidden wisdom . . . which none of the princes of this world knew . . . nor the wisdom of this world. Eye hath not seen nor ear heard . . . but God hath revealed them unto us by His Spirit" (Walther, *G. u. E.*, p. 7; Iowa, 1880, p. 17). See also Rom. 16:25-26.

Because only the Law and nothing of the Gospel is known to natural man, the art of dividing between the two is not a natural trait possessed in a greater or less degree by every human being. It is an aptitude which the Holy Ghost alone can and must impart. Luther says that he who understands this art should have the title of doctor of theology (Walther, 5), thus emphasizing the difficulty and importance of properly dividing Law and Gospel. Only the Holy Spirit can teach us the proper distinction between Law and Gospel. Man is self-righteous by nature. He seeks salvation by the works of the Law. Only the Holy Spirit can turn him away from the demands of the Law to find perfect righteousness and complete justification in his Savior Jesus. That is the lesson which the Holy Ghost must continually teach the believing children of God lest they relapse into self-righteousness or sink into despair when their conscience accuses them of having transgressed the holy Law of God (F. Pieper, *Christl. Dogm.*, III, p. 284).

Another difference between Law and Gospel regards their contents. The Law contains commandments as to what men are to do and not to do. The Gospel contains no such commandments, but reveals only what God has done for our salvation. The Law deals with our works, the Gospel with God's works. The Law is full of demands: "Thou shalt"; "Do this"; "Do not"; while the Gospel asks and encourages and empowers us to take and enjoy what God freely offers to us, grace and life and salvation.

A third difference between the Law and the Gospel pertains to their promises (Kansas, 1892, p. 17). While both promise eternal life, the Law promises it conditionally, and only the Gospel promises it freely. "The Law is not of faith, but the man that doeth them shall live in them" (Gal. 3:12). "This do, and thou shalt live" (Luke 10:28). The Law promises life, but only to one who really fulfills the Law in thoughts, words, and deeds. Compare Lev. 18:5; Deut. 27:26; James 2:10. But note the free and unconditional promises of the Gospel, Mark 16:16. "He that believeth," that is, he who accepts God's grace in Word and Sacraments through faith "shall be saved." Faith is not a work or a condition to be fulfilled by man, it is not a meritorious work; faith is merely acceptance and trust (Eph. 2:8-10; Iowa, 1880, p. 20).

A fourth difference, intimately connected with the former two, pertains to threats and warnings. The Law asks for perfect fulfillment, and if there is no perfect fulfillment, it pronounces its curses and threats (Gal. 3:10). Wherever there are curses or threats in the Bible, you can be sure that there you have Law. For the Gospel knows of no curses; it has only promises and comforting assurances. Whenever there is threatening in connection with the Gospel, that is Law.

A fifth difference pertains to the office and purpose of both Law and Gospel. We ask, What is the office of the Law? According to our Catechism and Article VI of the Formula of Concord the purpose of the Law is: "first, that thereby outward discipline might be maintained . . . secondly, that men thereby may be led to the knowledge of their sins . . . thirdly, that after they are regenerate . . . they might . . . have a fixed rule according to which they are to regulate and direct their whole life" (*Triglot,* p. 805, 1).

In the first place, the Law is to serve as a curb by preventing in a measure the coarse outbursts of sin. God knows that wherever the evil nature inherent in man should be allowed to have full sway, a veritable deluge of sin and vice and crime would sweep over the world. For that reason God inscribed into man's heart His holy Law, which tells man that every transgression of this Law will be punished and that he must live in accordance with this Law if peace and order is to rule on earth. Where this Law is observed, even in its outward works, conformity with this divine rule results in the welfare of individuals and committees. But only too frequently even the voice of the natural Law is set aside. The inherent evil breaks through the curb, and sin and its evil consequences will cause unrest, disorder, sorrow, death.

A second, and the chief, purpose of the Law is to serve as a mirror. "By the Law is the knowledge of sin" (Rom. 3:20). If a man carefully studies the Law of God and compares his own life and deeds with God's demands, he will realize that he has not kept the Law. Even the natural Law written in his heart will convict him of his sinfulness and of the necessity of regaining God's favor. And acquaintance with the Law as revealed in its full scope in Holy Scripture will serve only to deepen the sense of guilt, may fill man's heart with abject terror. In his agony he will exclaim, "What must I do to be saved?" To this question the Law has no other answer than the demand of perfect obedience (Deut. 27:26; Gal. 3:10; Rom. 6:23; Ezek. 18:20). This inexorable demand of the Law, its unrelenting curse, and his own helplessness will either plunge man into black despair, or he will set himself in defiance against God, will charge Him with harshness, cruelty, and injustice, and show his defiance against God by choosing a life of sin and vice and wickedness. So the Law will work wrath (Rom. 4:15); will kill, because it is the ministry of death, of condemnation (II Cor. 3:6, 7, 9).

A third purpose of the Law is to serve the regenerate as a rule for good works. This is the third use of the Law according to Article VI of the Formula of Concord. There it is stated that believers are not without the Law but should exercise themselves in it day and night (Ps. 1:2; 119). "Even our first parents before the Fall did not live without Law, who had the Law of God written into their hearts" (*Triglot,* p. 805, 2; Nebraska, 1916, p. 37).

What is the office and purpose of the Gospel? Since the Gospel is the glad tidings of great joy that God sent His own Son to deliver man from sin and death, the office and purpose of the Gospel is to forgive sins, give heaven and salvation as a gift of free grace. The Gospel is the means of grace which in spite of sin and condemnation gives salvation to him who believes. "The Gospel is a power of God unto salvation to everyone that believeth." The Gospel is the "Word of Life" in a perverse and crooked nation. The Gospel not only offers all heavenly blessings but also effects the acceptance of these gifts, which is faith. It produces peace of heart, for the person knows he is reconciled to God. It changes the heart, regenerates man, gives him the new life, and now he begins to love God, whom he formerly hated (Iowa, 1880, p. 23).

A sixth difference between the Law and the Gospel regards the persons to whom the one or the other is to be applied. The Law is not to be preached to the terrified sinners, those who weep over their sins, for that would drive them to despair and to destruction without ever having known the all-forgiving Savior. The Gospel, on the other hand, must not be preached to those who are proud, secure, self-righteous, for that would lull them into self-satisfaction. They would never be led to repentance and would die in their sins.

Because the Law and the Gospel differ so essentially, the Church of Christ and all its members, teachers, and pastors must learn to distinguish and differentiate between these two doctrines of the Bible. Luther says in his sermon on the difference between Law and Gospel (1532) that where this difference is not understood one cannot tell the difference between a Christian, a heathen, or a Jew (F. Pieper, *Christl. Dogm.*, III, p. 286; Kansas, 1892, p. 22f.).Without this distinction the Christian religion is robbed of its distinctive character and its distinctive comfort. This will become increasingly clear to us as we proceed in our study.

IV. PURITY OF LAW AND GOSPEL

The purity of the Law is destroyed when the scope of the Law is not correctly understood and defined. If we had only the natural Law, we would not know the full extent of the Law, for in the fall of man the full knowledge of the Law was in a large measure obscured. Only the Bible can teach us just how far the compass of the Law extends and what are its limits. If we abide with the Bible, we shall never have trouble in determining the extent of the Law (Nebraska, pp. 23, 58f.; Iowa, 1880, p. 52f.).

On the one hand, there are those who increase the area of the Law by adding man-made laws under the guise of binding religion. Things not forbidden they forbid; adiaphora are raised to the level of binding laws. Here belong the Pharisees of all ages, those who insist on the keeping of ceremonial and sabbath laws, the advocates of blue laws, and those who legalistically bind the consciences of men by making matters obligatory which God has not commanded.

On the other hand, the full extent of the Law is impaired when not all divine Laws are regarded as having equal importance. We

dare not divide the Law of God into minor and major commandments; such a distinction is unwarranted (Nebraska, 1915, p. 59).
We become guilty of vitiating the Law when we think lightly of
"small sins," habitual sins, sins of weakness, sins of the times. While
the Bible makes a difference between deliberate sins and sins of
weakness, or unknown sins (Luke 12:47-48; Matt. 11:16-24), yet
it does not differentiate in the sense that God punishes only deliberate sins and merely winks at others. Every sin is a rebellion against
God and worthy of death (Gal. 3:10; Deut. 27:26; James 2:10;
Matt. 12:36). Therefore a pastor must mention in his sermons not
merely national sins, crime in general, but he must warn diligently
and particularly against those sins that are quite common in his congregation, and point out very definitely the lesson Christ teaches so
often, that evil thoughts and desires are truly sins, transgressions of
God's holy Law.

To keep the Law pure, one dare not weaken its threats. God's
threats are total threats (Ex. 20:5; Ps. 5:5; Ezek. 18:4). God is
serious about these threats; He is the enemy of sin. But there are
always those who wish to take the teeth out of God's Law by
toning down either its demands or its threats, or both; who try to
sweeten the Law, as when they say that God is satisfied as long as
people do as well as they can, or that God will not damn eternally,
or that hell will not be as hot as it is pictured. The Catholic doctrines of purgatory and the treasury of the works of the saints
weaken the threats of the Law.

The Law is binding upon all people, and a denial of its universal
obligation vitiates and destroys the purity of the Law. All are
subject to the Law; there is no exception. The rich are not excused
from its demands, nor are the poor; neither saints nor sinners;
neither pastor nor people. Every soul that sinneth shall die. We often
hear people say that youth must be allowed to "sow its wild oats."
What is that but granting youth an exemption from the Law and
common decency? Some would excuse the rich from the Law. Laymen might be tempted to say, Because I am not a pastor, I can take
greater liberties than the clergymen. Pastors must reprove not only
the sins of the poor (theft, covetousness) but also the sins of the
rich(greed, pride, miserliness); not only the sins of youth but also
those of old age. In pastoral work the influential members must be
confronted with the Law as well as others. In school the children

of the so-called pillars of the church or children from the parsonage must not receive favors before others (Nebraska, 1915, p. 60f.).

The purity of the Gospel is likewise to be carefully guarded. When its free character, its universality and certainty, are denied, its purity is impaired. God's grace is absolutely free, not in any way dependent upon the worthiness of man. When we preach the Gospel, we must preach it pure, not make grace subject to conditions and accomplishments of men; for by such admixture of Law we rob the Gospel of its sweetness and change it into a second Law (Nebraska, 1915, p. 67f.; Kansas, 1892, p. 39.).

With like zeal we must guard the universality of grace proclaimed in the Gospel. Free grace is also universal grace (I Tim. 2:4; II Pet. 3:9; Ezek. 33:11). If our Gospel is not universal, it is not the pure Gospel.

Finally, the certainty of the Gospel must not be impaired. Our Christians must be told that because of God's unchanging grace all believers may be sure of their salvation, for God's Word and promise is sure. He who denies this and would have men live in constant uncertainty as to their justification, makes God a liar (Rom. 8:38; Phil. 1:6). Pietists, enthusiasts, and others who base the certainty of their salvation on certain feelings, or emotions, on the experience of special depths of sorrow or heights of joy, cannot inspire certainty of salvation. For the heart is an undependable and moody thing. Today it may soar in ecstasy; tomorrow it will fall into a state of sorrow and melancholy. Feeling, experience, can never produce lasting assurance. That can be effected only by the sure Word of Scripture, the unchanging Gospel of the never-failing grace of God (Nebraska, 1915, pp. 65-72).

V. LAW AND GOSPEL OPERATIVE IN CONVERSION

Our Confessions clearly distinguish between the effect of the Law and that of the Gospel in the conversion of the sinner. The Smalcald Articles state: "This office of the Law is the thunderbolt of God by which He strikes in a heap both manifest sinners and false saints, and suffers no one to be in the right, but drives them all together to terror and despair. This is . . . true sorrow of heart, suffering and sensation of death. This, then, is what it means to begin true repentance; and here man must hear such a sentence as this: You are all of no account, whether you be manifest sinners or saints; you must all become different and do otherwise than you now are and are doing, whether you are as great, wise, powerful, and holy as you may. Here no one is godly" (*Triglot,* p. 479f., 2, 3). The Formula of Concord reads: "Therefore God, out of His immense goodness and mercy, has His divine eternal Law and His wonderful plan concerning our redemption, namely, the holy, alone-saving Gospel of His eternal Son, our only Savior and Redeemer, Jesus Christ, publicly preached; and by this preaching collects an eternal Church for Himself from the human race, and works in the hearts of men true repentance and knowledge of sins and true faith in the Son of God, Jesus Christ" (*Triglot,* p. 901, 50).

Conversion consists of contrition and faith. Conversion is not possible without true sorrow worked by the hammer of the Law, but the actual change of heart, or renewal, is effected only by the Gospel. A man is regenerated only by faith, and saving, regenerating faith is wrought only by the operation of the Holy Ghost through the Gospel. The Law is to hammer to pieces the spirit and to work sorrow and mortification and despair. During the state of this sorrow and mortification there is no faith, and therefore the actual renewal has not yet taken place. But the moment that one receives the Gospel into his heart and a desire for grace, a spark of faith and confidence, be it ever so faint, is begun there, he has been renewed, or converted, but not before. The Gospel is the seed of regeneration, the power of God unto salvation (Rom. 1:16, 17). Paul states that faith cometh by hearing the Gospel (Rom. 10:16, 17), and Christ says that we believe in Him through the word of the Apostles, the Gospel (John 17:20). At the same time it is true that grace and faith will not inhabit any other but a broken and contrite heart; only such a heart is ripe for comfort and forgiveness. The Law must break the ground, prepare the field of the heart, so that the seed of the Gospel, if it is planted there, may actually have a seedbed in which it can take root and grow.

If the sinner is terrified by the Law, longing for help will arise in his heart. Is this longing for help a part of conversion? It is necessary to distinguish between longing and longing. Real longing for the grace of God in Christ is truly the first evidence of saving faith, created by the Gospel and its message of grace. But there is also the longing which is merely a desire for freedom from fear, from restlessness, from the burden of an evil conscience. The latter is one of the products of the Law, which terrifies the sinner so that he begins to look for help. But the Law does not know of any other way to salvation than that of perfect fulfillment of all its demands. At the point where the sinner, terrified by the Law, no longer knows where to turn, the Gospel enters and shows him the new light of the grace of God. The Gospel follows immediately upon the Law; what the Law has cast down the Gospel raises up. The Gospel by its glorious message of full salvation through the merits of Christ changes the fear and despair caused by the Law to faith and trust and joy in the Savior.

In conversion, therefore, the Gospel is the life-giving factor. With the terrors of the Law, God intends to prepare the heart for the consolation of the Gospel and vivification. Thus the Law should be thought of as only a servant in the house of God, while Christ with His Gospel is the Master. The most important revelation of God is the Gospel of the love of God in Christ Jesus (Gal. 3:15ff.; *L. u. W.,* 33, pp. 191-205; Kansas, 1892, p. 50).

VI. THE GOSPEL OPERATIVE IN JUSTIFICATION

The Law must be entirely eliminated from the doctrine of justification. The righteousness of God, that righteousness which alone is acceptable to God, "is without the Law," "by faith of Jesus Christ" (Rom. 3:21-22). If a man is justified at all, he is justified without the deeds of the Law (Rom. 3:28); in other words, either he is justified without the Law, or he is not justified at all.

The Law and its demands must be excluded from justification entirely and completely. God's declaration that the individual's sins are forgiven must not be made dependent even upon a single praying of the Lord's Prayer, as Luther observes; for that would make salvation dependent on a deed of the Law, and the Christian would at once and completely be deprived of the certainty of his salvation, since no Christian, because of his sinful flesh, can perfectly and sinlessly pray a single Lord's Prayer (F. Pieper, *Christl. Dogm.,* II, 661).

The Law may be mixed into justification in various ways: 1. when some natural goodness in man is regarded as the cause, in full or in part, on account of which God justifies an individual; 2. when justifying faith is looked upon as a virtue or good deed; 3. when justification is ascribed to faith in so far as, or because, faith is the beginning or source of sanctification and good works; 4. when justifying faith is looked upon as a work demanded by the Law; 5. when any warning against carnal security is regarded as part of the Gospel (F. Pieper, *Christl. Dogm.*, II, 659).

The very nature of justification as defined in Scripture excludes the Law and leaves the Gospel as the only means whereby God justifies the sinner. Justification, according to God's own Word, is a judicial act of God, based on the fact that God was in Christ reconciling the world unto Himself, not imputing their trespasses unto them; for God made Him to be sin for us who knew sin, that we might be made the righteousness of God in Him (II Cor. 5:19-21). The Gospel is no more than the word of this reconciliation, the glad news that Christ was delivered for our offenses and raised again for our justification (Rom. 4:25). As soon as the sinner believes this Gospel, accepts by faith the forgiveness and justification offered to him in the Gospel, then the general justification is applied personally to him without the deeds of the Law. Only in open defiance and denial of these clear statements of Scripture can the sinner's justification be made dependent on any work of the Law.

"Here again Lutheranism fully measures up to the sinner's need. He obtains justification by distinguishing between the Law and the Gospel, by fleeing from the Law and its threats and casting himself upon the promise of the Gospel" (*Popular Symbolics*, p. 5f.).

VII. LAW AND GOSPEL OPERATIVE IN SANCTIFICATION

We have heard that both the Law and the Gospel must be preached and applied to the Christian also. That is true in particular with regard to the Christian's sanctification, his daily life in holiness and good works. If the Christian would no longer have to contend with his sinful flesh, if he would be altogether a new man in Christ, he would no longer need the Law. Then his knowledge of the divine Law would be perfect (Col. 3:10) and his willingness to do God's will would equal his power to lead a life of flawless holiness (Eph. 4:24). The Formula of Concord says that then "they would do of themselves, and altogether voluntarily, without any instruction, admonition, urging, or driving of the Law, what they are in duty bound to do according to God's will . . . just as the holy angels render an entirely voluntary service" (Formula of Concord, Thor. Decl., VI, 6; *Triglot*, p. 965-6).

The constant inhering of the old Adam, who knows not the things of the Spirit of God and in whom dwells no good thing, makes daily study and application of the Law of God a matter of urgent necessity for every Christian. From the Law of the Holy God as revealed in the Scriptures the child of God must learn day by day to know and understand more thoroughly the will of his heavenly Father, his own sinfulness and helplessness, the need of daily whipping his old Adam into submission and of keeping under his body and bringing it into subjection (I Cor. 9:26-27). The strength for this daily putting off of the old man and of putting on the new man he receives not from his study of the Law. With this power and willingness the Holy Spirit endows him by holding before his eyes in the Gospel the Redeemer who, for love of man and in obedience to His holy Father, took upon Himself the enormous guilt amassed by the Christian, suffered the torment of hell which the Christian has deserved a thousandfold, procured for him the favor of God, the forgiveness of all his sins, sweet comfort in all the ills and woes of this life, and the assured prospect of a resurrection of the flesh and life everlasting in the glory of heaven. The glad news of what Christ has done for him, still is doing, and will do fills the Christian's heart and soul with gratitude and the unwavering determination to be and remain the loyal servant of His Lord and Redeemer. Thine I am, O my Savior! For me to live is Christ! (Phil. 3:4-14; Col. 3:1—4.)

VII. LAW AND GOSPEL OPERATIVE IN MINISTERIAL PRACTICE

Clergymen are called "ministers of the Gospel." This is not an accident, for it is the Gospel which is to give their service its character. The predominant tone in the clergyman's preaching should be comfort and salvation, not terror and damnation. If the minister is going to be true to his calling, he must "preach Christ." "It should be remembered that the Gospel, not the Law, is the most important doctrine of the Bible. The Holy Book was written because of the Gospel and not because of the Law. . . . Though necessary for diverse reasons, the preaching of the Law in the Bible is always incidental and subordinate to the teaching of the Gospel." (J. Schaller, *The Book of Books*, p. 5.)

"Every sermon which the pastor preaches should contain both Law and Gospel: Law to stir sinners to repentance and to instruct the believers in regard to their conduct, Gospel to bring sinners to faith and comfort the penitent. A pastor who omits either the Law or the Gospel is not doing his full duty. Cp. Acts 20:27-28; II Tim. 4:2" (*Concordia Bible Teacher*, 1945, 135; Walther, *G. u. E.*, p. 397).

The Gospel should have the foremost place in our preaching; yet we must be careful not to exclude the Law. The Law must be included, but it must be presented in such a way that it will prepare a way for the Gospel. It must break ground and prepare the soil of the heart as a bed for the seed of the Gospel. Often we hear the criticism that in the preaching in our Church there is too much justification or Gospel and not enough Law and thunder. The people are said to have gone to sleep. Where this criticism is in place, the fault is not too much Gospel, but it is a sign that neither the Law nor the Gospel has been presented in the right manner, in the right relation to each other. There has not been a right division of the Word of Truth. If people are asleep, then the thunder of the Law is in place. There must be warnings against satiety, hypocrisy, wickedness. Souls must be preached into condemnation. And only after they ask, What shall we do? is the time ripe for following up with the assuring comforts of the Gospel; not before. If there has been little or no warning against those sins prevalent in that particular congregation, if the assurances of the Gospel were brought before a feeling of regret could be created in the heart of the hearer, if Law preaching takes the form of mere pious admonition to good works, or if Law and Gospel are not presented in their right sequence, then the criticism that our Gospel preaching anesthetizes hearers might be justified (Kansas, 1892, p. 47f.; Iowa, 1880, p. 55f.).

In his pulpit work the pastor should not endeavor to divide his hearers into various classes, but simply preach Law and Gospel as presented in the Bible and leave it to God to work upon the individual hearts. He should not anxiously try to divide his audience, but should conscientiously divide the Word of Truth. Thus each hearer will receive the portion of food his soul needs. For the Word which condemns the godless person is the same as that which is needed to strike down the Christian's old Adam. The Word which regenerates the disobedient is the same as that which gives the Christian the power to lead a godly life (*L. u. W.*, 33, p. 274; Nebraska, 1916, p. 58).

In private pastoral care and counseling the pastor should carefully study the spiritual condition of the individual with whom he is dealing and endeavor to ascertain whether he is a terrified sinner or a secure sinner. The former must be told the Gospel, the latter the Law (Nebraska, 1916, p. 49f.). Calmly but firmly the sinner should be shown the error of his way, and when sorrow becomes evident, he should be told that God in His grace, for the sake of the atoning sacrifice of Christ, forgives every sin. When the sinner seeks to justify himself, he must be rebuked more severely with the Law. But the pastor must never forget that only the sweetness of the Gospel can change the stubborn sinner.

When the Commandments are studied in adult or children's instruction classes, the minister should not delay the teaching of the Gospel until the Commandments are finished. In that case the class would hear only Law for several months. The Gospel can be conveniently brought in during the study of every Commandment.

At the sickbed the pastor has the opportunity to draw near to the infirm, the sick, the suffering, the sorrowful, primarily with a word of comfort, the Gospel. Often the pastor will find that the patients are already distressed by the threats and the curses of the Law and the wrath of God; in that case he should not terrify them anew with the Law, but console and strengthen them with the full sweetness of the Gospel. If the pastor is called to the deathbed of a Christian with whom he cannot speak many words, he should comfort him with the Gospel. If the dying one lived a godless life, the pastor should bring such passages to his attention as contain both Law and Gospel, such as I Tim. 1:15; I John 1:7; John 3:16.

CONCLUSION

God gave His Word to us that thereby all men might be made "wise unto salvation through faith which is in Christ Jesus." Why, then, does the Word of God in so many cases not accomplish this purpose? We cannot mention all reasons, but there is no doubt that one of the reasons is the failure to understand and correctly apply Law and Gospel. If any man, pastor or layman, teaches the Word of God, let him "rightly divide the Word of Truth." Incorrect use of God's Word prevents the result it should have when correctly used; yes, it bars the way to faith and salvation.

With God's help let us use God's Word correctly. In the school of the Scriptures and of experience, where the Holy Ghost Himself is the Tutor, let us learn how to divide God's Word properly. Under God that will minimize the loss of souls due to a wrong use of the Word of Life.

VIII

The Decalog and the
Close of the Commandments

PART ONE: THE DECALOG IN GENERAL

G OD's children delight to do the will of their Father. Having experienced His manifold grace and unmerited loving-kindness, they ask, What shall I render unto the Lord for all His benefits toward me? (Ps. 116:12.) God has not left His children to grope in darkness as to the important question how they ought to walk and to please God (I Thess. 4:1). He has revealed to His children His holy will in His Law, found scattered throughout the pages of the Bible. In order to make it convenient for them to know His will, He has kindly summarized it in a brief code, the Ten Commandments, as He Himself calls them (Ex. 34:28; Deut. 4:13; 10:4). The ancient Greek Bible calls them "deka logoi," and therefore the term Decalog is frequently used to designate the Holy Law of God. As the heading indicates, we shall not study each Commandment separately, but consider the Decalog in general and turn our attention especially to its origin, its contents, its purposes, and its fulfillment.

I

Its Origin

1. *The Natural Law.*—The Decalog originated not on Mount Sinai, but in the Garden of Eden. It belonged to Paradise and was the greatest paradisaical joy of man. Adam found the highest delight in loving his Creator, in speaking to his God, and in hearing His Word. He had no parents and no other fellow human being than Eve, his wife. But how tenderly he greeted her; how perfectly he

loved her! How they together enjoyed the garden and all the earthly goods which their Maker had given them as wedding presents! How they rejoiced in God! And so perfect were they in all holy desires that "they were both naked, the man and his wife, and were not ashamed" (Gen. 2:25). Having both been created in God's image, they took it for granted: "Ye shall be holy, for I, the Lord, your God, am holy" (Lev. 19:2). Indeed, it could not be otherwise, for "God saw everything that He had made, and behold, it was very good" (Gen. 1:31). Therefore the Apostle writes: "Put on the new man, which after God is created in righteousness and true holiness" (Eph. 4:24). That man possessed perfect righteousness and holiness proves that he knew God's will, that the Law of God lived in his heart. When God created man, He wrote the Law into his heart. To do the will of God, to comply with the natural Law of God, was natural to him.

Now, did this moral, natural Law in man's heart disappear with the Fall? Not altogether. Why did Adam and his wife hide themselves when God came to see them? Because they knew they had disobeyed Him; because their conscience accused them of the sin against the first and greatest commandment. Why did Cain try to conceal his murder? Because his conscience told him: "Thou shalt not kill." Why did Joseph flee from Potiphar's wife? Because his conscience warned him: "Thou shalt not commit adultery." And why do the heathen, who have no written Law, do by nature the things contained in the Law? Because the word of the Law is written in their hearts; because their conscience bears them witness as to what, according to the will of God, they should do and not do (Rom. 2:14-15). No man can deny his conscience with a good conscience. We may disregard its voice, but we cannot silence it. When we have done well, it approves; when evil, it reproves. It acts as a killjoy whenever we violate it. Scruples of conscience are bad; stings of conscience are worse.

Of course, as the keen edge of a knife becomes dull by constant and willful abuse, so by the abuse of continued sinning man's conscience has become blunted. The Pharisees saw the bloody dagger labeled "murder," but could no longer read the dulled inscription "hatred." Therefore the Lord sharpens their conscience by telling them what St. John wrote later: "Whosoever hateth his brother is a murderer" (I John 3:15). And because of sin the knife of conscience sometimes cuts in the wrong direction. Often people have an erring conscience, regarding as good something that is evil, or imagining something that is good or at least not sinful to be evil. There is only one remedy for an erring conscience: it must be corrected according to the Word of God.

In order to remedy this sad condition due to man's blunted conscience, the Lord God reminded men again and again of His holy will by appealing to their conscience and by sharpening it. When Cain asked defiantly: "Am I my brother's keeper?" the Lord God, by questioning him: "What hast thou done?" answered him: Indeed thou art, for thou shalt love thy neighbor as thyself. When Sarah mused, "Thoughts are free," the Lord reproved her doubts about His Word and promise, saying: "Wherefore did Sarah laugh? . . . Is anything too hard for the Lord?" (Gen. 18:13-14.) And when Laban thought that since he had hired Jacob for wages, he would get all the toil and labor out of him that he possibly could, the Lord appeals to his conscience through Jacob, who tells him: "Thus I was; in the day the drought consumed me and the frost by night; and my sleep departed from mine eyes" (Gen. 31:40).

2. *The Revealed Law.*—However, in order to make His people, whom He had brought forth out of idolatrous Egypt, worship only Him, Jehovah, the only true God, and in order to make Israel unto Himself a peculiar treasure above all people and a holy nation, the Lord God repeated His holy will in its entirety, speaking with His own voice from Mount Sinai the holy Ten Commandments (Ex. 20:1-17). This Decalog is repeated by Moses in Deut. 5:6-21 with slight variations. Later, God commanded Moses to come up to the mount, and there God communed with him, giving him further instructions and ordinances. At the end of forty days God gave unto Moses "two tables of testimony, tables of stone, written with the finger of God" (Ex. 31:18), as He had promised Moses when he ascended the mountain (Ex. 24:12). "The tables were written on both their sides; on the one side and on the other were they written. And the tables were the work of God, and the writing was the writing of God, graven upon the tables" (Ex. 32:15-16). They were called the "two tables of testimony" because they were to be placed (Ex. 25:21) into the "Ark of the Testimony" (Ex. 31:7), with the mercy seat above, of which place the Lord God had said: "And there will I meet with thee, and I will commune with thee from

above the mercy seat, from between the two cherubims which are upon the Ark of the Testimony, of all things which I will give thee in commandment unto the children of Israel" (Ex. 25:22). And among all these things the Decalog certainly occupies not only a conspicuous, but the most prominent place (Matt. 22:34-40). Therefore also the whole Sanctuary is sometimes called "the Tabernacle of Testimony" (Num, 1:50)—the place from which God spoke to Israel His Word, both the curse of the Law as contained in the Decalog and the blessing of the Gospel as symbolized by the mercy seat (Ex. 20:24).

These two tables, however, Moses, in his holy wrath, broke in pieces when he came down from the mountain (Ex. 32:19). But the Lord told him: "Hew thee two tables of stone like unto the first; and I will write upon these tables the words that were in the first tables, which thou brakest" (Ex. 34:1). "And he hewed two tables of stone like unto the first" (v. 4). "And he was there with the Lord forty days and forty nights" . . . "and He wrote upon the tables the words of the covenant, the Ten Commandments" (Ex. 34:28). "He" here refers to God (Deut. 10:4). For when we read Ex. 34:27: "And the Lord said unto Moses, Write thou these words; for after the tenor of these words I have made a covenant with thee and with Israel," the covenant in the preceding section (vv. 10-27) is meant.

Now, Luther says somewhere: "The Ten Commandments are given to the Jews, not to us." That sounds heterodox, and yet it is true. If Luther had said these words of the entire Law of Moses, we would readily understand; for, in addition to the Ten Commandments, the Lord had given Israel hundreds of other laws and ordinances. Some concerned the Church of the Old Covenant: the various ceremonies of offerings and sacrifices, washings and purifications, Sabbaths and other festivals, meat and drink. All these had been given to the people of the Old Testament only, and they have been expressly abolished in the New Testament by Christ (Col. 2: 16-17). That was the Ceremonial Law.—Then there were ordinances which concerned the government of Israel, the theocracy, in which God Himself was their King and Ruler, as, for instance, the punishment of a thief (Ex. 22:1-4), safety measures (Deut. 22:8), and the like. A summary of both of these laws follows the Decalog immediately in Ex. 21-23 (chapters 19-24 are called "The Book of the Covenant," 24:7). With the disappearance of the Jewish nation as such also this Political Law has ceased to exist.

But Luther makes his remarkable statement of the Ten Commandments, or the Moral Law in general. And yet his statement is true. For in that form in which we find the Ten Commandments (Ex. 20:1-17), they had been given not to us, but to the Jews, as is evident from the very introduction: "I am the Lord, thy God, which have brought thee out of the land of Egypt, out of the house of bondage." The Decalog contains ceremonial laws, and these Luther, with wise judgment and divine authorization, either has omitted altogether from his Catechism or else adapted to New Testament conditions. Even the prohibition of iconolatry, attached to the First Commandment: "Thou shalt not make unto thee any graven image or any likeness of anything that is in heaven above or that is in the earth beneath or that is in the water under the earth. Thou shalt not bow down thyself to them nor serve them"—iconolatry which Israel had daily witnessed in Egypt—Luther omits, since his German people were hardly in danger of committing such heathen sins as Israel actually did commit only forty days after the giving of the Law. The divine threat and promise ending the First Commandment Luther takes for the Close of the Commandments, since both concern all the commandments. For the same reason he also omits the special threat attached to the Second Commandment: "For the Lord will not hold him guiltless that taketh His name in vain." In the Third Commandment Luther gives only the gist of the precept: "Thou shalt sanctify the holy day," or, "Remember the Sabbath Day, to keep it holy," omitting all the following ceremonial ordinances: "Six days shalt thou labor and do all thy work. But the seventh day is the Sabbath of the Lord, thy God. In it thou shalt not do any work, thou, nor thy son, nor thy daughter, thy manservant, nor thy maidservant, nor thy cattle, nor thy stranger that is within thy gates. For in six days the Lord made heaven and earth, the sea, and all that in them is and rested the seventh day; wherefore the Lord blessed the Sabbath day and hallowed it." In the Fourth Commandment, "Honor thy father and thy mother," Luther gives the attached promise "that thy days may be long upon the land which the Lord thy God giveth thee" the New Testament version: "That it may be well with thee, and thou mayest live long on the earth" (Eph. 6:2-3). And in the Tenth Commandment Luther contracts the words "nor his ox, nor his ass," animals concerning which special political laws had been given, into the expression "nor his cattle." (In a similar manner the German Catechism deviates again and again from the original Decalog in the Close of the Commandments; but since the English version is identical with the King James text, we need not here enter upon this discussion.)

We know that there are Ten Commandments (Ex. 34:28); but God did not number them. Hence men have numbered them differently. The important thing, however, is not their arrangement, but their fulfillment. Neither do we know for certain how many commandments were written on the first table of stone and how many on the second table. Also here various divisions have been made (5:5; 4:6; 3:7). We have, however, a hint in Matt. 22:34-40, where Jesus speaks of the love toward God and the love toward our neighbor as of "two commandments." In conformity with this statement we put the first three Commandments on the First Table of the Law and the seven others on the Second Table. But even with this division the Hebrew text of the First Table is about three times as long as that of the Second.

Now that this Decalog, stripped, of course, of all these ceremonial ordinances, is binding upon all men, is evident from its repetition, in different forms and arrangements, in the New Testament and from the fact that this New Testament Decalog conforms with our conscience. The Moral Law is the only norm and rule of man's life, not habit, custom, style, public opinion, government laws, or church ordinances, but the Moral Law first, last, and always.

II

Its Contents

1. *Its Clearness.*—The Decalog is the Moral Law. "Law" in the Bible has various meanings. Sometimes it stands for the entire divine Revelation (Ps. 1:2; Ps. 119); again, it represents the Old Testament (John 15:25; I Cor. 14:21); sometimes it means the Pentateuch (Luke 24:44); and, again, it signifies the Gospel (Is. 2:3). Even in its strictest sense we distinguish between the Moral, the Ceremonial, and the Political Law, as we have seen.

The contents of the Law, of the Decalog, are pre-figured and foreshadowed in these extraordinary phenomena: "Mount Sinai was altogether on a smoke, because the Lord descended upon it in fire; and the smoke thereof ascended as the smoke of a furnace, and the whole mount quaked greatly. And when the voice of the trumpet sounded long and waxed louder and louder, Moses spake, and God answered him by a voice. And the Lord came down upon Mount Sinai on the top of the mount, and Moses went up" (Ex. 19:18-20). And after he had come down again, we are told: "And God spake all these words, saying." Though invisible, yet God Himself spoke the Decalog. Majestically the first words sound forth like peals of thunder: "I am the Lord, thy God"—*the Lord*. Others are lords in a restricted sense: lords over a country, over an institution, over a household, etc.; God is the absolute Lord, "the Lord of Lords and King of Kings." As Lord He has the right to give us laws, to issue His commandments. The Law of God is His will toward us. And since God is holy, His will is holy: "Wherefore the Law is holy, and the commandment is holy and just and good" (Rom. 7:12). And where there is a legislator, there is a judge. But this Lord also says: "I am the Lord, *thy God*," the same God that has created you and that through His continuous creation daily provides for you and cares for you, feeds, clothes, protects, and preserves you. Out of gratitude toward Me you ought gladly to do My will in all things. Now, with the exception of the Third and Fourth Commandments, God begins every Commandment thus: "*Thou* shalt not!" Throughout the Decalog He speaks in the singular and not in the plural, as He might have done. The Law of God is something that concerned every Israelite, man, woman, and child, and that also today concerns every person of every age and sex, era and clime, race and color, language and nationality; it concerns also you and me. It is the most impressive form in which God could address us.

"Thou *shalt* not." The strongest possible grammatical forms in Hebrew are used in these prohibitions. What God enjoins in the Law, is not only His wish or desire, but a clear-cut demand or commandment, with all the authority of the majesty of God and with the threat of the severest divine punishment standing behind the Law. The Decalog demands of us unconditional obedience.

Again, with two exceptions, all commandments are given in the negative form: "Thou shalt *not*." That is the usual form of our laws, making something a crime, the commission of which shall be punished by law. But it has pleased God to give the Third and Fourth

Commandments an affirmative form to indicate thereby that every commandment contains something that we should not do and something that we should do. "Remember the Sabbath day" includes: Do not forget it. Honor thy parents implies: Do not dishonor them. On the other hand: "Thou shalt not speak false witness" enjoins upon us that we speak the truth. "Thou shalt have no other gods before Me" demands of us that we worship the Lord our God and serve Him only, and so forth throughout all the Commandments. Therefore our Catechism always speaks of a prohibition and of an injunction.

That is the clear content of the Law: it tells us what we should do and should not do; how we are to be and not to be. We should not be wicked and ungodly, not curse and blaspheme, not set our hearts upon the things of this earth, not be self-willed and disobedient, not full of hatred and revenge, not unchaste and impure, not greedy and avaricious, not practicing lies and deceit, not jealous and covetous, not lustful and concupiscent; in short, at no time and place, under no conditions and circumstances, to no extent, not even in the last degree, should we be unholy, unjust, unrighteous, bad, or sinful.

On the other hand, God's Decalog demands of each and every one of us that we should at all times and places, under all conditions and circumstances, perfectly and to the fullest extent love Him, His holy name, and His saving Word; and that, for His sake, we also love all of our fellow men whether it be father or mother, husband or wife, Jew or Gentile, American or Australasian, friend or enemy, in short, that we be holy, just as holy as He, "the Lord our God," is Himself.

2. *Its Inexhaustibility.*—What inexhaustible contents of the divine Decalog! We cannot here refrain from quoting the opening paragraph of the Introduction to an essay on the Fourth Commandment (Minnesota and Dakota District, 1899, 22-23): "Considering the holy Ten Commandments: their succinct brevity, their wonderful arrangement, and their great and manifold contents, the conviction is forced upon us that no creature in heaven or on earth could have possibly composed this Decalog, on the exposition of which the holy Prophets, though themselves immediately inspired by the Holy Spirit, have spent a lifetime and upon which, as upon an infallible norm, they based their doctrine. In our infirmity we cannot fathom,

even with our mere thoughts, the depths of the wisdom revealed in the order, form, and contents of the Decalog, and we imagine we have understood much of it, while we have but scratched its surface. —However, since even the last of the Prophets, Malachi, concludes his prophecies and the Old Testament with these words: 'Remember the Law of Moses, My servant, which I commanded unto him in Horeb for all Israel, with the statutes and judgments' (Mal. 4:4); since also the Lord Jesus and His holy Apostles base their doctrine on the Old Testament; and since Paul asserts that he was 'saying none other things than those which the Prophets and Moses did say should come,' we also have based our doctrinal discussions at our District conventions on that summary of sound doctrine . . . in order that both pastors and hearers may be led to the source and always be found within the boundaries of the divinely revealed, sound doctrine. For when convening to hear and consider the doctrine of the Catechism, what are we doing but gathering in the Paradise of God around the tree of the knowledge of good and evil, there by the Law to be reminded of the sad fall of our first parents with its disastrous consequence, the total depravity of our human heart, and then out of God's own mouth to hear the glad tidings of the Gospel concerning the promised woman's Seed that has appeared in the flesh that our wounds may be healed and our hearts comforted through faith in God's grace and the merit of Jesus Christ, that we call upon God in the name of our Savior in all our trials and tribulations and learn to strengthen our faith by the doctrine and the use of the holy Sacrament? . . . May God grant us that through His Holy Spirit for the sake of Jesus Christ! Amen."

III

Its Purpose

That the purpose of the Law is not to save man is clearly stated in Gal. 2:16: "By the works of the Law shall no flesh be justified." But that does not make it purposeless. Wool does serve us not for food but for clothing. So the Law of God, though it does not lead to salvation, has other good purposes. Unless we know the real purpose of the Law, we shall not use it properly but rather abuse it shamefully. It is an old division, at least as old as the Formula of

Concord (Article VI), that the Law is to serve 1) as a curb, 2) as a mirror, 3) as a rule, and we shall here follow this method.

1. *As a Curb.*—The Law of God is to serve, in the first place, as a curb "that the unregenerate may be kept under external discipline and thus restrained from outward gross sins." It will check, at least to some extent, the coarse outbursts of sin and thereby help to keep order in the world. For where no law is, there is no transgression and no punishment. But the Law of God, the voice of man's conscience, restrains many a murderer from committing the outward act, warning him: "Thou shalt not kill," and if you do, God will visit your iniquity. "We know that the Law is good if a man use it lawfully; knowing this, that the Law is not made for a righteous man, but for the lawless and disobedient, for the ungodly and for sinners, for unholy and profane, for murderers of fathers and murderers of mothers, for manslayers, for whoremongers, for them that defile themselves with mankind, for menstealers, for liars, for perjured persons, and if there be any other thing that is contrary to sound doctrine" (I Tim. 1:8-10). True, believers also need such a check at times because of their old Adam; however, they are rather admonished: "Be ye not as the horse or as the mule, which have no understanding, whose mouth must be held in with bit and bridle lest they come near unto thee" (Ps. 32:9).

2. *As a Mirror.*—As such the Law should be used by all men; but it is chiefly the Christian who uses it as a mirror. Viewing himself in the mirror of the divine Law and beholding there an exact picture of himself, he cannot but see: "We are all as an unclean thing, and all our righteousnesses are as filthy rags" (Is. 64:6). This mirror of the divine Law shows us blemishes not only on, but deep beneath our skin. Indeed, it exposes all the diseases of our sinful heart and thus leads us to a true knowledge of our sins. "By the Law is the knowledge of sin" (Rom. 3:20). And since the mirror is perfect, the reflected image is exact. In the Law we recognize even our evil thoughts and desires as sin: "I had not known sin but by the Law; for I had not known lust except the Law had said, Thou shalt not covet" (Rom. 7:7). And what is God's wise purpose in making us sin-conscious? "The Law was our schoolmaster to bring us to Christ that we might be justified by faith" (Gal. 3:24). The unwelcome reflection of our sinful image in the mirror of the divine Law should move us to go to the fountain of the Gospel, which is filled with the

blood of Christ, the Son of God, that cleanseth us from all sin, that fountain in which the dying malefactor on the cross cleansed and refreshed himself in his dying hour. Then shall also we return rejoicingly and triumph:

> And there have I, as vile as he,
> Washed all my sins away.

3. *As a Rule.*—Now that we have been cleansed and refreshed by the Gospel, through faith in Christ, we are ready and willing to work for Him. With the Messiah we say: "I delight to do Thy will, O My God; yea, Thy Law is within My heart" (Ps. 40:8). For, returning to the same mirror of the Law, we are delighted now to see ourselves beautiful and glorious, "holy and without blemish," "not having spot or wrinkle or any such thing" (Eph. 5:27). Now we make another use of the Law, adopting it as a rule and norm of our life, of our good works, to which also the Psalmist's words apply: Lord, "Thy Word is a lamp unto my feet and a light unto my path" (Ps. 119:105). And what a path! It is not only plain and straight to follow in all states and conditions of life, but also long enough to walk on it all the days of our years: to trust God, "though He slay me"; to continue instant in prayer, though it seem of no avail; to do for God's Word and Church whatever is in our power; to submit our will to any and all human authorities; to be merciful, meek, and forgiving toward all our fellow men; to be chaste and pure in deed, thought, word, and desire; to give with rejoicing; to think and speak well of others and to wish them the best gifts for this life and for that which is to come. But what a pleasant path to follow through the dreary desert of this loveless world, with the mild sunshine of divine blessings smiling down upon us, with the oases of mutual love, which is hallowed and sanctified by the Holy Spirit until it will be perfect in the celestial Paradise, refreshing us, and with the greatest joy which consists in seeing God, who is Love, and the blessed communion of all the saints of God in the exercise of perfect love, the fulfilling of the Law, awaiting us at the journey's end.

IV

Its Fulfillment

1. *By Christ.*—God demands a perfect fulfillment of the Law: "Cursed is everyone that continueth not in all things which are

written in the book of the Law to do them" (Gal. 3:10). Such perfection includes, of course, the fulfilling of the Law not only in word and deed, but also in thought and desire. It consists in doing the works of the Law with all our heart and with all our soul and with all our mind (Matt. 22:37). It presupposes that we have never once failed to fulfill a single commandment in a single point, though but in a fleeting thought or a subconscious desire. "Whosoever shall keep the whole Law and yet offend in one point, he is guilty of all" (James 2:10). For the Ten Commandments always march in company, the first one leading the way, the two last ones, the military police, watching that the path is kept straight and that there is not the slightest deviation either to the right or to the left. Such fulfillment, moreover, implies not only the avoiding of all that is sinful but also the doing of all that is good. "Therefore to him that knoweth to do good and doeth it not, to him it is sin" (James 4:17). The priest and the Levite in Luke 10:31-32 are striking illustrations. Such doing good is demanded of us not now and then, but always; not here and there, but everywhere; not in some degree, but fully, perfectly.

Now no one has fulfilled the Law of God in this way. The so-called perfectionists may lay claim to that, but they tell us only their dreams and visions. Their very claim is a sin (I John 1:8). They are being contradicted by the holy patriarchs, by Moses, David, and all the Prophets, by the Evangelists and the Apostles, by all the saints of God. "There is not a just man upon earth that doeth good and sinneth not" (Eccl. 7:20). We may think only of David's murder and adultery when he asks the Lord God: "Enter not into judgment with Thy servant"; however, he adds: "for in Thy sight shall *no man living* be justified" (Ps. 143:2).

Therefore all men are transgressors of the Law, are sinners, for "sin is the transgression of the Law" (I John 3:4). And though someone should be either so holy or so ignorant that he could not recall a single sin in deed or word or thought, yet he is conceived in sin, shapen in iniquity, and born of the flesh; yet already this inborn, original, and inherited sin condemns him before the divine tribunal in time and eternity, according to Eph. 2:3: "We were by nature the children of wrath, even as others." Is it not remarkable that St. Paul makes no difference at all in this respect between Americans and African Negroes, Greeks and barbarians, Jews and Gentiles, when he writes: "There is no difference, for *all have sinned* and come

short of the glory of God"? (Rom. 3:22-23.) And the sinner, standing before the judgment seat of God, cannot appeal to a higher
court, much less to a lower one, to that of his fellow men, offering
all kinds of vapid excuses. The strength of the Law is too powerful
for anyone to weaken by appealing to God's mercy and leniency,
by minimizing his sins, by comparing them with those of greater
transgressors, by stating his good intentions, by laying claim to
having been a victim of circumstances, by pointing to his imagined
or imaginary virtues, by promising future amendment, by good resolutions, by an open confession, by the vain hope of escaping somehow the detection and punishment of God, by the illusory mirage
of repentance after this life and of a final salvation for all sinners.

Therefore, according to the Law, all sinners are subject to God's
punishment in this world, to temporal death, and to eternal damnation. No Christian who has ever heard or read the appalling list of
the divine threats to a disobedient people (Lev. 26:14-43 or Deut.
28:15-68) can deny that God resorts also to temporal punishments
of sin nor fail to make the proper application to himself. And "the
wages of sin is death" (Rom. 6:23). And "cursed be he that con-
firmeth not all the words of this Law to do them" (Deut. 27:26).

> Holy and righteous God! Holy and mighty God!
> Holy and all-merciful Savior! Eternal God!
> Save us lest we perish in the bitter pangs of death.
> Have mercy, O Lord!

But *Christ* has kept the Law. In order to fulfill all righteousness,
he kept in all points even the Jewish *Ceremonial Law*. God, the Lawgiver, is above all laws, and cannot even keep the Law, though He
is holy. He has, for example, no parents whom He could obey. He
has no higher being to worship. But Christ, having assumed the
human nature into His own Person, now could, and did, fulfill the
Law. Some would deny that Christ's fulfilling the Law belongs to
His redemptive work, that He did it for us. They say that it is
self-evident that Christ fulfilled the Law perfectly, since He was
without sin and as God-Man could not sin. That, however, is contradicting Gal. 4:4-5, which says that Christ was "made under the
Law to redeem them that were under the Law." For, let us see: Was
it really necessary that the young Infant Jesus had to be circumcised
on the eighth day as far as the Child Itself was concerned? Lev.
12:3 we read: "If a woman have conceived seed and born a man

child, then shall she be *unclean* seven days . . . and in the eighth day the flesh of his foreskin shall be circumcised." But who will apply this Ceremonial Law to Him who was conceived by the Holy Ghost and born of the Virgin Mary? (Luke 1:35.) Likewise, the same chapter in Leviticus speaks of the purification of the mother and of the offering for the infant that has been born in the same manner, namely, that was conceived and born in sin. And yet, "when the days of her purification according to the Law of Moses were accomplished," the Infant Jesus was presented to the Lord, and an offering was made for Him, and Mary and Joseph did not return until "they had performed all things according to the Law of the Lord." And why did John the Baptist yield to Jesus' request to be baptized? Because Jesus wished to fulfill all righteousness, because He stood there before all the world as one who was under the Law and bound to keep it. We can trace Christ's keeping the Law throughout His entire life.

And He likewise fulfilled even the *political laws* of the Jews, though, as the Son of God, He was exempt from them. He paid His taxes to the Roman government (Matt. 22:21), to the Roman emperor, who had obtained his scepter from God (Rom. 13:1).

But above all did Jesus fulfill, for all men, *the Moral Law* of God. Though God slew Him and delivered Him to the pangs of hell, yet He trusted in Him unflinchingly, still calling Him on the Cross: "*My* God, *My* God!" And what better example of prayer have we in the entire Bible than that of Jesus, who, on the mountain, spent all night in prayer? What higher model is there for us all, especially for our youth and children, than Jesus, who, in the Temple of Jerusalem, was about His Father's business? What greater object lesson for our children could we find than Jesus' going down to Nazareth and being subject, obedient to his parents, even to his foster father, Joseph, and that until the age of thirty years, when He left His parental home? What higher perfection of love and kindness is there than He exhibited when He prayed for His enemies in the hours of extreme agony: "Father, forgive them!"? What finer pattern of perfect purity and decency could be given us than His discussion of the marital relation, or of the process of digestion, or of eunuchs? How He had compassion on a hungry multitude that had nothing to eat! And who could find a more fitting illustration of putting the best construction on everything than Jesus' saying to that woman caught in the very act of adultery: "Neither do I condemn thee. Go and sin no more"? And though Jesus had not where to lay His head, how fully contented He was at all times, rejoicing in Spirit and having His delight in the Lord, His heavenly Father! And all this for us—an entire lifetime devoted exclusively to the service of love, which is the fulfilling of the Law!

And, in addition to that, Christ bore the punishment for our transgressions of the Law, for our sins. He suffered and died for us (I Cor. 15:3). "Christ has redeemed us from the curse of the Law" (Gal. 3:13). "Christ is the end of the Law for righteousness to everyone that believeth" (Rom. 10:4). *Christ* has fulfilled the Law.

2. *By the Christian.*—The slave, emancipated by his loving master, now knows no other freedom than to serve him with a thankful and willing heart. The Christian, set free by Christ from the curse of the Law and its terrible punishments, now makes the will of Christ, His Savior, the norm of his life. Christ's good and gracious will is, first of all, our eternal salvation. "This is the will of Him that sent me, that everyone which seeth the Son and believeth on Him may have everlasting life" (John 6:40). But His will is also our sanctification, "that we, being delivered out of the hand of our enemies, might serve Him without fear, in holiness and righteousness before Him, all the days of our life (Luke 1:74-75). And for such a norm of life the Christian applies the rule of the divine Law, of the holy Ten Commandments, not in order thereby to be saved, but because through Christ he has been saved. What a chance to show our appreciation and to express our gratitude to Him! What an opportunity to do good and to love Him again who has first loved us: to trust every word and promise of Him who laid down His life for us; to speak to Him whenever we labor and are heavy laden; to sit at Jesus' feet and hear His Word; to love our parents, by whom He gave us life and living and to serve our country, in which He has placed us; to deal our bread to the hungry, to dry tears, and to pray for our enemies; to make our house and home a picture of the heavenly mansion which we shall occupy; to labor for His kingdom in the pulpit or at the school desk, in the factory or in the office, in the field or in the kitchen; to make our lips instruments of truth and our heart a maker of friends; to serve one another by love and to have our delight in the Lord! Oh, that we might at all times sow such seeds of love to the glory of God, for "we are His workmanship,

created in Christ Jesus unto good works, which God hath before ordained that we should walk in them" (Eph. 2:10).

But alas! No Christian can render a perfect fulfillment of the Law. Not only our good works but our best accomplishments are mixed and mingled with sin: "All our righteousnesses are as filthy rags" (Is. 64:6). We cannot pray a single Lord's Prayer with perfect devotion. When thinking of such poor Christian efficiency, one might despair. However, we must not forget that even the holy Apostle complained in a similar strain: "For we know that the Law is spiritual; but I am carnal, sold under sin. For that which I do I allow not; but what I hate, that I do," etc. (Rom. 7:14.) Rom. 8:1 he writes: "There is therefore now no condemnation to them which are in Christ Jesus, who walk not after the flesh but after the Spirit," and then sets forth, in this glorious eighth chapter, the blessed, happy state of the believers, God's beloved children and rich heirs of eternal salvation, whom no one and nothing can separate from the love of God, which is in Christ Jesus, our Lord. Indeed, for His sake, the Father accepts the sin-stained and imperfect service of His children, as a loving earthly father will smile at the feeble, sometimes even awkward and clumsy service of his little child, though through it all he sees, and rejoices in, the loving heart of his little son or daughter.

But a loving child will grow and increase in such service, will observe more and more perfectly the father's will and command. And so we children of God must not give up the study of God's will, nor quit the continuous practice of His service, but strive to improve upon our sanctification day by day, like the Apostle, who writes: "Not as though I had already attained, either were already perfect; but I follow after, if that I may apprehend that for which also I am apprehended of Christ Jesus" (Phil. 3:12).

No sane genius in music, art, literature, medicine, engineering, mathematics, or any other science or profession gives up because, after all, there is no human perfection. Should a child of God, a soldier of Jesus Christ, lay down his arms and surrender to the enemies of our soul just because Christian warfare, though it has the infallible promise of ultimate victory, is fraught with errors and mistakes? God forbid! For this reason we have again studied the Law of God that our heavenly Father may write it anew into our hearts "not with ink, but with the Spirit of the living God; not in

tables of stone, but in fleshy tables of the heart" (II Cor. 3:3), for
Only one life—'t will soon be past;
Only what's done for Christ will last. Amen.

PART TWO: THE CLOSE OF THE COMMANDMENTS

Immediately after the First Commandment the Decalog continues:
"For I, the Lord, thy God, am a jealous God, visiting the iniquity of
the fathers upon the children unto the third and fourth generation
of them that hate Me and showing mercy unto thousands of them
that love Me and keep My Commandments." Very appropriately
these words follow the prohibition of iconolatry, which Israel had
seen daily in Egypt; however, they refer to all Ten Commandments,
as the text clearly shows. After an introduction these words contain
a threat and a promise; and since we find a special threat in the
Second and a special promise in the Fourth Commandment, Luther,
in his Catechism, in order to emphasize that these words refer to
the entire Decalog, has, as a good teacher and pedagog, put these
words at the close of the Commandments and asks: "What does
God say of *all* these Commandments?" Lev. 26 and Deut. 28 prove
conclusively that this divine threat and promise concern all Commandments. If we ask what entitled Luther to do this, we have the
examples of Christ and of Paul, who both deviated from the order
of the Commandments in conformity with their specific purposes
(Matt. 19:18; Rom. 13:9).

1. *The Introduction.*—"For I, the Lord, thy God, am a jealous
God." Every word is significant. *"For"*: You had better serve Me
only and no other god, since you will be rewarded or punished
accordingly.—*"I, the Lord,"* Jehovah, the one eternal, unchangeable
God (Ex. 3:14; Rev. 1:4); I, the Father and Owner of all creatures,
the supreme Legislator, who have the right to give you commandments according to My will, the "one Lawgiver, who is able to save
and to destroy" (James 4:12).—*"Thy God,"* Elohim, plural, the
Triune God, whom you owe obedience as your Creator, Redeemer,
and Comforter. The Gospel should move us to obey Him. *"Thy*
God": That calls upon our faith: You have received so many benefits
from your God; now is it not your duty to thank and praise, to serve
and obey Him?—I, the Lord, thy God, *"am a jealous God."* Divine
jealousy differs from human jealousy in that it is never sinful, but
always holy and just. As a husband is justly jealous over the faith-

fulness of his wife, so with a jealous eye God keeps constant watch over all men to see whether they love Him, do His will, and keep His Commandments or whether they commit spiritual adultery by loving and lusting after other gods (Is. 50:1).

2. *The Threat.*—God threatens to "visit the iniquity." "Iniquity" is a suitable synonym for "sin": that which is not according to human equity and divine justice. God announces His visit to sin; He will pay man a visit, not inasmuch as He is His creature, but inasmuch as he is a sinner, a transgressor of His Commandments, for "sin is the transgression of the Law" (I John 3:4). God sometimes visited and visits man with His grace: "I have surely visited you. . . . I will bring you up out of the affliction of Egypt" (Ex. 3:16-17). But when God visits sin, He visits in His wrath: "In the day when I visit, I will visit their sin upon them" (Ex. 32:34), *i. e.,* I will punish them. Indeed, "God threatens to punish all that transgress these Commandments." "Cursed is *everyone* that continueth not in all things which are written in the book of the Law to do them" (Gal. 3:10). Not a single war criminal against God shall escape His justice.

God threatens to punish the sins "of the fathers upon the children unto the third and fourth generation of them that hate Me." "The iniquity *of the fathers,*" by way of a synecdoche, of course, includes also that of the mothers as well as of the forefathers and foremothers. Transgressors are those "that hate Me." The primary cause of the transgression of the Law is hatred of God. Inherited, original, sin is enmity against God (Rom. 8:7). The hatred against God is common more or less to all transgressors (Luke 14:26). That God threatens remains true in spite of the Gospel (Rom. 3:30-31).

God threatens to *punish*: 1. With His wrath and displeasure (Gal. 3:10). The sinner may laugh at this threat, since he does not care for God's friendship; but behind the threatening finger of God stands an unnumbered host of heavenly soldiers that excel in strength, that do His commandments, harkening unto the voice of His Word (Ps. 103:20). When He sends out a single one of them to attack the sinner, the result is terrible, for then follow:

2. God's temporal punishments, as enumerated in Lev. 26:14-39 and Deut. 28:15-68. All these temporal punishments have come later upon an ungodly nation of Israel that hated Him and transgressed His Commandments. We need only translate these national

and individual disasters into modern terms, and we stand in awe of the threatening finger of God.

3. Death: spiritual, temporal, and eternal death (Rom. 6:23; Gal. 3:10). Adam's day of disobedience was the day of his death (Gen. 2:17). That very day all spiritual life in him was killed: he accuses both God and his wife and has lost all sense of truth and decency. His soul is separated from God. And then follows for all sinners temporal death, the separation of body and soul, and the awful feeling that he must now face God's judgment (Heb. 9:27). And finally there comes eternal death, the everlasting separation of both body and soul from the presence of God. "God be merciful to me, a sinner!"

God threatens to punish the sins of the fathers "upon the children . . . of them that hate Me" (Jer. 15:1-4; 16:11-13; Is. 14:21; 43:26-28; 65:7; Jer. 32:18). Ezek. 18 harmonizes perfectly with this threat, which states "upon them that hate Me." But does this threat harmonize with God's justice? Yes, for these children have not profited by the warning of the evil examples of their parents (I Cor. 10:6-11). After all, God remains just (Ps. 51:4b).

"Unto the third and fourth generation." How true this is! How often we see that in our own circles, in our own community! We see a drunkard, who cannot make his living. "His father used to be like that. I remember that even his grandfather did the same." Here is an unhappy divorcee. "Already her mother had troubles with her husband and lived a miserable life. And people say the same about her grandmother." "Be not deceived; God is not mocked" (Gal. 6:7).

Since these threats concern the Moral Law, they are valid also in the New Testament. In fact, we can elaborate on and specialize the general threat by quoting two threats for the transgressors of each Commandment, one from the Old and the other from the New Testament: 1. Jer. 17:5—Phil. 3:19. 2. Lev. 24:15, 16—Gal. 6:7. 3. Hos. 4:6—John 12:48. 4. Prov. 30:17—Luke 15:14. 5. Gen. 9:6—Matt. 26:52. 6. Lev. 20:10—Heb. 13:4. 7. Hab. 2:6—I Thess. 4:6. 8. Prov. 19:5—Rev. 22:15. 9. Is. 5:8—I Tim. 6:9-10. 10. Ps. 81:12—James 1:15.

Why has God added this threat? Luther answers: "Therefore we should fear His wrath and not act contrary to His Commandments." Experience teaches that most sinners are not deterred from sinning even by these terrible threats of God. What, then, do these threats profit? They help, to some extent, to prevent the unbelievers, and also the old Adam of the Christians, from the coarse outbursts of sin (I Tim. 1:9-10). But they are to be especially our schoolmaster to bring us to Christ, to cause us to despair of our own righteousness and to flee to the Savior (Gal. 3:19), who will awaken us to a childlike fear, and make us truly 'God-fearing.' Only then shall we "fear His wrath and not act contrary to these Commandments."

3. *The Promise.*—"And showing mercy unto thousands of them that love Me and keep my Commandments." God, the Lord, thy God, promises. "He promises grace and every blessing," *i. e.,* He shows mercy, grace. Men are obligated to do God's Law (Luke 17:10). But, though they have not deserved it, He promises grace and every blessing, promises to do them good here in time and hereafter in eternity. But to whom? "To all that keep these Commandments." "Unto them *that love Me* and keep My Commandments. The promise of the Law is a conditional one. The condition is love. "Love is the fulfilling of the Law," a perfect fulfillment. "This do, and thou shalt live!" (Luke 10:28.)

But God promises "grace and every blessing." First of all, grace, which is forgiveness of sins, not because *they* have kept the Law, but because Christ has kept it for them. And therefore He promises them "every blessing," also temporal blessings (Lev. 26:3-12; I Tim. 4:8). Again we specialize the divine promise, quoting two distinct promises for each Commandment, one from the Old, the other from the New Testament: 1. Jer. 17:7—I Pet. 5:7. 2. Ps. 50:15—Matt. 7:7. 3. Is. 66:2—Luke 11:28. 4. Ex. 20:12—Eph. 6:2-3. 5. Prov. 21:21—Matt. 5:5, 7, 9. 6. Ps. 128—John 2:11. 7. Prov. 3:9, 10—Luke 6:38. 8. Ps. 15:1, 2—John 3:21. 9. Ps. 145:19—Matt. 6:33. 10. Ps. 37:4—I Tim. 4:8.

Now whereunto should these precious divine promises move us? "Therefore we should also love and trust in Him and willingly do according to His Commandments." This promise should have three distinct consequences:

1. That we love God. God owes us nothing, yet He promises. Since He shows us His love and has long ago shown us His unbounded love in Christ Jesus, we should love Him again: "We love Him because He first loved us" (I John 4:19).

2. That we trust in Him. He continually shows us the fulfillment of His promise. He never promises but what He fulfills (Ps. 33:4). Therefore we should always trust in Him, because He is faithful.

3. That we willingly do according to His Commandments. God could command without promising. But He says: If you do that, I will bless you and your children unto a thousand generations. God's wrath reaches the third and fourth generation; His mercy, the thousandth. We believers are still blessed in Abraham, our father (Gal. 3:9).

Fear, love, and trust in God is the goal that this conclusion puts before our eyes. That reminds us of the First Commandment: "We should fear, love, and trust in God above all things." But the Law can never effect this, only the Gospel (II Cor. 3:16).

But what is the purpose of this promise? Through faith in Christ a sinner's attitude toward the Law becomes an altogether different one. He now need no longer fear its damning curses. And he is eager to do the Father's will. For Christ's sake God will reward his good works with temporal and eternal blessings.

Therefore Christians may comfort themselves with such promises, although they must confess that they are not worthy of God's doing them good and that all their new obedience is but patchwork and no perfect fulfilling of the Law; that therefore Christ stands in the center and that through faith they have become God's children. Thus, through Christ, the Law is established and with it its promise, as St. Paul writes Rom. 3:31: "Do we then make void the Law through faith? God forbid! Yea, we establish the Law."

Let us thank God for this precious gift, His holy Law, that it may forever be our beloved schoolmaster to bring us to Christ; and then let us love Christ, our Redeemer, in doing His will gladly, continuously, and conscientiously all the days of our life, guided by the clear and accurate rule of His holy Ten Commandments. And if we are lacking the necessary strength, let us call upon Him daily for more power in the prayer He Himself has taught us, assured that He will fulfill abundantly every one of our petitions. And when we feel our weakness and inability to serve Him as we should, let us refresh ourselves with the fact that in the washing of regeneration and renewing of the Holy Spirit He has made us to be without spot or wrinkle, holy and without blemish; comfort ourselves again and again in His word of absolution: "My son [my daughter], be of good cheer; thy sins be forgiven thee," and often feast at His Table of Grace for the strengthening of our faith, the increase of our love, and the confirmation of our Christian hope until that day when He shall drink anew with us in His Father's kingdom. For:

> Only one life, 't will soon be past:
> Only what's done for Christ will last. Amen.

IX

Forgiveness of Sin

It is neither presumption nor yet an exaggeration when we say that our Lutheran Church is the Bible Church. There are two distinguishing characteristics in particular that confirm this claim. As the Bible Church we insist unwaveringly, and without qualification or reservation, that only the Bible, that is, the canonical books of the Old and the New Testament, is the divinely inspired and infallible Word of God. In opposition to those who in a greater or lesser measure add to this Word, subtract from it, or substitute for it, we hold, teach, and confess that the Bible is the only standard and rule by which questions of faith and life must be judged (*sola Scriptura*). As the Bible Church we furthermore glorify the central teaching of the Scriptures, the all-sufficiency of Jesus Christ as the one and only Savior of the world. In opposition to all who minimize the complete and perfect atonement of Jesus Christ by mixing human works in the article of Justification, saying that further sacrifices for sin are needed or that man must be his own savior and justify himself before God through good works or moral conduct, we confess with the clear teaching of Holy Scriptures that men are justified before God, not by works, but by grace, for Christ's sake, through faith (*sola gratia*).

These two fundamental doctrines, the supremacy of the Scriptures and the all-sufficiency of Christ, are the foundation of our faith. They have always been and, by the grace of God, will continue to remain the glory of our Lutheran Church. To relinquish the first would mean to sever ourselves from the only source of divine revelation; to forfeit the second would mean a denial of the central teaching of the Bible and apostasy from the Christian religion, which is the only divinely revealed and the only saving religion in the world. Both of these truths are basic in relation to the subject before us, which deals with *the forgiveness of sins,* for this subject forms the very heart and center of all Scriptural teaching.

"My sins! My sins!! My sins!!!" This was the despairing cry of Luther in the cloister when he could find no comfort for his conscience. Today, as in the past, and for all future time, man's greatest problem is the problem of sin. And today, as in the past, and for all future time, man's greatest need is the forgiveness of sins which God in his boundless grace and mercy has provided for all through Jesus Christ and which He freely offers to all men in the Word of the Gospel. It is upon this subject, which forms the chief article of the Christian religion, that we shall now center our attention: the forgiveness of sins.

I. THE UNIVERSAL NEED OF THE FORGIVENESS OF SINS

That all men are in need of forgiveness of sins is a fact that is repeatedly and emphatically stated on the pages of the Scriptures both of the Old and the New Testament, which declare that all men are conceived and born in sin and that all are guilty of actual transgressions of God's holy Law. Sin is described in Holy Scriptures as "the transgression of the Law" of God (I John 3:4). Other names for sin used in Holy Scriptures are "disobedience" (Rom. 5:19), "debts" (Matt. 6:12), "iniquity" (Ex. 34:7), "fault" (Matt. 18:15), "trespass" (II Cor. 5:19), "unrighteousness" (Rom. 6:13), and "wrong" (Col. 3:25). Taken together, these expressions occur in Holy Scriptures more than a thousand times. (The most common terms are "iniquity," 290 times; "transgression," 170 times; "sin," more than 600 times.)

Sin was brought into the world by the devil, who was once a holy angel but fell away from God (II Pet. 2:4; Jude 6), and by man, who of his own free will yielded to the temptation of the devil. Holy Scriptures expressly declare: "The devil sinneth from the beginning" (I John 3:8). It is therefore blasphemy to say that God is the author of sin. Since God's very essence is holiness (Lev. 19:2) and since all His works are done in righteousness and truth (Ps. 33:4; 145:17), God can no more be the author of sin than light is the author of darkness (James 1:13).

The story of the appearance of sin in the world is carefully recorded in the opening book of the Bible, in which we are told how our first parents, Adam and Eve, whom God had created in perfect righteousness and holiness after His own image (Gen. 1:26, 27; Eph. 4:24, Col. 3:10), disobeyed the commandment of God and yielded to the devil's temptation to eat of the forbidden fruit (Gen. 3:1-7). (Augsburg Confession, XIX, *Triglot*, p. 53.) Since God is almighty, some have criticized Him for permitting sin to enter the world. But they overlook the fact that God created man as a free moral agent. Accordingly, God did not compel man to resist the temptation, since a righteousness resting on compulsion and not having the support of man's own approval would be no righteousness at all. But neither did God compel man to yield to sin. On the contrary, man yielded to the devil of his own free will; his sinning was a matter of his own choice.

As the first people on earth Adam and Eve were the progenitors of the whole human race. From them all mankind originated, even as the Apostle declares: God "hath made of one blood all nations of men for to dwell on all the face of the earth" (Acts 17:26). In his relationship to God, Adam was not merely a single person, but the representative of all his descendants by ordinary generation. His person was the fountain of theirs, and his will the representative of theirs. He being the father of all, the whole human race was virtually in his loins, so that the whole human race sinned in him and suffered with him the consequence of sin. Therefore, Holy Scriptures declare: "By one man sin entered into the world, and death by sin; and so death passed upon all men, for that all have sinned" (Rom. 5:12). And again, "By one man's disobedience many were made sinners" (Rom. 5:19).

The hereditary guilt which all men have inherited from their first parents is commonly called "original sin." It is not only the guilt of Adam's sin imputed to his offspring, but also the corruption of man's nature, which took place when sin entered and which ever thereafter has inhered in the human will and inclination (Formula of Concord, I, *Triglot*, p. 863). Original sin, then, is not an activity, but a quality, a state, an inherent condition, which affects all men by birth and nature, as Jesus said: "That which is born of the flesh is flesh" (John 3:6), and as the Psalmist confessed: "Behold, I was shapen in iniquity; and in sin did my mother conceive me" (Ps.

51:5; see also Gen. 5:3; Job 14:4; 15:14). By reason of original sin all men are without true fear, love, and trust in God; all are without righteousness and inclined only to evil; all are spiritually blind, dead, and enemies of God; all are lost and condemned, ruined in body and soul. Thus it is written: "There is none righteous, no, not one. There is none that understandeth, there is none that seeketh after God. They are all gone out of the way, they are together become unprofitable; there is none that doeth good, no, not one" (Rom. 3:10-12; Is. 1:5, 6). "The imagination of man's heart is evil from his youth" (Gen. 8:21; 6:5). "The carnal mind is enmity against God" (Rom. 8:7). "The natural man receiveth not the things of the Spirit of God, for they are foolishness unto him; neither can he know them, because they are spiritually discerned" (I Cor. 2:14). Moreover, Holy Scriptures describe men in their natural state as being "dead in trespasses and sins" (Eph. 2:1), as being "by nature the children of wrath (Eph. 2:3), and as "having the understanding darkened, being alienated from the life of God through the ignorance that is in them because of the blindness of their heart" (Eph. 4:18; F. C., Epitome, I, *Triglot,* p. 781 f.).

Original sin, in addition to being dreadful, deadly, and damning in itself, is the "root and fountainhead of all actual sins." It is their parent, and they are its offspring. It is the silent, unseen cause; they are the effects. Actual sin is every act against a commandment of God in thoughts, desires, words, and deeds. The Moral Law, or the Ten Commandments, reveals to man God's holy will. It is that doctrine of the Bible in which God tells us how we are to be and what we are to do and not to do. Holy Scriptures tell us that the work of the Law was written in the heart of man from the time of creation (Rom. 2:14-15). But because this natural Law, inscribed in man's heart, was largely effaced by sin, God gave His holy Law a second time, in written form, arranged in Ten Commandments, and published it through Moses (Ex. 19 and 20). Actual sins are all acts committed against this Law. They include doing that which God has forbidden (sins of commission) as well as failing to do that which God has enjoined (sins of omission).

That all men are guilty of actual sins follows as a natural consequence of original sin. Since all are spiritually corrupt in body and soul, all are inclined only to that which is evil in God's sight. Even as a corrupt tree cannot bring forth good fruit (Matt. 7:17), so likewise every imagination of the thoughts of man's natural heart is only evil continually (Gen. 6:5). Speaking of man's natural heart and ascribing to it the origin of all actual sin, Jesus said: "Out of the heart proceed evil thoughts, murders, adulteries, fornications, thefts, false witness, blasphemies" (Matt. 15:19). That all men are guilty of actual sins is also clearly and emphatically stated in such passages as the following: "All have sinned and come short of the glory of God" (Rom. 3:23). "There is not a just man upon earth that doeth good and sinneth not" (Eccl. 7:20). "There is none that doeth good, no, not one" (Ps. 53:3). "The Scripture hath concluded all under sin" (Gal. 3:22; Rom. 3:9; F. of C., Ep., I, *Triglot*, pp. 783, 785).

The necessary consequence of sin is guilt on the part of man and righteous wrath and punishment on the part of God, whose divine majesty, righteousness, and holiness have been outraged. The countless cataclysms in the realm of nature, the unrelenting striving for existence among creatures, the consciousness of guilt and the vain efforts on the part of natural man to appease the wrath of God, the covetousness, greed, hatred, immorality, rivalry, and warfare among individuals and nations, the existence of sickness, sorrow, and suffering, and the billions of graves scattered over countless cemeteries throughout the world, all bear mute testimony to the universal presence, the terrifying power, and the indescribable consequence of sin. Wherefore the Bible not only tells us that all the world is guilty before God (Rom. 3:19), but it also tells us that "God is angry with the wicked every day" (Ps. 7:11; 5:5; 90:11) and that "the wrath of God is revealed from heaven against all ungodliness and unrighteousness of men, who hold the truth in unrighteousness" (Rom. 1:18; Eph. 5:6; Gen. 6:7ff; 19:24ff, etc.). Moreover, the Bible makes it plain that the consequence of sin does not only involve every evil of body and soul to which the human race has fallen heir in this world, but that it results in temporal death and, unless atoned for, in eternal death and damnation in the world to come. Thus it is written: "The wages of sin is death" (Rom. 6:23; 5:12; I Cor. 15:56; James 1:15). "The soul that sinneth it shall die" (Ezek. 18:20). "Cursed is everyone that continueth not in all things which are written in the book of the Law to do them" (Gal. 3:10). "Know ye not that the unrighteous shall not inherit the Kingdom of God?" (I Cor. 6:9; Ps. 92:7; Heb. 10:31; 12:29; Rev. 21:8.)

Such is the unspeakably terrible consequence of sin. And, foras-

much as sin constitutes a transgression against the infinite righteousness of God, there is nothing that man, as a finite creature, can do
to atone for it. Left to themselves, all are helplessly, hopelessly, and
eternally lost. None can save himself or another. Thus it is written:
"None of them can by any means redeem his brother nor give to God
a ransom for him" (Ps. 49:7). "Though thou wash thee with nitre,
and take thee much sope, yet thine iniquity is marked before Me,
saith the Lord" (Jer. 2:22; Job 9:30-31). All of man's efforts to free
himself are in vain. "By the deeds of the Law," says the Bible, "there
shall no flesh be justified in His sight" (Rom. 3:20). "All our righteousnesses," writes the Prophet, "are as filthy rags" (Is. 64:6):

> Enslaved by sin and bound in chains,
>   Beneath its dreadful, tyrant sway,
> And doomed to everlasting pains,
>   We wretched, guilty captives lay.
>
> Nor gold nor gems could buy our peace,
>   Nor all the world's collected store
> Suffice to purchase our release;
>   A thousand worlds were all too poor.

Such is the pitiable state of all men by nature. An insurmountable
mountain barrier of sin separates them from God (Is. 59:2). Their
sins represent a debt enormous beyond computation or calculation
(Matt. 18:23ff.). All must confess in the words of the Psalmist:
"Innumerable evils have compassed me about. Mine iniquities have
taken hold upon me, so that I am not able to look up. They are more
than hairs of mine head; therefore my heart faileth me" (Ps.
40:12). All must implore the Lord: "Enter not into judgment with
Thy servant, for in Thy sight shall no man living be justified" (Ps.
143:2). All must confess: "If Thou, Lord, shouldest mark iniquities,
O Lord, who shall stand?" But, thanks be to God, everyone can also
add in the words of the Psalmist, "There is forgiveness with Thee,
that Thou mayest be feared" (Ps. 130:3, 4).

Yes, Holy Scriptures assure us that the Lord is "merciful and
gracious, long-suffering, and abundant in goodness and truth, keeping
mercy for thousands, forgiving iniquity and transgression and sin"
(Ex. 34:6, 7; Ps. 130:7). There are numerous passages in both the

Old and the New Testament which assure us of this most comforting truth. They tell us that our sins have been taken away (John 1:29), that they have been forgiven (Ps. 85:2; Matt. 9:2; Col. 2:13), pardoned (Is. 40:2; 55:7; Jer. 33:8), remitted (John 20:23), atoned (Rom. 5:11), covered (Ps. 32:1; 85:2), purged (Is. 6:7; Heb. 10:2), washed (Ps. 51:2; I Cor. 6:11; Rev. 1:5), cleansed (I John 1:7). They assure us that God has redeemed us from all iniquity (Tit. 2:14), that He no longer imputes our iniquities unto us (II Cor. 5:19), that He has blotted out our sins as a thick cloud (Is. 44:22; Col. 2:14), that He has removed our transgressions from us as far as the east is from the west (Ps. 103:12), that He has cast our sins behind His back in the depth of the sea (Is. 38:17, Micah 7:19), and that He remembers them no more (Jer. 31:34; Is. 43:24, 25).

How God effected this full and free forgiveness of our sins is the wonderful truth that we shall next consider.

II. GOD'S WONDROUS PLAN FOR THE
FORGIVENESS OF SINS

Although God did not decree man's fall into sin, yet in His omniscience He foresaw it and therefore planned, even from eternity, to provide a way for man's redemption and salvation (II Tim. 1:9). This wonderful, heart-cheering, soul-saving, and life-giving truth is set forth in that part of the Bible known as the Gospel. The Gospel is the message of good will which tells us how full and free forgiveness of sins has been procured for all men through the atoning work of Jesus Christ (F. C., Thorough Declaration, V, *Triglot,* p. 959).

To make forgiveness of sins possible for His fallen creatures, God in His infinite wisdom already in eternity conceived a plan which would at one and the same time both satisfy His justice and exercise His love (Rom. 3:24-26). The sins of man had to be punished; God's justice demanded this. At the same time, however, God's loving grace found ways and means to help His fallen creatures, who could not help themselves. Holy Scriptures speak of the plan conceived by God as a mystery, because it is hidden to natural man and is revealed only through the Gospel (I Cor. 2:7-10; I Cor. 2:14; Eph. 1:7-10).

God's wondrous plan for the redemption of the world involved a Substitute who would take the place of the entire human race and render divine satisfaction for sin in their behalf. Since no such substitute could be found among men, seeing that all were in like condemnation, God chose His own Son Jesus Christ to be the world's Redeemer. And Jesus Christ, whose will ever conforms to that of the Father (John 6:38; 14:31; Heb. 10:9), voluntarily offered Himself for this work (John 10:11, 17, 18; 15:13; Eph. 5:2).

Immediately following man's fall into sin, God announced His plan of redemption by promising to send a Helper who would free men from the bondage of Satan, whose slaves and servants they had now become (Gen. 3:15). As the centuries passed, the promise was repeated to Adam's descendants again and again. Like a golden thread we find it interwoven throughout the Old Testament Scriptures. Then, long after the Fall, when God chose the Israelites as His peculiar people, He prescribed for them many laws, ordinances, rites, ceremonies, and sacrifices which, in a symbolical and typical way, associated their entire religious life with the coming of His Son, whom they were wont to speak of as the promised Messiah (*e. g.*, Ex. 12; Lev. 4:5, 16). Down through the long centuries of waiting the Lord sent His messengers, the Prophets, to His people, and all of them bore witness to the Savior, who was to come (Acts 10:43). These Prophets spoke of the person of the Redeemer (Deut. 18:15; Ps. 110:4; Zech. 9:9), of the time and the place of His birth (Gen. 49:10; Micah 5:2), and of the nature and purpose of His work, sometimes speaking of it with such certainty that they referred to it as a fact that had already been accomplished (Is. 53).

Then, when the fullness of the time was come, the Savior was born (Gal. 4:4). In keeping with the wondrous plan of salvation the circumstances surrounding His birth were so infinitely amazing and wonderful that they transcend all human thought and elicit the songs and praises of angels. (Luke 2). The Savior was not a mere human child, but the very Son of the living God, who had now become incarnate by taking the human nature into His divine Person, thus appearing in human flesh without sin. Many centuries before, the Prophet Isaiah spoke of this miracle of the ages, saying: "Behold, a virgin shall conceive and bear a son and shall call His name Immanuel" (Is. 7:14). When the fullness of the time was now come, God sent an angel to the Virgin Mary, at Nazareth, in Galilee, saying: "The Holy Ghost shall come upon thee, and the power of the Highest shall overshadow thee; therefore also that holy thing which shall be born of thee shall be called the Son of God" (Luke

1:35; see also Matt. 1:18f.). Referring to this transcendent event and overcome by profound awe and wonder, the Apostle Paul exulted: "Without controversy great is the mystery of godliness: God was manifest in the flesh" (I Tim. 3:16). Similarly the Evangelist St. John wrote: "The Word was made flesh and dwelt among us (and we beheld His glory, the glory as of the Only-Begotten of the Father), full of grace and truth" (John 1:14). Thus He, the eternal and only-begotten Son of God. who is of one substance with the Father, for us men and for our salvation came down from heaven, and was incarnate by the Holy Ghost of the Virgin Mary, and was made man (Phil. 2:7; I John 1:1-3). In Him all the fullness of the Godhead dwelt bodily (Col. 2:9); in the wondrous person of this God-Man Jesus Christ, the divine and the human nature dwelt in undivided, mysterious, personal union.

In the accomplishment of God's wondrous plan of salvation it was necessary that the Savior should be a sinless man, that so He might serve as the Substitute for men. Only by being a man could He take our place under the Law, and only in this way could He suffer and die in our stead. But it was also necessary that the Savior should be true God, for only then could His fulfilling of the Law be sufficient for all men, only in this way could His sinless life and His vicarious death be a sufficient ransom for the redemption of all, and only thus could He be able to overcome death and the devil for all men (Ps. 49:7-8; Heb. 7:11-28; 9:1-28).

That the sinless God-Man, Jesus Christ, the heaven-sent Savior of the world, accomplished these purposes in every detail and thus served as the perfect Mediator between God and men (I Tim. 2:5) is a fact that is clearly stated in numerous passages of Holy Scripture. "When the fullness of the time was come," says the holy writer, "God sent forth His Son, made of a woman, made under the Law, to redeem them that were under the Law, that we might receive the adoption of sons" (Gal. 4:4, 5). Because we were unable to keep God's Law, Christ became our Substitute and fulfilled all the righteousness of the Law in our stead (Matt. 3:15). He did no sin, and in Him was no sin (John 8:46; I John 3:5). His perfect obedience fully compensated for our disobedience. His perfect righteousness fully atoned for our unrighteousness, as it is written: "Christ is the end of the Law for righteousness to everyone that believeth" (Rom. 10:4; see Rom. 8:3; Heb. 5:8-10). It is upon this ground that the Apostle

Paul institutes a parallel between Adam and Christ, saying: "As by one man's disobedience many were made sinners, so by the obedience of one shall many be made righteous" (Rom. 5:19). As Adam in his transgression was the representative of the entire human race, so Christ in His perfect fulfillment of the Law was the Substitute for all mankind (*active obedience*).

But far more than this was needed for securing our eternal welfare. Not only must God's Law be kept, its transgressions, too, must be removed. Our many sins stood between God and us, and these had to be atoned for. Since we were in no wise able to make this atonement, God laid all of our sins upon His sinless Son (Is. 53:6). As our all-sufficient Savior, Christ bore our sins in His own body (I Pet. 2:24). *In* Him was no sin, but *on* Him were laid the sins of all mankind. As the Lamb of God He took away the sin of the world (John 1:29). As our perfect High Priest He offered Himself for us on the altar of the Cross and thereby suffered the full punishment and paid the entire debt of our sins (Heb. 7:27; 9:26; 10:14; *passive obedience*).

This transcendent truth is stated in many passages of Holy Scripture too simple to be misunderstood and too beautiful to be forgotten. The leading thought, the predominant note, the ever-recurring phrases "for us," "for our sins," for all," is apparent throughout. Here are but a few of the passages: "Christ hath redeemed us from the curse of the Law, being made a curse for us" (Gal. 3:13). "Christ died for our sins according to the Scriptures" (I Cor. 15:3). "Christ also hath once suffered for sins, the just for the unjust, that He might bring us to God" (I Pet. 3:18). He "gave Himself for us" (Tit. 2:14; Eph. 5:2; Gal. 2:20). He "gave Himself for our sins" (Gal. 1:4). "He laid down His life for us" (I John 3:16; I Cor. 5:7). He "gave Himself a ransom for all" (I Tim. 2:6; Matt. 20:28). God "hath made Him to be sin for us, who knew no sin, that we might be made the righteousness of God in Him" (II Cor. 5:21). "He was wounded for our transgressions, He was bruised for our iniquities. The chastisement of our peace was upon Him, and with His stripes we are healed" (Is. 53:5). "He is the propitiation for our sins; and not for ours only, but also for the sins of the whole world" (I John 2:2). God "spared not His own Son, but delivered Him up for us all" (Rom. 8:32; I John 4:9, 10).

Because the sinless Christ was Himself both the Sacrifice and the

Priest, His offering for the sins of the world was complete, perfect, and effectual for all time. By this one offering "He hath perfected forever them that are sanctified" (Heb. 10:14; 7:27; 9:26). His blood, being the very blood of God incarnate, was all-sufficient to atone for all sins of all men of all times. Speaking of that precious blood, Holy Scriptures declare: "By His own blood He entered in once into the holy place, having obtained eternal redemption for us" (Heb. 9:12). "The blood of Jesus Christ His Son cleanseth us from all sin" (I John 1:7). In Him "we have redemption through His blood, the forgiveness of sins, according to the riches of His grace" (Eph. 1:7; Col. 1:14). "Ye know," says the Apostle, "that ye were not redeemed with corruptible things, as silver and gold . . . but with the precious blood of Christ, as of a lamb without blemish and without spot" (I Pet. 1:18, 19). Thus, while God's wonderful plan of salvation bestows forgiveness of sins upon us as a free gift, that forgiveness is not the result of a mere fiat of God's divine will, but is based upon the most precious ransom of Christ's innocent suffering and death and the shedding of His holy blood.

The precious words "for us, for our sins, for all," assure us that God now regards us as though we ourselves had fulfilled the Law, as though we ourselves had atoned for the guilt of sin, and as though we ourselves had endured sin's punishment and paid its debt. "Because we thus judge," says the Apostle, "that if one died for all, then were all dead" (II Cor. 5:14; I Cor. 1:30). In the words of Luther every person in the world can now exult: "Thou, Lord Jesus, art my righteousness, and I am Thy sin: Thou hast taken what was mine, and hast given me what was Thine." In the words of the hymn even the vilest sinner can now joyfully sing:

> Chief of sinners though I be,
> Jesus shed His blood for me;
> Died that I might live on high,
> Lived that I might never die.

The ineffably wonderful, transcendingly glorious, and infinitely enduring nature of Christ's vicarious satisfaction gives us the incontrovertible assurance that the whole world of mankind is now reconciled to our holy, just, and righteous God, the whole world, all of whom had outraged His divine majesty by their sins. Thus it is written: "God was in Christ, reconciling the world unto Himself, not imputing their trespasses unto them" (II Cor. 5:19). The Law has been fulfilled, and we have been redeemed from its curse. The debt of the world's sins has been paid. Man's guilt has been atoned. Sin's power and dominion have been forever destroyed; its dreadful, deadly, and damning consequences have been removed. Satan's shackles of slavery have been broken (I John 3:8; Heb. 2:14, 15). Salvation full and free has been prepared for the world. The door to heaven and eternal life has been opened to all men. It is all an accomplished fact. *"It is finished!"* (John 19:30). Christ *"was* delivered for our offenses, and *was* raised again for our justification" (Rom. 4:25). Henceforth, and to all eternity, no further sacrifices for sins are needed, for, "where remission of these is, there is no more offering for sin" (Heb. 10:18).

This is the very heart and center of all Scriptural teaching. All the Prophets of the Old Testament gave witness to Christ (Acts 10:43; Luke 24:25-27, 44-46). All testified beforehand the sufferings of Christ and the glory that should follow (I Pet. 1:10, 11). In like manner, the suffering, death, and resurrection of Christ is the central theme of the New Testament Scriptures (Luke 24:46, 47; Acts 26:22, 23; I Cor. 2:2; Gal. 1:8, 9, etc). Because of the complete redemption wrought by Christ, God has justified the entire human race; all are declared righteous in His sight. The world, each individual, is now reconciled unto God. By the resurrection of Jesus Christ from the dead, God placed His stamp of approval upon the sacrifice of His Son and thereby declared that all men have been redeemed, that their sins are forgiven, that they are justified, declared righteous (Rom. 4:25; 5, 18; *objective justification*).

In this wondrous plan of God for the redemption of the human race, man contributed nothing. On the contrary, it is written: "When we were *enemies,* we were reconciled to God by the death of His Son" (Rom. 5:10). The act of justifying, or declaring the world of mankind righteous, was an act that occurred in the loving heart of God. It is not something that occurred *in* man, but rather something that occurred *for* man. The verb *justify* as it occurs thirty-eight times in the New Testament is always a forensic term, meaning "to hold or declare righteous." Like the creation of the world, justification is an event that took place outside of man, an act on the part of God alone. Therefore Holy Scriptures speak of it as a free gift which has come upon all men by the righteousness of Christ (Rom. 5:18).

But while God declared the whole world of mankind justified through Christ's vicarious atonement, this comforting fact would never be known unless God would reveal it; like a precious buried treasure its existence would be concealed. Accordingly, God's wondrous plan of salvation also embraces the purpose to tell mankind of the redemption that He has prepared for them so that they might appropriate its blessings unto themselves.

Let us therefore also consider, thirdly, the manner in which forgiveness of sins is appropriated by the individual.

III. THE INDIVIDUAL APPROPRIATION OF THE FORGIVENESS OF SINS

Left to himself, no man ever would, no man ever could, know that he has been redeemed. Therefore God Himself makes this soul-saving truth known to man. The means which God employs for this purpose is the Gospel. "Therein," says the Apostle, "is the righteousness of God revealed" (Rom. 1:17). In Holy Scriptures this Word of the Gospel is called "the word of Reconciliation" (II Cor. 5:19), for it is the Word which proclaims reconciliation between God and sinners. It is also called "the Gospel of the grace of God" (Acts 20:24), because it flows from God's free love and mercy. It is spoken of, furthermore, as "the Gospel of Christ" (Rom. 1:16), because Jesus Christ is the Heart and Center of it. And, again, it is spoken of as "the Gospel of peace and salvation" (Rom. 10:15; Eph. 1:13), because it publishes peace with God.

The Gospel also includes the Sacraments, Holy Baptism and the Lord's Supper, because these receive their saving power through the Word of the Gospel which they proclaim. Holy Baptism is expressly called "the washing of regeneration and renewing of the Holy Ghost" (Tit. 3:5). Because the water of Baptism is the water comprehended in God's command and connected with God's Word, it has the heavenly power to wash away sins (Matt. 28:19; Mark 16:16; Acts 2:38; Gal. 3:26, 27; Eph. 5:25, 26). So, too, the holy Sacrament of the Lord's Supper not only seals the forgiveness of sins, but also conveys this forgiveness by virtue of Christ's words in which He tells us that His body was given for us and that His blood was shed for the remission of our sins (Matt. 26:26-28; Mark

14:22-24; Luke 22:19, 20; I Cor. 11:24, 25). These means, the Word and the Sacraments, are called "the means of grace," for through them the grace of God merited by Christ is conveyed into the sinner's heart.

Being the very Word of God, the Gospel possesses heart-changing, soul-converting, and life-giving power. It is spoken of as "spirit and life" (John 6:63), as "the power of God unto salvation to every one that believeth" (Rom. 1:16), as an "incorruptible seed" which possesses the power of spiritual regeneration (I Pet. 1:23), and as the Word which is able to save souls (James 1:21; Rom. 10:17). It is through this "Word of Reconciliation" that God announces to men that He has reconciled the world unto Himself through the death of His Son, that their sins are no longer imputed to them, and that their redemption is an accomplished fact. Through this Word the Holy Spirit extends the gracious invitation: "Come; for all things are now ready" (Luke 14:17).

This is God's wondrous plan for making the glad tidings of salvation known to the world. St. Paul writes: God "hath committed unto us the Word of Reconciliation. Now, then, we are ambassadors for Christ, as though God did beseech you by us; we pray you in Christ's stead, be ye reconciled to God" (II Cor. 5:19, 20). This was the solemn charge that the Savior gave His chosen disciples who themselves had received forgiveness of sins through His Word (John 15:3). After His resurrection He said unto them: "Thus it is written, and thus it behooved Christ to suffer and to rise from the dead the third day; and that repentance and remission of sins should be preached in His name among all nations, beginning at Jerusalem" (Luke 24:46, 47). Shortly before His ascension into heaven He gave them the great commission to "go into all the world and preach the Gospel to every creature" (Mark 16:15). And, in His High-Priestly prayer He included a petition for all who would, in the centuries to come, believe on Him through the Word of the Gospel, which should be preached to them (John 17:20; see also Acts 13:38; Is. 40:9).

But man is not saved by merely hearing that Christ has obtained full and free pardon for him, just as little as a mortally sick person will regain his health by hearing that a cure for his illness has been found. The remedy will not benefit him who is sick unless he takes it. Even so the salvation wrought by Christ will in no wise avail the sinner unless it is appropriated by him individually and personally.

Because of his totally corrupt spiritual condition natural man has neither the desire nor the ability to accept the salvation which God offers him in and through the Gospel (I Cor. 2:14). However, in and through this life-giving, heart-changing, and soul-saving Word, the Holy Spirit performs His gracious work in man's heart. Through the Law He leals man to the knowledge of his sins and to repentance, and thus makes man feel the need of forgiveness (Rom. 3:20; Acts 2:37). Then, by means of the Gospel, the Holy Spirit creates faith in the heart so that man trusts in the grace and mercy of God and appropriates forgiveness of sins unto himself by accepting the gift of righteousness merited for him by Christ (Rom. 10:17; I Cor. 2:4, 5; Eph. 1:19; 2:8; Phil. 2:13; I Thess. 2:13). With the hand of faith man reaches out and takes the forgiveness of sins which has been prepared for him by Christ and which God freely offers in the Gospel. The very moment in which the sinner believes in Christ and accepts Christ as his personal Savior he is justified in God's sight; in that very moment he has full and free forgiveness of all sins, just as a person comes in possession of the gift that is handed to him the very instant he reaches out and takes it (*subjective justification;* F. of C., Thor. Decl., II, *Triglot,* pp. 903, 919; Apol., A. C., IV, *Triglot,* p. 125).

Justification being an accomplished fact, it can be appropriated only by faith. Whenever Holy Scriptures speak of works in connection with faith, these works are always spoken of as the result and never as the cause of faith (Rom. 6:4; 8:1; II Cor. 5:17; Gal. 2:20; Eph. 2:8-10; Tit. 2:11-14; I Pet. 2:9-12; F. of C., Thor. Decl., III, *Triglot,* pp. 923, 925, 928). Faith, and faith alone, appropriates the free gift of forgiveness. In this all holy Scriptures agree. In one and the same voice the Scriptures of both the Old and New Testament declare that the sinner is justified before God, not by his works, but freely, by grace, for Christ's sake, through faith. Thus the Old Testament Prophet Habakkuk wrote: "The just shall live by his *faith*" (Hab. 2:4; Rom. 1:17; Heb. 10:38). This was also the theme of all the other Prophets of the Old Testament, for thus it is written: "To Him (Christ) give all the Prophets witness, that through His name whosoever *believeth* in Him shall receive remission of sins" (Acts 10:43). Again, with reference to the Old Testament, it is written: "If Abraham were justified by works, he hath whereof to glory; but not before God. For what saith the Scripture? Abraham *believed*

God, and it was counted unto him for righteousness. Now, to him that worketh is the reward not reckoned of grace, but of debt. But to him that worketh not, but believeth on Him that justifieth the ungodly, his faith is counted for righteousness. Even as David also describeth the blessedness of the man unto whom God imputeth righteousness without works, saying, Blessed are they whose iniquities are forgiven and whose sins are covered. Blessed is the man to whom the Lord will not impute sin. . . . *Therefore it is of faith, that it might be by grace;* to the end the promise might be sure to all the seed" (Rom. 4:2-8, 16; Ps. 32:1, 2). Again, it was with reference to the Old Testament that St. Paul wrote to Timothy: "From a child thou hast known the Holy Scriptures, which are able to make thee wise unto salvation *through faith which is in Christ Jesus*" (II Tim. 3:15; see also Is. 55:1; John 5:39; Gal. 3:6). Even more clearly and emphatically we read in the language of the New Testament writers: "By the deeds of the Law there shall no flesh be justified in His sight, for by the Law is the knowledge of sin. But now the righteousness of God without the Law is manifested, being witnessed by the Law and Prophets, even *the righteousness of God which is by faith of Jesus Christ* unto all and upon all them that believe; for there is no difference, for all have sinned and come short of the glory of God, *being justified freely by His grace through the redemption that is in Christ Jesus,* whom God hath set forth to be a Propitiation *through faith in His blood,* to declare His righteousness for the remission of sins that are past, through the forbearance of God; to declare, I say, at this time His righteousness; that He might be just and *the Justifier of him which believeth in Jesus.* Where is boasting then? It is excluded. By what law? of works? Nay, but by the law of faith. Therefore we conclude that *a man is justified by faith without the deeds of the Law*" (Rom. 3:20-28). Again, we read: "Not by works of righteousness which we have done, but according to His mercy He saved us by the washing of regeneration and renewing of the Holy Ghost, which He shed on us abundantly *through Jesus Christ our Savior; that being justified by His grace,* we should be made heirs according to the hope of eternal life" (Tit. 3:5-7). All human efforts are without avail. All of man's boasted works of self-righteousness —good behavior, moral conduct, virtuous life, noble intentions, fastings, penances, pilgrimages, prayers, rites, ceremonies, sacrifices, intercession of saints, and similar acts—are rejected. In language that cannot be misunderstood Holy Scriptures declare: "*By grace are ye saved through faith; and that not of yourselves; it is the gift of God, not of works, lest any man should boast*" (Eph. 2:8, 9; see also Rom. 5:15, 18; 11:6; Gal. 2:16, 21; 3:10; 5:4; Phil. 3:9; etc.; Augsb. Conf., IV, *Triglot*, p. 45; Apol., Augsb. Conf., IV (II), pp. 131, 133; Apol., Augsb. Conf., III, 171; F. C., Ep., III, p. 793; F. C., Thor. Decl., III, p. 919).

> By grace! None dare lay claim to merit;
> Our works and conduct have no worth.
> God in His love sent our Redeemer,
> Christ Jesus, to this sinful earth;
> His death did for our sins atone,
> And we are saved by grace alone.

When we receive the precious gift of forgiveness of sins, appropriated by faith, we become partakers of all the unspeakable spiritual blessings of heaven (I Cor. 3:21; Eph. 1:18; 2:6, 7; Phil. 4:19; I John 3:2). "Being justified by faith, we have peace with God through our Lord Jesus Christ" (Rom. 5:1). God now regards us as His dear children, and as such we are also the heirs of heaven and eternal life, for where there is forgiveness of sins, there is also life and salvation (Gal. 3:26; Rom. 8:14-17). Clothed in the garment of Christ's righteousness, God now looks upon us as being holy, and we, as new creatures in Christ, delight to do God's will (Eph. 2:19; Rom. 1:7; I Pet. 2:9; Rom. 6; Gal. 2:20; 5:24; Eph. 4:32; I John 2:3; 4:19). Our hearts are filled with new love for our fellow men, and in gratitude for God's forgiveness to us we heartily forgive and readily do good to those who sin against us (Matt. 6:15; John 13: 35; Col. 3:13; Eph. 4:32; I John 3:14). Loving God and loved by Him, we live in a state of grace. All things work together for our good, and there is nothing that can separate us from the love of God, which is in Christ Jesus, our Lord (Rom. 8:28-39). We not only have forgiveness for past sins, but for present sins as well, as the present tense of the verbs in the following passages declare: "The blood of Jesus Christ His Son *cleanseth* us from all sin" (I John 1:7). "Behold the Lamb of God, which *taketh away* the sin of the world" (John 1:29; see also Ps. 103:3). As our exalted and glorified Savior, Christ ever lives to intercede for us at the throne of grace (I John 2:1, 2; Rom

8:34; Heb. 7:25, 9:12), and the Holy Spirit continues to perform His gracious work in our hearts by daily and richly forgiving us all sins (Eph. 1:7; Phil. 1:6; I Pet. 1:5; I John 1:9). Washed, sanctified, and justified in the name of the Lord Jesus and by the Spirit of our God (I Cor. 6:11), we daily live under an open heaven in which the sun of divine grace constantly shines and from whence, as from an inexhaustible storehouse, it unceasingly sends forth its healing and saving rays of forgiveness. Daily, hourly, constantly, the never-failing stream of refreshing, life-giving water of forgiveness flows. Where sin abounds, God's grace and mercy and forgiveness in Christ doth much more abound (Rom. 5:20).

> Though great our sins and sore our woes,
> His grace much more aboundeth;
> His helping love no limit knows,
> Our utmost need it soundeth.

Yea though our sins be as scarlet, they shall be as white as snow; though they be red like crimson, they shall be as wool, for "the blood of Jesus Christ, His Son, *cleanseth* us from all sin" (I John 1:7; Is. 1:18).

Such is the wonderful manner in which the individual appropriates the forgiveness of sins merited by Christ. It is God's earnest desire, confirmed by the solemn oath that, as He lives, all men should share in this forgiveness. He would have all men to be saved and to come unto the knowledge of the truth. He is not willing that any should perish, but that all should come to repentance (Ezek. 33:11; I Tim. 2:4; II Pet. 3:9), and Jesus Himself declared: "God so loved the world, that He gave His only-begotten Son, that whosoever believeth in Him should not perish, but have everlasting life" (John 3:16; Luke 19:10; Matt. 18:14). To this end the Savior also causes His Gospel to be proclaimed in all the world (Mark 16:15; Luke 24:47; Acts 1:8). To all who hear this Word the gracious invitation is extended, "Come; for all things are now ready" (Luke 14:17), and once more, at the very close of the Scriptures, the gracious invitation is extended in the words: "The Spirit and the bride say, Come. And let him that heareth say, Come. And let him that is athirst come. And whosoever will, *let him take the water of life freely"* (Rev. 22:17; F. C., Thor. Decl., XI, *Triglot,* p. 1071, 1073).

The fact, therefore, that many do not receive the forgiveness of sins is by no means to be attributed to any unwillingness on the part of God. Rather, the cause lies entirely within men themselves who refuse to accept the free gift which is offered them, who stubbornly resist the work of the Holy Spirit, and who therefore perish by reason of their own fault (Hos. 13:9; Luke 14:18; Matt. 23:37; Acts 7:51; F. C., Thor. Decl., XI, *Triglot,* p. 1077). In the satanic blindness of their sin-perverted and self-righteous hearts those who are lost reject Jesus Christ, the only Savior from sin, and are therefore damned because of their unbelief. For while forgiveness of sins has been prepared also for them, yet it cannot be appropriated but by personal faith. "He that believeth not," says the Savior, "shall be damned" (Mark 16:16). Again it is written: "Neither is there salvation in any other, for there is none other name under heaven given among men, whereby we must be saved" (Acts 4:12). "He that believeth on the Son hath everlasting life; and he that believeth not the Son shall not see life; but the wrath of God abideth on him" (John 3:36; 3:18; I John 5:12).—The Bible speaks of one sin that cannot be forgiven: the sin against the Holy Ghost (Matt. 12:31, 32; Mark 3:28, 29; Luke 12:10; Heb. 6:4-6; I John 5:16). This sin is unpardonable not because of any unwillingness on the part of God, nor because the merits of Christ are not sufficiently great, but because in consequence of man's persistent rejection of the Word of the Holy Spirit the final obduration is pronounced upon him; the Holy Spirit forsakes him utterly, and repentance becomes impossible.

CONCLUSION

The doctrine of the forgiveness of sins not only forms the heart and center of all Holy Scriptures (Apol., Augsb. Conf., XX, *Triglot,* pp. 339, 341; F. C., III, pp. 917, 919), it is also the article which distinguishes the Christian religion from false religions, all of which teach that man can be his own savior and that he can justify himself before God by his own works (F. Pieper, *Christliche Dogmatik,* I, pp. 15-16). Next to, and in conjunction with, the perversion of the doctrine of the sole and supreme authority of Holy Scriptures in all questions of faith and life, it was against the perversion of this article of justification that Martin Luther raised his voice in solemn protest when he condemned the sale of indulgences for the remission of sins and thus began the great battle of the Reformation. Having restored this article to its Scriptural place, Luther earnestly contended for it and did all in his power to preserve it inviolate. "Of this article," he said, "nothing can be yielded or surrendered (nor can anything be granted or permitted contrary to the same), even though heaven and earth, and whatever will not abide, should sink to ruin. . . . If this only article remains pure on the battlefield, the Christian Church also remains pure and in goodly harmony and without any sects; but if it does not remain pure, it is not possible that any error or fanatical spirit can be resisted" (Smalc. Art., p. 461; F. of C., *Triglot,* p. 917). In speaking thus Luther was merely re-emphasizing the statement of the inspired Apostle, who wrote: "Though we or an angel from heaven preach any other gospel unto you than that which we have preached unto you, let him be accursed" (Gal. 1:8; I Cor. 2:2).

The supreme importance of this article is emphasized, furthermore, by the fact that only the heaven-confirmed truth which it teaches gives enduring comfort to penitent sinners (Apol., A. C., IV, pp. 137, 147; Art. XII, p. 277; Art. XX, pp. 338, 341; Large Catechism, Petition V, pp. 723, 725; F. C., Thor. Decl., III, p. 925). It was here, in the righteousness won for him by Christ, that Luther found abiding comfort for his troubled soul. This truth opened for him the gates of paradise. And it is likewise here that every troubled soul can find the only satisfying answer to the all-important question: What must I do to be saved?—in the words: "Believe on the Lord Jesus Christ, and thou shalt be saved. . . . Be of good cheer; thy sins be forgiven thee" (Acts 16:30, 31; Matt. 9:2). Here, in the heart-cheering, soul-comforting truth that the wondrous plan of our salvation was conceived in the loving heart of God from eternity, that our salvation is based solely and alone upon Christ's completed work of redemption, that it is bestowed upon us by the gracious work of the Holy Spirit, that it is from beginning to end the work of the Triune God, and that it is rooted and grounded in the unerring Word of God, which liveth and abideth for ever, is the greatest assurance that God has given to us in this life. Here, in the immutable counsel of God's will, confirmed by His solemn oath, all who flee to the Savior for refuge have an anchor for their soul which is both sure and steadfast (Heb. 6:17-20; I John 3:20; 5:9, 10). Yea,

How firm a foundation, ye saints of the Lord,
Is laid for your faith in His excellent Word!
What more can He say than to you He hath said
Who unto the Savior for refuge have fled?

Finally, the doctrine of the forgiveness of sins gives all glory to God (Apol., Augsb. Conf., pp. 163, 179; XII, p. 275; XX, p. 339; XXVII, p. 423, 425). Since this article sets forth that salvation is the free gift of God in Christ, without any merit or worthiness on our part, it ascribes the glory for our deliverance from eternal damnation to God alone (Acts 4:12; Rev. 5:12). "If it be taken away," says Luther, "as is done by the Jews, or if it be perverted, as the papists pervert it, the Church cannot endure, and God does not receive His honor. For this is His honor and glory: He is gracious and merciful, willing to forgive us our sins for the sake of His Son and to save us" (on Gen. 21:17).

Surely, then, it is our paramount duty to keep this article inviolate and to earnestly contend for it (F. Pieper, *Christl. Dogm.*, II, p. 670 f.), that it may forever be preserved in its spotless purity for ourselves, for our children, and for all generations as yet unborn (Jude 3). Nor is it possible to overemphasize the fact that today, as in the past, and for all future time, the preaching and teaching of this truth is the Church's one and only divine commission and the world's first and foremost need. *God has no other plan for the salvation of the human race.* "Thus it is written, and thus it behooved Christ to suffer, and to rise from the dead the third day; and that repentance and remission of sins should be preached in His name among all nations" (Luke 24:46, 47). "This Gospel of the Kingdom," says the Savior, "shall be preached in all the world for a witness unto all nations; and then shall the end come." (Matt. 24:14; 28:19, 20; Mark 16:15, 16.)

May God preserve us and our Church steadfast in this truth! May He grant each of us grace to repeat in the words of Luther: "One thing alone shall rule in my heart, namely, this one article of faith in my dear Lord Jesus Christ; He also shall be the beginning, the middle, the end, and the object of all my spiritual thoughts by day and by night!" And, may the Holy Spirit inspire our hearts and tongues to join the saints on earth and in heaven in the paean of praise: "*Unto Him that loved us and washed us from our sins in*

His own blood and hath made us kings and priests unto God and His Father; to Him be glory and dominion for ever and ever. Amen." (Rev. 1:5, 6.)

X

Conversion

THE doctrine of conversion is a doctrine of paramount importance in the total body of Scriptural teaching and Christian belief. It deals with the all-important question of how the gracious salvation won for us by our Savior Jesus Christ is brought into the possession of the individual sinner for his soul's eternal salvation.

I. THE NECESSITY OF CONVERSION

Conversion is, as shall be explained more fully later, the bestowal of saving faith in our Lord and Redeemer Jesus Christ. It is deliverance from the power of darkness and translation into the kingdom of the Son of God. It is something that no human being can achieve for himself. St. Paul says, "Ye were dead in trespasses and sins" (Eph. 2:1); and we confess in the words of Luther's Small Catechism: "I believe that I cannot by my own reason or strength believe in Jesus Christ, my Lord, or come to Him." Without conversion and faith there can be no sharing in the merits of the Savior's blessed redemption, and without the regenerating activity of the Holy Spirit there can be no conversion. Salvation comes to man through the free grace of God, and the faith that grasps this grace can come only through a conversion that is wrought by God.

It is the good and gracious will of God that every human being shall be saved and enter eternal life. Paul bears testimony to the universal grace of God when he says, "God will have all men to be saved and to come to the knowledge of the truth" (I Tim. 2:4). God's love and favor extend to all men without exception. "The grace of God that bringeth salvation hath appeared to all men" (Tit. 2:11). And since all mankind is in need of salvation, God, out

168

of love for all the world, gave His only-begotten Son that whosoever believeth in Him should not perish, but have everlasting life (John 3: 16). Jesus Christ, the eternal Son of God, by His incarnation became "the Lamb of God, which taketh away the sin of the world" (John 1:29). Jesus, our Savior, fulfilled the Law in our stead, and in His spotless life and His atoning death on the Cross He provided a sufficient ransom for our redemption from sin, death, and the devil. He has taken away all guilt and suffered all punishment, and He has won freedom from the slavery of sin. As man's Substitute He has atoned for sin by paying the penalty of the world's guilt. He has redeemed all lost and condemned mankind, and His glorious resurrection is witness to the fact that the Father has accepted the sacrifice of His Son for the reconciliation of the world. To all mankind now is extended the gracious invitation to accept and enjoy the fruits of the Savior's work, the forgiveness of sins and the hope of eternal life. "Come, for all things are now ready," is the gracious invitation that is extended to all mankind.

But although the invitation to share in all the blessings of the kingdom of heaven and of eternal salvation is extended to all human beings, yet the condition of the heart and mind of man under sin is such that it is not within the power of anyone to take for himself the fruits of Christ's redemption. There was a time in the history of the human race when human nature was so constituted that the grace and favor of God were its natural possession. For man was created in the image of God, *i. e.*, in a true and thorough knowledge of God and of spiritual things and in perfect righteousness and holiness (Eph. 4:24; Col. 3:10). Man in his primeval state was God's perfect child and in possession of all heavenly blessings. But when sin came into the world through the disobedience of our first parents, when man's decision ran counter to the holy will of God, the divine image was lost. The immediate consequences of this act of disobedience were not only those which came upon the first sinners themselves; but, as Paul says, "By one man sin entered into the world" (Rom. 5:12). Sin entered the human race, so that all men, all descendants of Adam and Eve, are sinners. The original perfect righteousness, goodness, and holiness granted to man as a gift in creation is irrevocably gone for this life, and hereditary corruption and depravity has entered human nature as a result of the Fall.

The consequences of this first disobedience were tremendous for the entire human race. Man lost his perfect knowledge of God. His mind and understanding were darkened in spiritual things and reduced to blindness. To be sure, man can yet perceive the eternal power and wisdom of God in the works of creation. He can see that there is a God, great and mighty, for "the heavens declare the glory of God, and the firmament sheweth His handiwork" (Ps. 19:1). Man also remains conscious of the eternal holiness and justice of God, for the Law of God is written in his heart, and his conscience holds him accountable to the divine Law. But even this innate natural knowledge of God is fragmentary and imperfect, as Paul says, "For we know in part, and we prophecy in part, but (only) when that which is perfect is come, then that which is in part shall be done away" (I Cor. 13:9-10). The mind of man that has accomplished so many wonders in the things of this life lacks all understanding and power in spiritual things. To know God as He really is, as the God of love, who in the suffering and death of His Son has graciously provided salvation for all mankind, is beyond man's natural powers of understanding. God's plan of salvation cannot be discovered by the questing mind of man acting with its own natural powers. The wisdom of God is, as Paul says, "the wisdom of God in a mystery, even the hidden wisdom . . . which none of the princes of this world knew; for had they known it, they would not have crucified the Lord of glory." On the contrary, "eye hath not seen, nor ear heard, neither have entered into the heart of man the things which God hath prepared for them that love Him" (I Cor. 2:7-9).

Furthermore, the mere hearing of the message of God's love in Christ, the outward knowledge of the facts of God's plan of salvation, which is possible for everyone through the revelation of God's Word in the Scriptures, does not carry with it the ability to accept this message in saving faith. Man after the Fall is still a rational being, having an understanding and a will, and can acquire an intellectual knowledge of the truths of the Gospel by hearing the Word of preaching, by reading and study, by all the natural processes of learning; he can, as the Formula of Concord says, "hear the Gospel and to a certain extent meditate upon it, also discourse upon it, as is to be seen in the Pharisees and hypocrites" (Thorough Declaration, II, 24). But this does not include a spiritual grasp that accepts, believes, and trusts in what has been heard and learned. Many people know the truths of the Gospel and perhaps even know them well, still they do not believe them and do not put their trust in them; they may even strongly oppose them. To the Jews the crucified Jesus was, as Paul says, a stumbling block and to the Greeks foolishness (I Cor. 1:23). So unconverted man, even though he may pay his outward respects to the Bible and to Jesus as the world's greatest moral teacher, yet regards the truths of the Gospel, the message of salvation through faith in Jesus Christ, the Savior, and the forgiveness of sins, as far as he pays any attention to them at all, as foolishness, and he cannot believe them. It is impossible for natural man in his unconverted state to receive the truths of the Gospel with a believing heart and to put his trust in them. Paul sums up the situation when he says, "The natural man receiveth not the things of the Spirit of God, for they are foolishness unto him, neither can he know them, because they are spiritually discerned" (I Cor. 2:14). Man, *i. e.,* carnal-minded man, as a result of the Fall, utterly lacks the spiritual sense, the spiritual equipment with which to apprehend and make his own the things of the Spirit of God, particularly the blessed message of salvation in Christ Jesus.

The Fall brought not only darkness of the intellect; it also brought corruption and enslavement of the will. The will of man is in spiritual things held in the bondage of sin. To be sure, the will of man is free in worldly affairs, *i. e.,* the ordinary affairs of everyday life, and also to some extent in the exercise of "civil righteousness." The Apology of the Augsburg Confession says: "The human will has liberty in the choice of works and things which reason comprehends by itself. It can to a certain extent render civil righteousness, or the righteousness of works; it can speak of God, offer to God a certain service by an outward work, obey magistrates, parents; in the choice of an outward work it can restrain the hands from murder, from adultery, from theft. Since there is left in human nature reason and judgment concerning things subjected to the senses, choice between these things and the liberty and power to render civil righteousness, are also left" (XVIII, 76). But in spiritual matters the Word of the Savior holds good, "No man can come to Me, except the Father, which hath sent Me, draw him" (John 6:44). There is nothing in the mind and heart of natural man that could incline his will towards God. On the contrary, "The imagination of man's heart is evil from his youth" (Gen. 8:21), his mind is set on carnal things (Rom. 8:5), his inclinations and desires are toward evil. The natural sinful con-

dition of man directs his will towards those things which God hates
and forbids. Natural man, as much as in him lies, does not want to
come to God, he is afraid of Him, he flees and hates Him, his mind
and will are set against God. An influence from without is necessary
to produce in him a change of heart and mind, a *metanoia*, before
he can be willing to come to Christ and accept His blessed salvation.

This corruption of mind and will goes even deeper. Natural, unconverted man no longer possesses even a greater or lesser remnant
of the divine image, of his original spiritual powers, nor is it right
to say that man is merely "very far gone from original righteousness."
The Scriptures tell us that man after the Fall is wholly and completely corrupted. He is as a block of wood or stone in spiritual
things. Nothing God-pleasing either of thought or word or deed can
come out of him. His outward good works, to which Paul also refers
when he says that the Gentiles "do by nature the things contained
in the Law" (Rom. 2:14), will be duly rewarded in this life, but
since they are only a matter of external obedience and not the true
obedience which flows from faith and love toward God, the individual that does them, being yet outside of the Kingdom of Grace,
is still "without God in the world" (Eph. 2:12), and without the
hope of salvation (Mark 16:16). The state of natural man is described by Scripture as spiritual death with all that this word implies.
One who is dead cannot think the thoughts and perform the deeds
that are a part of life. As far as any life is ascribed to this condition,
the Scriptures speak of it as enmity against God. This state is not a
mere passive one, but even behind the outward appearance of a life
of good deeds there is a fundamental opposition to the true God
and a rejection of His grace. It is surprising with what strong language the Scriptures describe this utter helplessness of man, the
degradation of his intellect, the bondage of his will, the complete
subjection of his whole nature under the power of sin. He cannot
know, and if he knew, he cannot accept; and if he could, he would
not want to accept, because enmity against God fills his heart and
dominates his being.

The Formula of Concord devotes a large section to a very thorough discussion of this subject of man's spiritual death and helplessness in the article on "The Freedom of the Will." Of the many
quotable passages only a few shall be added here.

Thor. Decl. II, 7: "In spiritual and divine things the intellect, heart, and will of the unregenerate man are utterly unable by their own natural powers to understand, believe, accept, think, will, begin, effect, do, work, or concur in working, anything, but they are entirely dead to what is good, and corrupt, so that in man's nature since the Fall, before regeneration, there is not the least spark of spiritual power remaining nor present by which of himself he can prepare himself for God's grace or accept the offered grace, nor be capable of it for and of himself, or apply or accommodate himself thereto, or by his own powers be able of himself, as of himself, to aid, do, work, or concur in working, anything towards his conversion, either wholly or half or in any, even in the least or most inconsiderable, part; but he is the servant of sin (John 8:34) and a captive of the devil, by whom he is moved. (Eph. 2:2; II Tim. 2:26.) Hence the natural free will according to its perverted disposition and nature is strong and active only with respect to what is displeasing and contrary to God."

Thor. Decl. II, 12-14: "Therefore the Scriptures deny to the intellect, heart, and will of the natural man all aptness, skill, capacity, and ability to think, to understand, to be able to do, to begin, to will, to undertake, to act, to work, or to concur in working, anything good and right in spiritual things as of himself." (II Cor. 3:5; Rom. 3:12; John 8:37; 1:5; I Cor. 2:14; Rom. 8:7; John 15:5; Phil. 2:13).

Thor. Decl. II, 20, 21: "In spiritual and divine things, which pertain to the salvation of the soul, man is like a pillar of salt, like Lot's wife, yea, like a log and a stone, like a lifeless statue, which uses neither eyes nor mouth, neither sense nor heart. For man neither sees nor perceives the terrible and fierce wrath of God on account of sin and death, but ever continues in his security, even knowingly and willingly . . . All teaching and preaching is lost upon him until he is enlightened, converted, and regenerated by the Holy Ghost."

This Scriptural doctrine has ever been a stumbling block to the reason of man. The history of human thought and philosophy and the history of Christian doctrine are full of examples of philosophers and teachers of the Church who attempted to find other definitions of this basic human nature. There are those who deny entirely the fundamental corruptness of human nature, who think of human nature as fundamentally good with only remnants of evil which education and the natural processes of human development will eventually throw off. This misguided optimism and unrealistic trust in a fundamental goodness of human nature has suffered severe blows particularly in this generation, in which the deep baseness and corruptness inherent in human nature have been so thoroughly demonstrated. Others admit a corruption, but only a partial one; they say that there yet remains some fundamental goodness in man, a divine spark that may be fanned, an inherent moral foundation upon which it is possible to build a development of sound character, and a natural reaching out towards God joined with an ability to appropriate the fruits of His love and grace, etc. But from the foregoing it has become evident that Scripture leaves no room for such appraisals of human nature. Natural man, dead in trespasses and sins and corrupted by sin in his intellect, his will, and his entire nature, cannot, as Luther says in the explanation of the Third Article, "believe in Jesus Christ, my Lord, or come to Him." A complete change is necessary, a change that is brought about only by the almighty power of God working through the means of grace. This change takes place in man's conversion, and we shall study the nature of this conversion in the second part of this essay.

II. THE NATURE OF CONVERSION

The word *conversion* (*epistrophe, epistrephein*) is taken from the Scriptures. It is used, *e. g.,* in Acts 3:19: "Repent ye therefore and be converted that your sins may be blotted out" (cf. also Ps. 51:13; Is. 60:5; James 5:19-20; etc.). More frequently the English Bible uses the words *turn* and *turning* for the same Greek words, a turning of the heart of man from sin to grace, as in Acts 11:21: "A great number believed and turned unto the Lord" (cf. also Acts 9:35; 14:15; 26:18; II Cor. 3:16; I Pet. 2:25; etc.). Luther's Bible translation commonly uses the words *bekehren* and *Bekehrung*. Various synonyms for *conversion* are also used in the Scriptures, with only slight differences in meaning determined by the point of view from which they depict the sinner's turning to God. All of them designate the act of divine grace by which the sinner is delivered from the power of darkness and translated into the kingdom of Christ (Col. 1:13). These terms are *regeneration, awakening, illumination, call, repentance,* etc. The word *conversion* itself is used in the Scriptures in a wider and a narrower sense. In the wider sense it designates the entire process whereby man is transferred from his carnal state into a spiritual state of faith and grace and then enters upon, and under the continued influence of the Holy Spirit continues in, a state of faith and spiritual life. It includes within its scope both faith itself and the fruits of faith. In its narrower sense, the sense which will occupy us in this essay, the term is restricted to the work of God by which man is through the Gospel brought from his natural state of sin and wrath and spiritual death into the state of spiritual life and faith and grace, *i. e.,* the creation or bestowal of faith.

In general usage the word *conversion* is used in various meanings that are not in accord with the Scriptural use of the word. Conversion is not just a change of mind, a turning over of a new leaf, an attempt to make amends for sins and to appease the wrath of God by works, or sorrow over, and disgust at, sin coupled with a solemn resolution to bring about a moral reformation in one's life; nor is it, as in the theology of some revivalists, the rousing of certain definite or indefinite emotions in the sinner. All of these experiences lie to a greater or lesser extent also in the powers of an unconverted person, who may improve his life externally and may suppress certain vices and cultivate certain virtues. But outward good works are not conversion in the Biblical sense of the word, for such a "conversion" does not mean deliverance from the kingdom of sin and Satan and entrance into the kingdom of heaven.

Conversion, according to the Scriptures, taking the word in the narrower sense, is essentially the bestowal of faith in God's promise of salvation for Christ's sake (*donatio fidei*). It takes place in the heart and consists in this that the heart which is broken and contrite because of sin comes to faith in Christ and trusts in Christ for grace and forgiveness. In Acts 11:21, conversion is described as follows: "A great number believed and turned to the Lord" (polus te arithmos ho pisteusas epestrepsen epi ton kurion). The turning, or conversion, to God by the great number was accomplished by faith in the preaching of the Gospel of the Lord Jesus. The Lord Jesus was preached, a great number believed the Gospel of Christ and thus turned to, or was converted to, the Lord. Conversion took place when the Holy Spirit engendered faith in the hearts of penitent sinners (cf. also John 1:45-50; Acts 8:34-38; 16:30-34; and F. Pieper, *Christliche Dogmatik,* II, p. 545ff., and J. T. Mueller, *Christian Dogmatics,* p. 337). In accord with these passages of Scripture Luther defines conversion as follows: "To be converted to God means to believe that Christ is our Mediator and that we have eternal life through Him" (St. L. XIII:1101); and the Formula of Concord says, "Faith is kindled in us in conversion; this lays hold of God's grace in Christ, by which man is justified." In order to effect the change of heart, which is conversion, the Holy Ghost convinces man of his sinful depravity, offers to him God's grace in Christ Jesus, and works faith. A person then is truly converted when he believes that God has graciously forgiven his sins for Christ's sake, and conversion takes place in that moment when the Holy Spirit engenders faith in the heart of the penitent sinner. Conversion thus is in no way an achievement of the converted sinner. Man is purely passive in conversion; he is unable to contribute anything. It is all a gift of God's free grace.

The conversion of the sinner is not effected immediately through some kind of direct operation of the Spirit of God, but through definite, divinely ordained means, namely, the Word of God and the Sacraments, the preaching and hearing of God's Word. The Word of God is the divinely appointed means which the Holy Spirit employs for the regeneration and conversion of the human heart. Through the Gospel God offers to man His grace; the Gospel is the carrier of the promises of God, and the Gospel is also the means through which God works faith in the hearts of men, the acceptance of God's grace in Christ and the merits of Christ's redemption. The Gospel thus is, on the one hand, the object of the sinner's faith, the thing which he believes, and it is, on the other hand, the means of creating this believing acceptance of God's gifts, the means of working conversion. In it God not only offers to man the merit of Christ, but He also works the faith that accepts and trusts in the promises of God. So Paul says, "Faith cometh by hearing, and hearing by the Word of God" (Rom. 10:17). The explanation for this double function of the Gospel of presenting the message of God's grace and also working believing acceptance of the message lies in the fact that the Gospel is not just an ordinary human proclamation of interesting or cheering fact, on the level with many human proclamations, but that it is a living witness, full of power. The Savior says John 6:63: "The words that I speak to you, they are spirit and they are life." The Holy Spirit is always active in the Word and works through it to implant faith in the divine promises in the human heart. Therefore Paul calls the Gospel "the power of God unto salvation to everyone that believeth" (Rom. 1:16); and Isaiah says: "For as the rain cometh down and the snow from heaven and returneth not thither but watereth the earth and maketh it bring forth and bud, that it may give seed to the sower and bread to the eater, so shall My Word be that goeth forth out of My mouth; it shall not return to Me void, but it shall accomplish that which I please, and it shall prosper in the thing whereto I sent it" (55:10-11). Luther says: "Such is the efficacy of the Word whenever it is seriously contemplated, heard, and used, that it is bound to be never without fruit, but always awakens new understanding, pleasure, and devoutness, and produces a pure heart and pure thoughts. For these words are not inoperative or dead, but creative, living words" (Large Catechism, Third Com., p. 100). The Gospel is the divinely appointed effective means by which the Holy Spirit works faith or conversion in man; and because the Gospel is connected with Baptism and the Lord's Supper, also the Sacraments are effective means through which the Holy Spirit works faith and thereby converts sinners or confirms and preserves in faith those who are already converted.

In conversion not only the Gospel but the entire Word of God, both Law and Gospel, is effective. It is the Gospel by which the Holy Spirit works faith or conversion in man, but the divine Law is used by God to prepare the sinner for conversion. The sinner must be convinced of his sinfulness and his state of wrath and damnation before there can be faith in the gracious promises of God. There must be true repentance; this repentance includes both contrition, *i. e.*, the sorrow over sin and the terrors of conscience effected by the Law, and the faith in Christ's promises of grace and forgiveness which is worked by the Gospel. So the preaching of the Gospel must be preceded or accompanied by the preaching of the Law. The proclamation of the Law and of the Gospel must go hand in hand, both in their proper connection and with the proper distinction of the purposes which each of them serves. In God's guidance and direction of the ways of an individual human being this preaching of the Law is often supported and furthered by crosses, afflictions, and misfortunes which come upon man, or it may be that God uses an abundance of earthly blessings to lead an individual to repentance (Rom. 2:4: "Or despisest thou the riches of His goodness and forbearance and long-suffering, not knowing that the goodness of

God leadeth thee to repentance?"). But neither the manifestations of God's wrath nor of His goodness can take the place of the preaching of the divine Word. They are only, as it were, preparatory exercises, a kind of schooling, imposed by the hand of God; the Word of God alone remains the means through which the Holy Ghost operates in man toward his conversion. So Hollaz sums up the matter: "Conversion, taken in a special sense, is that act of grace by which the Holy Spirit excites in the sinner sincere grief for his sins by the word of the Law and kindles true faith in Christ by the word of the Gospel, that he may obtain remission of sins and eternal salvation" (*Doctr. Theol.*, p. 466). Thus the blessings of conversion are brought about by definite, divinely appointed means. Luther says: "Deus non dat interna nisi per externa. Spiritum Sanctum non mittit absque Verbo." God does not give the internal (gifts) except by external (means).

There has been much discussion and argument over the process of conversion in an attempt to describe just what takes place in the heart of a human being in conversion. Since we are here dealing with a divine miracle that is beyond the grasp of human reason, it will not be of much value to attempt to ascertain the truth through psychological observation or introspection. Conversion is not on the same level as the natural mental phenomena with which the psychologist deals. The psychologist can note only natural concomitants which will vary with different individuals, but he cannot get at the heart of the matter. Nor can we understand how our intellectual knowledge of the Gospel works spiritual knowledge or faith in our hearts. In these questions we must go to the Scriptures themselves for an interpretation. Scripture does speak of distinct "motions" or "movements" which occur in the heart (*motus interni, quibus conversio absolvitur*). The sinner, alarmed on account of his sins which he has learned to know from the divine Law ("by the Law is the knowledge of sin," Rom. 3:20), experiences the terrors of conscience, true fear and anguish of heart that come from the realization of being a lost and condemned creature, of having offended the holiness of God and having incurred His wrath and punishment. So the jailer at Philippi cried out, "Sirs, what must I do to be saved?" (Acts 16:30.) But the terrors of conscience, though necessary, are not in themselves of any value or merit, as we see from the case of Judas. As long as the alarmed sinner does not hear and believe the

Gospel, he remains unconverted in spite of his knowledge of sin and the wrath of God. But when the Gospel is preached, the Holy Spirit implants in his heart true faith in God's gracious promises of forgiveness, and through this second "motion," the implicit faith and trust in Christ, the sinner is converted and finds rest and relief for his troubled soul and conscience.

So these two "motions," contrition and faith, are found in every true conversion. They are portrayed in vivid language in the experience of David as recorded in Psalm 32: "When I kept silence, my bones waxed old through my roaring all the day long, for day and night Thy hand was heavy upon me; my moisture is turned into the drought of summer. Selah. I acknowledged my sin unto Thee, and mine iniquity have I not hid. I said, I will confess my transgressions unto the Lord, and Thou forgavest the iniquity of my sin." The Formula of Concord says: "In genuine conversion a change, new emotion, and movement in the intellect, will, and heart must take place, namely, that the heart perceive sin, dread God's wrath, turn from sin, perceive and accept the promise and grace in Christ, have good spiritual thoughts, a Christian purpose and diligence, and strive against the flesh. For when none of these occurs or is present, there is also no true conversion." (Thor. Decl. II, 70.)

But when contrition and faith are present in the heart, conversion has taken place. This is true even though the believer's knowledge of his sin is yet rudimentary and his trust in divine grace is still weak. The converted person should of course strive to grow in his knowledge both of sin and grace, but the Scriptures nowhere demand a specific degree of contrition or faith. True contrition exists wherever the sinner, like the jailer of Philippi, considers himself as eternally lost because of his sins, and true conversion has taken place wherever there is but a spark of faith, a mere longing for the love and forgiveness of God in Christ Jesus. For saving faith exists in the heart, and conversion has taken place, as soon as the penitent sinner longs for or desires the divine grace in Christ Jesus, as soon as he has a mere spark of faith. The man in the Gospel had such a faith who said, "Lord, I believe; help Thou mine unbelief" (Mark 9:24); and the Savior heard his prayer; and Isaiah assures us, "A bruised reed shall He not break, and the smoking flax shall He not quench" (Is. 42:3).

Regarding contrition it must also be said that it does not form the beginning of, or one-half of, conversion, nor does it in itself produce a better spiritual condition in the sinner. Least of all is conversion a matter of the emotional intensity of contrition or the outward manifestations of this emotion. Contrition of itself with all its terrors can lead only to despair, as in the case of Judas, for "the sorrow of the world worketh death" (II Cor. 7:10); but it is the indispensable preparation for conversion. There must be the prayer of the publican, "God be merciful to me, a sinner" (Luke 18:13); for faith cannot enter the proud and secure heart.

The converted person may be sure of his conversion. So Paul says to the Corinthians, "Know ye not your own selves how that Jesus Christ is in you, except ye be reprobates?" (II Cor. 13:5); and John says, "We know that we have passed from death unto life because we love the brethren" (I John 3:14). This knowledge, again, is not based upon or dependent upon any particular emotional reaction; it rests wholly on faith in the promises of God. The Formula of Concord says: "Concerning the presence, operation, and gifts of the Holy Ghost we should not and cannot always judge *ex sensu* (from feeling) as to how and when they are experienced in the heart; but because they are often covered and occur in weakness, we should be certain from, and according to, the promise that the Word of God preached and heard is truly an office and work of the Holy Ghost by which He is certainly efficacious and works in our hearts" (II Cor. 2:14ff.; 3:5ff.; Thor. Decl. II, 56).

Closely related to the question regarding the "motions" in the heart involved in conversion is the question whether conversion is gradual or instantaneous. Conversion is sometimes spoken of as being gradual; but in that case the term is used in a wider sense to include certain outward acts which commonly precede conversion. Such acts are the inculcation of the divine Law, the conviction of the sinner of his guilt and condemnation, the awakening of the terrors of conscience, the logical and historical understanding of the Gospel. But these acts do not in reality convert the sinner; they only prepare him for conversion. Conversion only takes place when the alarmed and despairing sinner becomes a rejoicing believer in Jesus Christ. And this kindling of faith is the matter of an instant, the moment when the Holy Spirit through the means of grace engenders faith in the contrite heart. As soon as the penitent sinner possesses the first spark of faith or even longing for faith, he is converted. Strictly speaking, therefore, conversion is instantaneous rather than gradual. It is the moment when the saving activity of the Holy Spirit enters; the outward acts which are included in the so-called gradual conversion are things which lie in a measure also within the power and reach of unregenerate man. But there is no middle state between conversion and non-conversion. Scripture recognizes only two classes of men, children of God and children of darkness. There is no middle ground between belief and unbelief, between spiritual life and spiritual death. Those who reject the instantaneous character of conversion and insist on gradual conversion, during which the sinner is at first enlightened, then awakened, and finally brought to a decision to accept Christ, frequently connect this view with some form of the teaching that man somewhere and in some manner cooperates in his conversion, either from powers which he naturally possesses or which the Holy Spirit is said to have bestowed on him. In these views conversion is in the last analysis the work of man, in which man converts himself.

In this connection we may discuss the question whether it is necessary to know the exact moment of one's conversion. Some Christians are able to do so, as the Apostle Paul. For others the working of spiritual knowledge and faith is rather like "the seed that springs and grows up, he knoweth not how" (Mark 4:27); for many of us it was effected in Baptism. It is not essential that we should know; it is, however, important and necessary to know that we are converted, and this we can know by relying on the promises of God.

Several other items pertaining to the Scriptural doctrine of conversion must be noted. The first of these is that God's grace in conversion is resistible. In conversion, God, according to the Scriptures, works through His mighty power. So Paul says, "And what is the exceeding greatness of His power to usward who believe according to the working of His mighty power" (Eph. 1:19), and, "For God, who commanded the light to shine out of darkness, hath shined in our hearts, to give the light of the knowledge of the glory of God in the face of Jesus Christ" (II Cor. 4:6). In conversion, God exercises His omnipotent power through the means of grace; and when God's power is exercised through means, it can be resisted. Scripture records examples of such resistance, *e. g.*, when the Savior speaks of Jerusalem: "How often would I have gathered thy children together even as a hen gathereth her chickens under her wings, and ye would not" (Matt. 23:37); and when Stephen says to his Jewish hearers, "Ye stiff-necked and uncircumcised in hearts and ears, ye do always resist the Holy Ghost; as your fathers did, so do ye" (Acts 7:51). There is no such thing as conversion of the elect only by irresistible grace, for God "will have all men to be saved and to come unto the knowledge of the truth" (I Tim. 2:4). Neither dare we, from the ability of the sinner to reject divine grace, draw the conclusion that he can co-operate with the Holy Spirit in his conversion. Paul says, "For it is God which worketh in you both to will and to do of His good pleasure" (Phil. 2:13).

In some passages of Scripture God is said to convert man, and in others man is said to convert himself. Jer. 31:18 we read, "Turn Thou me and I shall be turned, for Thou art the Lord my God"; but Jer. 24:7 we read, "And I will give them an heart to know Me that I am the Lord . . . for they shall return unto Me with their whole heart (sie werden sich von ganzem Herzen zu mir bekehren)." Acts 3:19 Peter says to his audience, "Repent ye, therefore, and be converted that your sins may be blotted out." There are many such passages in which man is called upon to repent. In spite of the seeming difficulty caused by these two ways of speaking, there is no real difficulty between them, for man converts himself only when God converts him. One and the same act in which God alone is the efficient cause is described by both expressions. It is Scriptural to say that man converts himself, not as though God begins and then man accomplishes and completes conversion, but only in the sense that conversion is entirely the work of God; for it is God alone who "worketh in you both to will and to do," and the Savior says, "No man can come to Me, except the Father, which hath sent Me, draw him" (John 6:44). On this question Baier says the following: "The word *conversion* is taken in a double sense in the Scriptures, inasmuch as at one time God is said to convert man and, at another, that man is said to convert himself, although as to the thing itself the action is one and the same."

Also believers in Christ may fall from grace. In the Scriptures we have the examples of David and Peter, and Paul speaks of some of his fellow workers as follows: "Holding faith and a good conscience; which some having put away, concerning faith have made shipwreck, of whom is Hymenaeus and Alexander" (I Tim. 1:19). This is not just a temporary loss of the exercise of faith, as is claimed by those who teach that faith once gained can never be lost, but is a real loss of faith itself. Those who have thus fallen from the faith are again in the status of the unconverted, and, unless the sin against the Holy Ghost has been committed, they may again be converted and brought to faith. This is called "reiterated conversion." "Since, however," as Mueller says in his *Christian Dogmatics*, p. 354, "man can only in rare cases definitely know who has committed the sin against the Holy Ghost, it is the duty of the Christian Church to preach repentance and faith to all men as it has opportunity (Ezek. 18:23-32; 3:16-21). . . . The Church should not withhold, but bestow the grace of the Gospel as long as men are ready to receive it, in accordance with the Lord's command, Mark 16:15, 'Go ye into all the world, and preach the Gospel to every creature'."

It would lead too far if we attempted in this brief essay to enter into the details of the errors in various types of teaching regarding conversion that persisted in one form or another through the centuries and continue to the present day, namely, Pelagianism, Semi-Pelagianism, or Arminianism, and the various forms of synergism, or if we undertook to discuss in detail the issues of the controversy which disrupted a large section of our Lutheran Church in America in the last century. In all these controversies, ranging from broadest Pelagianism, which denies the fundamental corruption of man and ascribes to him full power of decision to work out his own conversion, to the most subtle form of synergism, which would yet ascribe to man even some small degree of co-operation in conversion and faith, such as refraining from deliberate or malicious resistance, the issue is whether it is God alone who converts us and to whom therefore alone shall be the glory for our eternal salvation or whether man can make some contribution towards his own salvation. These matters are discussed at great length in the publications of our Church on which this essay is based. In Dr. J. T. Mueller's *Christian Dogmatics*, p. 355, there are listed ten objections that have been advanced against divine monergism in conversion, that is, against the doctrine that God alone converts man, together with the answers to them. A few of them may be summarized here.

1. Since God in His Word demands repentance or conversion of man, he must be able, at least in part, to convert himself.—But one may not from the divine demand draw a conclusion with respect to man's ability to comply with God's will. The divine commands and

exhortations are the means by which God works that which He demands. He works true knowledge of sin through the commands of the Law, and He works true faith through the Gospel exhortations.

2. Unless man co-operates in his conversion, his conversion becomes an act of coercion or force; in other words, in that case man is converted by irresistible grace, an assumption which Scripture condemns.—But it is the very nature of conversion that in it God through the means of grace changes the unwilling into such as are willing; it is not an unwanted act which God thrusts upon the sinner, but it is a gracious divine drawing, a working in him "both to will and to do." Luther says that God does not draw him as the hangman draws a criminal to the gallows, but by "softening and changing his heart" through the means of grace.

3. God works the ability to believe, but not the act of faith, or He prepares man for conversion, but does not accomplish it, since the final decision rests with man himself.—But according to Scripture the very act of faith is God's work and gift; "For unto you it is given (echaristhe) in the behalf of Christ not only to believe on Him, but also to suffer for His sake" (Phil. 1:29). God does work in man the ability to believe, but this ability is part of the spiritual life that has been planted in the heart in conversion. The person who can accept the offered grace is already regenerate; the man who is not regenerate resists God altogether.

4. If God alone works conversion in man, then it cannot be maintained that He really desires the salvation of all men; for actually He does not convert all.—But Holy Scripture teaches both doctrines: a. that God alone converts and saves sinners; b. that He earnestly desires to save all sinners. The perplexing problem, "Why, then, are not all saved?" is one which human reason cannot solve; for human reason is not a source of divine truth. The Christian is bound to Scripture as the only source and rule of faith, and Scripture does not give the answer to the question, "Why some rather than others?" Scripture affirms that God is the sole cause of man's conversion and salvation and, on the other hand, that unregenerate man is the sole cause of his damnation; but it does not explain why of two sinners who are in the same guilt (David, Saul) the one is saved and the other is not. The explanations which human reason offers for this mystery either involve the denial of God's universal grace, as in Calvinism, or, as in synergism, they deny the doctrine that salvation

is by grace alone, and thus repudiate the central doctrine of the Scriptures. The Formula of Concord clearly points out the position which the Christian must take when he faces the mystery of election and conversion, when it says: "Since God has reserved this mystery for His wisdom and has revealed nothing to us concerning it in His Word, much less commanded us to investigate it with our thoughts, but has earnestly discouraged us therefrom ("O the depth of the riches both of the wisdom and knowledge of God! How unsearchable are His judgments and His ways past finding out!" Rom. 11:33), we should not reason in our thoughts, draw conclusions, nor inquire curiously into these matters, but should adhere to His revealed Word, to which He points us." (Thor. Decl. XI, 54-58.)

III. THE EFFECTS OF CONVERSION

Through conversion and faith the believer is made a child of God. "For ye are all the children of God by faith in Christ Jesus" (Gal. 3:26). He enters into the Kingdom of God and becomes a partaker of all its blessings. Since faith is the acceptance of God's gracious offer of salvation, the child of God is justified, *i. e.*, God the Father for Christ's sake declares him just, holds, and pronounces him fully absolved from all guilt and punishment. To him now apply the words of Paul, "Therefore we conclude that a man is justified by faith without the deeds of the Law" (Rom. 3:28), and he can say, "Who shall lay anything to the charge of God's elect? It is God that justifieth" (Rom. 8:33). His iniquities are forgiven and his sins are covered; they have all been cast into the depths of the sea.

We, the converted children of God, now being justified by faith, have peace with God through our Lord Jesus Christ. We have access by faith into this grace wherein we stand, and we rejoice in the hope of the glory of God. By the forgiveness of our sins we have a good conscience, for in Christ we have boldness and confidence in the presence of God. We have joy in our hearts through our Lord Jesus Christ. We have comfort and consolation in affliction. We can say with Paul, "We glory in tribulations also, knowing that tribulation worketh patience, and patience experience, and experience hope, and hope maketh not ashamed, because the love of God is shed abroad in our hearts by the Holy Ghost which is given unto us" (Rom. 5:3-5). Justified by His grace, we have been made heirs of the hope of eternal life, for as sin has reigned unto death, even so grace reigns through righteousness unto eternal life by Jesus Christ, our Lord (Rom. 5:21). Having been called, we are also justified; having been justified, we also have the hope of eternal glory (Rom. 8:30).

But the Holy Spirit, who creates justifying faith in the heart of the sinner, also, from the moment that this faith has been wrought, sets in motion the divine work of sanctification. The children of God, having been quickened from death in trespasses and sins, now enter into a new life that unfolds itself in the service of God. So Paul says, "Being, then, made free from sin, ye became servants of righteousness" (Rom. 6:16). In this new life the love towards God which was destroyed in the Fall is restored, the love which, as Paul says, manifests itself in the fulfilling of the Law (Rom. 13:10). For when faith is kindled, the Holy Spirit enters the heart; yes, Christ the Savior Himself takes up His abode in the heart, as Paul says (Gal. 2:20): "Yet not I live, but Christ liveth in me." The children of God therefore are led by the Spirit of God (Rom. 8:14). The Holy Spirit through the faithful use of the means of grace not only supplies the strength to overcome the temptations of sin; He also actively directs and promotes the putting on of the new man in daily contrition and repentance, the restoration of the lost divine image in the increase of knowledge of divine truth and in the unfolding of a life of progressive sanctification in the true worship of God, in prayer, in the spreading of the Gospel, in a rich abundance of good works that are in harmony with the will of God. And He continues this blessed work until the time when in eternal life, in the Church Triumphant, the struggle between the spirit and the flesh, between the new man and the old evil nature, will have been brought to a victorious conclusion. Then the divine image of perfect righteousness and holiness, the soundness of mind and will which was lost in the Fall, will be completely restored in "the spirits of just men made perfect" (Heb. 12:23).

The chief point of emphasis in our whole discussion of the doctrine of conversion has been the utter helplessness and inability of man to contribute anything to his salvation. By grace are we saved, through faith, and that not of ourselves; it is the gift of God, not of works, lest any man should boast (Eph. 2:8). Therefore we say: All glory be to God for His love and mercy toward us and all lost and condemned sinners. We owe all to His unbounded grace. He has redeemed us. Through Him we have come to know that we are sinners, bound under His wrath and subject to eternal punishment. But He opened our hearts that we learned to know and accept Jesus as our Savior. He also will graciously preserve us in this saving faith and lead us to the fulfillment of our hopes in everlasting life. The grace of God will be the content of our psalms and hymns to all eternity. We too shall sing with all the saints in heaven a new song, saying, "Thou wast slain and hast redeemed us to God by Thy blood out of every kindred and tongue and people and nation and hast made us unto our God kings and priests . . . Worthy is the Lamb that was slain to receive power and riches and wisdom and strength and honor and glory and blessing" (Rev. 5:9-12).

> All blessing, honor, thanks, and praise,
> To Father, Son, and Spirit,
> The God that saved us by His grace,
> All glory to His merit.
> O Triune God in heaven above,
> Who hast revealed Thy saving love,
> Thy blessed name be hallowed.

> We thank Thee, Christ; new life is ours,
> New light, new hope, new strength, new powers.
> This grace our every way attend,
> Until we reach our journey's end.

XI

Faith

THE Christian religion is unique inasmuch as it is the one religion of salvation. Its message is the glad tidings of salvation. The central figure in the message is Jesus Christ; the central theme, the love of God; the central purpose, the salvation of the world through Christ's atonement; the central miracle, justification by faith, or the forgiveness of sins; the central means of imparting God's grace, the Word and the Sacraments; the central goal, the rebirth of the soul here and the new life it brings, glorification in the world to come, and everlasting life in the eternal presence of God. Christianity's message of salvation, then, is centered in and founded on the Christ of God, who is "the Savior of the world," John 4:42. By true and trusting faith in the Christ of the sacred Scriptures the individual enters into that right relation to God which the all-atoning work of Christ has established for the entire world of men.

It is therefore a superlatively great and vast subject which engages our attention, a subject which in one sense is most comprehensive and all-embracing and in another respect definitely concentrated and specific. In every respect, however, this subject is of transcendent significance and value, both as to its essence and content and as to its scope and objective.

I. THE NECESSITY OF FAITH

The Christian religion is a religion of grace and faith. As such, the Christian religion is designed to bring salvation to men. The very term "salvation" implies man's need of it. In fact, Christianity presupposes this need. It can be productive of blessing only to those who recognize and acknowledge this need. "They that be whole," says its divine Author and Founder, "need not a physician, but they that are sick. I am not come to call the righteous, but sinners to repentance" (Matt. 9:12, 13). The need thereof is universal. It is a positive delusion which causes many to ignore or even to deny this need. "The truth is not in them," is the verdict of St. John (I John 1:8).

This great need of mankind is summarized in the word "sin." This term denotes estrangement from God, who is perfect holiness and righteousness in the very essence of His being and in whom there can be no sin. The term "sin" also embraces God's wrath, which makes itself felt in the accusations of the sinner's conscience. In its last dire and disastrous effect it includes the certain prospect of everlasting perdition. Moreover, sin, in the Christian conception of the term, must be viewed not only as an act, but as a congenital and inveterate condition in the human heart. The Sacred Record not only recognizes and identifies sinful deeds and actions, but also "a body of sin," in which "there dwelleth no good thing" (Rom. 6:6; 7:18). It views man born of the flesh as "flesh" (John 3:6), as "evil from his youth" also in "the imaginations of his heart" (Gen. 8:21). Sin in its true nature is a habitual inclination to that which is evil and a habitual disinclination to that which is good in the sight of the holy and just God; it is enmity against God, spiritual death (Rom. 8:6-8; Eph. 2:1).

This destructive and fatal element, called sin, is recognized by all known religions. All known religions declare it to be a barrier to a happy fellowship and free communication between the offended Deity, whose laws have been transgressed, and offending man, who has transgressed them. In recognition of this deplorable condition and situation virtually all religions also make an attempt to devise means and ways for its removal or correction. Only the Christian religion, however, teaches the true nature of sin, and only the Christian religion has been successful—and it has been eminently successful—in finding a remedy for the fatal disease of sin.

"By grace are ye saved," St. Paul declares to the Ephesians (Eph. 2:5, 8). Out of this wholly unexpected and undeserved disposition of God towards the sinner issues the first thought as well as the possibility of a salvation for man. God, not man, originates and places into operation this superhuman act and process. God proposes to restore man and does not wait for man to rehabilitate and restore himself with God.—Saving grace is something in God. It is necessary to emphasize this because a tendency developed very early within the Christian Church to transfer a saving quality to man and to call that grace. This teaching of Pelagius, which has found its most forceful and consistent exposition in the Church of Rome, subverts the foundation of the Christian religion. Saving grace is not something which God requires in man, but which He offers man. Therefore St. Paul not only declared, "By grace are ye saved," but added, "and that not of yourselves" (Eph. 2:8). Under no condition can grace be human merit winning and obtaining the favor of God, but, as Luther said, "it is a thought which God entertains in His own mind and by which He prompts Himself to approach the sinner." It is obvious that Christianity relapses into paganism the moment this meaning of grace is inverted.

This gracious disposition on the part of God is disclosed in the Scriptures. God's Word calls it a "revelation" (Eph. 1:9). The fact that God entertains this gracious and benevolent attitude towards the sinner is a mystery to the mind of natural man. No system of religious thought or philosophy has ever anticipated or even remotely approached the idea of saving grace in an offended God. Paul calls the revelation of this grace the wisdom of God, which God ordained before the world unto our glory; yet it is a hidden wisdom, which none of the princes of this world knew, which hath not entered into the heart of man, which even after its revelation is foolishness unto natural man (I Cor. 2:7-14).

In every age the genius of man has wrestled with the problem of his own rehabilitation and restoration to the favor of God. All of these efforts have resulted in complete failure. Their failure is inscribed upon every religion which has been brought forth by human thought. Every humanly devised system and endeavor which has as its purpose the appeasement of an offended Deity advances a proposal which man makes to God and in which man lays down conditions and terms to God which He is expected to accept and with which He is expected to be completely satisfied. Divine truth, however, as revealed in the Scriptures, sweeps all such conjectures and speculations aside and focuses our thought and attention upon the grace of God, which tells us in effect that we do not possess the ability, or capacity, to solve the problem involved in man's relationship to God; that we cannot surmount the barrier which separates man from lasting peace and happiness; that all the intellectual and moral resources at our command cannot negotiate or effect our acceptance with God for one moment.

Since, therefore, salvation is not by works,' since God offers full salvation to all sinners as a free gift of grace, all that is needed for receiving salvation is to accept it as what it is intended and offered by God, as a free and unmerited gift of divine grace. Such acceptance is called faith. And the very fact that salvation is by grace proves that it is through faith, proves the necessity of faith for salvation. Says Paul: "For the promise that he should be the heir of the world was not to Abraham or to his seed through the Law, but through the righteousness of faith. For if they which are of the Law be heirs, faith is made void, and the promise made of none effect, because the Law worketh wrath; for where no Law is, there is no transgression. Therefore it is of faith that it might be by grace, to the end the promise might be sure to all the seed; not to that only which is of the Law, but to that also which is of the faith of Abraham, who is the father of us all" (Rom. 4:13-16). This necessity of faith will become increasingly clearer to us as we continue our study of faith.

II. THE CONCEPT OF FAITH

As we contemplate the concept of faith, we must, of course, confine ourselves to the Scriptural meaning of the term "faith." Profane usage is scarcely relevant in an effort to determine the exact significance of "faith" in the Scriptures. Classical Greek and Biblical Greek differ widely in their use of the term. Both the Greeks and the Romans recognized and even worshiped *pistis*, *fides*, faith; but the meaning which they connect with this term, when used in its passive sense, is "reliability, trustworthiness, fidelity, credibility of matters and persons"—or, when used in its active sense, "confidence, trust, conviction," either as bestowed upon others or as enjoyed from others. Even when used with reference to religious matters, Roman and Greek writers express by "faith in the gods" merely the universal or national recognition of the existence of deities and the acceptance of their power and supernatural influence. The expression is never used to express or to designate personal trust in divine favor and mercy. "Faith in the gods" with them never signifies firm reliance upon and confiding trust in a gracious God. Rather does it represent the commonplace idea and attitude over and against the Unseen, the Supernatural. The Roman goddess Fides was by no stretch of the imagination a personification of the Christian faith.

There is a very large number of Scripture texts in which the term faith and cognate terms are used. As not germane to our subject we eliminate from this number, first of all, those which predicate faith of God, as Rom. 3:3; II Tim. 2:13; secondly, all those texts which speak of faith in the economy of purely human affairs, as for example Matt. 23:23; Luke 12:42; and, finally, we eliminate the faith of the satanic spirits of which St. James declares: "Thou believest that there is one God; thou doest well: the devils also believe and tremble" (2:19). Our interest and attention at the moment are concentrated exclusively on that Biblical and theological quantity which enters into, and acts, a precise and well-defined part in the divine act of justification and which is known as "saving faith," *fides salvifica, fides justificans.*

It is most helpful and satisfying to know that the Scriptures not only employ the term "faith" but that the Scriptures themselves clearly and expressly present the exact significance of that term. Our Lord graciously accommodates Himself to the processes of human thought and uses ordinary imagery to portray and describe faith. He relates the Parable of the Great Supper, in which "a certain man sent his servant at supper time to say to them that were bidden, 'Come, for all things are now ready'" (Luke 14:17). Without further interpretation, we have here the gracious invitation of the blessed Christ: "Come! I have prepared an elaborate banquet for you; everything is in readiness; you need bring nothing with you; you need not fear that the supply of food will be exhausted. Nothing remains for you to do save to come and partake of that which is bountifully prepared." Faith is here portrayed as "a coming to Christ" and "a partaking of His blessings."—Faith is also pictured as a "seeing or beholding of Christ." Jesus declares: "This is the will of Him that sent Me, that every one which seeth the Son and believeth on Him may have everlasting life; and I will raise him up at the Last Day" (John 6:40). Obviously, our Lord is not speaking of a bodily seeing, but a seeing with the eyes and vision of faith, a seeing with heartfelt joy and happy anticipation of eternal blessedness. Faith is also presented as a trustful and obedient hearing of the divine Word. Jesus says: "My sheep hear My voice, and I know them, and they follow Me; and I give unto them eternal life" (John 10:27, 28). The wolf also hears the voice of the shepherd, but is terrified thereby and takes to flight. The sheep, however, hear His voice with joy and respond with readiness and eagerness. Faith, accordingly, is a glad, happy, eager, desirous hearing and acceptance of Christ's Gospel promise of salvation.—Faith, moreover, is described as a keeping of the Word of Christ. "Verily, verily, I say unto you, If a man keep My saying, he shall never see death" (John 8:51). The believer accepts the promises of the Gospel, trusts in, and relies upon, these promises, which assure him of life everlasting, and thus does not really die—his death is but a sleep—for all such pass through death triumphantly into that life which is perfection in the unending presence of God.

St. Paul continues the imagery and writes: "Lay hold on eternal life, whereunto thou art also called" (I Tim. 6:12). Here faith is called "a laying hold of." To "lay hold of" is an activity of the hand, and the inspired Apostle directs this to spiritual activity and urges us "to lay hold on eternal life," offered to us freely in the Gospel.— Finally, faith is also presented as "a winning of Christ." "But what things were gain to me, those I counted loss for Christ. Yea, doubtless, and I count all things but loss for the excellency of the knowledge of Christ Jesus, my Lord; for whom I have suffered the loss of all things, and do count them but dung, that I may win Christ" (Phil. 3:7, 8). To "win Christ" apparently is nothing else than to believe in the Christ of God as the Heaven-sent Savior and Redeemer and to come into possession of His priceless riches and treasures (*cp.* v. 9).

How truly delightful and satisfying it is that God's Word portrays and describes Christian faith by means of such attractive pictures and winsome expressions in order that we may recognize its nature and content and purpose and through such Christ-centered faith long for, and eventually obtain, the end of our faith, even our soul's salvation.

When the concept of faith is studied as a soteriological factor, as *fides salvifica,* saving faith, the conventional division of its aspects demand our attention. These conventional divisions are: knowledge, assent, and confidence. In the concept of saving faith these three aspects merge into one another. In any true act of saving faith none of these three aspects ever exists without the other two. In those texts of Scripture which express the act of faith in terms of knowing or of approving, we recognize merely metonymical statements, the element of confidence, or trust, always being connoted. Hence it is better to speak of knowledge, assent, and confidence as being "three separate and distinct definitions of faith," each of them complete in itself and therefore synonymous with the other two. As we may look at a triangular column and view it from three different angles, so that we see a different side each time and yet the same column, so we would look at faith from three viewpoints and yet see the same faith each time.

a. Faith as Knowledge

The Gospel is the divine offer of grace and blessing in Christ Jesus. Faith is the acceptance or possession thereof. Since this acceptance is a mental, not a physical act, it is also described as knowledge. "To know" is to grasp with the mind, to have or obtain mental possession of that which is communicated. St. Paul asks: "How shall they believe in Him of whom they have not heard?" (Rom. 10:14.) There is no question about the answer. They cannot believe. In order that a person may believe in God, it is necessary that he should first hear of Him. We must know who God is and what His thoughts and desires and promises are toward us. Such knowledge is obtained by means of the Word. "Faith cometh by hearing, and hearing by the Word of God" (Rom. 10:17). And when our Lord says: "This is life eternal, that they might know Thee the only true God, and Jesus Christ, whom Thou hast sent" (John 17:3), this is of the same import as "The just shall live by faith" (Rom. 1:17), and "that, believing, ye might have life through His name." Of this saving knowledge, as man's acceptance of what God in His mercy offers and communicates, St. Peter states: "His divine power hath given unto us all things that pertain unto life and godliness through the knowledge of Him that hath called us to glory and virtue" (II Pet. 1:3). This is the knowledge of salvation with which is connected the remission of sins, as Zacharias so eloquently foretold in the Benedictus that the "Prophet of the Highest" would "give knowledge of salvation unto His people by the remission of their sins" (Luke 1:77). Appropriate also is St. Paul's familiar statement: "God will have all men to be saved and to come unto the knowledge of the truth" (I Tim. 2:4). Through the knowledge of the truth as it is in God and revealed through Christ, man shall be saved. This means clearly that man is saved through faith in Him who declared: "I am the Way, the Truth, and the Life, no man cometh unto the Father but by Me" (John 14:6).

This salutary knowledge, saving faith, is not a mere intellectual acquaintance with the object known. Such knowledge, commonly referred to as "knowledge of the head" is condemned by St. James in the words: "Thou believest that there is one God; thou doest well: the devils also believe and tremble" (2:19). Judas Iscariot, for example, had such knowledge of the head. He had been in the privileged company of, and in intimate association with, the Master for almost three years, had received His blessed instruction from day to day, and had been favored with the exceptional opportunity of hearing words of wisdom and truth from the lips of Him who spoke as never man spoke. With his physical senses Judas had heard and perceived, and with his mind he knew, what his Lord had preached and taught. But he did not know Christ with his heart, or if he had believed in Him as his Savior, he had fallen from faith. Otherwise this disciple would not have betrayed and sold his own Savior, and he would not have given way to utter despair of God's mercy and plunged himself into perdition. Job, however, knew his God. In the deepest depths of sorrow and affliction, forsaken by all men, he confidently looked to God for sustaining help and comfort, saying: "I know that my Redeemer liveth," etc. (19:25). Paul, knowing that the time of his departure was at hand, exclaimed with full confidence of heart: "I know whom I have believed" (II Tim. 1:12).

Nor is this salutary knowledge an intellectual or technical knowledge which man acquires by the application and exercise of his own abilities and capacities. An individual person may be ever so brilliant and successful in the areas of scientific research and accomplishment, but in the realm of things spiritual he possesses no such inherent, latent, or acquired abilities. "The natural man receiveth not the things of the Spirit of God; for they are foolishness unto him; neither can he know them, because they are spiritually discerned" (I Cor. 2:14). When we, therefore, speak of knowledge in relation to things that pertain to man's salvation, we are speaking of a knowledge which is a gift and product of divine grace, which man does not possess by nature. It is a gratuity and an accomplishment of the Holy Spirit. "Now we have received . . . the Spirit which is of God, that we might know the things that are freely given to us of God" (I Cor. 2:12). The God "who commanded the light to shine out of darkness hath shined in our hearts, to give the light of the knowledge of the glory of God in the face of Jesus Christ" (II Cor. 4:6).

We pause, as a matter of practical reflection, to emphasize the paramount importance of this saving knowledge of God in the teaching and preaching ministry of the Church. How necessary and essential that particularly the children and the youth be thoroughly instructed in the truths of the Word and that by such process of instruction their minds, through the gracious operation of the Spirit of God, be filled with enlightenment and understanding concerning the unsearchable riches in Christ. The highest knowledge to be imparted to them is that they know the true God and Jesus Christ, whom He has sent. This likewise emphasizes the urgent necessity of Christian instruction by means of our preaching ministry, ever remembering that the Scriptures are "profitable for doctrine." Our preaching must be definite, positive, and instructive. It must be lucid and substantial doctrinal and expository preaching and not merely a presentation of admonitions and exhortations. It must be our concern and purpose to aid our Christian people, both the matured and the inexperienced, towards an ever increasing comprehension of the life-giving, life-building, and life-preserving verities of the everlasting Word. And all this not merely for the sake of intellectual acquaintance and mental satisfaction. Not knowledge for its own sake, but knowledge for the sake of the acquaintance with, and the acceptance of, God's boundless mercies and infinite love in Christ, the Redeemer. Such knowledge is saving faith since it accepts and appropriates what God communicates in the Gospel, and thereby the believer makes that his own which is extended to him, firmly clinging to what he has thus appropriated to himself.

b. Faith as Assent

When the subject matter of faith is proposed to a person for his acceptance and appropriation, there is an appeal made not to the intellect alone, but also to the will. The will of the carnal mind, this intensely hostile factor, is asked to surrender, to lay down its arms, to cease in its attacks upon the strange but sacred truths proposed for acceptance. Faith, therefore, from the first moment of its existence, is assent to the new and exalted phenomena presented to the mind. The efforts of divine grace toward the unbeliever seek to effect this result. The preaching of faith is not simply a system of plain factual statements, logical reasoning, and rigid conclusions, but it is hortatory, pleading, persuasive in its message. It presents and conveys an earnest and authoritative appeal to the affections and to the will, rather than merely submitting a statement of fact to the judgment of the intellect. This is illustrated and exemplified by such Scriptural expressions and declarations as these: "Repent and believe the Gospel." "Be ye reconciled to God." Come unto Me." "Turn ye, turn ye; why will ye die?" These urgent appeals and invitations are addressed to man for the purpose of exciting faith in him. The yielding to such calls, the accepting of the invitation that is being extended, the willing embracing of that which is being offered, is the essence of faith. In accord herewith the activity of the Apostles in preaching the Gospel is described as "persuading the things concerning the kingdom of God" (Acts 19:8); "persuading one to be a Christian" (Acts 26:28); "persuading men concerning Jesus" (Acts 28:23). During Paul's residence in Rome he "expounded and testified the kingdom of God, persuading his hearers concerning Jesus." As a result a division occurred among the people. "Some believed the things which were spoken and some believed not" (Acts 28:24).

The verb "to persuade" implies indecision, unwillingness, resistance, in the person to whom it is being applied. Its purpose is to remove that resistance and to create willingness in the place of reluctance, firmness in the place of wavering, decision in the place of doubt and hesitancy. An example from secular affairs recorded in the Scriptures may serve to illustrate this thought. In their effort to avert the threatened invasion of Herod the delegation from Tyre and Sidon proceeded to gain the good will of Blastus, the king's chamberlain. We are told they "made him their friend" (Acts 12:20). They broke down his opposition and won him over. The Word of God, which proclaims and offers the things of the Spirit of God, meets a similar hostile attitude in unregenerated man. The degree of intensity with which the Gospel is resisted and the manner in which such resistance is manifested vary. From the malicious scoffer, who rants and rages at the mere mention of the divine name, to the politely indifferent, who decline the Gospel with specious excuses, there are many varieties of spiritual and moral opposition and hostility to divine grace. In fact, no two persons are absolutely identical in this respect, as little as in any other. Resistance, like every other expression of a person's attitude toward God, is individual and singular. These differences, however, are of no moment, because they are all essentially exhibitions of that fatal unwillingness which is natural and congenital to all who are born of the flesh and therefore enemies of God. This resistance stamps the individual as "disobedient," that is, a person who will not suffer himself to be persuaded.

It was the divinely appointed mission of the forerunner "to turn the disobedient to the wisdom of the just" and in this way "to make ready a people prepared for the Lord" (Luke 1:17). John preached the remission of sins (Luke 3:3). His preaching was received by some and rejected by others (Luke 7:29, 30). There is every reason to assume that John was well understood by his hearers. This is corroborated by the great sensation which his preaching created. Nor should we suppose that only the lowly or simple folk were attracted to him. The significance of his stirring message and the import of his mission were understood by the scribes and others in high places. He also succeeded in gathering an interested audience at Herod's court. Obviously, these people did not reject the Gospel because the necessary data or information for the knowledge of faith had not been offered to the conception of their intellect. They knew, but they did not want to know. They had been ushered into the saving light of grace but had closed their eyes. Our Lord, comparing His own mission with that of John, explained the true cause of the Pharisees' unbelief when he charged them after the miracle of Bethesda: "Ye sent unto John, and he bare witness unto the truth. . . . He was a burning and a shining light; and ye were willing for a season to rejoice in his light," namely, if they had succeeded in allying John with the Jewish church council. "But I have greater witness than that of John. . . . And ye have not His (God's) Word abiding in you" (John 5:33 ff). These words of Christ plainly and directly charge the Jews with insincerity, and declare their insincerity to be the cause of their unbelief. Since their affections remained perverse and their will obstinate, the knowledge which was conveyed to them through the Spirit-filled preaching in their day only served to increase their guilt, so that Christ said to one of their group: "This is the condemnation, that light is come into the world and men loved darkness rather than light because their deeds were evil" (John 3:19). It is evident, therefore, that unbelief, also called disobedience, has its seat not in the intellect, but in the will and in the affections.

Faith is acceptance of God's gracious gift; unbelief is rejection of that same gift. In both acts the will of man is operative. The believer is yielding; the unbeliever, obstinate. The believer's will is merged in the will of God; the unbeliever's will is set up in defiance of God's will. As the believer by the knowledge of his faith thinks the thoughts of God, so he desires by the assent of faith the good pleasure and wills the will of God. It is his own desiring and his own willing that is going on within him, and he is conscious of it and pleased with it. He does not act under compulsion or like an automaton. His assent is a free and joyous act. The unbeliever, on the other hand—since he refused the knowledge of faith, refused to bring into captivity his thought to the obedience of Christ—continues to grope in spiritual darkness, ever evolving new errors and new follies from his unenlightened mind. And because the unbeliever clings to his natural appetites and desires, scorns the blessings and delights which the grace of God proposes to him, and continues to be governed by his selfish motives and passions, he finds the Gospel presentation of grace repulsive since its acceptance implies the acknowledgment that his natural desires and will are wicked and must be abandoned.

In much of our present-day theological literature it is quite the popular thing to define faith as "man's self-surrender to God." The idea underlying this view of faith is that of entrusting oneself, yielding oneself up, to someone. The act of faith, thus understood, virtually becomes an act of giving oneself to God. In the Scriptures, particularly in the epistles of Paul, however, faith never has this meaning because of the absolute exclusion of the works of man from the business of justification, which is by faith. Faith, understood as man's yielding or submitting himself to God, would be a work of the Law, such as the trust, or entrusting of oneself, which God requires in the Decalog. If faith is interpreted to mean man's self-surrender to God—to Christ—the distinction between faith and love is erased. Faith and love are both occupied with Christ, but each in a distinct manner. Faith beholds in Christ the sole means for obtaining the cancellation of guilt, while love gives itself up to the contemplation of Christ as the most lovable object and to the service of Christ as its greatest Benefactor. In the very nature of the case such love can exist only after faith has confidently embraced Christ as the answer to man's need. Love is the daughter of faith. It endeavors to make returns for the gifts received from Christ. Evangelical faith, faith in the Gospel, never gives to God, but accepts and receives from God.

Fact of the matter is that man cannot of his own will surrender to God or cease hostilities against Him. Natural man is dead in trespasses and sin (Eph. 2:1), and remains enmity against God as long as he is flesh (Rom. 8:7). There is none that seeketh after God (Rom. 3:11). Any cessation of hostilities is not an accomplishment of man's endeavors, but ever and always exclusively the work of the divine Spirit. Christian faith, also in this aspect of assent to, and acceptance of, the grace of God in Christ, is wrought and brought forth solely and alone by the miracle-working power of the Holy Spirit. St. Paul thanked God for the faith of the Thessalonians when he commended them for "receiving" his teaching. Having done so, he significantly added these words: "Which effectually worketh also in you that believe." The impelling and originating cause of faith is God. When God operates and works, the result is a work for which He must be given full credit. Our Lord thus declared to the Jews: "This is the work of God, that ye believe" (John 6:29).

Assenting faith is saving faith. Its value and blessedness endure not only for the moment or for the period of need and emergency, but for all time. It reaches into eternity. When Paul preached the faith in Christ to Felix, he in the same connection spoke of the Judgment which is to come. Assenting faith accepts from the hands of the sin-atoning and death-conquering Christ the full and free acquittal of the just, the heritage of the saints in glory, and the life which endures through all the endless ages of eternity. And this assent, here and now, communicates to the heart safety, strength, and security against the doubts and fears and anxieties which assail God's people in hours of spiritual conflict and infirmity. Again and again the believer turns to his Lord, who has befriended him, and renews his loyalty and allegiance, affixing his own heart's endorsement to the glad news: "Be of good cheer; thy sins be forgiven thee."

c. Faith as Confidence

The fiduciary character of faith as saving or justifying faith next engages our attention. The writer to the Hebrews speaks of it in the familiar text: "Now, faith is the substance of things hoped for, the evidence of things not seen" (11:1). We hope for that which we in the present do not as yet see or enjoy, but which we have good reason to expect. The things which the Christian hopes for are those things which are promised him in the Sacred Record. Our hope for earthly, material things is always connected with some measure of doubt and uncertainty until we actually have or possess the things themselves, the substance, and then are enabled to see and feel and touch what we have hoped for. Now, we are told that with regard to those things of which God's Word speaks "faith is the substance." This means to say that faith is that certainty, that assurance, which is as great and as firm as though we actually had them in our possession, as though we could see, feel, handle them, as though we had not only the prospect, but the substance of these things. Moreover, the inspired writer declares faith to be the "evidence of things not seen." When in material affairs we are told that a costly, desirable gift is prepared for us, we desire the evidence, or proof, that such is truly the case. The evidence, or proof, gives us the assurance and certainty that what we have been told is true. So in the realm of spiritual things, in those things which God tells us in His Word, "faith is the evidence," that is, faith is the assurance and certainty of the truth and promises of the Word. Such certainty as to the truth of the divine promises is also called confidence. Christian faith, therefore, is the confident persuasion and trustful assurance that I am by the grace of God, for the sake of the atoning sacrifice of my Savior Jesus Christ, a child of God and an heir of salvation as surely as God is God and His Word and promise are eternally true.

On the basis of Scripture, Luther and his followers taught confidence, or trust, as the great and decisive element in saving or justifying faith and insisted in stressing this truth in spite of the opposition of Rome. Already at Augsburg the confessors wrestled with the authors of the Confutation, who would not admit that confidence is the very essence of saving faith. (Apology, Art. IV, 48-60: "What Is Justifying Faith?") In its Sixth Session the Council of Trent passed the following resolution: "If any one saith, that justifying faith is nothing else but confidence in the divine mercy which remits sins for Christ's sake; or, that this confidence alone is that whereby we are justified; let him be anathema" (Canon XII). Roman dogmaticians such as Bellarmin rose to defend this thesis: *"Actus fidei est credere, non confidere"* (The act of faith is to credit something, not to confide in it). Bellarmine, *e. g.,* argued in this manner: "If believing is in the Scripture taken for trusting, we will be compelled to interpret very many passages of Scripture in a most absurd and foolish manner. E. g., "Believest thou not that I am in the Father and the Father in Me?" (John 14:10.) "I believe that Jesus Christ is the Son of God" (Acts 8:37). "With the heart man believeth unto righteousness" (Rom. 10:10). "If thou shalt believe in thine heart that God hath raised Him from the dead, thou shalt be saved" (Rom. 10:9). These and similar passages cannot, except in a very foolish manner, be understood of confidence."

Gerhard answers: "On the contrary, the general argument which Bellarmin deduces from a particular fact is most foolish. For it does not follow that because in some places of Scripture believing cannot be interpreted to mean trusting, therefore that meaning cannot occur in any place, and hence faith cannot mean confidence. Nor would it be absurd if some one were to say that in the passages cited confidence is connoted. Christ does not want this to be believed with a mere assent that the Father is in Him and He in the Father, but He commands us to come to the Father with confidence in the heart through Him as the Mediator. Accordingly, He says in the beginning of the chapter: 'Ye believe in the Father, believe also in Me,' which Stapleton (a Catholic writer) paraphrases thus, 'Have confidence in God and in Me.' The eunuch did not simply believe that Jesus is the Son of God, but he reposed all the confidence of his heart in Him as the Mediator who had been promised and exhibited. Nor is that historical faith by which we believe that Christ was raised from the dead efficacious for righteousness and salvation, because even demons believe this; but what is required of us to that end is that we believe, according to Rom. 4:25, that 'Christ was delivered for our offenses and raised again for our justification'." So far Gerhard (*Loc.* XVII: 3, 1. 81).

The Church of Rome is not alone in its officially avowed opposition to the Scriptural doctrine that justifying or saving faith is essentially confidence, trust, in the atoning work of Christ as set forth in the Gospel. No Church, however, save the Roman, has gone to the extreme of cursing and damning this teaching, which represents the very heart of the Christian religion. Nevertheless, the quality and character of saving faith is vitiated by the teaching of other religious groups, particularly by those which have grown out of the Socinian and Armenian movements in the 16th and 17th centuries, as well as by more than a few contemporary leaders and spokesmen in the religious world. Among the latter the Liberalists stand in the forefront. The position and attitude of Modernism is a matter of public record. The position of our present-day "neo-orthodoxy" is of a more subtle and refined nature. This movement speaks in seemingly orthodox fashion of trust in the Passion and sacrifice of the Lord, but upon closer observation it is evident that they regard the sacrifice of the Son of God not as expiatory and vicarious, but merely as a fulfillment of the word of prophecy and as a striking example of obedience and self-sacrificing service. Modern ecclesiastical spokesmen are most articulate when speaking of inner justification in opposition to the external justification—that forensic act of declaring a sinner righteous which the true Church of the Reformation regards as justification—and proclaim the "Christ in us" as of greater importance than the "Christ for us." All such views ultimately destroy all saving faith. Faith, in the final analysis, in all such teachings will be found to be a moral act of man and a work of merit. This is not the evangelical faith and can never save.

Faith is confidence. The very word—faith—by its very etymology rules out all manner of uncertainty and doubt. The Greek "pistis," the Latin "fides," the English "bond," the German "Bund," and many other formations indicate firmness, unwavering confidence, full assurance. Thus Jesus says: "They have known surely that I came from Thee, and they have believed that Thou didst send Me" (John 17:8). To believe means to accept as true (John 1:26; Luke 22:67; I John 5:1); to confide in, to rely on (II Tim. 1:12; Rom. 10:14; Gal. 2:16). When God speaks in His Word, the believer responds with a confident affirmation. Thus we read that the disciples of Christ "believed the Scriptures and the Word which Jesus had said" (John 2:22). When God promises His grace and blessing, offers forgiveness of sin, life, and salvation in the Gospel, the believer does not question the truth or sincerity of such promises, but accepts the offer and confidently relies on the promise and assurance tendered in the means of grace. Abraham's faith is thus described: "He staggered not at the promise of God through unbelief, but was strong in faith, giving glory to God and being fully persuaded that what He had promised He was able also to perform" (Rom. 4:20). As there can be no confident reliance without something to rely on, so there can be no faith without a divine assurance or promise. God is true, and His Word toward us is not yea and nay, but "all the promises of God in Christ are yea and in Him amen" (II Cor. 1:18-20). Faith, then, is the believer's "yea and amen" based upon this divine "yea and amen," which by its very nature excludes all doubt and uncertainty.

The difference between the assurance, or confidence, of faith and the certainty of human knowledge, which is based upon the testimony of the senses and on experience, is that faith is more certain than any merely human assurance can be, for the foundation whereon it rests is far more firm and reliable than the facts, and also the fancies, underlying a mere human assurance.

This must be especially maintained with regard to Christian hope. We have previously stated that "faith is the substance of things hoped for, the evidence of things not seen" (Heb. 11:1). Now, hope is the well-grounded expectation of things desired, and the ground of Christian hope is the Word of divine promise. Thus Christian hope is essentially faith concerning things to come (Rom. 8:24; Titus 3:7; I Pet. 1:3, 13); as Abraham "believed in hope" (Rom. 4:18), confidently relying on the promise of God, "being fully persuaded that, what He had promised, He was able also to perform" (Rom. 4:20 ff). This is also a purpose of the written Word, "that we through patience and comfort of the Scriptures might have hope" (Rom. 15:4). Whatever would pass as Christian hope must prove its genuineness and validity by the Word of divine promise laid down in Scripture. Peter tells us: "Be ready always to give an answer to every man that asketh you a reason for the hope that is in you" (I Pet. 3:15). Without a word of divine promise such readiness is impossible. Without such promise there is no reason for hope and, in fact, no hope, but an idle dream. The hope in which we are to "rejoice" (Rom. 5:2); by which we "are saved" (Rom. 8:24), as in "hope of eternal life" (Titus 1:2); the hope unto which God has begotten us again as "unto a living hope" (I Pet. 1:3), could not

prevail and endure in the tempests of life and in the billows of
death if it were based on any foundation less firm and abiding than
the sure and certain promises of God in the Scriptures, which are
ever yea and amen in Christ (II Cor. 1:20). How true, therefore,
the words of Paul: "Whosoever believeth in Him shall not be
ashamed" (Rom. 9:33).

This is the Christian's trust and confidence. It is built upon the
sure and firm foundation of the eternal and infallible Word. It rests
upon the unchangeable God, who ever remains faithful and true.
It relies upon the vicarious atonement accomplished by the eternally
triumphant and glory-crowned Christ as our only hope and help
and refuge in every condition and circumstance—in the depths of
sin and guilt, under the curse of the Law, in our struggles and conflicts with the enemies of our souls, in all the vicissitudes of life, in
the prospect of death, in view of the approaching eternity and the
happy reunion before the throne of the Lamb. "Which hope we have
as an anchor of the soul, both sure and steadfast" (Heb. 6:19).

III. FAITH AS A STATE

Faith is also conceived as a state. In this respect faith is viewed
as the continued possession of the gifts and blessings of God, in
and through Christ, through an enduring, abiding confidence in His
all-complete and all-sufficient redemption. "Examine yourselves
whether ye be in the faith," is the earnest admonition of the Apostle
(II Cor. 13:5). In sacred history we read of those who are "established in the faith" (Col. 2:7); who "continue in faith" (I Tim. 4:7);
whose "faith is increased" (II Cor. 10:15). We also read of those
who "for a while believe" (Luke 8:13). The great Apostle in acknowledgment of God's sustaining and preserving mercies rejoiced:
"I have kept the faith" (II Tim. 4:7), and the Savior spoke most
appealingly to Peter, in view of the approaching crisis: "I have
prayed for thee that thy faith fail not" (Luke 22:32). The Christian's
life is a life of faith. He makes the language of that great hero of
faith his own and declares: "The life which I now live in the flesh,
I live by the faith of the Son of God, who loved me and gave Himself for me" (Gal. 2:20). Even in a state of unconsciousness, when
he is incapable of performing any voluntary act, as when in profound
sleep or in the delirium of fever or in narcosis under the surgeon's

knife, the Christian is in a state of grace, for the child of God is at all times and everywhere bound up with Christ by faith. The divine Savior not only sojourns, but actually "dwells in our hearts by faith" (Eph. 3:17). He dwells in the heart of the Christian by means of an enduring faith, which has and holds Christ and all the treasures of His redeeming, reconciling love as an abiding possession. The believer's heart has by faith become the dwelling place of Christ.

Christian faith is capable of growth and increase (II Cor. 10:15). It will grow and increase as more of the saving truth of God comes within the embrace of the heart or as such apprehension becomes more firm and retentive. Of Abraham we are told that he was "strong in faith" (Rom. 4:20), and of others that they were "weak in the faith" (Rom. 14:1). Our Lord and Master reproved His disciples for being "of little faith" (Matt. 6:30). Their faith was deficient in vigor, in firmness and intensity. While they had every reason to be certain of their security and safety in the presence of their omniscient and omnipotent Lord, they were fearful and terrified. When Peter saw the wind boisterous, he was afraid. Although he was not entirely devoid of faith, he manifested a woeful weakness thereof when he cried, "Lord, save me!" Despite this serious and altogether inexcusable infirmity Jesus said to him in tones of gentle, but firm rebuke: "O thou of little faith, wherefore didst thou doubt?" (Matt. 14:30 ff.) Again, the Syrophoenician woman exhibited a firmness and persistency of faith which gained for her the Master's approving testimony: "O woman, great is thy faith" (Matt. 15:28), and of the heathen centurion's faith the Lord said with profound admiration, "I have not found so great faith, no, not in Israel" (Matt. 8:10). Theirs was a faith that could not be shaken by any doubt or uncertainty as to the Savior's power or willingness to grant their petitions. They possessed such an exemplary faith because it rested upon, and confided in, the assuring promises of the Word of Christ.—Lord, give us such a faith as this.

Even as our faith should grow and increase in intensity, so it should also increase in extension. Its extent and scope should be steadily enlarging that we be "enriched in all utterance and in all knowledge" (I Cor. 1:5). This also is accomplished by continued and diligent training and instruction in the faith-building truths of the Word. For this purpose Christ has established the ministry of the Word, and He gives to His Church pastors and teachers to instruct the people "till we all come, in the unity of the faith and of the knowledge of the Son of God, unto a perfect man, unto the measure of the stature of the fullness of Christ, that we henceforth be no more children, tossed to and fro and carried about with every wind of doctrine" (Eph. 4:13, 14).

The duty and obligation which all this places upon Christians is apparent. We need to be diligent and attentive hearers of the Spirit-filled Word in the public services of God's house. We need to encourage and foster a more determined and generous participation of our people of all ages in well-organized and systematic Bible-class work. In many of our churches we probably need to confess a regrettable weakness and neglect in the field of parish education. Only too often this is limited and confined to our youth groups. In addition, we need to place more emphasis upon the urgent necessity of study of the faith-nourishing and faith-strengthening Word on the part of the individual in his own private life as well as in home and family life. "Let the Word of Christ dwell in you richly," is the apostolic appeal and admonition. As we do so, we shall by the power and agency of the Spirit of God go from strength to strength, from victory to victory, in all matters pertaining to Christian faith and life.

Standing in grace by faith does not mean that the Christian should give way to a state of complacency. We are assured of our salvation by faith, but this does not exclude the possibility of falling from grace. Falling from grace is a possibility which even earnest Christians must at all times envisage. The Scriptures teach this possibility conclusively. Job was warned by God Himself in no uncertain language. Christ cautioned even His Apostles against any feeling of self-security, as though eternal life were already in their possession. Paul declared: "I keep under my body and bring it into subjection, lest that by any means, when I have preached to others, I myself should be a castaway" (I Cor. 9:24). Peter warns: "If the righteous scarcely be saved, where shall the ungodly and the sinner appear?" (I Pet. 4:18.) "For if after they have escaped the pollutions of the world through the knowledge of the Lord and Savior Jesus Christ, they are again entangled therein and overcome, the latter end is worse with them than at the beginning. For it had been better for them not to have known the way of righteousness than, after they have known it, to turn from the holy commandment delivered unto them" (II Pet. 2:20, 21).

The Christian guards against such self-complacency and self-security, knowing that we must "work out our salvation with fear and trembling," as the Apostle admonishes. He looks away from self, from all spiritual pride and self-sufficiency, to the sure mercies of God, pledged to us in His Word, guaranteed to us by the sin-atoning death and triumphant resurrection of Christ, and confirmed in our hearts by the testimony of the indwelling Spirit of God. "The Spirit itself beareth witness with our spirit that we are the children of God" (Rom. 8:16). And this is the witness of God: "These things have I written unto you that believe on the name of the Son of God, that ye may know that ye have eternal life and that ye may believe on the name of the Son of God" (I John 5:13). "For I am persuaded that neither death, nor life," etc., "shall be able to separate us from the love of God which is in Christ Jesus our Lord" (Rom. 8:38, 39). For its assurance, faith looks back to Calvary for the finished and accomplished redemption. It looks to the heart of the Bible, the Gospel, for the certainty of forgiveness. And thus it looks into the heart of God for a promised hope which is sure and final, the crowning glory of all faith, resurrection from the dead, immortality of the soul, and life everlasting. Thus the Christian's assurance of continuance in the state of faith rests upon the Scriptures, which certify that "as God has in time called us by the Gospel, enlightened, sanctified, and kept us in the true faith, even so He has from eternity chosen us unto the adoption of children and unto life everlasting, and no man shall pluck us out of His hand."

It will be appropriate at this point to give particular prominence to the means, or instruments, through which the act of faith, together with the entire process thereof—its growth and development, its continuation, as well as its fruits and accomplishments—are produced and effected. The Church has but one mission to perform and but one message to proclaim. The Church exists for the purpose of directing the world of men to Calvary and to proclaim the reconciliation of sinners with God through the blood-stained, glory-crowned cross of the victorious and ever-living Redeemer. "God was in Christ, reconciling the world unto Himself, not imputing their trespasses unto them," says St. Paul, and in order to show how the individual may personally participate in this reconciliation, he continues: "And hath committed unto us the Word of Reconciliation. Now, then, we are ambassadors for Christ, as though God did beseech you by us; we pray you in Christ's stead, Be ye reconciled to God" (II Cor. 5:19, 20). Accordingly, God in His mercy has established and ordained an instrument of power by means of which He appeals to the sinful heart of man and induces him to accept what Christ through His life of perfect obedience, His sin-atoning death, and triumphant resurrection has accomplished for all sinners. This instrument is variously termed in Scripture "Word of Reconciliation," "Word of Life," simply "The Word," etc. Its most common designation is "Gospel."

This Gospel alone—there is none other—is "the power of God unto salvation" (Rom. 1:16). This Gospel "effectually worketh" in men (I Thess. 2:13). This Gospel is the means of grace, whereby God seeks entrance into the hearts of men, causing them to understand His gracious purposes concerning them, to conceive a delight in such knowledge, to acquiesce in His declaration of pardon and peace, and to appropriate the work of Christ, rendered vicariously and in their behalf. From the Gospel issue strong, persuasive influences which attack the natural deadness, coldness, and indifference of the sinner's heart relative to the well-being of his soul. This power of constraining love lays hold upon the human will, which is full of pride and conceit and obstinately opposes the proposition that man can be saved only like a pauper, by the mercy of God. This miracle-working power overcomes the reluctance, the diffidence, the doubts and fears of the alarmed sinner, who supposes he is not worthy of such grace, and transforms his hesitancy and unwillingness into a joyous readiness and acceptance of, and trust in, the heavenly Father's full pardon and unconditional acquittal.

The promises of the Gospel have been attached also to certain ordinances of our Lord's appointment in which there is, besides the spoken Word of grace, some visible element connected with the Word. These sacred ordinances, Holy Baptism and the Lord's Supper, have the same purpose and design as the written and spoken Word. They offer, convey, confirm, and seal the saving grace of God to the sinner. Holy Baptism is the means of the new birth, the generation and creation of faith, and therewith of a new spiritual life. In Holy Communion the Lord gives His body and blood as a pledge and seal of His mercy and forgiveness to strengthen our faith, refreshes our souls, and gives us greater assurance and certainty in our spiritual estate.

God, however, at no time exerts the majestic and irresistible power of His divine omnipotence, compelling the sinner by means of force to yield to His entreaties and invitations. This would be a self-contradiction and would leave the sinner—convinced against his will—to be of the same opinion still. But there is a mighty moral persuasion exerted through the Gospel, and the Gospel ordinances, which effectually calls the sinner from darkness to light, renews his heart, produces true and trusting faith, makes him an heir of God and a coheir with Christ, and which nourishes and sustains him in the faith and the joyful service of his God, and which preserves him in this state of grace and faith unto the day of his final and complete glorification. "Ye are kept by the power of God through faith unto salvation" (I Pet. 1:5).

IV. FAITH AND RATIONALISM

Men of learning and repute have long endeavored to set forth what they term the "reasonableness of Christianity." They have tried to explain away the "mystery of Christianity." It must be conceded that all such have been victimized by the theories and speculations of rationalism. It is true that Christianity is mysterious. The Gospel of Christ is a "hidden mystery" unless it be revealed to the minds of men. No amount of observation and speculation of human reason, no process of induction or deduction, from whatever analogies or premises, can determine or establish one single article of the Christian faith. It was a fundamental error in medieval Scholasticism that men endeavored to exhibit the reasonableness of Christian dogmas before the tribunal of human understanding. Thus Anselm, generally recognized as the "father of Scholasticism," endeavored to prove that "God was made man by necessity," and to prove it in such a way "as to satisfy by reason alone both Jews and Gentiles."

While we are aware of the fact that Christianity is and must remain a revealed religion and as such is above human reason and philosophical demonstration, it must be maintained that Christianity is not against sound reason, or nonsensical. The doctrine of the Holy Trinity, for example, cannot be established by a mathematical formula; but no mathematical truth is incompatible with this doctrine, so that the one must fall if the other should stand. The doctrines of inspiration, of the deity of Christ, of conversion, of the

atonement, of justification, of predestination, are in no wise unreasonable. It has been well said that "unreasonableness is not on the
side of faith but on that of unbelief." Also here that most expressive
statement of the Psalmist has a direct application, "The fool hath
said in his heart, There is no God" (Ps. 14:1).

Atheism, the most aggravated form of unbelief, certainly is not
reasonable. It involves the denial of a first cause, of a supreme will,
of moral responsibility, and, ultimately, of reason itself. This form
of unbelief is unreasonable not only because of its radical character.
It differs from other forms of denial of religious truth only in degree
of unreasonableness. The denial of the doctrine of verbal plenary
inspiration, a fundamental error of modern theology, is as truly
unreasonable as any other form of unbelief and involves its proponents in a maze of inconsistencies and absurdities. We teach and
believe that the Bible is the written Word of God, given by inspiration of the Spirit of God. This is an article of faith, not a product or
conclusion of logical reasoning. Nevertheless it is certainly not unreasonable that God, the supreme Intelligence, the Lord over all
creation and the Savior of a fallen world, should communicate with
His rational creatures, should make His will known to His subjects,
should teach those whom He would rescue from bondage and
oppression for a blessed eternity the way of salvation, and to do all
this in a manner which would insure the achievement of His exalted
design and purpose. What is reasonable in intelligent men, in
earthly sovereigns and legislators, in philanthropists, benefactors,
and instructors is certainly not unreasonable in God.

In this connection it must be constantly emphasized and distinctly
understood that we do not believe and accept even one doctrine of
the Christian religion because it is not unreasonable. While we deem
it more reasonable to accept in trusting, confident faith what we find
in a volume which stands unconvicted before the tribunal of sound
reason than to agree with rationalism, or unbelief, contrary to sound
reason in theory and practice; yet our test of the truth of a doctrine
is not its compatibility with human reason but rather its conformity
with divine truth.

Faith listens to the voice of God speaking through the Sacred
Scriptures. Faith listens to no other voice. It will not listen to the
voice of rationalism. It is rationalism which denies the absolute
inerrancy of Scripture. The rejection of verbal, plenary inspiration

and the denial of the absolute inerrancy of the Scriptures proceed from rationalistic considerations. All who advocate such criminal heresy are guilty of placing reason above Scripture. They stand indicted by their own testimony. A spokesman for so-called modern scientific theology stated: "No statement can be accepted as true because it is in the Bible . . . all its teachings must be subjected to the authority of reason and conscience." Voltaire declared that he could not accept the accounts of God's strange and supernatural dealings with the Israelites in Egypt and in the desert "because they are revolting to reason." Another (J. De Witt) insisted that reason has the right to correct Scripture. "If, besides the divine truth that Scripture embodies, it also contains partial truths, which are sometimes as misleading as falsehood, and moral incongruities and monstrosities from which our souls recoil, how shall I separate the gold from the dross? By the use of my reason? Would you have me become a rationalist? Yes, rather than be a sophist or a simpleton. . . . Our enlightened moral instinct rejects it"—the old inspiration—"unreservedly and forever." The voice of rationalism is heard again when Walter M. Horton states: "To rely upon revelation apart from other truth is as bad as to rely upon prayer apart from action or upon providence apart from intelligent forethought. Revelation is no substitute for reason. If reason without revelation is blind, revelation without reason is a dazzling, unintelligible light."

The advocates of this position do not hesitate to assert that Holy Scripture itself promotes the principles of rationalism and insist that its statements and teachings must be processed through the crucible of reason. We quote S. P. Cadman: "The authority of the Bible is established by divine revelation, but it is also addressed to human intelligence. The Book itself invokes finite reason and appeals to its decisions. . . . Plainly, the Scriptures do not outlaw man's judgment on their contents. Why should we do so?" And N. R. Best, who writes on "The Mirage of Inerrancy," gives chapter and verse for that statement. "Utterly vain it is to talk of not employing reason on the Bible. . . . When did the Creator ever brand man's reason as unholy, unfit to handle the sacred things of either His deeds or His words? . . . Every page of the Bible might be justly inscribed with the invitation which stands in living letters on the first page of the Prophet Isaiah: 'Come now and let us reason together, saith Jehovah.' Reason is God's joy—not His black beast."

It should also be noted that even some theologians of the conservative group are afraid that Scripture cannot hold its own against advanced scholarship and "modern scientific theology." They fear that the inerrancy of Scripture might be disproved by the scientists and the historians and the philosophers. Hence they look to human scholarship to establish the divine authority of the Word and its plenary inerrancy. Instead of resting their faith in the truthfulness of the Word alone, they also base their belief on the conclusions of science and the assent of reason. This is subtle rationalism, but rationalism nevertheless. The *Journal of the American Lutheran Conference*, December, 1938, states: "How can we know the human framework of the Bible is true—the history, the geography, the biography, the science . . . ? We not only may but we must study these things critically, to see if the Bible statements are supported or contradicted by known facts from other sources. . . . It is my growing conviction that it is possible to arrive at a reasonable faith in the substantial truthfulness of the human framework of the Bible." This Lutheran theologian finds himself constrained to call upon critical investigation and human wisdom to help out the Bible. He is concerned about a "reasonable faith." This is certainly a rationalistic aberration. Our own Dr. Walther said of those who admit the possibility of errors in the Scripture and thus make it their self-appointed responsibility to sift the truth from error in order to establish the truth of Scripture that they are "introducing a rationalistic germ into theology." If such incipient rationalism is not checked, it will develop into the malignant form.

It follows quite logically that rationalism is greatly troubled about the "Christ problem." To the scientific thought of the modern theologian Christ is a most perplexing problem. This is true in a twofold respect. The first relates to His singular personality. Who is He? Is He actually the strangely composite being portrayed to us in the Sacred Record? He is explicitly called, described, and exhibited in the Word as the Son of God and Son of Man, and we, in full harmony with the Scriptures, confess Him to be "true God, begotten of the Father from eternity, and also true man, born of the Virgin Mary." Needless to say, this unique personality is incomprehensible to man's natural reason. Equally incomprehensible to the scientific thought of modern man is Christ's peculiar and avowed mission. Why did He come among men? Why did He live as He did, in amazing humiliation and complete self-forgetfulness, which eventually culminated in a strange suffering and death? Was it merely a life grossly misunderstood and filled with the pathos of such misunderstanding? Did His life end in defeat when His own nation turned against Him, when chosen friends forsook Him, and when the highest powers of the day rejected and condemned Him? We realize, of course, that the difficulties discovered by the critical mind of modern man are not new discoveries. In every age since the Incarnation the minds of men have been troubled by doubts concerning the person and the mission of the Christ of God.

Every attempt to solve the "Christ problem" has proved most unsatisfactory. The most popular solution offered is that Christ is the perfect Man and that His life is the paragon of morality. He is acclaimed as the supreme Pattern of moral and spiritual excellence which we should strive to emulate. This solution is altogether disappointing. It is disappointing because it denies the deity of our Lord. Christ as the perfect Man is at best "only half the Christ of the Bible." Essentially this means that He is not the Christ of the Scriptures at all, but rather a product of human fancy. Moreover, if the deity of Christ is conceded, it would appear illogical, even cruel, to exhibit Him to us as no more than perfect Man. Above all, it remains true that the saving element is eliminated from Christ's work if the purpose of His mission was to show men by a practical example what God requires of them in the way of proper moral conduct.—There is only one satisfactory solution for the "Christ problem," and that is the solution presented by the Scriptures themselves. This connects directly with the essence and the object of faith and the plan of salvation. Christ declares that He came "to give His life a ransom for many" (Matt. 20:28); that He had come "to seek and to save that which was lost" (Luke 19:10). The work of Christ is substitutionary work. "God made Him to be sin for us who knew no sin, that we might be made the righteousness of God in Him" (II Cor. 5:21). The element of obedience which is made so prominent in His life is necessary to complete the picture of Him as the Savior from sin and death. "He was obedient unto death, even the death of the cross" (Phil. 2:8). Actively fulfilling the demands of the Law, passively submitting to every punishment of the Law, He has procured a perfect salvation. He died because of our sins. We live because of His atonement for sin. Only as man believes that, can he appreciate Christ.

Dr. G. A. Buttrick, president of the Federal Council of Churches in 1940, did not hesitate to make this amazing statement: "Probably few people who claim to 'believe every word of the Bible' really mean it. That avowal, held to its last logic, would risk a trip to the insane asylum." Pray God that we may ever remain among those who believe every word of the Bible and really mean it. Such faith is the product of God's Word, wrought by the Holy Spirit, and "the faith produced by the Word is divinely convinced that the Word, every word of Scripture, is the divine truth."

This is the attitude which God requires of the Christian. "To this man will I look that . . . trembleth at My Word," Is. 66:2. As Christians we look upon the Bible as a most holy thing. It is clothed with divine majesty. It determines all articles of faith for us. It is the norm and rule in all matters of faith and life. What we read in this Sacred Book we receive "not as the word of men but, as it is in truth, the Word of God" (I Thess. 2:13). So Luther regarded it. "To me God's Word is above all, and the majesty of God is on my side" (XIX:337). "You must follow straight after Scripture and receive it and utter not one syllable against it, for it is God's mouth" (III:21). "As for me," says Luther, "every single Bible text makes the world too narrow for me" (XX:788).

V. FAITH AND LIFE

The sinner is justified by grace, through faith in Christ Jesus. A result of justification is a moral change and transformation which is effected in the powers and processes of the soul. A new relationship has been established, and in consequence thereof new attitudes, new desires, new objectives, and new ideals are produced and activated. God and all things divine have now become lovable objects to the sinner who previously disliked, even detested, them. His judgment and evaluation of things are not only changed, but completely reversed. He is motivated by new and noble impulses and henceforth finds pleasure and delight in doing God's will. Life itself has assumed a new purpose and direction and now becomes a privileged and cherished opportunity for rendering an exalted service to God and man. St. Paul expresses the beauty and nobility of this condition and life when he says: "I live; yet not I, but Christ liveth in me; and the life which I now live in the flesh I live by the faith of the Son of God, who loved me, and gave Himself for me" (Gal. 2:20). This life, too, is the outgrowth, the fruit, of that faith which at first grasped the pardoning hand of divine mercy and which continues to retain its hold on that hand. It is a life which is manifested in a thousand forms in the routine of our daily tasks. It determines every view of duty; it prompts every holy, generous, charitable resolve; it develops a prolific activity in the field of everything that is true, everything that is honest, everything that is just, everything that is pure, everything that is lovely, everything that is of good report, everything that is virtuous and praiseworthy (Phil. 4:8). It teaches us "that, denying ungodliness and worldly lusts, we should live soberly, righteously, and godly in this present world, looking for that blessed hope and the glorious appearing of the great God and Savior, Jesus Christ" (Titus 2:12, 13).

True faith, therefore, is a living power, an energizing, motivating, vitalizing power, which propels, drives, and urges to action. As such, living faith is functional, active, operative. It is God-begotten energy. Our Lord reveals the possibilities of such a living and functional faith when He declares: "All things are possible to him that believeth" (Mark 9:23). Because the disciples did not have the faith to meet the challenge of the man possessed of a dumb spirit, Jesus chides them: "O faithless generation, how long shall I be with you? How long shall I suffer you?" (Mark 9:19.) In this very connection He tells His disciples: "Verily, I say unto you, If ye have faith as a grain of mustard seed, ye shall say unto this mountain, Remove hence to yonder place, and it shall remove; and nothing shall be impossible to you" (Matt. 17:20). Repeatedly, Jesus gave the promise that "all things are possible to him that believeth." The blessed Savior desired to emphasize that Christian faith is a power which can break through the strongest barriers as though they were a spider's web. Christian faith has this power because it is rooted in God. By faith we may rise above, and become victorious over, every earthly adversity and distress. Faith is a cord which connects divine omnipotence to our impotence and draws the power of the infinite God down to our earthly needs and limitations. Faith harnesses the problems and cares of the trusting believer to the all-sufficient wisdom and love of God. It is also for this reason that God wants His people to have a courageous, valiant, and triumphant faith, a faith that overcomes all obstacles. Such were the lives of the heroes of faith in the past, and neither fire nor famine, neither sword nor dungeon, neither the gallows nor horrible death could silence their testimony. By faith the ancient saints of God walked through storms and fire unafraid. By faith Moses passed through the Red Sea. By faith Daniel stopped the mouths of lions. By faith Paul conquered mountainous problems. By faith Luther confessed Christ as Savior and King before kings and princes. By faith we know that God is for us and with us. Through Him we are more than conquerors.

The Scriptures ascribe world-conquering power to Christian faith. "Whatsoever is born of God overcometh the world, and this is the victory that overcometh the world, even our faith" (I John 5:4). The Apostle does not attribute world-conquering power to every and any kind of faith. The plague of a "humanistic faith" has been and still is resting upon this world of men. This faith, so prevalent and widely acclaimed, is centered in humankind, in man's ability to conquer self, sin, evil habits, social wrongs, and all the problems of our present-day economy. Modern thought has been captured by the philosophy of humanism. Through science, education, and ethical culture, men had hoped to build a superrace of men and a world of lasting peace and plenty. Confident of the abounding goodness of man and of his highly developed skills and techniques, men dreamed of an accomplishment which in a generation or two would turn all swords into plowshares and bring freedom from want and freedom from fear to all the world. This fond and idealistic expectancy has already ended in tragic disillusionment. The gigantic problems of world peace, world justice, social equality, just distribution of wealth, must be recognized as being essentially the problem of the inherited depravity of man. Since man by nature is sinful and corrupt, his most noble efforts and endeavors in the direction of moral and social progress of the race will inevitably again and again meet with the stumbling block of man's innate greed, selfishness, and lust for dominance and power. Moral and social disappointment and defeat are therefore unavoidable.

Christian faith produces a living, functional, and dynamic Christianity. A living Christianity is a life where the principles of self-denial and Christlike living constantly prevail. Where Christ is lived, genuinely lived in the daily lives of His followers, there ungodliness and worldly lusts will be denied and fought against and conquered in His name, and those who live their lives in His name will constantly live their lives, too, in righteousness and sobriety, in true godliness and piety.

Christians are urged to be diligently engaged in the pursuit of exalted virtues and noble practices. The urgency thereof is particularly compelling in our day. We are a part of a generation which thought it could exist without God and without obedience to His will. Such godlessness must lead to chaotic futility and despair. All over the world the children of men have been sowing the seeds of unbelief and rebellion and fear and suspicion and hatred and violence and unbridled passion. And they have largely forgotten that what a man sows he shall also reap. We cannot sow ungodliness and reap godliness. We cannot sow worldly lusts and reap lasting pleasures of body and soul. We cannot sow intemperance and reap sobriety. We cannot sow immorality and reap purity. We cannot sow suspicion and reap good will. We cannot sow strife and contention and rebellion and revolution and war and reap security and prosperity and progress and national and international understanding and peace. We cannot sow unbelief and reap faith in a merciful and loving and saving God. Therefore the insistent call comes to the people of God, living in a world desperately in need of reclamation and redemption, to live as the sons and daughters of God in the devotion and valor of a Heaven-born faith; to live soberly and righteously and godly, forsaking all iniquity, purifying and sanctifying themselves daily, always cognizant of the truth that all who are Christ's and all who would live in Christ are a peculiar, a separated people, a royal priesthood, who by word, deed, and example are zealous of good works and are concerned to show forth, or emphasize to others, the praises of their eternal God and Savior-King, whose they are and whom they love and whom they would serve in the obedience of faith.

In this faith, which in all the complex conditions and circumstances of life lays hold of the redemption by Christ and which fills the most ordinary actions of believers with the spirit of love and gratitude, lie the mainsprings of true morality. It is this faith which overcame the world in the days of the Apostles which has since changed the face of human affairs. Its silent but effective influences have gone out into all ranks and stations of men. In every age and generation, critics and opponents have asserted its decadence and pronounced it a failure. It is true that in its visible manifestations this faith exists and functions in much weakness. The pride of reason scorns it; but it proceeds quietly, unostentatiously, efficiently, and successfully with its work of revitalizing and rebuilding the children of men and fashioning them for an eternal triumph and victory. It possesses perennial youth, immortal vitality, unconquerable strength.

Not so long ago the assertion that the influence of Christianity was waning drew from Edward Thomsen this eloquent rejoinder: "While Christianity is speaking in languages more numerous, by tongues more eloquent, in nations more populous than ever before, shrinking from no foe, rising triumphant from every conflict, shaking down the towers of old philosophies that exalt themselves against God, emancipating the enslaved, civilizing the lawless, refining litera-ture, inspiring poetry, giving godlike breath and freedom and energy to the civilization that bears its name, elevating savage islands into civilized states, leading forth Christian martyrs from the mountains of Madagascar, turning the clubs of cannibals into the railings of the altars before which Fiji savages call upon Jesus, repeating the Pentecost 'by many an ancient river and many a palmy plain,' thundering at the seats of ancient paganism, sailing all waters, cabling all oceans, scaling all mountains, in the march of its might, and ever enlarging the diameter of those circles of light which it has kindled on earth—you call it a failure? Nay, indeed, this faith never fails." . . . "Its merciful mission to the disconsolate, where'er they languish, goes on despite the hypocrisy of false adherents, the feeble-ness of its true disciples, and the might of earth's powers that are arrayed against it. It will continue to win souls, even from the ranks of its most outspoken opponents, until with the final return of our Lord it will pass into the vision beatific and the peace and glory which it has promised its followers."

In his grand triumphal procession a king was asked: "What is wanting to make this perfect?" With a sigh of regret the king replied: "Continuance." Through faith in the Christ of God, our benign Savior and King, we have the assurance of that continuance. We live "in the hope of the glory of God" and are confident "that He which hath begun a good work in us will perform it until the day of Jesus Christ" (Phil. 1:6). Then our faith, here attended with much weak-ness and imperfection, will be translated into sight, our hope into joyous experience, and our experience shall be the experience of the eternal and unchanging presence of God. In the complete and perfect enjoyment of that continuous beatific vision "we shall be like Him," and "we shall see Him as He is."

XII

The Certainty of Salvation

WERE we to mention a distinguishing characteristic of our Lutheran fathers, we could do no better than to point to their "certainty." In matters of religion they were not at sea. They were "not carried about with divers and strange doctrines" (Heb. 13:9). They were "no more children tossed to and fro" (Eph. 4:4). They were sure of what they taught. Abiding by the Word, they spoke as the oracles of God. Knowing the Scripture to be verbally inspired and infallibly true, they regarded its statements final. As Luther once said: "Here I stand, here I stay, here I make my boast, here I triumph, here I defy the Papists, the Thomists, the Heinzists, the Sophists, and all the gates of hell; God's Word is above all, the divine majesty is on my side."

With this certainty of doctrine, however, our fathers received and possessed also the certainty of salvation. Their hearts were filled with "assurance." They lived in the firm persuasion of being in a state of grace. They were not only able to say: we are sure of our *teaching*, but also: we are sure of our *salvation*. They were certain of having not only the doctrine of grace, but also grace itself. Joyously and triumphantly sure they were of being in Christ Jesus God's redeemed, justified children, predestinated to eternal life and glory. They were certain of their salvation.

As we study this doctrine, we shall consider the Christian's assurance as the touchstone of Christian truth, as a treasure to be safeguarded, as the dynamic of Christian living.

I

Christian Assurance, the Touchstone of Christian Truth

221

A. WITH REGARD TO JUSTIFYING FAITH

With the Scripture we hold that "a man is justified not by the works of the Law, but by the faith of Jesus Christ" (Gal. 2:16). But what is this "faith of Jesus Christ"? Is it a purely intellectual apprehension of the facts of His Gospel? Or is it some vague mental wish with continued uncertainty about His offer of salvation? Indeed not! The faith that justifies is itself a certainty of salvation. Its essence is "a being sure of God's grace in Christ Jesus." Its core and kernel is assurance, firm reliance. It is what the theologians call *fiducia cordis*—the confidence of the heart.

The Scripture plainly teaches: "Faith is the *substance* of things hoped for, the evidence of things not seen" (Heb. 11:1). For "substance" the Revised Version has "assurance"; Luther: *eine gewisse Zuversicht.* Yet the difference is not important, since in any case faith is here described as certainty. The "unseen things hoped for" become so certain by faith in God's promises as though we had the very substance of them in our hands here and now. In faith there is no uncertainty in spite of the invisibleness of its objects. Faith is the antonym of doubt. And while, of course, it presupposes some intellectual knowledge of Christ and salvation, it is essentially a trusting of the heart, as also the oft-repeated Gospel phrase: "He that *believeth on the Son* hath everlasting life" (John 3:36) indicates. Believing is being certain. And the certainty of faith is the certainty of salvation.

A classic summary of this is given in the statement of our Apology: "That faith which justifies is not merely a knowledge of history . . . but it is *the certainty,* or the firm, strong confidence in the heart, when, with my whole heart, I regard the promises of God as *certain and true,* through which there are offered to me, without my merit, the forgiveness of sins, grace and salvation through Christ the Mediator" (*Triglot,* p. 135, § 48). "Faith," says Luther in his glorious Introduction to Romans, "is a living, moving confidence in God's grace—*so certain* that for it one could die a thousand deaths."

Like a touchstone this emphasis on a believer's certainty quickly brought to light all perverted views of faith. Catholic polemics, especially, turned full fury upon the Lutheran assertion that faith is essentially a certainty of God's grace. A psychological impossibility . . . a chimera . . . a "monstrum" they called it. The assembled bishops and patres at the Council of Trent hurled anathemas upon it. (Sess. VI; Can. XII.) The Jesuits proclaimed over against it the virtue of doubt. Confidence and certainty they denounced as presumption. Bellarmine called it pride. "It is intolerable," he said, "that men ordinarily become certain of grace, because certainty produces pride . . . uncertainty generates humility." And in line with this superficial argumentation, they actually stripped justifying faith of its essential meaning. From a matter of the will, they reduced it to an exercise of the understanding. Justifying faith they taught to be a mere knowing of the intellect,—a purely mental agreement to or acquiescence, and even less than that. An assent to the teachings of the Church and Scripture *without knowing what these are* they deemed sufficient. Who can fail to see that in this way they have made of faith a human work, robbed believers of God-given certainty and in the spirit of Antichrist perverted the article of justification by faith alone?

Already in his day Dr. C. F. W. Walther bewailed the fact that while most so-called Lutherans had some vague hope that God might be gracious unto them, they were not certain. "Either people are spiritually dead," he said (*Festklaenge,* p. 419), "and therefore careless and think they will surely get to heaven; or they are anxious and uncertain. How many meet death with the thought: Will I reach heaven or not? That is a terrible faith, a form faith. No, faith must be certain!" Justifying faith is not questioning the salvation earned for us by Christ Jesus and given freely by God's grace; it is with the will accepting and appropriating it; it is making it one's own and having possession of it. It is the "*substance* of things hoped for"; it is itself the certainty of salvation.

To this, however, many object on the ground that believers are still afflicted with uncertainty. This was the chief argument of the Papists against the Lutheran doctrine of certainty. It was also employed by our fathers' opponents in the nineteenth-century controversy on election. But our fathers refused to accept this as a proof. Though they acknowledged the presence of doubts in a believer, they were careful to make the proper distinction. True, they said, believers still have doubts. But far be it from us to praise these doubts as evidence of humility. They are not to be regarded as virtues, but as vices. They do not belong to the nature of faith, but to the nature of unbelief. They are not a part of the new man in us, but of the old, who also with this weakness must be drowned with daily contrition and repentance.

To praise doubt and make it a part of faith leads finally to a subversion of the whole article of justification by faith alone! Not by doubt or uncertainty are we justified, but by faith, which, in its essence, is certainty.

B. WITH REGARD TO SAVING GRACE

In treating the article of Christian certainty as a touchstone, we must regard it also in *its relation to saving grace*. For, it is evident there can be no certainty where the doctrine of grace is unknown or misunderstood. Without let or hindrance it must be faithfully reemphasized that "by grace we are saved" (Eph. 2:5). And to avoid all misunderstanding, it is necessary to ask, What is this "grace" by which we are saved? Is it a gracious virtue, power, or "charity" which God pours into a man's soul (*gratia infusa*)? Indeed not. It is not something subjective, in man's heart, but something objective, outside of man, in God's heart. It is the good will and favor of God, His unmerited love and mercy, which moved Him to send His Son to redeem all sinful mankind and for Christ's sake to declare judicially (justify) all the world to be forgiven.

This is the incalculably precious doctrine of grace, so beautifully summarized by St. Paul in the inspired words: "All have sinned and come short of the glory of God, being justified freely by His grace through the redemption that is in Christ Jesus, whom God hath set forth to be a propitiation through faith in His blood, to declare his righteousness for the remission of sins that are past, through the forbearance of God" (Rom. 3:23-25). And to show how completely our salvation rests upon this grace of God, and how definitely it excludes even the tiniest particle of human merit, St. Paul adds the challenge: "Where is boasting, then? It is excluded!" (V. 27.) And for fear that some might even look upon their faith as a meritorious work, he adds: "Therefore, we conclude that a man is justified by faith without the deeds of the Law!" (V. 28.) On nothing, nothing in our souls and lives, but only and solely on the free, universal grace of God does our salvation depend. And unless this is understood and maintained, there can be no certainty of salvation.

"That our hope of eternal life may not waver, but be certain," declares our Apology (Art. III, § 212, *Triglot,* p. 15), "we must believe that God gives us eternal life not on account of our works or merit, but through grace alone by faith in Christ." And to this Dr. F. Pieper once remarked: "It does not merely depend upon whether we have the doctrine of grace in more or less adulterated form; the result is always the same—an uncertainty of grace and salvation, if we do not oppose with all seriousness even the seemingly most trivial perversion of the doctrine of grace" (Iowa, 1885, p. 55).

"Seemingly trivial," says Dr. Pieper. Actually, there is no trivial perversion; every change of it is gross, pernicious, and disastrous for immortal souls. To the world it may appear as a trivial matter that the Church of Rome has defined grace as "the charity which is poured forth in their hearts by the Holy Ghost," and in the same canon of the Council of Trent (Sess. VI, Can. XI) has condemned the true Scriptural meaning that "the grace whereby we are justified is only the favor of God." It may seem a little thing that still today millions of dear children are being taught from the Catholic Catechism that "actual grace is that help of God which enlightens our minds and moves our will to shun evil and do good . . . and without this grace we can do nothing to merit heaven." It may be thought a minor matter that most of modern Protestant theology deflates the glorious word "grace" in the same way and defines it as an "inner light," "the indwelling of the Spirit," "the Christ in us," a "gracious experience." It may be deemed insignificant by some that Reformed theology denies the universality of grace, and so forces the seekers of salvation to look for assurance in their own experience. All this may appear to the untrained as trivial. But of all the miserable perversions of truth this poor world has suffered, these are the most pernicious, for they are an attack upon the very heart of Christianity, which is *God's grace.* They are destroying mankind's only hope and comfort, which is *God's grace.* And in no more deadly, vicious way could this be done. The word "grace" is still used; but it is divested of its Scriptural meaning. It is turned and twisted until it conveys the very opposite of what Paul intended. Grace is made synonymous with works. Justified by grace is said to mean justified by personal experience. Grace is interpreted as merit, and the result? O tragedy of tragedies! Precious souls are driven back to slave under the lash of the Law, where there is no certainty of salvation, nay, where there is no salvation at all!

A religion of works is always a religion of doubt and fear. Witness the pitiful uncertainty of adherents of the Church of Rome which condemns the *sola gratia* and consequently preaches the *monstrum incertitudinis*. Witness the attitude of synergistic and modernistic theologians, who speak of "human self-determination," "man's co-operation," "less resistance" as necessary to salvation, and then smile disdainfully at all claims of certainty. This proves that only a pure view of grace, and grace alone, God's grace, free grace, universal grace, unlimited grace through Christ's redemption can make the heart certain of salvation. Do we find a church, therefore, in which no one is certain and members are willfully kept in a state of doubt whether they are forgiven, redeemed and justified,—we may be sure that the cause of the uncertainty lies in some adulteration of the doctrine of grace. Is there an individual among us who never enjoys a bit of assurance of salvation, we may look for the trouble in some misunderstanding or oversight of the Scriptural fact of God's grace. Like a touchstone the certainty of salvation tests the purity of a person's or church's view of saving grace.

Nor ought we hesitate to apply this test constantly to ourselves. Even where the true doctrine is confessed, a misconception can arise, and that particularly through a false emphasis on faith. The too insistent demand: "Believe on Christ," repeatedly urged without careful explanation of what this implies, can lead to a dreadful annihilation of grace. Quickly the people can gain the impression that their "believing in Christ" is a meritorious work, a kind of part payment for their guilt. And this is the exact error of modern theologians, who also speak of being "justified by faith," but call faith "a doing of our inner self," "an ethical deed of the will." They, like so many, make of faith a virtuous, heaven-meriting work.

But for the careful preservation of the precious doctrine of grace, it must plainly and repeatedly be emphasized that saving faith is nothing of the kind. It is not a meritorious work; Scripture places it in opposition to works. Faith saves, justifies, not because of what faith is, but of what it apprehends. As the hand that accepts a free gift does not merit the treasure, so faith cannot merit salvation, but only accept it. Never dare we make a Christ out of our faith and think of it as though it were the source of our salvation. Our certainty is found in looking unto Jesus, not in looking to our own faith. Certainty of salvation does not rest on faith. Certainty is faith;

it cannot be built upon itself. Its one, firm, unshakable foundation is grace and grace alone.

C. WITH REGARD TO THE MEANS OF GRACE

Certainty of salvation as a touchstone of truth must be viewed also in its relation to *the means of grace*—the Word and the Sacraments. Without these God might have ever so much grace in store for us, but we would not know it, nor could we avail ourselves of it. Certainty would be impossible. Not only to offer and convey, therefore, but also to seal and assure unto us the grace which Christ has merited, has He given these precious means.

What a remarkable confirmation of this lies in St. John's simple statement (I John 5:8): "There are three that bear witness in earth: the Spirit [referring to the Word], the water [meaning Baptism], and the blood [the Lord's Supper]." "And," he adds, "these three agree in one"; that is to say, they agree in having one and the same purpose. They are designed to "bear witness on earth," and bear witness of the fact "that God," as he says in verse eleven, "hath given to us eternal life and this life is in His Son." Not only do they inform us of this blessed, saving truth, but also "bear witness" of it, render positive and powerful testimony with the purpose of making us sure of it. Therefore, also St. Paul wrote to the Thessalonians: "Our Gospel came not unto you in word only, but also in power, and in the Holy Ghost, and in much assurance" (I Thess. 1:5). And so the Gospel, both in the Word and the Sacraments (*verbum audibile et visibile*), comes to us still today. Its effectual purpose is to assure, seal, and make us certain of our salvation. The means of grace are the means of certainty.

Vast multitudes in Christendom continue to neglect and despise God's Word and His Sacraments in spite of the fact that God Himself has ordained and the Holy Spirit Himself has condescended to use them as means of creating certainty in the hearts. Ignoring the express purpose of the Gospel, the Church of Rome takes the lead by maintaining that certainty is possible only to privileged characters like Peter and Paul and then only through special revelations. It presents the Gospel, not as a means of assuring the penitent of forgiveness, but as a new commandment requiring works; the benefit of Baptism it confines to original sin and transgressions preceding it; the Lord's Supper it has changed into a sacrifice. And in like manner, Reformed theology goes on tampering with the means of grace. It still regards them as empty symbols of what the Spirit does. It denies their power to regenerate the soul and stresses the operation of God's Spirit apart from the means. It claims that the Spirit works without means and irresistibly, and it opens the door to all the crude extravagances of revivalism and emotionalism. As means of attaining certainty they speak, like the Romanists, of "special revelations," or "inner light," or "second conversions," or "inner Word," and advocate praying, agonizing, and wrestling with God. Nor is Modern Theology far removed from these crudities when it insists on assurance through inner experience. The net result of all this theoretical and practical rejection of God's ordained means is a welter of doubt and uncertainty about that which is to be the Christian's chief joy and comfort: the grace of God. It is blocking the gracious channel through which God is pleased to grant, create, and sustain the certainty of salvation.

This unspeakable tragedy arises from man's natural inclination *to feel* something of divine grace. The tendency is strong also in us. We want to sense, to feel, to experience. Our hearts are not naturally inclined to rely simply upon God's Word. As we sense the things of earth, so we crave to sense the things of the spirit. But that is a dangerous trend. In fact, we must thank God and marvel at His wisdom in not surrendering us to the vagaries of human feelings. For, as Luther already pointed out, our sense perceptions are very deceptive. We see something, and still do not see it aright. We hear something distinctly and still misunderstand. We feel something, and before long we feel it not. If, then, our certainty had been made by God to depend upon our imperfect sense and transient feelings, what a pitiful condition would be ours! How could we be sure that we were not deceiving ourselves? But faith, which has and keeps God's Word before it, does not deceive itself. It could deceive itself only if God's Word of grace were a lie. But as it is the incontrovertible, eternal truth, there can be in all the world and in all the realm of human thought or experience, no certainty greater and better than this which is founded upon God's Word.

Of course, when we reject our emotions, experiences, and feelings as the basis of certainty, we do not mean to say that a Christian's feelings are without value and import. Devout feelings of joy, peace, love, and hope are extremely precious. It is altogether unbiblical and un-Lutheran to ignore them. Just because we as a Church have been careful to reject the fanatical extravagances of a purely emotional type of Christianity, we must exercise care not to lapse into a cold, intellectual, feelingless type of being. It is an error of a dreadful nature to imagine that he who regards Biblical Lutheran doctrine as true is a sound Christian, irrespective of whether he ever experiences anything of the joy and peace of the Holy Ghost. Feeling is to be sought, but in the right way. It is not to be drummed up through emotional artifices. If anyone wishes to *feel* the grace of God without or before heeding the means of grace, he is building a barrier between himself and God. And what is more, the more he insists on such feelings without regarding the Gospel and the Sacraments, the less will he attain it. For, genuine feeling is a fruit of faith and certainty, which God generates only through His ordained means.

It has been said that this doctrine of the means of grace is "the peculiar glory of Lutheran theology." To this central teaching it owes its sanity and strong appeal, its freedom from sectarian tendencies and morbid fanaticism. That the Word of God is not only the sole authority in matters of faith and conduct, but also the sole means of all the regenerative influences of the Holy Spirit, has been properly called the "formal principle of the Reformation." And when we notice how intimately this principle is associated with the precious truth of faith and certainty, we can understand that this is no exaggeration. The crowning point of our teaching is that we can be certain of our salvation. But this glorious certainty can be and remain our possession only with a proper view and use of the means of grace.

If He, the Spirit of grace and truth, condescends to use the means of grace, what shall we say of ungrateful mortals who disdain to employ them for their own spiritual enrichment? No wonder they are without certainty of salvation. Their uncertainty reflects a misuse or neglect of the ordained means, even as it reflects fundamental misconceptions of saving grace or justifying faith. For, as we have repeatedly stressed, the certainty of salvation is a touchstone. It touches, tries, and tests the purity of men's view of these essentials. If they deny that a Christian can and should be certain of salvation, it is because they entertain false conceptions of faith and grace. If they are in continuous doubt and uncertainty, it is because the precious means, whose mighty purpose is to "bear witness" and make us sure that in Christ we have eternal life, are being kept from their hearts.

May this touchstone, whenever applied to us, individually or denominationally, show forth the gold of doctrinal purity!

II

Christian Assurance, a Treasure to be Safeguarded

A. A FAITHFUL REGARD FOR THE PROMISE OF GRACE

Of Abraham, the father of all them that believe, Scripture says: "He staggered not at the promise of God through unbelief, but was strong in faith . . . and fully persuaded" (Rom. 4:20-21). True, everything earthly seemed to militate against his assurance. All the arguments of sense, reason, and experience which often support a man's hope were against him. His feelings, his senses, his physical condition and that of Sarah, his wife, belied all hope of becoming the father of many nations. Yet, "against hope, he believed in hope." He was "not weak in faith, but strong in faith." He was "fully persuaded," a term which metaphorically implies that he was like a ship coming into harbor under full sail, fearing no wind, dreading no storm, sure of making port, carried on with unwavering assurance. Wonderful confidence and certainty of Abraham! How did he acquire, and amid so many vicissitudes preserve, this treasure? Answer: "He staggered not at the promises of God." He did not dispute them. He did not admit argument or debate as to the truthfulness of the promises. Great as they were, he did not stumble at them, but continued to venture all upon them. Has my God said it? That settles it; He cannot lie! Thus, with faithful regard for the promises, Abraham kept his treasure of certainty!

It is true, of course, that the promises themselves are staggering to our reason. That the infinite Creator should regard us finite, sinful creatures with such favor as to send us a Savior, atone for our sins, declare us forgiven, bring us to faith, grant us His Spirit, keep us in grace, and, having predestinated us, at last translate us to glory—all without our merit—is a promise so astounding that the human mind easily stumbles at it. Unbelief says, It cannot be. Sense and feeling dwell on the difficulties and seeming impossibilities. They stagger at the promises, not because they are so small and ordinary, but because they are so astonishingly great and glorious. Yet they are not too good to be true; they are too good not to be true. Their transcendent greatness ought to be recognized as a proof that they originated not in the little heart of man, but in the illimitable soul of God. He gave them; He inspired their writing. Nor have all the centuries of furious skepticism been able to uncover the slightest reason to discredit them. Neither will ages to come, however blasphemous their pretension may be. Heaven and earth shall pass away, but not the promises of divine grace.

"This," St. Augustine comments, "God has said, this He has promised. Is that not enough for you, then listen, this God has also sworn to." "As I live, saith the Lord God" (Ezek. 33:11). "Verily, verily, I say unto you, He that heareth My Word and believeth on Him that sent Me hath everlasting life and shall not come into condemnation, but is passed from death unto life" (John 5:24). By a greater than Himself the Lord cannot swear. And being an oath for confirmation (Heb. 6:16-18), ought that not put an end to all strife, doubt and questioning of this matter in our hearts? Says St. John, "He that believeth not God hath made Him a liar" (I John 5:10); and in his characteristic way Luther adds, "Yea, not only a liar, but also a perjurer!" Divinely inspired, oath-bound promises of grace God Himself has given as the depository for the safeguarding of the priceless treasury of certainty.

This, however, must not only be acknowledged in theory, but also carried out in practice. There are still timid souls in the Church who trouble themselves night and day with the question: "Am I really forgiven? Is the grace of Christ also mine? Am I an elect child of God? Will I really persevere and obtain eternal life?" Such thoughts, not infrequent among Christians, can poison the whole spirit, because they arise from the common but dangerous fallacy of ignoring the promises. We can and should be sure of our salvation with all it implies: redemption, justification, election, perseverance, and eternal glory; very sure, without ascending into heaven; unmistakably sure, without a special revelation; positively sure through the written Gospel promises of universal grace. These promises are written to settle the matter and make us a thousand times surer than if our names with all initials were printed among the elect in the Bible, surer than if our spirits were drawn out of the body and translated for a few days into the third heaven.

We are all, of course, more or less subject to moods of depression. Days come upon us when our spirit languishes, and in our desolation we may be inclined to sigh: "If only I felt different; if I could have some feeling of elation and feel my Savior near, then I would be certain of salvation." Where is the Christian who has not sometime felt like the man who on Monday went to his pastor with the sore complaint: "Yesterday I was filled with joy in the service, but now all is gone and I do not know what to do. All is dark as night." But this minister with more than psychiatric insight said: "I am glad!" "Glad?" asked the astonished man, "Glad? What do you mean?" "Yesterday," was the answer, "God gave you joy, and today He sees you are resting on your emotions instead of on the promises of Christ." He understood that our feelings are like the weather; they change from time to time. Moods come upon us so unexpectedly that they have been called "our subjective climate." And it is well to remember that the mental depressions which strike us so often after periods of elation, have multiple causes—largely physical, such as the exhaustion of the neurones. Nor ought we regard such gloomy spells as positive indicators of our spiritual state. We must learn to disregard our moods and rise above our feelings, whatever they may be, to throw ourselves, as Luther once said, "blindly upon God's evangelical promises." Our rock is God's promise, and it is not the rock which ebbs and flows, but the sea of our feelings and emotions. Would we even in our lowest moments safeguard our certainty and keep it, then let us not listen to the unstable testimony of inward emotions, but to His clear, written words of grace. "Be my feelings what they will, Jesus' promise I have still." Like Abraham, hold to, and stagger not at, the promises.

It is true that from the crucibles of adversity has often emerged a purer and stronger faith. But we dare not overlook that affliction is also used by Satan to assail a Christian's confidence. Not infrequently sorrow comes like a bolt out of the blue, smiting us to the very earth in an awful shock of grief and shaking our faith to its very foundations. Such experiences try the innermost soul and wring from the heart the bitter cry: "Where is now my God? Where is His mercy?" And since all of us are liable to meet such temptations, it is well to consider in advance what is to be done in those moments of affliction to safeguard our inner certainty of salvation.

It is well to remember the example of the dear Christian girl who when facing death was asked, "Are you not afraid?" and in answer pointed to the Bible at her side and said: "No, for you see, I have Christ there!" Like Abraham, stagger not at the promises of God.

O brethren, have any among us been in Doubting Castle? Have any of our dear ones been beaten and plagued by Giant Despair? Let us tell them: there is no need to suffer longer. There is a key that unlocks the dungeon doors. It is the key of God's promises. Take that blessed key, unlock the dungeon door, leave the gloomy haunts of sadness, come into the daylight splendor, up into the Delectable Mountains of Trust, Confidence, and Certainty, where the Good Shepherd will make you to lie down in green pastures, lead you beside still waters, restore your soul and bring you at last to dwell in the House of the Lord forevermore!

B. A CAREFUL DISTINCTION BETWEEN LAW AND GOSPEL

To preserve the treasure of Christian certainty, there is another important factor demanding our attention. That is a careful distinction and proper application of the Law and the Gospel. Anxious that hearers be not "subverted," but strengthened in their faith, St. Paul admonished Timothy, the young preacher: "Study to show thyself approved unto God, a workman that needeth not to be ashamed, rightly dividing the Word of Truth" (II Tim. 2:15). Study, he says, not to secure a degree in philosophy and gain the plaudits of men, but study to divide correctly the Word of Truth, which consists of both Law and Gospel. Not that minister needs to be ashamed who is without a college degree, but that preacher who cannot or will not properly divide the Law and the Gospel. Such a one is not approved of God, because by his confusion and misapplication of the two, precious souls will be deprived of the treasure of certainty. Also in cultivating and cherishing the certainty of our salvation, it is vital to speak the terrors of the Law to whom terrors belong and to speak Gospel comfort to whom comfort belongs. The Word of Truth must be rightly divided, expounded, and applied.

It would, therefore, involve a tragic misapplication to treat all cases suffering from uncertainty of salvation alike. Whether we are dealing with our own hearts or that of someone entrusted to our care, it is of utmost importance to look to the cause of the uncertainty. An attempt must be made to peer beneath the surface and ferret out the actual reason. If the uncertainty arises out of a growing carnal security, that is, out of an irregular use of the means of grace, or a careless, worldly, and unspiritual life, it would be wrongly dividing the Word of Truth to apply the Gospel. What is needed is the Law, such as St. Paul's admonition: "Examine yourselves whether ye be in faith; prove your own selves" (II Cor. 13:5). But, if the uncertainty arises out of the fears of a guilty conscience, it would be nothing short of disastrous to apply the Law. What, then, is needed is the unadulterated Gospel without the slightest admixture of the Law, stressing the objective justification and the universal grace, telling that "where sin abounded, grace did much more abound" (Rom. 5:20). Only when we observe this distinction in dealing with our own or others' uncertainty, can the true certainty of salvation be cultivated and preserved.

Dr. Walther, in his *Gesetz und Evangelium*, relates an enlightening experience of his own. As a young student, deeply concerned about his soul's salvation, he was greatly taken up with the pietistic writings of Fresenius. To an older candidate he remarked that Fresenius had it all over Luther. Though the candidate was an arch-pietist, *that* was a little too much for him. "Yet I in my blindness," says Walther, "meant it sincerely. Luther speaks only and always of faith. But Fresenius, that is the man who gives a recipe, following which I can be cured. And I can assure you, I carried out his rules of praying, watching, and reading conscientiously, but I was not cured; I only became more miserable, more despondent." That is always the result when anxious souls are offered an abbreviated Gospel, hemmed in and hedged about by all manner of precepts and conditions. To the aroused, concerned sinner there must be no more preaching of the demands and threats of the Law, no talk of agonizing and wrestling in prayer as though these were a means of achieving certainty, no mention of the necessity of experiencing special sweet feelings of grace before one can be sure of his salvation, but only the glad tidings that God for Christ's sake has forgiven and already declared him just. Any admixture of precept and works would destroy rather than upbuild in his heart the certainty of salvation.

Still, it would be equally disastrous for a minister to operate on the idea that believers do not need the Law. The Antinomian spirit, which holds that the Law must not be preached to a congregation of Christians because it will only tend to make people uncertain about their salvation, is still abroad in the world. If we are to make people certain, some may argue, then we must present nothing but the Gospel and say nothing about the threats of the Law. But as the fathers have often retorted, a preacher who would pursue that method must first provide himself with members who are impeccable. This he cannot do. All Christians, including himself, are still weighted with the flesh, that old nature which is constantly inclined to self-righteousness, pride, carnal security, and worldliness. It is in continuous need of the Law. To withhold the applications of the Law from our old Adam would be giving false comfort. It would be encouraging carnal security. And carnal security is something radically different from a believer's certainty of salvation. It is a self-confident, arrogant spurning of God's favor, a self-reliance and not a Christ-reliance, the very opposite of justifying faith. It is not of the new man, but of the old. And he it is that needs the Law. A Christian, therefore, who resents the preaching of the Law and will not let himself be warned is himself contributing to the destruction of his faith and certainty of salvation. Likewise, a preacher who will not warn and admonish in the manner of the Apostles, "Work out your own salvation with fear and trembling" (Phil. 2:12), is unfaithful in his office. By not rightly dividing the Word of Truth he becomes a soul plunderer, stealing away the priceless treasure of certainty.

Indeed, the careful and correct distinction and application of Law and Gospel cannot be emphasized too strongly in its relation to our subject. When we think how easily souls may be prevented from attaining certainty or how readily they may be deprived of it through a careless, unprepared presentation and division of the Word of Truth, all of us who are leaders in the Church have reason to exercise care and engage in study. Best of all is the counsel of Dr. Walther: "All this you must finally note for your own souls. Divide and apply the Law and Gospel rightly to yourselves. Use the Law with the purpose of being and remaining poor sinners, and condemn every work of your own which in sanctification you still do by inner compulsion. Seek, moreover, to warm your heart at the fire of divine love in Christ Jesus." Then, by God's grace we shall walk in newness of life and hold the treasure of certainty. Nor shall we fail in our counseling of souls with regard to this priceless gift.

C. A DILIGENT STRIVING AFTER GODLINESS

The exhortation of St. Peter (II, 1:10): "Make your calling and election sure," gives unmistakable confirmation of this. Its context shows that before and after the apostle impresses upon the Christians the importance of sanctification, both in performing good works and in avoiding the evil. "Give diligence," he writes, "to add to your faith, virtue; and to virtue, knowledge; and to knowledge, temperance; and to temperance, patience; and to patience, godliness; and to godliness, brotherly kindness; and to brotherly kindness, charity. For if these things be in you and abound, they make you that you shall neither be barren nor unfruitful in the knowledge of our Lord Jesus Christ. But he that lacketh these things is blind and cannot see afar off and hath forgotten that he was purged from his old sins. Wherefore, the rather, brethren, give diligence to make your calling and election sure; for if ye do these things, ye shall never fall."

Doing what things? Adding to our faith, striving after godliness. This will make us sure of our salvation. These good works will make us certain of our calling, election, and perseverance not, of course, in the sense that they will merit God's grace for us, but in the sense that they will serve us as witnesses of the faith and Spirit in us. They cannot make God sure; for to Him it is sure; but they can make *us* sure. The more we abound in the fruits of righteousness, the greater will be our certainty. The more barren we are, the greater will be our uncertainty. Hence the admonition: safeguard your certainty, make your calling and election sure, by a diligent striving after godliness.

It is well, however, to distinguish, as our fathers have done, that "sanctification is not the foundation, but the witness of our certainty." The Apology (Art. III, § 155; *Triglot*, p. 199) calls the good works of a believer *signa et testimonia*, signs and testimonies, of the forgiveness of sins. While faith itself—the positive consent of our hearts to the Gospel promises—is the *direct, inner* witness of the Holy Spirit, all the visible, noticeable fruits of faith, such as love of God, desire for His Word, kindness to our fellow man, hatred of sin, avoidance of evil, are the *indirect*, external witness of the Spirit. These are what Dr. F. Pieper has called the evidences of a second order (*zweiter Ordnung*), that "the Holy Ghost has begun the good work in us and will perform it until the day of Jesus Christ." Though our certainty of salvation does not rest upon them, we are to regard them as signs and proofs that we are in a state of grace.

It is true, of course, that periods of trial may come when the Christian is so harassed by doubt and dejection that he cannot view them as such. His best works may appear vile to him. In such perplexity the Christian soul must naturally be referred back to the objective promises of God's universal grace in Christ Jesus. But, for all of that, the importance of this secondary witness dare not be overlooked. Good works are to be wrought, cultivated, and re-garded as a powerful witness of "the Holy Spirit of God whereby we are sealed (made certain) unto the day of redemption" (Eph. 4:30).

If, then, we prove our faith in Christ by heeding His will; if we hate the things that displease Him; if we love the things He loves; if we are desirous of adding to our faith temperance, patience, brotherly kindness, charity; if we, for His sake, avoid the old sins from which He has purged us, and if we are repentant, when through the weakness of our flesh it happens that we grieve Him; then let us not hesitate to take that as a witness of the Spirit that we are called, elect children of God. In fact, that is a witness a million times stronger than if we saw our names and addresses recorded in the Holy Book, better than if a thunderous voice from heaven declared us to be chosen. And even if our hearts were desolate and cried nothing but: Lost, lost, you are lost, and we would experience something of the chilling terror of the damned—still we can and should be able to say: It is not true. Through Christ, who has not only justified but also sanctified us, we are sure that we are His called and elect children.

On the other hand, if there is in our life no evidence of sanctification, no striving after godliness, no attempt to add to our faith, no purging ourselves from the old sins, no love of God and the Savior, no desire for His Word, only a cold lip service, and no effort to keep separate from the world—we can be sure that any claim we make to the certainty of being saved is a delusion.

Any pretensions we make about being sure of our salvation, while we consciously continue in sin, will come to a sorry end. And even if on a bright day we would see an angel in celestial glory coming to us with the announcement: "Behold, I bring you tidings of great joy, You are a child and heir of heaven; it is certain you will never fall"—we can be sure that is not Gabriel, but Satan in disguise. Away with such certainty that would let us continue in sin! That was never the design of God's Word. On the contrary, it declares: "He that saith, I know Him and keepeth not His commandments is a liar and the truth is not in him" (I John 2:4).

III

Christian Assurance, a Dynamic for Christian Living

A. THE DYNAMIC OF CHRISTIAN WORSHIP

How true this is may be seen, first of all, in the matter of *worship*. To praise God, to pray, sing, and give thanks at home and in the congregation is a vital part of the Christian life. Its omission is a major spiritual tragedy. The decline of true, genuine, regular worship on the part of members is one of the Church's most vexing problems. What can be done to reinstitute the custom of family worship? What can inspire Christians to a more devoted prayer life? What remedy can be applied to the ever-growing callousness toward transgressions of the Third Commandment, neglect of the divine services, and indifference to public worship? What can be done to develop congregations that worship in spirit and in truth, joyously and eagerly?

The Scriptures give the answer repeatedly, but not more strikingly than in St. Paul's exhortation "to teach and admonish one another in psalms and hymns and spiritual songs, singing with grace in your hearts unto the Lord" (Col. 3:16). This apostolic counsel is prefaced with the remark: "Let the Word of Christ dwell in you richly in all wisdom." The Word of Christ is the Gospel of grace. Not as a servant but as a master this is to "dwell," or "keep house," in our hearts, constraining and impelling us to sing with grace unto the Lord. "With grace" means by the help and power of divine grace. Hearts that are made sure of grace by the Word of Christ possess the only real incentive to genuine worship. And the more certain believers are of their salvation in Christ Jesus, the more spontaneous and sincere, the more ardent and faithful will be their adoration of God. Certainty is the dynamic.

Last year (1944) the Director of the American Institute of Public Opinion, George Gallup, published a religious survey under the heading: "Americans Believe in God, but Millions Skip Church." His inquiries revealed that while ninety-six per cent of those questioned believed in God, forty-two per cent had not attended a religious service within a month. This supports the contention that a theoretical faith in God does not make regular, devout churchgoers. A mere lip acknowledgment of the existence of a deity does not move the heart to joyous praise and adoration. Something more is needed. Would we like to see our churches regularly crowded with eager, zealous worshipers, we dare not content ourselves with convincing them of God's existence; we must strive through the Scriptural means to make them sure of God's grace. True, there must be no withholding of the Law with its scathing denunciations of the church despisers and worship neglecters, but it must be realized that the Law can give them no power to love God's house and sing His praises there. With the Word of Christ we must wisely and prayerfully lead them out from under the Law into the realm of grace. With unmitigated zeal we must combat their doubts and make them certain that God for Christ's sake has forgiven and justified them. The surer they are of this, the more faithful will be their attendance at public and private worship. Then will they "enter in His gates with thanksgiving, and into his courts with praise."

Speaking of worship, however, it needs to be noted that Protestantism of our day is being swept by a trend toward ritualism. By some this tendency is viewed with alarm; by others it is hailed as an advance; among us there is no dispute about the value of an orderly, reverent, dignified service. Yet in the present trend toward order and form it is well to be constantly reminding ourselves that ritualism, at its best, is only a medium through which religious impulses are expressed; it is not the impulse itself. The settings, however appropriate, the music, be it ever so stately, the choirs, the vestments, the architecture, the arrangements, the postures, the bowings and bendings, even if they be in line with Scriptural truth and usage, are not a dynamic for true Christian worship. A service may be very solemn, and still not truly spiritual. Another may be crude, "without form and void," and still be a genuine adoration of God. Incessant care must be exercised that our people do not mistake a feeling of mysticism artificially created by ritualistic externals for genuine, wholehearted worship. A burning candle on the altar cannot set naturally cold hearts aglow with the fervor of true praise. What can? Only one thing, the certainty of salvation.

And how could it be otherwise! Looking into our own spiritual experiences, let us ask, When has our worship of God been most ardent and sincere? Has it not been in those hours when we were most certain of our salvation in Christ Jesus? What! I, a wretched sinner, willful and ungrateful, meriting no particle of grace, am completely absolved by the Almighty, cleansed by the Redeemer, predestined to eternal life, and now, above all this, am commanded by His illimitable goodness to be sure that when I close my eyes in death I will see no condemnation, but only blessedness and glory without end? Ah, then let come what may; though seasons of sorrow may lie ahead, my soul will again and again break forth in exultation, to sing with grace in my heart unto the Lord!

B. THE DYNAMIC OF CHRISTIAN SERVICE

But worship is only a part of the Christian's life; another, inseparably linked to it, is *service*. To honor the Savior with Christian graces, to advance His cause with selfless deeds of charity, is the God-appointed aim of the disciples. Yet all quarters of Christendom are bewailing the inertia, the passivity, and the serious unconcern of professing Christians toward all forms of welldoing. What can be done, they cry, to re-activate that huge preponderance of church members now retarding and almost annihilating the efforts of the faithful few? What can empower even these to make a more conscious and consistent effort to grace their lives with the meekness, patience, firmness, and other virtues of Christ? What can fan the fires of consecration and induce the young as well as the old to lay down their lives, their talents, their money, upon the altar of Christian world service?

We answer, with Scripture: the certainty of salvation. That is the needed dynamic. After restating that men are not saved by their works, but are made heirs of eternal life by the justification of grace, St. Paul tells the young preacher Titus (3:8): "This is a faithful saying, and these things I will that thou affirm constantly that they which have believed in God might be careful to maintain good works." So grace, justification were to be Titus' ever-repeated sermon themes. By "constantly affirming" these, his hearers were to be made sure of their salvation. And the greater their certainty, the greater would be their care and desire to maintain good works. Certainty was to be the dynamic. And it was.

Proscribed Christianity of the first centuries witnessed an amazing expansion in the Roman Empire. The little group of believers shed an influence that still stands as a marvel in history. Their holy daring, their fearless witness-bearing, their sacrificial living and dying for the cause of Christ belong to the most thrilling stories of the Church. And in analyzing the reasons of their zealous and successful efforts, even Edward Gibbon, the historian, has come rather near the secret. He mentions, among others, their unshakable confidence in immortal life. Their hearts were so sure of God's grace and so attached to His heaven that it was easy for them to renounce the plaudits of this world and render with joy the difficult, heroic services those pagan days required.

Is it not laughable, therefore, when some of our moderns tell us with an air of superior social consciousness that the Church of today must be more interested in earthly tenements than in heavenly mansions, and that for its own expansion and reconsecration it must preach a Gospel of social security rather than of spiritual certainty? Nothing could be farther from the truth. Those who sneer at St. Paul's "faithful saying" of grace and refuse to affirm it constantly to the assurance of their hearers are divesting the Church of its great Scriptural and historic dynamic. They are cutting the throat of Christian service. They are thwarting the very end they boast to accomplish. As Luther once said: "You must have heaven and be already saved before you can do good works; the good works do not earn heaven, nay, just the contrary,—it is heaven, given to you by God's grace that does the good works" (St. L. XII:136).

Also stewardship secretaries and finance officers, grappling with the ever-wearying problem of raising funds for the Kingdom needs, must keep this in mind. Justly they lament the fact that still two thirds of the Church's membership has little learned the art of Christian giving. Though, often, the situation is desperate, they refuse to become professional promoters with devices and gadgets that are a scandal to the cause of Christ. To develop methods, plans, and systems that do not infringe upon Scriptural principles is their duty. But the machinery itself has no power. As someone has said: "Bluff a man into giving, and you subtract fifty per cent from his next gift. But convince him of God's love and make him certain of his salvation, and you add one hundred per cent to the second and one thousand per cent to his tenth contribution."

On the base of a little white phosphorescent cross appears the instruction: "If you want it to shine, keep it in the sunlight!" Never does that little emblem glow with such brilliance in the dark room, as when it has stood all day in the rays of the sun. Nor will our congregations shine brightly, glorifying the Father with good works, unless we keep them in the sunlight of Christian certainty. This must be our aim. Of this doctrine we must not be afraid. In our certainty of salvation we must glory. It is God's dynamic for Christian service.

C. CHRISTIAN SEPARATION

But it is well to observe that the same is true of what we may call *Christian separation,* a separation which the Scriptures commend to the believers in the word: "Come out from among them, and be ye separate . . . and touch not the unclean thing."

"The grace of God," writes St. Paul, "that bringeth salvation hath appeared to all men, teaching us that denying ungodliness and worldly lusts we should live soberly, righteously, and godly in this present world" (Titus 2:11-12). Grace teaches that; saving grace, universal grace educates the soul effectually to separate itself from the sinful practices and philosophies of the world. A life of separation is, in other words, made possible by the certainty of salvation. Contrary to popular opinion, Christian assurance is not a license to sensual liberty. Making the heart sure of God's love, forgiveness, and salvation, is a check to licentiousness. It causes the love of God to displace the lust of the world. Also here, certainty is the dynamic.

Over eighty per cent of children and young people in our country are gazing upon scenes of filth and social sewage poured out by the vulgar worldly press and cinema. They are fed on utterly false and distorted views of moral conduct. They are confronted with viciously conflicting patterns of behavior, with the result that their sense of wrongdoing is dulled and their hearts are fired with the lure of the world. Round about the standards of moral decency, modesty, and purity have been blasted away. And to keep our youth from throwing themselves into the world's wild delirium of indulgence—what a task! "Who is sufficient for this?" Where is the youth counselor, pastor, parent, or teacher who does not tremble at this social problem? To cope with it, a flood of printed counsel has been poured upon the market. Institutes of juvenile research, staffed with experts, have been founded for the more acute cases. Occasionally a lonely voice is raised against the commercialization of amusements which places the door receipts above the moral welfare of the young. Nor need we frown upon these well-intentioned efforts. We ourselves dare not swim with the stream, but must brave the tidal wave of worldliness. With unwearying devotion to the young we must continue to lecture, preach, and warn against all the apparent and not so apparent forms of ungodliness. But if that is all that we can do, we might as well confess defeat. For in all the lectures of the Law there is no power to give new life and to change hearts.

We must remember that the protests and denunciations of the Law, while they have their place, cannot rescue the young from the encircling waters of worldly lusts. Any plan of education or youth counseling that does not incessantly aim to bring and keep the young on the solid ground of Christian certainty is doomed to failure. Only as the youthful hearts become sure of God's infinite love and mercy to them in Christ Jesus, will they have power to resist the vicious worldly influences about them. It is the certainty of being saved for the better, perfect world above that weakens affection for this godless world below. If we, the adult members in the Church, and above all, their parents in the home would but consistently show ourselves absolutely and unshakably certain of divine love, grace, salvation, and heaven, our children would have an invincible encouragement to give their hearts to things spiritual, and so overcome the strong lure of things material.

Here we are brought face to face with an essential cause of youth's inordinate attachment to the world. The youth problem is an adult problem. Children and young people get to see all too little spiritual certainty, and, as a consequence, all too much wanton worldliness— in their elders. Much more quickly than we imagine do they perceive whether their parents' affections are set on things in heaven or on things on earth. Youth has a strangely acute faculty for sensing the presence or absence of genuine spiritual qualities in its seniors. And what is it sensing at present? There is no need here to enter upon that which is so commonly known. It is "the materialism of middle age," remarked an eminent minister, "which appears as our greatest danger." Everywhere also in our homes and circles among the middle-aged and even the older, the encroachments of the world are discernible, not necessarily in the pursuit of flagrant lusts, but chiefly in a tremendous overemphasis on the frivolous side of life, the love of luxury and ease to the neglect of consecrated spiritual activity. How easily even the love of blameless things of earth can stifle the spiritual life! What an enemy of the Spirit is the love of the world! How shall we march and fight against this rabid foe?

There is no question that we must continue to inveigh with righteous candor against the lusts of the world. There is constant need of diagnosing the cancer and catching it in its earliest stages. But thereby we are not removing or healing it. We are giving no power to overcome it. If we want to pry men's souls loose from this earth, we must bind their hearts to heaven. We must preach "the certainty of salvation." This is the dynamic. This will make them "otherworldly." This will free them and us from lusts that should never get even the countenance of our toleration, to say nothing of our indulgence. This will clear our vision of this day's impassioned pursuit after things unworthy of our dear Redeemer.

D. CHRISTIAN STEADFASTNESS

In concluding, however, it is profitable to observe that certainty of salvation, as a dynamic for Christian living, also creates true *steadfastness*. To endure affliction without murmuring, to suffer persecution without yielding, to face opponents without compromising, to meet death without shrinking—is an ideal set before us with many words of Scripture. "Be ye steadfast, unmovable" (I Cor. 15:58). "Blessed is the man that endureth temptation" (James 1:12). Yet our flesh rebels against this; our reason stumbles at it. Trials and temptations appear unnecessary and intolerable. To our old nature loyal endurance is impossible. What, then, can make it possible? What can embolden us to be steadfast in adversity as well as prosperity?

Look to the man who gloried in his infirmities—St. Paul, the Apostle who was "in labors more abundant, in stripes above measure, in prisons more frequent, in deaths oft." Reference to his sufferings on behalf of the Gospel he makes also in his final letter to Timothy. Even while writing this Epistle, he lay in prison, awaiting a martyr's death, knowing that the time of his departure was at hand. But does he wail and moan? Does he look back upon life's course with regret? Does he now tremble, begin to vacillate, and think of compromise? Not he. "I am not ashamed," he writes. Not chagrined, not regretful, even though his executioner might be sharpening the ax. And why? Because, he explained in holy triumph, "I know whom I have believed and am persuaded that He is able to keep that which I have committed unto Him against that day" (II Tim. 1:12). Oh, the power of Christian certainty! What triumphs over fear, what victories over cowardice, what boldness, firmness, steadfastness it gives!

Not long ago a youthful layman said: "Pastor, you hardly know the terrific pressure that is daily brought upon us to deny our faith!" The minister agreed, but at the same time he thought, I wonder how many members of the church realize what cunning and no less potent influences are at work to deter the pastors from faithful Scriptural teaching and practice? For both clergy and laity the pressure is increasing. Who is the man among them that can stand fast beneath the withering crossfire of mockery, ridicule, scorn, hatred and the countless other forms devised to shake their faith and riddle their character? Answer: It is the man who, like Paul, is sure of the salvation of his soul and its preservation to eternal life! It is the man of certainty, who says in his inmost soul: "I know whom I have believed and am persuaded that He is able to keep." Sure that his eternal destiny is lodged with the best Trustee, Christ Jesus, certain that he is the redeemed, justified, elect child of God—what does he care what men will do unto him? With his certainty of God's grace, he is the one who is dwelling in the secret place of the tabernacle of the Most High; he, of a truth, is in the pavilion of the Almighty. And though all the world be in arms against him, he is in perfect peace. Though a host rise up against him, he is not dismayed. He is no cringing, fawning timeserver, who bends like the willow. He is an oak that can stand the storm. Do friends despise and forsake, because of his quiet, but firm adherence to the truths of God, and does a universal hiss come up against him from the world about —he does not yield but says to himself: "*I* compromise my principles? *I* change my doctrines? *I* lay aside my Biblical views? *I* hide what I believe to be true? No, never! Since I know and am sure God's grace is upon me, His love is about me; His heaven reserved for me, in the teeth of all men shall I speak and act God's truth." Indeed, nothing makes the Christian so bold, firm, and serene even amid dread opposition as this blessed certainty.

On the eighteenth day of February (1946) it was exactly four hundred years that our revered Dr. Martin Luther closed his eyes in death. That we possess the precious truth of Christian certainty is, under God, a result of his rediscovery of it. Having unearthed this priceless treasure, he never ceased to proclaim it. His writings, in essays, sermons, hymns, and expositions, still stand as an incontrovertible witness to the fact that a Christian can and should be certain of his salvation. And that he himself rejoiced in this assurance cannot be denied. It was this that gave character to his monumental life. This was the dynamic of his unflagging zeal, his consecrated boldness, his iron steadfastness.

Nor did it fail him in the fight against the last dread enemy—death. For some days previous he had felt its approach. Repeated attacks of dizziness and pain kept him in a state of expectancy, but not alarm. His composure and even his good humor did not leave him. "Oh, how ill I am," he exclaimed a few hours before to Jonas, "I feel I shall remain in Eisleben, where I was born and baptized." Medicines were of no avail. For a while his attendants rejoiced that some warm applications had caused him to break out in a sweat. But he cherished no delusions. "It is the cold sweat of death; I shall yield up my spirit," he said, but not gloomily. For in the same breath he gave thanks aloud to God, who had revealed to him His Son. "Take my poor soul into Thy hands," he prayed. "Although I must leave this body, I *know* that I shall ever be with Thee." No moaning, no sadness here, because he had the certainty of Paul. He knew whom he had believed and was persuaded that He was able to keep that which was committed unto Him against that day.

"Reverend Father," said his weeping friends, "wilt thou stand by Christ and the doctrine thou hast preached?" "Yes," was the dying answer, the last words of those lips which have so eloquently preached to us—the certainty of salvation!

Steadfast unto the end!

XIII

Prayer

THE current conflict has again focused the attention of thinking people upon prayer. Stories emanating from foxholes, naval vessels, lifeboats, and planes reveal experiences that rival some of the miraculous answers recorded in the Bible.

These must have jolted the brain-centered intellectuals who in ponderous language spoke of prayer as "spasm of words sent into cosmic indifference"; "a voice projected into a silent world from which comes no answer"; "a great delusion."

They brought uncomfortable moments to the so-called liberals who in disdain rejected the authority of the Scriptures and then, with superior insight, proceeded to build a view gained from the sciences, such as physics, anthropology, and history. What was the result? The miracle of the tower of Babel was repeated: they spoke in different tongues. Prayer itself was so distorted that it resembled some of the dizzy creations of modern art. Most of the writers restricted its sphere so that its purpose is to "discover the divinity within ourselves," "to call our own resources into play," "to throw open the doors and windows of the soul to the gracious influences which stream in from the life and light of God."

Many professing Christians must have made the startling discovery that they had been strangers to the power of prayer. For them it had been a part of a mechanical routine, an emergency measure, a fire escape to which they ran in the hour of need.

But also the most devout Christian must have sensed that he had but touched the periphery of an amazing glory. Greater things lay ahead for those who had the faith to venture deeper into its sanctuary.

For these reasons a restudy of prayer is timely. We shall travel

over ground that seems familiar, the Word of God and synodical
essays of bygone days. As we do, however, we may discover much
that has eluded us and emerge with a deeper appreciation of the
power of prayer than we have ever had before.

We therefore begin our task with the prayer:

O Thou by whom we come to God,
The Life, the Truth, the Way,
The path of prayer Thyself hast trod—
Lord, teach us how to pray.

WHAT IS PRAYER?

Thesis I

Prayer is a vital phase of Christian life.

Neither the Augsburg Confession nor the well-known Lutheran
theologian Baier in his *Dogmatics* treats prayer in a special section.

Does this mean that the Lutheran Church regards it as an incidental appendix to Christian doctrine? Not at all. Whatever their
reason for assigning to it a seemingly unimportant position, the men
who wrote these historic documents lived and worked in the atmosphere of prayer and knew it intimately as an indispensable working
force.

The Word of God reveals that the doctrine of prayer is an
essential part of divine revelation, in which all truths are so interrelated and interdependent that one cannot disregard or distort one
phase without affecting the pattern. Yes, all divine truths touch it at
some point and determine its character and value.

The Bible breathes the spirit of prayer and reveals it in action in
the history it records. In it, at every turn, one sees children of men
with eyes upturned to the skies.

The patriarch, expectantly looking forward to the coming of the
promised Woman's Seed, gathers his own about the altar under the
skies. He offers a sacrifice. He prays. Moses, the statesman of God,
bearing the crushing responsibility of leading a homeless people
through the desert to the Promised Land, pleads for divine guidance
and support through ever-recurring crises. David, the obscure shepherd, the king-elect, the exile, the ruler, the disillusioned and
restored sinner, in his psalms takes us into a scope of prayer un-

dreamed of by many. Daniel in a strange land risks his future as a scientist and statesman, yes, life itself, by kneeling three times a day before a window that faces toward the Holy City. Saul, thwarted in his murderous career by the vision near the gates of Damascus, having by the grace of God found in Jesus of Nazareth his Lord and Savior, prays. Blinded, he now learns to see; crushed to the ground, he rises to enter a career that will take him through conflict and persecution to unrivaled achievements in the kingdom of God.

Above all, Jesus, man's Substitute, placed under the Law, exemplified the meaning of prayer. The desert and the mountaintop stood by in reverence as He time and again broke their midnight silence with prayer. Bearing the weight of mankind's sin, He poured out His burdened soul and drew on an inexhaustible source of power. As a result the face that on the evening before bore the lines of fatigue returned to the disciples in the morning radiant with joy and strength. The latter in amazement therefore pleaded, "Lord, teach us to pray."

All of this leads Luther to say that "what the pulse is to the physical life, that prayer is to the spiritual life; to cease to pray means to cease being a Christian." Dr. Walther, in *Gnadenjahr*, writes: "To be a true Christian and to pray are so inseparably united that a person cannot think of one without the other. As crying is the first sign of life in a newly born child, so prayer is the first sign of life in a reborn Christian. As soon as Saul was converted, we read of him, 'Behold, he prayeth'." Still another calls it "a thermometer of spiritual life."

Yes, prayer is a vital phase of Christian life. Through it a child of God gives expression to his many needs and his response to divine mercies. Conscious of his own utter unworthiness, he confesses his sins to his offended God and pleads for forgiveness. Facing life's tasks and experiences in a difficult and dangerous world, he implores Him who is his Refuge for help and sustaining strength. Lost in wonder as he beholds the miracles of divine power in nature, he praises. Noting how this power in goodness reaches out into the life of the smallest creature, he combines reverence and love with his praise and thus blesses his Maker. Seeing divine mercies stream into his own life, he thanks the Giver of all.

However, though prayer is essential, we must guard against the error of many Reformed theologians, who call it a means of grace.

They regard it as a means through which a wrestling soul gains the exhilarating feeling that he is converted, or through which a groping soul receives a supernatural revelation independent of the Word of God and the Sacraments.

This is contrary to Scripture. Nowhere does Scripture make man's salvation contingent upon his feelings. Job was a child of God, even though in the hour of greatest need he seemed to reach out in vain through the deepening gloom for the presence of God. Job 23:3, 8-10: "Oh, that I knew where I might find Him, that I might come even to His seat! Behold, I go forward, but He is not there; and backward, but I cannot perceive Him; on the left hand, where He doth work, but I cannot behold Him; He hideth Himself on the right hand that I cannot see Him." Then, with a faith that looks through appearances to the promises of God, he continues: "But He knoweth the way that I take; when He hath tried me, I shall come forth as gold."

As regards the second point, Scripture plainly points to the Word and the Sacraments as the means through which the Holy Ghost creates and sustains faith in man. Rom. 10:17: "So, then, faith cometh by hearing, and hearing by the Word of God." This revelation is adequate for all purposes of spiritual life. II Tim. 3:16, 17: "All Scripture is given by inspiration of God and is profitable for doctrine, for reproof, for correction, for instruction in righteousness, that the man of God may be perfect, throughly furnished unto all good works."

Lutheran theologians, distinguishing between the means of grace and prayer, speak of the one as the hands of God extended to man, and the other as the hands of man extended to God.

Thesis II

Prayer is commanded by God.

Samuel Johnson once was asked what he regarded as the strongest argument for prayer. He replied, "Sir, there is no argument for prayer." The famous writer's own practice as well as his recorded prayers showed what he meant. Many years before him Cicero wrote: "No tribe is so barbarous, no one of all peoples so fierce, that the idea of God has not filled the mind." He therefore calls prayer "a law of nature." The archaeologist, the anthropologist, and the historian confirm this. Thus the individual who sneers at prayer has broken with the religious view of the world, yes, with something that is inherent in his own nature, something that in the hour of need may break through his defense mechanisms and force him to his knees in tearful pleas.

But prayer has a firmer foundation than instinct.

I Chron. 16:11 we read: "Seek the Lord and His strength, seek His face continually."—This is a command.

Ps. 50:15: "Call upon Me in the day of trouble."—This is a command.

Matt. 7:7: "Ask, and it shall be given you; seek, and ye shall find; knock, and it shall be opened unto you."—This is a command.

Phil. 4:6: "In everything by prayer and supplication, with thanksgiving, let your requests be made known unto God."—This is a command.

So the Psalmist understood the Word of God. He therefore writes: "When Thou saidst, Seek ye My face; my heart said unto Thee, Thy face, Lord, will I seek" (Ps. 27:8).

The cumulative effect of these and many other passages induces Luther to write in the Large Catechism. "My prayer is as precious, holy, and pleasing to God as that of St. Paul or of the most holy saints. This is the reason: For I will gladly grant that he is holier in person, but not on account of the commandment; since God does not regard prayer on account of the person, but on account of His word and obedience thereto. For on the commandment on which all saints rest their prayer, I, too, rest mine." (*Triglot.* p. 701, 16.)

Thesis III

Prayer is endowed with promises of a faithful God, who "is able to do exceeding abundantly above all that we ask or think."

The command to pray is found in a setting of promises that amaze the believer who takes time to analyze and evaluate them.

John 16:23 we read: "Verily, verily, I say unto you, Whatsoever ye shall ask the Father in My name, He will give it you."

Ps. 91:15, 16: "He shall call upon Me, and I will answer him; I will be with him in trouble; I will deliver and honor him. With long life will I satisfy him and show him My salvation."

James 5:16b: "The effectual fervent prayer of a righteous man availeth much."

These promises, marvelous in character and scope, have as their guarantor Him of whom the Bible says (Heb. 10:23b): "He is faithful that promised." The Word of God, yes, the entire history of the human race, is an unbroken testimony to this fact.

, Add to this the consideration that these promises are an integral part of a covenant, a contract, of which God Himself assures us (Is. 54:10), "The mountains shall depart and the hills be removed; but My kindness shall not depart from thee, neither shall the covenant of My peace be removed, saith the Lord, that hath mercy on thee."

In the midst of these covenant-supported promises the inspired Apostle Paul places the Cross as the supreme guarantee when he writes (Rom. 8:32): "He that spared not his own Son but delivered Him up for us all, how shall He not with Him also freely give us all things?" What does that mean? Nothing less than this, that God in His infinite love has already presented the greatest gift in His possession, Him who was nearest and dearest to Him, His only-begotten Son. All that we have a right to expect on the basis of the promises made for this life and that which is to come is small in comparison with what we have already received.

Can God do more to reassure us?

But God is not only willing. He "is able to do exceeding abundantly above all that we ask or think" (Eph. 3:20). There are no limits to His power. No situation may arise that will defy His ability to help.

Many, however, question this. Among the objections that loom up most frequently in the discussion of the power of prayer is the following: The universe is under the control of fixed laws, representing the highest wisdom of the Creator. It is therefore presumptuous for me, an insignificant speck in this vast world, to suppose that through prayer I can induce God at some point to interfere with this world order to help me.

These critics pretend to know something which they cannot know within their present limitations. Perfect knowledge of the universe would be needed to declare that any phenomenon is opposed to its laws.

Their objection makes God a prisoner of His own creation. Still worse, it reduces Him to a mechanic who can do no more than watch the world operate as a machine in accordance with its own inherent laws, deaf to the cries of man, who time and again requires a help not possible within its ordinary processes.

As a matter of fact, Jesus has placed the term "Our Father" at the very entrance into the sanctuary of prayer. This term is the key to the character of God and the promises which He has made. Just what does that mean? Some of you delegates are business executives. As such you establish an order of the day. Let's imagine that your schedule calls for an important conference of departmental heads at 11 o'clock in the morning. You instruct your secretary to see to it that you are not disturbed. At 11:30 your secretary summons you to the telephone. It is a message from your wife. Your little son has been critically injured in an accident and is being rushed to a hospital. What happens? The business executive is forgotten. The father comes to the fore. The higher law of love overrules the lower law of business efficiency. You rush to the hospital in order to be at the bedside of your son and render whatever aid you can.

Such is God, only infinitely more so. As a result there is no story more intriguing than the story of prayer. Moses, David, Elijah, Daniel, Peter, John, Paul, and many others prayed. In answer the earth, the sea, the sky, the human body, the animal kingdom, yes, even death, suspended their laws. Nor has prayer lost any of its power since then. Luther through it called back to health two faithful co-workers, Melanchthon and Myconius, when they already had begun to walk through the valley of the shadow of death. August Hermann Francke in Halle, Germany, and George Mueller in Bristol, England, built institutions of mercy that are monuments to the miraculous power of Him who answers prayer. Add to this the story of our own prayerful lives, and we cannot do otherwise than face the critics with the undeniable truth: "God is able to do exceeding abundantly above all that we ask or think."

WHAT ARE THE ESSENTIAL CHARACTERISTICS OF PRAYER?

Posture is not of the essence of prayer. The paralyzed, the drowning, the troubled workman in the midst of the day's activities, may pray even though they may not conform to externals usually associated with prayer. Yet normally posture is important. The person who is really conscious of being in the presence of the Most High will somehow express his reverence. When the ancients lifted their hands toward heaven, they therewith dramatized their faith that all good gifts come from above. "Folding of hands in our day is an expression of trust and confidence in God, to whom, conscious of our own weakness, we surrender ourselves unconditionally. Some liturgists likewise point out that when the hands are folded, hands and fingers form the shape of a cross." (Meusel's *Handlexikon.*) Kneeling symbolizes humility in our approach to God.

The place is not vital to prayer. Usually we ought to pray in the setting of prayer, "the closet" (Matt. 6:6) or "the congregations" (Ps. 26:12). But when conditions do not permit this, faith may create a setting of prayer "everywhere" (I Tim. 2:8). Jacob's dream of the ladder must give to all of us the courage to turn the workshop, the sickroom, the sea, the desert, the mountaintop, the plane, the tank, into a house of God, a gateway to heaven.

Prayer has been defined as a conversation of a Christian with God. Yet the voice does not belong to its nature. It may be only "the soul's sincere desire, unuttered." But it may have the eloquence of a cry. When the Israelites were trapped between the Red Sea and the Egyptian army, God said to Moses: "Why criest thou unto Me?" And this, even though Moses is not reported to have spoken a single word.

The hymn writer aptly characterizes such prayer in the following lines:

> Prayer is the burden of a sigh,
> The falling of a tear,
> The upward glancing of an eye,
> When none but God is near.

What, then, is essential?

Thesis IV

Prayer, to be valid, must be offered to the Triune God in the name of Jesus.

In a broad sense any plea directed to a power supposedly higher than man may be regarded as prayer. The Word of God, however, definitely limits the term.

I Sam. 7:3 Samuel exhorts the house of Israel: "Prepare your hearts unto the Lord, and serve Him only."

Is. 42:8 God says: "I am the Lord; that is My name; and My glory will I not give to another, neither My praise to graven images."

No room here for worship of idols, no matter what their form or nature. But what about such vague terms as Supreme Being, the Great Spirit, the Architect of the Universe, the All-Father, terms which are designed to include God somehow, regardless of the concept of the person praying?

Let us see. The God of the Old Testament is invariably the Covenant God, who said to Abraham: "In thy seed shall all the nations of the earth be blessed" (Gen. 22:18 a). He is the God who promised the Messiah, whom Isaiah identifies in the startling prophecy "Unto us a Child is born, unto us a Son is given; and the government shall be upon His shoulder; and His name shall be called Wonderful, Counselor, The Mighty God, The Everlasting Father, The Prince of Peace" (Is. 9:6).

He is the God who has identified Himself in every passage that expressly teaches or implies the deity of Jesus Christ and of the Holy Ghost. He is the God who at the baptism of Jesus revealed Himself as Father, Son, and Holy Ghost. He is the God whom Jesus describes in unmistakable terms in the great commission given to His Church: "Go ye, therefore, and teach all nations, baptizing them in the name of the Father, and of the Son, and of the Holy Ghost" (Matt. 28:19).

To all who deny the deity of Jesus Christ, such as the Jew, the Unitarian, the Christian Scientist, the Spiritualist, and others, as well as to those who would hide God's real identity behind a mist of vagueness, the Lord says: "All men should honor the Son even as they honor the Father. He that honoreth not the Son honoreth not the Father, which hath sent Him" (John 5:23).

This Triune God reserves for Himself alone the honor of being worshiped. Jesus in His memorable battle with the devil quotes Deut. 6:13 freely in the challenge "Thou shalt worship the Lord, thy God, and Him only shalt thou serve" (Matt. 4:10).

No room here for saint worship. The Catholic Church, in trying to justify the practice, professes to distinguish between worship described in Greek as *douleia* and worship characterized as *latreia*. The one may be used to signify respect, reverence for man; the other means worship such as belongs to God exclusively. Saint worship, they assure us, is merely of the former character.

We wish it were. As a matter of fact, prayer to the saints is primarily a plea for mediation: "Pray for us." But in many instances it is a worship which can hardly, if at all, be distinguished from that which God reserves for Himself alone. One need but examine such books as Liguori's treatise *The Glory of Mary*, endorsed by Pope Pius IX, to realize the full implications of saint worship. Thus Luther confesses that when he as a young man faced death because of an accidental injury, he pleaded to Mary for mercy. "But for the grace of God," he continues, "I would have died placing my trust in Mary."

It may be well at this point briefly to summarize other objections to saint worship as raised in the synodical essays of former years. Scripture nowhere commands it. Scripture nowhere gives an instance of such worship. Scripture, contrasting God with saints of the Old Testament, says: "Doubtless Thou art our Father though Abraham be ignorant of us and Israel acknowledge us not; Thou, O Lord, art our Father, Our Redeemer; Thy name is from everlasting" (Is. 63:16). Saint worship implies an inadequate atonement. It credits the saints with greater mercy than Him who gave His life for us on Calvary's cross. It clutters up the way to the Father's heart and to that extent crowds Him into the background. The rosary calls for seven Ave Marias to one Pater Noster. Saint worship of necessity imputes to the saints divine characteristics, such as omnipresence and omniscience. Saint worship, in multiplying mediators, clearly does so in violation of such clear Scripture passages as John 14:6: "I am the Way, the Truth, and the Life; no man cometh unto the Father but by Me," and I Tim. 2:5: "There is one God, and one Mediator between God and men, the Man Christ Jesus."

Jesus Himself therefore has said: "Verily, verily, I say unto you, Whatsoever ye shall ask the Father in My name, He will give it you" (John 16:23).

What does He mean with the term "in My name"? It is evident from the very nature and purpose of His message to mankind that He wished to say, pleading His merit, relying fully upon His atoning work.

This does not require that in every prayer the words "in the name of Jesus" must occur. If that were true, it would exclude from the category of Christian prayer the Lord's Prayer, a masterpiece of divine wisdom, which is to serve as a model for our prayers. Let us bear in mind that it came from the heart and mind of Jesus. What do such terms as "Our Father," "Thy name," "Thy kingdom," "Thy will," "trespasses," and "forgive" mean when spoken by Him? The same as they always mean to Him as He unfolds the divine plan of salvation which centered in His death on Calvary. The Lord's Prayer and all other God-pleasing prayers therefore, whether they expressly use the term "in My name" or not, are in the setting of the atonement.

The Lord's Prayer spoken by the anti-Trinitarian and all others who deny the substitutionary atonement is not a Christian prayer, because under the guise of Christian terminology it has been stripped of all that is included in the expression "in My name." This holds true also of the prayers of Masonry, the mother of lodgery, and the large number of secret organizations which in varying degrees mimic her.

We are fully aware of the claims of Masonry that it does not interfere with the religious beliefs of any of its members. It merely requires as basic a belief in a Supreme Being. Who the latter is, every worshiper may determine for himself, whether he be Christian, Jew, Mohammedan, Buddhist, or Confucianist. A Christian therefore is free to give to the prayers spoken his own meaning and direction.

It is not as simple as that. To understand Masonry, one must know its fundamental objectives as compared with those of the Word of God. Both aim to save: one through a righteousness which the individual achieves for himself in harmony with the principles of Masonry, the other through faith in Jesus Christ, the divine Savior from sin. Both aim to unite in a spiritual fellowship: the one does so on a basis on which all, Christian, Jew, Mohammedan, Buddhist, Confucianist, and others may worship together as spiritual brothers, regardless of differing religious beliefs; the other has as its goal one fold, one Shepherd, in other words, a union in Him who has said: "I am *the* Way, *the* Truth, *the* Life; no man cometh unto the Father but by Me," a union in Him of whom Peter says: "Neither is there salvation in any other, for there is none other name under heaven given among men whereby we must be saved" (Acts 4:12). These objectives are mutually exclusive. The twain as such can never meet. Since these objectives give to the prayers their content and meaning, no Christian dare worship at the altar of Masonry or any of the organizations patterned after it.

Thesis V

Prayer must proceed from faith.

Jesus says: "All things whatsoever ye shall ask in prayer, believing, ye shall receive" (Matt. 21:22).

James 1:6, 7 we read: "Let him ask in faith, nothing wavering. For he that wavereth is like a wave of the sea driven with the wind and tossed. For let not that man think that he shall receive anything of the Lord."

How can we do otherwise than pray in faith when we bear in mind that God has promised to hear, that He has given His own character as security, and that He has assured its value through the sacrifice of His only-begotten Son? How can we fail to believe if we view every Christian prayer in the setting of Bethlehem, Gethsemane, Calvary, and Olivet?

Prayer, therefore, is not a leap into the dark. It is not to be put upon an experimental basis. Dr. Walther says: "What the kernel is in the shell, the soul in the body, that faith is in prayer." Another essayist states that "believing prayer is a key with which a Christian unlocks heaven, yes, the father heart of God." Luther therefore advises: "Do not leave prayer until you have thought or said, 'This prayer has been heard by God. This I know for a certainty. Amen'."

This faith is a creation of divine grace, a work of the Holy Spirit. "No man can say that Jesus is the Lord but by the Holy Ghost" (I Cor. 12:3). The latter also assists and guides in prayer. "Likewise the Spirit also helpeth our infirmities; for we know not what we should pray for as we ought, but the Spirit itself maketh intercession for us with groanings which cannot be uttered" (Rom. 8:26). Believing prayer has therefore been called an art learned in the school of the Holy Ghost.

There are times, however, when the experiences of life seem to belie the promises of God. The distressed heart cries out time and again, but there is silence. It re-echoes the plea of the Messiah rejected by man and forsaken by God: "My God, My God, why hast Thou forsaken Me? Why art Thou so far from helping Me, and from the words of My roaring? O My God, I cry in the daytime, but Thou hearest not; and in the night season, and am not silent" (Ps. 22:1, 2). It gives expression to the anomalous prayer: "Lord, I believe; help Thou mine unbelief." For the comfort of such a sufferer Luther says, "It is not faith that doubts, but the believing Jacob." He himself exemplifies this battle of the believer with doubt in such prayers as the following: "O Thou, my God! Do Thou, my God, stand by me, against all the world's wisdom and reason. Oh, do it! Thou must do it! Yea, Thou alone must do it! Not mine, but Thine, is the cause. For my own self, I have nothing to do with these great and earthly lords. I would prefer to have peaceful days and to be out of this turmoil. But Thine, O Lord, is this cause; it is righteous and eternal. Stand by me, Thou true, eternal God! In no man do I trust. All that is of the flesh and savors of the flesh is here of no account. God, O God, dost Thou not hear me, O my God? Art Thou dead? No. Thou canst not die; Thou art only hiding Thyself. Hast Thou chosen me for this work? I ask Thee how I may be sure of this, if it be Thy will; for I would never have thought in all my life of undertaking aught against such great lords. Stand by me, O God, in the name of Thy dear Son, Jesus Christ, who shall be my Defense and Shelter, yea, my mighty Fortress, through the might and strength of Thy Holy Spirit. God help me. Amen." In this plea one almost hears Luther saying with the German hymn writer, "Ich glaub', was Jesu Wort verspricht; Ich fuehl' es oder fuehl' es nicht."

Faith by its very nature, however, excludes willful sin. There is not room in any heart for both. Thus willful sin invalidates prayer.

Is. 59:12: "Behold, the Lord's hand is not shortened that it cannot save, neither His ear heavy that it cannot hear; but your iniquities have separated between you and your God, and your sins have hid His face from you, that He will not hear."

Prov. 29:8: "He that turneth away his ear from hearing the Law, even his prayers shall be an abomination."

Ps. 66:18: "If I regard iniquity in my heart, the Lord will not hear me."

This may account for many unanswered prayers.

Thesis VI

Prayer must be conditioned by the will of God.

Prayer is not a blank check which the petitioner fills in indiscriminately and then presents at the Throne of Grace. In that event man would rule the world. The result would be conflict, chaos, disaster.

Thoughtful parents have a plan for their children, one that is designed for their welfare. Within the scope of this plan the wishes and requests of the latter are granted.

Our heavenly Father has a plan of love and wisdom for us. This embraces invaluable blessings such as freedom from the guilt and the power of sin, membership in His family, a character and a walk "worthy of the vocation wherewith we are called," partnership in building up His Kingdom of Grace, eternal life in heaven.

Within this area, prayer is answered. I John 5:14: "This is the confidence that we have in Him, that if we ask anything according to His will, He heareth us." Everything that is essential to this will, such as faith, love, hope, strength to overcome the enemies of our soul, power and wisdom to serve Him, will be granted without reservations. Everything that is incidental to this plan, such as food, clothing, health, freedom from distressing circumstances, must be left to the discretion of God in such terms as, "If it be Thy will."

The supreme example of the latter prayer is given by the Savior Himself in the Garden of Gethsemane. Three times He pleads: "Father, if Thou be willing, remove this cup from Me." The answer to this most fervent of all prayers ever uttered by human lips was Calvary with all its suffering and shame, because it was essential to God's plan for man's salvation. But with that answer came another: a calm strength which even Calvary could not break.

Similarly we may pass through the very experiences which we hoped to ward off through prayer—sickness, bereavement, financial losses, trying personal and home situations. When that happens, we have God's assurance that the cup does not contain poison, but medicine wisely chosen by the Great Physician of souls for our eternal welfare. "We know that all things work together for good to them that love God, to them who are the called according to His purpose" (Rom. 8:28). A higher good, in harmony with God's plan, may result: a purer, stronger, and expanded faith, a deeper love, a more consecrated and a larger service to God and man. And throughout the trial there is vouchsafed to us "the grace that is sufficient."

Thesis VII

The scope of prayer must be as broad as living mankind.

In prayer faith speaks in the singular and appropriates God as if

He belonged to the individual alone. Rightfully so, for God says: "Fear not; for I have redeemed thee; I have called thee by thy name; thou art Mine" (Is. 43:1). Faith, accepting this promise at face value, confidently rejoices: "The Lord is my Shepherd; I shall not want. He maketh me to lie down in green pastures; He leadeth me beside the still waters" (Ps. 23:1, 2).

But love also speaks. It expands the scope of prayer as it says in the plural: "Our Father who art in heaven." It includes the members of one's family—father, mother, son, daughter, brother, sister. It reaches out and includes "all saints," the members of the household of faith. On the lips of Moses it becomes a plea for the nation for which he is willing to have his name blotted out from God's Book if that will save his people. Yes, it goes beyond national and racial boundaries. I Tim. 2:1 we read: "I exhort, therefore, that, first of all, supplications, prayers, intercessions, and giving of thanks be made for all men."

Nor does Christian prayer limit itself to friends. Jesus commands His disciples: "Pray for them which despitefully use you and persecute you." He exemplifies this love when He on the altar of the cross pleads, "Father, forgive them, for they know not what they do." Stephen the Martyr in the spirit of the Savior prays: "Do not hold this sin against them." One of the essayists therefore concludes that prayer is "a blessing of which we should not even deprive our enemies."

The scope of prayer, however, is limited to the living. Heb. 9:27 we read: "It is appointed unto men once to die, but after this the Judgment." When the today of God's saving grace has come to a close for an individual, the tomorrow of judgment and an eternal destiny begins. All the pleas of the living cannot affect his fate. Mass for the dead therefore is a futile effort.

THE PLACE OF PRAYER IN THE LIFE OF THE CHRISTIAN

Thesis VIII

In the life of the individual, prayer must be more than an emergency measure, a way of escape from troubles and difficulties that distress. It must be a working force that reaches out for the more abundant life promised by our Savior.

We do not possess any truth of God's Word until we use it and weave it into the pattern of our life. A person may be a Christian by profession but an atheist in practice. One may pay glowing tribute to prayer while at the same time a stranger to its power.

The commands "Pray without ceasing" (I Thess. 5:17) and "Continue instant in prayer" (Rom. 12:12) require that prayer be the atmosphere in which we live and work.

For many it becomes this in times of stress. The Christian father who in the morning left some member of the family critically ill at home, during the long working hours will time and again utter what Luther calls a *Stossgebet*.

But prayer is to occupy a larger place in our existence. It is to be the atmosphere of all of our days. How can it be otherwise when we bear in mind that each day we are making important decisions affecting our destiny as well as that of others? How can it be otherwise in the life of a pastor who is conscious of his responsibility as shepherd of immortal souls? The telephone rings. A hysterical voice in broken sentences and half-sentences tells him that tragedy has come to his or her home. He is wanted at once. Instinctively his heart goes out in prayer that God may enable him to say what should be said, in order that comfort may be brought to the stricken hearts. —His desk calendar tells him that within a few minutes someone will come to him for counsel. From what he knows, he will be called upon to perform an operation upon a human soul more delicate than that which the heart surgeon must perform. A prayer rises from his heart as he faces the interview.

It is a good custom to include in the schedule of the day stated times for prayer where we are alone with our God and Savior and pour out our heart to Him, hold sweet communion with Him in prayer.

While praying, we "in everything by prayer and supplication, with thanksgiving, are to let our requests be made known to God." Note that the Word of God makes no exception. All of our life is to come within the range of prayer.

That means that we are to go into the presence of God with our greatest problem, the root of all other problems, sin. Failure to do so spells disaster here and hereafter. We may try to ignore it; we may try to weaken its guilt by streamlining the divine Law, by setting up false moral standards, by using terms that hide its real nature; we may try to forget it in a life of gaiety; we may try to crowd it down whenever it threatens to cause trouble. David tried it, but in vain. Ps. 32:3, 4 he writes: "When I kept silence, my bones waxed old through my roaring all the day long. For day and night Thy hand was heavy upon me; my moisture is turned into the drought of summer."

There is but one safe way out. Sin must come to the surface. It must come to the surface in the presence of a forgiving God, who for Jesus' sake is able to say: "Come now and let us reason together. Though your sins be as scarlet, they shall be as white as snow; though they be red like crimson, they shall be as wool" (Is. 1:18). David also tried this method. He writes: "I said, I will confess my transgressions unto the Lord; and Thou forgavest the iniquity of my sin" (Ps. 32:5). The result was the peace of God which passeth all understanding.

Through prayer we shift the focus of our thoughts from self to God. The Christian lifts his eyes unto the hills from whence cometh his help. He says with the Psalmist: "Unto Thee, O Lord, do I lift up my soul." As his weakness turns toward the almighty power of God, demoralizing cares vanish, and a quiet strength replaces them. Dr. Hyslop, one-time superintendent of Bethlehem Royal Hospital, at an annual meeting of the British Medical Association, said: "As an alienist and one whose whole life has been concerned with the sufferings of the mind, I would state that of all hygienic measures to counteract disturbed, sleep-depressed spirits, and all the miserable sequels of a distressed mind, I would undoubtedly give the first place to the simple habit of prayer."

This means that the Christian who gives to prayer a vital part of the day's schedule faces life's tasks and opportunities, its ordinary experiences and its crises calmly, free from the frictions that break souls not so liberated. He draws from above a power that is adequate for every need. In response to specific prayers he time and again receives help that is denied the prayerless man. The *Altenburger Bibelwerk* therefore says: "Reverent and believing prayer is the surest and most powerful medicine in all need, also in the midst of duty."

Our Savior needed it; and though burdened with a schedule that defied human strength, He found time to retire into solitude for prayer.—Luther's capacity for work amazes. How did he manage?

He tells us that at times he was so busy that he required three hours of prayer in a day. No wonder that a historian speaks of the Reformation as having been born and sustained in the prayer closet of Luther.—Dr. Walther was a man of prayer. He must have been. His calm strength and his historic achievements in the kingdom of God were possible only to a man of prayer.

We as individuals therefore plead: "Lord, teach us to pray."

Thesis IX

Prayer must be an integral part of the home if it is to function according to God's plan.

The home is a gift of a loving and wise Creator. Its influence is far-reaching, deeply affecting the future of the individual and through him the course of the Church, the nation, and the world at large. Only the frivolous and the spiritually blind can fail to make their motto that of Joshua: "As for me and my house, we will serve the Lord."

Prayerfully young people, about to establish a home, ought to build their plans for the future. Prayerfully they ought to make the adjustments which will enable them to blend their lives into one. Prayerfully they ought to build the resources of the home, bearing in mind that "except the Lord build the house, they labor in vain that build it."

When their home is blessed with children, they ought to pray for the wisdom and patience that will enable them to guide the growing lives into the pathway of Christian faith, achievement, and eternal happiness. As soon as possible, they will cultivate within the children habits of prayer, so that they may for themselves draw on the rich blessings which a loving God has in store for them.

Every day at a suitable time parents and children will assemble for Bible study and prayer. The result will be that family life will be on a higher level. The ties that bind will be strengthened. Problems will be met with the help of God. Christian stewardship will direct the talents and the family income into channels of Christian service.

Such a home will give to Church and State men and women who

will be invaluable assets through their life and work. Yes, it will enrich heaven itself with blood-bought souls.

We therefore plead: "Lord, teach our homes to pray."

Thesis X

Prayer is essential to the Church in its life and functions.

Someone has said: "Our generation is marked by practical efficiency and spiritual shallowness." This is true of many churches. Organize, deputize, supervise, these are the magic key to success. Methods that rival those of the business world have been adopted and put into action in the hope of accomplishing larger things.

Machinery is important. God is a God of order. In His Church He wants everything done decently and in order. But machinery without power is ineffective, futile. Back of it there must be the indispensable power of the Holy Spirit.

When on the first Pentecost the Holy Spirit burst upon the disciples with light and power, they became a force that "turned the world upside down." This power is also available to us. Our Savior has said: "If ye, then, being evil, know how to give good gifts unto your children, how much more shall your heavenly Father give the Holy Spirit to them that ask Him?" (Luke 11:13.)

But why corporate prayer? Can't each person pray for himself in the privacy of his home? A vocal solo may be beautiful; but a choral or an oratorio sung in harmony by a balanced chorus is more so. That is also true of prayer. The same Savior who urged us to "enter the closet" when we pray has also said: "Again I say unto you, That if two of you shall agree on earth as touching any thing that they shall ask, it shall be done for them of My Father which is in heaven. For where two or three are gathered together in My name, there am I in the midst of them" (Matt. 18:19, 20).

Congregational prayer, if genuine, also tends to unite hearts and minds. It lifts the life of the group above that which is petty into the atmosphere of Christian love.

Add to this the specific blessings for which the congregation prays. It pleads that the Lord may give to the pastor "utterance," that He may "open to him doors." The pastor, in turn, implores God that his congregation may be "strengthened with might by His Spirit in the inner man," that it may "grow in grace and knowledge." Pastor and people present the special needs of individual members and families to the Throne of Grace.

These are not pious platitudes. They are prayers directed to Him who answers prayer. As a result, here are blessings that will enrich beyond understanding the congregation that has the faith to pray for them, blessings granted by the grace of Him who has become our Father in Christ Jesus.

Corporate prayer reaches out into the life and work of all congregations united by a common bond of faith. Think of what it means to a District when the congregations within its area pray for each other and for their joint tasks. Then enlarge that circle to include all of Synod. Here is potential power that will strengthen the bonds of unity and weld Synod into a mighty army, moving forward to great victories for Him who died for us.

We as congregations, as a District, as a Synod, therefore pray: "Lord, teach us to pray."

XIV

The Holy Christian Church

DEFINITION OF THE TERM

THE derivation of the word "church" is not certain. It may be derived from the Greek word *kyriake,* which means of or belonging to the Lord (*kyrios*). In this sense John uses the word *kyriake* in connection with the "day" (*hemera*) in Rev. 1: 10: "I was in the Spirit on the Lord's day." But if the derivation of the word "church" is uncertain, the thing for which it stands is not. The doctrine of the Church is clearly and firmly established in the Scriptures. It is as glorious and comforting as it is important. Its importance is underscored by the attention given to it by Christ and His holy writers in both the Old and the New Testament. This doctrine invites the Christian to peer into the eternal councils of God and leads him from Gabbatha to the right hand of God's majesty, "far above all principality, and power, and might, and dominion, and every name that is named, not only in this world, but also in that which is to come; and hath put all things under His feet, and gave Him to be the Head over all things to the Church, which is His body, the fullness of Him that filleth all in all" (Eph. 1:21-23).

The word used most frequently in the original Greek to designate the Church is *ecclesia*. This, in its ordinary classical sense, usually meant an assembly called out by some legitimate authority. It is thus used of the assembly which was stirred up by Demetrius at Ephesus. When the town clerk had spoken, "he dismissed the assembly" (*ecclesia*) (Acts 19:41). The holy writers in the New Testament, however, clothed this word with a more exalted meaning. Only a few times did they use it in its classical sense; over one hundred times they used it in the sense of Church. In the Gospels it occurs on only two occasions, each time in St. Matthew ("On this rock will I build My Church," 16:18; "Tell it unto the Church," 18:17). Elsewhere the Evangelists use synonymous terms. St. Matthew speaks of it as "the kingdom of heaven," or, occasionally, as "the kingdom of God." St. Mark and St. Luke use the expression "kingdom of God." St. John uses this once. None of these three use the expression "kingdom of heaven." St. Matthew frequently refers simply to "the Kingdom." Other expressions are found in the Gospels, as, Christ's flock (Matt. 26:31; John 10:1), but the idea of the kingdom predominates. It was the Apostles who popularized the term "*ecclesia*" in their epistles.

The doctrine of the Church is one which must be believed. This is due as well to the character of faith as to the nature of the Church. "Now faith is the substance of things hoped for, the evidence of things not seen" (Heb. 11:1). The Church is invisible. Therefore we confess: "I believe in the Holy Christian Church." To explain what we mean with the word "Church," we add the words, "the communion of saints." So we are not speaking of a church building in the Creed, some structure erected of wood or stone and called a church because the church assembles in it. Such a building can be seen. Nor do we speak of the church service or the people in the pews, whom the ushers count. We do not mean the numbers listed in the *Statistical Yearbook*. We confess that in the midst of those who occupy the pews and are included in the figures of the *Statistical Yearbook* the Church is hidden. The word "communion" as used in the Creed is not generally understood in that sense today. Our Catechism substitutes the word "congregation." It answers the question: "What is the Church?" thus: "The congregation of saints, that is, all Christendom, the whole number of all believers; for *only* believers, and *all* believers, are members of the Church." Here the Church is identified with the congregation of saints, with all Christendom, and with the whole number of all believers. Saints, believers, Christians, and members of the Church are the same people.

The term "believer" does not, however, mean the same thing to all people. It does not mean to some what it does to true Christians. Faith is said by some to be important, but not the object of faith. It matters little what one believes, as long as one believes fervently. This false conception of faith makes it necessary to define the object of faith in the Christian religion; for only that faith which trusts in the correct object of saving faith makes one a Christian, a member of the Church. For the correct object of the Christian faith we turn to Luther's explanation of the Second Article, where we confess that Jesus Christ "has redeemed me, a lost and condemned creature, purchased and won me from all sins, from death, and from the power of the devil, not with gold or silver, but with His holy, precious blood and with His innocent suffering and death, that I may be His own, and live under Him in His kingdom, and serve Him in everlasting righteousness, innocence, and blessedness." Faith in these words makes a person a member of the Church. But now "no man can say that Jesus is the Lord, but by the Holy Ghost" (I Cor. 12:3), because "the natural man receiveth not the things of the Spirit of God" (I Cor. 2:14), being dead in trespasses and sins (Eph. 2:1), and the carnal mind being enmity against God (Rom. 8:7); therefore we furthermore confess: "I believe that I cannot by my own reason or strength believe in Jesus Christ, my Lord, or come to Him; but the Holy Ghost has called me by the Gospel, enlightened me with His gifts, sanctified and kept me in the true faith; even as He calls, gathers, enlightens, and sanctifies the whole Christian Church on earth, and keeps it with Jesus Christ in one true faith." As the Holy Ghost regenerates one sinner after another with the Gospel, which "is the power of God unto salvation to everyone that believeth" (Rom. 1:16), He adds stone to stone in the structure of the Church. Paul writes to the Ephesians: "But God, who is rich in mercy, for His great love wherewith He loved us, even when we were dead in sins, hath quickened us together with Christ (by grace ye are saved), and hath raised us up together, and made us sit together in heavenly places in Christ Jesus: that in ages to come He might show the exceeding riches of His grace in His kindness toward us through Christ Jesus" (Eph. 2:4-7). In doing this, God built the Church. Still writing to the Ephesians, Paul declares: "Now therefore ye are no more strangers and foreigners, but fellow citizens with the saints and of the household of God; and are built upon the foundation of the Apostles and Prophets, Jesus Christ Himself being the chief Cornerstone; in whom all the building fitly framed together groweth unto an holy temple in the Lord: in whom ye also are builded together for an habitation of God through the Spirit" (Eph. 2:19-22). A beautiful description of the Church! How this building, framing together, and growing unto an holy temple in the Lord actually proceeds, we are told in Acts. When Peter had preached to the multitude on Pentecost Day, "then they that gladly received his word were baptized, and the same day there were added unto them about three thousand souls" (Acts 2:41). Note that only those who received his word and were baptized were added. Again, when Peter and John preached in the Temple, "many of them which heard the word believed; and the number of the men was about five thousand" (Acts 4:4). Again the believers are counted. So, then, "believers were the more added to the Lord, multitudes both of men and women" (Acts 5:14). Thus was the prayer of the Lord Jesus heard: "Neither pray I for these alone, but for them also which shall believe on Me through their word" (John 17:20). Faith in Christ, in His Word, makes men members of the Christian Church—the faith that they are "being justified freely by His grace through the redemption that is in Christ Jesus (Rom. 3:24).

This faith alone, and nothing else, makes one a member of the Church. Membership in any visible organization, no matter what it may be called, does not. One may be a voting member or a communicant member in a Christian congregation without being a member of the Christian Church. Ministers and priests, elders and deacons, bishops, cardinals, and popes—none of these is by virtue of his office a member of the Church. Church attendance, partaking of the Sacrament, liberality in giving to the Church or to the poor —all of these together do not guarantee membership in the Church.

That only believers in Christ as the Savior are members of the Church is affirmed by such expressions as these: "the house of God, which is the Church of the living God" (I Tim. 3:15); "God's building" (I Cor. 3:9); "the temple of God" (I Cor. 3:16); "the temple of the Holy Ghost" (I Cor. 6:19); "His body, the fullness of Him that filleth all in all" (Eph. 1:23); and John could say that Jesus "should gather together in one the children of God that were scattered abroad" (John 11:52). Only believers are children of God, "for ye are all the children of God by faith in Christ Jesus" (Gal. 3:26). Unbelievers walk "according to the course of this world, according to the prince of the power of the air, the spirit that now worketh in the children of disobedience" (Eph. 2:2). They are decidedly not a part of the Church. Christ has no concord with Belial (II Cor. 6:15). And he that believeth has no part with an infidel (*ibid.*).

CHARACTERISTICS OF THE CHURCH

The Church Is Invisible

A unique body like the Church must have distinctive characteristics. What these are Christ tells us in His Word. The properties or attributes of the Church are clearly described by Him and the Apostles; the adjectives may be our own. Since only believers in Christ are members of the Church but faith is invisible, the Church is invisible. It is not, however, a mere Platonic idea; it is very real and concrete. It is invisible only to man, not to God. Faith always bears fruit in sanctification, but outward appearances may deceive. It may be impossible to distinguish the tares from the wheat, a false show of goodness from true sanctification. Therefore it is not possible to conclude that those who act like Christians are such in reality. "And when He [Jesus] was demanded of the Pharisees, when the kingdom of God should come, He answered them and said, The kingdom of God cometh not with observation: neither shall they say, Lo, here! or, lo, there! for, behold, the kingdom of God is within you" (Luke 17:20, 21). The kingdom of God does not come like a conquering army under a visible commander-in-chief, with banners flying and clashing arms. The Christian has the kingdom of God hidden within his heart. Where the power of the Gospel is exerted, there the Church will be found, but to man it will still be unknown to whom the Gospel has been a power of God unto salvation. Not so to God. He understands my thoughts afar off; He sees my faith, "for there is not a word in my tongue, but, lo, O Lord, Thou knowest it altogether" (Ps. 139:4). No one need worry that God might not recognize him as a believer, a member of the Church, for "the foundation of God standeth sure, having this seal, The Lord knoweth them that are His" (II Tim. 2:19). When Elijah, the great prophet, disheartened by recent experiences, thought that the Church had been totally destroyed, that only he was left, God knew that He had seven thousand in Israel who had not bowed their knees to Baal (I Kings 19:8-18). Yet what is clearly seen by the omniscient Lord, the faith in the heart of men, which alone makes them members of the Church, must by its very nature remain invisible to mankind, and therefore we must say that the Church, the communion of saints, is invisible to human eyes.

Some modern Lutherans speak of a visible side of the Church, referring to the marks of the Church: Word and Sacraments. They contend that inasmuch as the Church can be found only where these are to be found, they must belong to the essence of the Church. However, the means of grace are no more a part of the Church than the tools of the builder are a part of the finished structure. It stands to reason that those denominations which do not have a correct conception of the working of the means of grace cannot understand the Biblical doctrine of the Church. To Roman Catholicism the Church is a visible body. Bellarmine, one of the greatest theologians of the Roman Catholic Church, says, "The Church is a society as visible and palpable as is the state of Rome, or the kingdom of France, or the republic of Venice" (Bellarmine, *Lib.* 3, *De Eccl. c.* 2). J. F. di Bruno writes, "The true Church of Christ on earth is the union of all the faithful, who communicate one with another by profession of the same faith, by participation in the same sacraments, and who are subject to their own bishops, and in a special manner to the Roman Pontiff, who is the visible center of Catholic unity" (*Catholic Belief,* chap. XXV). While God has His own children also in the Church of Rome, yet they are children of God and members of the true Church not because they hold membership in the Church of Rome, but by virtue of their faith in the atoning sacrifice of Christ Jesus. But who is able to pick them out from the vast membership of this far-flung organization? Here, too, only the Lord knows them that are His.

The Church Is One

Since it is only the faith in Christ as the Savior that makes one a member of the Church, there can be only one Christian Church; for there is no "other name under heaven given among men, whereby we must be saved" (Acts 4:12). To the Ephesians Paul wrote: "There is one body, and one Spirit, even as ye are called in one hope of your calling; one Lord, one faith, one baptism, one God and Father of all, who is above all, and through all, and in you all" (Eph. 4:4-6). And to the Corinthians: "For by one Spirit are we all baptized into one body, whether we be Jews or Gentiles, whether we be bond or free; and have been all made to drink into one Spirit" (I Cor. 12:13). There may be many members, but there can be only one Church, "for as we have many members in one body, and all members have not the same office, so we, being many, are one body in Christ, and everyone members one of another" (Rom. 12:4, 5). Jesus Himself expressed it thus: "And other sheep I have, which are not of this fold: them also I must bring, and they shall hear My voice; and there shall be one fold and one Shepherd" (John 10:16). This perfect unity of His people Jesus purchased with a price, for He was slain and has redeemed us to God by His blood out of every kindred, and tongue, and people, and nation, and has made us unto our God kings and priests (Rev. 5:9, 10).

This one Church can neither be divided nor multiplied. There can be only one Church, which, however, is catholic or universal. It is limited neither by time nor space. The Church in the Old Testament and that in the New constitute one Church. The faithful in the Old Testament believed in the Messiah who was to come; those in the New believe in the Christ who has come. The Messiah of the Old Testament and the Christ of the New is one and the same Person. Peter declared in the house of Cornelius: "To Him [Christ] give all the Prophets witness, that through His name whosoever believeth in Him shall receive remission of sins" (Acts 10:43). Luke adds: "While Peter yet spake these words, the Holy Ghost fell on all them which heard the Word. And they of the circumcision which believed were astonished, as many as came with Peter, because that on the Gentiles also was poured out the gift of the Holy Ghost" (Acts 10:44, 45). Why should they of the circumcision be astonished? "Is He the God of the Jews only? is He not also of the Gentiles? Yes, of the Gentiles also: seeing it is one God which shall justify the circumcision by faith, and the uncircumcision through faith" (Rom. 3:29-30). It is the same faith that makes Jews and Gentiles members of the one Church. In his Epistle to the Galatians Paul links up the Gentile believers of the New Testament with Abraham, the father of believers, stating: "Even as Abraham believed God, and it was accounted to him for righteousness. Know ye therefore that they which are of faith, the same are the children of Abraham" (Gal. 3:6, 7). And again: "And if ye be Christ's, then are ye Abraham's seed, and heirs according to the promise" (Gal. 3:29). There was a church at Jerusalem, Antioch, Corinth, Rome, and at many other places—all together constituting one and the same Church, as the Church B. C. is the same as the one A. D. Faith in Christ is the tie that binds all the members into one body under Christ the Head.

The Church Is Christian

The fact that Christ is the Head of the Church or also the chief Cornerstone or Foundation makes the Church the Christian Church. It "is His body, the fullness of Him that filleth all in all" (Eph. 1:23). "For as we have many members in one body, and all members have not the same office; so we, being many, are one body in Christ, and everyone members one of another" (Rom. 12:4, 5; cf. Eph. 4:12). Christ is "Head over all things to the Church" (Eph. 1:22; 4:15). "Christ is the Head of the Church" (Eph. 5:23). "And He is the Head of the body, the Church: who is the Beginning, the Firstborn from the dead, that in all things He might have the pre-eminence" (Col. 1:18). Christ is the Head of the Church, as the father and husband is the head of the family (Eph. 5:23), but He is more than that. As the head directs the body, so Christ the Church. His will guides it. He is its life. Without this Head the Church would be a lifeless body, it would not and could not exist. He admonished His disciples: "Abide in Me, and I in you. As the branch cannot bear fruit of itself, except it abide in the vine; no more can ye, except ye abide in Me" (John 15:4). Again, Christ is the chief Cornerstone of the Church (Eph. 2:20). Peter wrote "to the strangers scattered throughout Pontus, Galatia, Cappadocia, Asia, and Bithynia, elect according to the foreknowledge of God the Father" (I Pet. 1:1, 2), in other words, to the Church: "Wherefore also it is contained in the Scripture, Behold, I lay in Sion a chief Cornerstone, elect, precious: and he that believeth on Him shall not be confounded" (I Pet. 2:6). He is the Church's foundation, "for other Foundation can no man lay than that is laid, which is Jesus Christ" (I Cor. 3:11). This Church is in truth the Christian Church.

It is also the *holy* Church—twice holy! It is holy, because the blood of Jesus Christ, God's Son, cleanses it from the guilt and the power of sin (I John 1:7). The Christian may sing:

> Let the water and the blood
>   From Thy riven side which flowed
> Be of sin the double cure,
>   Cleanse me from its guilt and power.

On the one hand, the believer is found in Christ, not having his own righteousness, which is of the Law, "but that which is through faith of Christ, the righteousness which is of God by faith (Phil. 3:9). The Church is holy also because it serves God with holy works which God Himself calls good and holy (Rom. 12:1; Eph. 2:10). Sin no longer has dominion over the believer, for he is not under the Law, but under grace. (Rom. 6:14.) The holiness of the Church is beautifully expressed in these words: "Christ also loved the Church, and gave Himself for it; that He might sanctify and cleanse it with the washing of water by the Word, that He might present it to Himself a glorious Church, not having spot, or wrinkle, or any such thing; but that it should be holy and without blemish" (Eph. 5:25-27).

Because the Church is "built upon the foundation of the Apostles and Prophets" (Eph. 2:20), it is also called the Apostolic Church. This is no other foundation than Jesus Christ. (I Cor. 3:11.) Jesus told His disciples: "He that heareth you heareth Me" (Luke 10:16). He prayed for His disciples, but also for them which should believe on Him through their word. (John 17:20.) Therefore the early Christians "continued steadfastly in the Apostles' doctrine" (Acts 2:42). That was the positive side; on the negative side, they avoided errorists. (Rom. 16:17.) Error has a dilapidating tendency and causes ruin and decay in the building of the Church. It strikes directly at the Church's foundation, the foundation of the Apostles and Prophets, and at Christ, the chief Cornerstone.

This Church is indestructible.

> Though there be those that hate her,
> False sons within her pale,
> Against both foe and traitor
> She ever shall prevail.

To every believer who confesses his faith in Jesus with the words of Simon Peter, "Thou art the Christ, the Son of the living God" (Matt. 16:16), Jesus can say: "Thou art Peter, and upon this rock I will build My Church; and the gates of hell shall not prevail against it" (Matt. 16:18). Peter is one who partakes of the nature of a rock. Simon Peter was such a man, because he was built up on Christ as the chief Cornerstone. Likewise every believer who is built upon this rock, upon Christ or upon the words of Peter's confession, which is the same thing as being built upon Christ, is a lively stone in a spiritual house, the Church. The Pope's interpretation of this passage in Matthew is untenable. The Pope makes Simon Peter the rock on which Christ builds His Church; but Christ is Himself the Foundation. (Cf. Matt. 16:19; 18:18; John 20;21-23). The important point here is the fact that the most powerful forces of hell cannot overthrow the Church.

Since there is only one Church, there can be only one saving Church. Outside this Church there is no salvation. Faith in Christ makes one a member of the Church; only believers are members. Faith saves; unbelief damns (Mark 16:16). This explains the statement that there is no salvation outside the Church. But this cannot be said of any so-called visible church. The Pope makes this claim for his Church. He is wrong. It cannot be said of his Church any more than of the Lutheran Church or of any other denomination. (See below.)

Paul speaks of the Church as a glorious Church (Eph. 5:27). It is that. Its Head is a great king. The angel Gabriel said to Mary: "Thou shalt conceive in thy womb, and bring forth a son, and shalt call His name JESUS. He shall be great and shall be called the Son of the Highest; and the Lord God shall give unto Him the throne of His father David; and He shall reign over the house of Jacob forever; and of His kingdom there shall be no end" (Luke 1:31-33). Zechariah foresaw this King's triumphal entry into Jerusalem centuries before the first Palm Sunday. He cries out: "Rejoice greatly, O daughter of Zion; shout, O daughter of Jerusalem: behold, thy King cometh unto thee: He is just, and having salvation" (Zech. 9:9). "Pilate therefore said unto Him, Art Thou a king then? Jesus answered, Thou sayest that I am a king. To this end was I born, and for this cause came I into the world, that I should bear witness unto the truth. Every one that is of the truth heareth My voice" (John 18:37). What a glorious Kingdom! What if Pilate cynically asks: "What is truth?" (John 18:38.) The King remains glorious; "the light shineth in darkness; and the darkness comprehended it not" (John 1:5).

THE SOVEREIGNTY OF THE CHURCH

To this glorious King the members of the Church are subject; but as His subjects, all things are theirs. Why kneel down to a so-called visible head of the Church, though he wears a triple crown and is surrounded by all the pomp and glory of the earth? Paul warned the Corinthians: "Therefore let no man glory in men. For all things are yours; whether Paul, or Apollos, or Cephas, or the world, or life, or death, or things present, or things to come; all are yours; and ye are Christ's; and Christ is God's" (I Cor. 3:21-23). Would you rather hear Christ Himself? He told His followers: "Be not ye called Rabbi: for one is your Master, even Christ; and all ye are brethren. And call no man your father upon the earth: for one is your Father, which is in heaven. Neither be ye called masters: for one is your Master, even Christ" (Matt. 23:8-10). This glorious sovereignty the Church must defend. Paul exhorts the Corinthians: "Ye are bought with a price; be not ye the servants of men" (I Cor. 7:23). Christians must remember the glorious sovereignty of the Church in view of the pretensions of "that man of sin," "the son of perdition: who opposeth and exalteth himself above all that is called God, or that is worshiped; so that he as God sitteth in the temple of God, showing himself that he is God" (II Thess. 2:3-4). Against the false glitter of the papacy Christians must exalt the true glory of the Church: Christ is its Head; all members are brethren.

The glory of the Church is such that a wise man will gladly exchange everything else for it. Jesus said: "The Kingdom of heaven is like unto treasure hid in a field; the which when a man hath found, he hideth, and for joy thereof goeth and selleth all that he hath, and buyeth that field. Again, the kingdom of heaven is like unto a merchant man seeking goodly pearls: who, when he had found one pearl of great price, went and sold all that he had, and bought it" (Matt. 13:44-46).

VISIBLE MARKS OF THE CHURCH

The visible marks which indicate the presence of the invisible Church are the means of grace. Roman Catholicism will point to its hierarchy. The Anglican Church will mention the so-called apostolic succession of its bishops. But neither the one nor the other is a mark of the Church's presence. Nor are domes and spires, bells and organs, such marks. The only true marks are the Word and the Sacraments. Wherever the Gospel is preached and the Sacraments are administered according to Christ's institution, the Church is certain to be: "for as the rain cometh down, and the snow from heaven, and returneth not thither, but watereth the earth, and maketh it bring forth and bud, so shall My Word be that goeth out of My mouth; it shall not return unto Me void, but it shall accomplish that which I please, and it shall prosper in the thing whereto I sent it" (Is. 55: 10, 11). This is God's promise. Therefore we are certain that the Church was present in Jerusalem when the first Christians "continued steadfastly in the Apostles' doctrine and fellowship, and in breaking of bread, and in prayers" (Acts 2:42). Jesus illustrated the origin and the growth of the Church with various parables. That of the Sower of the Seed shows how the Gospel operates (Matt. 13:1-9; 18-23). Also the Parable of the Mustard Seed and that of the Leaven (Matt. 13:31-33). The means of grace generate and preserve the Church, because God's Spirit works through them. Shall we say that they are the high-tension line over which God's power flows? Irrespective of illustrations, it is important to remember that the Church is God's work alone. "Know ye that the Lord He is God: it is He that hath made us, and not we ourselves: we are His people, and the sheep of His pasture" (Ps. 100:3). The Church is that chosen generation, royal priesthood, holy nation, and peculiar people whom God called out of darkness into His marvelous light (I Pet. 2:9). Why can we not select a definite group of people and either by threat or promise persuade them to agree to be believers? If that could be done, we might point to such a group as a visible communion of saints. The answer is simple: We cannot make such a decision, "for by grace are ye saved through faith; and that not of yourselves; it is the gift of God: not of works, lest any man should boast. For we are His workmanship, created in Christ Jesus unto good works, which God hath before ordained that we should walk in them" (Eph. 2:8-10). Over the completed structure of Christ's Church we must write the words: "All glory be to God on high!" Be it stated here, however, that the grace of God is not irresistible. Jesus would have gathered Jerusalem's children together, "even as a hen gathereth her chickens under her wings," but He had to lament: "Ye would not!" (Matt. 23:37.) The stiff-necked and uncircumcised in heart and ears at Jerusalem always resisted the Holy Ghost (Acts 7:51). The Lord had to complain: "O Israel, thou hast destroyed thyself" (Hos. 13:9). This explains why in spite of the power of the Gospel the Church remains invisible. "Many are called, but few are chosen" (Matt. 22:14).

THE VISIBLE CHURCH

In a figurative sense, however, we may also speak of the visible Church or churches. The visible Church, according to our Catechism, includes "the whole number of those who profess the Christian faith and are gathered about God's Word, but among whom, besides the true Christians, there are also hypocrites." The sovereign unit in the visible Church is the local church or congregation. The holy writers speak of local churches. To the Corinthians Paul wrote: "The churches of Asia salute you" (I Cor. 16:19). Again, "Unto the church of God which is at Corinth" (I Cor. 1:2). Luke speaks of "the church which was at Jerusalem" (Acts 8:1). To the Romans Paul wrote: "The churches of Christ salute you" (Rom. 16:16). He says: "But if any man seem to be contentious, we have no such custom, neither the churches of God" (I Cor. 11:16). Such local churches can be addressed. Their membership can be counted. They have elders to minister unto them, and they come together for public worship. Paul admonished the elders of the church at Ephesus: "Take heed therefore unto yourselves, and to all the flock over the which the Holy Ghost hath made you overseers, to feed the church of God, which He hath purchased with His own blood" (Acts 20:28). Of a bishop he says: "For if a man know not how to rule his own house, how shall he take care of the church of God?" (I Tim. 3:5.) Paul and Barnabas "ordained them elders in every church" (Acts 14:23). At Antioch they gathered the church together and rehearsed all that God had done with them, and how He had opened the door of faith unto the Gentiles (Acts 14:27). Paul speaks of the whole church's coming together into one place (I Cor. 14:23). And Christ commands: "Tell it unto the church" (Matt. 18:17).

The number of those who are members of such a local church may include hypocrites. To the human eye these may appear as sanctified, as the true believers. Their hypocrisy may eventually become manifest, or it may not. That of Ananias and Sapphira did. So did that of Judas. Some may believe for a while, but later drift away. Such are called apostates. After one of Christ's sermons, "many of His disciples went back and walked no more with Him" (John 6:66). Col. 4:14 we read: "Luke, the beloved physician, and Demas greet you." Philemon 24 Paul calls Marcus, Aristarchus, Demas, and Lucas his fellow laborers. But II Tim. 4:10 he complains: "For Demas hath forsaken me, having loved this present world, and is departed unto Thessalonica." Many a one receives the Word with joy, "yet hath he not root in himself, but dureth for a while; for when tribulation or persecution ariseth because of the Word, by and by he is offended" (Matt. 13:21). Some seeds fall by the wayside, some upon stony places, some among thorns (Matt. 13:4-7).

As only the believers in Christ's salvation constitute the invisible church at large, so in reality only the true Christians constitute the local congregation. When we speak of all people of a local congregation as a church, we do so in a synecdochic sense, putting the whole for a part. However, not to the unbelieving members of the local church, but only to all believers has Christ given the Office of the Keys. Paul, writing to the local church at Corinth, addresses his Epistle, "Unto the church of God which is at Corinth, to them that are sanctified in Christ Jesus, called to be saints, with all that in every place call upon the name of Jesus Christ our Lord, both theirs and ours" (I Cor. 1:2). This address excludes the hypocrites. All the rights, privileges, and powers of a Christian congregation presuppose faith on the part of the members. Members of the church are to let the Word of Christ dwell in them richly in all wisdom; teaching and admonishing one another in psalms and hymns and spiritual songs, singing with grace in their hearts to the Lord (Col. 3:16). They are to put away from among themselves a wicked person "in the name of our Lord Jesus Christ . . . with the power of our Lord Jesus Christ" (I Cor. 5:4). They are to watch over the doctrine of their pastor, as Paul reminds the Colossians: "And say to Archippus, Take heed to the ministry which thou hast received in the Lord, that thou fulfill it" (Col. 4:17). They are to show forth the praises of Him who hath called them out of darkness into His marvelous light (I Pet. 2:9).

Only true believers can sanctify the Lord God in their hearts and be ready always to give an answer to every man that asketh them a reason of the hope that is in them with meekness and fear (I Pet. 3:15). Hypocrites are not members of the Church, but of the world. They must be told, like all unbelievers: "Repent ye therefore, and be converted, that your sins may be blotted out" (Acts 3:19). The local church, then, in the strict sense, is the congregation of believers who, at a specific locality, have gathered about the Word of God and the Sacraments.

THE LOCAL CONGREGATION DIVINELY INSTITUTED

The local church is a divine institution. God did not leave it to the free choice of a Christian whether or not he wants to join a local congregation which insists on purity of doctrine and correct Biblical practice. Christ commands not only to search the Scriptures, but also pronounces His blessing upon them that hear the Word of God and keep it (Luke 11:28). He says: "He that is of God heareth God's words" (John 8:47). He instituted His ministry for the preaching of the Word and the administration of the Sacraments in public worship. The local congregation calls, ordains, and installs its pastor; it therefore also provides him with a living worthy of his honorable calling. It is, however, the duty of every hearer of God's Word to contribute to the economic support of the preacher and teacher. Paul instructed the Galatians: "Let him that is taught in the Word communicate unto him that teacheth in all good things" (Gal. 6:6). Again, a Christian is not merely to tell his brother his faults alone, or with one or two more; but, in case the brother remains impenitent after the first two grades of admonition, he is also to join the other members of a church in giving him a final admonition; he should be one of those to whom Christ declares: "Verily, I say unto you, Whatsoever ye shall bind on earth shall be bound in heaven; and whatsoever ye shall loose on earth shall be loosed in heaven" (Matt. 18:18). (Cf. I Cor. 5:13; II Cor. 2:8.) Finally, among other reasons for communing, we approach the Lord's Table also in testimony of the communion of faith, "for we, being many, are one bread, and one body: for we are all partakers of that one bread" (I Cor. 10:17). The first Christians have set an example to be emulated for all times, continuing steadfastly in the Apostles' doctrine and fellowship, and in the breaking of bread, and in prayers (Acts 2:42). They did not forsake the assembling of themselves together, as the manner of some is. (Heb. 10:25.) It follows that a Christian cannot resign from a Christian congregation, as he may from a purely secular club or society, but that he may ask to be transferred from one congregation to another.

SYNOD

For practical reasons a number of sovereign congregations may unite to form a larger organization. Synod's constitution lists eight objects which would be quite difficult or even impossible for an individual congregation to attain. These are: "(1) The conservation and promotion of the unity of the true faith (Eph. 4:3-6; I Cor. 1:10) and a united defense against schism and sectarianism (Rom. 16:17); (2) the joint extension of the Kingdom of God; (3) the training of ministers and teachers for service in the Evangelical Lutheran Church; (4) the publication and distribution of Bibles, churchbooks, schoolbooks, religious periodicals, and other books and literature; (5) the endeavor to bring about the largest possible uniformity in church practice, church customs, and, in general, in congregational affairs; (6) the furtherance of Christian parochial schools and of a thorough instruction for Confirmation; (7) the supervision of the ministers and teachers of the Synod with regard to the performance of their official duties; (8) the protection of pastors, teachers, and congregations in the performance of their duties and the maintenance of their rights." Article III, Object.— Or a number of synods may join in a larger body, as the Evangelical Lutheran Synodical Conference of North America, whose purpose and object are stated thus in its constitution: "An expression of the unity of the spirit existing among the respective synods; mutual encouragement as to faith and confession; promotion of unity as to doctrine and practice and the removal of any threatening disturbance thereof; co-operation in matters of mutual interest; an effort to establish territorial boundaries for the synods, provided that the language used does not separate them; the uniting of all Lutheran synods of America into *one* orthodox American Lutheran Church." Article III, Purpose and Object.—Beneficial as such larger church bodies as these are, they are not commanded in Scripture. Therefore, "in its relation to its members the Synod is not an ecclesiastical government exercising legislative or coercive powers, and with respect to the individual congregation's right of self-government it is but an advisory body." Article VII, Relation of Synod to Its Members.—And "the Synodical Conference is only an advisory body with respect to all things concerning which the synods constituting it have not given it authoritative power." Article IV, Authority.—For sufficient reason a congregation may withdraw from a larger church body, or such a body may be dissolved. In this matter reason and common sense, tempered by charity, must decide. (I Cor. 13:11; 16:14; Rom. 13:10.)

Inasmuch as a larger union of local churches is not demanded by God, it is futile to look for any ready constitution or a blueprint for the organizational structure of such a body in the Bible. Christ did not give His Church a visible head; He is its only Head. The dogma that the Pope is the visible head of the Church is a medieval figment of which the early Church knew nothing. The Roman Catholic hierarchy, consisting of bishops, archbishops, metropolitans, and the like, has no basis in Scripture. In the New Testament the terms "elders" and "bishops" are used as synonyms. The New Testament knows nothing of a visible monarchy, aristocracy, or democracy in the church at large. (Matt. 23:8-10; 20:25-26; I Cor. 3:5-7; I Pet. 5:3; II Cor. 8:8.) In some countries the State has usurped authority over the Church (Caesaropapism); in others the Church has attempted to control the State (Papocaesarism). Neither the one nor the other meets with Christ's approval (Matt. 22:21; Acts 5:29). Christ has given no consistory, presbytery, or synod any authority over the Church. Whatever authority such groups have has been given them by men and can extend only to external matters which do not involve conscience. No body or individual has the right to legislate in matters of doctrine. The Church has only one authority, namely, the Word of God. The Bible is the Church's fundamental law. Any doctrine or practice which conflicts with it is, to use a term borrowed from political science, unconstitutional. "Should not a people seek unto their God?" (Is. 8:19.) "To the Law and to the Testimony: if they speak not according to this Word, it is because there is no light in them" (Is. 8:20). Peter warns: "If any man speak, let him speak as the oracles of God" (I Pet. 4:11). In His Word Christ, moreover, speaks directly to every believer. He has appointed no one infallible interpreter of His Word, whose interpretation would be binding on the Church. It was Peter who wrote these words: "We have also a more sure Word of prophecy: whereunto ye do well that ye take heed, as unto a light that shineth in a dark place, until the day dawn, and the Daystar arise in your hearts; knowing this first, that no prophecy of the Scripture is of any private interpretation" (II Pet. 1:19-20). All Christians have the right of the

Bereans, who "searched the Scriptures daily, whether those things were so" (Acts 17:11).

With respect to the relation between the Church Universal and the local churches, Scripture teaches clearly that these are not two different churches or two different kinds of churches, but the Church Universal consists of all true believers who are found in the local churches, together with all individual believers who on account of peculiar circumstances do not hold membership in a local church.

ORTHODOX AND HETERODOX CHURCHES

The visible Church may be divided into an orthodox and a heterodox church. Inasmuch as the Church is "built upon the foundation of the Apostles and Prophets, Jesus Christ Himself being the chief Cornerstone" (Eph. 2:20), it must adhere firmly to the Word of Christ and of the Apostles, who were His witnesses and spokesmen. To those Jews who believed on Him Jesus said: "If ye continue in My Word, then are ye My disciples indeed; and ye shall know the truth, and the truth shall make you free" (John 8:31-32). Before leaving His disciples, Jesus gave them the command to teach all nations to observe all things whatsoever He had commanded them. (Matt. 28:20.) This was not a temporary command, for He added the words: "And, lo, I am with you alway, even unto the end of the world" (*ibid.*). Christ wants His Word taught in truth and purity. Puny man is not arrogantly to add his own thoughts in conflict with the divine Word or to deny any part of it. False prophets, however, do this very thing. Already in the Old Testament the Lord had to complain: "I have not sent these prophets, yet they ran; I have not spoken to them, yet they prophesied" (Jer. 23:21). Paul instructed Timothy to charge some "that they teach no other doctrine" (I Tim. 1:3). Again, "If any man teach otherwise, and consent not to wholesome words, even the words of our Lord Jesus Christ, and to the doctrine which is according to godliness; he is proud, knowing nothing, but doting about questions and strifes of words, whereof cometh envy, strife, railings, evil surmisings, perverse disputings of men of corrupt minds, and destitute of the truth, supposing that gain is godliness: from such withdraw thyself" (I Tim. 6:3-5). Purity of doctrine is, therefore, the criterion for orthodoxy. This implies the preaching, teaching, and profession of divine truth in all its purity, and the administration of the Sacraments in full accordance with their divine institution. The church which does this is an orthodox church. To the extent that any church does not do this, it is a heterodox church. This difference must never be ignored, particularly in our time when the slogan "Not creeds, but deeds" is so generally adopted and religious indifference and the spirit of unionism are rampant, frequently cloaked in the guise of charity.

To qualify as an orthodox church, a church must be faithful to all the doctrines of the Bible. This presupposes that its creeds or public confessions must be Scriptural. This is true of the Confessional Writings of the Lutheran Church. According to these, the Lutheran Church is an orthodox Church. Churches which subscribe to creeds that in any manner depart from the truth of Scripture are heterodox churches. The public confessions of such churches are the fruits by which they are to be known. Jesus uttered this warning: "Beware of false prophets, which come to you in sheep's clothing, but inwardly they are ravening wolves," adding the words: "Ye shall know them by their fruits" (Matt. 7:15-16). The term "ravening wolves" is not too harsh. Every error in doctrine is a peril to the soul, and its teacher partakes of the nature of a ravening wolf. However, the formal subscription to a true creed or confession is not enough in itself. There are those who by formal resolution, in convention assembled, subscribe to all the Lutheran Confessions, but who in their teaching and practice depart from them. The claims of such to orthodoxy are a mockery. Not merely the official creed of a church but its actual daily profession and application determines the extent of its orthodoxy. Jesus says: "*Teaching* them to observe all things." Certainly not the official creed of a church standing on some shelf will work faith, but the lesson taught in school and the sermon preached from the pulpit. Be it added that Lutherans should subscribe to their Confessions, not *in so far* as they agree with the Bible, but *because* they do that.

A church does not become a heterodox church at once if false doctrine occasionally disturbs it. From the days of the Apostles to our own this has happened. Paul could truthfully say to the elders of Ephesus: "For I have not shunned to declare unto you all the counsel of God" (Acts 20:27), but he found it necessary to warn them: "Also of your own selves shall men arise, speaking perverse

286 The Abiding Word

things, to draw away disciples after them" (v. 30). This eventuality did not make the church at Ephesus a heterodox one. The Ephesian church would have become so under such circumstances if the elders had not heeded the words of the Apostle: "Therefore watch, and remember that by the space of three years I ceased not to warn every one night and day with tears" (v. 31). A church stands to lose its orthodoxy as soon as it ceases to watch and to warn against error in all seriousness.

Persistent false teaching makes a church a sect. An orthodox church is not a sect. A false church is a church to the extent that it adheres to the truth, a sect to the extent that it departs from it. Errorists cause divisions contrary to the Apostolic doctrine, thereby creating sects. Calling a church a sect is an indictment of its errors and an admonition to accept the truth in its entirety.

The orthodox visible church is not the only saving church. When faithful pastors warn against the errors of a heterodox church, they do not thereby impugn the Christianity of the believers in such a church. Wherever the Gospel is to be found and sinners put their trust in it, there Christians are to be found. As a matter of fact, they may be veritable paragons of Christianity, since they must retain their faith under great difficulties. Christ had His disciples during the centuries of spiritual darkness which preceded the Reformation, when there was no orthodox visible church on earth. Paul says: "A man is justified by faith without the deeds of the Law" (Rom. 3:28). By which faith? Jesus answers: "Whosoever believeth in Him [God's only-begotten Son] should not perish, but have everlasting life" (John 3:16). Whoever believes that, is saved, no matter to which denomination he belongs.

UNIONISM

The presence of true Christians in heterodox churches, however, does not justify fraternization with such churches on the part of an orthodox church. Nor is an orthodox Christian justified in joining a heterodox church because there are still Christians in it. God's command simply says: "Avoid them" (Rom. 16:17). It is not a charitable act to confirm anyone in error by apparently ignoring it; but this is done when churches join in ecclesiastical functions without first eliminating offensive doctrinal errors, or when an individual joins a heterodox church in public worship. The emphasis here is on joining in worship. The mere presence of a true believer in a heterodox assembly need not in itself be an act of worship. He may, for example, attend the burial service in a heterodox assembly merely as a mark of respect to the deceased.

Joint worship where difference in doctrine demands separation, is unionism; separation and division where God's Word does not demand it, is schism. This word denotes a formal division or separation in the Christian Church or the offense of seeking to produce division in a church. Schismatics are those who create or take part in schism, and a group of them constitute a schismatic body. Schismatics cause a separation on non-divisive grounds (adiaphora) for personal, hence sinful, reasons. Some may do this out of malice, others out of weakness or ignorance. Because God demands it, separation on account of false doctrine may not be classified as schism.

RIGHTS AND POWERS OF THE CHURCH

The rights and powers of the Church have already been mentioned elsewhere, but they are important enough to be considered separately. They may be summarized as the right and power of preaching the Gospel, the administration of the Sacraments, especially the application of the keys of heaven by loosing and binding in the name of God. To Peter, the spokesman of all the disciples in a public confession of faith in Christ the Son of God, Jesus gave the keys of the kingdom of heaven to bind and to loose. (Matt. 16:19.) This power He gave to the local church. He says: "Tell it unto the church; but if he neglect to hear the church, let him be unto thee as an heathen man and a publican. Verily, I say unto you, Whatsoever ye shall bind on earth shall be bound in heaven: and whatsoever ye shall loose on earth shall be loosed in heaven" (Matt. 18:17-18). To His disciples He gave the command: "Go ye into all the world, and preach the Gospel to every creature. He that believeth and is baptized shall be saved" (Mark 16:15-16). Here Jesus combines the preaching of the Gospel with the administration of the Sacrament. On the evening of His resurrection He breathed on His disciples and said: "Receive ye the Holy Ghost: whosesoever sins ye remit, they are remitted unto them, and whosesoever sins ye retain, they are retained" (John 20:22-23). A manifest and impenitent sinner is to be excluded from the Christian congregation; therefore Paul writes to the Corinthians concerning such a one: "Put away from among yourselves that wicked person" (I Cor. 5:13). These are the rights and powers of the Church which every local congregation is to exercise. Whatever else a church may do either serves their effective execution or is the blessed fruit of faith. The congregation may build a church or school to help the preaching and teaching in its midst; it may engage in eleemosynary activity. Such things are by-products of the real purpose of the Church: to save souls. The church in Jerusalem presents this example: "Then the Twelve called the multitude of the disciples unto them and said, It is not reason that we should leave the Word of God, and serve tables. Wherefore, brethren, look ye out among you seven men of honest report, full of the Holy Ghost and wisdom, whom we may appoint over this business. But we will give ourselves continually to prayer, and to the ministry of the Word" (Acts 6:2-4). In order to stir up the congregation at Corinth to contribute to the saints, Paul wrote: "Wherefore show ye to them [the messengers of the churches], and before the churches, the proof of your love, and of our boasting on your behalf" (II Cor. 8:24). The Church is not founded for the purpose of being an institution for social welfare, but individually and collectively its members do a great deal of blessed social work, thereby letting their light shine before the people as Christ has commanded them to do. (Matt. 5:16.)

SOME PRACTICAL APPLICATIONS OF THE DOCTRINE OF THE CHURCH

What, now, are we to do about the doctrine of the Church? In the first place, we are to take heed to be and remain members of the invisible Church. That simply means that we are to remain penitent sinners, who, in daily contrition, turn to Jesus for forgiveness. In view of the Lord's Parable of the Sower—the fowls, the stony places, the thorns—we must heed Paul's admonition: "Examine yourselves whether ye be in the faith; prove your own selves" (II Cor. 13:5). Faith being engendered and preserved by the means of grace, we must be found in the congregation of God's saints. This implies that we support the Gospel ministry, for "the Lord ordained that they which preach the Gospel should live of the Gospel" (I Cor. 9:14). Christians cannot keep the joy of their salvation to themselves; they cannot but speak the things which they have seen and heard (Acts 4:20). Like the shepherds at Bethlehem they must make known abroad the saying which was told them concerning the Christ Child. (Luke 2:17.) They want Christ's Church to grow. And inasmuch as false doctrine is poison to the soul and hinders the growth of the Church, they avoid false teachers (I John 4:1). They are anxious to be translated from the Church Militant on earth to the Church Triumphant above; they want to advance from Christ's Kingdom of Grace to that of Glory. And they want others to do that. Paul expresses their attitude in these words to Timothy: "Therefore I endure all things for the elect's sakes, that they may also obtain the salvation which is in Christ Jesus with eternal glory" (II Tim. 2:10).

When the last one of the elect has been added as a member to the Church, Christ's body, the end will come. The Church Militant will cease to exist; the Church Triumphant will remain. Christ's Kingdom of Grace will be no more; His Kingdom of Glory will continue forever. "And the ransomed of the Lord shall return, and come to Zion with songs and everlasting joy upon their heads: they shall obtain joy and gladness, and sorrow and sighing shall flee away" (Is. 35:10). "But the God of all grace, who hath called us unto His eternal glory by Christ Jesus, after that ye have suffered awhile, make you perfect, stablish, strengthen, settle you!" (I Pet. 5:10.)

XV

The Evangelical Lutheran Church, the True Visible Church of God

OUR topic was chosen by Dr. Walther as the title of one of his outstanding works. Originally published in *Der Lutheraner* as the basis for the doctrinal discussions of Synod at its convention at Fort Wayne, 1866, it was by resolution of Synod published in book form, and a brief explanation of the Scripture proof showing the pertinency of the passages was added.

This Scripture proof is followed by testimonies, consisting of quotations from the Symbolical Books of our Church, from Luther, and from other great teachers of the Lutheran Church, which prove that the truth expressed in the theses on the basis of Scripture has been generally taught within the Lutheran Church.

This book was to serve the Districts as the basis for a thorough discussion of the theses at their conventions and at the same time was to enable their members to acquaint themselves in advance with the subject matter. Three Districts followed the suggestion made at their conventions in 1867. The Western District continued the discussion of the previous year up to Thesis Six; the Central District continued the discussion and completed Thesis Ten; in the Eastern District Thesis Thirteen was finished. In the same year the Northern District discussed "The Principles of the Lutheran Church on the Interpretation of the Bible" on the basis of twenty-nine theses. For this reason Theses Fourteen to Sixteen of Walther's book were not discussed (see *Walther's Letters*, II, p. 101). In 1868 the Western District began with Thesis Seventeen and finished part of Eighteen. The Central District spent all of its time on the same thesis, particularly on Points B and C, and the Eastern District in the same year discussed Point C of this thesis and began Point D, finishing the discussion of C and D at the convention held in 1871.

Naturally much of the material contained in the later theses was anticipated in the discussion at these meetings. Some of the material contained in the later theses had already been discussed at earlier conventions. In 1858, for instance, the Western District had discussed the proper attitude towards the Symbolical Books of the Church on the basis of Walther's famous paper: "Why Are the Symbolical Books of Our Church to be Subscribed to Unreservedly by Those Who Wish to Be Its Servants?" The theses prepared by Walther are accessible in the book *Walther and the Church*, edited by Dr. Th. Engelder in collaboration with Dr. W. Dallmann and Dr. W. H. T. Dau. To each thesis some comment is added. The Scripture proof is merely indicated, and there are some references to the testimonies.

Our presentation accordingly will not be a connected exposition of Walther's book, but a brief summary of the doctrinal essays read at various synodical and District conventions and the ensuing discussions. In many cases we shall hear Walther himself giving the implications and applications of the material he had prepared.

Thesis I

The one holy Christian Church on earth, or the Church in the proper sense of the word, outside which there is no salvation, is, according to God's Word, the total of all that truly believe in Christ and are sanctified through this faith.

The discussion at Fort Wayne, Ind., in the year 1866 was introduced by a statement of Dr. Walther giving the reasons for the preparation of these theses. Till now, he stated, we have been compelled to emphasize the doctrine of the invisible Church and to combat the error that the visible Lutheran Church is the one holy Christian Church. Because of this controversy we have been looked upon and suspected as people who disparaged the true visible Lutheran Church, and who because of unionistic inclinations considered it immaterial to which visible church body one belonged. This battle has now been victoriously completed. Lately nobody has dared to state publicly that the visible Lutheran Church is the one holy Christian Church, outside which there is no salvation. In order, however, to meet the objection that we care nothing for the true visible Church, we shall now gladly present the doctrine of the

Evangelical Lutheran Church as the true visible Church of God on earth and discuss this doctrine jointly on the basis of Holy Scripture and the Confessions of our Church. This will serve to establish us in the joyous assurance that we are not members and servants of a false Church but of the true Church and therefore are building the true Zion.

Christ says, "On this rock I will build My Church" (Matt. 16:18). This rock is Christ (I Cor. 3:11; Eph. 2:19-22).

Eph. 5:23 emphasizes these truths: "Christ is the Head of the Church"; "He is the Savior of the body"; "The Church is subject unto Christ . . . in everything"; "Christ has cleansed to Himself a glorious Church, not having spot, holy and without blemish."—Only he who has been justified through faith in Christ Jesus is united with Christ and belongs to the Church of Christ. This doctrine is not only a matter of interest to theologians, but is at the same time an urgent call to repentance. If we are silent on this doctrine, or if we preach an opposing false doctrine, all hypocrites may think that they are members of the true Church, since they outwardly belong to the Lutheran Church. This doctrine is also a source of great comfort for people living far away from any church. Such people may think they are outside the Church; but if such a person has Christ in his heart through true faith, he is in the Church and enjoys the most intimate communion with all the saints and the blessed. Martin Luther stayed in the Church of the Pope as long as he did only because he did not understand the doctrine of the Church. Finally he realized: the believers are the Church; by leaving the Papacy I am not leaving the Church.

Heb. 3:6 states: "But Christ as a Son over His own house; whose house are we if we hold fast the confidence and the rejoicing of the hope firm unto the end." Though people who remain in the true faith for only a time may be called members of the Church during that time, only those may in the strict sense be called members of the Church who remain steadfast in faith.—The remark was made from the floor: "The sectarians claim that whoever departs from their teaching thereby separates from Christ. Such a claim, to be sure, is erroneous, because the people who leave the sects thereby separate from false doctrine; but certainly we Lutherans can say that whoever separates from the visible Lutheran Church is lost and separates from Christ." Walther answered that we can make such a statement only if we can add that he stubbornly separated from the Lutheran Church against better knowledge and if we have sure and infallible proof that this person has also lost faith in Christ or has never been a Christian. We must admit that there are true believers among the sects and that we cannot, for instance, condemn or excommunicate all Methodists. If we were to consider all people who have left the Lutheran Church children of death, we should have to prove that nobody could leave his Church because of an erring conscience. We must indeed condemn the action, but not the person, unless we are sure that he has utterly departed from the Word of God.

Walther's first testimonies for this thesis were taken from the Augsburg Confession. Article VII reads: "The Church is the congregation of saints, in which the Gospel is rightly taught and the Sacraments are rightly administered." Article VIII states: "Although the Church properly is the congregation of saints and true believers." Article VII first contains a definition of the Church and then states the marks whereby the Church may be recognized. This interpretation is proved by the statement in Article VIII and conclusively determined by the Apology, which repeatedly states that this is the proper understanding of Article VII. Wherever there are believers, there we have the Church. We dare not follow the error of Romanizing Lutherans, who contend that the Church is the visible assembly of believers about the Word and the Sacraments. According to the Apology the marks indicate not what the Church is, but where it is. We must admit that the Church is found among heterodox bodies, who do not have the pure Word and Sacrament. We do not say that people should join such bodies. We are not the champions of false teachers, but of the children of God who are hidden in this body.

A lengthy section from the Apology (*Triglot*, p. 229f.) led to an emphasis on the spiritual nature of the Church. It is inconceivable how Lutheran theologians can declare that wicked men are members of the Church. They contend that Christ wished to establish an external religious kingdom similar to the kingdoms of this world, with a hierarchy of officers, *i. e.*, pastors and other rulers, and with the distinction of those who rule and those who obey. They assert that the difference between these two kingdoms consists only in this, that the kingdoms of this world concern themselves with temporal matters, whereas the Church concerns itself with religious matters. But according to Scripture the true Church of Christ is invisible because it consists only of true believers and faith is invisible. Two men may give a gift to a poor person, but I do not know which one is doing this act in faith as a Christian and which one is not doing it in true faith.—As the Head of the Church is invisible, so also His body, the Church, is invisible. It is therefore not proper to speak of two sides of the Church, one visible and one invisible. Strictly speaking, the Church is invisible and will be invisible until it is revealed with Christ in glory. We should not say that the Church is visible, but only that its existence can be determined by certain marks.

Thesis II

Though the one holy Christian Church, as a spiritual temple, cannot be seen but only believed, yet there are infallible outward marks by which its presence is known; these marks are the pure preaching of God's Word and the unadulterated administration of the holy Sacraments.

According to Thesis I the Church is invisible. This might lead us to think that it is immaterial whether we belong to a congregation or which church we join. Therefore our second thesis states that the invisible Church has infallible marks and that it can easily be found and recognized.

Three passages: I Pet. 2:5, II Tim. 2:19, and Gal. 4:26, are adduced as proofs for the fact that the Church is invisible. A special note is added to Gal. 4. False Lutherans interpret the words "Jerusalem which is above" as referring to the Church Triumphant. But we must bear in mind that Scripture, when speaking of the kingdom of heaven, does not use the terms "above" and "below" in a local sense, but that "above" means heavenly and "below" means earthly. For St. Paul writes Col. 3:1, 2: "Seek those things which are above.". . . "Set your affections on things above, not on things on the earth." The Jerusalem which is above is the holy Christian Church because it is heavenly in its nature.

Scripture shows us that the preaching of the Word is the infallible mark of the Church. The first proof is found in Mark 4:26, 27: "And He said, So is the Kingdom of God, as if a man should cast seed into the ground, and should sleep and rise night and day, and *the seed should spring and grow up,* he knoweth not how." According to verse 14 "the sower soweth the Word"; Matt. 13:38 states, "The good seed are the children of the Kingdom." The seed grows, although the sower does not know how; but in spite of all weeds the sower, having sowed the seed, knows where his field of wheat is. Similarly, no man can see the believers grow as the plants of God; but the seed of the Word which has been sown is the sure mark whereby the field of the Church may be recognized; for the seed of the Word not only bears the children of the Kingdom or the true believers in itself as a germ, but according to Christ's own words it will spring and grow up.

The Romanists try to ensnare people by pointing to marks of the Church which are either false or fallible, such as the unity and holiness of the Church, the name Catholic, the age of their Church, miracles which supposedly have been wrought in the Roman Church. Not all characteristics of the Church are also infallible marks of the Church, since many of these characteristics are found also in other groups. Similarly, the Methodists claim to possess certain infallible marks of the Church, as, for instance, purity of life, missionary zeal, zeal in prayer, etc., but these also are not infallible marks. The Word, however, is an infallible mark.

In connection with Matt. 28:18-20 it was remarked that Word and Sacrament are not marks of the Church because a visible religious institution is established wherever Word and Sacrament are in vogue. In this sense even the opponents of the true doctrine admit that Word and Sacrament are marks of the Church because they consider Word and Sacrament as essential parts of the definition of the Church. This, however, is an utterly un-Lutheran notion. They are the infallible marks of the Church because the Church is born through the Word.

St. Paul states in I Cor. 12:13: "For by one Spirit are we all baptized into one body, whether we be Jews or Gentiles, whether we be bond or free; and have been all made to drink into one Spirit." Gal. 3:27: "For as many of you as have been baptized into Christ have put on Christ." Where the two holy Sacraments are administered according to Christ's institution, there believers are to be found, and a church exists. The administration of the Sacraments is therefore also an infallible mark of the Church.

To prove that this is Lutheran doctrine, Article VII of the Augsburg Confession was quoted as well as several sections from the Apology referring to the same matter. The last sentence in one quotation reads, "And we add the marks: the pure doctrine of the Gospel (the ministry of the Gospel) and the Sacraments." The German original has the word *Predigtamt*. This remark called forth the statement that the Apology does not use this word in the sense of Grabau, who always identifies the ministry with the pastoral office and claims that no one could obtain faith or forgiveness of sins or salvation without the pastoral office.

Thesis III

In an improper sense Scripture applies the term "churches" also to all visible communions which indeed do not consist only of believers and persons sanctified by faith, but to whom hypocrites and wicked are admixed, among whom, however, the Gospel is preached in its purity and the Sacraments are administered according to the Gospel.

Thesis I shows what the Church really is; Thesis II, whereby we may know it and where we may find it. The question may be asked, How does it happen that the Bible frequently uses the word "church" not of a communion of saints, but of a group of people of whom evidently not all are holy? Human language uses most words in more than one sense, and therefore the Bible also does. Such visible bodies bear the name of church by synecdoche, the whole receiving its name from the part which really alone deserves the name, just as we call a ring a gold ring even if it contains some copper, and a field a field of wheat even though weeds grow on it.

Matt. 18 the Lord says, "Tell it unto the church." Evidently this is not the Church Universal, but the local congregation. In a similar manner Paul calls those inhabitants of Corinth who after his preaching had formed a visible congregation "the church of God which is in Corinth." In such churches in which the Word of God is regularly preached there may be and usually are also unchristians and hypocrites. Yet a church is not called a church because of the hypocrites within it, but because of the believing children of God found where the Gospel is being preached. People, therefore, who leave a church because of its wicked members, because, as they say, it consists only of hypocrites and is no church, are slandering the children of God within that congregation and thereby the Lord Jesus Himself.

The theological axiom "Outside the Church there is no salvation" applies only to the invisible Church and not to the visible Church. This truth must be maintained against Grabau and the Roman Church, which calls itself the only saving Church, and against the sects who claim that they are perfectly holy.

This truth is taught also in the Augsburg Confession, Article VIII: "Although the Church properly is the congregation of saints and true believers, nevertheless, since in this life many hypocrites and evil persons are mingled therewith, it is lawful to use Sacraments administered by evil men, according to the saying of Christ 'The scribes and the Pharisees sit in Moses' seat,' etc. (Matt. 23:2). Both the Sacraments and Word are effectual by reason of the institution and commandment of Christ, notwithstanding they be administered by evil men." These hypocrites and evil persons are not in reality members of the Church, but are members only in name, as even the Canon Law of the Roman Church admits. They have connection with the Church in outward rights, titles, and offices. They may even be pastors, or teachers, or elders, but they have no real communion with the real believers. There are hypocrites among the Christians because the devil sows tares among the wheat, but Christ sows only the wheat. This truth should cause all of us to examine ourselves whether or not we are really true believers, whereas the doctrine that hypocrites are real members of the Church leads men to carnal security.

Also the dogmaticians of the Church teach the same doctrine, and the Formula of Concord condemns the erroneous doctrine of the Anabaptists "that that is no true Christian congregation in which sinners are still found."

Thesis IV

In Scripture the name "church" is given even to those visible congregations which have become guilty of a partial lapse from the true doctrine, as long as they hold God's Word essentially.

The previous thesis stresses the fact that we may call visible congregations churches, although they contain unbelievers. But since we know that there are Christians even where the doctrine is not pure, our fourth thesis tells us that the Church exists also where it is tyrannized by false teachers. An example of such tyranny is the Papacy; even there God maintained His Church, so that the gates of hell could not prevail against it. Elijah believed that he alone was left, but the Lord assured him that seven thousand in Israel had not bowed unto Baal. Wherever, therefore, the Word of God is still essentially present or where the defection is only partial, as long as parts of the saving truth are still present, the Church still exists, and we find Christians.

The important words in this thesis are, "as long as they hold God's Word essentially," that is, as long as they hold and confess the Bible to be God's Word. Even though false teachers do not present all doctrines of Scripture correctly, if they still testify that the Bible is the book from which everyone may learn the way of salvation, their hearers still have the criterion whereby they can distinguish the wrong from the true. But if false teachers declare the Bible to be a book of fables, as the Socinians, Universalists, and Rationalists do, then God's Word is no longer essentially held. They sometimes say that the Bible is the Word of God, but their further explanation shows their deception. To declare the Bible to be the Word of God means more than to utter these words. It means to declare the Scripture to be the sole judge in matters of faith. The Reformed and the honest Catholics believe this, and therefore the Church still exists in their midst. It is also to be noted that the word "essentially" modifies the word "hold" and not "God's Word."

The Scripture proof for this thesis is taken from the Letter to the Galatians. Paul calls the Galatians "the churches of Galatia" (Gal. 1:2), and still he has to tell them that important doctrines of the Scripture have been falsified among them. Gal. 3:1: "O foolish Galatians, who hath bewitched you that ye should not obey the truth?" and 5:4: "Christ is become of no effect unto you, whosoever of you are justified by the Law; ye are fallen from grace." Still the Galatians held God's Word to be God's Word, and since the seed of regeneration was still among them, there were Christians in their midst.

A quotation from the Introduction to the Book of Concord shows that although we must condemn every false doctrine, "it is in no way our design and purpose to condemn those men who err from a certain simplicity of mind, but are not blasphemers against the truth

of the heavenly doctrine, much less, indeed, entire churches"
(*Triglot*, p. 19).

In connection with other quotations the fact was emphasized that
we must also bear in mind that there are degrees of purity in doctrine.—Article VII of the Augsburg Confession contains the statement: "in which the Gospel is rightly taught and the Sacraments
are rightly administered." Our Confessions do not wish to teach that
the Church does not exist where the Word is not taught entirely, in
its full purity. Gerhard states that definitions, rules, and laws must
be taken from the ideal. The Church can still exist where enough of
the Scriptural truth is proclaimed that people may come to faith. A
church body administers Baptism correctly if it still confesses the
Triune God, even though its doctrine regarding the benefit of the
Sacrament may be erroneous. Though we admit this truth, we agree
with Loescher that we dare not practice church fellowship with
people who do not proclaim the Word of God in its truth and purity.

Thesis V

*Communions still holding God's Word essentially but erring
obstinately in fundamentals are, in so far as they do so, not churches
but schisms or sects, i. e., heretical communions.*

Dr. Dallmann complains that he found it hard to make the very
German Walther speak English. We notice this difficulty in connection with our thesis. The German word rendered schisms is *Rotten*.
This word has a connotation absent from the word "schism," that of
mutiny and factiousness, and at times approaches the idea of our
modern *gang*. A sect in English is either a group of persons who
follow a particular school of thought or a group cut off from a larger
body, from an established or a parent church, by differences in the
interpretation or application of what all regard as the same revelation. The German *Sekte* implies a heretical group which has accepted false doctrine and for this reason has separated from the
Church.

The lengthy discussion of this thesis revolved about the controversies and problems of the time. Grabau and others had ridiculed
Synod's doctrine of the Church and accused the fathers of making
the sects component parts of the Church. Therefore great emphasis
is placed on the statement "in so far as they do so." When we use the

term "the Reformed Church," we disregard all who mock and blaspheme the truth; but in so far as a heterodox Church is a sect and holds fast to error, it surely does not belong to the Church. In so far as there are Christians among the Reformed, they are a Church; in so far as false teachers among them degrade the pure doctrine, they are a sect. If a member of the Reformed Church rejects the false doctrine of the Lord's Supper, of Baptism, of absolute predestination, etc., we accept him as a brother. If, however, such a person, though he appears to be a Christian, confesses his acceptance of these false doctrines, we cannot acknowledge him as a brother and must let the Lord judge whether he is a Christian or not.

Grabau continually bestowed the name of sect and heretical communion upon our Synod without, however, ever proving that we erred in a single doctrine. As soon as any person or group opposed him even in a slight degree, he called them sectarians or heretics.

As our Lutheran theologians understand the term, a heretic is a person who maintains his false doctrine in spite of repeated admonition, who attacks the pure doctrine and causes divisions and offenses and thus deceives the souls by soul-destroying error. A heretic is a person, and a heretical communion is the group that follows him. A sect is more than a mere division in the Church, it is a communion founded by false teachers, privily brought into the Church, a group in which destructive, damnable, fundamental errors are being circulated.

Luther calls attention to the famous statement of Augustine: "I shall possibly err, but I shall not be a heretic," because he was willing to acknowledge his error and to have it shown to him. Some famous Church Fathers erred and built wood, hay, and stubble upon the foundation which is Jesus Christ, but they were either not admonished or cast their false doctrine aside in the hour of death. Such men should not be called heretics. Heretics refuse to accept admonition and persist in their false doctrine as Arius did.

A congregation or a denomination becomes a sect when it persists in false doctrine in spite of admonition. The Papacy is the worst example of a sect. But even in this corrupt group some Scriptural doctrines are still in evidence, though not in their purity. When a child is baptized in the name of the Triune God in this Church, we behold the Church; when, however, the doctrine is preached that he who sins after Baptism is lost, we see the sect. The Roman Church is full of damnable errors, and a Christian should know these errors, to be able to bear witness to the truth.

This thesis should not be abused to foster what was called syncretism in the 17th century and what we now call unionism. The following argument is used by unionists: Since God has His believers in all churches, let us all unite and form one large brotherhood. This theory rests on a fallacy. We believe that Christians are to be found among the sects, but we do not know them. When a person adheres to a false doctrine, I do not know whether he is a Christian and a believer.—We are obligated to preach the pure doctrine, and this obligation involves testimony against false doctrine. For twenty years we have been testifying against false doctrine, and God has blessed our witness. The Papacy and unionism are the two most dangerous forces. The Pope makes salvation doubtful; unionism makes truth doubtful. Let us be filled with a holy hatred against the Pope and against unionism.—Nobody dare say, I dislike controversy. A Christian is called to battle and controversy. God has called us to a ministry of reproof; God's Word is profitable for reproof, for the reproof of false doctrine. God tells us, Reprove; the world says, Do not reprove. Whom are we to obey? Christ did not hesitate to reprove error, and called the errorists by name. Error is always dangerous. If we give the devil the little finger, he will soon take the whole hand. True love for the souls living in error requires that we show them their error.—Finally, we must not overlook the fact that not only error, but also errorists are not to be tolerated.

THESIS VI

Communions destroying the unity of the Church through nonfundamental error or on account of personalities or ceremonies or life are, according to God's Word, schismatic or separatistic communions.

Thesis V speaks of people who separate from the true Church because they hold fundamental errors. In Thesis VI the reason for separation is a different one. Individuals or groups leave the true Church because they disagree in secondary doctrines or even on account of persons who have incurred their displeasure or, in their opinion, have offended them. Some separate on account of ceremonies, because the pastor chants the liturgy, because the chorals are sung rhythmically, because wafers are used in the celebration of the Lord's Supper, because the communicants kneel at the altar. Others leave on account of life, claiming that the congregation consists of godless people or of unconverted people. Such a separation is not called a sect but a schism in ecclesiastic parlance.

The Biblical proof for this thesis is found I Cor. 11:18, 19: "For first of all, when ye come together in the church, I hear that there be divisions among you; and I partly believe it. For there must be also heresies among you, that they which are approved may be made manifest among you." Such divisions and separations do not occur on account of doctrine, but on account of persons, or when people withdraw from public services and from association with their fellow Christians for reasons other than doctrine. Heb. 10:24, 25 states: "Let us consider one another to provoke unto love and to good works, not forsaking the assembling of ourselves together, as the manner of some is, but exhorting one another, and so much the more as ye see the day approaching."

An example of separation on account of nonfundamental doctrines was given. If members were to leave our Synod because they no longer believe that the Pope is the Antichrist, they would be causing a separation. For this doctrine is not a part of the foundation of our faith. We do not believe in the Pope, but in Christ. This error is not a fundamental error, but it is a dangerous error. We would not call those who leave us heretics, but we would not have fellowship with them.

Such separations, or schisms, have disrupted some congregations. Later immigrants have joined this schismatic group in ignorance simply because their relatives belong to it. We should apply the term "schismatic" only to those who have caused the division. In refusing to practice church fellowship we are not declaring such people to be excommunicated.

Many immigrants are not accustomed to genuine Lutheran ceremonies, as we use them. If they leave a congregation merely on account of such ceremonies, they commit a grave sin. Because of the objections of such people not all congregations have introduced these ceremonies. A congregation need not refrain from such introduction because one or two members object, but must indeed permit them to refrain from making use of them. (They may stand while receiving Communion). Uniformity in ceremonies should be considered a goal to strive for and steps should be taken to educate the people.

Thesis VII

Communions calling themselves Christian but not accepting God's Word as God's Word and therefore denying the Triune God are, according to God's Word, not churches but synagogs of Satan and temples of idols.

Since Christ commands that all who are to be received into His Church are to be baptized in the name of the Triune God, the Father, the Son, and the Holy Ghost (Matt. 28:19), all communions denying the mystery of the Trinity are outside the Church. Since John writes, "Whosoever denieth the Son, the same hath not the Father" (I John 2:23), all worship of people who deny that Jesus is the true Son of God, is not worship of God, but idolatry. John says, "Christ is the true God and eternal life. Little children, keep yourselves from idols" (I John 5:20, 21), and thereby shows that the worship of those who deny the deity of Christ is pagan idolatry. Now that Christ has appeared, the Jews are no longer a people and Church of God, but the synagog of Satan. So also all communions that, together with the Jews, deny the Word of God of the New Testament and deny that Jesus is the Christ, are not Christians, not God's people, not a church, but a synagog of Satan (Rev. 2:9).

This declaration does not deny the Christianity of the congregations in Germany upon whom rationalistic wolves were foisted by the State during the time of Rationalism. The congregations never approved of the blasphemy. But congregations which of their own free will refuse to have the Christian faith and Baptism are in a different position. Unitarians, Socinians, Swedenborgians are outside the pale of Christendom. Such people pray to idols. The passages here quoted apply also to the Masons. A question was asked regarding the validity of the baptism performed by the pastor of the Free Protestant Church in Cincinnati, who denied the Trinity. Since the congregation evidently agreed with its pastor, the Lutheran congregation was advised to notify the Protestant congregation that it would not consider its baptism valid.

Thesis VIII

Occasionally theologians apply the name "true," i. e., "real Church", in distinction from nonchurches, to all communions that

*still retain the Word of God essentially; yet, when we use the term
without reservations and in contrast to erring churches or sects, the
true visible Church is only that Church in which God's Word is
preached in its purity and the holy Sacraments are administered
according to the Gospel.*

Theologians use the word "true" in a twofold sense. 1. We may say
a communion has the essential characteristics of the Church. In this
sense we may call the Reformed and other churches true, or real,
churches. 2. The word "true" indicates the possession of all the
virtues which a person or an object could and should have to be
perfect. Our thesis uses the term in the second sense. Our Church
possesses all of the virtues which a visible Church can have. "True"
therefore means as much as orthodox.

Our thesis also uses the expression "without reservations." When
we speak of other churches in which false doctrines are current, we
must always add a limitation; we must say that they deserve the
name "church" only with certain reservations.

The well-known passage in John 8:31: "If ye continue in My
Word, then are ye My disciples indeed," shows that the true Church
continues in Christ's Word, hears His voice, follows Him in every
way, and flees from the strangers who teach a different doctrine. We
admit that there are Christians in heterodox groups, but we do not
tell them, "Stay where you are." The Lord tells them, "Continue in
My Word." Error is like any sin. If I commit a sin without knowing
that it is sin, I may still remain in the state of grace. If I later realize
that my deed is sinful and still continue in it, I sin against conscience
and am lost.—We should be grateful that we are Lutherans. False
doctrine is a poison and spreads farther and farther, unless a man
frees himself of it. Our Lutheran Church with its insistence on pure
doctrine has been a blessing also to errorists and has kept them
from proceeding farther in their false doctrine. It is the duty of our
Church to raise its voice aloud in defense of the divine truth.

The passage I Cor. 1:10: "I beseech you . . . that ye all speak the
same thing and that there be no divisions among you, but that ye be
perfectly joined together in the same mind and in the same judgment," testifies against men who subscribe to the Confessions without a reservation, but later ask for the privilege of interpreting
them as they please.

Since many people contend that agreement in all doctrines is not necessary, the Formula of Concord was quoted: "Thus the churches will not condemn one another because of dissimilarity of ceremonies when, in Christian liberty, one has less or more of them, provided they are otherwise agreed with one another in the doctrine and *all* its articles, also in the right use of the holy Sacraments" (*Triglot,* p. 1063).

A Church is considered a true Church, even though error is found in it, if the error is not maintained publicly and if it is reproved.

Thesis IX

Though according to the divine promises it is not possible for the one holy Christian Church ever to perish, it is yet possible, and at times it has really happened, that there did not exist a true VISIBLE *Church in the absolute sense, that is, a Church in which through an uncorrupted public ministry the preaching of the pure Word of God and the administration of the unadulterated Sacraments held sway.*

There is a reason for placing this thesis here. When the Lutherans declared to the Papists, "Your Church is corrupt; you no longer are the true Church," they received the reply, "Where was the true Church if ours was not the true Church?" Only those who retain the correct doctrine of the invisible Church can refute this argument. The Lord has indeed promised that the invisible Church will never perish, but He has not promised that the Church would always be in a flourishing condition. There have been times when there was no true visible Church. The picture which the Lord presents of the last days is a gloomy one. In those days it surely will seem as though the Church had ceased to exist.

The condition of the visible Church among the ten tribes of Israel at the time of Elijah was quoted as a proof for the thesis. At the same time, however, there was a flourishing Church in the Kingdom of Judah. The prophecies concerning the last days found in Matt. 24 and Luke 18 are clear statements foretelling a general apostasy. There is no Scriptural warrant for the assumption that the true visible Church of a pure confession and an unadulterated public ministry will exist for all times in this world.

Thesis X

The Evangelical Lutheran Church is the total of all who unreservedly accept all canonical books of the Old and New Testaments as God's revealed Word and who confess agreement with the teaching again brought to light through Luther's reformation and presented concisely in writing to Emperor and Empire at Augsburg in 1530 and repeated and expanded in the other so-called Lutheran symbols.

In the original form of the thesis Dr. Walther had not included any statement regarding the acceptance of the Old and New Testaments as God's Word, since he had intended to stress only that which is specifically Lutheran. In response to a request at the convention of the Central District in 1867, he added such a statement, and the expanded thesis was adopted in the form given above.

Only he has a right to call himself a Lutheran who accepts the doctrine contained in the Symbolical Books of the Lutheran Church. The so-called "American Lutheranism" of the General Synod is not truly Lutheran.

Some clearly revealed doctrines of Scripture are not treated in the Confessions. These doctrines are Lutheran because they are Biblical, for the Lutheran Church has publicly acknowledged the Old and the New Testament as God's Word. The majority of Scriptural doctrines, however, have been publicly confessed by the Lutheran Church either by the adoption of the ancient confessions or by accepting new ones. With such as profess to be Lutherans we must not dispute, for instance, about the doctrine of justification. If a professed Lutheran denies this doctrine, we must tell him, "You are no Lutheran," for this doctrine has been clearly defined in our Lutheran Confessions.

Thesis XI

The Ev. Lutheran Church is not the one holy Christian Church outside which there is no salvation, though it has never separated from the same but acknowledges it alone.

This thesis draws a conclusion which everyone must accept who has assented to the previous theses. No Bible passages are adduced, and the testimonies do not present any new thoughts. The discussion of this thesis began in the Eastern District only a few months after the Buffalo Colloquy had been held. The majority of the Buffalo pastors had come to an agreement with our Synod, but a few refused to accept our doctrinal position; the leader of these was Pastor von Rohr. Grabau had been deposed by his own synod, but still had some adherents. The discussion was polemical, and many ideas expressed in connection with earlier theses were repeated.

Thesis XII

If the Ev. Lutheran Church has these marks, namely, pure Gospel preaching and unadulterated administration of the holy Sacraments, it is the true visible Church of God on earth.

Attention was called to an objection raised against the title of the book, which claimed that the Lutheran Church is *the* visible Church. The critics would substitute the indefinite article. But we ask, Where is there another church body on earth which is orthodox to the same extent as the Lutheran Church is? We do not deny the possibility, but at present we know of none. Therefore we shall retain the definite article until we are convinced of the opposite.

Thesis XIII

The Ev. Lutheran Church acknowledges the written Word of the Apostles and Prophets as the only and perfect source, rule, norm, and judge of all teaching—a. not reason, b. not tradition, c. not new revelations.

Scripture is the only source of doctrine. There is nothing besides Scripture which can be a source; it is the perfect source; nothing besides Scripture is needed. It is very necessary to hold fast to this truth since many German theologians accept the Bible as the norm and judge of divine truth, but not as the only source. For them the real source is the Christian self-consciousness, which is transmitted in the Church. The function of the Bible is merely to restrain any excess or, as Hofmann puts it, to wash and cleanse ourselves in the water of Holy Scripture if we have defiled ourselves.

That Holy Scripture has the authority ascribed to it in this thesis is proved by statements of the Bible.

Deut. 4:2: "Ye shall not add unto the Word which I command you, neither shall ye diminish aught from it." This Book was to be the only source for the Jews; if there were other sources, this com mand would have been unnecessary.—The objection was raised that something had been added. But men have not done it; God Himself has added something through the Prophets and the Apostles.—If we dare not diminish aught, it is clear that the Bible contains nothing that is superfluous.—This passage is important, because the opinion is gaining ground that the doctrine of the Church is the product of a gradual development and that it increases in volume as the Church grows older. But we are not to *develop* doctrine with the result that *new* doctrines are produced, but we are to exercise our intellectual powers to *understand* and *grasp* the doctrines which the Church has always possessed.—This truth is repeated in Josh. 23:6.

Isaiah preaches against those who go to the dead for the living and urges them: "To the Law and to the Testimony; if they speak not according to this Word, it is because there is no light in them" (Is. 8:20). Whoever seeks heavenly truth outside the inspired Word remains in darkness, finds only lie and error, and will be lost forever. In the New Testament the same direction is given: "They have Moses and the Prophets; let them hear them." Luke 16:29.

The passage II Tim. 3:15-17 is added principally because of the word "perfect": "that the man of God may be perfect." Paul wishes to say, If you wish to be perfect, be satisfied with Scripture. Do you wish saving doctrine? Holy Scripture is sufficient for every true and saving doctrine. Do you wish to reprove? Holy Scripture offers you all the means to refute false doctrine. Do you wish to correct? Holy Scripture offers you sufficient means and ways to make a frail life perfect. Do you wish to instruct for a pious and holy life? Holy Scripture suffices for instruction in righteousness.

Reason cannot be the source of pure doctrine. I Cor. 1:21: "For after that in the wisdom of God the world by wisdom knew not God, it pleased God by the foolishness of preaching to save them that believe." The way to salvation is barred by nature not only to the foolish and simple, but also to the wise. The wisdom of the world leads men away from God and conceals God instead of revealing Him. The wisest men of antiquity did not know the true God, much less his attitude of affection toward us, least of all the way to God. In the eyes of natural man the Gospel is foolishness; in reality it is heavenly wisdom.

I Cor. 2:4, 5: "And my speech and my preaching was not with

enticing words of man's wisdom, but in demonstration of the Spirit and power, that your faith should not stand in the wisdom of men, but in the power of God." God's Word alone, not human persuasiveness, can work and give faith; faith cannot be engendered by arguments of reason. It is foolish, yes, sinful, to by-pass or deny what is offensive to human reason in Scripture.

Christianity indeed is not unreasonable, but it not only transcends human reason, which is corrupted by sin, but it is also contrary to this corrupt reason. Whoever wishes to make the "foolishness" of the Cross of none effect in the eyes of the world, makes the Cross of Christ of none effect. To make concessions to the unbelievers in order to win the educated is treason against the sanctuary. The only proper use of reason in connection with Scripture is that of an instrument; reason cannot produce any divine truths.

We recall the well-known statement in I Cor. 2:14: "Natural man receiveth not the things of the Spirit of God; for they are foolishness unto him, neither can he know them, because they are spiritually discerned." God's Holy Spirit alone can illuminate our heart. Therefore Paul warns the Colossians: "Beware lest any man spoil you through philosophy and vain deceit, after the tradition of men, after the rudiments of the world, and not after Christ" (Col. 2:8).

Tradition is not the source or judge of doctrine. Christ says, Matt. 15:9: "In vain they do worship Me, teaching for doctrines the commandments of men." If anybody is to be sure and happy in his faith and furnished unto good works which are to please God, he must have his roots in the Word of God. An example of basing one's faith on tradition instead of on God's Word is found in Grabau's and the Episcopalian doctrine of the necessary succession of the apostolic office requiring ordination. These people can never be assured by any official act of their pastor, since they can never be sure that this succession has never been interrupted; and yet they believe that neither preaching nor the administration of the Sacraments is valid and efficacious if these acts are not performed by a validly ordained pastor. According to Pastor von Rohr's argument, the power of the Word and of the Sacraments is not inherent in the Word itself, but in the qualification of the man who administers it. This error stems from an erroneous conception of the Scriptural idea of the ministry, which in reality is a service, serving men with the Word and the Sacraments.

New revelations are not the source and norm of doctrine. Heb. 12:26–28, quoting Hag. 2:7, proves this point. "Whose voice then shook the earth; but now He hath promised, saying, Yet once more I shake not the earth only, but also heaven. And this word, Yet once more, signifieth the removing of those things that are shaken, as of things that are made, that those things which cannot be shaken may remain. Wherefore, we receiving a kingdom which cannot be moved, let us have grace whereby we may serve God acceptably with reverence and godly fear." People ask, Why should we not expect new revelations? This passage answers questions of this type. Whereas in the Old Testament God continued to give new revelations, the doctrinal complex, or the body of doctrine, of the New Testament is unchangeable and cannot be enlarged.

II Pet. 1:19: "We have also a more sure Word of Prophecy, whereunto ye do well that ye take heed, as unto a light that shineth in a dark place, until the day dawn, and the Day Star arise in your hearts." In v. 16 Peter had declared that he had not followed cunningly devised fables, but had seen Christ's glory and had heard the Father's voice. But the Word of Prophecy is even more sure. Christ resisted the devil not by new revelations but by using the powerful "It is written." Luther too rested his whole case on "It is written." We thank God when He permits us to *feel* His gracious presence, but we cannot build our hope of salvation on our emotions. God's Word alone can be our anchor; it remains clear, true, and sure forever.

Theses XIV, XV, and XVI were not discussed; we add them here for the sake of completeness.

Thesis XIV

The Ev. Lutheran Church holds fast to the clearness of Scripture. (There are no "views" and "open questions.")

Thesis XV

The Ev. Lutheran Church acknowledges no human interpreter of Scripture whose interpretation must be received as infallible and binding on account of his office—1) not an individual, 2) not an order, 3) not a particular or general council, 4) not a whole Church (nicht eine ganze Kirche).

THESIS XVI

The Ev. Lutheran Church accepts God's Word as it interprets itself.

THESIS XVII

The Ev. Lutheran Church accepts the WHOLE written Word of God (as God's Word), deems nothing in it superfluous or of little value but regards everything as needful and important, and also accepts all teachings deduced of necessity from the words of Scripture.

The Bible proof is found Matt. 5:18, 19: "For verily I say unto you, Till heaven and earth pass, one jot or one tittle shall in no wise pass from the Law till all be fulfilled. Whosoever, therefore, shall break one of these least commandments and shall teach men so, he shall be called the least in the kingdom of heaven; but whosoever shall do and teach them, the same shall be called great in the kingdom of heaven." Rev. 22:18, 19: "For I testify unto every man that heareth the words of the prophecy of this book, If any man shall add unto these things, God shall add unto him the plagues that are written in this book; and if any man shall take away from the words of the book of this prophecy, God shall take away his part out of the Book of Life and out of the Holy City and from the things which are written in this book." The passages given for Thesis XIII were also quoted.

This is the glory of the Lutheran Church that it accepts God's Word in its entirety, whereas other church bodies have only parts of it.

Modern theology is based on the principle "The Bible is not God's Word, but merely contains God's Word." This principle is contrary to the Bible, entirely un-Lutheran, a refined rationalism, not a rock but a seesaw, which does not permit the heart to become firm.

Before the Reformation nobody wishing to be considered a Christian dared to deny the verbal inspiration of the Bible. Now we are considered a narrow-minded synod, because we still believe that every word of Scripture is given by inspiration of God. But we remember Luther's statement: When Scripture lost its authority, the storm of Antichrist broke and flooded everything.

In the Papacy the Word of God is still valid in theory, but in practice it has been eliminated (1) by the assertion that there are various meanings in Scripture, (2) by making tradition equal in authority with Scripture, (3) by forbidding the laity to read the Bible and to pass final judgment on the basis of Scripture. This truly is Antichrist; here we behold the mystery of iniquity.

Our thesis states that everything is needful. God does nothing unnecessary, and therefore there is nothing unnecessary in the Bible. We may not know why many of the statements of the Bible are necessary, but God knows why He included them. An old pastor of Synod was delivered from great spiritual distress by the words: "O Lord, thou preservest man and beast" (Ps. 36:6).

Because in the distribution of the Lord's Supper we use the words "This is the true body," the objection has been raised against us that we add to the Word of God. When we consecrate, we use the very words of Scripture; in the distribution, however, we confess our faith, so that nobody may doubt what we believe.

Whoever denies one Word of God knowingly in the sight of God denies the whole Word of God. It is wrong to say, If the statement denied is not an article of faith, the denial is of no importance. Faith means to accept something because God has stated it. We are not permitted to declare any clearly revealed doctrines to be open questions, as the Iowa Synod asked us to do. The Church dare not declare anything concerning which Scripture has rendered a decision to be a matter of indifference. The fact that the Lutheran Church accepts the entire Word of God is the surest proof that it is the true visible Church; but if it were to depart from the Word of God in one point, it would be a sect. Let us be on our guard against deviating in one point. At Luther's time the doctrine of the Lord's Supper was denied; the progress in denial has finally led many to atheism. We should not worry about the accusation of exclusiveness and lack of charity. God has made this order: First the glory of the Word and then love; not: First love in external union and then doctrinal arguments for all eternity.

The last part of the thesis states: "and also accepts all teachings deduced of necessity from the words of Scripture." The Lord quotes the words "I am the God of Abraham and the God of Isaac and the God of Jacob." From this Biblical statement He deduces in the following sentence: "God is not the God of the dead, but of the living," the doctrine of the resurrection, and yet He says to the Sadducees: "Ye do err, not knowing the *Scriptures* nor the power of God." Here the Lord Jesus calls the doctrine of the resurrection deduced from Scripture words "the Scripture." The word "triune" is not to be found in the Bible, and still all Christians believe the doctrine of the Holy Trinity on the basis of Scripture. The Baptists state, No passage in the Bible commands that children be baptized. However, the Bible says, "Baptize all nations." Since children belong to the nations, we make the proper deduction that children also are to be baptized. This principle of our Lutheran Church is accepted and used by all denominations. If, for instance, they wish to prove the deity of Christ, they quote not only those passages in which He is called God but also passages in which divine names, divine attributes, and divine works are ascribed to Him, and then conclude: Therefore He must be God.

This principle is of vital importance for our personal faith. Nowhere does the Bible state expressly that Jesus is *my* Savior. It does state, however, that Christ is the Savior of the world. I belong to the world; therefore He is my Savior. This principle is important also for our Christian life. The Bible, for instance, nowhere says expressly, You are to go to synodical conventions, but it does state: "endeavoring to keep the unity of the Spirit" (Eph. 4:3). If I am to endeavor to keep the unity, I must make use of all means to accomplish this purpose. Synodical meetings are a means to maintain this unity; therefore I should attend them.

The proper use of this principle is very necessary, but we dare not abuse it. We do this if we draw our deductions not from the Word of God, but from our reason. Scripture states: Christ ascended into heaven. The Reformed now argue: Therefore according to His human nature He can no longer be on the earth. This deduction has its basis in human reason and not in Scripture.

Thesis XVIII

The Ev. Lutheran Church gives to each teaching of God's Word the place and importance it has in God's Word itself.

A

It makes the teaching of Christ, or of justification, the foundation and the very heart and essence of all teaching.

Four Bible passages are quoted as a proof. I Cor. 3:11: "For other

foundation can no man lay than that is laid, which is Jesus Christ";
I Cor. 2:2: "For I determined not to know anything among you
save Jesus Christ, and Him crucified"; Rev. 19:10: "For the testimony
of Jesus is the spirit of prophecy"; and I Cor. 15:3: "For I delivered
unto you, first of all, that which I also received, how that Christ
died for our sins according to the Scriptures." The discussion of these
passages in the Western District, 1868, is a classic which deserves
to be translated in its entirety. We can, however, indicate only a few
important points. The doctrinal revelation of the Bible may be compared to a very artistic building. In erecting such a building we do
not start at the top, but we begin with the foundation. The foundation of Christian preaching must always be the doctrine of Christ,
or of justification. If a pastor preaches all other doctrines but does
not preach Christ as the only Savior of sinners, he preaches in vain.
When we demand that people preach Christ as the Savior from sin,
people frequently reply, Why demand this? Is this not self-evident?
But because it is so self-evident, it is left undone by only too many.
Look at the sermon books of our time. You will find how little this
fundamental doctrine is treated in them. The more zealous a
preacher is, the more he is inclined to overlook the doctrine of justification. He may even think if he preached Christ and the redemption procured by Him without any reservation, no one will get to
heaven. But he should bear in mind that it is not his duty to make
a fence around Mount Calvary as Moses had to make one around
Mount Sinai, but it is his obligation to proclaim to the people the
peace which God has made with them.

Some preachers think that one dare not be too liberal with the
preaching of the Gospel lest the people become spiritual anarchists.
Such an attitude is the real delusion of the last days. It seems to be
very pious, but in reality it is crucifying Christ anew and is utterly
un-Lutheran. It is characteristic of the Evangelical Lutheran Church
that it tries to produce faith, childlike trust, by all its teaching and
activity. Whatever is necessary for salvation has already been done.
Man need only dip into the great storehouses, which never become
empty, and take what he lacks. We must not try to make people
pious before we preach Christ to them, but we should preach Christ
to those for whom He died, to the sinners. Whoever makes anything
else the basic doctrine, as Pietism did, no longer preaches Lutheran,
that is Biblical, sermons. Some people think that it is easy to preach

justification, but in fact it is difficult. Unless one has experienced the marvelous grace of God in his own heart, one cannot properly understand and preach this doctrine and will again and again adulterate the preaching of the Gospel with the Law. To be sure, we must preach the Law; and when we preach the Law, we must preach it as though there were no Gospel. But when we preach the Gospel, we must preach it as though there were no Law. When we preach sanctification, we must remember that only the Gospel gives Christians the strength to live as Christians. Also when we preach sanctification, we can accomplish our purpose only by preaching Christ into the hearts of our people.

B

The Ev. Lutheran Church distinguishes sharply between the Law and the Gospel.

The Lutheran Church not only says that the distinction must be made, but it actually makes this distinction. The Bible itself makes the distinction. John 1:17: "For the Law was given by Moses, but grace and truth came by Jesus Christ." Rom. 10:4: "Christ is the end of the Law for righteousness to everyone that believeth." Paul admonishes Timothy to be a workman "rightly dividing the Word of Truth" (II Tim. 2:15). This doctrine is confessed by our Church in the Formula of Concord and by Luther. To observe this distinction in practice is not easy. Many preach, "You are redeemed if you believe." They should say, "You are redeemed in order that you may believe." We hear people preach, "God's Son has come into this world and made it possible for God to accept men as His children if they change"; but Christ *has* accomplished everything, and we should make it our own through faith; and when this faith comes into our heart, *we are changed* and are willing to serve God, not in fear or with the idea of securing a reward, but out of love for Him who first loved us. The art of rightly dividing the Word can be given to us only by the Holy Spirit. Our one purpose in preaching the Law to the impenitent must be to fill him with fear and anguish; but when he asks, What shall I do to be saved? the Gospel, and the Gospel alone, dare be preached.

The most serious danger is that of introducing the Law into the preaching of the Gospel, but we can also commit the opposite mistake. When we expound the Ten Commandments, we are inclined to say, Don't think that God expects us to do all of this; we are too weak, and God will be satisfied with our good intention. The latter statement is true, but it belongs into the Gospel. When we explain the Ten Commandments, we must do so as though there were no Gospel, no grace, but only a zealous God. We must tell people that God does not remit the least of His demands in the Law. Whoever does not keep the Law entirely is lost. In this manner men are brought to a realization of their sin and are driven into the Gospel.

The Law is introduced into the Gospel if, for instance, we try to make a Christian who is not producing many fruits zealous by laying down the Law to him. The Apostles admonished people through Jesus Christ and by the mercies of God. It is also a mixture of Law and Gospel if we in a legalistic manner demand that people believe, or if in festival sermons we demand that people should rejoice. We should rather preach in a manner which will cause the people of their own accord to begin to rejoice. We do not reject admonition and urging, but we must reject legalistic demand. When we preach justification, we should encourage the people by showing them that Christ has promised to send the Holy Ghost to create faith also in their hearts. Luther's sermons are excellent models of the division of Law and Gospel. God grant us His grace that we become more and more proficient in this division.

C

The Ev. Lutheran Church distinguishes sharply between the fundamental and the nonfundamental articles of doctrine contained in Scripture.

This section was discussed somewhat briefly in the Central District, which, however, could not complete the discussion. The Eastern District took up the discussion and began again with Point C. We shall list the high spots of the discussion. The purpose of this discussion was not to show in which doctrines unity was unnecessary. In the previous discussions it had been emphasized again and again that the Church cannot declare any doctrine unnecessary or not binding.

We distinguish between fundamental and nonfundamental doctrines because we must determine what is the minimum which a man must know to have saving faith. What is the absolute minimum requirement of saving knowledge? This has been stated excellently by Quenstedt in the following manner: "God, one in essence, triune in person, out of His unspeakable love toward the fallen human race forgives sins to every sinner who acknowledges his sins, through and for the sake of Christ, the Mediator, and His merit, which is proclaimed in the Word and grasped by faith; He ascribes to him the righteousness of Christ and gives him eternal life." Whoever knows these truths may be saved. Of course, if such a person is permitted to live, he will not be satisfied with this minimum of knowledge, but will strive to grow in the knowledge of the sacred truth.

Any error in this minimum of doctrine is a fundamental error. We may also call a fundamental error every error which, carried through consistently, either overthrows the merit of Christ or makes it superfluous. But in passing judgment upon individuals we must bear in mind the inconsistency which is frequently found in men, when their heart still believes what their intellect rejects. Thank God for this happy inconsistency!

On the basis of quotations from the dogmaticians the distinction between primary and secondary fundamental articles of faith was pointed out. Primary fundamental doctrines are doctrines which everybody must know in order to be saved. Secondary fundamental articles are such regarding which a person may be ignorant without harming his faith, but which one may not deny, much less oppose, if he should know them. For instance, the doctrine that God is infinite and omnipresent, etc. Finally, there are nonfundamental articles of faith which may be unknown to a person and may even be denied by him without utterly losing faith. It is understood, of course, that if a person knows that such doctrines are revealed in God's Word and still denies them, he is in great danger; for he thereby is undermining the so-called instrumental basis of faith, the Word of God itself. Among these nonfundamental doctrines we find such doctrines as that of creation, of the immortality of man before the Fall, of Antichrist.

This thesis speaks of articles of faith. The definition of Hollaz was adopted. An article of faith requires, first, that it be revealed in the Word of God; secondly, that it concern the salvation of man; thirdly, that it be intimately connected with the other doctrines of faith; fourthly, that it be inevident, that is, that it cannot be learned or understood by the light of nature, but only by the supernatural

light of revelation. From these we distinguish mere doctrines of
Scripture which indeed are revealed in the Bible but do not meet
all of these four points. For instance, the Bible tells us that Pontius
Pilate was governor when Christ suffered, that Balaam's ass spoke.
We believe these truths because they are revealed in God's Word,
but if we knew nothing of them, the connection of Scriptural doctrine would not be disturbed.

We also speak of theological problems. These are questions which
arise in connection with the Scriptural record or with certain doctrines, questions on which the Bible itself either gives no information
or makes no conclusive statement. Such a problem, for instance, is
the question regarding the day and the year of the birth of Christ,
whether Mary after the birth of Jesus always remained a virgin, and
other questions. We may indeed argue about such questions, but we
dare not present our opinions as the Word of God. Furthermore, if
our opinions on such questions are contrary to some clear statement
of the Bible, we dare not hold to them. If, for instance, somebody
believes that great numbers of Jews will be converted, we have a
theological problem. But if somebody dreams about a glorious
future of the Jews as a separate nation and of a general conversion
of this nation, he is contradicting plain statements of Scripture; for
instance, I Thess. 2:16 and Matt. 24:34.

D

*The Ev. Lutheran Church distinguishes sharply between what
God's Word commands and what it leaves free. (Things indifferent
[adiaphora], church government.)*

This section was discussed briefly in the Eastern District in 1868
and again taken up at the meeting of the Central District in 1871.
This marked the conclusion of the discussion of Dr. Walther's Theses.

The distinction between matters commanded in the Word of God
and things left to our Christian liberty is an important characteristic
of our Lutheran Church. This is a matter of great practical importance and also affects church polity.

A Christian as such has no master except Jesus Christ. This is the
plain statement of Matt. 23:8: "One is your Master, even Christ; and
all ye are brethren." This truth is further emphasized in Gal. 5:1:
"Stand fast, therefore, in the liberty wherewith Christ hath made us

free, and be not entangled again with the yoke of bondage." This truth is not contradicted by Heb. 13:7: "Remember them which have the rule over you, who have spoken unto you the Word of God," for obedience is due pastors only when they are able to say, "It is written; therefore do it." Our Synod owes its flourishing condition to its understanding and recognition of this truth. Therefore it is organized not as a legislative body but as an advisory body. Our congregations know that we do not demand obedience except the obedience to the Word of God. Therefore they have willingly offered their gifts for the Kingdom of God as they have done.

We must be careful how we deal with a person whose conscience is still bound in indifferent matters. If he is bound because of ignorance, we should avoid giving him offense and should instruct him. If, however, he will not listen to our instruction, we must stand fast in our Christian liberty.

A congregation must remember that its rules and resolutions do not have the force of divine commandments. We may indeed appeal to the love of the members, but we dare not make the observance of such rules a matter of conscientious obligation.

On the basis of these and similar Bible passages Article VII of the Augsburg Confession states: "Nor is it necessary that human traditions, that is, rites or ceremonies instituted by men, should be everywhere alike."

Many church bodies make the form of church government a matter of conscience, for instance, the Episcopalians, Presbyterians, etc. The Lutheran Church has prospered under various forms of church government, but we are happy that we are able to follow the form of government found in the Apostolic Church. This fact makes it necessary for all members of the congregation to take a lively interest in the affairs of the congregation.

Some rites and ceremonies are confessional rites. Because the Reformed insist that the bread in the Lord's Supper must be broken, we use wafers and do not break the bread. Because the Baptists insist that immersion is the only correct form of baptizing, we do not immerse in baptism.

There are certain indifferent matters which usually are connected with something sinful. Here we should not and dare not insist on our liberty, for St. Peter says: "As free, and not using your liberty for a cloak of maliciousness, but as the servants of God" (I Pet. 2:16).

The question was asked, How are we to deal with a man who refuses to pay toward the pastor's salary? May a certain fixed sum be imposed as a tax? The taxing system in congregations is a shameful and unfair practice, but provision for the physical needs of the pastor is a matter of divine command, as the Table of Duties shows. Every member who is not the object of charity must contribute to this support. Before we, however, institute disciplinary proceedings against people who contribute too little, their stinginess must be a public matter, for only the manifest and impenitent sinners may be excommunicated.

Thus the Ev. Lutheran Church by sharply distinguishing between what God's Word commands and what it leaves free and by giving to each teaching of God's Word the place and importance it has in God's Word itself, manifests the marks which, together with the other marks, prove that it is the true visible Church of God on earth.

Note—The reader will find the remaining theses in *Walther and the Church*, pp. 126–128.

XVI

The Universal Priesthood of Believers

A<small>LL</small> Christians are royal priests through faith in Christ Jesus. Accordingly we may speak of the universal priesthood of believers. This doctrine is clearly taught in Holy Scripture. It is a precious dotrine. It tells the believers in Christ how highly blessed they are—blessed with priceless spiritual rights and powers. But —and this they must not overlook—these rights and powers entail duties and responsibilities on their part which they must not shirk. And because the priesthood of the believers in Christ is a gift of God, hence of eminent importance, the enemies of God and of His people strive with might and main to deprive the believers of this doctrine.

Many nations have had a priesthood. Convicted by their con- science that sin has estranged them from the holy God, the sinners look about for someone who will mediate between them and the offended deity. When the Israelites saw the lightnings and the mountain smoking and heard the thunderings and the noise of the trumpet at Sinai, they removed and stood afar off. "And they said unto Moses, Speak thou with us, and we will hear: but let not God speak with us, lest we die" (Ex. 20:19). By their words and action they expressed the fear of the unrighteous in the presence of the righteous God. Because of this fear they pleaded for a mediator to stand between themselves and God.

In the Old Covenant, God gave His chosen people a particular order of priests. These were to direct the believers of their time to the Messiah. They were also to foreshadow the priesthood of Christ and of the believers in Him. God describes the nature and the func- tions of this priesthood so elaborately and in such detail in the Law of Moses that we may turn to it for adequate terms and illustrations when speaking of the priesthood of Christ and the believers.

The priesthood of the Old Covenant was a shadow of things to come (Col. 2:17). The shadow may be a silhouette of the body that casts it. So the outlines of the New Testament priesthood may be seen in that of the Old Covenant. But the Holy Spirit does not depend on man's ability to draw a true picture of a body from its shadow. He knows how illogical man is in the things of the Spirit of God (I Cor. 2:14). Therefore He tells us Himself in the New Testament what a priest is and does. He says: "For every high priest taken from among men is ordained for men in things pertaining to God, that he may offer both gifts and sacrifices for sins" (Heb. 5:1). Three marks of a priest are here noted: 1. He must be taken from among men, must be a man himself, so that he may appear before God as man's representative and substitute; 2. he is ordained for men in things pertaining to God, that is, in things which pertain to the relationship between God and man, thus serving as a mediator between them; 3. he may offer both gifts and sacrifices for sins. Luther, the great protagonist and defender of the doctrine of the universal priesthood of believers, describes a priest in these words: "A priest is a person who has been ordained for the sake only of sinners and must care for them by mediating between God and them, reconcile them, and pray for them" (St. Louis, V:1025). Again, "A priest is a person, as the Scripture pictures him, who is ordained by God and is commanded to mediate between God and men in such a manner that he may proceed from Him, bringing and teaching us His Word, and, again, turn to God to sacrifice and pray for us, etc. Therefore three things belong to the office of a priest, namely: to teach and preach the Word of God, to sacrifice, and to pray, etc., all three of which are often mentioned in the Scripture" (St. Louis, V:1018). In his commentary on Genesis, Luther says: "So the office of a priest is a twofold one. First, he must face God and pray for himself and his people. Secondly, he must face about from God to the people in the Word and doctrine" (St. Louis, I:456). In other words, a priest is a mediator between God and men.

There was, indeed, a priesthood of believers before God instituted the Levitical order of priests, even as there is one now, after God has abolished the latter. In the days of the patriarchs, the fathers were the priests of their household. Noah built an altar unto the Lord and offered burnt offerings on it (Gen. 8:20). Abram dwelt in the plain of Mamre, which is in Hebron, and built there an altar unto the Lord (Gen. 13:18). He planted a grove in Beersheba and called there on the name of the Lord, the everlasting God (Gen. 21:33). When God had chosen Israel as His own peculiar people, He told them through Moses: "Now, therefore, if ye will obey My voice indeed and keep My covenant, then ye shall be a peculiar treasure unto Me above all people, for all the earth is Mine. And ye shall be unto Me a kingdom of priests and an holy nation" (Ex. 19:5, 6). All believing children of God in the commonwealth of Israel were priests before God.

When God, however, led His chosen people out of Egypt, He instituted also a separate order of priests. For this purpose He set apart the tribe of Levi and in this tribe the house of Aaron. This official priesthood should mediate between the holy God and His sinful people. Under the priests of this order His people were as children "under tutors and governors until the time appointed of the father" (Gal. 4:2). The high priest was taken from the house of Aaron. He had to be without blemish physically. The Lord said unto Aaron: "Thou and thy sons and thy father's house with thee shall bear the iniquity of the sanctuary, and thou and thy sons with thee shall bear the iniquity of your priesthood. And thy brethren also of the tribe of Levi, the tribe of thy father, bring thou with thee, that they may be joined unto thee and minister unto thee" (Num. 18:1, 2). The Lord instructed Moses: "No man that hath a blemish of the seed of Aaron, the priest, shall come nigh to offer the offerings of the Lord made by fire" (Lev. 21:21).

Aaron and his sons were consecrated to the priesthood in an elaborate ceremony. Moses washed them with water and clothed them in their priestly garments. He sanctified the tabernacle and its contents by anointing them with oil. He poured of the anointing oil upon Aaron's head and anointed him to sanctify him. A bullock was slain for the sin offering, and its blood was applied to purify the altar. A ram was brought for the burnt offering and another for a ram of consecration. Blood had to be shed. Aaron and his sons had to be sanctified by the sprinkling of the oil and the blood. The innocent sacrificial animal had to die in the place of guilty man. Moses said to Aaron and his sons: "As he hath done this day, so the Lord hath commanded to do, to make an atonement for you" (Lev. 8:34). So Aaron and his sons were consecrated to an official priesthood which was distinct from the universal priesthood of believers in Israel.

Before Solomon's Temple was built, the priests officiated in the

Tabernacle of Testimony; later in the Temple at Jerusalem. In the Holy of Holies of either place was the Ark with the Mercy Seat, whereon the blood of the yearly atonement was sprinkled by the high priest.

The official duties of the priests consisted in teaching, but particularly in sacrificing. Blessing the Levites, Moses said: "They shall teach Jacob Thy judgments and Israel Thy Law. They shall put incense before Thee and whole burnt sacrifice upon Thine altar" (Deut. 33:10). Malachi emphasizes the teaching function of the priests in these words: "For the priest's lips should keep knowledge, and they should seek the Law at his mouth: for he is the messenger of the Lord of Hosts" (Mal. 2:7). But the priests should be holy particularly, "for the offerings of the Lord made by fire and the bread of their God they do offer" (Lev. 21:6). Among the sacrifices the most important was the sin offering for atonement. There the priest appeared as the mediator between man and God, reconciling God by the shedding of blood, so that He would dwell among the children of Israel and be their God (Ex. 29:42). The culmination of the offerings for sin was reached on the Day of Atonement, on which the priest made an atonement for the people, to cleanse them, that they might be clean from all their sins before the Lord (Lev. 16:30: Yom Kippur). On this day the priest went into the Holy of Holies and sprinkled the blood of the bullock and the goat of sin-offering upon the Mercy Seat.

This Old Covenant priesthood, then, with its teaching and sacrificing, particularly the high priest with his expiatory sacrifice on the Day of Atonement, was a shadow of things to come, of Christ, the true High Priest, and of His perfect expiatory offering on the Cross, which alone lent expiatory efficacy to the sacrifices of the Old Testament (Heb. 10:1). "For it is not possible that the blood of bulls and of goats should take away sins" (Heb. 10:4). Because this was so, the Redeemer came. He said: "Lo, I come to do Thy will, O God. He taketh away the first that He may establish the second. By the which will we are sanctified through the offering of the body of Jesus Christ once for all" (Heb. 10:9, 10). In Christ, then, the shadow has disappeared in the body; the imperfect has vanished before the perfect. In Him the Old Covenant priesthood with its various ceremonies attained its highest fulfillment and culmination.

The realization of the Old Covenant type in Christ is clearly apparent in the New Testament. According to Heb. 5:1, every high priest was taken from among men in order to represent men before God. No angel could do that. This mediator between God and men, moreover, should be such a person as could sympathize with the infirmities of sinners. He had to be one who could "have compassion on the ignorant and on them that are out of the way, for that he himself also is compassed with infirmity" (Heb. 5:2). Christ, our High Priest, is true man, as He had to be to fulfill the Law of God and to suffer and die in man's stead. "When the fullness of the time was come, God sent forth His Son, made of a woman, made under the Law, to redeem them that were under the Law, that we might receive the adoption of sons" (Gal. 4:4, 5). Says the writer to the Hebrews: "Forasmuch then as the children are partakers of flesh and blood, He also Himself likewise took part of the same, that through death He might destroy him that had the power of death, that is, the devil, and deliver them who through fear of death were all their lifetime subject to bondage. For verily He took not on Him the nature of angels; but He took on Him the seed of Abraham" (Heb. 2:14-16). As a true man of whom Isaiah could say (53:4), "Surely He hath borne our griefs and carried our sorrows," Christ was not "a High Priest which cannot be touched with the feeling of our infirmities, but was in all points tempted like as we are" (Heb. 4:15). Surely He will be merciful and will hear us when we call upon Him in the day of trouble.

The Old Testament high priest had to be called of God, as was Aaron (Heb. 5:4). Not everyone could be a high priest. "So also Christ glorified not Himself to be made an High Priest; but He that said unto Him, Thou art My Son, today have I begotten Thee" (Heb. 5:5). God called His Son to be a High Priest. David says in the Spirit: "The Lord hath sworn, and will not repent, Thou art a priest forever after the order of Melchizedek" (Ps. 110:4). In obedience to this call of the Father, the Son approached the altar where He was to be both the High Priest and the Offering. In the night of His betrayal He said: "But that the world may know that I love the Father; and as the Father gave Me commandment, even so I do" (John 14:31). In all that He did and suffered He sought not His own will, but the will of Him who sent Him (John 5:30), for He came down from heaven, not to do His own will, but the will of Him who sent Him (John 6:38). Christ, indeed, was not only the

High Priest, but also the Sacrifice. John the Baptist could say: "Behold the Lamb of God, which taketh away the sin of the world" (John 1:29). The Old Covenant high priest was consecrated to his office by washing and anointing with oil. So Christ also was washed and anointed. The Psalmist says: "God, Thy God, hath anointed Thee with the oil of gladness above Thy fellows" (Ps. 45:7). At His Baptism, God's Spirit came down upon Christ. "God anointed Jesus of Nazareth with the Holy Ghost and with power" (Acts 10:38).

But primarily in His act of atonement did Christ match the pattern of His Old Testament prototype. The high priest went into the Holy of Holies on the great Day of Atonement and brought before God the expiatory blood of the atonement. Thus Christ went to the Father (John 16:16). But He brought His own blood, and His own body was the tabernacle, for "Christ being come an High Priest of good things to come, by a greater and more perfect tabernacle, not made with hands, that is to say, not of this building; neither by the blood of goats and calves, but by His own blood He entered in once into the holy place, having obtained eternal redemption for us" (Heb. 9:11, 12). Yes, He entered into the Holy of Holies, into heaven itself, "for Christ is not entered into the holy places made with hands, which are the figures of the true; but into heaven itself, now to appear in the presence of God for us" (Heb. 9:24). What is that to us? "Having therefore, brethren, boldness to enter into the holiest by the blood of Jesus, by a new and living way, which He hath consecrated for us, through the veil, that is to say, His flesh, and having an High Priest over the house of God, let us draw near with a true heart in full assurance of faith, having our hearts sprinkled from an evil conscience and our bodies washed with pure water" (Heb. 10:19-22). The atoning work of our great High Priest assures us that all believers will also enter the Holy of Holies, heaven itself, for "for this cause He is the Mediator of the New Testament that by means of death, for the redemption of the transgressions that were under the first testament, they which are called might receive the promise of eternal inheritance" (Heb. 9:15).

The Levitical priests were teachers of the Law and instructed the Israelites in the true meaning of its various ceremonies, particularly of the expiatory sacrifices. So Christ also teaches in His Word and instructs those who search it with regard to His person and work. The Father spoke from heaven, saying: "This is My beloved Son, in whom I am well pleased; hear ye Him" (Matt. 17:5). And as God was in Christ, reconciling the world unto Himself, not imputing their trespasses unto them, so He has committed unto us the Word of Reconciliation (II Cor. 5:19).

Aaron bore the names of the twelve tribes of Israel upon his shoulders for a memorial before the Lord (Ex. 28:12). Thus Christ brings the names of His people into remembrance before God. He does that to this day, for He will never cease to be our High Priest. "The Lord hath sworn, and will not repent, Thou art a Priest forever" (Ps. 110:4). In the Holy of Holies, in heaven, He prays for them whom the Father has given Him (John 17:9), for them who believe on Him through the Word of the Apostles, which is His Word (John 17:20). Christ, who died, yea rather, who is risen again, who is even at the right hand of God, He it is who maketh intercession for us (Rom. 8:34). "And if any man sin, we have an Advocate with the Father, Jesus Christ, the Righteous" (I John 2:1). He ever liveth to make intercession for His people (Heb. 7:25).

In this, as well as in other respects, Christ, the body, far surpasses the Levitical priesthood, the shadow. The Old Covenant priests did not live forever. They died and were succeeded by others. Christ also died, but He rose again. As High Priest He is like Melchizedek, who appears in the Bible as having neither beginning of days nor end of life. In this respect Melchizedek was made "like unto the Son of God" (Heb. 7:3), "whose goings forth have been from of old, from everlasting" (Micah 5:2). Therefore Isaiah says: "Who shall declare His generation?" (Is. 53:8).

Christ was, indeed, a true man like the priests of the Old Covenant, but, unlike them, He was "holy, harmless, undefiled, separate from sinners, and made higher than the heavens; who needeth not daily, as those high priests, to offer up sacrifice first for His own sins and then for the people's; for this He did once when He offered up Himself. For the Law maketh men high priests which have infirmity; but the word of the oath, which was since the Law, maketh the Son, who is consecrated forevermore" (Heb. 7:26-28). However, Christ is also God. He is the Son. And God was in Christ, reconciling the world unto Himself. How inestimably precious was therefore His blood with which He entered the Holy of Holies!

But in another respect the superior excellence of Christ as our High Priest is manifest. The Old Testament high priest approached the mercy seat to sprinkle it with blood; Christ is Himself the Mercy Seat, sanctified with His own blood. We are "justified freely by His grace through the redemption that is in Christ Jesus, whom God hath set forth to be a propitiation through faith in His blood" (Rom. 3:24, 25). He "gave Himself a Ransom for all, to be testified in due time" (I Tim. 2:6). Therefore "He is the Propitiation for our sins" (I John 2:2). So Christ, sacrificing Himself, was at one and the same time Priest, Sacrifice, and Mercy Seat.

Christ truly was able to reconcile God and man, and He was the only one who could do that, "for there is one God and one Mediator between God and men, the Man Christ Jesus" (I Tim. 2:5). Knowing, then, that we have such a High Priest, "let us therefore come boldly unto the throne of grace that we may obtain mercy and find grace to help in time of need" (Heb. 4:16).

All that has been said regarding Christ as our High Priest is basic for the universal priesthood of believers. Save for the priesthood of Christ there could be no believers, for Christ died for our sins according to the Scriptures and was buried and rose again the third day according to the Scriptures (I Cor. 15:3, 4). "And if Christ be not risen, then is our preaching vain, and your faith is also vain" (I Cor. 15:14). Hence Christian faith, as well as Christian preaching, is based on the death and resurrection of Christ, our High Priest.

Now, as the Old Testament priesthood foreshadowed Christ, so it was also a shadow of the universal priesthood of believers. According to prophecy, Christ was to have a following, a priesthood of believers, who through faith in Him would be His own, have free access to God through Him, and would serve Him in holiness and righteousness. Addressing the eternal Priest after the order of Melchizedek, David declares: "Thy people shall be willing in the day of Thy power" (Ps. 110:3). God's people of the New Testament are told (Is. 61:6): "But ye shall be named the priests of the Lord, men shall call you the ministers of our God." Speaking of the time when the Levitical priesthood would be no more, God says: "For from the rising of the sun even unto the going down of the same, My name shall be great among the Gentiles; and in every place incense shall be offered unto My name and a pure offering, for My name shall be great among the heathen, saith the Lord of Hosts" (Mal. 1:11). With these words He predicts a priesthood not of the tribe of Levi or the house of Aaron.

In the New Testament we see the fulfillment of these prophecies. All believers in Christ, but only these, are priests of the Most High. There is no doubt about it. Peter, contrasting believers and unbelievers, addresses the former with the words: "Unto you therefore which believe He [Christ, the chief Cornerstone] is precious: but unto them which be disobedient, the Stone which the builders disallowed, the same is made the Head of the corner, and a Stone of stumbling, and a Rock of offense, even to them which stumble at the Word, being disobedient; whereunto also they were appointed," and now he continues: "But ye are a chosen generation, a royal priesthood, an holy nation, a peculiar people, that ye should show forth the praises of Him who hath called you out of darkness into His marvelous light" (I Pet. 2:7, 8, 9). These words include all to whom Christ is precious, that is, all believers. These are the same people to whom Peter had said previously: "Ye also, as lively stones, are built up a spiritual house, an holy priesthood, to offer up spiritual sacrifices, acceptable to God by Jesus Christ" (I Pet. 2:5). Indeed, by washing us with His blood, Christ, our great High Priest, has made us priests. Surely we must join in the words of John: "Unto Him that loved us and washed us from our sins in His own blood and hath made us kings and priests unto God and His Father, to Him be glory and dominion forever and ever. Amen" (Rev. 1:5, 6).

All who by faith in Jesus Christ as their Redeemer and Mediator have forgiveness of sins are priests before God. Since sin no longer separates them from God, they have free access to Him. They may approach Him personally. Thus the name "priest" belongs to every believer. It is no longer reserved for any particular order within the Church. And this name is not a mere empty title; it gives expression to the rights and powers of Christ's people. It also reminds them of their duties and responsibilities.

We saw how the Old Covenant priesthood foreshadowed that of Christ; it is also a shadow of that of His believers. The Old Covenant priesthood was instituted by God Himself, and its personnel was chosen by Him. So God, who has saved us, called us with an holy calling (II Tim. 1:9). Thereby we became a chosen generation, a royal priesthood (I Pet. 2:9), "elect according to the foreknowledge of God the Father, through sanctification of the Spirit, unto obedience and sprinkling of the blood of Jesus Christ" (I Pet. 1:2). The Levitical priests were consecrated by washing, investiture,

and anointing. The believers are washed, sanctified in the name of
the Lord Jesus and by the Spirit of our God (I Cor. 6:11). As many
as have been baptized into Christ have put on Christ (Gal. 3:27).
God has clothed them with the garments of salvation and covered
them with the robe of righteousness (Is. 61:10). As the Levitical
priests were clothed in white, so the believers have washed their
robes and made them white in the blood of the Lamb (Rev. 7:14).
The Old Testament priests were anointed. God shed the Holy Ghost
on us abundantly through Jesus Christ, our Savior (Tit. 3:6). The
faithful have an unction from the Holy One (I John 2:20). In Christ
the believers were sealed with that Holy Spirit of promise (Eph.
1:13). That is their consecration to the priesthood. All of this was
accomplished already in their Baptism, the washing of regeneration
and renewing of the Holy Ghost (Tit. 3:5). As the chief task of the
Old Testament priests consisted in sacrificing, so the New Testament
priests bring their offerings before God. These, indeed, are no longer
expiatory offerings, since Christ, our great High Priest, has long ago
reconciled God with the sinner by His sacrifice on the Cross. As an
holy priesthood they offer up spiritual sacrifices, acceptable to God
by Jesus Christ (I Pet. 2:5). Of these the writer to the Hebrews
says: "By Him [Christ] therefore let us offer the sacrifice of praise
to God continually, that is, the fruit of our lips, giving thanks to His
name. But to do good and to communicate forget not, for with such
sacrifices God is well pleased" (Heb. 13:15, 16). Paul sums up the
entire ministry of these New Testament priests in the words, addressed to the believers at Rome: "I beseech you therefore, brethren,
by the mercies of God, that ye present your bodies a living sacrifice,
holy, acceptable unto God, which is your reasonable service" (Rom.
12:1). How this may be done in particular, God also tells us in
His Word.

It would be surprising indeed if this precious doctrine of the
universal priesthood of believers went unchallenged by the enemies
of truth. As a matter of fact, the Pope teaches that there still is,
in the New Testament Church, a peculiar official priesthood, established by God, set over the laity, repeating the sacrifice of Christ
in the Mass to expiate the sins of the living and the dead, having
judicial powers in confession, and, in general, serving as the only
effective mediation between God and the sinners, without which no
one can come to God. The Council of Trent declares: "If any one

saith that there is not in the New Testament a visible and external priesthood; or that there is not any power of consecrating and offering the true body and blood of the Lord and of forgiving and retaining sins; but only an office and bare ministry of preaching the Gospel; or that those who do not preach are not priests at all; let him be anathema" (*Canons and Decrees*, Session XXIII, Chapter IV, Canon I). Luther effectively refuted the Roman dogma of the sacrament of holy orders and showed how it undermines the cardinal principle of the Christian religion: justification by faith in the atoning work of Christ. The Roman dogma concerning the priesthood, moreover, deprives the believers of privileges which Christ has given to all and reserves them for a special order of priests. Protestants may beware; they, too, are not immune to this error, as the history of the Lutheran Church in this country proves. Therefore Paul's warning to the Galatians is in place also with regard to this matter: "Stand fast therefore in the liberty wherewith Christ hath made us free, and be not entangled again with the yoke of bondage" (Gal. 5:1).

As priests the believers not only enjoy great rights and privileges, but also have important duties and responsibilities. Through Christ they have access by one Spirit unto the Father (Eph. 2:18). They may appear before Him in the Holy of Holies with their offerings of prayer, to pray, praise, and give thanks. But having done that, they step out of the Holy of Holies, as it were, to minister unto those without. The services which they render under their responsibilities as priests may be regarded conveniently as being performed within three spheres of activity: the church, the family, and the world.

As a *local church*, or congregation, the believers exercise their priestly powers by calling preachers and teachers. It is important that we remember that preaching and teaching were some of the chief duties of the priests, not only of the Levitical priests, but of all the believers in the Old Testament. Peter calls Noah a preacher of righteousness (II Pet. 2:5). God honors Abraham by calling him a Prophet (Gen. 20:7). The believers, as a royal priesthood, should show forth the praises of God (I Pet. 2:9). Jesus gave the believers the command: "Teach all nations, baptizing them in the name of the Father and of the Son and of the Holy Ghost, teaching them to observe all things whatsoever I have commanded you" (Matt. 28:19, 20). Again, "Go ye into all the world, and preach the Gospel

to every creature" (Mark 16:15). Jesus breathed on His disciples
and said unto them: "Receive ye the Holy Ghost: whosesoever sins
ye remit, they are remitted unto them; and whosesoever sins ye
retain, they are retained" (John 20:22, 23). These words, quoted
from Matthew, Mark, and John, were not limited to any particular
order of priests like the Levitical priests of the Old Covenant; they
were addressed to all believers. The words in Matthew, for instance,
were not limited to the eleven disciples, for Jesus added the words:
"And, lo, I am with you alway, even unto the end of the world"
(v. 20). In Mark He adds the words: "And these signs shall follow
them that believe" (Mark 16:17). Hence the persons to whom
Christ gave His command to preach are the believers. Christ gave
the power to remit and to retain sins to the entire congregation,
however small it may be. He declared: "For where two or three
are gathered together in My name, there am I in the midst of them"
(Matt. 18:20). Because of these powers and privileges given to the
New Testament believers, the Prophet exclaims: "O Zion, that bringest good tidings, get thee up into the high mountain; O Jerusalem,
that bringest good tidings, lift up thy voice with strength; lift it up,
be not afraid; say unto the cities of Judah, Behold your God!"
(Is. 40:9.)

However, "God is not the author of confusion, but of peace"
(I Cor. 14:33). The work of preaching and administering the Sacraments cannot be carried out by the congregation as a body. And if
every individual member of the congregation would insist that he
has the right to preach in public worship, that would inevitably
cause confusion, disorder, strife. Therefore in His wisdom God has
established the holy ministry for the public administration of the
priestly rites belonging properly to all believers.

That the holy ministry is a divine institution is clearly stated by
Paul when he tells the pastors of Ephesus, "Take heed therefore
unto yourselves and to all the flock, over the which the Holy Ghost
hath made you overseers, to feed the church of God, which He hath
purchased with His own blood" (Acts 20:28). I Cor. 12.28 we read:
"And God hath set some in the Church, first Apostles, secondarily
prophets, thirdly teachers, after that miracles, then gifts of healings,
helps, governments, diversities of tongues." Eph. 4:11, 12 Paul says·
"And He [Christ] gave some, Apostles; and some, prophets; and
some, evangelists; and some, pastors and teachers; for the perfecting

of the saints, for the work of the ministry, for the edifying of the body of Christ."

Therefore Paul writes (I Cor. 4:1): "Let a man so account of us as of the ministers of Christ and stewards of the mysteries of God." Pastors are ministers, servants of Christ, placed into their office by the appointment of Christ, the Head of the Church. And they are to be stewards, householders, of the mysteries of God: God's gifts for our salvation embodied in the Gospel and the Sacraments. These gifts, of course, are given to the entire congregation. But they are to be publicly administered by the pastor whom God gives to the congregation. For this reason the office of the pastor is called the public ministry. It may be well to note that the term "public" is here used not as distinguished from "private," the public administration being restricted to all acts performed in the presence of the Christian congregation, the private to those acts performed in the privacy of the home, at the sickbed, etc. The term "public" is used here in the sense in which it is used, *e. g.*, in the term "notary public," a notary appointed by the public to do certain work in the name and by the authority of the public. In like manner the pastor is the public administrator of the ministry not only in public worship, but whenever he as the representative of the congregation performs the duties of his office. Through him the congregation and every individual represented by him preaches, teaches, baptizes, administers the Sacrament.

For this reason the members of the congregation in calling a pastor do not give up in the least any of their rights as kings and priests. "They have signed away nothing when they have elected a pastor. They never had the right to infringe upon the equal rights of others and never were appointed to the ecclesiastical office. When the work of the congregation is to be done, according to the Lord's direction they appoint some one to do it in their behalf, because it is impossible for each individually to discharge the duty directly in his own person. But the work which is thus done according to the Christian people's call is their work, for the public performance of which they have made the minister their agent. For the right conduct of such ecclesiastical office they hold him responsible to the church whose representative they have called him to be; and as the work which they have called him to do is that which the Lord has primarily consigned to them and for which He has given the necessary instructions, He holds them responsible to Him for its performance according to His revealed will. He is thus at once the minister of Christ and of His Church. As the congregation is thus responsible for the discharge of the public office according to the Lord's will, it is manifest why the Church must insist that no one should publicly in the Church preach or administer the Sacraments unless he be rightly called" (Loy, *The Augsburg Confession,* pp. 777, 778).

The minister is, therefore, the servant of Christ through whom Christ bestows His blessings upon the congregation. But lest a minister because of this fact become proud and overbearing, let him remember that, after all, he is a minister, or servant. If he would glory, let him say with Paul: "Most gladly therefore will I rather glory in my infirmities, that the power of Christ may rest upon me" (II Cor. 12:9). On the other hand, lest the layman despise his pastor because the latter is a minister, or servant, of the congregation, let him heed the words of Scripture: "Let the elders that rule well be counted worthy of double honor, especially they who labor in the Word and doctrine" (I Tim. 5:17). But he must not stop here. The Apostle adds: "For the Scripture saith, Thou shalt not muzzle the ox that treadeth out the corn, and, The laborer is worthy of his reward" (I Tim. 5:18).

Since all believers are priests and, as such, preachers and teachers and since they exercise these functions publicly through the called servants of the Word, therefore it follows that they are responsible to God for the correct practice and the purity of doctrine of their respective ministers. As the elders are overseers over the flock, so the members of the flock are overseers over the elders. To the believers John writes: "Beloved, believe not every spirit, but try the spirits whether they are of God, because many false prophets are gone out into the world" (I John 4:1). Jesus warns the believers: "Beware of false prophets, which come to you in sheep's clothing, but inwardly they are ravening wolves" (Matt. 7:15). What, then, should the believers do when they have found teachers who are spreading false doctrine? Paul instructs the Romans: "Now, I beseech you, brethren, mark them which cause divisions and offenses contrary to the doctrine which ye have learned, and avoid them" (Rom. 16:17). The Bereans have given us a standing example how laymen should judge the doctrines of their preachers and teachers. Of them it is said: "These were more noble than those in Thessa-

lonica in that they received the Word with all readiness of mind
and searched the Scriptures daily whether those things were so.
Therefore many of them believed; also of honorable women, which
were Greeks, and of men, not a few" (Acts 17:11, 12). Here the
believers exercise their prerogative as priests to judge the doctrines
of the great Apostle. All did this—men and women, Jew and Greek
—all priests!

Though the laymen of a congregation do not by virtue of their
priesthood have a call to teach and preach publicly in the congregation, they do have a responsibility with regard to the welfare of
their neighbor's soul. They must not say with Cain: "Am I my
brother's keeper?" (Gen. 4:9.) The believers' duty in this respect is
described by Paul in these words: "Wherefore comfort yourselves
together, and edify one another, even as also ye do. And we beseech
you, brethren, to know them which labor among you and are over
you in the Lord and admonish you and to esteem them very highly
in love for their work's sake. And be at peace among yourselves.
Now we exhort you, brethren, Warn them that are unruly, comfort
the feeble-minded, support the weak, be patient toward all men, see
that none render evil for evil unto any man, but ever follow that
which is good, both among yourselves and to all men" (I Thess.
5:11-15). The believers should, indeed, heed their ministers, who
admonish them publicly; but what these do publicly, that is to say,
by virtue of their call extended to them by the whole congregation,
they are to do by virtue of their priesthood, into which God has
called them. How the believers are to admonish each other, Paul
indicates with these words: "Let the Word of Christ dwell in you
richly in all wisdom; teaching and admonishing one another in
psalms and hymns and spiritual songs, singing with grace in your
hearts to the Lord" (Col. 3:16). The content of the admonition
must be the Word of God. This admonishing is done conjointly with
teaching. It may be done in the most pleasant manner, in psalms and
hymns and spiritual songs. The specific aim of such admonishing is
indicated by the writer to the Hebrews in these words: "And let us
consider one another to provoke unto love and to good works, not
forsaking the assembling of ourselves together, as the manner of
some is; but exhorting one another and so much the more, as ye
see the Day approaching" (Heb. 10:24, 25).

Yes, to provoke unto love and to good works. James says: "Pure religion and undefiled before God and the Father is this, to visit the fatherless and widows in their affliction and to keep himself unspotted from the world" (James 1:27). The following words will not be spoken only to the ministers, who call on the afflicted by virtue of their office: "Come, ye blessed of My Father, inherit the Kingdom prepared for you from the foundation of the world. For I was an hungered, and ye gave Me meat; I was thirsty, and ye gave Me drink; I was a Stranger, and ye took Me in; naked, and ye clothed Me; I was sick, and ye visited Me; I was in prison, and ye came unto Me" (Matt. 25:34-36). These words are addressed to all believers, who have manifested their priestly office in priestly service of their fellow men.

The task of dealing with the trespassing brother is clearly described by the Lord Himself (Matt. 18:15-17). First there is individual admonition, then in the presence of one or two witnesses, finally—if the trespassing brother will not repent—the church must act. "Tell it unto the church," says Jesus (v. 17). When an incestuous person was to be put away from among the Christians at Corinth, Paul instructed them to take action when they were gathered together (I Cor. 5:4). The congregation was to act in such a case of excommunication. The congregation may be large or small, its powers as a gathering of priests remain the same, "for," says Jesus, "where two or three are gathered together in My name, there am I in the midst of them" (Matt. 18:20). Thus Paul writes to the Corinthians: "In the name of our Lord Jesus Christ when ye are gathered together" (I Cor. 5:4). Where men are gathered together in the name of the Lord Jesus Christ, there is a congregation which can bind or loose the sinner.

In matters which are neither commanded nor forbidden in the Bible, such as mere outward ceremonies (adiaphora), the members of a Christian congregation may exercise their prerogatives as priests by making such arrangements as they consider most acceptable. The minority will accede to the wishes of the majority. Charity will be the guiding principle.

In the family the believers are active as priests particularly in two respects. We may speak of the family altar, where the father is the priest and the mother the priestess. Then, too, believing parents are to bring up their children in the nurture and admonition of the Lord (Eph. 6:4). Since it is God's will that every believer should preach the Gospel to his neighbor, he must surely proclaim it to the members of his own household, particularly to his own flesh and blood. Thus the Old Testament patriarchs were priests within their households. They preached the name of the Lord to all, but particularly to their own family. So we are told of Abraham: "And the Lord said, Shall I hide from Abraham that thing which I do, seeing that Abraham shall surely become a great and mighty nation and all the nations of the earth shall be blessed in him? For I know him that he will command his children and his household after him, and they shall keep the way of the Lord, to do justice and judgment, that the Lord may bring upon Abraham that which He hath spoken of him" (Gen. 18:17-19). God was so greatly pleased with Abraham that He decided to confide a momentous secret to him. Why? Because God knew that Abraham would faithfully command his children and his household after him, and they should keep the way of the Lord. This presupposes that Abraham acquainted the members of his household with the way of the Lord. In other words, Abraham had exercised his prerogative as priest within his own household. What else should we expect of the father of believers? God later expressly enjoined Israel to teach the words of the Law to the children, yes, to make them the subject of constant discussion. Deut. 6:6, 7 we read: "And these words, which I command thee this day, shall be in thine heart; and thou shalt teach them diligently unto thy children and shalt talk of them when thou sittest in thine house and when thou walkest by the way and when thou liest down and when thou risest up." That covers every possible opportunity of inculcating the Law of God.

In the New Testament the Lord Jesus Himself singled out the homes for the planting of His kingdom. When He sent out His twelve disciples, He bade them: "And when ye come into an house, salute it. And if the house be worthy, let your peace come upon it: but if it be not worthy, let your peace return to you" (Matt. 10:12, 13). Again, when He sent out the seventy, He instructed them: "And into whatsoever house ye enter, first say, Peace be to this house. And if the son of peace be there, your peace shall rest upon it; if not, it shall turn to you again. And in the same house remain" (Luke 10:5-7). We know that the early Christians met in the homes to study the Word of God. Surely here, too, the admonition of St. Paul to the Colossians applies: "Let the Word of Christ dwell in you richly in all wisdom" (Col. 3:16).

Fathers must be priests particularly towards those who need their spiritual fostering most—their own children. These know God's Word less than adults; hence they must be instructed in it. Scripture is very clear on this point. Writing to the Ephesians, Paul exhorts: "And ye fathers, provoke not your children to wrath, but bring them up in the nurture and admonition of the Lord" (Eph. 6:4). These words imply a twofold duty on the part of the fathers. They must nurture their children, that is, feed them with the Word of God. They must also admonish them, set them right. This latter task brings to mind the parental authority of the fathers: they have power to administer the Law. They are *royal* priests.

When the children reach school age, the teacher assumes part of the duties of the parents to bring up the children. The children entrusted to their care by the parents, Christian teachers are to bring up in the nurture and admonition of the Lord. This, however, does not absolve the parents of their duty. They cannot evade their responsibility as priests towards their children by engaging teachers. Though the teachers assume that responsibility in the school, the parents must exercise it in the home and elsewhere. They must, indeed, be mindful of it in co-operating with the teacher in the school. Where believers are forced by unfavorable circumstances to send their children to a school in which God's Word does not rule, they must bear the full responsibility of their spiritual priesthood towards them by teaching them God's Word diligently and thoroughly at home.

This responsibility of parents as priests does not cease with confirmation. Not only will believing parents set a good example for their children in attending divine services regularly, thereby encouraging their children to do the same, but they will also set a good example in searching the Scriptures at home, thereby encouraging their children also in this priestly function. Here, too, the words of Jesus apply: "Search the Scriptures, for in them ye think ye have eternal life; and they are they which testify of Me" (John 5:39). Timothy was a richly blessed youth because he was taught God's Word in his childhood. Paul writes to him: "And that from a child thou hast known the Holy Scriptures, which are able to make thee wise unto salvation through faith which is in Christ Jesus" (II Tim.

3:15). Indeed, Timothy was a highly favored child. But to whom did he owe this favor? Paul points to Timothy's mother and grandmother. He says: "When I call to remembrance the unfeigned faith that is in thee, which dwelt first in thy grandmother Lois and thy mother, Eunice, and I am persuaded that in thee also" (II Tim. 1:5). Here two women are mentioned. Let us remember that in the priesthood of believers there is no difference between male and female—both are priests.

A glance at Luther's Small Catechism shows how the great Reformer stressed the duty of the parents as priests in their own household. At the head of the First Chief Part we find these words: "The Ten Commandments, as the head of the family should teach them in all simplicity to his household." Each Chief Part is headed by a similar admonition. Let us note, too, how he holds the father responsible for teaching his family to pray. He introduced the section on morning and evening prayer with the words: "How the head of the family should teach his household to pray morning and evening." Again, he says: "How the head of the family should teach his household to ask a blessing and return thanks." Thus by constant repetition Luther thoroughly inculcates the duty of believing parents as priests in their own household. That is a duty which believing parents cannot evade.

With respect to the world, believers have the priestly duty to declare the Word of God to the unbelievers and to pray for the government and for all people. Believers exercise their priestly rights and powers in the congregation and the family; a third sphere, not included in these first two, is the unbelieving world. Believers are indebted also to the latter. They must confess Christ to the unbelievers, so that some of these may become believers and thus priests themselves. Only through the Gospel's power can this be brought about. In other words, believers as priests must also be missionaries. What else could these words mean: "That ye should show forth the praises of Him who hath called you out of darkness into His marvelous light"? Having been called out of spiritual darkness into the marvelous light of Christ Jesus, believers must now strive with all their might to call those who still sit in darkness into that same light. We have already quoted the words of Jesus which bid the believers to teach or make disciples of all nations, baptizing them and teaching them to observe all things whatsoever He has commanded them (Matt. 28:19, 20), also His command: "Go ye into all the world, and preach the Gospel to every creature" (Mark 16:15). These words, as we have seen, are addressed to all believers. It is of great importance that believers confess their faith while in the world. This is evident from the words of Jesus: "Whosoever therefore shall confess Me before men, him will I confess also before My Father, which is in heaven. But whosoever shall deny Me before men, him will I also deny before My Father, which is in heaven" (Matt. 10:32, 33). The context shows that here confession before the world is meant, namely, before those who kill the body but are not able to kill the soul (v. 28).

Verbal confession, however, must be proved sincere by the confession of a Christian life. Jesus puts it thus: "Let your light so shine before men that they may see your good works and glorify your Father, which is in heaven" (Matt. 5:16). The meaning of these words is clear. Peter says: "Dearly beloved, I beseech you as strangers and pilgrims, abstain from fleshly lusts, which war against the soul; having your conversation honest among the Gentiles, that whereas they speak against you as evildoers, they may by your good works, which they shall behold, glorify God in the day of visitation" (I Pet. 2:11, 12). The good works of believers are the fruits and the proof of their faith. Their Christian life is a powerful testimony to the world; it proclaims the strength and value of their faith. Christians are different; they are not like the world. On the one hand, they know that whosoever will be a friend of the world is the enemy of God (James 4:4); on the other hand, by their good works they induce the world to investigate the source of their Christian life. Peter urges the believers: "But sanctify the Lord God in your hearts, and be ready always to give an answer to every man that asketh you a reason of the hope that is in you with meekness and fear" (I Pet. 3:15).

The duty to confess Christ to the unbelievers is incumbent also upon the entire congregation of believers. In its church and school the congregation confesses Christ. And what a single congregation may be unable to do, it can assist in doing by joining a group of believing congregations in a larger church body, such as our Synod. Such an organization enables the believers, these spiritual priests, to confess Christ in all the world. Thus the Lutheran Church is now confessing Him on every continent on the earth. This confessing is done by sending out missionaries, by preaching the Gospel by radio, and by disseminating Christian literature. In this manner the believers do the works of their great High Priest, who Himself has given them the promise: "Verily, verily, I say unto you, He that believeth on Me, the works that I do shall he do also; and greater works than these shall he do, because I go unto My Father" (John 14:12).

Is it necessary at all to say anything here of Christian giving? Our great High Priest has said: "Give, and it shall be given unto you" (Luke 6:38). Believers, New Testament priests, offer gladly and willingly. David, addressing our great High Priest, says: "Thy people shall be willing in the day of Thy power" (Ps. 110:3). They need not be driven.

And now prayer for the government and for all people. We have already considered the privilege of believers as priests to appear before God in prayer. They pray for themselves, for the Church, for their dear ones; they must also pray for their enemies, for such as do not as yet believe. Paul writes to Timothy: "I exhort therefore that, first of all, supplications, prayers, intercessions, and giving of thanks, be made for all men, for kings, and for all that are in authority, that we may lead a quiet and peaceable life in all godliness and honesty. For this is good and acceptable in the sight of God our Savior, who will have all men to be saved and to come unto the knowledge of the truth" (I Tim. 2:1-4). This praying is to be for the welfare of the world. Those who do not as yet believe are to come unto the knowledge of the truth. Thereby enemies are made friends, and the number of God's priests on earth is increased.

Blessed are those believers who remain conscious of their privileges and duties as God's priests! In the same measure as they exercise their priestly functions, their own faith will be strengthened and their love increased. They will grow in grace. Here, too, the words of Christ apply: "Give, and it shall be given unto you" (Luke 6:38).

"Now the God of Peace, that brought again from the dead our Lord Jesus, that great Shepherd of the sheep, through the blood of the everlasting covenant, make you perfect in every good work to do His will, working in you that which is well pleasing in His sight, through Jesus Christ, to whom be glory forever and ever. Amen" (Heb. 13:20, 21).

XVII

The Office of the Keys

THE Office of the Keys is of incalculable importance and value to the Church, because it is a doctrine which is clearly revealed in the Bible, a doctrine which gives to every Christian the power to forgive sins and the glorious assurance and comfort of the forgiveness of his own sins and a doctrine which establishes and preserves the equality and liberty of all believers.

I. THE DEFINITION OF THE OFFICE OF THE KEYS

The expression "Office of the Keys" does not occur in the sacred Scriptures. The word "office" signifies a set of duties which one has to perform. "All members have not the same office." The office of a judge is to hear cases and make decisions in court; the office of a minister is to take care of the flock God has given into his charge.

The term "keys" is frequently used in both Testaments of Scripture as a symbol of power. "I will give unto thee the keys of the kingdom of heaven," Jesus said to Peter (Matt. 18:19). "I am He that liveth and was dead, and, behold, I am alive forevermore, Amen, and have the keys of hell and of death" (Rev. 1:18). Although Scripture here employs metaphorical language, not figurative but real power is meant and conveyed. The keys signify the power which enables a person or an institution to perform certain tasks, the power which can make men inexpressibly happy or inexpressibly wretched.

The metaphor of the keys is used in Holy Scripture because the locking or the unlocking of the gates of heaven is concerned and because sins are chains which can be loosed or locked by means of keys. The plural of the word "key" is used to indicate the twofold power of the keys. There are both a binding key and a loosing key.

The phrase "Office of the Keys" is a pictorial description of the peculiar power of the Church. It signifies the plenary power which the Lord has handed to His Church on earth. Luther's Small Catechism defines the Office of the Keys as "The peculiar church power which Christ has given to His Church on earth." The Smalcald Articles state: "The keys are an office and power given by Christ to the Church" (Part III, VII, I). The Office of the Keys is a peculiar, special, unique, spiritual power given by the Lord to the Christian Church to distribute the promises of the Gospel.

The doctrine of the Office of the Keys, as defined above, is a distinctively Lutheran, or Biblical, teaching, one which distinguishes the Lutheran Church from other churches. In some heterodox churches this doctrine has been misused and misinterpreted or not even recognized. The Church of Rome contends that the keys lie only in the hands of the official clergy and that they convey both spiritual and earthly power to the Papacy (Augsburg Confession, XXVIII, "Of Ecclesiastical Power"). Some of the Reformed churches hold that the power of the Church is to be controlled by the higher orders or ranks of the clergy, that the Church is empowered to make laws that bind the consciences of its members, but that the Church has no actual power to remit or to retain sins. But the Lutheran Church believes and teaches the doctrine of the Office of the Keys as it was taught and practiced by Jesus Himself and as it was taught and practiced by the Apostles of Christ. Any abuse or misuse of this doctrine will lead the Church away from the safe moorings of Scripture.

II. THE SOURCE OF THE CHURCH'S POWER

The Church receives the power of the keys, not from any human, but solely from a divine, source. The Lord Jesus Christ not only founded the Christian Church, but endowed it with power and authority to execute its peculiar work. In His capacity as Head of the Church the Lord clothed the Church with power. It was He who said to Peter and to the Apostles and disciples and to the whole Church on earth, "*I* will give thee the keys of the Kingdom." Hence the Lutheran Catechism says that the Office of the Keys is "the peculiar church power which *Christ* has given to His Church on earth."

The question may be raised whether Christ had the right and

the power to bestow the Office of the Keys upon the Church. Jesus had earned and obtained the power of the keys by His death and resurrection (Rev. 1:18). As a result of His complete and perfect fulfillment of His sacerdotal work, God made Him "both Lord and Christ" (Acts 2:36), and Jesus had employed both the binding key and the loosing key on numerous occasions (Matt. 23:33; Luke 7:48). As Lord and Head of the Church, Jesus had the right and the power, not only to execute the Office of the Keys in His own person, but also to grant the same power to His Church on earth. He has handed the keys to His followers on earth, who are to use them for Him. "All power is given unto Me in heaven and in earth. Go ye, therefore, and teach all nations", the Lord had declared in His valedictory (Matt. 28:18-19). Thus the power of the keys has been bestowed upon the Church by the Lord of the Church Himself.

A heavy emphasis should be placed upon the fact that the Church receives its power to act in a spiritual capacity from the Lord and not from any human beings. The Church may indeed receive certain powers from the State, but whatever authority the State grants the Church can be only material and not spiritual in nature, for the State possesses no spiritual powers and hence cannot bestow any.

The Church receives its peculiar power and authority from the Lord through the medium of His Word. It is true that Jesus told His Apostles on Ascension Day, "Ye shall receive power after that the Holy Ghost is come upon you" (Acts 1:8). But it is just as true that the Word of God is the channel through which the Holy Spirit operates. In his First Epistle Peter writes that men are "born again . . . by the Word of God." In his Epistle to the Ephesians Paul recommends that every Christian should "take . . . the sword of the Spirit, which is the Word of God" (Eph. 6:17). When Jesus commissioned the Twelve and sent them out to carry on His work in a hostile world, the Lord told them, "When they deliver you up, take no thought how or what ye shall speak; for it shall be given you in that same hour what ye shall speak. For it is not ye that speak, but the Spirit of your Father which speaketh in you." (Matt. 10:19-20).

There is, of course, a tremendous power even in human words. Look into history, and you will see how human words have molded and shaped the lives and affairs of men.

But there is a far greater power inherent in the Word of God because the Holy Spirit is divinely operative in it. Jesus says: "It is the Spirit that quickeneth; the words that I speak unto you, they are spirit, and they are life." (John 6:63). Of Peter's preaching the Word of God in Caesarea, the Sacred Record says, "While Peter yet spake these words, the Holy Ghost fell on all them which heard the Word" (Acts 10:44).

The Church has no other spiritual power than that which the Word grants it. In its ministrations the Church must therefore not go beyond the Word. (Gal. 1:8; 3:10). Whoever goes beyond the Word of God insults the majesty of God, does irreparable harm to the Church, and creates disorder and confusion. The Church is bound to obey the Word of God unconditionally and for all times (John 17:20), and it is commanded to avoid those who teach doctrines contrary to those laid down in the indelible pages of the Sacred Volume (Rom. 16:17). Whoever adds to, or subtracts from, God's Word stands condemned by the Lord, who says, "Behold, I am against the prophets that use their own tongues and say, He saith" (Jer. 23:31). "In vain they do worship Me, teaching for doctrines the commandments of men" (Matt. 15:9).

Since the spiritual power of the Church comes from the Lord through His Word, it follows that Christ is the only spiritual ruler in the Church and that His Word is the only means of control over the doctrines and religious practices of the Church. The question of church government Jesus Himself decided when He said, "One is your Master, even Christ; and all ye are brethren" (Matt. 23:8). Though the Lord empowers men to preach the Gospel and to administer the Sacraments, He does not empower them to rule over the consciences of men. If some people quote the New Testament injunction "Obey them that have the rule over you, and submit yourselves" (Heb. 13:17), the reply must be made that this passage requires all believers to obey their pastors when the latter proclaim the Word of God. In view of the clear instructions of the Master, the Church must never allow any human authority to dictate to it what its doctrines and creeds should be, nor should the Church ever accommodate itself in doctrine to the demands of science and culture. Such a procedure is suicidal. "Beware," says the Apostle Paul, "lest any man spoil you through philosophy and vain deceit, after the tradition of men, after the rudiments of the world, and not after Christ" (Col. 2:8).

The possession of the Office of the Keys does not depend upon the numerical size of a congregation or upon its wealth and prestige. Whether a congregation has the size of the first Christian church in Jerusalem or consists of only two or three persons gathered together in the name of Christ, each receives the same church power from the Lord.

The objection is often advanced that there are some things in church work and in church life which are not specifically ordered by the Word of God, as for example, cremation, smoking, playing cards, church liturgy, and other open questions. In adiaphora every congregation can make its own decisions, but these matters are to be decided in accordance with the law of brotherly love and in accordance with the recommendations of Scripture, "Let all things be done decently and in order" (I Cor. 14:40; Formula of Concord, X, 1-3, *Triglot*, p. 1053), and, "Keep the unity of the Spirit in the bond of peace" (Eph. 4:3). If the question is asked, "What difference does it make if in adiaphora the Church makes rules and regulations for itself that are binding upon its members?" the Apostle Paul answers, "Stand fast in the liberty wherewith Christ hath made you free" (Gal. 5:1), and, "Let no man judge you in meat or in drink or in respect of an holyday or of the new moon, or of the Sabbath days, which are a shadow of things to come; but the body is of Christ" (Col. 2:16-17). Those churches which hold that rules and regulations made by their church bodies, provided they are not in conflict with express statements of the Bible, are binding upon the consciences of all, become guilty of putting the commandments of men on a par with the commandments of God (Matt. 15:9).

The contention is sometimes made that while it may be good theory to say that the Word of God is the supreme source of power in the Church, this idea does not work out well in practice. But the rule of the Word does work out well among those who are Christians. Jesus once said, "He that is of God heareth God's words" (John 8:47). Those who refuse to submit themselves to the rule of the Word of God are enemies of God. True Christians will be satisfied to be ruled by the Word of God. Even though Christians have the sinful flesh, which often forgets the Word of God and rebels against it, the rules and regulations formulated by men will not make them pious and God-fearing people.

Christians enjoy the marvelous privilege of having Christ as their supreme Lord and Master and of having His Word as the supreme source of power in the Church on earth. Persons who contend or pretend that they have been commissioned by God to control and to govern the doctrines and religious observances of the Church are branded as false prophets by Scripture, which declares, "If any man teach otherwise and consent not to wholesome words, even the words of our Lord Jesus Christ, and to the doctrine which is according to godliness, he is proud, knowing nothing, but doting about questions and strifes of words, whereof cometh envy, strife, railings, evil surmisings, perverse disputings of men of corrupt minds and destitute of the truth, supposing that gain is godliness; from such withdraw thyself" (I Tim. 6:3-5). The Apostles of Christ claimed that their preaching was based not upon their own wisdom and power, but upon the power of God. The Apostle Paul told the Corinthian Christians, "My speech and my preaching was not with enticing words of man's wisdom, but in demonstration of the Spirit and of power, that your faith should not stand in the wisdom of men, but in the power of God" (I Cor. 2:4-5; cp. Acts 20:32). If the Church draws its religious power only from the Lord through His Holy Word and does not seek to obtain power for performing its religious functions from any other source, the Church will be really powerful, and its acts will be successful and will redound to the glory of God. The Smalcald Articles say: "The Church can never be better governed and preserved than if we all live under one head, Christ, and all the bishops, equal in office (although they be unequal in gifts), be diligently joined in unity of doctrine, faith, Sacraments, prayer, and works of love" (Part II, Art. IV, 9; *Triglot*, p. 473f.).

III. THE NATURE OF THE CHURCH'S POWER

The power that the Office of the Keys grants to the Church is exclusively a spiritual power. "The weapons of our warfare are not carnal," says Holy Writ (II Cor. 10:4). "Put on the whole armor of God . . . and take the sword of the Spirit, which is the Word of God" (Eph. 6:10-17). On more than one occasion did Jesus intimate that the administration of His kingdom involved a spiritual and not a civil power. "Ye know," He said to the Twelve, "that the princes of the Gentiles exercise dominion over them and they that are great exercise authority upon them. But it shall not be so among you" (Matt. 20:25-27). "My kingdom is not of this world; if My kingdom were of this world, then would My servants fight" (John 18:36).

Since the power given to the Church by the Lord is purely spiritual, the Office of the Keys does not empower the Church to use physical force and compulsion over against human beings or to inflict physical penalties and capital punishment upon its members for any breach of the divine law or to enact laws that bind the consciences of men. Though the Church is empowered to preach the laws of God (Matt. 28:20), and to exercise whatever disciplinary measures God Himself enjoins and permits (Matt. 18:15-17), it does not have temporal power and authority to prescribe all manner of rules and regulations that bind the consciences of men, beyond those defined in the Scriptures. The Church has the power of the Word, not the power of the sword. Every attempt to convert the spiritual power of the church into a worldly power is unevangelical and dangerous.

Which powers does the Office of the Keys grant to the Church? The opinion is commonly held that the Office of the Keys grants only the dual power of remitting and retaining sins. While this function is one of the most important powers bestowed upon the Church by the Lord, the spiritual power of the Church is much more comprehensive. The Office of the Keys is a concept which includes the possession and the practice of all the spiritual powers, rights, duties, and privileges necessary for the welfare and promotion of the Church on earth. The keys of the kingdom of heaven are keys of God's house. Whoever has the keys of a house or a building ordinarily has power over everything in it and the authority necessary for its complete control and management. The final instruction of Jesus to His men was couched in these words: "Teach them to observe all things whatsoever I have commanded you" (Matt. 28:20). In whatever ways the Gospel of Christ is taught and applied to mankind, the Office of the Keys is put to employment. The Office of the Keys gives the Church the plenipotentiary power to proclaim the Word of God, to administer the Sacraments, to remit and to retain sins, to exercise church discipline, and to perform all other rights and duties pertaining to the well-being of the Church on earth. To the Church in Corinth Paul wrote, "All things are yours, whether Paul, or Apollos, or Cephas, or the world, or life, or death, or things present, or things to come: all are yours" (I Cor. 3:21-22; cp. Acts 20:27).

In His goodness God has given to the Church the power of conveying His grace to mankind in various ways. Since in the Christian religion everything depends upon man's assurance of receiving the forgiveness of sins, the Gospel gives counsel and aid against sin in several ways: "First, through the spoken Word, by which the forgiveness of sins is preached . . . in the whole world; which is the peculiar office of the Gospel. Secondly, through Baptism. Thirdly, through the holy Sacrament of the Altar. Fourthly, through the power of the keys, and also through the mutual conversation and consolation of the brethren, Matthew 18:20" (Smalc. Art., III; IV; *Triglot*, p. 491). In other words, every application of the Gospel of Christ conveys the grace of God to men with the same power and effect. In answer to the question why God has given men so many different ways of obtaining forgiveness, the statement may be made that God is so rich in grace that He bestows a variety of means whereby men may obtain forgiveness of their sins. Because of the weakness of man's faith God gives men reassurance by repetition.

In particular, the Office of the Keys empowers the Church to remit and to retain sins, both original sin and the actual sins of men. The Smalcald Articles state the fact that "The keys are an office and power given by Christ to the Church for binding and loosing sins, not only the gross and well-known sins, but also the subtle, hidden, which are known only to God" (Part III, VII; *Triglot*, p. 493). The words of Jesus are clear and unmistakable: "Whosoever sins ye remit, they are remitted unto them; and whosoever sins ye retain, they are retained" (John 20:23).

Do these words of Jesus authorize the Church merely to announce and to declare to men that God is willing and ready to forgive their sins, or do these words of Jesus empower the Church actually to convey forgiveness to the sinner? A proper understanding of these words of Jesus is of inestimable importance to every Christian. Many misunderstand and misinterpret the plain commission of the Lord. Some of the Reformed and liberal churches hold that no human being can forgive sins and that men can only announce the fact that God stands ready to forgive men their sins. The Jamieson-Fausset-Brown *Commentary* supposes that "the power to intrude upon the relation between men and God cannot have been given by Christ to His ministers in any but a ministerial or declarative sense" (p. 169). The reason why the power of the keys is a stumbling block to many people is that they do not believe or understand the doctrine of objective justification, namely, that God has been fully reconciled by the atoning work of Christ and that forgiveness of sins has been won by Christ for every sinner, as is shown by the statement of Scripture, "God was in Christ, reconciling the world unto Himself, not imputing their trespasses unto them, and hath committed unto us the word of reconciliation" (II Cor. 5:19).

From the words of Jesus in John 20:23 it is apparent that the church has the power not merely to announce and to declare to men the remission or the retention of their sins, but actually to give forgiveness to penitent sinners and to deny forgiveness to impenitent sinners. By His sacrificial death and by His resurrection Jesus not only obtained the possibility of forgiveness and justification, this possibility becoming a reality as soon as the sinner comes to faith. No, by His vicarious suffering and death the Lord won full absolution for all people. He "was delivered for our offenses and was raised again for our justification" (Rom. 4:25). "As by the offense of one judgment came upon all men to condemnation, even so by the righteousness of one the free gift came upon all men unto justification of life" (Rom. 5:18). And Jesus not only has redeemed and reconciled the world, but He also has given His followers the power to confer upon all people the forgiveness won by Him. He tells His followers not simply to announce the fact that God will forgive them, provided that they believe, but He tells them actually to remit and to retain sins.

Opponents of this view argue that since God alone can forgive sins, man becomes guilty of blasphemy if he presumes to do so, and that therefore ministers can only announce or declare to sinners the forgiveness that Christ has won for them. But ministers and other Christians do not forgive sins on their own authority, but in the name and by the authority of Christ. Thus St. Paul emphasizes the fact that "if I forgave anything, to whom I forgave it, for your sakes forgave I it in the person of Christ" (II Cor. 2:10).

In the *Liturgy and Agenda* of the Lutheran Church one of the formulas for pronouncing absolution reads as follows: "Upon this your confession, I, by virtue of my office, as a called and ordained servant of the Word, announce the grace of God unto all of you, and in the stead and by the command of my Lord Jesus Christ I forgive you all your sins, in the name of God the Father, God the Son, and God the Holy Ghost." If a minister were merely to announce the fact that God is willing to forgive, the hearer could not be certain about receiving absolution and hence would be deprived of the comfort of the forgiveness of his sins. "When a messenger comes to a prisoner and says, 'I announce unto you that the governor pardons you,' the prisoner would have reason to say, 'Thank you for the announcement. When will the governor's pardon arrive?' But when the messenger says, 'In the name of the governor and by his command I pronounce you a free man,' that leaves no room for the prisoner to doubt." (F. Kuegele, *Theological Quarterly*, 1905, p. 56).

The doctrine of the Roman Catholic Church that only a priest can forgive sins and that every sinner must make an enumeration of his sins to the priest in order that the latter may in a judicial capacity impose proper penalties is contrary to Scripture, requires what is impossible and unnecessary, and makes the clergyman a judge over his fellow men. "The objection, made by some, that a judge ought to investigate a case before he pronounces upon it, pertains in no way to this subject; because the ministry of absolution is favor or grace, it is not a legal process, or law. (For God is the Judge, who has committed to the Apostles, not the office of judges, but the administration of grace, namely, to acquit those who desire, etc.) Therefore ministers in the Church have the command to remit sin; they have not the command to investigate secret sins. And, indeed, they absolve from those that we do not remember; for which reason absolution, which is the voice of the Gospel remitting sins and consoling consciences, does not require judicial examination." (Apology, Art. VI, 6-8; *Triglot*, p. 282f.) When in the Lutheran Church communicants are asked the familiar three preparatory questions, the minister does not act as a judge, but as a pastor who desires to help the communicants prepare for a worthy reception of Holy Communion.

The contention is made by some people that when Jesus says in John 20:23, "Whosoever sins ye remit, etc.," the Lord means that ministers should state the conditions upon which God will remit or retain sins. If this idea were correct, no one could ever be sure of obtaining actual forgiveness, because no one could know whether he had satisfactorily fulfilled the conditions. This thought, which declares that absolution is conditioned by the works of man and thus denies the full satisfaction rendered by Christ, is a complete perversion of the words of Christ, for His words do not establish conditions for obtaining absolution, but they authorize the actual transmission of forgiveness to sinners. The Apostles of Christ understood the words of Jesus in a literal and authoritative sense, and they exercised the dual power granted them every time they preached the remission of sins in the name of Christ (See, *e. g.,* Acts 2:38; 3:6; 5:1-5; 10:43).

When the Church exercises its power of granting absolution, it makes a special application of the Gospel of Christ to individuals or to groups of individuals. The whole Gospel of Christ is an absolution. Absolution may be defined as the special form of administering the Gospel in which a minister or other Christian forgives the sins of others. Absolution is not a power which exists outside the Gospel, but it is the application of the Gospel to mankind. In the general absolution the grace of God is conveyed to a whole congregation, and in the private absolution the grace of God is applied to the individual. "The power of the keys administers and presents the Gospel through absolution, which proclaims peace to me and is the true voice of the Gospel" (Apol., Art. XII, 39. *Triglot,* p. 261).

Every proclamation of the Gospel is an absolution, for every time the Gospel is circulated, it distributes the forgiveness that is deposited in the Word of God. Although the whole world has been absolved by the death and resurrection of Christ more than 1900 years ago, the news of this absolution must be conveyed to man, and at the same time conferred upon man, through the Gospel in order that man may become aware of and accept the forgiveness that has been obtained for him by the Lord. The world that was absolved by the work of Christ nearly two millenniums ago is not absolved all over again by the preaching of the Gospel, but the fruits of the redemption are thereby applied to men.

Private absolution does not confer upon the sinner a better or more powerful or another kind of forgiveness than that given by the preaching of the Word, but it makes a special application of the Gospel to men, and it gives the individual a greater comfort and certainty that forgiveness has been conferred upon him personally; thus, for example, the angel of the Lord told the women at the empty tomb of Christ to go and tell the news to His disciples and to Peter, for Peter needed to hear the news especially (Mark 16:7).

By believing in Christ a person obtains forgiveness of his sins (Acts 10:43), but absolution gives a person reassurance and renewal and repetition of forgivenes. While Jesus was at dinner in the house of Simon, the Pharisee, He said about the woman who had anointed His feet, "Her sins, which are many, are forgiven," and yet the Lord gave her a special absolution by saying to her, "Thy sins are forgiven" (Luke 7:47-48).

The fact that the whole world has been redeemed and reconciled by Christ is not an indication of the fact that all the world will ultimately gain eternal salvation; man must by faith accept and appropriate the Gospel or be lost forever.

There is no such thing as a twofold absolution, one pronounced by man and the other by God; for the absolution spoken by men is God's absolution which is pronounced by men in God's stead and by His command (John 20:23).

When a person reads the promises of the Gospel, he applies the absolution of the Gospel to himself and in effect absolves himself. Since absolution is a special application of the Gospel which confers the grace of God upon mankind, it may be called, in a wider sense of the term, a means of grace.

IV. THE PERSONS INVESTED WITH THE POWER OF THE KEYS

The power to remit and to retain sins belongs, strictly speaking, to the Triune God alone. When at the time of the healing of the man sick of the palsy the scribes of Israel raised the question, "Who can forgive sins but God only?" (Mark 2:7) they expressed a truth revealed in the Old and New Testaments (cf. Is. 43:25; Mark 2:7). All sins are committed, either directly or indirectly, against God; hence only God can remit sins, and only God can retain sins. But God exercises this prerogative of His not immediately or directly, but only through His Word which He commands His followers to proclaim to every creature (Matt. 28:19-20; John 15:3; Eph. 5:25-26). In other words, God commands His believing disciples to grant forgiveness or to deny forgiveness as His representatives, for He tells them, "Whosoever sins ye remit, they are remitted unto them; and whosoever sins ye retain, they are retained" (John 20:23).

The doctrine that men can forgive sins in the name of God has met and still meets with vehement opposition. When Jesus said to the man sick of the palsy, "Thy sins be forgiven thee," the scribes objected and protested (Mark 2:1-7). Like those scribes many argue that man cannot forgive sins, but that man can only declare that it is now possible for God to forgive man sins. Others contend that when men attempt to forgive sins, they make themselves equal with God, interfere with God's rights, and commit an act of blasphemy and sacrilege. But God has commanded men to forgive sins in His name and in His stead. Though the keys open and close the gates of heaven, they are on earth in the hands of men whom God has appointed as His agents.

The original possessor of the keys of the kingdom of heaven is Jesus Christ. He is the true God, who has all power in heaven and in earth, including the power of the keys. When a palsied man was brought to the home of Jesus in the city of Capernaum for cure, the Lord said to the dissenting scribes there present, "That ye may know that the Son of Man hath power on earth to fogive sins . . ." (Mark 2:10). This power is still, of course, in the possession of Jesus. Though He has given the power of the keys to men, He has not given it away, but He continues to wield this power through the agency and instrumentality of men.

The Office of the Keys was first transmitted by Jesus to the Apostle Peter, to whom Christ said, "I will give unto thee the keys of the kingdom of heaven" (Matt. 16:19). Were the keys intended for the use of Peter alone? Certainly not; for in that case, with the death of Peter, the power of the keys would have become invalidated. The Roman Church teaches that Jesus gave the keys only to Peter, who then conveyed them to his successor, and that the incumbent of the papal chair, as the successor of Christ and Peter, is the sole holder of the power of the keys and of supreme authority in the Church of Christ. This claim is both Scripturally and historically baseless.

The reasons why the Petrine theory is fallacious and false are fully stated in the Smalcald Articles ("Of the Power and Primacy of the Pope," 1-82). The Bible nowhere teaches that Peter was appointed the vicar of Christ on earth, but it prohibits any one Apostle from exercising lordship over the others (Luke 22:24-26; Matt. 18:1-4). Peter never claimed, never exercised, and was never accorded supreme power in the Church of the Apostolic Era. In fact.

on one occasion the advice of James was accepted by the Church as of equal value with that of Peter (Acts 15:7-30), while on another occasion Peter was even rebuked by Paul (Gal. 2:7-11), which would never have occurred if Peter had received the supremacy in the Church from the Lord. Peter calls himself only a fellow elder (I Pet. 5:1), recognizes the supreme authority of Scripture rather than his own (II Pet. 1:19), was ordered about by the Church of his day (Acts 8:14), and the Scriptures expressly state that *all* of the Apostles constitute the foundation of the Christian Church (Eph. 2:20). The Council of Nicaea in 325 A. D. did not recognize the superiority of the Roman pontiff, and many ancient synods were held in which the Pope did not preside. Hence the ancient Church did not acknowledge the primary or superiority of the Pope.

A study of the context of the passage in which Jesus handed the keys of the kingdom of heaven to Peter (Matt. 16:13-20) will clearly show that the Church of Christ is to be built, not upon the person of Peter, but upon the confession of faith as uttered by Peter at that time. In Matthew 16:18 Jesus makes an exalted play upon words and says in effect, "Your name is *Petros,* "Rock," and upon your rocklike confession of faith I will build My Church." If Jesus had intended to make Peter the foundation of, and the supreme authority in, the Church, He would no doubt have said, "Thou art Peter, and upon *thee* will I build My Church." Since Peter was the first of the Twelve to make a confession of faith in Christ, he was the first to receive the power of the keys, which was intended for all the Apostles and was expressly extended to all of them in other passages of Scripture (John 20:23; Matt. 18:18), to all of them in equal measure with Peter. And every believer in Christ who makes Peter's confession his own also obtains the power of the keys from the Lord. Of all Christians the Scriptures declare, "Ye are a royal priesthood" (I Pet. 2:9), and ye are "kings and priests unto God" (Rev. 1:6). To all Christians Paul writes, "All things are yours, whether Paul, or Apollos, or Cephas" (I Cor. 3:22).

That Christ endowed not only Peter, but all of the Apostles and all believers with the power of the keys is quite evident from the words spoken by the risen Lord on the day of His resurrection to a large group of His adherents: "Receive ye the Holy Ghost; whosesoever sins ye remit, they are remitted unto them; and whosesoever sins ye retain, they are retained" (John 20:23). The words previously spoken by the Lord to Peter in the singular number are here repeated, in essence, in the plural.

The power of the keys has not been given only to the Apostles of Christ, nor to Apostles and their successors only and later transmitted and transferred by them to their successors in the clerical office. The assumption that Christ granted the power of the keys only to the Apostles, only to the clergy, fails to take into consideration the fact that at that meeting in Jerusalem on Easter Sunday night the Lord addressed not only the ten Apostles, but also some others who were present. St. Luke informs us that not only the ten Apostles, but also the two Emmaus disciples and some other disciples were present at that time (Luke 24:33-35). Did Jesus deliberately disregard and ignore the other disciples and grant the keys only to the ten Apostles before Him? The power of the keys transmitted on that momentous occasion was not reserved for the Apostles alone, for they, including Peter, have died long ago, and the grant of power would have died with them, since there is no evidence in Scripture or in history that the Apostles were empowered to impart this power to others. The original apostolate ceased with the death of the Apostles. As eyewitnesses of the work of Christ and as inspired teachers of the Church the Apostles had no successors, although as preachers of the Gospel all Christian ministers are successors of the Apostles. But there is no need of insisting upon an unbroken line of successors to the Apostles, for the inspired Word of the Apostles is the basis of all doctrine in the Church of Christ (John 17:20; Eph. 2:20).

That the power of the keys was intended by the Lord to every believer is shown by the words of Christ spoken in the Temple, "He that believeth on Me, as the Scripture hath said, out of his belly shall flow rivers of living water. (But this spake He of the Spirit, which they that believe on Him should receive. . .)" (John 7:38-39). Every person who has received the Spirit of God, every believing Christian, receives the keys as a precious gift of God and as a solemn trust from God. In the power of the Holy Spirit every believer is authorized not only to proclaim the message of God's forgiveness, but also to grant to people the forgiveness of their sins in the name and by the authority of God. With this understanding the Apostles and the Christians of the Apostolic Era exercised the power given them by the Lord—exercised it every time they preached the Gospel (Acts 3:19; 8:35; 9:20).

The Office of the Keys was given by Christ not only to the Apostles and disciples, but also to the whole Church on earth. "The keys belong not to the person of one particular man, but to the Church, as many most clear and firm arguments testify. For Christ, speaking concerning the keys (Matt. 18:19), adds, 'If two or three of you shall agree on earth, etc.' Therefore He grants the keys principally and immediately to the Church" (Smalc. Art., "Of the Power and Primacy of the Pope," 24; *Triglot,* p. 511). That Christ has given the power of the keys to the Church as a whole is clear from several passages of Scripture (Matt. 16:18-19; I Cor. 12:28; Rev. 5:9-10). The Church Triumphant, which has been translated into glory and is without sin, does not, of course, need the Office of the Keys. Unbelievers, non-Christians, heathen, hypocrites, and others of that stripe do not belong to the Church Universal and hence do not have the Office of the Keys. Nor does God want them to use the keys, for He says to them, "What hast thou to do to declare My statutes, or that thou shouldest take My covenant in thy mouth, seeing thou hatest instruction, and castest My words behind thee?" (Ps. 50:16-17.) But every believer who has received the Holy Spirit is a royal priest who possesses all the rights and privileges of the Office of the Keys.

Every local church of God, whether it is large or small, rich or poor, European or American, white or black, or whether it contains a mixture of believers and unbelievers, if God's Word is proclaimed and taught in its midst, has the Office of the Keys because of the believers that are included in its membership (Matt. 18:17-20). The fact that individual local congregations in the Apostolic Era possessed and practiced the Office of the Keys indicates the correctness of the teaching that the power of the keys has been entrusted to every local congregation. Thus Paul asked the local congregation in Corinth to use the binding key against an incestuous man, and later the Apostle asked the same congregation to employ the loosing key to reinstate the man who had repented of his grievous sin (I Cor. 5:4-5; II Cor. 2:6-10).

Since the power of the keys has been given by the Lord to every believer, this privilege belongs also to Christian ministers in their capacity as believers as well as in their capacity as called and ordained servants of the Word. The Office of the Keys belongs also to Christian women (Gal. 3:26-28), and the specific duties of Christian women are outlined and defined in the Scriptures (I Pet. 3:1-6; I Tim. 5:4-5). Although Christian women possess all the rights and privileges and duties of the Office of the Keys, the Scriptures place some limitations upon their exercise of these rights in public (I Tim. 2:11-12; I Cor. 14:34-35).

That the Office of the Keys has been bestowed upon human beings and that God remits and retains sins through men is thus a definite doctrine of Scripture. The statement of Scripture that God "has given such power to men" (Matt. 9:8) led Luther to make the comment that God does not forgive sins on earth except through men.

V. THE PUBLIC ADMINISTRATION OF THE OFFICE OF THE KEYS

Although the Office of the Keys belongs to all believers in Christ, it is to be exercised publicly by the ministers of Christ, to whom the Church delegates and transfers the rights, powers, duties, and privileges of the spiritual priesthood by means of a divine call. The office of the ministry, charged with the public administration of the keys, is not a mere human arrangement or idea, nor does it create a special class of believers over and above other Christians, but it is a divine institution, the highest and most honorable office in the Church, all other offices being subordinate to it. The ordination of called ministers with laying on of hands is not a divine institution, and does not qualify men for office, but it is a good custom of the Church which gives public confirmation of the call.

The public administration of the Office of the Keys is treated in a separate article, pp. 366-387.

VI. THE EFFICACY AND VALIDITY OF THE OFFICE OF THE KEYS

Whenever the called ministers of Christ administer the Office of the Keys publicly in the name of the congregation, or whenever any believer employs the binding key or the loosing key in private, they do not perform an ineffective and inoperative act, but their acts are as effective and valid and certain in the sight of God as though Christ Himself had performed them. God approves, recognizes, sanctions, and accepts the absolution pronounced by Christians in

His stead and in His name as though He Himself had pronounced it. The Augsburg Confession says: "Our people are taught that they should highly prize the absolution, as being the voice of God, and pronounced by God's command" (Art. XXV, 3; *Triglot*, p. 69). The forgiveness bestowed by men upon penitent believers is as effective and valid, both in heaven and on earth, as though Christ had bestowed it in person. Jesus says to His followers, "Whosesoever sins ye remit, they are remitted unto them; and whosesoever sins ye retain, they are retained" (John 20:23). The Lord does not say, "Whose-soever sins ye remit, I shall then also remit; and whosesoever sins ye retain, I shall then also retain." These words of Jesus declare in clear and unmistakable terms that the absolution granted or denied by men in the name of God is effective and valid before God. Luther wrote: "He says thus: When you bind and loose on earth, I will at the same time bind and loose in heaven. When you execute the work of the keys, I also will do the same; when you do it, it is done, and I do not need to do it again. Whatsoever you bind and loose, that will I no more bind and loose, but it shall be bound and loosed without My binding and loosing. My work and your work shall be the same work, and not two different works. My keys and your keys are the one and the same set of keys, and not two different sets of keys; when you have done your work, My work also is done; when you bind and loose, I also have done the binding and loosing. He obliges and binds Himself to our work, so that He entrusts to us the execution of His own work." (Luther, *On the Keys*, 1530, Weimar Edition, 30, II, 497f. Quoted by Prof. Uuras Saarnivaara, *The Power of the Keys*, 1945, p. 19f.) Since the Office of the Keys, when administered by men, is accepted as effective and valid by God, it should be accepted and respected as valid also on earth in the congregations.

If people wonder how a minister or any other Christian, who is himself a sinful person, can actually and effectually grant forgiveness to others, they should be reminded of the fact that God's Word orders him to do so and that God's Word continues to be effective even when spoken by sinful lips. As a matter of fact, even if an unbelieving minister of a Christian Church pronounces absolution, or even if a Christian minister pronounces absolution upon an unbeliever who pretends to be a Christian, the forgiveness spoken in such instances is still effective and valid before God, even though it is not accepted by the unbeliever.

The efficacy and validity of the absolution pronounced publicly by a minister or privately by any believer do not depend in the slightest degree upon the faith, repentence, worthiness, good works, satisfaction, feelings, experience, attitude, co-operation, conduct, or intention of any person or of any minister. The power to forgive lies in the Word of God, not in any human being. Even if the minister of a Christian congregation were a hypocrite or a heretic, his acts performed in the name of God and of the congregation would still be both efficacious and valid; and even if Satan were to come and take the minister's place for a day, the absolution spoken by him would be effective and valid. The Apology of the Augsburg Confession gives the opinion that "Neither are the Sacraments without efficacy for the reason that they are administered by wicked men" (Art. VII, VIII, 3. *Triglot*, p. 227). All those who announce the grace of God in Christ Jesus to mankind never make a mistake by so doing; for there is no such thing as an erring key.

If the objection is offered that a minister cannot really forgive sins because he cannot look into the hearts of men and determine whether they are truly repentant believers, the reply must be made that absolution is not conditioned upon man's behavior. True, absolution is not to be pronounced upon manifestly impenitent persons, though God's absolution is not ruined by the absence of faith in a person, for Scripture says, "What if some did not believe? Shall their unbelief make the faith of God without effect?" (Rom. 3:3.) Accordingly, absolution must never be pronounced conditionally, but always unconditionally, as Jesus did. Jesus did not say to the palsied man, "If you repent and believe, your sins will be forgiven," but He said simply, "Thy sins be forgiven thee" (Matt. 9:2). The forgiveness of sins does not rest upon any goodness or quality in man, but only upon God's gracious disposition toward sinners for Christ's sake. To say that forgiveness depends upon something in man is to commit the error of synergism. God actually offers and gives the forgiveness of sins to all sinners, whether they believe or not. Through Christ's redemption of the world God has been reconciled to all the world; the unbelief of man cannot annul this fact. Man's unbelief does not make God's forgiveness null and void, ineffective, and invalid (Rom. 3:3).

Although the efficacy and validity of the Office of the Keys do not depend upon anything in man, forgiveness is *received* only through faith. "Whosoever believeth in Him shall receive remission of sins" (Acts 10:43). In absolution one must distinguish between the means of transmission and the means of acceptance, which are, of course, correlatives. Romanism teaches that no receiving means is required on the part of a person, since, as the Roman Church holds, the grace of God is infused into a person by his mere physical contact with God's means of grace (*ex opere operato*). But anyone who desires to receive the benefits of the Gospel, of Baptism, of Holy Communion, must accept these gifts of God through faith. What does the most precious gift of God benefit a person if he refuses to accept it? A person who refuses or neglects to believe that God has forgiven his sins fails to receive absolution, but the fault is entirely his and not that of the Word. Unbelief effectively prevents the heart from receiving the grace of God. "Unto us was the Gospel preached," says the Epistle to the Hebrews, "as well as unto them; but the Word preached did not profit them, not being mixed with faith in them that heard it." Luther wrote in his pamphlet *On the Keys*: "Many people do not believe the Gospel, but the Gospel nevertheless does not lie. A certain king gives you a castle: if you do not accept it, the king has yet not lied nor deceived, but you have deceived yourself, and the fault is yours; the king has surely given it." (Quoted by Saarnivaara, *op. cit.*, p. 34.) "Concerning the righteousness of faith before God we believe, teach, and confess unanimously, in accordance with the comprehensive summary of our faith and confession presented above, that poor sinful man is justified before God, that is, absolved and declared free and exempt from all his sins and from the sentence of well-deserved condemnation and adopted into sonship and heirship of eternal life, without any merit or worth of our own, also without any preceding, present, or any subsequent works, out of pure grace, because of the sole merit, complete obedience, bitter suffering, death, and resurrection of our Lord Christ alone, whose obedience is reckoned to us for righteousness. These treasures are offered us by the Holy Ghost in the promise of the holy Gospel; and faith alone is the only means by which we lay hold upon, accept, and apply, and appropriate them to ourselves. This faith is a gift of God by which we truly learn to know Christ, our Redeemer." (F. of C., Thorough Declaration, III, 9-10, *Triglot*, p. 919.) To obtain the glorious benefits of the Gospel, faith is necessary, for "without faith it is impossible to please God" (Heb. 11:6).

IX. THE OBLIGATIONS AND RESPONSIBILITIES ENTAILED BY THE POSSESSION OF THE OFFICE OF THE KEYS

The exercise of the Office of the Keys, given to all Christians, includes a large number of solemn duties. The Church must exercise the power of the keys by the administration of the Word and Sacraments and by the establishment of Christian churches, both at home and abroad, for the conversion of sinners, in accordance with the great commission given by the Head of the Church in His valedictory (Matt. 28:18-20) and for the edification of the saints, in accordance with the inspired instructions left by the Apostle Paul (Eph. 4:12-13).

The Church has the duty, not only of proclaiming the Word, but also of preserving the Word of God. While powerful hostile forces are arrayed against the Word and while the spirit of error pervades the world, the Church must bend every effort, under God, that God's truth does not perish from the earth and that the indelible pages of the Sacred Volume be preserved and perpetuated in their purity, so that there may never arise on earth a generation of men which knows not the Lord nor the works which He hath done (cp. Judg. 2:10). The Church's duty as keeper of the precious deposit of the divine truth is given in the words of Scripture, "O Timothy, keep that which is committed to thy trust" (I Tim. 6:20).

The possession of the Office of the Keys obligates the Church to formulate creeds and confessions in order to awaken in its membership a clear conception of what it believes and teaches and in order to offer to those that are without a definite understanding of its doctrines and practices (Rom. 10:9; Matt. 10:32-33).

Since the Lord has given all Christians a loosing key and a binding key, He expects all Christians to employ both keys in their respective capacities. Many Christians are altogether too quick to employ the binding key and too slow to use the loosing key, too quick to retain, and too slow to remit, the sins of their fellow men. But Holy Scripture strongly urges Christians to use the loosing key with alacrity and with avidity. In the Lord's Prayer Jesus teaches Christians to pray, "Forgive us our trespasses as we forgive those who trespass against us." When Peter once came before the Lord with the question, "Lord, how oft shall my brother sin against me, and I forgive him? till seven times?" the Lord replied, "I say not unto thee, Until seven times, but, Until seventy times seven" (Matt. 18:21-22). And thereupon the Lord related the Parable of the Unmerciful Servant, adding the application and the admonition, "So likewise shall my heavenly Father do also unto you if ye from your hearts forgive not everyone his brother their trespasses" (Matt. 18:23-35). Paul the Apostle also recommends the use of the loosing key when he declares, "Be ye kind one to another, tenderhearted, forgiving one another, even as God for Christ's sake hath forgiven you" (Eph. 4:32; cp. Gal. 6:1).

But Christians are also charged with the duty of employing the binding key when occasion demands. Several passages of the New Testament indicate the fact that the Church of the first century exercised this power (Matt. 18:17; I Cor. 5:2-5; I Tim. 1:20; Tit. 3:10-11). Does the Church of the twentieth century exercise church discipline and practice excommunication? A theologian of the Christian Reformed Church charges that also the Lutheran Church does not practice church discipline and excommunication. He avers: "At present there is in the Churches round about us a noticeable tendency to be lax in discipline, to place a one-sided emphasis on the reformation of the sinner through the ministry of the Word and—in some instances—through personal contacts with the sinner and to steer clear of any such measures as excluding one from communion with the Church" (L. Berkhof, *Syst. Theol.*, p. 601). Are his charges true about the Lutheran Church? It should be carefully borne in mind that the Sacred Volume strongly emphasizes the obligation of using the binding key against manifest and impenitent sinners (cp. I Cor. 5:13).

Another obligation resting upon all Christians in consequence of their possession of the keys is the duty of judging the doctrine of the Church. Jesus admonishes His followers to "beware of false prophets" (Matt. 7:15). The Apostle John urges Christians to "try the spirits whether they are of God" (I John 4:1). Paul beseeches all Christians: "Mark them which cause divisions and offenses contrary to the doctrine which ye have learned; and avoid them" (Rom. 16:17). Christians of today might well emulate the example of the early Christians in the village of ancient Berea, who, even when the great Apostle Paul preached to them, "searched the Scriptures daily, whether those things were so" (Acts 17:10-11).

The exercise of the Office of the Keys includes many other duties, which can only be listed and mentioned in this place, such as the establishment and the proper maintenance of the Christian ministry, Christian schools, Christian colleges, and Christian publishing houses; the cultivation of the study of theology in order that a deeper knowledge and understanding of God's Word may be gained by men; mutual exhortation and encouragement on the part of brethren in the faith; the application of Christian charity and benevolences; intercessory prayer for friend and foe; the preservation of salutary church customs, ceremonies, and festivals; the organization of synods and of Christian societies for fellowship; the promotion of the Christian life as it becometh the Gospel of Christ; and whatever other functions are necessary or salutary for the welfare and the promotion of the Church on earth.

If the Church of God were to be derelict in the performance of any of its various solemn duties, it would be unfaithful to its Lord and Master, would impoverish its spiritual life, and would bring upon itself swift destruction.

X. THE PROPER USE OF THE OFFICE OF THE KEYS

The enormous power contained in the Office of the Keys has been given to the Church by the Lord with the intention that it be used, and used properly. If this peculiar church power is rightly used and administered, inestimable blessings will result for the church, for the community, and for the whole country (cf. Gen. 30:27; 39:3-5; 12:2). But if this power is abused and misused, neglected and omitted, the most serious consequences will ensue. The abuse and misuse of power always eventuates in disaster. If civil officials do not use their power properly, the people in their area of activity will suffer; if a general does not use his power wisely and well, his armies will be defeated; and if Christians do not use the power of the keys and use it properly, they will be guilty, to state the matter mildly, of a serious sin of omission.

The peculiar power entrusted to the Church is to be employed in accordance with the instructions of the Master, who has entrusted the Church with the keys. This power is by no means to be employed according to the whims and caprices of men, according to the desire and option of man, or according to man's free will. The specifications of the Lord are clearly stated in the pages of His revealed Word. If Christians wield the power of the keys in accordance with the directions of the infallible Word of God, they will make a proper use of the keys.

Someday the Lord of the Church will demand an account of the way in which men have used the power of the keys. "Everyone of us shall give account of himself to God," says the Apostle Paul (Rom. 14:12; cf. also II Cor. 5:10; Eccl. 12:14). All of the activities of men are being recorded, with photographic exactness and distinctness, upon the ledger of God; and when all nations shall be summoned to appear before the tribunal of God, every individual will have to give to the Great Auditor a full account of the way he has spent his life and has employed the gifts of God. And, of course, the more anyone has received and enjoyed in his lifetime, the greater will be his accountability and responsibility (Luke 12:48).

For the high privilege of having the Office of the Keys every Christian owes praise and thanks to God, from whom cometh down every good gift and every perfect gift (James 1:17). Luther once made this comment: "The keys are the real sanctuary and the noblest and holiest treasure of God, Christ, and the Church, since they are sanctified by Christ's blood and still every day administer the blood of Christ. . . . Both of these keys (the binding and the loosing key) are necessary to such an extent in Christendom that one can never thank God enough for them." (*On the Keys,* quoted by Saarnivaara, *op. cit.,* p. 3.) Like the people of Capernaum who witnessed the healing of the man sick of the palsy and who saw an actual demonstration of the use of the keys by the Lord Himself, every Christian has abundant reason to "glorify God, who has given such power to men" (Matt. 9:8). *Soli Deo Gloria!*

XVIII

The Call into the Holy Ministry

The call to the ministerial office is the act of God, operating either immediately or mediately, by which He sends, separates, and chooses men to perform the work necessary for the proper functioning of the ministry of the New Testament either in its pastoral or in its missionary function.

ACCORDING to the Scripture all incumbents of the ministerial office are *called by the Lord.* This truth is very clearly taught in Rom. 10:15: "And how shall they preach except they be sent?" According to Holy Scripture preaching without a divine call is a mark of false prophets. Speaking through His prophet Jeremiah, God condemns the false prophets: "I have not sent these prophets, yet they ran" (23:21). The statement of Heb. 5:4: "And no man taketh this honor unto himself, but he that is called of God" states a fundamental principle which applies not only to the office of the high priest, but also to the ministry of the New Testament.

Accordingly Scripture emphasizes the fact that the incumbents of the ministerial office are *sent by God.* To the Apostles, whom He had called *immediately,* the Lord says: "As My Father hath sent *Me,* even so *send I you*" (John 20:21). Before His ascension He gives them the grand commission, "Ye shall be witnesses unto Me both in Jerusalem and in Judea and in Samaria and unto the uttermost part of the earth" (Acts 1:8). Paul writes of himself: "Paul, an Apostle, not of men, neither by man, but by Jesus Christ and God the Father, who raised Him from the dead" (Gal. 1:1).

The same truth holds good of the servants of the Church who had

366

been called *mediately*, through the congregations. Paul tells the elders of Ephesus: "Take heed therefore unto yourselves and to all the flock, over the which the Holy Ghost hath made you overseers, to feed the Church of God, which He hath purchased with His own blood" (Acts 20:28). To the congregation of these elders St. Paul writes: "And He gave some, apostles; and some, prophets; and some, evangelists; and some, pastors and teachers" (Eph. 4:11). "And God hath set some in the Church, first apostles, secondarily prophets, thirdly teachers" (I Cor. 12:28). Therefore the Lord exhorts the believers of all times: "Pray ye therefore the Lord of the harvest, that He will send forth laborers into His harvest" (Matt. 9:38). Scripture also emphasizes this truth of a divine call in the sending out of missionaries: "As they ministered to the Lord and fasted, the Holy Ghost said, Separate me Barnabas and Saul for the work whereunto I have called them" (Acts 13:2).

What is implied in this divine act of calling? The answer is apparent from the various terms that the Lord uses when He calls such persons for this service. Rom. 10:15: "And how shall they preach except they be *sent?*" The word translated "sent" is the word from which the noun "apostle" is derived and means to send forth as one's agent, representative, ambassador, to act and to speak in the name and with the authority of the one who has sent. Therefore Paul writes: "Now then we are ambassadors for Christ, as though God did beseech you by us: we pray you in Christ's stead, Be ye reconciled to God" (II Cor. 5:20). Another term used to describe the call is to "separate." The Holy Ghost commands the church at Antioch: "*Separate* me Barnabas and Saul for the work whereunto I have called them" (Acts 13:2). In calling men the Lord separates them for His special service to which they are to devote themselves. Scripture also uses the term "*choose*"; "And of them He chose twelve, whom also He named Apostles" (Luke 6:13). The Lord selects some of His servants for special work in His kingdom. This idea is expressed by Beyer in his third thesis, "Whosoever has accepted such a call has no right to relinquish it unless God Himself recalls him from office."

The call to the ministerial office differs from the call of the spiritual priests. It is the call to a specific service or ministry in the Church. Dr. Walther in the second part of his book *On the Church and the Ministry* points out the difference between the priestly office and the holy ministry. See Walther and the Church, pp. 71, 72.

The fathers of our Synod very definitely distinguished two different forms of the office of public preaching: that of the missionary and that of the pastor. Since all Christians are priests and kings before God, they all have the duty to show forth the praises of God also to such as are still strangers from the covenants of promise, to do mission work (Matt. 28:18-20; Acts 1:8). Hence all Christians, individually or collectively, in the form of a congregation or of a group of congregations (as a synod or a synodical district) have the right and the duty to call missionaries who are to preach the Gospel to the heathen, and by the grace of God to establish Christian congregations. "This call," says Dr. F. Pieper, "is not a human call but a divine call, and they who have received and accepted this call as missionaries have received and accepted a divine call just as surely as they who have been called for pastoral activity by already existing congregations" (*Lehre und Wehre*, vol. 71, p. 425).

Yet our fathers insisted on distinguishing the office of the missionary from that of the pastor. "This pastoral office," we read, "can exist only after a congregation has come into existence, because no call can be issued before there are persons who may call." And again: "When Christian congregations have come into existence . . . whose members all have the same rights and powers, no one among them may administer the public ministry of teaching in public office" (as representative, in the name and by the authority of the congregation) "without conferment of such office, without a proper call." (*Lehre und Wehre*, vol. 9, p. 179.)

Like all doctrines of Scripture, the doctrine of the divinity of the pastor's call is of immense practical value for both pastor and congregation. Pastors and others called by the Lord for service in His church will not seek their own honor, but the honor of their Lord. They will preserve the proper willing joyfulness in their work in spite of all difficulties, will be strong and courageous, diligent, faithful, and careful, and will realize that their sufficiency must come from the Lord. The congregations, on the other hand, will diligently hear their pastors and accept their preaching as God's Word. They will acknowledge that the servants sent to them by the Lord are the very ones whom the Lord wants them to hear. They will honor them as servants of Christ and cheerfully provide for their physical needs and will never expect of them that they become the servants of men.

THESIS II

The Lord requires the congregation to establish and maintain the pastoral office in its midst and has given the congregation the right to establish as many auxiliary offices as its needs require. The right to call workers in the congregation is inherent in the congregation.

In this thesis we consider the ministerial office in the congregation. We begin with the parable that Dr. Zorn used. A farmer in the West had a very large farm of 4,000 acres. In making his will he decreed that his farm should belong to his eight sons, not in eight equal shares, but undivided. In order to avoid strife, the sons were to choose one out of their midst who was to administrate the farm in their name. After the death of the father the sons acted in accordance with his last will and chose one of the brothers to be the administrator. They did this because the father had commanded it and because they were the owners of the farm. Which powers did this administrator have? Being one of the sons and heirs, he was a joint owner, but as administrator he was not the owner, but a servant who in the name of all the heirs was to administer the property. The brothers, indeed, had the right to supervise the work, but the administration itself was the obligation of the administrator. If he had become negligent in his work or had acted contrary to the provisions of the will, they could depose him from his office. If the work increased, the brothers could provide aid for him, but he still remained the administrator.

The application of this parable is clear. Our Lord Jesus Christ by His bitter suffering and death has secured for us forgiveness of sins, the adoption of sons, life and salvation, the keys of heaven and has placed all of these treasures into the Gospel. It is the will of Christ that all of these gifts belong to all believers and be used for the profit of all, as we read in Eph. 4:12-16.

In order that these gifts may be properly administered, the Lord requires the congregation to establish and to maintain the pastoral office in its midst. The institution of this office is not a mere ordinance of the Church, as a number of theologians held in the last century. They contended that the Church had instituted this office without any special divine command, because of the particular needs of the time. Against such teaching, in *The Church and the Ministry,*

Walther wrote the Third Thesis, which reads as follows: "The ministry of preaching is not an arbitrary office, but its character is such that the Church has been commanded to establish it and is ordinarily bound to it till the end of days. Proof from the Word of God: Thus speaks the Lord, Matt. 28:19-20: 'Go ye and teach all nations,' etc., 'teaching them to observe all things whatsoever I have commanded you. And, lo, I am with you alway, even unto the end of the world.' From this it is evident that by the command of Christ the Apostles' ministry of preaching was to endure to the end of days. Now, if this is to be the case, the Church must continually to the end of days establish the orderly public ministry of preaching and in this ordinance administer to its members the means of grace" (p. 211-212).

This is very evident from the statement of St. Paul to Titus: "For this cause left I thee in Crete, that thou shouldest set in order the things that are wanting and ordain elders in every city, as I had appointed thee" (1:5). Congregations had been founded by Paul and Titus in Crete. When Paul had to leave Crete, some things were still wanting. Therefore Paul had Titus stay in order to set these things in order. The most important thing was to ordain elders in every city (ordain, of course, does not mean ordain in our present sense, but to put somebody in office as a steward, or as a king, and the like). Titus was to do this as Paul had appointed, directed, commanded him to do. This command Paul gave by inspiration of the Holy Ghost. It is God's command, God's appointment and direction. Therefore Paul immediately adds the divine qualifications for an elder or bishop.

Because it was the will and the command of the Lord, the church at Jerusalem had instituted this office of the public ministry. We read in Acts 15:22: "Then pleased it the Apostles *and elders*, with the whole Church, to send chosen men of their own company to Antioch." On their first missionary journey Paul and Barnabas, after completing their preaching mission in various cities, returned again to the place where the seed had been sown and "ordained them elders in every church" (Acts 14:23). The Greek word used here for ordain indicates the manner in which these elders or pastors, as we call them, were placed in their office, by the election of the people; for the word translated "ordained" means to choose by a show of hands, a common form of election. The congregation at

Ephesus had such elders; they came to Miletus to take leave from Paul (Acts 20:18). Paul writes to the Philippians: "Paul and Timotheus, the servants of Jesus Christ, to all the saints in Christ Jesus which are at Philippi, with the bishops and deacons" (1:1). St. Peter writes: "The elders which are among you I exhort, who am also an elder" (I Pet. 5:1). Accordingly Dr. Walther writes in *The Church and the Ministry*: "Our Church teaches, according to the Word of God, that God has commanded the whole true holy Christian Church to proclaim and make known His precious Gospel. Where, therefore, a small group of believing Christians or a true church is found, this church has the command to preach the Gospel; but if it has this command, it self-evidently also has power, yes, the duty to designate preachers of the Gospel." (P. 33.)

The duties of the incumbent of the pastoral office in the congregation have been excellently summarized by Dr. Walther in Thesis VII of *The Church and the Ministry*: "The holy ministry is the authority conferred by God through the congregation, as holder of the priesthood and of all church power, to administer in public office the common rights of the spiritual priesthood in behalf of all." Whatever God has given to the spiritual priesthood, the pastor is to administer in public office. He is to teach the Word of God, to administer the Sacraments, to be the overseer of the flock over which the Holy Ghost had made him overseer (Acts 20:28). He is to be steward of the mysteries of God (I Cor. 4:1) and must answer to God for the souls entrusted to his care (Heb. 13:17).

Our thesis adds this statement: "and has given the congregation the right to establish as many auxiliary offices as its needs require." There is no direct command of God obligating the congregation to establish any office except the office of the pastorate in its midst. However, when the need arose in the congregation at Jerusalem to establish the office of deacon, the Apostles presented the situation to the people and suggested the election of seven men to provide for the poor in the congregation. The congregation adopted the suggestion. Other congregations also had deacons (Phil. 1:1). This auxiliary office must have been quite common in the early Church, for in the First Epistle to Timothy, St. Paul states the qualifications not only for a bishop, but also for a deacon. The Church at Cenchrea had a deaconess (Rom. 16:1). When the need for such offices no longer existed, they were abolished.

The authority to establish such offices is implied in the well-known statement: "For all things are yours; whether Paul, or Apollos, or Cephas, or the world, or life, or death, or things to come; all are yours" (I Cor. 3:21-22).

Not all of the auxiliary offices are on the same level. It is not necessary for the congregation to issue a call to all people who are assisting the pastor in his work in the congregation. If we bear in mind that calling involves separation to the Lord, that the persons called are to devote themselves to the work in the congregation and that their work involves the proclaiming of the Word of God, we can readily draw the line. Our teachers, for instance, are to assist the pastor in his work. They are to teach the Word of God to the children, and therefore it is entirely in accordance with the spirit of the New Testament to call them to such service. This call, of course, does not make them pastors of the congregation and does not remove the responsibility for the souls of the children from the pastor, but it does very emphatically assure both teachers and congregation that the teachers are doing their work in response to the command of the Lord of the Church.

Likewise, when the need arises, the congregation has the perfect right to call an assistant to its pastor. Such an assistant performs his work as a servant of God. The congregation also has the right to determine which work is to be assigned to him, although it is not contrary to any statement of Scripture for the congregation to leave the division of labors to the pastor or to the agreement of both. When the need for such office ceases, the congregation may vote to discontinue it. The congregation is indeed obligated to maintain the pastorate in its midst, but is nowhere required to have the work distributed between two men.

Who has the right to call workers in the congregation? Not the Pope, as the Roman Catholics teach; not the bishops, as the Episcopalians think; not the clergy, as Romanizing Lutherans hold; not the head of the government, the consistory, or the patrons, as is the practice in Germany, but the Christian congregation, the congregation of believers.

This is the clear doctrine of Scripture. To prove this we may adduce several groups of Scripture passages. In the first place, the ministry is the office of the public proclamation of the Gospel and of the administration of the Sacraments. Who is originally charged with the proclamation of the Gospel and the administration of the Sacraments? Jesus says, Matt. 28:19-20: "Go ye therefore and teach all nations, baptizing them in the name of the Father and of the Son and of the Holy Ghost, teaching them to observe all things whatsoever I have commanded you." Lest anyone think that only the Apostles are addressed here, the Lord immediately adds: "And, lo, I am with you alway, even unto the end of the world." The Apostles did not live to the end of the world, but the congregation of believers remains unto the end of the world. It is this congregation which here receives the commission. This congregation of believers is the body which is to put the Word of God into circulation. Accordingly it is the right and the duty of the believers to choose persons who are to do this preaching in the name of the believers. Individual persons in the church have the right to perform the functions of this office only when they have been called to do so by the people who have received the original commission. (Cf. Smalcald Articles, § 67; *Triglot*, p. 523.)

Even though the Apostles were called immediately by Christ, Scripture speaks in such a manner as to make it clear that the Christians are the people to whom the office of the Word belongs really and originally. St. Paul tells all believers: "All things are yours, whether Paul, or Apollos, or Cephas, or the world . . . all are yours" (I Cor. 3:21-22). The Word and the office which these Apostles had belong to the believers. Therefore the Holy Ghost also commanded the *congregation* of Antioch to separate Paul and Barnabas for their missionary work (Acts 13:2-3), and when they returned from their journey, they reported to the *congregation* (Acts 14:27).

There is a second line of argument. We ask: To whom have the keys of heaven been entrusted by Christ? Who has been commissioned originally by the Savior to forgive and retain sins? Whoever has received this commission is also commissioned to establish the ministry and to appoint servants of the Word of God, for the forgiveness and retention of sins is effected by the use of the Word of God. The congregation of believers has received this commission. Accordingly all Bible passages in which the keys of heaven, the power to forgive and retain sins, are awarded to all believers also prove that the believers are required to establish the ministry, through which the keys are administered publicly.

The Office of the Keys is not given merely to a few persons in the

Church, but to all believers. To be sure, in Matt. 16:19 the Lord says to Peter: "And I will give unto thee the keys of the Kingdom of Heaven; and whatsoever thou shalt bind on earth shall be bound in heaven; and whatsoever thou shalt loose on earth shall be loosed in heaven." It is evident from the connection that Peter does not come into consideration as an Apostle, but as a believer. When in reply to the question of the Lord about the faith of the disciples Peter had confessed his faith with the words "Thou are the Christ, the Son of the living God," the Lord gives him the keys of heaven. Whoever believes as Peter did possesses the keys of heaven. Any doubts on this score are removed by the Lord Himself in Matt. 18:18, where He expressly grants to all believers the power which He had given to the believing Peter. He says: "Whatsoever ye"—ye believers, ye members of the congregation—"shall bind on earth shall be bound in heaven: and whatsoever ye shall loose on earth shall be loosed in heaven."

Our Small Catechism, therefore, answers the question: What is the Office of the Keys? in the following manner, "It is the peculiar church power which Christ has given to His Church on earth, to forgive the sins of penitent sinners unto them, but to retain the sins of the impenitent as long as they do not repent." (Cf. Smalc. Art., § 24, *Triglot*, p. 511.)

These Scripture passages also show us that every local congregation possesses all spiritual powers and therefore also the right to call (not, as some would have it, only the entire Christian Church or the Church of a certain country); every local congregation, that is, the believers at a certain place, even if there were only two or three of them, has the power and the right to call a pastor. For a congregation possesses all spiritual powers not according to its size, but because it consists of believers.

A third group of passages. I Pet. 2:9: "But ye are a chosen generation, a royal priesthood, an holy nation, a peculiar people; that ye should shew forth the praises of Him who hath called you out of darkness into His marvelous light." Who are these people whom the Lord has commissioned to show forth the praises of Christ, to preach the Gospel? Not the Pope, cardinals, and bishops, not the consistory, the patrons, or the clergy. No, they are the believers who have been called out of darkness into His marvelous light. The whole chapter speaks of believers, and these believers are entrusted with the preaching of the Gospel. They therefore have the right and the duty to appoint pastors who are to administer the duties of the spiritual priesthood in public office.

The Smalcald Articles say: "Here belong the statements of Christ which testify that the Keys have been given to the Church, and not merely to certain persons, Matt. 18-20: Where two or three are gathered together in My name, etc."

"Lastly, the statement of Peter also confirms this, I Ep. 2:9: Ye are a royal priesthood. These words pertain to the true Church, which certainly has the right to elect and ordain ministers since it alone has the priesthood." (*Triglot*, p. 523f.)

Our Confessions also refer to the calling of pastors by the congregation as to a common custom of the Church. The Smalcald Articles state: "For formerly the people elected pastors and bishops" (*Triglot*, p. 525).

The Pope deprived the Church of the right to call its preachers. Through his creatures, the bishops, he assigned pastors to the Christians. He claimed that he had been given the keys of heaven and thereby the right to call. Luther exposed this robbery and insisted that the right of calling be restored to the congregations. Let us diligently preserve this gift which God has restored to His Church through the services of Luther and which had to be gained anew for the congregations in our own country. A Christian congregation should not surrender the right to call its pastor. To be sure, a call is valid even if the right to call a pastor has been delegated to certain persons or a group within or without the congregation. But if this manner of calling were to become customary, people would again forget that the right to call is inherent in the Christian congregation. We might again have papistic, Church-State, or Methodist conditions, and have popes, consistories, patrons, conferences impose pastors upon the congregations of God according to their pleasure. The calling of a pastor is a matter of great concern to the entire congregation and to every member. Therefore the congregation itself should carry out the calling of its pastors through its natural representatives, the voting members. When calling, a congregation should be willing to accept advice, much advice, but should execute the call itself.

The Christian congregation has the right to call. According to Scripture a congregation exists where a number of Christians are gathered together in Jesus' name for the purpose of having the Gospel preached and the Sacraments administered in their midst. Our new Catechism makes the following statement: "A local church, or congregation, is a group of professing Christians who regularly assemble for worship at one place." It is not essential that they have formally organized as a congregation, have elected officers and adopted a constitution. In the report of Synod, 1851, page 15, we read: "Since the Sheboyank Indians have expressed the sincere desire that Missionary Auch come to them, and accordingly a call by this Indian Christian congregation has been issued to him, Missionary Auch will follow this call."

Your essayist received his first call to a field in Home Missions where no organized congregations existed. The call was issued by the Mission Board of the Minnesota and Dakota District *in the name of a number of Christians* at various places in this field. Where a group of Christians regularly assembles for worship and, especially, if they have celebrated the Lord's Supper in their midst, they are truly a local congregation in the sense of the Scripture and have the right to call a pastor.

Where congregations are subsidized by a mission board, it is only right and proper that they consult with the mission board before issuing a call. They are dependent upon the financial assistance of their fellow Christians for the maintenance of the Gospel ministry in their midst. They need the advice and counsel of the board which these fellow Christians have elected for the supervision of this work and which is responsible for the proper administration of the funds which they contribute.

Another question may be asked here. For many years congregations desiring to call a candidate from the seminary have sent this call to the College of Presidents and have authorized this body to insert the name of the candidate. Does this practice deprive the congregation of its right to call? Another question has been asked in this connection. A candidate has received a call from this Committee on the Distribution of Calls. The same candidate receives a second call in which his name has been placed by some congregation because a pastor has recommended him to the congregation, and in this manner his name has been immediately entered into the call. Does this factor make the second call more important than the first one? Dr. Pieper answers "No" to both questions. In both cases the man to be called was personally unknown to the congregation. In both cases the congregation made use of other persons in order to find a suitable person. The synodical committee can perform this service as well as a pastor, to say the least. We must also consider this fact that people, who have no official obligation to recommend pastors and often possess very little judgment, recommend candidates who perhaps are more suitable for and more necessary at some other place. Synod has adopted this procedure after careful deliberation. Everybody should consider whether he can answer to God for interfering with this orderly arrangement. Every congregation should and must retain complete freedom of choice, but this freedom should also be used wisely and in the fear of God (I Cor. 14:33-40).

Thesis III

The missionary activity of the Church and the proper preparation of men for the work of the Church require the services of many workers. The right to call such workers is vested in the group or body to whom such power is delegated by the congregations.

It is proper for Christians to be motivated by self-interest when their salvation is at stake. The Apostle admonishes all Christians: "Work out your own salvation with fear and trembling" (Phil. 2:12). But every Christian must also observe the command which is equally valid for him: "Go ye into all the world and preach the Gospel to every creature." The Christians are the original possessors of the office of teaching. Because of this endowment they are obligated to let the light of the Gospel shine at as many places as possible. Indeed, according to the Lord's great missionary commission it should be their objective to have the preaching of the Gospel established at all places where the Word is not yet proclaimed. It should be their aim to establish pulpits in the cities and in the country wherever this is possible. Some people argue that if the people want to hear the Gospel, they can come to churches that already exist; they should not move to places where there is no church. This is an utterly wrong conception of the obligation resting upon us Christians. The Lord does not say to us, Wait until the people come to you, but He says, "Go and preach the Gospel to every creature." We must follow the example of the Lord and His Apostles. The Lord did not say, I shall stay in Nazareth; everybody knows where

I live, and whoever wishes to, can hear Me here. No, He went from place to place in Palestine preaching the glad message. He did not tell the apostles, Stay in Jerusalem and wait until the people come to you, but instructed them, "Ye shall be witnesses unto Me both in Jerusalem and in all Judea and in Samaria and unto the uttermost part of the earth" (Acts 1:8). In the field of Home Missions the Church should exercise due care not to found too many small congregations which are too close together and which do not require enough work of their pastor. That would be a waste of the gifts of the Lord. But though we may have made this mistake at times, we have committed another tragic mistake far more frequently, the mistake of not being sufficiently zealous about the work of the Lord. We have not measured up to our opportunities in our own country, and millions of heathen in foreign countries are still without the precious message of salvation through Christ. We Christians are obligated by the commission of our Lord to establish the office of teaching at such places.

But where are these preachers to come from? We need them for our own churches and schools. We need them in ever increasing numbers if we are to fulfill our missionary obligation. All Christians who are entrusted with the establishment of the ministry also have the obligation to provide for the training of pastors and teachers. The Lord has not promised that He would send the preachers in some supernatural manner, but it is His rule that the Church itself provide these preachers out of its own midst and prepare them for the work. The preparation of pastors and teachers is an integral part of the establishment and maintenance of the office of the ministry.

Who is to call the workers for this twofold vital activity of the Church? As far as the workers in the field of missions are concerned, let me remind you of the statement by Dr. Pieper, quoted above: "The Christian Church, that is, the Christians, has the missionary command 'Go ye into all the world and preach the Gospel to every creature.' Therefore we as Christians, or the already existing congregation, or a combination of congregations (synodical District, Synod) have the right and the duty to call competent persons for missionary activity. This call is not a human call, but a divine call, and they who have received and accepted this call, have received and accepted a divine call as well as they who have been called for pastoral activity by already existing congregations."

Regarding the call of professors at our institutions Pastor Beyer states, page 27: "The right to call is inherent in the congregation, and if the choice of the congregation is not in some respect the basis for his call, the person called can never be sure of his call. But as pastors and teachers are called by the congregation, so the choice of professors at our synodical institutions is effected by the congregations. All men called for the office of teaching at our synodical institutions are called by the group of congregations joined together in Synod. They have the right to appoint the men who are to issue the call. They have the right to nominate candidates and to confirm or reject the election." The last statement refers to the method of election formerly in vogue in our Synod. But the change in this one detail does not affect the basic principle.

Our Confessions also emphasize this duty of all Christians. The Smalcald Articles (*Triglot*, p. 525) state: "From all these things it is clear that the Church retains the right to elect and ordain ministers . . . (therefore, if the bishops either are heretics or will not ordain suitable persons, the churches are in duty bound before God, according to divine law, to ordain for themselves pastors and ministers)."

In this connection Dr. Pieper calls attention to the fact that the Lutheran Church made a promising start in America, but did not provide for the training of pastors; therefore the mustard seed never became a large tree. On the other hand, when the fathers of our Synod came to America, they started a school of the prophets although at the time they had enough pastors and had a surplus of candidates. Therefore the Word of God could have free course when the opportunity presented itself.

Thesis IV

Since it is the Lord of the Church who gives and places His servants in the Church, a call should not arbitrarily and in advance limit the duration of the service of the person called. However, where the Lord Himself in advance indicates that a certain service in the Kingdom is of a temporary nature, a call may be issued properly for a specific time.

In this section we intend to discuss the so-called permanent call. Strictly speaking, there is no such thing as a permanent call, because sooner or later everyone serving in the Kingdom of God must die.

However, the Bible does make some very definite statements on the duration of the call. I Cor. 12:28: "And *God has set* some in the church, first apostles, secondarily prophets, thirdly teachers, etc." Eph. 4:11: "And He *gave some,* apostles; and some, prophets; and some, evangelists; and some, pastors and teachers." According to these plain Scripture passages the time any person is to serve is in the hands of God, *He* is to determine how long a man is to serve in any special office. To make the service of a pastor or teacher a matter of contract, subject to termination by either side upon ample notice, is contrary to the Scriptural doctrine of the call.

From the very beginning our Synod had to take a definite stand on this question. Among the conditions of membership in Synod the following is listed: "Regular (not temporary) call of the pastor." Chapter V, paragraph 11, we find this statement: "Licenses to preach which are customary in this country are not granted by Synod because they are contrary to Scripture and to the practice of the Church." The committee which formulated the constitution at Fort Wayne in 1846 added two explanatory statements at the end explaining and justifying this position.

This has been the consistent practice of our Synod since that time and has been stated again and again in official papers presented at conventions and in our periodicals. Pastor Beyer presents the following thesis: "Those whom a congregation has called, God has called through that congregation, and a congregation has no right to remove them from office except in cases in which God Himself commands such removal." He concludes the paragraph with this statement: "A congregation has no right to call a pastor or a teacher or to dismiss him on the basis of a contract." (Pages 36-37.)

This statement is not to be understood, however, as meaning that every call for a fixed time is to be condemned. In the early history of our Synod, when malaria was a scourge in parts of our country, it often became necessary for pastors to take a leave of absence to regain their health. The congregations usually called a candidate to take charge of the congregation during his absence and he was duly ordained. When the pastor returned, the service of the supply pastor was at an end.

In 1898 Dr. Pieper was requested to answer some questions regarding the call to the ministry. He did this in *Lehre und Wehre,* 1898, pages 339 to 341. The first question is: What is the relationship between the call for temporary assistance in the ministry and the so-called temporary call? Answer: The call for temporary assistance occurs in various forms in our midst. If a pastor, as a result of illness for a time is totally incapacitated for the duties of his office or if, as a result of physical weakness or because of being overburdened with work, for instance, by taking over the District Presidency, he is not in a position to perform all the work connected with his office, the congregation calls an assistant for the pastorate with the express condition that the call is to have only temporary validity, that is, only as long as sickness or physical weakness or overburdening with work makes such help necessary. The question now is: Is the congregation empowered to issue such a call, or is such a call just as objectionable as a so-called temporary call? The answer is: The call for temporary help stays within the bounds of divine order and has nothing in common with the objectionable temporary call.

"The essence of the temporary call does not consist in this that a call is limited as to time, but in this that human beings arbitrarily limit a call as to time, that is, that they want to determine how long a pastor is to be active at a certain place. This is indeed contrary to the divinity of the call to the ministry. The ministry is divine not only in this sense that God has ordained it for all time, but also in this sense that unto the end of time God places the persons, who are to serve Him in the ministry, at the various places and determines the time during which they are to be active at a place. Congregations are merely the instruments of divine placing and transfer. Paul definitely states that the Holy Ghost had made the elders at Ephesus "overseers," although they were called mediately, by the congregation (Acts 20:28). But if God has placed them, men dare not transfer them at their discretion. God has reserved for Himself both the placing and the transfer of the servants of the Church. Congregations which cause the transfer or the deposing of pastors dare do nothing but carry out God's transfer or deposal. A transfer is governed by the divine rule in I Cor. 12:7: "But the manifestation of the Spirit is given to every man to profit withal." A deposal is governed by the Scripture passages that tell us which persons God does not wish to have as preachers. (Hos. 4:6; Rom. 16:17; I Tim. 3:2-7, etc.) If a congregation issues a so-called temporary call, that is, if it in advance and arbitrarily decides that the man to be called is to leave his place after one, two, three, or four years, it becomes guilty of encroaching upon God's office and work. Dr. Walther says: 'Neither is a congregation authorized to issue such a call, nor has a pastor the right to accept it.' Such a call is contrary to the divinity of a proper call to a pastorate in the Church as it is plainly taught in the Bible.

"But the call for temporary help as described above has nothing in common with this temporary call, as already stated. The factor of human arbitrariness is not present. Sickness, weakness, being overburdened with business, necessary temporary absence are sent by God, and the congregation which provides for temporary help for a presumably temporary need is not going its own way, but is going the very way which God is leading it. The congregation issuing such a call is acting altogether correctly, and the person called in such a manner is also acting correctly when he accepts such a call, and the man called temporarily for help is serving God in the public ministry no less than a man called for permanent service at the congregation. Therefore, if no other obstacles prevent the acceptance of the call, no person eligible for office dare decline to accept a call for temporary help." A similar statement is found in the Report of the Nebraska District, 1898, page 27.

THESIS V

The call may be terminated
a. by a call to another field of activity;
b. by deposing from office for persistence in false doctrine or refusal to repent or loss of good reputation;
c. by dismissal from office or resignation if the ability to serve in a certain field has ceased;
d. if the need for the services has ceased.

When a congregation calls a pastor or a teacher and the call is accepted, all parties should enter into their relationship with the distinct understanding that, as far as they are concerned, this relationship is to continue until the Lord clearly indicates that the call is terminated. Pastors or teachers viewing their charge as stepping stones to some more important position are acting as unworthy servants of the Lord. Congregations or individual members of the congregation who are constantly finding fault with the pastor or teacher and making life miserable for him in the hope that he will leave are transgressing the command of the Lord: "Touch not Mine anointed, and do My prophets no harm" (Ps. 105:15).

God, however, may terminate a call. This occurs most frequently by a call to another field of activity. We do not say that every call which a pastor or teacher receives is an indication that his present call is terminated. This question can be decided only after a prayerful comparison of both calls. But a congregation dare not say, We want to keep our pastor or teacher under all circumstances. Such a congregation would make itself superior to God. The Lord has not revealed an elaborate set of rules to cover all cases so that we could determine His will by a reference to rule 24 or 16. He has given us a general directive in I Cor. 12:7: "But the manifestation of the Spirit is given to every man to profit withal." If it is manifest that the abilities of the pastor or teacher would be used to a greater advantage at another place, or that a pastor no longer is able to perform his duties at his present charge, God evidently wishes to make a change, and both pastor and congregation should cheerfully submit to the will of God. Since in such matters we are inclined to view things too much from a personal angle, it is always advisable to secure the advice of competent men.

According to Scripture the call must be terminated for persistence in false doctrine, refusal to repent, or because of the loss of a good reputation. The Scriptures distinctly warn the Christians against false prophets. "But though we or an angel from heaven preach any other gospel unto you than that which we have preached unto you, let him be accursed" (Gal. 1:8). If any pastor persists in false doctrine in spite of admonition, the congregation must depose him from office no matter how well liked he may be personally. The Lord does not want any false prophets in His Church, and congregations must carry out the will of the Lord. The same step must be taken if a pastor or a teacher commits a sin and refuses to repent. Also the servants of the Word must daily pray the Fifth Petition. Congregations also must bear with the sins of their pastors and teachers, just as the pastor must bear with the sins of the congregation. But if a pastor or teacher will not repent of his sin, the congregation must take steps to remove such a person from the office which he has disgraced by his impenitence.

In certain cases the call must be terminated even if the pastor or teacher repents of his sin. The Lord plainly states in I Tim. 3:7:

"Moreover he must have a good report of them that are without." Certain sins make a person infamous. His continued presence in the work of the Church would be a constant stumbling block to the unchurched and make it almost impossible for the congregation to gain such people for Christ. Declaring such people ineligible for further service in the church is not passing any judgment on the sincerity of their repentence or on their Christian faith. Beyer states: "As the call to service in the Church makes men pastors and teachers, but not Christians, so the loss of this office does not in itself make a person a non-Christian."

The call may also be terminated by dismissal from office or resignation if the ability to serve in a certain field has ceased. There is a difference between deposal (Amtsentsetzung) and dismissal (Amtsabnahme). This difference is explained in the Report of the Wisconsin District, 1907, page 81: "The term *deposing*, when distinguished from dismissing, is used when the pastor is declared ineligible for office either on the basis of a gross offense, which also makes the person infamous before the world, or because of persistence in false doctrine or impenitence." Dismissal, however, merely signifies that the person should not continue to serve in his present field though he is eligible for service in some other field. In the Wisconsin case the pastor had forfeited the confidence of the overwhelming majority of his congregation. He was advised to resign, but refused to do so. He later refused to attend a meeting which had been agreed upon under his chairmanship and against which he did not protest. Thereupon he was dismissed from office. In 1889 a teacher in a congregation in the East was not able to meet the demand of the congregation for instruction in English. The congregation asked him to resign. When he stated that he could not do this, the congregation decided to dismiss him if he would not resign by September 1. The District did not fault the congregation for its action; it merely requested the congregation not to carry out its resolution at once, but to give the teacher time to accept another call. (Report of Eastern District, 1889, p. 50f.) Dr. Zorn states briefly: "The call of a pastor in a congregation ceases when he is no longer able to perform the essential, absolutely necessary duties of his office. This applies also to the call of the teacher." Ordinarily we attempt to solve such cases either by a transfer or by resignation. If neither can be effected, the congregation has the right to dismiss the man from office. In such cases the congregation will not act hastily and will seek the advice of District officials or other men able to counsel.

The call may be terminated also if the need for the services has ceased. Dr. Zorn, speaking of the duration of the call of a teacher, states p. 31f.: "If the *necessity* of this auxiliary office in the church no longer exists, there is no compelling reason why the congregation must keep the teacher."

During the mass movement of people caused by the war, some congregations have experienced such a loss in membership as to make it impossible for the congregations to maintain a separate pastorate. Two formerly independent congregations have been compelled to form one parish. Usually such a situation can be met by calling away one of the pastors and having the other take charge of the parish. If this is not possible, the call of a pastor may be terminated. A congregation formerly had a flourishing school with several teachers, but because of lack of children is no longer able to provide sufficient work for all of the teachers. Again the call of one or even more of the teachers may be terminated. The congregation should in such cases act wisely and charitably, but nobody dare deny the congregation the right to terminate the call.

A mission board has called a pastor to a certain place because the prospect warranted such an action. A decided change, however, takes place, many people move away, and there is no possibility of ever establishing an independent congregation. If there were absolutely no other possibility of providing these people with the Word of God and the Sacraments, we might be willing to continue subsidizing such a group indefinitely. If, however, the remaining people can satisfy their spiritual needs by joining a neighboring congregation or by being served by some neighboring pastor, the call of the pastor may be terminated.

Thesis VI

All persons concerned in the matter of a call should be conscious of the fact that the Lord of the Church is using them as His instruments and should consider this their one objective—to do the will of the Lord.

The subject matter referred to in this thesis might well serve as a paper during an entire convention. In the Texas District in 1915 Pastor Osthoff delivered a paper on the topic "Divine Principles and Rules for the Calling and Transferring of Pastors and Missionaries." For the present discussion, however, we shall restrict ourselves to the last thesis of Dr. Pieper's paper in the Western District which reads: "Although God calls through the Christian congregation, through men, calling remains entirely God's affair. Therefore both congregations and pastors, as well as all those who are active in matters of call, should guard most carefully against manifestations of human weakness" or, to use a cruder term for Dr. Pieper's "Menscheleien," "wire pulling." We shall briefly summarize his thoughts.

What are congregations and pastors to do in order that God's will and not their own be done? They must observe the divine instructions which God has given in His Word. We have heard who is to call. God also describes the persons who are to be placed in the ministry, and He has also given the rule according to which the calling and transferring of these persons is to be effected.

The congregation may call only orthodox pastors. Christ has commanded all Christians: "Teach them to observe all things whatsoever I have commanded you" (Matt. 28:20). See also the section "On Bishops" in the Table of Duties in our Catechism. No congregation should call a pastor or teacher not having the testimony of orthodoxy from the Church. If it calls a pastor or teacher already in office, it will insist on it that his name appear in our Annual or that he has been officially recommended after an examination. If a congregation wishes to call a candidate, it again will follow the synodical rule to call only a candidate who has successfully passed his examination. The man to be called must not only know the correct doctrine but must be able to teach and have a good reputation.

Another rule to be observed by the congregation calling a pastor is found in I Cor. 12:7: "But the manifestation of the Spirit is given to every man to profit withal." God distributes His gifts differently, and the needs of congregations are different. How are congregations to receive the names of men suitable for their needs? For very good reasons our congregations themselves have introduced the custom of having candidates for the office proposed by people who know the candidates and are also acquainted with the needs of the congregation. The *Synodical Handbook* makes it the duty of the District

President to suggest candidates to congregations calling, and congregations should consider these suggestions very carefully. Thereby the congregation does not give up any right, but proves itself conscientious and anxious that God's will be done. Pastors who are asked to suggest candidates should well consider the responsibility which they take upon themselves. They are not always in the position to give the proper advice since usually they do not know the candidates and lack the full understanding of the needs of the congregation calling and of the congregation served by the pastor recommended.

Similar care should be exercised when a congregation considers a call received by its pastor or teacher. The same general principle quoted above must guide all deliberations in such matters. Some congregations take the attitude that they are against any transfer of their pastor or teacher as long as he is working satisfactorily. I may add that some congregations do not properly respect a sister congregation in the matter of a call, but without giving any real consideration to the reasons advanced for the acceptance of the call simply vote to ask the pastor to return the call. Some even feel that they owe their pastor the courtesy of passing such a resolution, irrespective of the importance of the call. We need but reverse the situation to realize how unfair and unchristian such an action is.— If it is evident that the gifts which God has granted to the pastor or teacher could be used to a greater advantage at some other place, or that for other valid reasons a change is indicated—for instance, state of health, or inability to provide properly for the pastor or teacher, the congregation should cheerfully give its pastor a peaceful dismissal. God has called the pastor or teacher away, God will again provide for it. God has given the Christian congregations the right to call with the expectation that they will act in a God-pleasing manner in matters of a call.

Many questions might still be treated under this heading, but if all concerned are guided by divine principles and prayerfully attempt to determine the will of God and make use of the counsel of men qualified to give advice, such difficulties can be solved and the work of the Church can be done by men who in all difficulties may rely on this comfort: The Lord has called me into this field of activity. I am doing His work. To the best of my ability I shall be a faithful steward of the mysteries of God, knowing that my sufficiency is of the Lord. I shall plant and water, and God according to His wisdom will give the increase. I live not unto myself but unto Him who loved me and gave Himself for me and has made me, unworthy though I am, to be His messenger for the salvation of souls.

XIX

The Lutheran Pastor

As is indicated in the title, "The Lutheran Pastor," we wish to
study the qualifications and the proper conduct of the person
who has been called to be the pastor of a Lutheran congregation. We stress the word "Lutheran," because it at once brings us
into our proper field, eliminating from our discussion such misuses
of the office as are general in the Roman Catholic Church, on the
one hand, and in so many Protestant churches, on the other.

The Lutheran pastor is neither a mediator between God and men,
nor is he merely a regular Sunday-morning speaker who may base
his discussion on some book of history, science, or literature.

The Lutheran pastor fills an all-important office, instituted by God
Himself. He is called into this office by the congregation which he
serves, in accordance with the will of God. For both the office of the
ministry and the call of the pastor are subjects which are clearly
taught in the Scriptures. Our Lutheran Church has, therefore, made
a diligent study of each of these subjects. In our own Synod they have
often been discussed at conventions and conferences on the basis of
essays written by members of our Church.

As is fitting and proper, these essays are now being offered in
digest form, together with many others, as a testimony to our Synod's
doctrinal position and practice through the first century of her
history.

The essay before us also belongs to this group. It is a digest of
our Synod's description of her pastors, drawn from the earlier publications of our Church. We are, therefore, to concern ourselves with
the pastor himself, as the person who is to be, or has been, called
into the office of the ministry. However, before we begin our discussion, a few general remarks should be made.

389

According to the clear teachings of Scripture, a pastor, like all Christians, has been made a priest of God through Baptism and the Word. In this respect there is no difference between him and any layman. The Apostle Paul says of the Church: "There is neither bond nor free, there is neither male nor female: for ye are all one in Christ Jesus" (Gal. 3:28).

Applying that to ourselves, we may say, There is neither president nor pastor nor teacher nor layman. For all are one in Christ. All of us stand shoulder to shoulder in the royal priesthood of which all believers in Christ are members.

However, it is also the teaching of Scripture that some in the Church are to be called by their fellow believers, to exercise the office of the priesthood in their stead. Not all are to minister or to preach, for this would cause confusion and disorder in the Church. Pastors, therefore, gain a position of leadership in the Church by means of a call from the Lord through His Church.

In the third place, the Scriptures clearly teach that such a call cannot be given to every Christian. For the Lord has so fully described the essential qualifications of pastors as to rule out the appointment of many to this office. The qualifications are such that not every Christian may aspire to be a pastor. The Apostle Paul writes to the Romans: "As we have many members in one body and all members have not the same office, so we, being many, are one body in Christ, and every one members one of another, having gifts differing according to the grace that is given us" (Rom. 12:4-6a). The Apostle Paul clearly states in this connection that the gifts for the office of the ministry are given only to some. In his First Letter to the Corinthians he again mentions this fact and then puts the questions: "Are all prophets? are all teachers? do all interpret?" (I Cor. 12:29f.) The obvious answer is this: The Lord wants His Church to confer the title of pastor upon those whom He has qualified for the office.

It is for this reason that an essay dealing with the qualifications, the work, and the conduct of pastors should be discussed in open sessions and not behind the closed doors of a pastoral conference. For the congregations are not only entitled to know, but ought to know, what they may and must expect of their pastors. The conscientious pastor will also prefer to have such a subject openly discussed, for it will protect his office against abuse, inasmuch as it will also show what ought not to be expected of the servant of the Church.

Let us, then, briefly review our Synod's description of her pastors, drawing our propositions from earlier publications of our Church. Because of the wealth of material on hand and because of the need of brevity, we must confine our study to only a few of the articles and essays which have been published by our Synod in her first hundred years.

I

THE PASTOR'S ESSENTIAL QUALIFICATIONS

In the Table of Duties of Dr. Martin Luther's Small Catechism the first passage properly applies to bishops, pastors, and preachers. Pastor P. Andres, the essayist at the Michigan District convention in 1907, calls attention to this wise arrangement when he says: "Those who by virtue of their calling are to direct others to study the Table of Duties and are to exhort them faithfully to fulfill their obligations must be first and foremost to learn their own lesson, that it may be well with the house of God" (p. 13).

When we study the portion of the Table of Duties referring to pastors, we find that three of the qualifications listed are of such importance that they must be called essential, that is, they are so necessary that without them a person ought not to be called to be a servant of the Lord and of His Church. These three are faithfulness, ability, and blamelessness. It is proper that we begin our discussion with a study of these essential qualifications.

FAITHFULNESS

Faithfulness is an essential qualification of everyone who wishes to serve as a pastor.

The Lord says through the Apostle Paul: "It is required in stewards"—the word "stewards" in this instance being used of persons entrusted with the mysteries of God—"that a man be found faithful" (I Cor. 4:2). According to Thayer's *Greek-English Lexicon of the New Testament*, the Greek word denoting faithfulness is used "of persons who show themselves faithful in the transaction of business, the execution of commands, or the discharge of official duties."

God Himself makes this a requirement. Hence, unfaithfulness

bars a man from the ministry. It may be said in passing that this and all other requirements made of pastors in the Table of Duties apply equally well to our parochial school teachers, inasmuch as their office as teachers of the Word is a part, and a very important part, of the office of the ministry.

Since faithfulness is an essential qualification, only men of proved faith and character should be called into this office.

In support of this proposition, we refer to the fact that a pastor must not be a novice, that is, a person who has recently been brought to faith. Pastor Andres mentions the fact that "men should first give proof and evidence of their faith and zeal before they can be recommended as pastors." He, then, applies this to our own conditions, saying: "A candidate who is not yet mature, who can furnish no good recommendations, even though he confesses our common faith, should not be called into the office of pastor or teacher" (Mich. Dist., p. 47).

Such faithfulness demands serious application to all of the duties of the ministry.

Pastor F. Kuegele speaks of this matter in a rather lengthy article entitled "The Pastor in His Work," written for the *Theological Quarterly.* He states that "when a man is called to the office of the Christian ministry, he is not called to a life of leisure and enjoyment of days of ease; he is called to work. . . . Nor is the work of the ministry all of one and the same kind. It will not compare with the work of a factory hand who has only one thing to do day after day . . . The ministry requires work of mind and body, hand and brain. It wants the whole man. There is scarcely another calling which requires so many and such a variety of activities as does the ministry of the Gospel." (Vol. VIII, 1904, p. 47f.) For this very reason, pastors should consider their calling worthy of their best time and efforts.

Such faithfulness, however, does not imply constant and continuing effort without relaxation.

"The pastor, as well as others, should live according to God's order in nature," writes Pastor Kuegele, "using the day for labor and the night for rest. Nor is it wrong for the preacher, worn in mind and body, to take a vacation for recuperation, agreeably to the Lord's own example. . . . The Lord wants His laborers to work, but He does not want them to overwork themselves. . . . The minister who overtaxes his abilities sins in ruining his health and shortening his usefulness. Taking the needed time for rest is a duty." (*Theol. Quart.*, 1904, p. 49.)

Finally, such faithfulness will help the pastor to maintain a cheerful attitude toward his work.

The world does not know how to evaluate a pastor's work. Even Christians, at times, become guilty of misjudging a faithful pastor, charging him with negligence in office, where a consideration of human limitations would have suggested that they seek to lighten his burdens by relieving him of some of his work. Under such trying conditions the pastor can take heart, being encouraged by the fact that the Lord judges differently. He demands faithfulness, not superhuman effort. "I know thy works," says He, "and thy labor, and thy patience, and how thou hast borne, and hast patience, and for My name's sake hast labored, and hast not fainted" (Rev. 2:2-3). Such thoughts will drive out the despair of the heart, which especially in evil days might cause the pastor to grow restless, tired, and despondent. They will cause him to say instead: "Surely my judgment is with the Lord, and my work with my God" (Is. 49:4).

ABILITY

Ability is also required by the Lord of everyone who desires the office of a pastor, as is clear from I Tim. 3:2, where we read: "A bishop must be . . . apt to teach." This subject may well be summed up as follows:

In order to qualify for the office of the ministry, a person must thoroughly understand the Word of God.

While discussing this subject, Pastor Andres rightly argues that "the office of teaching can and shall be committed only to those who have a thorough knowledge of the divine truth. For how can he who has no thorough knowledge lead others to the knowledge of the divine truth? Every pastor and teacher must, therefore, be able to say confidently with the Apostle Paul, 'Ye may understand my knowledge in the mystery of Christ'." (Eph. 3:4; Mich. Dist., p. 37.)

In addition to a thorough knowledge of the Word, a pastor must also have the ability to teach it.

In proof of this proposition, we may again refer to Paul's words to Timothy, that "a bishop must be . . . apt to teach" (I Tim. 3:2), and to another passage in his Second Letter to Timothy, which reads: "The things that thou hast heard of me among many witnesses, the same commit thou to faithful men, who shall be able to teach others also" (II Tim. 2:2). Pastor Andres draws the following deductions from these passages:

"The ability and aptness to teach others must be found in special measure—and it is self-evident that it must be found—with those who are in the holy ministry and to whom the work of teaching is entrusted as a part of their office. He who does not have this aptitude may well have the right faith and be clothed with many Christian virtues, but he cannot and dare not be a pastor or teacher. If a person lacks teaching ability, he lacks the foundation which is necessary above all else." (Mich. Dist., p. 37.)

The same writer points out that "only he is apt to teach who gauges his teaching by the ability of the hearers to comprehend his message. All attentive hearers should be edified, established, and enlightened thereby." (Mich. Dist., p. 38.)

Dr. W. H. T. Dau gives pertinent advice on this point in an article entitled "The Pastor as a Model to the Congregation." He writes:

"In the important office of a pastor not only what is said, but also how it is expressed, is of great moment. As to the matter of his talks, public and private, that is furnished by the holy Scriptures. . . . As to the manner of his talks, his choice of words, the pastor, if he is a wise man, will choose that, too, from the Scriptures, and will stock his mind with a rich vocabulary of Bible words and phrases. For the mysteries of God cannot be expressed in more striking or apter terms than in the words to which the Spirit gave utterance." (*Theol. Quart.*, VI, 1902, p. 184f.)

The pastor who follows this suggestion of Dr. Dau will reach not only the ears, but also the hearts of his hearers, thereby proving that he is apt to teach.

BLAMELESSNESS

The sinful depravity of the human heart, the lying and deception of the old Evil Foe, and the many temptations of the wicked world make it necessary to speak of a third qualification, without which a man cannot serve the Lord as pastor or teacher. That third qualification is blamelessness. "A bishop must be blameless" (I Tim. 3:2), says the Apostle Paul. The Revised Version of the Bible translates it: "without reproach." A pastor must not be open to censure or attack, but irreproachable, having a reputation to which no taint of sin attaches. With reference to this qualification, the essays and articles studied suggest the following propositions:

Blamelessness and sinlessness dare not be confused. The former is demanded, the latter not even possible.

If only sinless beings were permitted to preach the Word of God, the Lord would have to delegate this work to the holy angels. For Jesus was the only man who dared to say even to His spying enemies: "Which of you convinceth Me of sin?" (John 8:46.) Though our synodical fathers often made mention of the "holy" ministry, they nowhere inferred that the ministers themselves were to be holy. The author of one of the essays, whose name is not given, is bold to say that the flesh of the pastors "is not one whit better than the flesh of the godless" ("Vom Privatstudium des Pastors," *Lehre und Wehre*, XLI, 1895, p. 223).

Blamelessness is bought with the price of constant vigilance, sobriety, and good behavior.

In an essay which concerns itself with the very necessary caution which a pastor should exercise in his daily life, Pastor Theodore Brohm, one of the Founding Fathers, puts every pastor on guard when he says:

"It should be apparent with what anxious care, yes, with what fear and trembling, a preacher should watch over his daily life. He who neglects to exercise caution becomes daring, and he who is daring becomes lax. A lax Christian, in turn, becomes a hypocrite, and a hypocrite turns into a heretic and an enemy of the truth." (Th. J. Brohm, "Von der einem Prediger hoechst noetigen Vorsicht in seinem Wandel," *Lehre und Wehre*, V, 1859, p. 111.)

Pastor Brohm's words are not an exaggeration of the facts. He had witnessed such a fall and, therefore, had cause to warn every pastor of the dangers threatening him. After alluding to that fall, Pastor Brohm says:

"I do not only have such gross and striking offenses in mind. I am thinking also of a large number of less conspicuous sins, which would hinder the ministry of the Gospel, would diminish its effectiveness, and would hamper the welfare of Christian congregations . . . if they were not at once brought under the discipline of the Spirit. . . .

"One pastor, because of his temperament, is given to wrath and related sins. If this sinful inclination is not checked by means of the chastisement of a gracious God, it becomes a habit and rule, so that at the least opposition a person is aroused, uses harsh words, becomes impatient, and, not knowing himself, mistakes his carnal anger for a holy zeal for the house of God. . . .

"Another is inclined toward pride and other sins of this type. The pastor who is greedy of honor would rather endanger the peace of the Church than relinquish the honor which he feels he deserves or give up his point of view. In fact, being urged on by pride, he will make statements which on another occasion he might have considered the grossest heresy. . . .

"Next to pride, no evil is a greater hindrance in the office of the ministry than greediness, which causes a man to flatter his parishioners and to refuse to rebuke them, that he himself may gain thereby. . . . The world will tolerate greed in others, but not in pastors. . . .

"Above all, a pastor must exercise great caution in his dealings with the opposite sex, that he may give himself no occasion to temptation and may give others no cause by his careless, though possibly guileless, behavior to spread false accusations, which, though readily believed, are not easily and successfully refuted." ("Des Pastors Vorsicht," *L. u. W.*, V, pp. 111ff.)

Dr. Dau mentions the fact that especially the young, unmarried pastors must be on their guard. The admonition of Paul to Timothy to deal with women in the congregation as mothers or sisters is mentioned by him as certainly proving "a great help to the pastor in his associations with the female members of his charge." The writer adds: "It will instinctively teach him the proper bearing and language on such occasions and suppress all thoughts of an inordinate nature." (*Theol. Quart.*, VIII, p. 213.) Thus the pastor must watch over his own soul, if he wishes to serve the Lord in the office of the ministry. "Everything about him should breathe purity" (*ibid.*).

We conclude this important proposition with a warning from L. Hartmann's *Pastorale Evangelicum* (1697), translated into the German by Dr. G. Schick. "The person," says he, "who wishes to enter the ministry without arming himself with a heroic and persistent determination to fight the good fight of faith, is deceiving himself. For no one will find the devil a worse foe. No one will more often be tempted. No one will suffer more and greater shame than the pious and faithful standard-bearer of the Church, whom God has determined, not for the enjoyment and pleasure, but for the hatred and disgrace of the world, as St. Paul says, Rom. 8:36; 'For Thy sake we are killed all the day long; we are accounted as sheep for the slaughter'." (*Lehre und Wehre*, VI, 1860, p. 99.)

According to God's Word, only he who is blameless is permitted to be and remain a pastor.

Pastor Andres sums up the whole matter as follows:

"If a person has committed a grievous sin, thus losing his good reputation, he can, if God gives him grace leading to repentance, be a member of a Christian congregation and will be able to serve God in another calling; but he can no longer serve as pastor or teacher of a Christian congregation. For in so doing, he would cause his office to be defamed and would give the adversaries occasion to look with scorn upon the Church.

"It does not rest with a congregation to decide whether or not a pastor who has lost his good name shall be permitted to remain in office. The Lord Himself says such a man may no longer be a pastor. . . . A congregation acting contrary to this prohibition of the Lord cannot hold membership in our Synod, for it is guilty of an open violation of God's Word." (Mich. Dist., pp. 28f.)

These, then, are the pastor's essential qualifications: He must be faithful in the performance of all the duties of his office, as the Lord grants him grace and strength thereto; he must have a thorough knowledge of the divine truths of Scripture and be able to impart the saving truth to his hearers in such a manner that they are edified thereby; and, thirdly, he must avoid all appearance of evil, so that his enemies will not be able to bring serious charge against him which would rob him of his good name in the community. Blessed is the man whom the Lord has so richly favored! For only by the grace of God can a pastor have these three essential qualifications for the ministry.

In our discussion of these qualifications we have already described the pastor as he is to conduct himself in his office. We have seen the need of constant diligence, of caution, and of temperance. We have also mentioned, at least in passing, the variety of activities required by his calling. These activities of the pastor will engage our attention in the remaining portion of this essay.

II

THE PASTOR AT HOME

Let us follow the pastor who is described in the publications of our Church, as he goes about his daily work. In order to do this, we must first of all enter his home. Coming into the pastor's home, we ought often find him in his study, occupied with his books.

THE PASTOR WITH HIS BOOKS

Most of the time which the pastor spends with his books should be devoted to the study of the Scriptures.

The one essential book in the pastor's library is the Bible. "The holy Scriptures are and always will be the source of our wisdom, the rule of our faith and life, the source of our own and our hearers' salvation. . . . We learn from the Scriptures how to carry out the duties of our office. Our sermons are derived from the Bible. . . . The Scriptures are the center about which everything revolves for the theologian." ("Vom Privatstudium," *L. u. W.*, XLI, p. 280.)

Naturally, as Hartmann rightly says, "The holy mysteries of God should not be read without a fervent prayer for the gracious gift of the Spirit to enlighten and teach the heart. A person should put himself into the proper frame of mind when approaching this blessed task and constantly keep in mind the purpose of the Book and of the passage of Scripture which he is reading." (*L. u. W.*, VI, p. 99.)

Finally, the Scriptures should be studied with pen in hand. The result of our Bible study should be a constantly growing collection of Bible truths, indexed according to subjects, interpreted by means of clear passages of the Bible itself. (*L. u. W.*, XLI, pp. 283-285.)

The Confessional Writings of our Church and the writings of Luther and other great teachers are next in importance.

"Luther is the Church reformer whose coming was prophesied in Scripture. He is, therefore, the most trustworthy teacher among those who were not directly inspired as were the Apostles and Prophets," says a writer in *Lehre und Wehre* (XLI, p. 331). Dr. Walther, Dr. Pieper, and other leaders in our Synod have said that, in their estimation, Luther's works are such an inexhaustible source of information for all branches of theology, that they can supplant a large library of other books, but cannot be supplanted by another library, no matter how large it might be.

That, however, does not mean that the pastor should neglect the study of other good books. The selection is not as great as it might seem to be. Our synodical fathers include in the list the writings of Augustine, Luther, Chemnitz, Gerhard, and Walther. Undoubtedly, later listing would also include Dr. Pieper's *Christliche Dogmatik.* These writings, together with the Confessions of our Church, ought to be studied by the pastor

Finally, the pastor should, if possible, be conversant with the original languages of the Bible as well as with logic, rhetoric, history, and pedagogy.

"Whoever is not master of the original languages must depend upon believing commentators, who have made use of the original languages, to give him the explanation. For the exposition of the Scriptures comes out of the original text," we read in *Lehre und Wehre* (XLI, p. 364). Luther once said:

"As dearly as we love the Gospel, so diligent let us be in the use of the languages; for God did not without good reason cause the Scriptures to be written in only two languages, the Old Testament in the Hebrew and the New in the Greek. Since God did not despise them, but chose them for His Word, we, too, should honor them above all others." (*Ibid.*, p. 365.)

The study of the other subjects mentioned will also prove helpful to the pastor who wishes to do his full duty in the best manner possible. Such a pastor will also choose three books which are not on his library shelf and diligently study them. From his own heart he will learn how to deal with others. Every person with whom he comes in contact will be a book from which and about which he will learn many things. Finally, the works of creation and preservation will furnish him with countless proofs of God's power, justice, mercy, wisdom, and faithfulness. Such reading will make him a full man.

But, oh, how difficult it is for the pastor to apply himself to this work as he ought to do!

A pastor is tempted by many hindrances and obstacles to neglect his studies.

Whenever private study is mentioned, our thoughts at once accuse or else excuse one another. For every pastor realizes how difficult it is to be faithful in the use of his books. Few pastors devote as much time to study as would be advisable, for there are so very many obstacles and hindrances to keep them from this blessed work. At least a few of them are mentioned in the essays and articles upon which this study is based.

First of all, the flesh is weak, given to laziness, having no delight in the Lord, seeking to dampen the spirit of the new man in us, tempting us to become restless, tired, and despondent, or haughty, overconfident, and self-satisfied.

Then, too, the work is so pressing. One pastor must spend many hours on the road as he travels from one station to another. His brother in the ministry is in school half of the day and, after making the most necessary calls, is too tired to study. A third man has a large congregation. His pastoral work alone is too much for one man. A fourth is troubled with ill health. Constant headaches keep him from his desk. There may also be sickness in the family. The weak brother is even hindered by the fact that he must spend so much time in the garden or the barn.

Need we still mention the fact that strife in the congregation, thanklessness on the part of many members, slander, and the like tempt many a pastor to forsake his studies? No wonder it is so difficult for a pastor to spend the right amount of time with his books!

The Lord, however, gives him many inducements to be faithful in the use of his books.

God makes it clear to the pastor that He wants him to "give attendance to reading" (I Tim. 4:13), and to "search the Scriptures" (John 5:39), that he may "grow in grace" (II Pet. 3:18), "increasing in the knowledge of God" (Col. 1:10), that he may "be filled with the knowledge of His will" (Col. 1:9).

The Lord also induces us to study by reminding us of the purpose of our work and the responsibility which goes with it. When we speak, we should do so "as the oracles of God" (I Pet. 4:11), preaching only what God has given us to say. We should preach the truths of God with "words easy to be understood" (I Cor. 14:9), that our preaching may profit the hearers. Moreover, we should "teach them to observe all things," whatsoever God has commanded us (Matt. 28:20), "rightly dividing the word of truth" (II Tim. 2:15). Pastor Kuegele points out that, in order to do this, "a careful and thorough distinction between Law and Gospel is indispensably necessary. (For) the distinction between these two doctrines is the key to the Bible. Any man who does not know that the Bible contains these two distinct doctrines will not and cannot understand its teachings; the Bible will appear to him a book full of contradictions." (*Theol. Quart.*, VIII, p. 175.)

The example of true teachers of all times should also inspire us to study as they did. Peter knew the contents of all the epistles of Paul. Paul himself, though well advanced in years, had men bring him books and parchments. David busied himself with the Law of God night and day, as he tells us in Psalm 119.

"If, then, these divinely inspired writers, upon whom the Holy Ghost poured out His richest gifts, nevertheless made diligent use of books, how must we blush with shame if we do not with all our powers apply ourselves to reading," says Hartmann in his *Pastorale* (p. 97).

There are also other inducements, which we mention only in passing, such as our feeling of humility, which should prompt us to read what others have written, the profit which we and our congregations will derive from our studies, the harm which we and our congregations would suffer, if we were to neglect them, yes, also the zeal of the enemies of the Church, who faithfully apply themselves to the task of suppressing the truth. In view of all these considerations, the faithful pastor must spend much time with his books.

THE PASTOR WITH HIS FAMILY

Having spent so much time in the pastor's study, we must make our visit with his family very brief. Yet even in a short time we shall be able to gain much helpful information and inspiration from our several sources on this important subject.

One of the pastor's greatest blessings is a wife who believes in, and respects, the Word of God.

The married estate was instituted for the welfare of man, and the pastor, above all others, profits by this divine institution. For "his efficiency in carrying out the obligations of his office, rather than being decreased, is increased by the married estate" (Mich. Dist., p. 30). By means of it, he and his wife can be a blessed example to the congregation. For a Christian wife "will, also in this day and age, honor her husband from the heart . . . in spite of his weaknesses and imperfections; for she respects the Word of God, which demands this of her . . . She will also, in cheerful agreement with the will of her husband, observe the proper moderation in social affairs, neither gadding about, nor constantly staying at home, and in her intercourse will avoid both idle gossip and an unnatural reserve." That is the description of the pastor's wife given by Dr. Wilhelm Sihler, one of the early leaders of the Missouri Synod. ("Was ist der Wille Gottes in Hinsicht auf das eigene Hausregiment der Diener der Kirche?" *Lehre und Wehre*, XXIV, 1878, p. 166.)

Though the pastor's wife dare never become an assistant pastor, she nevertheless holds an important position in the congregation.

We do not hear the pastor discuss the confessions of his members with his wife. She is not a pastor. If members seek to make her an assistant pastor, she will refuse the office. Pastor Brohm considers it the best trait of a pastor's wife "that she be deaf and dumb—deaf to all idle gossip, dumb to repeat what she has heard" (*L. u. W.*, V, p. 115).

However, her position is an important one. For, as Pastor Brohm points out, "In addition to being a helpmeet to her husband, she will serve as an example to all women in the congregation by her humble, loving, quiet, decent, mild manner of living and in this respect is, indeed, her husband's helper" (*ibid.*).

In Christian harmony the pastor and his wife bring up their children in the nurture and admonition of the Lord.

In true Christian humility, the pastor and his wife will see their own weaknesses reflected in the temperament of their children. But this will not deter them in the use of the Law, and that, at times, with the help of the rod, in impressing upon their children the seriousness and damning character of sin. (*L. u. W.*, XXIV, p. 167.)

Just as certainly, however, they will make constant use of the Gospel, in great love leading their children to the Savior through regular use of the Word of God at the family altar and all through the day, so that it will be apparent to all that the Word of God is not only taught in the home, but actually holds sway. Also in this manner they will be an example to all who know them. (*ibid.*)

THE PASTOR WITH HIS GUESTS

A word is in place on this subject because the Lord Himself tells us that a pastor should be "given to hospitality" (I Tim. 3:2). We submit the proposition that

The pastor is an example also when entertaining his guests.

In the early Christian Church the opportunity often presented itself to the pastor to befriend Christians who had left their homes because of persecution. Though such conditions no longer exist, the pastor does have occasion to welcome guests into his home. Incidentally, Pastor Andres reminds congregations to take this into consideration when building a parsonage, that their pastors may be able to practice hospitality in the true sense of the word. (Mich. Dist., p. 36.)

The "Table of Duties" also shows that the pastor should prove himself the ideal host. In his manners, his speech, and his conduct he should be a refined, courteous, polite gentleman. Such a walk of life is required of him not only for his own sake, but in the interest of his congregation as well. Such a walk of life is also possible for him if he makes his home a place of prayer and devotion. God give us such homes in abundance.

III

THE PASTOR IN THE CHURCH

As we follow the pastor from his home to the church, let us bear in mind that he is still a man—enlightened by the Spirit, it is true, but having also the evil flesh within him, privileged by God to carry out the most important assignment on earth, but having no sufficiency of his own to perform the task. Even in the pulpit, therefore, he will not and cannot reach perfection.

In Christian love his hearers will bear with him in his weaknesses, pray for him in his holy office, and, above all, humbly and penitently, willingly and cheerfully, lovingly and believingly hear the Word of God which he has drawn from the Bible and is offering them for the nourishment of their souls. The person who takes this to heart will be in the proper frame of mind to enter the church and there to listen to the pastor in the pulpit.

THE PASTOR IN THE PULPIT

The matter of the pastor's sermons depends almost entirely upon the amount of work which he has done in the study.

If the pastor has applied himself diligently to the study of God's Word in the home, he will preach Scriptural sermons in the pulpit, so that a "Thus saith the Lord" will introduce his statements.

If he has learned to realize the seriousness of his office, he will seek to provide for the temporal and eternal welfare of his hearers in every sermon.

If he has made a thorough study of the difference between the Law and the Gospel, he will not rob the former of its severity, nor the latter of its sweetness.

If he has studied the important doctrinal controversies on the basis of the Confessions and in other writings, he will be careful to set forth with all possible clearness the distinctive doctrines and customs of the Lutheran Church.

If he has kept abreast of the times, he will, naturally, preach sermons which are timely.

If he has made a thorough study of logic and rhetoric, he will not be in danger of preaching sermons which are so confusing that they do not hold the attention of the hearers and impart no clear knowledge of the plan of salvation.

Finally, if the pastor has looked into the book of his own heart, he will preach to himself before he enters the pulpit. Then, having preached unto himself, he will, with God's help, seek to practice what he preaches, lest he tear down what God has built up through his preaching.

The pastor's manner of preaching depends upon the amount of love which he has in his heart.

The pastor who has felt the healing power of the Word of God and, therefore, loves it with all his heart, can also preach it from the heart. If he truly loves his members and desires their salvation, he will also show that love in his manner of preaching, not adding a fleshly anger to the serious preaching of the Law, nor taking away some of the sweetness of the Gospel by preaching it in a matter-of-fact tone of voice. Instead, he will impress his hearers with the fact that he has a fatherly interest in his own and seeks their welfare.

THE PASTOR AT THE ALTAR

Also in the administration of the Sacraments, which is next in importance to the preaching of the Gospel, the pastor, as he is described in Synod's publications, will be an example to all men. As we discuss this point, let us bear in mind that we are dealing only with the pastor's practice as he administers the Sacraments. The voice of the Church with regard to the doctrines involved will be heard elsewhere. The following propositions briefly sum up the matter. (Cf. *Theol. Quart.*, VIII, pp. 229-237; IX, pp. 117-126.)

In administering the Sacrament of Baptism, the pastor, in a solemn manner, befitting this sacred act, and in a distinct voice, so that he may be heard by all, repeats the exact words of the baptismal formula, being careful to apply a sufficient amount of water so that the sponsors will be able to testify that the babe was truly baptized.

Before administering the Lord's Supper, the pastor does all in his power to assure himself that only those will receive the Sacrament whom the Lord calls worthy.

In the distribution of the Lord's Supper the pastor solemnly and expressly mentions the fact that the communicants are receiving the true body and the true blood of Christ.

THE PASTOR IN THE MEETINGS

In the congregation meetings the pastor is most likely to show his true nature and temperament. The wise and faithful pastor will, therefore, make a study of his own heart before each meeting and especially take note of the qualifications set forth in the Word of God. These may be briefly summed up in a single proposition.

The pastor is to be a leader, not a lord, in the church.

In explaining the Apostle Peter's statement that pastors are not to be "lords over God's heritage" (I Pet. 5:3), Dr. Dau says, "Peter here inculcates a paradox: the model pastor will rise in the estimation of his flock in proportion as he sinks in his own; his influence will be greatest when he avoids the appearance of wanting to exercise it" (*Theol. Quart.*, VI, p. 179).

A few remarks of Pastor Andres are also in place at this point. Discussing the word "striker" in the "Table of Duties," he mentions the fact that the pastor should not lash the members with his tongue, nor emphasize each word with his fist. He explains the word "vigilant" as meaning sober in mind and heart, careful, thoughtful, mentally alert, keeping one's temper. Finally, in connection with the word "patient," he brings out the thought that the pastor should give in rather than in a stubborn way seek to put through his own plans. (Mich. Dist., pp. 32-42.)

Pastor Kuegele speaks on the whole proposition when he says: "On the one hand, it is to be remembered that the pastor is the minister, the servant of the congregation, and not its lord and ruler; on the other hand, that he is the steward of Christ and can and dare do nothing in violation of his Master's Word and command." (*Theol. Quart.*, IX, p. 124.)

In pastoral conferences the faithful pastor gives evidence of humility, sincerity, and love.

It is self-evident that the faithful pastor will attend pastoral conferences, where he has the opportunity to attend Communion, to hear and discuss the Word of God, and thus to feed his soul. One of the essayists says that "he who finds conferences boring and profitless . . . may well ask himself, Why do I not make the conferences more interesting and profitable? and the answer will be, Because I do not study diligently enough." (*L. u. W.*, XLI, p. 237.) The pastors who do take an active part in the discussions must, however, be warned against becoming contentious, says Pastor Andres in discussing the term "brawler" in the Table of Duties (Mich. Dist., p. 43). Elsewhere we read that "different opinions and modes of expression ought to be avoided in the interest of the unity of the faith and the peace of the Church" (*L. u. W.*, XLI, p. 328).

IV

THE PASTOR IN THE HOME OF MEMBERS

The visiting which is done by the pastors of some church bodies would permit no distinction to be made between pastoral and social calls. For these pastors do not make pastoral calls. They have no conception of their duty toward the individual Christian. That, however, is not true in the Lutheran Church. The Lutheran pastor who wishes to make a pastoral call has a definite purpose in mind, namely, to bring the Word of God to an individual member of his congregation who has suffered bodily, mental, or spiritual harm. In his social calls he has no such purpose in mind and, on such occasions, is more a friend than a pastor in the home of his members, if this is correctly understood. Let us now accompany him as he makes his calls in the congregation.

THE PASTOR MAKING PASTORAL CALLS

Having obtained permission to accompany the pastor as he makes his pastoral calls—a permission which, in reality, is not granted to anyone—we are bound to the strictest secrecy. For much goes on between the individual member and the shepherd of souls which must forever remain hidden in the pastor's heart.

The propositions which deal with the pastoral calls will, therefore, be of a general nature. For we dare not break the seal of the confessional; nor do we wish to reveal too much of the disappointment, the grief, the heartache, yes, also of the fear and trembling of the pastor as he makes some of the more difficult calls, where the rescue of an immortal soul is involved.

The faithful pastor combines the use of the best virtues within him while making his pastoral calls.

He is patient with the weak member, but is firm in his stand on the Word of God. He is bold to rebuke the sinner, but inspires confidence in himself as one who will not betray the penitent. He shows a hatred toward sin, but a love toward the sinner. He ministers to the needs of others, but seeks nothing for himself. He feeds the fire of his zeal with the oil of mercy. He shows no undue familiarity in dealing with the individual, nor does he assume a professional reserve which would make him seem like a stranger to his own members.

The faithful pastor applies the Word which he has learned in accordance with the needs of his members.

Pastoral calls have their beginning in the study. Here the proper text for each case is carefully sought out. Here the proper methods outlined in his pastoral theology are diligently studied, so that each member receives the proper portion. The secure and self-righteous are brought low with the Law. The sorely tried and tempted are raised up with the Gospel. The person, however, who rejoices even in his infirmities, who maintains a confident trust in the Lord in the midst of the severest trials, strengthens his pastor's faith and hope as much as his own faith and hope are strengthened. God bless these cheerful, courageous Christians!

THE PASTOR MAKING SOCIAL CALLS

Though the pastor enters the homes of his members as a friend when making social calls, he is still their pastor.

When the pastor visits his members, they have one of the best opportunities to compare his teaching with his daily life. Let him, therefore, bear in mind that "in all things" he is to show himself "a pattern of good works" (Tit. 2:7). Pastor Andres derives the following from his study of the "Table of Duties."

The pastor is to be temperate in every form of enjoyment, not guilty of boisterousness, by no means guilty of questionable jokes, not even giving the appearance that he is a drinker, and giving no appearance of covetousness. (Mich. Dist., pp. 32-45.)

The Table of Duties states this positively when it tells the pastor to be vigilant, sober, and of good behavior, and it closes with the words,

> Let each his lesson learn with care,
> And all the household well shall fare

V

THE PASTOR IN THE COMMUNITY

In this last chapter we intended to speak of the pastor as pastor and then also as citizen. But where shall we draw the line? The only proposition which suggests itself is the following:

The pastor has only one calling in the world. He is the ambassador of Christ.

A pastor simply cannot divest himself of his office, not even for an hour a day. Whether on the street, or at the bank, or in the stores, or in the home of members or non-members, or on the golf course, or wherever he may be, he is still the Reverend Soandso. (*Theol. Quart.*, VI, p. 215.)

He has been called to work in the vineyard of the Lord. "It is, therefore, unfitting," says Hartmann, "that a pastor be a hunter, merchant, speculator, soldier, farmer, etc. For if it is not proper to leave the preaching of the Word to wait on tables (Acts 6:2), then, surely, it is less proper to leave the Word of God to have time for things of a different nature" (*L. u. W.*, VI, p. 100). That was also the position taken by Dr. Walther and other leaders of our Synod. Though this point does not rule out the right of a pastor to seek diversion, it surely warns him against the practice of some who gain favorable publicity by neglecting their all-important office in order to render some questionable service to the world. As has already been stated, the office of the ministry wants the whole man, a man of love and of faithfulness.

"What rigid self-discipline will be necessary to this end!" exclaims Dr. Dau. "From morn till eve, from the early Sunday devotion to the evening prayer on Saturday, at home and abroad, in his study or in his parlor, in the pulpit or at the homes of his parishioners, in his labors and in his recreations, the pastor should be the model of a Christian." (*Theol. Quart.*, VI, p. 215.)

Does the task seem too great? Are the burdens too heavy? Fear not, for the Spirit will uphold you. "And let him who grows weary with work look to the goal," says Pastor Andres. "There we shall rest from our labors. There Christ Himself will be our reward. . . . There the teachers 'shall shine as the brightness of the firmament; and they that turn many to righteousness, as the stars forever and ever'." (Dan. 12:3; Mich. Dist., p. 52.)

XX

Authority in the Church
With Special Reference to the Call

THE term "authority" is quite familiar to us. We meet with it in every field of human endeavor and in every area of human relationships. Nor is it of recent origin or a late development. It has always been; in fact, it dates back to the days of creation. God himself gave authority to man when he gave him dominion over all created things (Gen. 1:20). That authority was obviously intended by God to add to the bliss, enjoyment, and happiness of man on earth. But like all other good gifts of God, so authority, too, has become corrupt through sin's entering into the world. With its motives of selfishness, its lust for power, its utter disregard of the fellow man's rights and interests, authority has to a large extent become a veritable curse. Authority has been abused, it has been usurped, it has been misdirected. And high and low, groups and individuals in every area and station of civil, communal, and social trust, were guilty; and suffering, bloodshed, and ruin followed in the wake.

And yet authority properly constituted, legitimately exercised, and justly administered is a boon to human society. There must be authority if there is to be order and not chaos, civil decency and not social degeneracy, happiness and not distress, justice and not oppression, control and not licentiousness. It was therefore divine wisdom that again established authority in a world that had gone to pieces by giving to men the Fourth Commandment and thereby regulating family life; by instituting civil government and thereby guaranteeing a peaceful community life (Rom. 13); by defining the relationship between masters and servants and thereby solving the problem of capital and labor (Eph. 6). In that way the Lord, in His providential care, has most graciously safeguarded every relationship in life by surrounding it with authority sufficient to insure true happiness.

Ordinary human intelligence fully agrees with the divine order of things. Men of their own volition establish and subject themselves to authority. They are willing that such of their fellow men as they find to be competent should be given authority, authority to rule, to govern, to legislate, to lead, to direct, to teach, etc. Common sense dictates that. To be sure, since these are man-made arrangements, they have their shortcomings and their imperfections. Nevertheless they serve an essential purpose most eminently, and their deficiencies are far outbalanced by their efficiencies.

Thesis I

As in all spheres of human endeavor that impose or involve responsibilities, privileges, obligations, and duties, there is and must be authority, so there is authority also in the Church. This authority, however, is not of human origin, but was established and dearly bought by the blood of Christ and is given to the Church by the Master Himself, to be exercised by the Church as such or conferred by the Church on its individual members.

Our Thesis draws a parallel between the situation that obtains in the realm of the secular and that which prevails in the realm of the spiritual. As in the case of the former, so also in the instance of the latter there are those who are invested with responsibilities, obligations, and duties. And as this fact presupposes authority in the affairs of the world, so it presupposes authority in the affairs of the Church. There is, however, this difference: While the authority in the State, for instance, is essentially government by the consent or tolerance of the governed, *i. e.,* of all the citizens of the commonwealth, the nature and extent of authority in the Church is by divine grant to the believers, and to them only.

The Authority of the Office of the Keys.—Concerning this, Luther says in his Small Catechism: "It is the peculiar church power which Christ has given to His Church on earth, to forgive the sins of the penitent sinners unto them and to retain the sins of the impenitent as long as they do not repent." This is based on Scripture. In Matt. 16:19 the Lord addresses the following words to Peter: "I will give unto thee the keys of the kingdom of heaven; and whatsoever thou shalt bind on earth shall be bound in heaven, and whatsoever thou shalt loose on earth shall be loosed in heaven." That was granting Peter a sweeping authority, an authority, as Luther explained, "as valid and certain as if our dear Lord dealt with us Himself." Nor does that mean that the Lord gave this unique prerogative to Peter alone among the Twelve, for in John 20:19-23, He addressed these selfsame words to the assembled Eleven and others. And He outlines the entire scope and manner of this authority in Matt. 18:17-20. He lets it be clearly understood that He has the entire Church in mind, every local congregation of believers. "Tell it to the Church," He says. Tell what? This—and now he uses the selfsame words: "Whatsoever ye shall bind on earth," etc. This the Lord was anxious to impress upon his Christians ever and again, even to the very last. Just before He ascended to heaven, addressing for the last time all the believers that surrounded Him, He spoke these impressive words: "All power is given unto Me in heaven and on earth," and so, by this power, I now commission and authorize you and My Christians unto the end of the world: "Go ye and teach all nations, baptizing them in the name of the Father and of the Son and of the Holy Ghost, teaching them to observe all things whatsoever I have commanded you."

The Authority of the "Spiritual Priesthood."—What the Savior expressed in these unmistakable terms, the authority with which He honored and blessed His Church, St. Peter restates in these sublime and majestic words: "Ye are a chosen generation, a royal priesthood, an holy nation, a peculiar people." In one grand majestic sweep there are here delegated to the Church the spiritual, divine, and heavenly blessings, rights, powers, etc., all the performances, functions, and obligations of the household of God to make Christ known and to bring His blessings and gifts, the fruits of His redemption, to others. According to this all believers in Christ are "priests," God's priests, entitled to perform all the functions of the New Testament priesthood. And in addition to that distinction they also have royalty; not that common, ordinary, cheap human royalty, but a God-dispensed royalty. They are also "kings," God's kings. (Rev. 5:10.) They occupy an exalted position. The Lord has even elevated them above the angels. (I Cor. 6:2-3.)

The Authority of the Call.—"The congregation of believers—not the Pope, not the bishops, not the ministers—originally and immediately possess the keys of the kingdom of heaven; the congregation of believers is originally and immediately commissioned to preach the Gospel to every creature and administer the Sacraments; the congregation of believers is entrusted with the power of appointing 'overseers of the flock,' 'stewards of the mysteries of God,' pastors, ministers, who in their name preach, baptize, administer the Lord's Supper, absolve." (*Prooftexts*, pp. 102-103.)

And the congregation has the right not only to call, but also to supervise its pastor and teacher. When it called its pastor, it did not relinquish its priestly prerogatives; it merely delegated the public performance of such rights to its pastor. The congregation is, and always will remain, responsible for the proper administration of the various functions of the ministerial office. If false doctrine creeps into the church, the members may not fold their arms in sanctimonious innocency and deny responsibility, again resorting to the language of the first Adam: "The preacher, Lord, whom Thou gavest to be with us, he gave us of this doctrine, and we did eat." When false teachers entered the Galatian congregations, Paul did not address himself to these Judaizers, but spoke directly to the Galatian congregations and insisted that the congregations take the matter of purging themselves from this contamination into their own hands. (Gal. 3.) The people of Berea therefore set a good example when they subjected Paul's preaching to a thorough scrutiny, "searching the Scriptures daily whether those things were so" (Acts 17:11). Would any of us say: We certainly have nothing to fear from a pastor of the Missouri Synod? Friend, that might have been Eve's retort, too, when the Tempter spoke to her: "Would any strange voice be heard in God's own Paradise?" So then: "Beloved, believe not every spirit, but try the spirits, whether they are of God" (I John 4:1). Note that if the members are to judge doctrine, they must know doctrine. If they would know doctrine, they must search the Scriptures, in fact, be diligent, even daily students of the Word, and also read their church paper. (I Pet. 2:2.)

Authority vs. Obligations.—If God's people, all of them, are authorized to proclaim the Gospel, then all are also obligated to promote the course of the Gospel by training pastors and teachers; by establishing and supporting schools, colleges, and seminaries; by personally witnessing for Christ in their respective surroundings; by contributing of their material possessions so that missionaries can be sent to people still sitting in darkness; by faithfully, energetically, wholeheartedly, attending to the affairs and needs of the home congregation.

Authority Bought with a Price.—Those are indeed remarkable and strange things that constitute the basis for the authority which the Lord has established in His Church. No human mind would even have conceived of such a possibility, much less could any human ingenuity have elaborated a plan to bring about such results or provide such treasures or establish the authority of which we speak (I Cor. 2:9). We are dealing here with the hidden wisdom which God ordained before the world unto our glory. Yes, we are speaking of something that cost the Lord a tremendous price, even the precious blood of the eternal Son of God. No one recognized this better than Paul, who therefore told the elders of Ephesus that they were privileged to serve a cause, *i. e.*, feed the flock, "which Christ hath purchased with His own blood" (Acts 20:28). He tells Timothy the same things, in fact, recalls to Timothy's mind the bloody scene in the judgment hall of Pontius Pilate (I Tim. 6:13-16). And he does so with an emphasis that is overwhelming and irrefutable and leaves no doubt as to the source to which the Church is indebted for the authority it enjoys, namely, the redemption in Christ Jesus. Because Christ, who knew no sin, was made sin for us, we have been made the righteousness of God in Him and have received the *stewardship* of the riches of the household of God. Because we were reconciled unto God by Christ, there has been committed to us the Word of Reconciliation, or the *authority* to inform the world of its complete redemption. (II Cor. 5:18-21.) If that understanding is always present with us, then each and every one who holds any commission or authority by the dispensation of the Christian congregation, and be that ever so insignificant in the eyes of men, will serve in that capacity with the greatest personal devotion and joy.

Authority Not of the State; Not of Carnal Means.—There is a final point that we shall have to consider in this connection, namely, that this is a *spiritual* and *not a physical power;* an authority of the Word and not of the sword, of the Church and not of the State. "My kingdom is not of this world," the Savior told Pontius Pilate. When Peter drew his sword, the Lord bade him: "Put up again thy sword into its place," Matt. 26:52. (Luther, when offered the assistance of the military for the advancement and protection of the Gospel. *Triglot*, Augsburg Confession, Art. XXVIII, 8-14.)

If the Church invades the realm of the State, it need not complain if the State intrude upon the territory of the Church. If the Church demands that the State give the Church a voice in the regulation of the affairs of the State (in framing of "Sunday blue laws," in reforming social ills, in combating vice in its various forms, in prohibiting the sale and consumption of alcoholic drinks, in formulating peace plans, etc.), it need not be surprised if the State retaliates by proclaiming and trying to dictate to, and make demands on, the Church. With every special privilege the Church asks of the State it obligates itself for a like service in return. Let us understand once and for all that "authority in the Church" is definitely expressive of the most emphatic insistence on strict separation of State and Church. (*Lutheran Witness*, Vol. LIV, pp. 3, 18, 35, 50.)

We repeat, because we cannot overemphasize the fact that *authority in the Church is an authority of the Word and nothing else.* Whenever not the Word, but some other means are employed to achieve results in the Church, the Church is abusing its authority, it is leaving its moorings, it becomes disloyal to its trust. The Church therefore stoops to disgraceful tactics when it appeals directly or indirectly to outsiders for assistance either by soliciting outright contributions or by urging them to patronize their lunch booth at the fair or by inviting them to their church supper or appealing to the government for free textbooks, etc. (On bazaars, fairs, etc., see *Lutheran Witness*, LIV, p. 174, *Chicago Journal of Commerce.* In what respect may bazaars, church fairs, sales, etc., be unobjectionable? See *Lutheran Witness*, Vol. XL, p. 329.)

Thesis II

Authority in the Church therefore cannot, and must never, undertake to abrogate, detract from, add to, change, or misconstrue one iota of God's Word, but rather preach, teach, and confess, in short, uphold and defend, the majesty of the Word.

Not an Authority Over, but in Behalf of the Word.—The Church is the guardian of the Word. That, however, does not mean, and cannot mean, that the Word was placed under the jurisdiction of the Church. It cannot imply that the Church may accept or reject, preach or ignore statements and teachings of the Scriptures as it pleases; that it may adopt what appeals to the senses or fits into the modern picture, and discard what does not seem to be "expedient" or appears to be at variance with the findings of science or is out of harmony with the trends of the times; that it may accept what seems reasonable and reject what runs counter to human understanding. (Modernists.)

The Lord is very jealous of His Word. When He gave us His Word, He made it very clear that His Word is not to be tampered with. When therefore the Lord had terminated his divine commitments to the sons of men, He warned them, saying: "If any man shall add unto these things, God shall add unto him the plagues that are written in this Book; and if any man shall take away from the words of this prophecy, God shall take away his part out of the book of life and out of the Holy City and from the things that are written in this Book" (Rev. 22:18-19). "To the Law and to the Testimony," this motto of the Prophet Isaiah must also be the slogan of every true ambassador in the New Testament era. (Is. 8:20.) "If they speak not according to this word," the Prophet continues, "it is because there is no light in them," they lack understanding; they are not honest, neither with God nor with men; they are full of falsehood, there is wickedness in them, they are blind leaders of the blind. "He that hath My Word," the Lord admonishes by the mouth of the Prophet Jeremiah, "let him speak My Word faithfully" (Jer. 23:28). The Galatian Christians had yielded to "another Gospel." False prophets had "perverted the Gospel of Christ," and they had tolerated that. In rebuking the Galatians for that, Paul certainly minces no words. He is forceful, plainspoken, and scathingly direct. (Cp. Moses, Ex. 32:19.) In holy indignation, Paul, as it were, shouts the divine condemnation into the ears of the Galatians, and not once, but twice in short succession: "Though an angel from heaven preach any other Gospel unto you than that which we have preached unto you," nay, more than that: Paul says: "even if I myself" should dare to reverse my teaching and preach differently than I did before, "let him—and also myself—"be accursed" (Gal. 1:8). There must be no deviation whatsoever from the truth. Yea, the children of God are not only in a general way to abide by their Father's language, but they are to preach, teach, confess, and express the verities of God with the same words, using

the familiar language that the Holy Ghost used and scrupulously
avoid terminologies, expressions, and phrases that lack clarity or
may be misunderstood, or are ambiguous and misleading. The closer
we stay to the language of the Scriptures, the less will be the
possibility of error. "I beseech you, brethren," Paul therefore writes
to the Corinthians, "that ye all speak the same thing and that there
be no divisions among you" (I Cor. 1:10). Christ emphasizes that
in His high-priestly prayer when He says: "I have given them Thy
Word." That was the Savior's glory and divine satisfaction that He
had been true to the Father's Word and communicated nothing else
to the sons of men. That must also be the supreme satisfaction of
the Church. The Church becomes guilty of a breach of trust, of a
usurpation of authority, of a lese majesty, of a crime against the
sovereignty of God, yea, of high treason if it dares to criticize and
find fault with the Lord's Holy Word, or impugns and doubts the
reliability and veracity of certain Biblical statements. Leaders in the
Church will therefore be true guides and spiritual counselors of their
people, they will be using their authority aright, if they will follow
the advice the Lord gave Joshua, Josh. 1:6-8. (I Cor. 2:2, 13.)

The Lord is very much concerned that this be done. When in
the long ago the Lord wanted to send Jonah to the doomed city of
Nineveh, He gave him very definite instructions. We read: "And
the Word of the Lord came unto Jonah the second time, saying:
Arise, go unto Nineveh, that great city, and preach unto it *the
preaching that I bid thee*" (Jonah 3:1-2). That was definite language, indeed. Jonah was not to preach to Nineveh what he
wanted, but what God wanted, not his word, but the Lord's Word.

Turning to the New Testament, we find that the Lord is, perhaps,
even more uncompromisingly definite. Why should He not be? We
are enjoying a fuller glory, too. To Timothy, Paul writes: "I charge
thee therefore before God and the Lord Jesus Christ, who shall
judge the quick and the dead at His appearing and His kingdom:
Preach the Word" (II Tim. 4:1-2). And to Titus he wrote: "But
speak thou the things that become sound doctrine" (Titus 2:1).
Paul knew whereunto he had been called, namely, "to be the
minister of Jesus Christ to the Gentiles, *ministering the Gospel of
God*," nothing more, nothing less. Whence are heretical tendencies?
Whence erroneous interpretations? Whence false teachings in the
Church? Simply because men have assumed unto themselves the

authority to subject the Words of Scripture to the yardstick of human intelligence instead of searching the Scriptures for a self-interpretation of its statements. The church that arrogates unto itself the right to sit in judgment on God's revelations ceases to be a church of God. It is not even any longer a respectable human agency; for even among men it is a commonly accepted principle that the author of a book is its own authentic interpreter.

The Great Commission, from which there can be no deviation, reads: "Go ye and *preach the Gospel.*" To His Church, to His disciples of every clime and time, every race and place, this is the Master's ultimatum: "If ye continue in My Word, then are ye My disciples indeed" (John 8:31). Or as the Lord expressed Himself Matt. 10:27: "What I tell you in darkness, that speak ye in light; and what ye hear in the ear, that preach ye upon the housetops." They are to speak out fearlessly, holding nothing back, but publishing the whole counsel of God, all that He has revealed to them. In perfect accord with this injunction of his Lord, St. Peter admonishes the readers of his First Epistle: "If any man speak, let him speak as the oracles of God" (I Pet. 4:11). It cannot be emphasized too often and too strongly: Not the Church, and no one in the Church, has any authority at any time, in any case, under any circumstances to exalt or elevate human opinion above the Word or grant human philosophy the right to sit in judgment on divine revelation. Rather must the Christian's attitude be one of "casting down imaginations and every high thing that exalteth itself against the knowledge of God and bringing into captivity every thought to the obedience of Christ" (II Cor. 10:5).

Authority of the Word vs. the Scientists.—That, therefore, reduces to utter absurdity and folly the notion quite current with the unthinking public and the warped minds of the 20th-century wiseacres, who seem to think that because a scientist has demonstrated an extensive knowledge of the things that pertain to the particular field in which he has done intensive research work, he must also be an authority on matters religious. As if knowledge and understanding of spiritual things could be had without the Spirit's divine enlightenment and guidance, even without the most elementary knowledge of the Scriptures. The Scriptural truth will ever apply: "The natural man receiveth not the things of the Spirit of God, for they are foolishness unto him; neither can he know them, because they are spiritually discerned," I Cor. 2:14. (Burbank-Edison, *Lutheran Witness,* Vol. XLV, pp. 43, 349, 127; Vol. L, page 370.)

In this connection it will be highly proper to take cognizance of the efforts that are under way to bring about doctrinal unity between us of the Synodical Conference and the Lutherans of the American Lutheran Conference. Nothing would tend more to the glory of God; nothing contribute more to the healing of the "affliction of Joseph"; nothing bring greater joy to the hearts of distressed Christians; nothing aid more in removing the offense of doctrinal disruption between those who at one time were brethren of the same faith than if this were accomplished. We hope and pray for this, but must nevertheless stand firm in our resolve that this shall not be effected at the expense of the Word. Not a single divine truth must be sacrificed. There must be no compromising. There can be no yielding to halfway measures. There shall be no denying of a single clearly revealed Bible statement, no matter how insignificant it may seem to be. "The Scripture cannot be broken," John 10:35. (*Der Lutheraner,* May 15, 1945, Fuerbringer: "Eine Aufgabe unserer Lutherischen Kirche.")

We Must Not Tire of Hearing the Word.—May the *lay members* of our Christian congregations never tire of hearing the eternal truths of God. The danger of the alluring trends of the times, as in the days of Paul with the people of Athens, is that people are interested "in nothing else but either to tell or to hear some new thing" (Acts 17:21). They want to be entertained. They want to be thrilled. Even so, we fear, our people are all too often impressed with the flashy but meatless generalities of the modern pulpit orator. But let them not say like Israel in the desert: "Our soul loatheth this light bread" (Num. 21:5), but rather like the Psalmist: "Oh, how love I Thy Law! It is my meditation all the day. . . . Order my steps in Thy Word" (Ps. 119:97, 133), always remembering the inspired wisdom of St. Paul's advice to the Philippians: "To write the same things to you, to me indeed is not grievous, but for you it is safe" (Phil. 3:1); it saves you from error's maze and the pitfalls of science falsely so called, from the doubts of despair and other great shame and vice. May it be the prayer of every minister of the Gospel for himself and of the congregation for their pastor: "Take not the Word of truth utterly out of my (our pastor's) mouth" (Ps. 119:43), lest the Lord in His wrath "send them strong delusion that they should believe a lie," II Thess. 2:11. (Cf. *Theological Quarterly*, Vol. II, p. 505.)

"When the heart tires of God's Word," says Luther, "and no longer regards it as its most treasured possession, the devil has free access and may introduce all manner of errors and falsehood. . . . Who no longer finds the heavenly bread palatable will not last very long spiritually; his spiritual death is imminent" (III:1737).·

THESIS III

Authority in the Church must be in perfect accord with, can never be subversive of, or conflict with, that Christian liberty which is ours through the redemption in Christ Jesus.

Christian liberty is a glorious fruit of Christ's redemption. It is perfect freedom from everything that formerly held sin-troubled man in terror, fear, and spiritual bondage. By Christian liberty we mean freedom from the curse and dominion of the Law of God, freedom from the ceremonial and political laws of Moses, and freedom of conscience from all man-made, ecclesiastical ordinances, mandates, and regulations. (Cf. Western District, 25, 26; *Lehre und Wehre*, p. 15; Central, 5; Wisconsin, 8, 9; Canada, 15; Northern, 5.)

Freedom From the Curse of the Law.—In Gal. 3:13 we read: "Christ hath redeemed us from the curse of the Law." Hence "there is now no condemnation in them which are in Christ Jesus" (Rom. 8:1). Why is this so? And how can that be? Simply because Christ in our stead bore the curse, suffered the punishment, paid the guilt. Hence no accusations, no demands, no charges can be raised against us in the court of the Most High. (Rom. 8:33-34.) There is no possibility of the wrath of God to flare up anew, because it spent all its fury on our Substitute. There is no possibility of the Accuser to get a hearing against us, for, as John the Seer tells us in Rev. 12:10, there is no possibility of our guilt ever again engaging God's attention; for Christ has blotted out "the handwriting of ordinances that was against us, which was contrary to us, and took it out of the way, nailing it to the Cross" (Col. 2:14-15).

Free From the Dominion of the Law.—In the same manner all true believers in Christ are free from *the dominion of the Law*. In Rom. 6:14 we read: "Ye are not under the Law, but under grace." The Law is not our lord. The Law does not command, rule, regulate, govern our attitudes and actions. Christians have received "the adoption of sons." Most assuredly, the children of God are guided by the Law, but they follow it, they live up to it, they walk in it, not by coercion, but by willing, cheerful, love-prompted obedience, according to the motto of Paul: "I delight in the Law of the Lord after the inward man" (Rom. 7:22). The Apostle therefore calls the Gospel "the Law of the spirit of life in Christ" (Rom. 8:2), because it, and not the Law, is the motive power. It is the Gospel that gives life, initiative, willingness, and strength to the regenerate heart of the child of God. A Christian does not need to be driven.

The Law has never yet improved the attitudes of men nor ennobled their characters. True Christians you need only to "beseech by the mercies of God" (Rom. 12:1), and action will follow. The love of God is shed abroad in their hearts by the Holy Ghost. (Rom. 5:5.) "For ye have not received the spirit of bondage again to fear, but ye have received the Spirit of adoption, whereby we cry: Abba, Father" (Rom. 8:15). In other words, as free children of God they stand above the Law and no longer as unwilling slaves under the Law, "knowing this," as St. Paul writes to Timothy, "that the Law is not made for a righteous man, but for the lawless and disobedient, for the ungodly and for sinners, for unholy and profane," I Tim. 1:9. (*Triglot*, Formula of Concord, Art. VI, p. 962:5; Augs. Conf., XXVI, p. 90:51. Luther, XIX:1556f., 1559.)

Does that mean that a Christian has no further use for or need of the Law? Most assuredly not. Christians, and the best among them, are human beings with a double personality as long as they live in the flesh. Through faith in Christ Jesus they have experienced the new birth. They were regenerated. The Spirit of God has given them a new heart, a new mind, a new will. They have become new creatures. But what the Bible calls "the old man," so named because it is our inherited human depravity, was not changed, is incorrigible, was born a scoundrel, and will remain one until he will be put off when the image of God will be fully restored. And so Paul says: "I see another law in my members, warring against the law of my mind and bringing me into captivity to the law of sin which is in my members" (Rom. 7:23). "I find, then, a law," Paul had stated, "that when I would do good, evil is present with me." Thus a Christian is spirit and is flesh. According to the spirit he delights in godliness, according to the flesh he delights in wickedness. Of this state of affairs Paul is thoroughly ashamed and greatly distressed, and he expressed the utter disgust of every child of God with this traitor in his bosom when he exclaimed: "O wretched man that I am! Who shall deliver me from the body of this death?" For our old Adam therefore we still need the Law, and we ought to apply it vigorously and unsparingly. They that are Christ's are to crucify their flesh daily. (Gal. 5:24.) That is a painful operation, but it needs to be done if we would retain the precious liberty that cost Christ so dearly, for the old man "is corrupt according to the deceitful lusts" (Eph. 4:22). If permitted to have his way, he will soon lead us back into the slavery of our former lusts.

Freedom From Ceremonial Laws.—Our Christian liberty furthermore consists in perfect freedom of conscience from the ceremonial and political laws of Moses and also from all man-made ecclesiastical laws, regulations, and ordinances. Thus the ceremonial laws of Moses that governed and regulated all things pertaining to the worship in its various aspects were divine laws for the Jews during the Old Testament dispensation. But when the fullness of time was come and God sent the Messiah, whom all these laws and ordinances foreshadowed, these ceremonial laws ceased to have a purpose and were therefore abrogated and abolished by God Himself, as is evident from Col. 2:16-17. (The Seventh-Day Adventists.) The holy writer has the entire ceremonial system of the Old Testament in mind. First he does away with all the ordinances that regarded the consumption of meats and drinks. Then he speaks of the three types of Jewish festivals: "holy day," or yearly festivals; "new moon," or monthly festivals; "Sabbath days," or weekly festivals. And with regard to all of them he admonishes the New Testament Christians not to let anyone bind the observance of these matters upon their consciences or sit in judgment on and condemn them if they no longer observe them.

We do not observe Sunday because of any divine command, but in the free and unrestricted exercise of our Christian liberty. As Christ, when the Pharisees criticized Him for permitting the disciples to pluck the ears of grain on a Sabbath day and eat, told these pious legalists: "The Son of Man is Lord even of the Sabbath day," so those who through faith are one with Christ are in and with Christ also lords of the Sabbath. Luther: "He that believes on the Lord Jesus is a Lord over all laws and will not be accursed by any."

A lucid and most convincing illustration of this truth is recorded by Paul in Romans 14. The occasion was the issue that had risen in the congregation at Rome, which consisted of Jews and Gentiles, over such questions as: Is it lawful for Christians, in the public market, to buy meat that had originally been slaughtered for purposes of worship in the temples of the idols? Again: Should the Old Testament festive days still be observed or, at least, reverenced and remembered? In both instances Paul assures them that it is a matter of personal privilege and Christian liberty. Each may do as he pleases. In neither case can one set up a law or rule of conduct for the other. It is purely a question of private judgment. As conscience dictates, so must each behave himself. No law of God is involved, and the only guideline to be observed is that "every man be fully persuaded in his own mind," which means that each individual, irrespective of the course he follows, must be sure of his step and do nothing in a doubting spirit. If he eats the meat in question, let him make sure that he has no compunctions about it. If he chooses not to observe certain days or festivals, let him have the conviction that it is his prerogative. Luther: "Let him neither waver nor doubt, but be sure it is no sin before God whether he eat or do not eat." Concerning matters therefore that are neither commanded nor forbidden by God a Christian may act according to the measure of his faith, *i. e.,* according to his Christian understanding and the knowledge he has of the revealed truths of God, and according to the extent to which his action would be conducive and profitable unto godliness and promote the honor of God among men. (Augs. Conf., Art. X.)

Two points should, perhaps, receive a little more attention. The first concerns matters that are neither commanded nor forbidden in the Bible. In the terminology of the Church these are called *adiaphora*. We understand this term to apply to things that are of a neutral character, *i. e.,* of and by themselves neither good nor bad, because the Bible has neither bidden nor forbidden them, neither demanded nor condemned them. They are therefore a matter of Christian liberty. In the line of ecclesiastical "middle things" the Formula of Concord mentions ceremonies and church rites (Art. X), to which we might add the liturgy, the clerical garb, stole, surplice and gown, crucifix, candles, paintings, altar, statues, etc. In the sphere of secular, physical, and material things we may mention meats, alcoholic drinks, smoking, games, entertainments, our personal dress, etc. In the political realm, whether a country should be a democracy, a kingdom, or an empire, etc.

Though it is true that a Christian may use all these things with perfect freedom of choice and pleasure, it must nevertheless be remembered that an adiaphoron may and will cease to be an adiaphoron and become a forbidden thing to the individual user if and when he becomes guilty of flagrant abuse or sinful use of an adiaphoron.

Again, we have several times mentioned "conscience" in connection with the use of adiaphora. Conscience plays an important part in these matters. Conscience decides whether I may avail myself of an adiaphoron or not. (The case of working on Sunday, smoking, drinking, alcoholic drinks, playing cards, fire and life insurance, etc.) What, then, becomes our duty if we would have a peaceful conscience and preserve our Christian liberty? We must inform our conscience by being diligent readers of the Scriptures, thereby growing in Christian knowledge, by learning the will of God more perfectly, by correcting erroneous conceptions. Then, and then only, will we be able to take firm steps in every issue that confronts us. (I Pet. 2:2; Rom. 12:2; Phil. 1:10; Eph. 4:14.)

Freedom From Man-Made Laws.—If this Christian liberty implies perfect freedom even from all those ceremonial and political laws which in times past, *i. e.,* in the Old Testament, were God's very own laws, then it must be most obvious that no man-made ecclesiastical laws, regulations, and ordinances can be foisted upon the consciences of the free and sovereign people of God against their will and persuasion. Paul therefore admonishes the Galatian Christians: "Stand fast therefore in the liberty wherewith Christ hath made us free, and be not entangled again with the yoke of bondage" (Gal. 5:1). That danger has raised its ugly head at all times in the Church, already in the first church at Jerusalem and soon after Paul's first missionary journey when there were those who insisted that the Gentile Christians, concerning whom Paul and Barnabas reported, submit to circumcision and other Old Testament ordinances. This threatened to cause serious disruptions and even schism in the early Church until it was adjusted at the council in Jerusalem. Whoever attempts to burden the consciences of God's people with injunctions not commanded by God, or to put upon the

necks of the disciples the yoke of oppressive laws, or to force them
to yield to regulations of purely human coinage, causes confusion
of minds, distraction of souls, corruption and ultimate dissolution of
Christian liberty. "Ye are bought with a price," Paul warns the
Corinthians, "be not ye servants of men," I Cor. 7:23. (*Triglot,*
Augs. Conf., XXVIII, p. 90:53; XXVI, p. 72:21; Apology, VII-VIII,
p. 540:39; XV, p. 322:31; Smalcald Articles, p. 504:5.)

No pastor, church council, or synod has the authority to impose
upon a Christian congregation any legislation on which the congregation has had no vote or to which it has not consented Nor must
a congregation by intimidation or any kind of moral force be tricked
into consenting to measures that have been prepared for their
adoption. Nor must adoption of any resolution be sought before it
has become reasonably sure that all understand what they are voting
for. Such and similar tactics are a shameful effrontery to, and an
unpardonable infringement upon, the majesty of one of God's
sovereign congregations and a grave offense against the priceless
liberty that is their Christ-wrought, blood-bought prerogative.

Do such things actually happen? (Pastor Grabau of the Buffalo
Synod.) Even in our own circles during the dark days of the Saxon
colonies in Perry Co., Mo., our fathers passed through sad experiences of spiritual tyranny. In fact, there was little left of their Christian liberty. To this day we ought to recognize the lesson those
Saxon Christians learned for the blessed benefit of subsequent generations. Indeed, we should be thankful that it was upon the insistence of the St. Louis group of congregations that the paragraph
was written into the constitution of Synod that "in its relation to its
members the Synod is not an ecclesiastical government, exercising
legislative or coercive powers, and with respect to the individual
congregation's right of self-government it is but an advisory body."
Accordingly, resolutions passed by Synod at its triennial sessions
are not to be considered as automatically binding on the congregations of Synod and do not become law until a majority (in constitutional matters, two thirds) of the congregations, either by actual
vote or by acquiescence, have endorsed such resolutions. However,
if this is not to be a dead letter and if our congregations would
retain their priestly rights and their Christian liberty, it behooves
them, not negligently and carelessly to ignore or forget about the
Synod's resolutions or let others attend to them, but to discuss them

in their meetings and communicate the result of their deliberations to their proper authorities. Let us exercise our Christian prerogative. We often lose what we have by not using it.

Are, then, all laws incompatible with Christian liberty? What we have said with regard to any abuse of authority or any infringement upon our Christian liberty must not be understood to mean, or to give encouragement to the notion, that all laws and regulations in the Church are incompatible with, and a curtailment of, Christian liberty. To take that attitude would throw gates ajar for all manner of disorder, confusion, and chaos. No, the Church of God is not a lawless, disorderly body. Its motto, which the Lord Himself has given her, is rather: "Let all things be done decently and in order" (I Cor. 14:40). Let all regulations and laws governing adiaphora be the expression of the collective thought of the majority, arrived at in the unhampered exercise of their Christian liberty. It must never be said of a congregation—or of the Synod, for that matter—that a certain resolution was "railroaded through." On the other hand, however, if a resolution has the endorsement of a majority, the minority should cheerfully yield, rightly assuming that in a meeting of Christian brethren all have voted their honest conviction, that therefore the opinion of the majority best expresses, promotes, and safeguards the best interest of the cause. If therefore all will conscientiously observe these points, our Christian liberty will suffer no harm.

When Luther says that we cannot afford to give up or forego our Christian liberty, it follows of necessity that whoever does not insist on his Christian liberty is in grave danger of losing the certainty of his salvation. The sects impose much that in their opinion reflects an advanced stage of sanctified living and constitutes a closer approach to perfection. It is, however, of far greater importance that we retain our Christian liberty than have the reputation of being exceptionally pious people. For we cannot possibly preserve the certainty of our state of grace if we do not conserve our Christian liberty. Reference might be made here to Melanchthon, who also failed in this respect and to whom even Calvin wrote that he harmed the Church more by his partial weakening than a hundred others by their total apostasy. (Canada District, 1900, p. 36.)—It is interesting to note that the Reformed churches, when placing their anathema on alcoholic drinks, card playing, Sunday baseball, and so forth, often quote a passage in support of their pietistic claims that says the very opposite of what they would have it say. We refer to Col. 2:21.)

Abuses of Christian Liberty.—However, offenses against Christian liberty are not only committed by burdening the consciences of God's free children with rules and regulations without or against their consent, but also when Christians use their freedom in order to *cover up their sinful attitudes or habits.* That is done when church people say: I do not have to go to church every Sunday. I do not have to partake of the Lord's Supper frequently. I do not have to send my child to the Christian day school. I do not have to contribute in proportion to my income, etc. The Apostle has just such cases in mind when he says (Gal. 5:13): "Brethren, ye have been called unto liberty; only use not liberty for an occasion to the flesh." In a similar vein St. Peter warns: "As free, and not using your liberty for a cloak of maliciousness, but as the servants of God" (I Pet. 2:16). Under the same pretense others refuse to comply with congregational resolutions. (Rom. 14:10-13, 15, 20-21; I Cor. 6:12; 8:8-13.) Again, it is a gross but very common abuse of Christian liberty if it is used as an excuse for *shirking work* that we might do and should do. How may the pastor be guilty? the teacher? the voter? the elder? etc. "My brethren, these things ought not so to be" (James 3:10).

Thesis IV

Since in the last analysis all authority in the Church reverts back to the spiritual priesthood of all believers, of which, in fact, it is an emanation, those who have been given authority cannot lord it over the Christian congregation. They are stewards rather than masters, servants rather than lords, and accountable to their God and to their respective congregations.

In this thesis we touch, perhaps, on the main issue, or vital point, in connection with the question of authority in the Church. All authority in the Church, in the final analysis, has its origin in the spiritual priesthood of God's people. We have already touched on this in Thesis I, but shall have to view it here from a somewhat different angle.

Speaking of pastors first, we note that it is indeed a peculiar privilege and the greatest honor that can come to man to be called by God through one of his sovereign congregations as an ambassador of Christ and a pastor of His flock. Listen to what Paul has to say about his ministry: "I thank Christ Jesus, our Lord, who hath enabled me for that He counted me faithful, putting me into the ministry" (I Tim. 1:12), "according to the glorious Gospel of the blessed God, which was committed to my trust" (I Tim. 1:11). But he emphasizes it again and again that in this glorious office he is "*a minister*," that is, a servant of his people. (Col. 1:25-29.) And he realized that he must give account to God for his ministry. (Rom. 14:12.) No wonder that he writes Timothy: "If a man desire the office of a bishop, he desireth a good work" (I Tim. 3:1).

The same applies to the teachers in our Christian schools. A teacher is truly divinely called and by that call has received authority from the congregation, the authority to feed the lambs of Christ, which, after all, is the sacred responsibility of a *servant* of God's chosen people, as is evident from the heart-searching question of the Master: "Simon Peter, lovest thou Me?" (John 21:15.)

Then there are in the Christian congregation others that have been given authority, given authority because entrusted with the performance of essential tasks for the maintenance and general well-being of the Kingdom (elders, trustees, treasurer, Sunday school teachers, etc.). But again theirs is an authority which is a *privilege of serving;* the high honor which is *an opportunity for humble ministration* in the Church. All of them in their way and for their particular purposes and duties have received authority from the congregation, which, as far as it goes, must be respected by those who have established such offices, but which none of the incumbents must use to rule over the congregation. (I Pet. 5:3.)

Indeed, the members of the Church of Christ are an elite company. They have high standing, all are "free men." None of them therefore must be treated as serfs or slaves. They are sovereigns in their God-given rights which no one must shorten, shrink, or weaken. From them and through them all officers in the Church receive their right to function. How illogical, therefore, even from a purely human point of view, if such officers would want to dictate to, and rule over, the members of the household of God. But the Lord will not suffer such attitudes. When therefore the sons of Zebedee, in a moment of carnal ambition, requested seats of honor above the other disciples, the Lord administered a very stern rebuke to them. (Matt. 20:25-27.) At another occasion the Master expresses His warning in this fashion: "Be ye not called Rabbi; for one is your Master, even Christ, and all ye are brethren; and call no man your father upon the earth, for one is your Father, which is in heaven. Neither be ye called masters, for one is your Master, even Christ" (Matt. 23:8-10). The same warning is issued by St. Peter (I Pet. 5:3).

The Apostles themselves were very careful not to offend against this. When writing to the Corinthians in order to remind them of the collection the various congregations were to raise for the famine-stricken Christians at Jerusalem, St. Paul, in a very tactful way, tells those Christians: "I speak not by commandment, but by occasion of the forwardness of others and to prove the sincerity of your love" (II Cor. 8:8). Nor is there any ambiguity in these words of Paul: "Not for that we have dominion over your faith, but are helpers of your joy" (II Cor. 1:24).

Pastors Are Servants.—Pastors are stewards rather than masters, they are servants rather than lords, and should always be aware of the fact that they are accountable to God and to their congregations. (I Cor. 4:1; I Pet. 5:3.) Surely, of all the Apostles of the Lord none achieved greater results, none accomplished more than St. Paul, and none humbled himself more, none developed a deeper service consciousness than he. "Though I be free from all men," he tells the Corinthians, "yet have I made myself servant unto all that I might gain the more" (I Cor. 9:19ff.). Or as he puts it II Cor. 4:5: "We preach not ourselves, but Christ Jesus, the Lord; and ourselves your servants for Jesus' sake." The public ministry does not constitute a class or caste superior to the laity.

Pastors, then, have no right to demand obedience in purely external matters. They are exceeding their authority when they legislate, prescribe, dictate, impose innovations, customs, regulations, which are plainly the affair of the voting assembly or even of the various organizations in the congregations. The congregation remains the court of last resort and final authority. True, the pastor is, by reason of his position and training, the leader and guide, the counselor and adviser, the one to instruct and inform, to admonish and warn, to encourage and urge his people in behalf of a righteous cause, be it in the interest of the home congregation or the Church at large, but he must never lord it over his congregation.

Pastors Not Slaves.—That does not mean that pastors are slaves of the congregation. At times members of a congregation try to lord it over their pastor or teacher. That is just as improper and wicked, just as serious an abuse of authority as if the pastor usurped his position and standing. The members, too, must stay within their bounds. If they are "kings" before God, so is their pastor; if they are "priests," so is he; if they have rights which the pastor must respect, then the pastor, too, has rights which the congregation must hold sacred. Let them always bear in mind that while their pastor and teacher derive their authority to perform from the congregation, they at the same time are the Lord's ambassadors, the Lord's servants. When, therefore, certain members in the Corinthian congregation cast ugly insinuations and passed unfair and unwarranted judgment on Paul, he told them frankly: "With me it is a very small thing that I should be judged of you or of man's judgment; yea, I judge not mine own self . . . but He that judgeth me is the Lord" (I Cor. 4:3-4). Let us heed what we have learned from Luther's Small Catechism under the caption "What the Hearers Owe to Their Pastors." (Heb. 13:17.)

The Church of God is Intended by God to Be the Most Complete Democracy.—Here all are brothers, none is master, not even the pastor; all are servants, none are lords, not even the deacon who has been in office for twenty years. Here all have equal rights, no one is a privileged character, not even the wealthy Mr. Jones. (See James 1.)

In the Church there can and should be unity of spirit in the bond of peace, brotherly relationships, happy co-operation, communal interests (Eph. 4:3-6), mutual respect. All are laborers together with God," (I Cor. 3:9). *Cliques and parties* in a congregation are possible only where the authority has been abused, where carnal selfishness has replaced mutual spiritual helpfulness, considerateness, and love. The congregation at Corinth was on the very verge of disruption because divisions and contentions had made deep inroads and poisoned the minds of the members with jealousy and distrust (I Cor. 1:11ff.). The Gospel of Jesus Christ cannot thrive, the work of the Church cannot prosper, where such things are going on. "I beseech you, brethren," Paul pleads with these people, "by the name of our Lord Jesus Christ, that ye speak the same thing that there be no divisions among you, but that ye be perfectly joined together in the same mind and in the same judgment" (I Cor. 1:10). Things were in a similar sorry plight in the congregations of Galatia. Those congregations were cut asunder by arrogant, loud-mouthed Judaizers. False doctrine, carelessness in doctrinal matters, lukewarmness over against the truth, and weak-kneed tolerance of error will take the stamina out of any congregation, so that the works of the flesh, all of them, as enumerated by St. Paul—and, perhaps, foremost among them, envyings, factions, and divisions—will find that congregation an easy prey of the old evil Foe. (Gal. 4:19-21.) To the doctrinally well-informed Galatians, Paul therefore uses the ironical and sarcastic approach: "If ye bite and devour one another, take heed that ye be not consumed one of another" (Gal. 5:15).

THESIS V

Authority in the Church must be administered (1) in the fear of God, (2) for the welfare of the Church, (3) in the interest of our fellow men, and (4) unto the glory of God. All authority in the Church must therefore be faith-inspired, love-filled, service-minded, and performed in a spirit of sacrificing helpfulness.

1

Matt. 24:45-47; 25:21; Rom. 2:17-24; Eph. 5:15-16; Col. 4:17; I Tim. 3:1; I Tim. 6:20. St. Paul's example: I Cor. 8:12, 22, 23. All should be active "fellow citizens with the saints" (Eph. 2:19). None only "guests." No place for "drones" and "loafers."

2

The entire corps of workers must be motivated by a single purpose, the welfare of the Church. (Ps. 137:5-6; 84:10.) No organization (men's club) has a right to exist unless it serve pre-eminently the cause of the Gospel.

3

Moses (Ex. 32:33); Paul (Rom. 9:1-3); Ps. 139:23-24.

4

John the Baptist (John 3:30); I Pet. 4:11. John 5:44. It is not important that the pastor become famous, but that the Lord be glorified.—The church choir (soloists) that performs for personal glory is a nuisance in the service.

With the above motivations in mind, let us make a few practical applications.

Every congregation must observe some kind of system in the management of its financial affairs. That is in the interest of good order and plain ordinary fair dealing. Paul observed that, too, when he raised the collection for the famine sufferers at Jerusalem. The business matters of a congregation must also be handled in a businesslike manner, according to such methods as are applicable in a given congregation. That, however, does not mean that the procedure must be harsh, cold, and uncharitable. On the contrary, the law of Christian love must be the guide line in all financial transactions. It cannot be the purpose of this paper to enter into a detailed discussion or a minute investigation of various systems. Suffice it to choose a point or two at random to illustrate the application suggested in our thesis.

1. No system should become the accepted method of collecting funds until it has been discussed in a brotherly, thoroughly ample fashion and adopted, not by a scant majority, but by a good margin.

2. After this has been done, the law of Christian love would demand that the minority fall in line, and yet it will hardly be proper to invoke disciplinary procedure if a few individuals do not at once see fit to comply, for instance, in the case of the envelope system. Patience, tact, and the good example of the majority will eventually bring them around.

3. If a congregation employs the so-much-per-communicant taxing system, we feel that it has only itself to blame if it runs into all kinds of difficulties and perennial deficits. The members in the distant past may have been able to adopt such a system by general consent, but the system is legalistic and lacks the evangelical approach.

4. *Pledges.* The pledge system has its justification, yet meets with frequent disapproval and even with bitter antagonism. Why? Might it be that the congregation handled it in an unevangelical and even in an unreasonable manner? It has happened that a congregation demanded of a member who asked for a dismissal to a sister congregation that he first pay the full amount of his pledge, although only a few months of the year had elapsed. If such practice is indulged in, we need not be surprised if members become reluctant to pledge at all.

5. The *Christian day school* is a precious institution. It has rightly been called "the Church's little children's Paradise." There can be no question that it is the best means of giving children that careful Christian training demanded by the Lord when He admonishes parents to "bring up their children in the nurture and admonition of the Lord" (Eph. 6:4). And it is the most effectual agency for safeguarding the Church's future by reason of a well-indoctrinated laity. No Christian congregation ought to be fully satisfied until it has established a Christian day school in its midst, and no parents should feel quite at ease if they do not send their children to the Christian day school available for them. And yet, while a congregation ought to put forth every effort and offer every reasonable inducement to get all the fathers and mothers to send their children, failure on the part of parents to do so can hardly, of and by itself, constitute occasion for church discipline, unless absolute spiritual neglect of the child or open despising of the Word can be laid to the charge of such parents. You cannot legislate parents into the Christian educational system, you must evangelize them into it. After all, the parochial school is not a divine institution, but a human expediency.

6. Again it is eminently proper and should be the aspiration of every communicant male member of the congregation to become a voting member as soon as he has reached the stipulated age. But it is turning an essential Gospel privilege into a legalistic "must" when the constitution of a congregation states that at the age of 21 every young man of the congregation automatically becomes a voting member and is expected to attend the meetings of the voting membership.

7. The question of *confirmation age* often becomes a controversial issue because of some ironclad regulation on the statute books. If an age limit is desirable, let it come in the form of a flexible suggestion, which takes all circumstances into consideration, especially the child's maturity and its ability to grasp the Christian essentials, on which latter point the pastor as a rule is a more competent judge. A child of fourteen may be less ready to be confirmed than a child of twelve. This is not to be interpreted as meaning that we advocate early confirmations. We believe in maturity.

Thesis VI

We have reserved the closing chapter of our paper for a brief consideration of a phase of congregational authority that has not always received reverent and conscientious attention. We refer to the prerogative a congregation exercises in connection with the call of a pastor or a teacher. What authority does a Christian congregation have? If all Christians are a royal priesthood before God, then they have a right to say who of their fellow priests should perform the several functions of that priesthood in their behalf and in their stead. In other words, the members of a Christian congregation have the authority to choose the man, pastor or teacher, to whom they would entrust the public preaching and teaching of the Word and the public administration of the Sacraments. We cannot emphasize that fact too strongly. The calling of a pastor or a teacher is the sovereign right of the Christian congregation, though only two or three compose that congregation. (Matt. 18:20.) As certainly as all spiritual rights, powers, and keys belong to them, just as certainly they have the right to call for themselves one of the "evangelists, pastors, or teachers" which the ascended Lord has given as gifts to His Church and delegate unto him the work of the ministry. The Lord no longer calls immediately, as He did the Prophets and the Apostles, but mediately through the Christian congregation, as is evident from Acts 1:15-20; Acts 6:2-6; 13:1-3; II Cor. 8:19. If Titus 1:5 and Acts 14:23 seem to say that the Apostles without collaboration of the respective congregations "ordained elders," it might be well to take note of Chemnitz's comment on these passages. The expression "ordained" in the original signifies a stretching forth of the hand and by raising of hands to choose or elect. It is taken from the custom of the Greeks to cast their vote or to indicate their approval by raising the hand. Paul and Barnabas have therefore not forced these presbyters upon the congregations against their will or without their consent. (Texas District, 1915, page 30.) A congregation therefore dare not be denied the right to choose its own pastor or teacher. It is an infringement upon the God-given privilege of a congregation when in some Reformed Churches the bishop is given authority to delegate to the individual congregations the pastor who is to serve them for the next term or when in state churches the consistory assumes that function. In the Lutheran Church, particularly in our Synod, strict regard is had for the congregation's right to call. That is also scrupulously observed by our boards of missions. They are careful not to curtail the priestly rights of a congregation. They recognize the God-given privilege of the smallest congregation to call its own pastor. In many instances, however, the small mission congregations will find it to be more expedient, and even safer, to delegate to the Board of Missions the right to act in their stead and, in conjunction with the College of Presidents and the faculties of the respective seminaries, call the man whom they consider fit for their particular local needs. That is sensible. For in the vast majority of cases they would be completely at a loss to know whom to call. Even self-supporting congregations will do wisely if they take the District President into their confidence and let him suggest available men. That, of course, is no easy task for the District President, and he will have to exercise judgment and tact when he recommends candidates, lest he disappoint the respective congregations and thereby undermine their confidence in his good judgment.

We are here approaching a matter of a delicate nature and cannot emphasize too definitely and too earnestly the serious responsibilities that are involved. Christian consideration and love, frankness and fairness of heart and mind, unselfish attitudes, reasonable demands, a good understanding of their mutual interests and needs are some of the essential prerequisites for the God-pleasing handling of a call. These prerequisites need to be sought in fervent prayer. If calls have not been a success, if the wrong man go to the wrong place, may it have been that someone somewhere offended against one or more of the points mentioned? Was the congregation too exacting in its choice, too selfish in its demands, too inconsiderate in its expectations? Was their prayer for God's presence and guidance too superficial and formal to be sincere and thoughtful? Was there an unholy stubbornness on the part of a few, undue and tactless counseling of the vacancy pastor? Was there improper, because unsolicited or unwarranted, interference by "outside advisers"? Was there too much pressure from synodical officials? Were there even self-recommendations by men anxious to get the call? Did the congregation, contrary to its obvious needs, choose the man who was willing to serve for a smaller salary rather than to raise the salary to generally accepted and badly needed levels?

All these things amount either to a reprehensible curtailment of spiritual rights or to meddling with congregational affairs—or to a shameful abuse of congregational authority. May we be ever solicitous of the sovereignty of the Lord's people! "Know ye that the Lord He is God. It is He that made us (them) and not we ourselves (they themselves). We (they) are His people and the sheep of His pasture" (Ps. 100:3).

We take a peep into the meeting of a congregation which has lost its pastor. It is a solemn and a serious affair. They are therefore assembled in the fear of God, and beseeching the Lord to guide them in their choice of a new shepherd, they proceed to consider the various candidates *legitimately entered* upon the list of choosable men. Those are anxious moments in the life of a congregation. Humanly speaking, the future well-being of their congregation will depend upon the action it takes on that occasion. They bear a definite responsibility over against the present and even the next generation. And they are accountable to their God for the use they make of their authority. He will guide them if they will let Him. Let there be no doubt or misgivings about that, but they must conscientiously seek to do His will in every particular.

It must also be borne in mind that the calling congregation must not be content only to serve its own interests. It must also be *solicitous of the interests of the congregation whose pastor they plan to call*. We therefore ask: Will their will coincide with the will of the Lord if a congregation inconsiderately insists on calling a man who has but recently become the pastor of a sister congregation? Will they do the Lord's bidding if they let themselves be guided solely by monetary considerations, outward appearance, size of family? Is it wise to insist on calling a young man when size and prevailing conditions in the congregation clearly call for an experienced pastor? Is it a proper attitude when a congregation, financially well able, attempts to get a pastor or teacher at the lowest possible salary or refuses to call a man, admittedly recognized to have the necessary qualifications, because "he lives too far and transportation costs would be too high"? Is it right to stipulate in the call that the congregation will pay so and so much for traveling expenses, but that the pastor or teacher must take care of all that is over and above that sum? When calling a teacher, should not a congregation bear with the brethren of a sister congregation by stating that they will gladly permit the teacher to complete the school term before he transfer to them? This, by the way, is the policy adopted by the Texas District and also by Synod's College of Presidents.

Now let us turn to the congregation whose pastor or teacher receives the call. What will be their attitude? There are those who at once resent it that another congregation dares to "covet" their minister or teacher. They fail to understand that in certain circumstances they are duty bound to let their workers transfer to another part of God's kingdom. They have the idea that after a minister has once become their pastor, it is their privilege to keep him for themselves. So some are offended when their pastor gets a call. They become stubborn. They refuse to attend the meeting at which the call is to be considered and evaluated. On the other hand, others who usually don't attend the voters' meeting flock to this meeting, purposing under all circumstances to cut the matter short by simply demanding that the pastor or teacher stay. They argue: We do not want a change. But what if the Lord wants it? They say: We have a good pastor or teacher, one who is just the right man for us. But what if the Lord thinks he is even better fit for his flock at the other place? They say: If our pastor or teacher leaves us, this congregation will go to pieces; or the school will disintegrate. But we ask: Is your congregation dependent upon or built upon your pastor or upon Christ? Or is your pastor or teacher indispensable? Will the Lord be at a loss how to sustain you or provide for you, because your pastor left you? They say: We may have to wait a long time before we get another man; workers are scarce. But, O ye of little faith and slow to believe the divine promises, is the Lord mocking you when He says: "Pray ye the Lord of the harvest that He send forth laborers into the harvest"? Will He disappoint you? And even if you do have to wait, what of it? May the Lord not have something to do with that for your good? Or is He going to ask you, His children, to do something that will be harmful to you and His cause? They say: It cost us a lot of money to move our pastor or teacher down here several years ago. Can anyone expect us to incur such expenses anew? But didn't He who says: "All the gold and silver is Mine," supply the funds at the time? And can't He do it again? Aren't you ungrateful and extremely unappreciative of the spiritual blessings with which a bountiful and gracious God overshadowed you? But here is the climax of a pitiful attitude—they say: If our pastor or teacher leaves us, I am through with the congregation and with Synod likewise. Friend, your old Adam wags an ugly tongue!

What is the proper attitude a congregation is to take when its pastor or teacher receives a call? A sister congregation has approached them, has sent them an appealing letter. It is a case of the royal priests in one part of the Lord's kingdom addressing the royal priests in another part of the Master's domain. Brethren approach brethren in a matter that is vital in the Lord's work. They present their problem. It pertains to the same precious cause in which both are engaged, which both carry on, for which both labor and hope and pray, to which both are devoting their time, their talents, and their daily efforts, concerning which both express their ardent aims and the innermost longings of their heart when they approach the throne of grace and plead: "Our Father, who art in heaven, Thy kingdom come." The brethren of one area are presenting to the brethren of another area their specific problem. They have lost their pastor or their teacher, as the case may be. Perhaps the Lord removed him completely from this earthly sphere and translated him into His heavenly home. Perhaps the Lord, through one of His sovereign congregations has only called him away into another field of labor that was whiter unto the harvest or larger in extent or exposed to graver dangers. At any rate, at the Lord's bidding and for reasons that lay beyond their control, they have lost their shepherd. In perfect orderliness, as becometh God's children, they met in the fear of the Lord to call a new pastor. They asked the Lord to guide them and lead them aright. Unanimously they agreed on a certain man. They had every reason to believe that this man was the Lord's choice, because the Lord was in their midst. Whether they are correct in their assumption remains to be seen. If he was the man the Lord wanted this congregation to have, then the Lord would both convince and move the hearts of his congregation to grant him a peaceful dismissal. They sent the call to the man of their choice. They expect him to weigh their arguments prayerfully. But they also address a letter to the congregation and present their reasons for calling this man, calmly, soberly, truthfully, and in as detailed a manner as seems essential. They make no overstatements, neither do they omit pertinent facts. With a prayer they send the call on its way.

Let us see first what will be the reaction of the man who receives the call. Will he decide the matter of the call by himself, or will he present the call to the congregation? There is a letter accompanying that call. That letter comes from one of God's congregations and is addressed to another congregation equally as sovereign. Can a pastor or a teacher suppress or ignore that fact? What is the verdict of the fair-minded men of the world concerning such as deliberately fail to deliver a letter sent to someone else, but in their care? Pastors and teachers do not have the "authority" to withhold from their congregation such an important document as a call. We do not mean to establish an ironclad rule, but do believe that a solemn warning is in place against any unethical conduct in this matter. It may work like a boomerang. Your action may not remain a secret. The world is not so large after all. It is shrinking almost daily. Some day members of the congregation you high-handed may meet with members of your congregation and incidentally drop a remark about the call you suppressed. We need not explore the effects of that revelation. Let us be careful not to exceed or abuse our authority.

But to return to the congregation that is being asked to release its pastor or teacher to the calling congregation! What will be its reaction, procedure, and duty? Will the authority they have permit them to dismiss the plea of their brethren with the terse, harsh, and unbrotherly declaration: We move that the call be returned without any consideration or loss of time, no matter what arguments or reasons they advance? That would be a most flagrant abuse or misuse of their authority. They have no right to do that. It rather becomes their duty as a God-fearing "royal priesthood" to examine it carefully and with the full consciousness of the responsibility they owe God and their brethren in the faith. The reasons advanced by their brethren must be met, investigated, and satisfactorily, *i. e.,* with clear and convincing counterarguments refuted before they may return the call. If they cannot overcome the arguments, if in their consciences they must admit that the points made cannot be refuted, there is but one course left for them to pursue, namely, to grant their pastor or teacher a peaceful dismissal, even if this causes heartache and bitter tears. May we bear in mind that the calling congregation places an implicit confidence in the integrity and fair-mindedness of their brethren. They, the brethren of the calling congregation, have sent no representative to plead their cause. They felt that

that should not be necessary, and it shouldn't. They are dealing not merely with friends, but with brethren.

In the last analysis, however, it will be the pastor or the teacher who must speak the deciding word. Whatever his likes or dislikes, his personal inclinations and feelings, his conscience must be the judge. Least of all must pastor or teacher be swayed by glowing compliments and glittering promises of larger salaries, better accommodations, and the like, which, by the way, not only smatters of bribery, but is a very obvious admission that they cannot meet the arguments in the call. But pastor or teacher do not improve their judgment by listening to flattery. They do not clear their vision by accepting bribes. Be honest with yourself, your brethren, and your God. Never dare to stay or go with a bothering conscience. Stay, if the reasons for staying are convincing. Go, if the reasons for going are compelling.

Of course, a situation may develop, or circumstances may arise that make it extremely difficult to decide which is the more important call, the old one or the new one. In such doubtful cases the old call takes priority over the new one.

Perhaps it should also be stated in this connection that the responsible officials of the Church, the President of the District, the Vice-Presidents, the Visitors, the Board of Missions have the authority expressly vested in them to safeguard the interests of the congregations as well as of the workers under their jurisdiction by recommending a change of parishes or fields if circumstances clearly indicate this to be desirable, feasible, and salutary.

CONCLUSION

We have again brought to our remembrance precious Gospel truths. We have meditated on the important subject of "Authority in the Church." In so doing, we have also found that we have by no means exhausted that subject. We have rather found that the farther we progressed in our discussions of this subject, the vaster became the expanse of its doctrinal importance, the richer the depth of its practical implications. Authority in the Church, as we have learned to know it, is no longer a thing to be feared and dreaded, but to be fostered, exercised, and rejoiced over. "Authority in the Church"—O precious fact! for it is the authority to tell about the forgiveness of sins through the atoning blood of Jesus Christ; the authority to proclaim the world-embracing love of God and universal reconciliation and redemption; the authority to tell the world of salvation by grace through faith, without the deeds of the Law, and to apply the precious seals of the Gospel—Baptism and the Lord's Supper—to the individual sinner for the added confirmation and assurance of his state of grace. "Authority in the Church"—O sublime prerogative! for it empowers the individual congregation to call pastors and teachers without any meddling or interference from any source and to appoint whatever workers are needed to carry on the work of the Church. "Authority in the Church"—O blessed consciousness of every worker in the Kingdom, nay, of every member of the Christian congregation, that in whatever capacity they may be serving, they are engaged in the sublimest and noblest of human efforts: the saving of souls and the glorification of the Savior! That, friends, is purpose, aim, and privilege of all authority in the Church. Surely, the lines are fallen unto us in pleasant places, yea, we have a goodly heritage. Well might we feel overwhelmed by the grandeur of our happy lot and be constrained to exclaim with Moses, and with even greater propriety than he: "What nation is there so great, who hath God so nigh unto them as the Lord our God is in all things that we call upon Him for?" (Deut. 4:7.)

May the Lord preserve unto us this glorious authority! May He give unto pastors, teachers, officers, and laymen in the Church His Holy Spirit that all may be filled with an holy awe of the authority that is theirs, that they may protect it as "the apple of their eye"; that they may exercise it without fear or favor; that they may jealously guard it from any abuse and defend it against any infringement. And now our closing prayer is: "The God of peace, that brought again from the dead our Lord Jesus, that great Shepherd of the sheep, through the blood of the everlasting covenant, make you perfect in every good work to do His will, working in you that which is well pleasing in His sight through Jesus Christ, to whom be glory forever and ever. Amen" (Heb. 13:20-21).

XXI

Mission Work in the Apostolic Age
and Its Lessons for Today

The word "mission" means "sending," and a "missionary" is "one sent." Missionaries are the "sent ones" of the Lord Jesus, ambassadors of Christ.

MISSION work dates back to the days of Adam. We read in Gen. 4:26: "Then began men to call upon the name of the Lord." Noah was a missionary. In II Pet. 2:5 he is called a "preacher of righteousness." Abraham built an altar and began to tell the Canaanites of the one true God. It is true that God promised Abraham: "Salvation is of the Jews"; but at the same time He told him: "In thee shall all families of the earth be blessed" (Gen. 12:3). The Israelites were a select people, but only "that the blessing of Abraham might come on the Gentiles through Jesus Christ" (Gal. 3:14). Many of the Israelites never had this understanding of God and looked upon salvation as for the chosen people only and in the proud spirit of pharisaism despised the Gentiles. Others, however, knew that the coming Messiah was for all people, and they lived in the spirit of the aged Simeon.

Furthermore, we know from our Old Testament that the heathen became acquainted with the one true God and were believers; for example: the Syrian nobleman, Naaman, King Nebuchadnezzar, and the Ninevites. Throughout the Old Testament the Prophets and Psalmists sang of a Messiah for all people; Psalm 87:5: "And of Zion it shall be said, This and that man was born in her." That means all sorts of people. And Is. 60:3: "And the Gentiles shall come to thy light." What the believers of the Old Testament prophesied and yearned for, happened. "But when the fullness of the time was come, God sent forth His Son, made of a woman, made under the Law, to redeem them that were under the Law, that we might receive the adoption of sons" (Gal. 4:4, 5). And what the Lord prophesied through David, Ps. 19:3, 4, came true: "There is no speech nor language where their voice is not heard. Their line is gone out through all the earth, and their words to the end of the world." In the mission work of the Apostles we see clearly the fulfillment of Old Testament prophecy.

Soon after our Lord entered upon His prophetic office, He chose twelve disciples. With these He went into the cities and villages and rural areas, and when He looked upon the spiritual barrenness of His people, He cried: "The harvest truly is plenteous, but the laborers are few; pray ye therefore the Lord of the harvest that He will send forth laborers into His harvest" (Matt. 9:37, 38). Continually He said to His people: "The time is fulfilled, and the Kingdom of God is at hand; repent ye, and believe the Gospel" (Mark 1:15). When He sent His disciples forth with the same message, He gave them power to perform miracles, to heal the sick, to raise the dead, and to drive out devils. You will notice that He also told His disciples: "Go not into the way of the Gentiles, and into any city of the Samaritans enter ye not; but go rather to the lost sheep of the house of Israel" (Matt. 10:5, 6), and we read: "And they departed and went through the towns, preaching the Gospel and healing everywhere" (Luke 9:6). Their mission work at that time was limited to the lost sheep of Israel. It was after the Cross of Calvary and the work of salvation was finished as planned from all eternity by the Father, Jesus' victory over death, the devil and hell, final and complete, that He gave His disciples the command to preach the Gospel beyond the land of Israel, to all creatures throughout the world. The entire world became a mission field. His kingdom was to be established among all people. With that command He ascended on high, and their eyes beheld Him no longer. This was His testament; this was His great command; this was their great trust. The golden apostolic age was about to begin.

THE MISSIONARY COMMAND

The missionary command we find in St. Matthew and St. Mark. Matthew reads: "Go ye therefore and teach all nations, baptizing them in the name of the Father and of the Son and of the Holy

Ghost, teaching them to observe all things whatsoever I have commanded you; and, lo, I am with you alway, even unto the end of the world" (Matt. 28:19, 20). And Mark sums it up this way: "Go ye into all the world, and preach the Gospel to every creature. He that believeth and is baptized shall be saved; but he that believeth not shall be damned" (Mark 16:15, 16). The words may be different, the thought is the same. The meaning of the command is: I, the Lord Jesus, command you, My followers, in every age, to go out into all the world, teach all people, all nations, every creature, My Gospel. Make all people My disciples. Pay no attention to national boundaries. Go everywhere where people live, and the burden of your message is to be: "He that believeth and is baptized shall be saved; he that believeth not shall be damned." What a majestic command! No man would dare to make such claims but our Lord. He alone had the right. All power is given unto Him in heaven and in earth. He redeemed all people, every creature, with the price of His own blood. Every soul that ever lived or shall live has been redeemed. He, the Son of God, and He alone, is the Savior of every soul.

Yes, the missionary command was the manifesto of a King. Jesus was about to ascend to His throne, and as He did so, He proclaimed that all power was given to Him in heaven and earth. And therefore as the King of creation He sends forth His ambassadors to the nations of the earth to call all people into His kingdom. His followers, His redeemed people, are to carry out this commission until the end of the world. With this command is the promise of His personal presence and power, His providential presence in a special sense and manner. It is a presence which carries with it all the omnipotence of the Godhead, and it is a promise that none can claim in its fullness unless they are obeying the command that precedes it. The command also includes a commission to each individual to go to individuals. Every member of the human family is to receive the offer of heaven, and everyone has an equal right in redemption. All shall inherit all things in Christ.

This manifesto of our King is the most solemn and searching word on the subject of missions in the Bible. It will meet each one of us on Judgment Day. By a miracle of God's grace He wants to use sinners, those saved, to save others. We, not angels, are to proclaim the message of salvation. What a privilege and honor it is to carry out this manifesto of our King! No one dare despise this honor.

The motive that prompted our Lord's missionary command is love, God's gracious love for all mankind, His love to deliver every individual soul from the power of death and the devil; to deliver every individual soul from the awful corruption of sin; to reconcile all mankind with God and to bring to all the treasure of God's grace, forgiveness of sin, life and salvation, peace and joy. And we, God's redeemed ones, will show true gratitude for this love of God only when our hearts are filled with His love for all our lost fellow men. The world lies in the bondage of sin, in indescribable misery and corruption, without the Gospel. Nothing but the Gospel of Jesus Christ can lift the world out of this corruption. With hearts filled with a love that banishes all prejudice and selfishness, the whole Church of God must join hands to carry out the great manifesto of our King.

THE MEANS TO CARRY OUT THE MISSIONARY COMMAND

We come now to the means or equipment to carry out the missionary command of our Lord. When kings set out in ancient times to conquer the world, they equipped their soldiers with arms and military supplies. Our Lord has equipped us with only one thing to win the world for Christ: the Gospel. The command is: "Preach the Gospel to every creature." Baptize all nations. "He that believeth and is baptized shall be saved." To preach the Gospel includes Baptism. Baptism also is Gospel. It is the "visible Word," as our Apology says. Therefore our task is to preach the Gospel. Those who believe the Gospel are to be baptized. Baptism is the seal imparting certainty of God's grace, life, and salvation.

But someone will say, "Did not the Apostles also preach the Law?" The Apostles did preach the Law, but never did they preach it to bring salvation. There is no salvation in the Law. They preached the Law to awaken and arouse men to a knowledge of their sinfulness; to make men realize that they are under the condemnation of God; to bring men to repentance, to godly sorrow over sin. Their message of salvation was always: "Believe on the Lord Jesus Christ, and thou shalt be saved."

Only faith in Jesus brings salvation. Only faith in Him delivers from Satan and eternal death. This is the message of the Gospel. The great objective of all mission work is beautifully set forth in the words of the Apostle Paul before Agrippa when he speaks about his conversion and quotes the Lord Jesus, who said to him while a light from heaven shone round about Paul: "But rise, and stand upon thy feet; for I have appeared unto thee for this purpose, to make thee a minister and a witness both of these things which thou hast seen and of those things in the which I will appear unto thee; delivering thee from the people and from the Gentiles, unto whom now I send thee, to open their eyes and to turn them from darkness to light and from the power of Satan unto God, that they may receive forgiveness of sins and inheritance among them which are sanctified by faith that is in Me" (Acts 26:16-18). Through the Gospel alone men are delivered from the power of Satan, receive forgiveness of sin, are assured of the great inheritance in heaven, and are sanctified children of God here in time and hereafter in eternity.

It is essential that in our mission work we realize this one great objective. It is essential that we do not carry on mission work in order to gain earthly prestige or political influence. The Gospel is not given us for that purpose. Nor is it given us for the purpose of building up a great national organization. It is not given us merely to promote the good of a nation, to promote civilization, education, and culture. The purpose of our mission work is solely and only to bring eternal life to perishing souls; to build the Kingdom of God; to place living stones in the eternal temple of God. The results of our mission work will always be a better individual and a better nation. So-called Christian nations are blessed beyond anything we find in heathen lands. But the objective of all mission work, let us never forget, is always to deliver lost and condemned sinners from the bondage of eternal death and to bring them eternal life. This is the burden of the Gospel. That is the sole purpose for which our Lord has given us the Gospel.

THE MISSIONARIES

Soon after our Lord Jesus entered upon His public ministry He chose twelve men to be His disciples. They were humble, God-fearing men, uneducated, not great theologians, not great in the eyes of the world. Jesus became their Teacher. He taught them divine wisdom. One turned traitor, and he, Judas, was replaced by Matthias. The names of the others are recorded in Acts 1:13, "Peter, and James, and John, and Andrew, Philip, and Thomas, Bartholomew, and Matthew, James the son of Alphaeus, and Simon Zelotes, and Judas the brother of James." It was to these men that Jesus gave the missionary command on a mountain in Galilee previous to His ascension. Later Matthias joined them to make the twelfth Apostle, and to them the Lord Jesus Himself added the mighty Paul. Besides the Apostles we read of their pupils or assistants. Such men as Philip, the evangelist, Barnabas, Luke, the beloved physician, Timothy, Titus, Silas, John Mark, Apollos, Aquila and Priscilla, Onesimus, Epaphras, and others. We cannot review the work and activity of all the individuals of this noble band of apostolic missionaries, but we shall do well to note a few details concerning the life of some of them. We know that their work and activity covered the entire civilized world of their time. We do know that they also touched the barbarous nations round about them.

Peter worked for a time in Jerusalem, then in Samaria and throughout Asia Minor. Of James we know that for a time he presided over the church at Jerusalem. John was in Jerusalem with Peter. He was also with Peter in Samaria. He visited the churches in Asia Minor. For twenty years he resided in Ephesus. Under Emperor Domitian he was exiled to the Isle of Patmos, but he returned to Ephesus and died at an old age. It is said that Andrew preached the Gospel in Scythia and the regions of the Black Sea. Philip was among the company of Apostles in Jerusalem. From Jerusalem he is supposed to have gone to Phrygia. Thomas carried the Gospel to the regions of the Far East. Bartholomew, too, carried on mission work to the borders of India. Tradition tells us that Matthew went to Ethiopia. Judas, the brother of James, is considered to have been a missionary to Arabia and Mesopotamia. Simon Zelotes worked in Africa, and he is said to have preached the Gospel in Britain.

Scripture does not tell us much about the mission work of the Apostles. But what little we do know from Scripture and the history of the Christian Church, we have reason to believe that during their lifetime the little company of Apostles carried the Gospel far beyond their own land. They were not only home missionaries, but also foreign missionaries. They considered the whole world their mission field.

We have more information about Paul than any of them. Paul summed up in himself all the qualities, characteristics, and spiritual dynamics of missionary service. The one great feature which we wish to dwell upon is the fact that above all others he was a missionary pioneer. He was the great pathfinder in an unexplored realm of the heathen world. It was his task to blaze a road through the dark recesses of earth's benighted regions. His intense desire and his aim was to preach the Gospel "where Christ had not been named" and to press on to the regions beyond, to the uttermost parts of the earth. In the face of a thousand disadvantages with neither churches nor missionary boards to back him, in a single lifetime, this marvelous man carried the Gospel to so many cities and countries of the world that he is truly called the greatest missionary to the Gentile world.

We shall do well to take a glimpse at some of the work of the pupils and assistants of the Apostles. Philip, the evangelist, had been greatly honored of God as a soulwinner and an evangelist of the Apostolic Age. In the city of Samaria he was in the very midst of a great revival, and thousands of souls were being added to the Church. Suddenly there came a call to him to leave his fruitful work and go down to the desert road that leads from Jerusalem to Gaza. If ever a man could have been excused for staying at home and taking care of his present work, Philip was that man. Yet not a moment did he hesitate. Promptly he left his work and started out like Abraham, not knowing whither he went. Suddenly there is a cloud of dust on the distant horizon. Soon he is facing the chariot of a high official of the Ethiopian court who was returning from Jerusalem to his distant home with a hungry and disappointed heart. He had the Book of God, but he needed a living voice to interpret it. We are reminded of the words of Paul, "And how shall they believe in Him of whom they have not heard? And how shall they hear without a preacher?" (Rom. 10:14.) Philip speaks to the Ethiopian. It is not a long interview, but how momentous and decisive! A simple question, a simple sermon to a single hearer, and it is all about Jesus; a simple confession of faith and then the solemn rite of Baptism. He may have been the first heathen convert of the ages to have been won, and he was sent on his way rejoicing to the millions of Africa.

That is a great chapter in the Book of Acts, a great page in the missionary history of the early Church. How much it expresses. How many its lessons: prompt obedience to the missionary call, even if it seems to lead away from vital work; courage to go out into the unknown, personal work for the winning of souls, gathering them one by one, and then when they are won, entrusting them to the Lord Jesus and leaving them to go on their way rejoicing.

We have sufficient knowledge of the personal circumstances of the noble Barnabas to justify us in concluding that he was probably a successful businessman, certainly a man of wealth and property. Our first introduction to him tells us that "having land, (he) sold it and brought the money and laid it at the Apostle's feet" (Acts 4:37). The first fruit of his consecration was the giving of his means to the cause of Christ. How gloriously God honored him by taking not only his gifts, but himself and making him a little later the friend of Paul and the first missionary sent out by the church in Antioch to inaugurate the great work of foreign missions. Barnabas stands therefore for all that is most practical and devoted in the work of a Christian layman.

Luke was the faithful companion of Paul. Luke gave us the Book of Acts, and after he had written twenty-eight glowing chapters, he left the book unfinished for us to add in coming generations the remaining chapters of this story, not so much the Acts of the Apostles as the Acts of the Holy Spirit and the ascended Christ.

Mark was one of those ardent and enthusiastic young men who are eager to go under the first impulse, but when the real difficulties confronted him, he was just as eager to get home. But the story of Mark tells us about the patience of Barnabas and Paul. Later Mark was taken back by Paul, and Paul was able to say of him, "He is profitable to me for the ministry" (II Tim. 4:11). Mark teaches us that there is also a second chance in mission work.

And what shall we say of Aquila and Priscilla? They were just plain business people who took care of themselves, and as the providence of God moved them from city to city and land to land, they just let their light shine wherever they happened to be. The result was a glorious reflection of their lives in the lives of others and the calling of some of the most honored of the servants of Christ to the holy ministry. It was through them that Apollos was led to a full understanding of Christian doctrine. Speaking of them, Paul says that they "for my life laid down their own necks, unto whom not only

I give thanks, but also all the churches of the Gentiles" (Rom. 16:4). Sent by no church, not dependent on any church, they represent what we might call the self-supporting missionary, the Christian family transported to the heathen world and there reflecting the beauty and glory of Christ to all around.

Timothy is so close to Paul that he calls him his beloved, faithful son in the faith. Timothy is always willing to be Paul's humble helper if only God will use him for such great work as Paul is doing. Timothy stands forth as a faithful assistant. Paul always treats him as an equal. Paul is always praying for Timothy.

What a fine picture we have of Epaphras in Col. 4:12. "Epaphras, who is one of you, a servant of Christ, saluteth you, always laboring fervently for you in prayers that ye may stand perfect and complete in all the will of God." The language used about Epaphras is extremely strong. There are several Greek words used for prayer, but the one used about his prayer is the strongest of all. It expresses the kind of entreaty which presses its suit until it has "prayed through" the most difficult situation. "Laboring fervently for you in prayers" is the strongest kind of language used to describe Epaphras' prayers. Epaphras stands for the ministry of prayer. This is the ministry which will bring consecrated hearts and hands into mission work and open the doors of every land. It is the ministry from which none are barred. The aged mother, the worn-out preacher, the humble illiterate Christian, all can pray, labor fervently in prayer, for missions. And there is no missionary force more prevailing than prayer.

As we read the Book of Acts, several characteristics of this noble band of early Christian missionaries stand out very clearly. You will notice that above everything else they were all missionaries in the real sense of the word. They looked upon themselves as the "sent ones" of God to bring to their fellow men the risen and victorious Lord Jesus Christ, the only Savior of our souls. All that they did, all their activity, centered around this one great driving power in their lives. They were men of great faith. To them the risen Lord Jesus was very real. He was their very life. For Him they lived, for Him they were ready to die. Nothing was too hard for them, no sacrifice too great for them if only they could carry out the will of their Master. They looked for no honor or glory. Gold and silver held no attraction for them. Their souls were filled with a burning love for the souls of men. Like their Master, this love made them absolutely fearless. They knew the Lord Jesus was with them always; and filled with His divine power, they believed that their work would always accomplish God's gracious purposes. And the one great fact was that they believed God did it all through His Holy Spirit. When Paul reported about his missionary endeavors to the church at Antioch, we are told, "And when they (Paul and Barnabas) were come and had gathered the church together, they rehearsed all that God had done with them and how He had opened the door of faith unto the Gentiles" (Acts 14:27).

What an example this noble band of missionaries is for us!

THE MISSIONARY CHURCHES

The Book of Acts gives us some information about the churches of the Apostolic age. We know that the first one was at Jerusalem. On Pentecost 3,000 souls were added to the church at Jerusalem. Additional souls were added later. And of this great church we are told, "And they continued steadfastly in the Apostles' doctrine and fellowship and in breaking of bread and in prayers. And fear came upon every soul, and many wonders and signs were done by the Apostles. And all that believed were together and had all things common and sold their possessions and goods and parted them to all men, as every man had need. And they, continuing daily with one accord in the Temple and breaking bread from house to house, did eat their meat with gladness and singleness of heart, praising God and having favor with all the people. And the Lord added to the church daily such as should be saved" (Acts 2:42-47). And still, with all this spiritual beauty and glorious fellowship, we hear of Ananias and Sapphira. We hear of friction between the Grecians and the Jews over support of the widows; we hear of conflicts about keeping the Law of Moses. Yet with all this friction, this church becomes an example to all churches. It is a great missionary church!

Another great missionary church is the church at Antioch. It was founded by those who fled from Jerusalem. Barnabas comes here, needs help, and Paul comes. Itself the product of lay missionary endeavor, it speedily sends forth Paul and Barnabas to found other churches. The church at Antioch is a great missionary church.

We hear of the wonderful churches in Galatia, Ephesus, Colosse. In Galatia there was not only one church but a number of them

(Gal. 1:2). The church at Ephesus was founded in a great commercial city. Here was the seat of ancient idolatry, the temple of Diana, the seventh wonder of the world. The church at Colosse was founded by Epaphras, was disturbed by errorists; later the Apostle praises its faith. And we hear of the church at Philippi, founded by Paul upon the plea, "Come over . . . and help us." This church Paul calls his joy and crown. We hear of the church at Thessalonica, near Philippi, of which Paul says that it is an example to all churches in Achaia, "For ye are our glory and joy" (I Thess. 2:20). It is a great missionary church, for Paul says, "From you sounded out the Word of the Lord not only in Macedonia and Achaia, but also in every place your faith to Godward is spread abroad" (I Thess. 1:8). We hear of the church at Corinth. Paul founded this church at a strategic point. It was at the crossroads of the Roman Empire. "Be not afraid, but speak, and hold not thy peace; for I am with thee, and no man shall set on thee to hurt thee; for I have much people in this city" (Acts 18:9-10). Here the Lord's Supper was abused. Paul again is prompted to admonition. His admonition is accepted. "As also ye have acknowledged us in part, that we are your rejoicing, even as ye also are ours in the day of the Lord Jesus" (II Cor. 1:14). We hear of the great church at Rome, the capital of the world. Here is a church of all classes. Here people came and went. Of this church Paul says, "That your faith is spoken of throughout the whole world" (Rom. 1:8). Paul is anxious to know this congregation. He comes to it as a prisoner. He works here two years.

We learn some great lessons from these churches. We notice that they are not perfect. All sorts of imperfections were rampant, although they were founded by the Apostles. Over and over again their founders had to admonish the people of these churches in the spirit of Paul, "That ye put off concerning the former conversation the old man, which is corrupt according to the deceitful lusts; and be renewed in the spirit of your mind; and that ye put on the new man, which after God is created in righteousness and true holiness" (Eph. 4:22-24). After the churches were founded, their founders did not rest from their labors. Continually their founders and pastors preached the Law and the Gospel that their members might grow in grace and in the knowledge of their Lord and Savior.

As we make a study of these great churches, we find that with all their imperfections they were glorious churches; we find the Apostles found much to praise and much to thank God for. They praised the faith of their people; they believed that their people had accepted the Gospel; that their people were true Christians. They thanked God that their members daily grew in grace and in the knowledge of the Lord Jesus. They thanked God that the people of these churches were patient in tribulation, ready to endure persecution. They thanked God that the members of these churches loved one another, shared with one another, helped one another, that they lived as their Lord wanted them to live; that they came together for worship regularly; that they celebrated the Sacrament of the Lord's Body and Blood. Last but not least, who of us can read about these churches without noting how they were praised for their missionary zeal? They had experienced the power of the Gospel, tasted its sweetness, and they could not rest until they passed it on to others. This was not only the spirit of their pastors and teachers, but the spirit of the members. The members of these churches were personal missionaries to the Jews and Gentiles. Wherever they went, they carried with them the Gospel of their risen Lord and Savior. Indeed, the early churches were missionary churches!

We learn some lessons from the great churches of the Apostolic Age. We learn that we shall never find perfect churches. All our churches will have problems, members that are not always true to what our churches stand for; some will become backsliders. But we learn that as of old our teaching and preaching and admonition will always have its effect. Through the Word of God we can be certain that our people, too, will grow in grace and in the knowledge of our Lord and Savior Jesus Christ. We will always find much to praise and much to thank God for. We shall find that our people, too, love the Lord Jesus, love to worship with one another, love to help one another in need, love to read their Bibles, love to come to the Lord's Table. We shall find that our people will be fruitful in all good works, will be ready to support charitable endeavors, will be ready to care for the sick and the needy. We shall find in our churches people who are patient in tribulation, comforted in sorrow, ready to endure hardship. We can be certain that in our churches we shall have people who are true children of God, who are converted and enjoy the forgiveness of sin, life, and salvation. We shall find our people interested in missionary endeavors, zealous to spread the

Gospel, ready to carry out the will and command of our Lord Jesus, willing also to be personal missionaries if we do our part to train them. This is one of the most significant qualifications of a truly Lutheran congregation. No congregation can be truly spiritually alive unless it is forever committed to the missionary command: "Preach the Gospel to every creature."

We have the same means for our people to grow in grace as the early Christian churches—God's Word and His Sacraments. Let us lead and guide our people into a greater appreciation of the Word of God, a greater appreciation of God's grace and mercy. Let us bring home to their hearts the work of the Church, the need to share with God and pray for the expansion of His kingdom. It is for us to inform our people of the open doors, to tell them through sermons and talks, church periodicals and literature, about the things that God would have them do. We may rest assured that God will fill the hearts of our people with the same spirit as that of the early Christians, with the same missionary zeal and devotion. We have the assurance of God's divine power in our churches. We must labor to make our churches great missionary churches.

THE DIFFICULTIES OF MISSION WORK IN THE EARLY CHRISTIAN CHURCH

The missionaries began their work in Palestine among the Jews; from there they went out into all the world. The field of their activity covered a great area. This entailed great hardship upon the missionaries. In II Corinthians, ch. 11, Paul gives us some idea of the hardships involved in the mission work of that early age. He was continually in peril. He and his helpers were poor. They had to work for a living. They were not only the missionaries in the very beginning, they were often the sole supporters of their mission work. From neither Jews nor Gentiles they received a welcome. They were ridiculed, despised, and persecuted. The powers of darkness did everything possible to hinder their work. Wherever people gathered around the Gospel, the devil immediately got busy.

The difficulties of mission work today are no different. Missionaries must be ready to sacrifice. It is true today, especially in foreign lands, that our missionaries must often experience hardship in travel. It is just as true today as it was in the days of the Apostles that the

Gospel receives no welcome. True ambassadors of Christ must be ready to experience ridicule, must be ready to be despised, must be ready to endure hardship. In the glorious promise "Lo, I am with you alway" lies the only answer to every problem. Wherever our missionaries today gather people around the Gospel we must expect the devil to get busy immediately. He will always be the old evil Foe. Our Lord, let us always remember, is victorious over this old evil Foe.

THE BLESSED RESULTS OF MISSION WORK

The Lord Himself pictures to us the glorious results of mission work in the parable, Matt. 13:31-32. "The kingdom of heaven is like to a grain of mustard seed which a man took and sowed in his field; which indeed is the least of all seeds, but when it is grown, it is the greatest among herbs and becometh a tree, so that the birds of the air come and lodge in the branches thereof." The mission work of the early Christian Church started out as a small mustard seed indeed, but it was history-making in its results. How small the beginning at Jerusalem! From there the Gospel went into Syria. Soon it reached the islands of the Mediterranean; it spread over into Asia Minor and into Europe. All this happened in 30 years. During these few years, what glorious churches were founded. The Gospel of Christ Jesus conquered proud, self-righteous hearts. Countless heathen turned from their idols. The despised Gospel brought countless numbers out of sin and corruption to the Savior, and for the Savior they were ready to sacrifice everything if only their lives could glorify Him. In Him they lived; in Him they died.

God has signally blessed also our mission work. From the small beginning of our Synod in 1847, 22 pastors and 12 churches, our church has grown to 3,507 pastors and 5,658 congregations in 1944. When our Synod was founded, we had approximately as many souls in it as the church at Jerusalem. (Today, 1944, communicant members: 1,013,007; souls: 1,478,062.) We know that among all these souls there are those who love the Lord Jesus, look upon Him as their only Savior. For Him they are ready to live, for Him they are ready to die. We know that this great company of redeemed souls are always ready to carry out the trust committed to them, which is to preach the Gospel to every creature. And ours is the same great promise, "All power is given unto Me in heaven and in earth." In the power and spirit of the Apostolic age we can and will continue to do our mission work.

XXII

Christian Stewardship

THE topic of the essay which is to engage our attention and which we are to discuss these days is "Christian Stewardship." Advisedly the limiting adjective "Christian" has been placed before the pregnant noun "stewardship"; for there is obviously also a type of stewardship which is practiced by human beings who are not of the family of God. A banking institution, for example, whose board of directors does not include a single professing Christian, will nevertheless carry out painstakingly and conscientiously the terms of a will which establishes a trust fund to be administered by the bank's trust department. The sense of obligation and responsibility, which is a manifestation of civic righteousness, the stringent laws which govern the acts of an administrator, and fear of the consequences if the law is disregarded—these factors will combine to result in a stewardship that is honest, efficient, and advantageous as men judge these matters. But it is not *Christian* stewardship.

"Christian stewardship" is a phrase that has appeared with increasing frequency in our circles during the past decades. The fathers did discourse on this topic also, to be sure, and a few very exhaustive treatises which relate to the subject are found in our synodical literature, although somewhat strangely, the term *Haushalterschaft* is hardly ever used by the fathers who employed the German language. *Beruf* and *Arbeit* are the terms commonly found. But while under the heading "Stewardship" seven references were listed which were recommended to your essayist as source material, there were twenty under the heading "Ministry" and fifteen on the topic "Conversion." This is not as much out of proportion as may appear at first glance, when we remember the background of the fathers and their early struggle to clarify in their own minds the Scriptural teaching on the doctrine of the Church, and when we recall the later controversial discussions with other Lutherans as the doctrine of conversion came under dispute. But it may not be inappropriate to remark that the Church today does well to remind herself more frequently, as a corollary to the doctrine of justification, which will always remain the chief doctrine and the very heart of Christianity, that faith without works is dead (James 2:26) and that Christian stewardship provides an avenue to prove the faith that is in us.

Unfortunately, the term "stewardship" in our circles has received a connotation that too often is too distinctly financial. We have in our Synod today eighteen District stewardship bulletins and six full-time stewardship secretaries in addition to District stewardship committees. The health of the budget treasuries appears to be the major concern of this systematized effort (due, no doubt, to an ever-present need), although the full implication of *all* principles of Christian stewardship certainly is not left untouched. Nevertheless, the fact remains that frequently and almost automatically the mere mention of the term "stewardship" when used in our churches is identified among the members with the ingathering of funds. Now, who would deny that the giving of money is an important phase of Christian stewardship and that it records better than almost anything else the rate of progress being made in our overall stewardship life? But there is more, much more, to Christian stewardship than the signing of a pledge card or the placing of a check in the collection basket. Stewardship is an attitude, a way of life, which the Christian adopts by divine directive, or, as Julius Earl Crawford puts it: "Stewardship is the recognition and fulfillment of personal privilege and responsibility for the administration of the whole life in accordance with the will of Christ." May the Holy Spirit guide us, as we ponder what the infallible Word of our God tells us about Christian stewardship and draw some lessons from our study.

Thesis I

God, the Creator and Preserver, is also the Owner of all things. It is He who gives us physical strength, mental endowments, our property "and all that we need to support this body and life."

"In the beginning God created the heaven and the earth" (Gen. 1:1). This very first statement of Scripture is basic for a correct

understanding of the principles which underlie Christian stewardship. *God* created, not man; and God created *alone*. He did not set
into motion a force which finally, under its own momentum and
after countless ages, resulted in the universe. God is not a collabo-
rator with man in creating. He is the one and only Creator. And God
created *all*. After the first six eventful days had passed, there was
nothing left unfinished and incomplete. Down to the last detail the
world was in perfect condition, reflecting the wisdom and the power
and the glory of Him concerning whom the Scriptures say: "God
made the world and all things therein" (Acts 17:24). And it is
not self-exaltation, but the truth, the solemn truth, when God's
judgment on His own work is recorded in these words: "Behold, it
was very good" (Gen. 1:31). Man and beast, fish and fowl, trees
and grass, mountains and valleys, rivers and oceans, the greater and
the lesser lights of heaven—*everything*—was the perfect product of
the one and only Creator, and His work alone. The theory of evolution, also the deistic and diluted version, stands in conflict with the
basic tenet of Christian stewardship that God is the Creator of all
things, animate and inanimate.

And this same world created by God continues today. It has been
battered and bruised and its beauty marred by the impact of sin,
which has infiltrated like a poisonous, deadly gas wherever man
moves. Eden is lost; man earns his daily bread in the sweat of his
face; there is confusion of tongues; nations fight; blood is spilt; death
is commonplace and inevitable; but the world continues. Seedtime
and harvest, day and night, follow century after century in orderly
rotation. The trade winds continue to blow; men are born; they
mature; they pass from the scene. No force has ever been able to
destroy this world, for He who has created it "upholds all things by
the word of His power" (Heb. 1:3). "He giveth to all life and
breath and all things, for in Him we live and move and have our
being" (Acts 17:25, 28), is the all-embracing declaration of St. Paul.
Unbelievable ingenuity on the part of man has discovered how the
forces of nature may be harnessed and perverted to bring about
destruction. Atomic bombs have made their appearance. God suffers
all this. But He still retains absolute control of the entire situation
and preserves the world which He has created. He has not with-
drawn His hand from His creation, for then there would come upon
us immediate and utter disaster. He will not suffer the destruction

of His handiwork until in His own appointed hour "the heavens shall pass away with a great noise and the elements shall melt with fervent heat, the earth also and the works that are therein shall be burned up" (II Pet. 3:10).

It is logical to deduct that He who has created and who preserves this world and all the things that are therein must also hold title, *i. e.*, must own all things. But Christian people need not rely on their reason in this matter. Rather we turn to the Scriptures to determine the identity of the universal Property Holder. We are not surprised to find clear-cut statements on the question, "The earth is the Lord's, and the fullness thereof, the world, and they that dwell therein" (Ps. 24:1) declares David; "The silver is Mine, and the gold is Mine, says the Lord of hosts" (Hag. 2:8) cries the Prophet Haggai; "Every beast of the forest is Mine, and the cattle upon a thousand hills" (Ps. 50:10), saith the Lord, speaking through Asaph. And the statement of Abraham still stands: "I have lifted up mine hand unto the Lord, the most high God, *the Possessor of heaven and earth*" (Gen. 14:22).

God owns all. That is the burden of the foregoing paragraph. If that is true—and we have established it upon the basis of Scripture —then fundamentally and originally man really owns nothing. Whatever man now possesses has been given to him as a sacred trust from the hand of God. This statement is in complete accord with Scripture: "What hast thou that thou didst not receive?" asks Paul (I Cor. 4:7; compare also John 3:27). Yes, actually what have we that is not a gift of God? *My* body, so fearfully and wondrously constructed that even now men of medicine marvel at its intricate and well-balanced machinery—where did it come from? "I believe that *God* has made me and all creatures," the Church answers on the basis of Scripture. Scientists working feverishly in their laboratories cannot create a human being and endow it with a living soul. But God can and does.—*My* health, so carefully guarded and checked against disease in these vitamin-conscious days—but who renders germs harmless as they enter my system, and who has guided research workers to discover the sulfa drugs and penicillin to counteract deadly infections and to restore health? Great is the Lord, our God!—*Your* keen mind, which enables you to think rationally and to express your ideas in coherent speech, making it possible to associate normally with your fellow human beings—

where did that brain power come from? You inherited that from your parents, you say. Ah, yes! But that's not the whole story. "I believe that God has given me my *reason and all my senses*" supplies the final answer. *My* home and *my* farm, for which we have worked so industriously all these long years, I tilling the soil or working in the shop, my wife managing frugally to enable us to pay off our mortgage and to lay aside for a rainy day, you say. But, friend, who created the opportunity for you to find gainful employment in the fields, and who gave you the necessary skill and health to hold down a job? In the final analysis it is God who is the great Employer, not some personnel manager or government agent.—But *my* children whom *we* have reared, our pride and our joy as they walk in the paths of uprightness, untouched by the rising tide of juvenile delinquency, you insist. Ah, yes, but does not Scripture say very distinctly, "Lo, children are an heritage of the Lord" (Ps. 127:3)? And from what source do you receive the ability to counsel and to advise your children paternally, to find the right word at the proper moment, and to keep the happy balance between harshness and undue leniency in your child training? "Not unto us, O Lord, not unto us, but unto Thy name give glory" (Ps. 115:1). But *my* money, *my* savings account, *my* war bonds? Once again, friend, the same question confronts you: "Who gave you the opportunity to earn, who prospered your investments, who inclined the hearts of your friends to remember you with gifts and inheritances? And once again it is the same answer to summarize the thought we have attempted to develop: "All things come of Thee" (I Chron. 29:14). God is the Owner of everything and all I possess.

Now what has been said is not intended as agitation to bring about a revolutionary change in the manner in which we human beings express ourselves in this matter. We refer to *my* body, *my* health, *my* farm, *my* children, *my* business, *my* money, and in relation to our neighbor this is absolutely correct. The very fact that God says to you and to me in the Seventh Commandment: "Thou shalt not steal," presupposes that I am the owner of certain goods or properties—as far as *you* are concerned. I hold legal title to my automobile, and if you appropriate it without my knowledge and consent, you have taken *my property* and stand condemned as a thief in the sight of God and man. But when *you* move out of the picture and *God* moves into it, the situation is changed: *His* claim as the

Owner of all supersedes any legal title which the state has granted me. When we speak of "our" possessions, it is not so much the terminology which counts as the thinking behind the terminology. In an age which presents exceptional temptation to revel in materialism, at a time when false values are placed upon what men like to call the good things of life, and in a period when our people also share in the unprecedented upswing in earnings which has lifted national income from 40 billion dollars in 1932 to 144 billion dollars in 1943 (260 per cent), it is essential that we keep in mind very firmly this basic principle: "All that is in the heaven and in the earth is Thine" (I Chron. 29:11). Only then have we laid the solid and straight foundation upon which to develop Christian stewardship. The warning spoken by God in the days of Moses is definitely in place today; in an age of plenty He says to us: "Thou shalt remember the Lord, thy God; for it is He that giveth thee power to get wealth" (Deut. 8:18).

Thesis II

"Our" possessions come to us undeservedly through the mercies of God, the Owner, who distributes them according to His gracious will and gives us directions regarding their use. This stewardship relation to God is not a degrading experience but a privilege.

In the judicial branch of civil government there is a court known as a Court of Claims, where citizens may appear to petition for adjustment of property rights and establish legal title to those things which belong to them as a matter of human law and justice. Such an arrangement is essential for the protection of the citizens, and it is a fair procedure according to the natural law that prevails among men in their relationship to one another.

But this procedure is not workable at all if we step into the court of God to claim for ourselves, as a matter of right and justice, the properties and the talents which we now call our own. In fact, we would not even be tolerated in this court if we appeared in our own name; for it is an axiom that he who comes into court must come with clean hands. And our hands are not clean; they have been soiled by sin, and our right to file claim in our own behalf to that which is designated as our property does not exist. Yet here we are assembled, all of us having "clothing and shoes, meat and drink, house and home, wife and children, fields, cattle," and many goods, being provided for richly and daily with all that we need to support our body and life. We received it from God, we have been told. Yet in the same breath we are reminded that we have no claim on these things. What is the answer? Let the answer be given in the words which every member of the Church learns as a fundamental teaching of Scripture and to which all of us therefore subscribe: "All this purely out of fatherly, divine goodness and mercy, without any merit or worthiness in me." The everlasting mercies of God in Christ, our Savior and our Intercessor in the court of heaven, are new every morning. His grace faileth never and moves God not only to provide spiritual sustenance for our souls through the means of grace, but also to sustain us in our bodies by granting us, undeserving though we are, the multitude of things we like to call "our possessions." Truly, when we contemplate the vast extent of our belongings in these days of material prosperity and then remember that we have absolutely no claim upon God to give us anything at all, we re-echo the words of Jacob: "I am not worthy of the least of all the mercies and of all the truth which Thou hast showed unto Thy servant" (Gen. 32:10).

So here we, each one of us, find ourselves established in this world having by the mercies of God many things which are referred to as our possessions, and it is only human that we begin to compare our property and talents with those of our neighbors. Immediately we discover that some have more than others. There is no equality between men in respect to earthly possessions. In reality this should occasion no surprise. Scripture singles out, without disapproval, the riches of Abraham and the wisdom of Solomon. "The rich and the poor meet together; the Lord is the Maker of them all," says Solomon (Prov. 22:2). There is no Biblical warrant for that idealistic conception of human society in which a part of their property is arbitrarily taken away from those who have much in order to give it to those who have little, with the expressed intention of thereby establishing economic equality between all men. Experiments along such visionary lines are bound to fail in the long run, because they leave out of consideration human nature and the order which God Himself has established and permits when He chooses to entrust more to some and less to others. Capitalism as a system which recognizes a difference in the economic standards prevailing among men is not condemned by God. But let the unscrupulous steward of many things who oppresses the poor take no false comfort from this statement. No more devastating criticism against the *abuse* of capitalism, whether practiced in urban or rural communities, is found than the Bible pronounces when it says, "Woe unto them that join house to house, that lay field to field, till there be no place, that they may be placed alone in the midst of the earth" (Is. 5:8). Maldistribution which results from economic injustices and which causes misery and suffering is utterly contrary to the will of God and an interference with His divine plan of economics, which is always good, even though it is incomprehensible to us at times why certain ones should have five talents, others two, and some only one.

But whatever the extent of our earthly wealth and talents may be, we are not at liberty to make use of these things as we please. For remember, in reality they are not our property. They have been entrusted, loaned, lend-leased to us, if you please, and their disposition is not to be made according to our own conclusions, no matter how intelligent they may appear, and certainly not according to our whims and fancies, but according to the directive we shall consider in the next thesis. For the present we are only concerned with establishing the fact that we are not at liberty to do as we please with that which we call our own. We are the trustees, the managers, the caretakers, or the stewards. This relationship of trust which we have towards God is taken as an accepted fact when Paul declares, "It is required in stewards that a man be found faithful" (I Cor. 4:2). The fact that limitations are placed upon us should not disconcert us at all, for, to quote from an essay delivered many years ago on this subject, "it is part of the common law of every civilized country that a trustee must employ the trust funds according to the will of the trustor; that a steward must use his master's goods not for himself but only for his master as directed, and must ever be prepared to give an accounting; that an employee must rightfully use and preserve the materials belonging to his employer and must faithfully employ his strength and skill for the benefit of his employer . . . and this law of stewardship is clearly taught in the Scriptures and particularly by Jesus Himself, as applying to man's relation to God" (English District, 1915, p. 12f.).

The fear is sometimes expressed by such as have given only superficial thought to the stewardship relationship which exists between God and man that this relationship involves a degradation and a humiliating experience. Not so! A steward is not a slave. The connotation of the word "steward" is that of a responsible and honored official. In the Parable of the Unjust Steward (Luke 16) it is apparent that the master had placed a great deal of confidence in this man; no fettering regulations were imposed upon him; he had the privilege of using his own initiative; he was put on his honor. The same situation is observed in the Parable of the Talents (Matt. 25). The stewards are given their various talents, and it is left to their discretion how they are to be invested to the advantage of the master. This is a privilege and a high responsibility and certainly not a mark of degradation. The point has been aptly expressed in these words: "The colored chauffeur owns nothing of all that he handles for his wealthy employer. The auto he drives, the garage which he keeps clean, the uniform which he wears—nothing of all these things is his own, not even a brass button on his coat. Still he beams with pride when he opens and closes the door of the limousine and drives it in the service of his master. He does not feel resentful at the thought that the destination of the drive and even the route is not *his* choice but that of the master.—Should *we*, then, feel degraded because God, the eternal, almighty Creator, has given us body and soul, our members, reason, and senses, our food, clothing, shelter, our health of body and mind, our means of livelihood, and directs the use of all these things? God's ownership of our earthly blessings confers a sublime dignity on our stewardship and should be the source of great joy and the inspiration for songs of gratitude and praise. Not the doleful cry 'I am only a steward!' but the joyful exclamation 'I am honored of God to be His steward!' should issue from our hearts and lips by a contemplation of this truth" (Central District, 1936, p. 44).

Thesis III

Our possessions are to be used according to the will of the Owner. It is His will that we employ them in our secular calling and heavenly calling, which are interrelated. We are to use our possessions for the support of ourselves and our fellow men and, primarily, for the maintenance and expansion of God's kingdom.

We come now to the point in our discussion where we must consider the program which God had in mind when He entrusted to us as stewards that share of talents which in His judgment was desirable for us to have, or the directive He has transmitted to us. For certainly His gifts are not to be frittered away idly but must be put to the use which is pleasing to the Owner. It may be well if we remind ourselves at once that the Christian has a secular, or earthly, calling (*irdischer Beruf* in the theological literature of our fathers) and a heavenly calling (*himmlischer Beruf*). The earthly calling, in the words of Harless in his *Ethics,* is the station which life's calling for the individual occupies within human society, and through which the individual serves the natural human purposes of his own existence and that of the community. His activity as a member of the Church in the kingdom of God for his own and his fellow men's eternal salvation and for the extending of the Kingdom we may define as his heavenly calling. These two callings are not mutually exclusive; tney cannot be separated and kept apart as though they had no connection with each other. They are not two parallel, never-touching lines of activity. This situation is not always fully understood by all of God's people. They attempt vainly to make an artificial distinction: the heavenly calling, in their opinion, begins on Sunday morning, when they arise and make their preparations for attending divine worship; and their heavenly calling comes to an end, again in their opinion, after they have completed the visit to the house of God and once more begin to occupy themselves with secular occupations and pastimes. Their viewpoint is: "Christianity has nothing to do with my secular calling, my business affairs. Business and Christianity must be kept apart; the twain shall never meet; how I run my business is my own affair, and no church, no pastor, no deacon, should interfere."

It would be easier and much more convenient if the two callings could be disassociated so readily and so completely. But it cannot be done. "Whether, therefore, ye eat or drink, or whatsoever ye do, do *all* to the glory of God" (I Cor. 10:31) reminds us that our stewardship life is not a Doctor Jekyl and Mr. Hyde affair. Also within the limits of his secular calling the Christian is guided by the will of God to fulfill his heavenly calling. Uhlhorn writes: "Let us repeat: the secular calling and the heavenly calling lie not outside of each other, but within each other. . . . We fulfill the obligations of our heavenly calling only if we are faithful in performing the duties of our secular calling; and we discharge properly the duties of our secular calling if we are people who also in our secular calling serve God and work for His kingdom." The nature of the task which we perform in our secular calling has been left to our discretion and choice and will be determined by our environment, our opportunities, and our aptitudes. Thus we shall have farmers, business men, clerks, factory workers, tradesmen, professional men, employers, and employees. The only limitation which God places upon us in this respect is that we should occupy ourselves with honest work whereby mankind is benefited and He is glorified. Among those who are to be benefited as we go about the duties of our secular calling are, in first line, we ourselves as individuals. God has placed us into a secular calling that we might work and have the means to maintain ourselves as respectable members of the human family. A loafer is never a good steward but disgraces God, who directs, "If any would not work, neither should he eat" (II Thess. 3:10). Neither does the squanderer who is beset with the philosophy "They can't let me starve" find approbation of his way of life with God.—In the divine order of things we also have our families and immediate dependents, who are to benefit through our secular calling. "If any provide not for his own, and specially for those of his own house, he hath denied the faith and is worse than an infidel" (I Tim. 5:8) still finds its application today. But so does also that more general admonition: "Is it not to deal thy bread to the hungry, and that thou bring the poor that are cast out to thy house?" (Is. 58:7), which serves as a reminder that our concern for the physical welfare of men cannot be limited to those closely attached to us by consanguinity or affinity, but must include all who are brought into contact with us and who are in need of our help. The trend in our country, which is following the pattern so prevalent in other parts of the world, toward paternalistic government through old-age pension systems, unemployment insurance, and socialized medicine may tend to blur our obligations; but it cannot excuse the people of God from the responsibilities for the welfare of those belonging into the family circle or those brought unmistakably close to us as members of the human race.

We are well aware—to touch only upon one more point in this connection—of the complicated situation that exists in industrial life today, and we know that the labor-management relationship presents a very real problem, which is aggravated by such issues as technological employment, government regulations, and socialization of industry. Yet the basic principles of Christian stewardship in the secular calling continue to hold good for employer and employee even now. The Christian employee, as a part of his secular calling, is to use the talents of body and mind which God has given him industriously in the interest of those who give him employment; and the employer, on his part, is under obligation to use his gifts and opportunities also for the welfare and protection of the workman. We know this sounds like an over-simplification of a difficult problem. Yet these remain basic principles. That a practical application of the principles of Christian stewardship in our secular calling is possible for mutual benefit also in the complexities of the present day may be observed, for example, in Concordia Publishing House and doubtless in other business organizations staffed by Christian people who exercise forbearance toward one another, who are mutually concerned about each other's interests, and who thus, in their secular calling—in that smaller circle which rests within the larger circle of their heavenly calling—let their light so shine before men that their good works are seen and that their Father in heaven is glorified (Matt. 5:16). Such faithful stewardship in the menial tasks of life and in exalted positions will unconsciously elicit the question from unbelievers, "What manner of men are these Christians?" and will predispose them favorably to give audience to the messengers of Christianity. Also in this way is God glorified as His people go about their secular calling.

Possibly it is in place now to remind ourselves (if we need such a reminder) that it is not at all incompatible with Christian stewardship when God's people use His gifts and endowments also for pleasure and enjoyment which are in keeping with their dignity as children of God. The caricature which pictures the Christian a haggard, dejected individual, unable to smile, unwilling to enjoy the beauties of nature and the friendly companionship of men, opposed to permitting himself and others harmless pleasures and conveniences, is just that—a caricature which does violence to the real facts connected with Christian stewardship. God grants skills in the sciences and talents in the fine arts in order that we might derive pleasure from them. God provides His great outdoors, the invigorating tinge of winter, and the balmy breezes of summer in order that we might spend pleasant days relaxing and regaining our vitality to be fitly equipped for the demands of our calling. God has given us families and friends to enjoy the sociability of normal human beings. Good stewardship in our secular calling does not militate against using those things which God has provided for our pleasure.

But far more important than our earthly calling with its stewardship obligations is our heavenly calling, which we perform as members of the Christian Church for the express purpose of helping to build and to expand, through the preaching of the Gospel, the kingdom of our God into which we have been called by grace. This objective of our heavenly calling has priority, absolute priority, for the Savior says, "Seek ye first the kingdom of God and His righteousness" (Matt. 6:33). Maintaining and expanding the Kingdom, bringing men to Christ, which is the obligation and the privilege of our heavenly calling, is the most important task confronting us. It outranks and supersedes everything.

The children of the world dispute such a statement. Those who are benevolently inclined toward the Church and her members may concede that the existence of the Church and her widening influence are of some value. But at best it remains to them a side issue. Building a railroad empire, arranging international cartels, erecting world-famous structures and towers—such achievements rate high in their estimation. The building of Christ's kingdom, which is carried on without glamour, with little applause, often at great sacrifice, interests them little, if at all. Some of them are openly opposed to it. How could it be otherwise? God, heaven, hell, the hereafter—all this means nothing to them, for they are carnal-minded and have no understanding of spiritual matters.—But while this reaction on the part of unbelievers must be taken for granted, it is positively distressing to observe that also some professing Christian people become inoculated with this spirit of antipathy and indifference; that they too seem more interested in their daily bread than in the Bread of Life; that they too spend more time in deliberating how they may attire themselves strikingly and modishly than they do in pondering how the white robe of Christ's righteousness may be retained by them; that they too are willing to make heavy investments in order to acquire for themselves a modern and luxurious home, while they appear unmoved by the opportunities to make gilt-edge investments in the Kingdom which will give their King's Word an ever-widening audience.

We are here to remind one another, brethren, that our heavenly calling as members of the kingdom of Christ must claim our first attention. It therefore requires the intense and unselfish use of all the talents and the first fruits of all gifts which we receive from the hand of God. God is not satisfied with halfway measures; He does not tolerate divided loyalty. "Give Me thine heart" is the demand of Him who has created us, who has redeemed us unto Himself through the blood of the Lamb that was slain, who gives us His Holy Spirit to dwell in us through the means of grace. The Christians in Macedonia did this very thing: "they first gave their own selves to the Lord" (II Cor. 8:5). And we? If our heart belongs to God, then our endowments and our properties will be placed fully and freely at His disposal.—It will be worth our while to analyze the implications of this last sentence for a few moments by referring to a few particularized items of Christian stewardship as they play into our heavenly calling.

A

THE STEWARDSHIP OF OUR BODY
AND PHYSICAL SKILLS

It is God who gives us our body and makes us responsible for it. "I beseech you therefore, brethren, by the mercies of God that ye present your bodies a living sacrifice, holy, acceptable unto God, which is your reasonable service" (Rom. 12:1) is the exhortation of God. It is His expectation that we treat our body as a precious gift, guarding it against abuse, supplying it with the necessary food, rest, and relaxation in order that our physical strength and the skills which our hands develop may be placed into His service. Particularly in smaller congregations will be found opportunity to give service to the church in this way. The plumber can repair the leaking water pipe in the church basement; the carpenter may help fashion the needed items of church furniture; the electrician is ready to make necessary improvements in the lighting system; the landscape gardener is anxious to draw on his experience to beautify the church property; the seamstress will gladly busy herself in the task of preparing appropriate altar vestments for the seasons of the church year; the painter offers his professional skill to redecorate the buildings of his congregation, and so forth, ad infinitum. And even in larger congregations, where circumstances will make impossible the employment of the skills in such a personal and direct manner, there will remain opportunity, nevertheless, to employ these physical talents in an advisory capacity.

B

THE STEWARDSHIP OF MIND

God gives us reasoning ability; we are created to think, to comprehend, to remember. A good steward, who takes his heavenly calling seriously, will train his mental faculties to the degree that God gives opportunity. He will observe and read and study to improve himself. He will fight against the temptation to indulge in unseemly thoughts and shameful reveries and thus pervert his mental powers. Our thinking apparatus is to be used to meditate on the eternal mysteries of God's love in Christ, to appreciate ever more deeply the gracious providence of God, to ponder on the methods and the possibility of stretching forth the curtains of the habitations of God, and thus to carry out, in a measure at least, the injunction of our Lord, to be about our Father's business.

Is a local congregation confronted, for example, with the question of relocation or expansion—a question which involves far-reaching decisions? Then our best thought should be devoted to finding the correct solution of the problem. All our business acumen, our experience, our ingenuity, should be pooled with that of our fellow Christians to reach the decision which will benefit the kingdom of our Lord. Or is our Church engaged in discussing with other Christians the differences of doctrine and practice which separate us from them? Then no business merger could be more important; the same careful thought on the basis of the authoritative Word of the Senior Partner, God, the same conscientious evaluation of all the points involved, the same painstaking probing of all the evidence and all pertinent documents which we would give to a commercial partnership, yes, even more, will be devoted to the study of church union if we are good stewards of our mental powers.

C

THE STEWARDSHIP OF TIME

Certainly it is God who allots us our span of life. In the time He gives us—precious moments—the stewardship obligations of our heavenly calling must receive first consideration. We simply *must* find time, take time, make time, to place at the service of God in the building of His world-encircling empire. This presupposes that we use a part of our time to hear and meditate on His faith-creating Word in order that we ourselves will remain within His kingdom, "working out our salvation with fear and trembling" (Phil. 2:12) and avoiding the accusation that we, having preached to others, should find ourselves castaways (I Cor. 9:27). It is God-willed selfishness—if we choose to call it that—that our first concern is our own salvation; that we who proclaim the Redeemer's love to others, ourselves remain the beloved sons and daughters of God through a personal attachment in faith to the Savior; that we who urge others to hear the saving Word retain and increase our own familiarity with it.

But what use do we Christian people really make of our time? Are we good stewards? The answer is not altogether re-assuring. Figures are compiled to show, for example, that on the average only 50.4% of our people use their time fittingly by going to church on Sunday morning (for the North Nebraska District the figure is 61%). We are also disturbed by tabulations which show that during 1943 only one new member was gained, on the average, for every 115 communicants in our congregations. Undoubtedly one reason for this distressingly low figure will be found in a faulty use of our time—God's time. Complaints come frequently that church meetings are difficult to arrange because our people claim they have no time to attend; that it is discouraging to search for Sunday school teachers because prospects claim lack of time to give to this service. And what about the not infrequent shamefaced admission that there is no prayer in the family circle, the excuse being that there is no time? That important call on our neighbor to invite him to church is delayed on the pretext that this is not a convenient season for personal mission work. The church papers remain unread because we are too busy with keeping abreast of the affairs in Caesar's kingdom "Redeem the time because the days are evil" (Eph. 5:16), the

Apostle encourages us as stewards of God. His point is: Make good use of the short time at your disposal; plan to put first things first; arrange your day systematically; give a generous proportion of your time to the Lord's work; don't withdraw from the activities of the Kingdom on the plea "I have no time," but remember God's purpose in permitting you to remain on earth is that you serve Him also by giving and using generously for the extending of His kingdom the time He makes available.

D

THE STEWARDSHIP OF MONEY

This great medium of exchange we possess, all of us to some extent, as a trust from God. So much has been said and written about the stewardship of money that one begins to hesitate to add yet another chapter. Nevertheless completeness demands it, and misunderstanding and the reluctancy which prevail in many instances even today make it necessary.—The Church (God) needs money. This fact should be stated boldly and without apology. And since the work of the Church—bringing men to faith through the preaching of the Gospel and retaining them in the fold—is a great and continuous program, which lasts until the end of time and extends into every part of the universe, the Church (God) needs much money and will always need much money. The laborers we send forth in our name as God's ambassadors are worthy of their hire (salary); that takes money. The preparation of the workers in the days of their youth and their support during the period of waning strength takes money. The construction of the buildings in which our workers are trained costs money. The alleviation of physical misery in homes which Christian charity has established and in which the spirit of Christianity prevails (this is also a part of our calling as God's people) costs money. All this is according to the will of God, who could have His kingdom expanded without any financial assistance from us, but who decided that He would draw us into partnership and who directed that the first fruits of our material wealth should be used to promote the task which ranks first and holds a perpetual priority—the work of the Christian Church. From this point of view do we judge the situation. We are an honored people, occupying a preferred position in the world; for God does not approach His enemies or those who have turned their backs upon Him with a request to be His colaborers; He comes to us Christians, to every one of us, but only to us, as a matter of high privilege. And realizing this, we are anxious to discharge our obligations also in the stewardship of money, a matter which comes so close to us and which touches our lives as does almost nothing else. The Owner of our money supplies specific directions and answers anxious questions. We shall allude only to three broad questions.

1. In what spirit do we give money? Not under compulsion since there is no way to escape the collector; not as a matter of habit, because grandfather gave; but willingly, "for God loveth a cheerful giver" (II Cor. 9:7); intelligently, properly evaluating the opportunities and making a proportionate division of our funds; and in gratitude for innumerable blessings—as we shall see in the next thesis.

2. How often do we give money? According to a regular schedule. "Upon the first day of the week" (I Cor. 16:2) still remains the God-inspired advice of the Apostle. Even as God grants us the things which we need regularly, so should we, as faithful stewards of His resources, regularly make available our gifts for His kingdom.

3. How much of our money should we give? God tells us: "As I have prospered thee" (I Cor. 16:2), urging us to be generous. He encourages us to set aside a liberal proportion of our money, but He does not put us under a fixed mathematical obligation; rather He places confidence in us that we, His people, the stewards of His resources, will use our Christian liberty to reflect our blessed state, in accordance with the treasures bestowed upon us as trustees.

We may add, in closing this chapter, that just in connection with the stewardship of money many questions will arise which must be answered with a considerable latitude since they touch upon phases that have not been expressly stipulated by God. Experience has demonstrated, for example, that certain customs and practices have been extremely successful in helping Christian people to become better stewards (*e. g.,* the pledge system and the envelope system); but it would be going beyond Scripture to make acceptance of these definitely worth-while customs a *sine qua non,* or a matter of conscience, for a local congregation. And while the argumentation in behalf of tithing can and should be made very persuasive and appealing, and while God no doubt is pleased with a properly motivated tither, and while what constituted a mandate in the Old Testament may very well be accepted, followed and exceeded by the Christians of the New Testament as an example, yet the Scriptures of the New Testament contains no specific or arbitrary percentage demand, and the Church must therefore exercise caution that the conscience of her members is not bound or made uneasy, even by implication, in any matter where Christ has set them free.

THESIS IV

While stewardship is also a matter of obedience to God's command, the prime motive which dominates us as we discharge our stewardship obligations is gratitude to God and love for our fellow men.

What reasons move us to practice Christian stewardship? What is the proper motivation to place our physical strength, our mental endowments, our time, our property, and our money at the disposal of God, who has entrusted all things to us? Remember that we are concerned with *Christian* stewardship. Our relationship to God is not that which exists between slave and master, but that of a child to its father. It is not fear which dominates us and forces us to give time, effort, and gold. Neither do we place ourselves and our goods at the service of God in order to keep up appearances or to create a false front, for that would constitute deceit and fraud, and in such misleading maneuvers the Christian can have no part. And certainly we do not give for personal gain or profit. There is nothing Christian about taking time off in the office, at a sacrifice, in order to attend a meeting of the voters' assembly if our purpose is not to make a contribution to the advance of the Kingdom through our presence and counsel, but rather to win clients among brethren who are impressed with what seems to them to be our consecration and devotion to the Lord's cause. Among Christians the motive of fear, prestige, and personal gain must be ruled out, always and absolutely, if their stewardship is to ring true.

But we do act in obedience to God. "Honor the Lord with thy substance and with the first fruits of all thine increase" (Prov. 3:9) God tells us through Solomon. "To do good and to communicate forget not; for with such sacrifices God is well pleased" is the mandate of the Owner spoken through His Apostle (Heb. 13:16). "Charge them that are rich in this world that they be rich in good works, ready to distribute, willing to communicate" (I Tim. 6:17-18) is the specific instruction to Timothy. These statements are more than polite requests which leave it up to the decision of the individual whether compliance is agreeable to him or whether he would prefer to refuse. These are direct commands. They refer primarily to our money and earthly goods, it is true, but they cover also the whole range of talents and endowments and powers which God has given to us. Whatever, therefore, we have and call our own we place into God's service because He wants us to do so.

But it would be a pity indeed if the last word had now been spoken and if this statement closed the discussion on the motives which urge us to be good stewards. True it is, we give because *God* wants us to give; that in itself would be enough. But it would not be satisfactory to a Christian steward. We give, above all, because *we* want to. Gratitude to God is the great and compelling reason which animates us. Every other influence must fade into the background by comparison. What a debt of thanks we do owe God for the material blessings He showers upon us and for the great spiritual gifts He has made our own! This is a generalized statement which is always true and which has its application at all times among God's people. But today we, above others, can itemize to impress upon ourselves the force of this statement, which is so apt to be interpreted as a mere platitude. We are citizens of the only great nation in the whole world which has experienced no physical destruction of its homes, its factories, its public buildings; no bomb has fallen on our territory; God has given victory to our armies; we emerge from the war as a prosperous people materially, living a life of comfort and enjoyment which is without parallel on other continents or islands in this world of ours. We are again harvesting a bumper crop, which will yield enough to give us all that we need to support this body and life; and out of our abundance there will remain sufficient to supply millions who face deprivation and starvation. Our Government is stable and strong—in comparison with others—and able to carry on its functions in an orderly and constitutional manner. Who are we to deserve these blessings before others?

And then let us give more than a passing thought also to our

spiritual blessings. God forgives sins; all sin, every sin, to you and
to me. He does this by grace, finding in us nothing, nothing at all,
that would merit consideration. He does this because His love for
us sinners is so great that He willingly sacrificed His own dear Son
for our transgressions. And through the resurrection of His dearly
Beloved, in whom God could find no fault but who was made sin
for us—in Christ's resurrection the fact of accomplished redemption
is proved and divinely attested. God now presents to us—as an unconditional gift—this redemption in and through the means of grace.
In His Word He gives us the power to believe that

> Salvation unto us has come
>   By God's free grace and favor;
> Good works cannot avert our doom,
>   They help and save us never.
> Faith looks to Jesus Christ alone,
> Who did for all the world atone;
>   He is our one Redeemer.

Through the Sacrament He strengthens us in this faith. He assures
us that our salvation is certain, as certain as His word of promise
is true. He promises to sustain us in the hour of trial and doubt.—
This great central teaching of the Bible, yes, the entire Word,
unadulterated by any rationalizing, limiting amendments of men,
our Church has retained since her organization 100 years ago; these
precious truths are freely taught in our schools, preached with confidence and power from our pulpits, discussed without restraint in
our homes. No restriction in the freedom of our worship is placed
upon us. "What shall I render unto the Lord for all His benefits
toward me? I will offer to Thee the sacrifice of thanksgiving and will
call upon the name of the Lord. I will pay my vows unto the Lord
now in the presence of all His people" (Ps. 116:12, 17-18) must be
our unanimous and forthright answer. There we have the real
motivation which urges us to be good stewards of the manifold
gifts entrusted to us—sincere gratitude to Him who loved us before
the foundations of the world were laid and who continues to love
us in time and beyond time.

But he who is grateful to God and loves the Giver of all will
also love his fellow men. The two can be separated as little as the
flame of a candle can be without heat. "This commandment have we
from Him, that he who loveth God loveth his brother also" (I John

4:21), says the Apostle of love. As we see the physical destitution of mankind, the hopelessness and the despair which have engulfed millions, we are urged by love to them, who also have been created by the hand of God, to use God's entrusted gifts for their relief. Such opportunities are with us always, and particularly in the post-war era, when they are brought to us in a very striking manner. But if the physical distress of hopeless human beings gives us concern, as it should, what must be our reaction when we view the spiritual destitution of the masses? Without God means to be without hope in this world and beyond hope in the next. Yet these scores of millions (and now we are referring not only to the dislocated hordes roaming over devastated areas in Europe and Asia, but we are thinking also of the ungodly in our own country) are coredeemed with us through the atoning sacrifice of Christ; for them also His blood was shed on Calvary's hill, "for God so loved the *world* that He gave His only-begotten Son" (John 3:16). Love for those whom God also loves will move us to be good stewards and to use our powers and gifts to extend a helping hand in the distress of body and, particularly through our missionary expansion efforts, to offer the balm of Gilead for the ills of man's immortal soul.

Thesis V

It is not easy to practice good stewardship. But God strengthens us and enables us to make progress. He promises a reward of grace.

To the uninitiated it might appear as though good stewardship should be an easy matter. Christians want to serve their God and their fellow men; God has given them the means to do this; He also creates the opportunities for this service; the Christians recognize these opportunities—it all sounds quite simple.

But in reality it is not as simple as all that; there are complicating factors which prevent Christians from attaining sainthood in the days of their flesh. "For the good that I would I do not" (Rom. 7:19), complains even such a hero of faith as St. Paul. Our perverse nature, the old man, who is our constant and unwelcome companion, rebels when the new man within us urges that we make use of our stewardship privileges, and in Satan he has an able ally. In the most plausible manner we begin to argue with ourselves that charity begins at home; that we must give due concern to our health, for example, and husband our physical strength by remaining at our comfortable fireside rather than to be out on an errand of Christian service, when as a matter of fact a brisk walk would benefit our physical condition. The ineptitude and the inactivity of our fellow Christians become a smoke screen behind which we like to hide our own lack of interest in advancing the cause of the Savior and promoting the welfare of our neighbor. Worst of all, we permit Satan to interfere by separating us slyly from the supply line which feeds us the ammunition that is needed if we are to carry on as good stewards; we do not make abundant use of the means of grace. Neither do we resort frequently enough to the privilege of prayer, but we do give ear as the Evil One urges upon us the conviction that unusual circumstances and expediency make a neglect of our stewardship opportunities pardonable; that the demands made on our time, talents, and property are not to be taken as seriously as they sound; that God asks for much in the expectation of receiving at least a little. All this, and more, makes the practice of Christian stewardship difficult. All of us will realize this from our own personal experience. What to do?

The key to the problem, the solution, we find in these words of Christ: "Without Me ye can do nothing" (John 15:5) or, inversely, in the statement of Paul: "I can do all things through Christ, which strengtheneth me" (Phil. 4:13). The fact that we practice Christian stewardship at all is a result of God's work in us through the Holy Spirit, who gives us the power and the strength to begin a life of sanctification. And it is only fair to state that among our people as individuals and collectively as Christian congregations we do find case history after case history—and we think in increasing numbers —where the principles of Christian stewardship are not given mere lip service, but where they are translated into positive action which stirs the heart of every lover of Zion with gratitude. Thank God for that!

But the end is not yet. Perfection is a distant goal, always; but nevertheless it remains a goal. "Not as though I had already attained, either were already perfect; but I follow after" (Phil. 3:12), declares Paul. Even as the infant creeps, the young child waddles, the youth walks, and the man runs, so we children of God strive, in the power which God gives us, to become ever better stewards as we advance in years and as we increase in wisdom and knowledge.

We intensify our meditation of His Word; our prayers for wisdom to understand our opportunities and for courage to grasp them become more fervent; we train ourselves to be on the alert and to realize when the doors for service in the Church, and also in our secular calling, are opened to us. Our determination is stiffened not to be diverted from the privileges of our high and holy calling by other interests which are insidiously projected by sinister forces and adversaries. And the reassuring answer to our petition for strength comes distinctly and repeatedly: "Be not afraid"; "I am with thee"; "My strength is made perfect in weakness" (II Cor. 12:9). We take new courage and fight on confidently.

And we never ask, "What shall we have therefore?" (Matt. 19:27.) Even though the impossible should occur and we should finally develop into perfect stewards of the manifold gifts and talents which God entrusts to us, yet would we not have advanced beyond the admission: "We are unprofitable servants; we have done that which was our duty to do" (Luke 17:10). All thought of reward must be ruled out, and is gladly ruled out by Christian people who realize that stewardship, even the best stewardship, is and remains always an imperfect work of love to God and for humanity. Compensation may come to us frequently in the form of gratitude on the part of those who have been benefited by our stewardship life; temporal prosperity may be ours; joy and satisfaction in knowing that we are engaged in a God-pleasing manner will be experienced. But these items never constitute reward in the sense that if we would present these awards or recognitions in documentary form to our God, the doors of heaven would open automatically. So why talk about reward?

Nevertheless God does talk about a reward. To his faithful steward the master says in the parable: "Well done, thou good and faithful servant; thou hast been faithful over a few things, I will make thee ruler over many things; enter thou into the joy of thy Lord" (Matt. 25:21). What can this mean? It means that though we have deserved nothing, God holds out to us as recognition a reward of grace. All the acts of service we have performed, no matter how humble and insignificant they have appeared to us, have been observed and noted by our Lord. Our attempts to be faithful have not escaped His all-seeing eye. When everything is counted up—and there will be a day of accounting, when we must

report to God how we have discharged our stewardship opportunities and used our talents—the total will never earn us the right
to enter the dwelling place of the Most High and to taste the
glories of heaven. God demands perfection; nothing less will do.
Yet He is graciously pleased to accept the acts of our Christian
stewardship as proof that faith, saving faith, has dominated our
heart and life and to welcome us into our Father's house of many
mansions.

Let us look forward joyfully to that blessed day. As stewards we
stand in a privileged relationship to God. We know we are doing
His work; we are divinely certain of His protection, guidance, and
direction; though the path we now walk is uneven and we stumble
often, we continue on our way unafraid, upheld by our gracious
Lord, grateful for the opportunities of the present day, hopeful for
the privileges of tomorrow also, and awaiting expectantly that
blessed moment when we shall enter upon the state of perfected
stewardship which awaits God's people as the culmination of divine
grace.

XXIII

Dangers Confronting the Church Today

THE subject chosen for this discussion embraces many areas of Christian activity. Some dangers affect the life in Christ of the individual, others threaten the life of the entire Church. Some are at the very heart of the Christian Church; others lie at the outer edge, yea, outside the camp waiting for the opportune moment to enter. Some, like the poor, are always with us; others come, stay for a while, seem formidable for the moment, and then lose their cunning and vanish. They are clouds that pass in the night. Some dangers threaten those in the Church that are bubbling over with the energies of youth; others beset those who have reached the half-way mark on life's journey; and still others lie in wait for those who have reached the sunset years of their life.

Some dangers are basic; that is, they are at the bottom of the problems of the Church. They are the source from which your spiritual troubles and my spiritual troubles and the spiritual troubles of the entire Church come. Although they plagued the Church in the days of the Twelve, in the days of St. Augustine, and in the days of Martin Luther, they still must be given priority in any discussion of the subject.

These dangers are also basic in this respect, that they must be kept in mind in discussing any dangers impeding the progress of the Church. They are basic and confront the Church now, in our land, in our Church, in our congregations, in our homes, in our daily life.

I

UNBELIEF

Let us begin with the mother of all problems in the Church: unbelief.

482

The quality of faith in the hearts of its members should be the chief concern of the Church. "Your faith is the victory that overcometh the world" (I John 5:4-5). The Church, any church, any group of Christians, is just as strong as the faith of its members. "I can do all things through Christ, which strengtheneth me" (Phil. 4:13). Luther said he could scale walls with Christ. By contrast, the lack of faith is the source of all evil and of all weakness in the Church. Luther writes:

> Unbelief is really the chief sin in the world and the source of all evil. The heart that is under the spell of unbelief despises the Word of God and treats the Gospel as though it had been proclaimed by the devil. Furthermore, the heart that is under the spell of unbelief refuses to be obedient to father and mother and the government, lives in adultery and fornication and in every shame and vice. These are the fruits produced by the tree of unbelief. He who does not believe in Jesus Christ as his Savior does not have the Holy Ghost, and because the Holy Ghost does not dwell in him, he can have no decent thoughts (Erlangen ed., 3, p. 419f.).

Unbelief will increase in intensity and destructive power as the end of time draws nigh. "When the Son of Man cometh," our Savior says, "shall He find faith on the earth?" (Luke 18:8). At that time the temptation to unbelief will be so strong that, if it were possible, even the faith of the elect would be destroyed (Matt. 24:24). Speaking in a parable of those days, our Savior says that only the wise virgins will have oil in their lamps (Matt. 25:1-13). Unbelief is the dominant attitude of mankind.

Now what are the *various forms* which unbelief assumes? In the first place, we have the coarse, haughty denial of basic Biblical truths. "The fool hath said in his heart, There is no God" (Ps. 14:1). "How does God know? And is there knowledge in the Most High?" (Ps. 73:11). When our Synod was young, this was a widely prevalent form of unbelief. The aftermath of the French Revolution, the writings of Voltaire, Diderot, D'Alembert, and a host of lesser lights, produced a flood of atheism. Attacks upon the Church, upon the existence of God, upon the resurrection of the body, were common in the days of our Synod's youth. Newspapers published these attacks without the least bit of compunction. The great progress of the biological and physical sciences had revealed, so it was claimed, that Christianity is an outmoded way of life. That Dr. Walther often devoted much time and space to the defense of the Gospel against these coarse attacks was made necessary by the prevalence of coarse unbelief.

Today raucous expressions of unbelief are not as prevalent as they were in the first fifty years of our Synod's existence. Where is the Bob Ingersoll (1833-1899) in our time making fabulous sums lecturing on "The Mistakes of Moses" or on "The Benefits of Agnosticism"? Who of us has heard coarse, rough public attacks on Christianity? In fact, the Church is publicly acknowledged to be a most honored and revered institution. Returning generals are giving public expression to their belief in God. Chaplains are honored officers in the Army and the Navy. Public meetings are opened with prayers. Huge sunrise services are conducted on Easter morning. Our President struck a responsive chord in the hearts of millions when he urged the people to assemble for prayer in observance of V-E Day. Religion is honored in America as a general rule.

And yet there is much unbelief abroad in the land. The form has changed, the substance has remained. In fact the substance has become stronger and more destructive. The very subtleness of current unbelief makes it all the more deadly. Where is that absolute confidence in, that childlike reliance upon, God's Word? Who, like Martin Luther, is willing to stake everything on promises of God?

> The Word they still shall let remain
> Nor any thanks have for it;
> He's by our side upon the plain
> With His good gifts and Spirit.
> And take they our life,
> Goods, fame, child, and wife,
> Let these all be gone,
> They yet have nothing won;
> The Kingdom ours remaineth.

It is true, God's revelation to man is not specifically challenged, but the divine inspiration of the written Word is denied quite generally by leading men outside and inside the visible Church. Having found coarse and raucous attacks upon God ineffective, Satan has his minions bore from within. The attacks are more subtle and therefore more destructive. These subtle attacks cannot but undermine the faith of many. How can childlike reliance on the promises of

God be developed if the very character and nature of Scripture is called into question? If the written Word is only inspired in spots, who can tell what is and what is not a promise of God? Unless the individual knows this is God's inspired Word, he will forever dwell in uncertainty. His faith will be weak and frail. By the grace of God our church body has not become guilty of a theoretical denial of the divine inspiration of the Scriptures. We still profess publicly that every word in our Bible is given by inspiration of the Holy Ghost. May God grant His grace that we continue to do so! But our neglect of the Scriptures, our failure to act upon our professed belief, frequently amounts to a practical denial of this fundamental doctrine. Where are the Christians whose faith is buoyant and virile, who find real joy in any suffering which befalls them because of their faith in Christ? Where are the Christians whose greatest joy in this life is to work and give for Christ? How many are there in our time of whom St. Paul could say, as he did of the erstwhile Galatian Christians: "Where is the blessedness ye spake of? For I bear you record that, if it were possible, ye would have plucked out your own eyes and have given them to me" (Gal. 4:15).

> Rise again, ye lion-hearted
> Saints of early Christendom.
> Whither is your strength departed,
> Whither gone your martyrdom?
> Lo, love's light is on them,
> Glory's flame upon them,
> And their will to die doth quell
> E'en the lord and prince of hell.

Luther says: "The Word of God is preached to us, and we listen to it as though it were the word of a man, of a preacher, or of a chaplain. We do not believe that it is the Word of Almighty God" (Erlangen ed., 36, p. 344).

It is true, our salvation is not dependent on the strength of our faith. It is not the quality of your faith that makes you acceptable to God. We are justified by faith because faith is God's appointed way of accepting the merit of Christ. The finger that carries the precious diamond may be very weak, but the diamond is just as precious as if carried on the finger of a strong man. The little child is just as safe as the stouthearted mariner when both are in the boat that outrides the storm.—And yet there is great danger in a weak faith. "O ye of little faith" (Matt. 8:26). It was weakness of faith that caused Peter to sink, when he saw the wind boisterous. Weakness of faith that caused him to deny his Savior three times, and later to withdraw from the Gentile Christians for fear of the Jews. (Gal. 2:11ff.) Weak faith exposes the individual to dangers that may be fatal.

This is true not only when our faith concerns the promises of God's grace but also when it concerns the threats of His wrath. As it was in the days of Moses, so it is in the year 1945: "Who knoweth the power of Thine anger? Even according to Thy fear, so is Thy wrath" (Ps. 90:11). How many realize the hand of God in the misfortunes that befall us? How many are aware of the fact that this present war is a scourge of God for victors and vanquished alike? The complaint of the Almighty concerning the children of Israel recorded in Amos 4:9-10 could be made of our nation: "I have smitten you with blasting and mildew; when your gardens and your vineyards and your fig trees and your olive trees increased, the palmer worm devoured them: yet have ye not returned unto Me, saith the Lord. I have sent among you the pestilence after the manner of Egypt; your young men have I slain with the sword and have taken away your horses; and I have made the stink of your camps to come up unto your nostrils: yet have ye not returned unto Me, saith the Lord."

When Joseph had his brother Simeon put into prison, his brothers said one to another: "We are verily guilty concerning our brother, in that we saw the anguish of his soul, when he besought us, and we would not hear; therefore is this distress come upon us" (Gen. 42:21). The thief on the right said to the thief on the left of Christ: "Dost thou not fear God, seeing thou art in the same condemnation? And we indeed justly, for we receive the due reward of our deeds." The spirit of Joseph's brothers and of the thief on the right is rare in our day. There are too many among us who say: "We have done nothing amiss. The Germans, the Italians, the Japanese. Not we!" We are ready to examine the natural causes of calamities. We consume our energy in meditating upon the wickedness of other nations, but that is as far as we go. There is no energy, no will, left to examine ourselves. If we believed God's threats, we should examine ourselves and our deeds.

Now what are the *results of such unbelief?* One of the results is mentioned by our Savior in Luke 21:34: "Take heed to yourselves lest at any time your hearts be overcharged with surfeiting and drunkenness and cares of this life." The rich man, who neglected Moses and the Prophets, was clothed in purple and fine linen and fared sumptuously every day (Luke 16:19). St. Paul tells the Galatians that unbelief manifests itself "in envyings, murders, drunkenness, revelings, and such like; of the which I tell you before, as I have also told you in time past, that they which do such things shall not inherit the kingdom of God" (Gal. 5:21). Unbelief, whether it be the blatant brand of the professed agnostic or whether it be the practical kind of the professing Christian, promotes a softening-up process. That is, the individual does not practice self-discipline. Iniquity increases. It gains the upper hand. Evil becomes dominant; love waxes cold. The evil servant in the parable who was convinced that his Lord was delaying his coming began to smite his fellow servants and to eat and drink with the drunken (Matt. 24:49).

The question arises, Are these fruits of unbelief evident in our time? To ask the question is to answer it. Men are becoming increasingly indulgent over against themselves. A characteristic of our time is the softening-up process in self-discipline. "Eat, drink, and be merry" is the motto. Roadhouses and "beer joints" multiply. Since few believe that the Lord is a strong and jealous God, visiting the iniquity of the fathers upon the children unto the third and fourth generation, few think it necessary to live up to the demands of God's Law written in their hearts. The members of our churches are affected by the spirit of the times. It is difficult for our young men and maidens to swim against the current. While in Rome, it is so easy to do as the Romans do. If St. Paul had to say, "The good that I would I do not; but the evil which I would not, that I do," how much more do we have to say that in the year 1945! There is no denying the fact that as our Synod approaches its hundredth birthday, its members have become more worldly-minded.

But how about the lack of love for our fellow men? It is true, we contribute generously to the community chests. Our communities meet their quota for charity. The machinery of charity rattles along at high speed. But genuine, selfless charity, the thing which Christ had in mind when He said, "When thou makest a dinner or a supper, call not thy friends nor thy brethren, neither thy kinsmen nor thy neighbors, lest they also bid thee again and a recompense be made thee" (Luke 14:12)—this brand of charity is rare in our modern world. The world, during the last five years, has gone through a process of brutalizing that is horrible to contemplate. Our boys, boys from our churches, were taught fifty-seven different ways of killing a man without making any noise. Let no man think that the brutalizing effect of the war will leave our Church unscathed.

Closely related to unbelief and stemming from it is the general tendency in secondary and higher education of our land to raise doubt to the level of a virtue and to regard faith and conviction as a weakness. Far be it from us to decry the value of an open mind and the quest for facts no matter what the results may be. The Church need never stultify itself. We need not fear that the facts of science will ever prevail against the Church. Nor shall we ask God to discontinue to bless us in our efforts to promote "all pure arts and useful knowledge." But when the thousands of high school teachers are taught that the truth cannot be ascertained and that the truth or falsity of a statement depends on your viewpoint, in other words, that truth is relative and that Pilate's question "What is truth?" presents the ideal attitude of a modern scholar, the destructive power of such thinking must be evident to all. We oversimplify when we state that the theory of evolution is the gravest danger to which our children in the tax-supported high schools are exposed. The gravest danger is that in many places our children are taught systematically that no one should claim that he has the truth. Where this principle is applied, it works like an acid upon the faith of our youth.

This, then, is a description of one set of dangers which confronts our Church as it nears the century mark. Surrounded by an atmosphere of unbelief and doubt and living among people who are fast losing their ability for self-discipline, our Church is in danger of being softened up and of losing its power for good in a decadent world.

What is the remedy? What are we going to do about it? What can we do? We might try to escape. Monasticism had its origin in the effort to escape the evil effects of world currents. The early monks desired to live a life of faith unmolested by the evils of the present world. The attempt failed miserably, because it was a man-made approach to a spiritual problem, and it tried to get around a function which our Savior has assigned to all Christians. Our Savior's instructions are: "Behold, I send you forth as sheep in the midst of wolves; be ye therefore wise as serpents and harmless as doves" (Matt. 10:16). We are to remain in the world, not of the world (John 17:15). Christ prescribed struggle for those who are His, and promised a crown after successful combat. But the Christian "is not crowned unless he strive lawfully" (II Tim. 2:5). The weapons of our warfare are God-appointed. Weapons and methods selected by man contrary to those prescribed by God can only do harm.

What are the methods and weapons of warfare prescribed by God? Their chief characteristic is that they dissolve doubt and strengthen faith. The methods used rather frequently by our fathers in their strife with unbelief were those used at times by St. Paul. They used the apologetic approach. By this method the reasonableness of the existence of God is demonstrated. Romans I is the outstanding example of this approach. The writer of the Epistle to the Hebrews uses the same method. He writes: "Every house is builded by some man; but he that built all things is God" (Heb. 3:4). St. Paul's famous address on Mars' Hill, in which the Apostle speaks to the Athenians of the unknown God, "whom they should seek, if haply they might feel after Him and find Him, though He be not far from every one of us; for in Him we live and move and have our being" (Acts 17:27f.). All nature tells us that there is a God, that He is powerful and mighty and wise and good.

But saving faith is not created through the natural knowledge of God; neither is it strengthened thereby. The real source of faith is the Word of God, the Gospel of Christ crucified. "Faith cometh by hearing." Christian faith is always faith in the Word. Christian faith is nothing else than the acceptance of the Word. There are powers inherent in the Word, and these powers produce faith. The Gospel is a power of God unto salvation. Faith is not only produced by hearing, but it is also kept alive and virile by hearing. Where the Word of the Gospel is, there the Holy Ghost is and gives power to the Word. It is His way of producing and strengthening faith.

What, then, must we do to arm ourselves against the current modes of unbelief? What must you do if doubts arise in your heart regarding the trustworthiness of the Christian religion? What must you do if doubts arise in your heart concerning the question whether you are a child of God? What must you do if science seems to you about to triumph over the Church of your Savior? There is only one answer to all these questions. Use the Word in season and out of season. The Holy Spirit will testify to you that God's Word is the truth. Weakness of faith is caused by neglect of the Word, even as strength of faith is insured by the use of the Word. (Example of early Christians, Waldenses, Lollards, movement inside the Roman Catholic Church at beginning of 19th century, *i. e.*, Bishop Seiler in Regensburg, 1805, Leander Van Ess, 1807.)

II

INDIFFERENCE IN MATTERS OF DOCTRINE AND LIFE

Indifference in matters of doctrine is a mark of our day, and it is dangerous. It is closely akin to unbelief. The nonbeliever and the indifferent are brothers. Both stem from a common mother. The unbeliever says: "I will not accept anything on faith." The indifferent says: "It makes no difference to me what one believes or what one does not believe."

Almost every branch of the Church is found among the 250 religious groups in America. In addition, the United States has become a veritable incubator for religions, with new ones hatched periodically from the fertile minds of would-be reformers. Many are sincere although mistaken; others are glory- or money-seeking egoists. Even the ancient philosophies of the Orient are transplanted to our soil. Often it seems that the more fantastic the claims, the more zealous and successful are the sectarian advocates in winning adherents among the gullible listeners throughout the land.

Man is by nature religious. He knows that there is a God. He knows that this God punishes wickedness. Every man knows these two truths. These two truths bother every man. Questions of God and of salvation become real for every man at some time in his life. He tries to solve his problems by a process of trial and error. As a consequence we have a veritable surge of religions.

What attitude are we to take over against the multitude of religious organizations? Two choices are open to us. We can say: "It does not matter. They are all right. One religion is as good as another." In that case truth is relative and a matter of personal opinion. Or we can take the position that truth is absolute and unchangeable.

If truth is absolute, then any variance from the truth is error; and churches will be found to contain either all truth, no truth, or a mixture of truth and error.

The principle of tolerance and the principle of least resistance make many people choose the first of the two alternatives. They dismiss the whole problem by saying: "It doesn't matter so much what you believe as long as you are sincere"; "it doesn't make so much difference what your religion is as long as you live up to it"; "it doesn't make any difference to what church you go as long as you go to some church"; "one church is as good as another"; "we are all aiming for the same place anyway."

Let us examine this principle of indifference in belief. If this principle is true, then it makes no difference whether you believe in infant baptism or reject it just so you are sincere in either belief. Then it does not matter whether you are a Lutheran or a Roman Catholic, a Presbyterian or a Methodist, if only you are sincere. But then, it also doesn't matter whether you are a Lutheran or a Mormon, a Christian Scientist or a Seventh-Day Adventist, as long as you are a sincere Mormon, etc. Then it makes no difference whether you believe in a Christian God or the Mohammedan God, provided, of course, that you are sincere in your belief. Finally, it does not matter whether you believe in Jupiter and Mars, Odin or Thor, as long as you are sincere in your worship.

What is wrong with this principle? The fact is that it does make a difference what you believe. Our Savior said: "If ye continue in My Word, then are ye My disciples indeed; and ye shall know the truth and the truth shall make you free" (John 8:31f.). A lie cannot make you free. A lie to a condemned criminal that he is pardoned will not save him from the electric chair. It is cruel to tell such a man an untruth, because it prevents him from making preparation for death. Only a true word of pardon can set him free.

Jesus is Himself the Truth, the Teacher of the truth. "We beheld His glory . . . full of grace and truth" (John 1:14). "Grace and truth came by Jesus Christ" (John 1:18). Jesus said of Himself, "I am the Way, the Truth, and the Life" (John 14:6). And this truth is absolute. It is exclusive. Christ added, "No man cometh unto the Father but by Me." "To this end was I born, and for this cause came I into the world, that I should bear witness unto the truth. Every one that is of the truth heareth My voice" (John 18:37).

That Christ was speaking of absolute truth and not of relative truth may be seen from His warnings against the workings of Satan through false teachers. In foretelling the judgment of God upon Jerusalem and on the world, Jesus pointed out that the first sign would be the coming of false prophets. "For many shall come in My name, saying, I am Christ; and shall deceive many." "Many false prophets shall rise and shall deceive many." "There shall arise false Christs and false prophets, and shall show great signs and wonders, insomuch that, if it were possible, they shall deceive the very elect" (Matt. 24:5, 11, 24).

Years after Christ's ascension, the Apostle Paul continued these same warnings. In his charge to the elders of Ephesus he says: "Take heed, therefore, unto yourselves and to all the flock. . . . For I know this, that after my departing shall grievous wolves enter in among you, not sparing the flock. Also of your own selves shall men arise, speaking perverse things, to draw away disciples after them" (Acts 20:28-30).

"It makes no difference what you believe, as long as you do what is right." Let's examine the second half of this statement. This is a popular contradiction which has gained wide currency. The danger lies in this, that indifference is raised to the status of a virtue and that people who are indifferent in matters of faith will also be indifferent in matters of living. What you believe determines how you live. For example, what you believe regarding God determines how you live. If you believe that God is Love, you will have a certain boldness and joyousness whenever you think of God. You love God and find joy in running the ways of his command. Slavish fear will depart from your heart. If you believe that God is omnipresent, that will shape your behavior. If you believe that marriage is a lifelong union entered into by rightful betrothal, your wedded life will be entirely different from what it would be if you regarded marriage merely as a temporary contract made between two human beings without any reference to God.

Christ says people sin because they do not believe right (John 16:9): "The Holy Ghost reproves the world of sin because they believe not on Me."

Whether it be merely half belief or false belief, all unbelief is sin, and sin brings damnation. The judgment of Jesus upon wicked men is based upon their unbelief and their love of darkness rather than the light of truth (John 3:17, 19).

In this connection we ought to discuss the danger that false doctrine might arise in our midst. To many people this is merely an academic question. They cannot conceive of false doctrine arising out of the Missouri Synod. But isn't that possible? Pure doctrine is a gift of God's grace. We have pure doctrine because God has given it to us without any merit or worthiness on our part. Like all other gifts of God, purity of doctrine can be lost.

How could that happen in the Missouri Synod? There are various ways. At present we have faithful ministers and teachers, who preach and teach the Word in its truth and purity. They have received a thorough training in schools maintained by the members of our Church. For almost a hundred years our churches have taken a lively interest in these schools. They have paid the salaries of the professors and contributed liberally toward the maintenance of the buildings. As few church bodies in history, the Missouri Synod from its infancy has fostered and promoted the training of ministers and teachers.

As a result our members have been made rich in all knowledge and spiritual understanding. Even our children have received thorough training not only in this or that specific doctrine, but in all doctrines. The whole counsel of God for our salvation is made known to them.

Experience of the past shows us that in many cases churches which have enjoyed the gracious gifts of God in a rich measure either become complacent, self-righteous, or satiated.

This is a grave danger confronting the Missouri Synod right now. We have grown in numbers. We have become wealthy. Some of our church buildings are magnificent. We are being recognized. We are no longer an immigrant body. Our synodical machinery hums along.

And *we* have *pure doctrine*. The others do not have it. We are in danger of exhibiting pure doctrine as a young girl sports a diamond on her finger. We are in danger of becoming pharisees. Remember that the present generation has received the body of pure doctrine as a heritage. We did not have to battle for it. It was given to us. Even as the son of a rich man gets sick and tired of money, so we are in danger of becoming satiated.

You know the story of Israel in the wilderness. How graciously and bounteously God fed them with quail and manna! "Our soul loatheth this light bread" (Num. 21:5). They were sick and tired of the abundant food. There is a strange parallel between physical food and spiritual food. When spiritual satiety sets in, disintegration is not far off. Then such a person, such a congregation, such a synod looks around for other food. Spiritual vigor decreases, and the end is not far off.

What is the remedy for this condition? How can we meet the danger? The first step is recognition of the situation and as a consequence genuine repentance. Then must follow a deepening of our knowledge concerning doctrine. Our fathers called it *Vertiefung in die Lehre*. We must dig deep into doctrine. Occupy ourselves with doctrine. Increase our knowledge of doctrine. Remember, we know only in part. We are not masters. We are learners. That was a fine hint on the part of our Savior when He called those who followed Him "disciples," by which He wished to indicate that they would have to learn as long as they drew their breath. Dr. Luther knew Christian doctrine probably better than any other man since the days of St. Paul; yet what does he say concerning his occupation with doctrine? "I am an old Doctor of the Holy Scriptures, and yet I have not gotten beyond the simple truths of the Catechism. To say the truth, I do not completely understand the Ten Commandments, the Creed, or the Lord's Prayer. I am not able to say that I have mastered these parts of Christian doctrine. I use the Catechism every day in prayer with my son Hans and my little daughter Magdalene. How is a man going to understand thoroughly the first words of the Lord's Prayer: 'Which art in heaven?' If I really understood these words and believed them, I would at once draw the conclusion that I too am Lord of heaven and earth and that Christ is my brother" (Erlanger ed. 57, p. 14f.).

Digging deep into Christian doctrine will preserve us from false doctrine. The result will be a deeper knowledge of doctrine generally, a better understanding of the relationship between the various doctrines. Love of, and appreciation for, doctrine will take the place of satiety and ingratitude. Doctrine will be the pearl of great .price. We will see that each doctrine has something to do with our day-to-day living as Christians. Doctrine will come into its own, and the old age of the Missouri Synod will be like her youth.

Let us bring this section of our discussion to a close with a reference to the danger of weariness in the Kingdom. The men exposed to the danger of weariness in the work of the Kingdom are particularly the pastors and teachers and congregational officials. It is easy to be in high spirits when everything progresses according to plan and the congregational machinery hums with activity. Every new victory gives encouragement for the battles ahead. Nothing succeeds like success. The people hear the Word. Church attendance is good. The members are growing in all knowledge and in all utterance. The pastor is encouraged to dig deeper into Christian doctrine. As time goes on, he comes up with golden nuggets from the Word of God. The teacher notes the progress in faith and life of those entrusted to his care; he finds joy in his work and is moved to greater faithfulness in his work. The pastor and the teacher get along well with each other. The elders admonish a fellow Christian who is in danger of departing from the flock, and to the surprise of everyone he heeds the admonition and corrects the error of his way. The next case they take up with alacrity because they tasted success. Every success drives them on to new and nobler efforts.

But unfortunately that is not the situation in all congregations nor at all times in the same congregation. Failure is discouraging. The pastor prepares each sermon carefully. He delivers it well, but the progress in Christian living is infinitesimally and microscopically small The pastor begins to weary of his unfruitful labor. The temptation to resign grows by the hour. "What good is done through my preaching?" he asks. The teacher works hard for the children, but the opposition to the parish school increases. A committee called on an erring brother. They admonished him as tactfully and carefully as they knew how. What a storm broke loose! What a flood of hatred and bitterness! All of the relatives of the man were up in arms. You say, "Why should I stick my neck out?" You pull your neck in. Weariness sets in. You are tired. As a consequence, work that should be done by you remains undone. The progress of your congregation is slowed up and finally is brought to a snail's pace.

Now what can you do for this tired feeling? First of all, you can call to your mind that the cause is not yours but God's. You are a worker together with God. You owe God the best service of which you are capable. He assumes the responsibility for the ultimate success or failure of a mission. All that He requires of you is that you be found faithful, faithful in the use of those means which He has prescribed for the creation and development of faith in the hearts of men. The worker who feels that weariness is coming upon him as he labors in the Kingdom ought to ask himself two questions: First, "Am I using the means which my Lord wants me to use?" Secondly, "Am I using these means to the best of my ability?" He must use these means first in respect to himself. "The husbandman that laboreth must be first partaker of the fruits" (II Tim. 2:6). Weariness will tend to depart, and new vigor will begin to be in evidence.

III

SECONDARY DANGERS

In speaking of certain dangers as *secondary* we ought never to regard them as unimportant or insignificant. We are thinking of such dangers as threaten the health and strength of certain institutions; and the condition of these institutions, in turn, affects the health and strength of the Church. Whenever these institutions are weakened, the Church is weakened; and he who is interested in the well-being of the Church must be interested not only in the being but also in the well-being of these institutions.

The importance of the family is apparent from the fact that historically and objectively it is the primary social group. It has been called the "mother cell of society." The family determines the kind of citizens, the kind of neighbors, and the kind of church members that go into the making of a community. Human beings normally pass their infancy, their childhood, and much of their youth under the sheltering care of the home. Here they receive their first impressions from their environment and, I may add, the most lasting impressions; here they accumulate their first experiences in social conduct; here the foundations for their future philosophy of life are laid. In the family circle the traditions of the past become the building stones of the future, and the individual develops into the kind of social being that will determine his usefulness in Church and State.

God Himself created the family. In the wise dispensation of our heavenly Father an urge to sex life and love for his offspring has been implanted in man. As a matter of fact God has made the continuance of the human race dependent on these two factors. Unlike the irrational animal, man has been given an aptitude and a need for the more permanent union of domestic society. His very qualities of affection, tenderness, and parental love impel him to want a more lasting union than that afforded by a state of sexual promiscuity. God has so arranged things that man's nature craves for a more intimate companionship and love than that afforded by the uncertainties of ordinary social life. Moreover infancy and childhood need many years of care and help, and naturally postulate for parents a permanency of union. All this God put into His words when He said: "God created man in His own image, in the image of God created He him; male and female created He them. And God blessed them, and God said unto them: Be fruitful and multiply and replenish the earth" (Gen. 1:27, 28). "Therefore shall a man leave his father and his mother and shall cleave unto his wife; and they shall be one flesh" (Gen. 2:24). Christ utters the command "What God hath joined together, let not man put asunder" (Matt. 19:6).

The Christian ideal of marriage is emphasized by Christ in His reply to the Pharisees concerning divorce (Matt. 19:4-6; Mark 10:6-9). It is the union for life of one man and one woman in mutual love and faithfulness. They are one flesh, and God wants this union to last until death separates it. In its true nature, marriage is monogamous and indissoluble. Polygamy, though practiced in Old Testament times and by the heathen, is contrary to the divine order as established in the beginning (Matt. 19:8). It ignores the equal value of woman as a person, and makes of her only a chattel of man and a means for the gratification of lust.

The God-declared purposes of marriage are in keeping with the Christian ideal of marriage. According to the Scripture marriage was instituted for the promotion of human happiness (Gen. 2:18), for the orderly propagation of the race (Gen. 1:27), and for the proper care and education of children (Eph. 6:4).

Now, what are some of the modern factors affecting the solidarity of the family? Let us begin with the dangers which threaten the family and which lie in the changes that have come upon us through modern industrialization. With the coming of the machine in the modern factory system, first the working man was taken out of the home, then the working child, and now the working woman. Father and mother and the children do not live and work and play together as they did in olden times. They see relatively little of each other. Home life, which used to engender in the child homemaking qualities, is gradually changing, and for many families it has indeed undergone a complete transition. Children are now often brought up in apartment houses, where labor-saving devices and other amenities of our twentieth-century civilization obviate any training in domestic duties and hence eliminate the spirit of co-operation which such duties foster.

Many mothers are employed at remunerative work away from home during the daytime. The effects of such employment on family life and on the health and moral education of the children are obvious. It is impossible for a mother occupied all day away from home to perform her family duties and to give adequate care and supervision to her children. The result is only too often that a house is used by the entire family merely as a place in which to eat and sleep. When she is tired from her day's industrial work, it is well-nigh impossible for a woman to prepare nourishing meals, to keep the home attractive, and to give due attention to her husband and children. Infant mortality, poor health, broken homes, divorce, juvenile delinquency, are frequent results of a woman's occupying an industrial position. Modern industrialization poses a very serious threat directly to the home and indirectly to the Church.

Equally threatening to the home and the Church are the dangers which come from modern forms of thought. One of the outstanding characteristics of modern literature is the defense of moral laxity in sexual matters. Combined with this defense is the advocacy of free love and companionate marriage, the pagan adoration of the body and its beauty, the curtailment of feminine attire, the near nudity and the suggestive scenes of the moving pictures and the stage, the detailed newspaper accounts of sex irregularities perpetrated by men and women of the screen, who are heroes and heroines to many of our adolescent youth, the pornographic and near-pornographic stories in our pulp-paper magazines, and the smutty realism of many popular novels.

To bring up a family of clean and mentally and morally healthy boys and girls under such circumstances is a most difficult task. I know of no time in the history of the world when the family and family life was under pressure of more adverse influences than it is today.

What can we do about it? The real cure must come by a process of Christian education and the inculcation of Christian ideals. Faithfulness in the use of God's Word is the most necessary element in the preservation of the family and the Christian home. The Word of God is the channel through which the powers of the other world are led into this present world and brought to the heart of the Christian. Let everyone use the Word not for entertainment or for increasing one's knowledge or for criticism, but for edification, that is, with the intention of meditating upon it, following up its inner connections, and applying it to oneself that it may satisfy the longing of the soul for salvation, be profitable for doctrine, for reproof, for correction, for instruction in righteousness.

Let the Church lift up its voice with might and tell the world that marriage is a divine institution, not a mere temporary contract between human beings that may be broken at the will of either of the two contracting parties, that children are a heritage of the Lord (Ps. 127:3), and that parents should bring them up in the nurture and admonition of the Lord, that the spiritual well-being of their children must always be for Christian parents a matter of most vital moment. Let our young people's societies, our Sunday schools, and above all our Christian day schools be fostered by all the people of the entire congregation, and let these institutions remember that their worth depends upon the use which they make of the Word.

To the above we might well add the sincere and effective effort to cultivate a Christian family spirit. This is the invisible bond of union which ties the various members of the family together into a distinct group. It is a definite feeling of belonging together, of having mutual aims and interests, of reverence for family history, traditions, and customs.

How can this be done? For the cultivation of a Christian family spirit the establishment of a family altar is essential. By the family altar we mean that all the members of the household gather together at stated times before the Throne of Grace and that they unite their hearts and voices in praise and thanksgiving, in prayer and in intercession for each other, and cultivate the consciousness of the "unseen Friend" in every need. Furthermore, to cultivate the Christian family spirit, the parents ought to do all within their power to make home a place where the children like to be and where they will find appropriate entertainment (reading, music, radio).

In this connection it should be noted that the observance of family festivals, such as Christmas, Thanksgiving Day, birthdays, and other anniversaries will help much to establish fond memories of the home long after its sheltering walls have been left behind by the younger generation. One of the most beautiful sights on earth is that of a loving and harmonious Christian family.

Church-State Relationships

Our next topic for discussion concerns the relationship between the Church and the State. Whatever goes on in the State affects what goes on in the Church. The strength and health of the Church is a matter of vital concern to the State, and the strength and health of the State is a matter of vital concern to the Church. Strange as it may seem, this is an area of human activity in which there has been much muddled thinking almost during the entire Christian era. Some have wanted the State to be a servant of the Church, and others have wanted the Church to be a servant of the State. Some have glorified the State unduly, and others—well-meaning Christians—have denied to the State the right of existence. These latter people maintain that Christians should have nothing to do whatever with the affairs of the State and that they owe allegiance to no earthly power, that the act of saluting the American flag, for example, is a form of idolatry.

Scripture very definitely states that civil government is ordained of God and obedience to the government is a Christian's obligation. The government is God's servant for the punishment of evildoers and the protection of those that do well. It is not simply a human arrangement or a social contract (philosophical schools of Rousseau, Kant, Spencer, Hobbes, Locke, and others: Man surrendered some of his rights to the collective will or community. By so doing he transferred himself from a natural state into a civil state, and in the transfer under a social contract the civil state arose. After finding itself in a civil state, the collective will or community then proceeded to determine its form of government), but it is an ordinance of God for the maintenance of law and order and the furtherance of human welfare. Disobedience to the government is disobedience to God, whose agent the government is. So long as the laws of the State are not in conflict with laws of God, it is the duty of the Christian to render implicit obedience to them. Whenever the government ceases to be "a minister of God for good," "a revenger to execute wrath upon him that doeth evil"; when a government constantly violates every principle of right and justice and in fact becomes a minister of Satan for evil, it becomes the duty of every Christian to join with his fellow citizens to bring about much-needed reforms.

It will help us in the understanding of our problem if we bear in mind that the State has one sphere of influence and the Church another. The State has one set of functions and the Church quite another. The State has one set of means for obtaining its ends and the Church quite another. Though these spheres of influence differ from each other, though the functions of the State differ from the functions of the Church, they do affect in the case of Christian men and Christian women the same people.

What are some of the *functions of the civil government?* The main function of the government is to establish, preserve, and maintain the right of life, liberty, and the pursuit of happiness. We call these rights natural rights; that is, they are possessed by the individual by reason of the fact that he is a human being. The State does not confer them. It cannot confer them. God conferred them on the individual when He created him. The State merely guards and protects them.

The purpose of the State is not primarily economic, just as it is not primarily scientific, artistic, or religious. But since it is the business of the State to regulate the temporal affairs of its citizens to such an extent as is necessary for the protection of the general welfare, economic, scientific, artistic, and even religious questions come in for a large share of the State's attention.

The methods and means with which the State operates are carnal. Decisions must be made on the basis of reason. The stick, the revolver, the robot bombs, the B-29's, and the block busters, the atomic bombs, are the weapons of the State.

The task of the Church is spiritual. The Church is concerned primarily with the immortal soul of the individual. It is set for the evangelizing of the world (Matt. 28:19-20).

For this purpose it has been entrusted with the administration of the Word and the Sacraments. These are the means through which the Holy Ghost carries on His saving and sanctifying work in the hearts and lives of men. They are the means through which the saving grace of God comes to men. These means through which the Holy Spirit operates must be faithfully administered by the Church. In so far as she fails in any wise to measure up to this duty, the work of the Holy Ghost in the hearts and lives of men is impeded, and the evangelization of the world is retarded.

The Church must faithfully preach the Word (II Tim. 4:2), and she must preach it in its purity (Gal. 1:8). It pleased God by the foolishness of preaching to save them that believe (I Cor. 1:21). Unless she preaches the Word to men, they will not be brought to Christ, their Savior (Rom. 10:13-15), nor be built up in the faith (John 17:17). She must preach the real Gospel and not some substitute for it; otherwise men will go about to establish their own righteousness, instead of submitting themselves to the righteousness which is of God in Christ (Rom. 10:3).

The modes in which she administers the Word are public preaching, Bible class, Christian day school, Sunday school, young people's work, home missions, foreign missions, inner missions, bedside ministrations, religious publications, radio activity, and such other methods of proclaiming evangelical truth as may from time to time be advisable and necessary for the proper prosecution of her work.

It is very evident that the purposes and means and methods of the State vary greatly from the purposes and means and methods of the Church. These two sets of purposes, means, and methods must always be kept separate in our thinking.

It is quite evident even to the casual observer that a multitude of duties and functions have been added to those of the State in the past fifty years. Whether this trend is healthy or unhealthy I do not wish to discuss in this essay. For purposes of our present discussion it is sufficient to point out that functions which have been taken over by the government have been taken from individuals and corporations and thus affect our day-to-day life very materially. Problems that arise from the State-Church relationship are on the increase and will, I believe, continue to increase in the years which lie ahead.

In addition to the above trend in governmental thinking we of the Missouri Synod have an additional set of problems, arising from the fact that for seventy-five years we were an immigrant Church and that for the past twenty-five years we have gradually ceased being an immigrant Church. For about seventy-five years we had relatively little to do with Church-State relationships. We were German. Many of our people could not speak English, and many were dead set against learning English. Furthermore, many believed that outside of obeying the laws and paying their taxes Christians should have little to do with government. The danger of mixing Church and State was ever present in the thinking of our fathers. It was at times a convenient excuse for non-participation in governmental affairs.

Now the situation has changed. We have been in this country for three or four generations. Our Church is fast absorbing the traditions, the culture, and the language of America. The rate of absorption is steadily increasing, and Church-State relationships are increasing in complexity. Our people will participate more and more in governmental affairs. This is a good sign, but it means problems for the Church. The 140,000 young men and women who were uprooted and forced to spend from two to five years away from the influence of Christian home environment will have their thinking about social relationships deeply affected. We can expect our people to be affected more and more by currents of American political thinking.

We can expect that the evils of party politics and party fanaticism, the ever-present danger of graft and dishonesty, the tendency to disregard disagreeable laws, will be a constant threat to the spiritual life of our members.

What can the Church do? The Church must ever enlighten the conscience of her members on troublesome public questions. Keeping strictly within her sphere, the Church must put forth every effort that the nation within whose boundaries she exists become more and more permeated with the principles of social life laid down in the Word of God, the principles of righteousness, of justice, of tolerance and forbearance, of mutual helpfulness and co-operation.

She must do this not by futile efforts to control legislation or to direct the administration of government, but by laboring patiently and persistently to increase the number of those within the nation whose hearts have been regenerated by the Spirit of God and whose lives are directed by that Spirit. Not by invading political assemblies, but by entering the pulpit with an emphatic and convincing proclamation of the whole Gospel of Christ can the Church make a real contribution to the political well-being of our nation. The fact that the State and the Church are two separate and distinct organisms, that they have two separate and distinct spheres of influence, does not imply that they should assume an attitude of complete indifference toward each other; on the contrary, a mutual friendly recognition and a readiness on the part of each (within the limitations of its own scope and sphere) to aid and serve the other is indispensable to the peace and prosperity of both. "Let each his lesson learn with care, and all the household well shall fare."

A third set of dangers threatens our Church from our modern industrial employer-employee relationships, formerly called the relationship between capital and labor.

What does Scripture say about labor? In the beginning God gave man a dominant position in the world. The earth was man's dwelling place, and every creature was for his use and enjoyment. But even before the Fall, man was expected to work (Gen. 1:28-29; Ps. 8:6). After the Fall the sentence read: "In the sweat of thy face shalt thou eat bread" (Gen. 3:19). The mastery of nature was to take place through work. Work is the basis of all human progress and civilization.

The dignity of labor is a distinctly Christian achievement. In the pre-Christian Mediterranean world, labor, especially manual labor, was for slaves only. The free citizen devoted himself to intellectual pursuits and to politics.

The Bible speaks of labor not merely as a burden nor simply as a discipline, nor even as a means of obtaining a livelihood, but as a really God-pleasing service, no matter how mean and lowly it may be, if only it is rendered in the fear and love of God. I Cor. 7:20-22: "Let every man abide in the same calling wherein he was called. Art thou called being a servant? Care not for it; but if thou mayest be made free, use it rather. For he that is called in the Lord, being a servant, is the Lord's freeman; likewise also he that is called being free is Christ's servant." I Cor. 10:31: "Whether, therefore, ye eat . . . do all to the glory of God." Eph. 6:5-9: Employer-employee relationships. Labor is the orderly manner of life for a Christian. It is the only proper way to provide a living for themselves and those dependent upon them (I Thess. 4:9-12; II Thess. 3:6-13). Labor is the means to enable Christians to practice Christian charity.

Labor and property go together. Property represents the fruit of some form of labor. Labor may be said to be the divinely appointed method of acquiring property (Gen. 1:28; Ps. 128:2; Prov. 13:4; II Thess. 3:10-12), and the accumulation of property is one of the blessings God bestows upon labor.

One of the distinct characteristics of our modern age is the remarkable development of large industrial concerns with an almost endless variety of highly specialized occupations. We are living in a machine age. It cannot be denied that the development of the machine and its use in modern industry has brought uncounted blessings to man. But it has brought new tasks, new difficulties, new problems, and new dangers to the men and women and children who make up our congregations.

The development of the machine has brought about a radical change in the relationship between master and workman, employer and employee. In the pre-machine age manufacture was usually carried on in small shops, often connected directly with the home of the employer, who engaged only a small number of men to assist him in his work. These naturally entered into very close personal relationship with the master, who was responsible not only for the technical training of his apprentices but also for their social and civic education and their personal well-being.

Today we have production on a gigantic scale in enormous factories involving millions of dollars in capital investments. These investments belong to thousands of individuals who purchase them in the form of stocks and bonds. These people have no interest in the enterprise or in the way it is managed except a reasonable financial return on their investment. The relationship between the owners and workers is quite impersonal. It is in this situation that we must seek the origin of endless problems between capital and labor: the soulless machine, the detachment of management from ownership, and the highly developed profit motive of the capitalistic system.

It is not within the province of the Church to devise or endorse any particular economic or industrial system. The relationship between employer and employee is purely human.

What can the Church do in the matter? Must it sit idly by and twiddle its thumbs? There is grave danger in doing nothing. The Church may find it increasingly difficult to interest labor in its work if the Church is not interested in the problems of labor. Should the Church take sides? Many economic historians in our country claim that the Church is generally on the side of the biggest money bags. What ought the Church to do?

It is within the province of the Church to point out the fundamental principles on which all industrial relationships should rest according to the Word of God. The Church must point out the inherent worth of human personality, that everyone of us is his brother's keeper, that there is a stewardship of all earthly goods, including wealth, power, time, ability, and opportunity. Every man must someday give an account of his stewardship. As a fourth principle the Church must accentuate the undeniable principle that the laborer is worthy of his hire, a hire not simply sufficient to assure his physical existence, but one that will enable him to establish and maintain a home, raise a family, and look forward to the sunset days of his life with equanimity and confidence; a hire, too, that is in some proportion to the economic value of his service to the community, and, finally, the right of private property to be maintained.

In view of the deplorable physical and spiritual conditions so widely prevalent among the working people of our great industrial centers, the Church must develop an aggressive missionary activity in such centers. The Church must bring the Gospel of peace and love to those whose souls are starving for the Bread of Life and whose minds are poisoned with the bitterness of their economic struggle.

How this can be done in the most effective manner must be a matter of grave concern to individual Christians, to synodical officers, especially mission boards and mission secretaries.

The difficulties and dangers threatening our Church as we near the century mark of our existence are truly great. Unbelief, doubt, indifference, weariness in the work of the Kingdom, adverse conditions affecting our hearths and homes, evil influences arising from a rapidly industrialized state and materialistic society—all these tend by a process of attrition to destroy the strength of the Church. We are sent forth as sheep in the midst of wolves.

But our Lord and Master, the Overshepherd of the flock, has equipped us with powerful weapons. Our cause is not lost. The future is bright in Christ. "Finally, my brethren, be strong in the Lord and in the power of His might. Put on the whole armor of God, that ye may be able to stand against the wiles of the devil. For we wrestle not against flesh and blood but against principalities, against powers, against the rulers of the darkness of this world, against spiritual wickedness in high places. Wherefore take unto you the whole armor of God, that ye may be able to withstand in the evil day and, having done all, to stand. Stand, therefore, having your loins girt about with truth, and having on the breastplate of righteousness, and your feet shod with the preparation of the Gospel of peace; above all, taking the shield of faith, wherewith ye shall be able to quench all the fiery darts of the wicked. And take the helmet of salvation and the sword of the spirit, which is the Word of God" (Eph. 6:10-17).

"Therefore, my beloved brethren, be ye steadfast, unmovable, always abounding in the work of the Lord, forasmuch as ye know that your labor is not in vain in the Lord" (I Cor. 15:58).

XXIV

Civil Government

Iɴ His sacerdotal prayer Christ says that His disciples are not of
the world, that they no longer conform to the manner and ways
of the sinful and unbelieving world. Yet Christ has not taken them
out of the world. They are still within the world and as such have
the duty to shine as lights in the midst of a crooked and perverse
nation and to be blameless and beyond reproach also in their attitude
toward those ordinances which God has instituted for the preservation of order and discipline and peace in a world of sin. One of these
divine institutions is civil government.

Tʜᴇsɪs I

*Civil government is a divine institution comprising the whole
number of those persons through whom by divine ordinance the
legislative, judicial, and executive powers necessary for the governing of a commonwealth are administered in accordance with the
form of government obtaining within that commonwealth.*

Civil government is, as Scripture informs us, an institution of God.
God, who is good to all and whose tender mercies are over all His
works (Ps. 145:9), is also a God, not of confusion and disorder, but
of peace (I Cor. 14:33) and therefore has made provisions that
peace and order rule on earth as far as that is possible in a world
of sin and unrighteousness. How did God do that? Let us go back
to the day when Noah left the ark after the Flood, which had
destroyed every living thing from the face of the earth with the
exception of Noah and his family. Smelling the sweet savor of the
sacrifice which grateful Noah had offered to the Lord, God promised
never again to curse the ground for man's sake, never again to inter-

rupt the course of seedtime and harvest, cold and heat, summer and winter, day and night, while the earth remaineth. He blessed man and told him to replenish the earth and rule over it. And then He promised He would protect their most precious possession, their life. "Surely your blood of your lives will I require. At the hand of every beast will I require it, and at the hand of man. At the hand of every man's brother will I require the life of man" (Gen. 8:20; 9:5). But God did not intend to punish personally and immediately every infraction of man's right to live. He delegated this authority of avenging murder to human agents. "Whoso sheddeth man's blood, by man shall his blood be shed" (Gen. 9:6). Thus did God Himself institute in the rejuvenated world the authority and duty of man to safeguard the life of his fellow man and to punish the shedder of human blood by shedding his blood.

Here God instituted governmental authority, although He did not prescribe any special form of government. Noah, the father of the family, was the first head, the first ruler, the first government in the new world, vested by the Lord Himself with judicial authority, even the power of the sword, for the punishment of evildoers. A few centuries later we see Abraham, the housefather, ruling at the same time as the sovereign of the family, leading his servants into battle against the unjust and predatory kings in order to save his nephew, Lot. And he is not faulted, but blessed by the Lord (Gen. 14). God Himself called Moses to be the deliverer and ruler and lawgiver of Israel (Ex. 3:1-22) and Joshua as his successor (Num. 27:15-23; Josh. 1:1-9). It was God who chose Saul to be the first king over His people Israel (I Sam. 9:16), who rejected him (I Sam. 13:13, 14), and who chose David in his stead (I Sam. 16:1-13; II Sam. 7:8-11). And God did not only appoint the kings of Israel. At His command Hazael was anointed to be king over Syria (I Kings 19:15; II Kings 8:13). Daniel makes the general statement: God "removeth kings and setteth up kings" (Dan. 2:21), and tells Nebuchadnezzar, the mighty ruler of the world, that the God of heaven had given to this king of kings a kingdom, power, and strength, and glory (Dan. 2:37); and "that the Most High ruleth in the kingdom of men and giveth it to whomsoever He will and setteth up over it the basest of men" (Dan. 4:17; cp. vv. 25, 31, 32; 5:21). Christ tells wicked Pilate, the Roman procurator, who boasted of his authority which he so arbitrarily and unjustly used, "Thou couldest have no power at all against Me, except it were given thee from above" (John 19:10). Paul very emphatically teaches the divine institution of government, irrespective of its character or form, so long as it has power to rule. "Let every soul be subject unto the higher powers. For there is no power but of God; the powers that be are ordained of God. Whosoever therefore resisteth the power, resisteth the ordinance of God" (Rom. 13:1, 2). And three times (vv. 4, 5) he calls government the "minister of God," a servant, or attendant, who carries out the will of his Master, through whom God maintains order and discipline in the world.

Peter's statement: "Submit yourselves to every ordinance of man" (I Pet. 2:13) does not deny that government is divinely instituted. Irrespective of how we understand the term "ordinance of man," there is the clear demand that we should obey these ordinances, whether they be higher or lower authorities, "for the Lord's sake." God demands such obedience, because, as Paul says, they are *God's* ministers, divinely instituted.

Civil government remains a divine ordinance regardless of how individuals acquire their authority or enter upon their office. Ordinarily the agencies of government are set up, and the individuals for the offices chosen, through man. In some cases the son or daughter follows the parent in authority. Some are elected by groups or the entire people, some wrest this power unto themselves by force or cunning, but regardless of how the power was acquired, the government in power is still the "ordinance of God." We do not mean to say that God endorses or sanctions the evil methods of acquiring power, but He does often permit such governments to come into existence and to exercise authority as a chastisement upon the people so governed. For the same reason God permits evil rulers and evil administrations to continue in office, sometimes for many years.

The form of government may vary greatly in different nations or the world. What is suitable in one nation or for one people may not be suited at all to the needs of another. Although God gave to Israel its form of government and afterward permitted a change, He does not by any command or recommendation establish any particular form. Whether a form of government is imposed upon a people by individuals, by groups, by conquest, or by choice, it still remains an ordinance of God. And what is said of government in general applies also to every individual unit of government, whether separate state, city, country, borough, or township. Everyone connected with the administration of the law, with government, is placed there by divine authority. These men are the government through whom God regulates the affairs of men in this world; they are His representatives, for "the powers that be are ordained of God."

Thesis II

The duties of civil government are: to promote the general welfare of its people by protecting the individuals and groups in their civil rights and to defend the state against dangers from within and without.

The proper province of civil government is not the religious sphere; it has not been instituted for the spiritual welfare of man, nor for preparing him for eternity. That duty has been given by the Lord of the Church Himself to the Church, and He has clearly and definitely defined that duty. He therefore also has distinguished between Church and State and wants that distinction maintained. John 18:36 He says: "My kingdom is not of this world," and in Matt. 22:21 we read: "Render therefore unto Caesar the things that are Caesar's, and unto God the things that are God's." Civil government governs the state, and as the state is something tangible, visible, temporal, so civil government is confined to that same sphere. It deals only with such things as are subject to reason. The deputy of the Roman Empire for Achaia, Gallion, knew and practiced this distinction when he refused to judge in spiritual matters (Acts 18:12-17). The historic position of our Church is clearly attested in Article XXVIII of the Augsburg Confession, where we read: "Since the ecclesiastical power grants eternal things and is exercised only by the ministry of the Word, it does not interfere with civil government any more than the art of singing interferes with civil government. For civil government deals with other things than does the Gospel. The civil rulers defend not minds, but bodies and bodily things against manifest injuries; and restrain men with the sword and bodily punishments in order to preserve civil justice and peace. Therefore the power of the Church and the civil power must not be confounded." (*Triglot,* p. 85, § 10-12.)

The duty of government is to promote the welfare of the people, order, discipline, and peace within the commonwealth. When St. Paul admonishes Christians to pray for all in authority, he adds as the reason for such prayer "that we may lead a quiet and peaceable life in all godliness and honesty" (I Tim. 2:2). In these words the holy writer establishes as the essential duty of government the promotion of the general welfare by protecting each and every member of the state in his civil rights. For where law and order, peace and quiet prevail, there the members of the body politic individually as well as collectively may fulfill their duties toward each of the three divinely ordained institutions, Church, home, and state, and thus the entire commonwealth may prosper. The state is made up of many individuals differing as to their social rank, their profession, their economic standing, their abilities, their knowledge, their religion. These differences, however, are not to influence the government's attitude toward its citizens. The authority of the government is to be used and applied for the protection of all citizens alike, and even the violators of the law and condemned criminals are to enjoy this protection against violence. Government, therefore, has the duty, for the protection of the commonwealth and the promotion of the general good, to suppress mob violence, no matter in what manner or form it may rear its ugly head. Failure to do so makes the civil authorities themselves partners to the crime.

Government is also to protect the civil rights of its citizens, those rights which are the natural rights of every human being, the right of being what God made them and of owning what God gave them.

Chief among these rights is the right of life. God is the Author and Preserver of life, and, as we have seen in the first thesis, He has commanded man and particularly government to protect the life of man (Gen. 9:6; Matt. 26:52; Rom. 13:4). Under this head we may include the right and duty of government to safeguard the life and health of the individual by laws demanding the installation of proper safety devices in factories, of fire escapes, etc., in public buildings, by laws forbidding the contamination of the water supply, by traffic and speed laws, by quarantines in times of epidemics, and by the thousand and one regulations and ordinances needed to safeguard life and limb and health in the complex living conditions of our age.

Next to life, a man's honor and reputation is his most prized possession, and laws protecting his good name and directed against slander and libel are justly within the scope of state or national laws.

Another right to be protected by civil government is that of property, and the authorities are only doing their duty when they guard the property of the individuals or corporations against theft or destruction by individuals or groups organized for this purpose.

Every citizen unquestionably has the right to work, to earn his living by the labor of his hands or mind. When God says, "If any would not work, neither shall he eat" (II Thess. 3:10), He not only declares laziness, the unwillingness to work, a sin, but thereby establishes the divine order that material welfare, as a rule, be based upon labor. The right to choose an occupation, or calling, or work, and the right to be active in that calling must be granted every one, and civil authorities are to protect all their citizens in this right and permit neither capitalists nor labor agitators to curtail this right. "While the right of uniting for legitimate purposes, for the exercise of common right, for fellowship in labor or enjoyment, must not be impugned, banding together for illicit purposes, complicity in wrongdoing, or for infringing upon the rights of others, cannot be morally sanctioned. Laborers' unions are proper when by lawful means they assert their common rights; they are evil when by illicit means they assert their own rights, or when by any means they encroach upon the rights of others. And especially when they exercise coercion by means of force, they usurp rights which are not theirs, rights which are also of the civic sphere, the rights of civil governments" (*Theological Quarterly*, III, p. 429).

Other rights which government is in duty bound to protect are the right of freedom of speech and assembly and particularly the right of religious liberty and freedom of conscience. Since religion is a relation between man and his Maker, and since in matters of conscience man is to acknowledge but one norm, the will of God, no man has the right to dictate to his fellow man in matters of religion and conscience. Governmental interference in these matters is tyranny, and can under no circumstances be morally justified.

A further duty of civil government is to protect the state against dangers from within and without. The peace and welfare of the commonwealth is disturbed, of course, by every transgression of the law, but there are such dangers also as are a direct threat to the existing form of government, *e. g.*, when individuals, or organizations, or parties attempt to overthrow the government by violence.

It therefore is a duty of the government to be on the lookout against such subversive, seditious activities and to suppress them before they spread and work harm to the state. In our country we have the right of free speech, so that individuals as well as organizations may voice and spread their own views and ideas even about government, but the civil authorities may not tolerate any political or social or economic propaganda that has as its aim the overthrow by violence of the existing form of government or the constituted authorities. When disturbances of peace are created by any groups within the commonwealth it is the duty of the government in the interest of the peace and welfare of its loyal subjects to put down such disturbances, be they riots, mobocracy, or armed insurrection and revolution.

Since government must exercise its authority as "the minister of God to thee for good," and since it bears the sword as a revenger to execute wrath upon him that doeth evil (Rom. 13:4), it must use this authority also when the interests of individuals, or groups, or of the entire commonwealth are threatened from without, by foreign individuals, or groups, or states. Government, therefore, has the right to declare war if its efforts to safeguard these interests by peaceable means are not successful. In waging any war, however, the re-establishment of peace must be one of the chief aims of government, since it has no right to sacrifice the property and the lives of its subjects needlessly. Peace should be considered the normal state of the community, and the preservation or restoration of peace is to be the prime consideration of government.

Thesis III

In the administration of its duties government must make use of all ways and means necessary and suitable for the proper discharge of its obligations.

This is a truth so obvious that it really needs no proof. No one can achieve his purpose unless he possesses the necessary means and makes use of them. The functions of government being of so varied a nature and so wide a scope, the means needed in order to do justice to all these various functions must naturally vary greatly. What will well serve its purpose at one time and in one age may be altogether unsuited under changed circumstances, and what may be expedient and even necessary in one state may be entirely unsuitable and even detrimental in another. Yet there are certain basic requirements without which government could not adequately serve its purpose.

Civil government could not properly function without exercising some form of legislative, judicial, and executive power. This threefold authority is exercised by every government even when this power is not specifically named or defined in a constitution.

An essential means for government is legislation. Government is impossible without some form of law. Lawless government is not government, but disorder, confusion, anarchy. Laws are not made to be a dead letter; they are not enacted merely to be on record in the minutes of the legislative body or published in some form. Laws are made to regulate the life of the citizens of the commonwealth.

According to the laws enacted by the legislators, the actions and words of the citizens are to be judged. Therefore there must be judges, whose duty is to judge those who are guilty of any infraction of the law and to decide whether any one charged with neglect of or willful disobedience to the law is guilty or not. And if guilty, the penalty provided by the law must be inflicted by the proper authorities. In this manner the majesty of the law must be vindicated. "It is the duty of jurors and attorneys and judges to do what is in their power that every one who has, and no one who has not, offended against these laws may be promptly convicted and duly sentenced according to law and the nature and circumstances of the case, and it is the duty of the executive to let the law take its course in the execution of the sentence. Executive clemency, the pardoning of criminals, is not a matter of justice, but of policy. It is not the government's business to exercise mercy on criminals, but to protect society and its members against criminals, and only when this purpose is not thereby endangered may executive clemency have its way, and pardon may be granted where punishment was decreed. On the other hand, the defiance of the letter and spirit of the law by mercenary lawyers, the corruption of juries and judges and other judicial abuses, are moral offenses of extreme gravity which work the ruin of a people with fearful certainty." (*Theol. Quart.*, III, p. 436.)

What is the norm to be followed by the government in making use of the means supplied by its legislative, judicial, and executive powers? This norm is not the Moral Law of God as revealed in the Bible. "If it were, the laws of all nations would have been and would be today inadequate to their purpose, the law of Israel not excepted. For the Mosaic political law was not the Moral Law. The law of divorce which permitted a man to send his wife out of the house with a bill of divorcement, because she found no favor in his eyes (Deut. 24:1, 2) was certainly not in accordance with the Moral Law (Matt. 19:7-9), but came short of it, while numerous statutes of the Mosaic code went beyond the precepts of the Moral Law, which does not prohibit pork as an article of food (Deut. 14:8), or military service during the first year of married life (Deut. 20:7), or plowing with an ox and an ass together (Deut. 22:10), or fabrics made of wool and linen mixed (Deut. 22:11). Thus, also, the census law of Augustus was not a precept of the Moral Law; yet Joseph and Mary complied therewith (Luke 2:1ff.), as Jesus with the Temple-tax law (Matt. 17:24ff.). Paul claimed his rights under the Roman law as a Roman citizen (Acts 16:37ff.; 25:8; 22:25), not according to the Moral Law, which says nothing of the impropriety of beating a Roman (Acts 16:37; 22:25ff.), or of the right of appeal to Caesar (Acts 25:11, 21). There never was nor can be a civil court capable of judging according to the Moral Law, which requires an omniscient judge, before whom every evil thought and desire is manifest. Nor can the penalty imposed by the Moral Law be inflicted by a human executioner, but only by Him who is able to destroy both soul and body in hell (Matt. 10:28)." (*Theol. Quart.*, III, p. 434f.)

In carrying out its legislative, judicial, and executive functions government must follow the Natural Law as it is still inscribed in the hearts of natural man, and the dictates of reason, experience, and common sense.

Experience teaches that it is worse than useless to legislate far ahead of public opinion. It is a hopeless endeavor to try to raise the moral standard by mere legislation. In a state where just and unjust live side by side, where Christians are in the minority, where the natural aversion to legal coercion is unrestrained in the general public, the enforcement of a high moral standard is often impossible. Even in the commonwealth of Israel, Moses was obliged to permit a marriage to be legally severed by a divorce, the rightfulness of which was not sanctioned by the Moral Law of God. "Moses," says

Christ, "because of the hardness of your hearts suffered you to put away your wives; but from the beginning it was not so" (Matt. 19:8). Enforcement of a moral standard by legislation upon a people simply not willing to adopt that standard will only work harm. People will seek ways and means of evading the law, look for loopholes, will try to bribe the judges, and often succeed, and so this legislation, good as it may be in itself, will only breed and foster still greater contempt of all laws, produce lawbreakers. The best legislation in a commonwealth composed of good and evil people will demand a standard of morality above the general level of the populace, but not so far above as to make its enforcement impossible in that particular community.

Thesis IV

The relation of the members of a commonwealth to their government is that of subjects to a superior authority. As subjects of their government they are to render for conscience' sake due honor, obedience, and service to their government as far as this can be done without violating God's Law.

This thesis speaks of the relation and duties of the members of a state or commonwealth toward their government. Since government is called a power, an authority, it is evident that those ruled by these powers are their subjects. The duties of citizens as subjects of government are clearly defined in a number of Scripture passages and for the sake of convenience may be grouped under three heads: honor, obedience, service.

HONOR YOUR GOVERNMENT

"Render therefore to all their dues," Paul says, speaking of what we owe to the higher powers, the powers that be, the existing authorities; and he continues, "Honor to whom honor is due" (Rom. 13:7). We owe honor to all governmental persons, irrespective of their higher or lower rank. In the preceding verses Paul had pointed out the honor which is theirs by divine will. Not only are they vested with an office of divine institution, but every officer of the state, every person in an official position is ordained, assigned to his place by God, is appointed by God (Rom. 13:1), honored by God to be made His "minister," or servant, through whom God rules the community (v. 4, 5), and as such clothed by God Himself with the power and authority he holds in his particular office. *Therefore* render to all their dues. You owe honor to these men in office. Paul was well aware that most of the persons holding official positions in the Roman Empire were heathen, many of them dishonorable characters, unfit to be rulers. And still God wants them to be honored as His ministers.

What a lesson for Christian citizens! It is not always an easy matter to render due honor to officials, judges, legislators, whom we know to be disreputable men, companions of gangsters, dishonest, venal. Yet, however wicked and dishonorable his character, being one of the authorities that be, he has been honored by God to be His minister. This honor is his due, and God demands that we render to him his dues, honor to whom honor is due.

OBEY YOUR GOVERNMENT

A second obligation devolving on every member of the commonwealth, every subject of a government, is that of obedience. The very term "subject" implies this duty. To be subject to another means that one no longer has the right to do as he pleases, that he is placed under the will of another, that he must do as told by his superior or suffer the consequences. Reason and common sense regard it as self-evident that if government is to govern, to rule, it must insist on obedience and must be given the right to insist on being obeyed. Else it would cease to be what it is supposed to be, government. And again, God does not leave this matter of obedience to be decided by logical deduction and reasonable arguments. God demands of the subjects obedience to their government. "Put them in mind," Paul charges Titus, the bishop of Crete, "to be subject to principalities and powers, to obey magistrates" (Tit. 3:1). To the Romans he writes: "Let every soul be subject unto the higher powers. . . . Wherefore ye must needs be subject, not only for wrath, but also for conscience' sake" (ch. 13:1a, 5). And Peter says: "Submit yourselves to every ordinance of man for the Lord's sake" (I Pet. 2:13). There can be no doubt, if we want to obey God, we must obey our government, for God demands such obedience. Need we repeat that such obedience is due to government as government, irrespective of the character of the individual incumbents? Or need we reiterate that obedience is due to all governmental officials, to all persons in authority, be they president, or senators, or aldermen, or policemen, or health officers? God makes no distinction. Neither may we.

Neither is obedience to be limited to such laws as are to our liking, with the liberty of disregarding laws with which we do not agree, which we regard as inadequate, or unwise, or which for any other reason do not find our approval. Of course, if a law conflicts with God's Law and obedience to that law would be disobedience against God's command, the word of Peter applies: "We ought to obey God rather than men" (Acts 5:29; 4:19).

And again, if the constitution under which the government operates permits citizens to seek a change of the existing laws, we may make use of all legal ways and means to effect such a change, to abrogate insufficient, unwise, impractical legislation and substitute for it legislation really serving the best interests and welfare of the community. But as long as a law exists, the citizens of the commonwealth which through its legislators has enacted it must render obedience to it.

Obedience to the laws is not restricted to those laws only that flow from or are in agreement with the Natural Law, but also such laws and regulations must be obeyed that government issues or enacts in matters that do not come under the scope of the Natural Law. As examples of such we might mention rationing, control of markets and prices, traffic laws and regulations, hunting and fishing laws, and similar measures.

SERVE YOUR GOVERNMENT

A third duty of citizens as subjects of their government is service. Wherever a Christian has an opportunity to serve his government by word or deed, it is his bounden duty to do so. As a Christian, he will include his government in his daily prayers. Particularly in these critical times he will ask God to grant to those in authority wisdom and understanding to guide the ship of state safely through storm and breakers. "I exhort, therefore," says the Apostle, "that, first of all, supplications, prayers, intercessions, and giving of thanks be made for all men; for kings and for all that are in authority; that we may lead a quiet and peaceable life in all godliness and honesty. For this is good and acceptable in the sight of God, our Savior"

(I Tim. 2:1-3). In a letter addressed to the Jews deported to Babylon, Jeremiah exhorts them to do their full duties as citizens of the country into which the Lord had caused them to be carried away captives, and then exhorts them: "Pray unto the Lord for it" (Jer. 29:1-7). Christians ought never to forget to pray for their government.

A Christian will serve his government by making use of his right of suffrage and will carefully and conscientiously cast his vote for such candidates or such legislation as will best serve the welfare of the commonwealth and its authorities. Says Jeremiah, "Seek the peace of the city . . . for in the peace thereof shall ye have peace" (Jer. 29:7). The Christian will not shirk his duties as a citizen, such as serving on a jury, on committees to promote public welfare, or to prevent the spread of public dangers, epidemics, famines, floods, etc. Needless to say, a Christian should be ready to serve in any public office, and as a public servant of the state seek not his own political, or social, or financial advantage, but let his chief regard be the welfare of his commonwealth.

Since government has the right to wage war, if that become necessary to defend its authority and rights, a Christian will gladly render military service to his country. When Roman soldiers came to John the Baptist, saying, "And what shall we do?" God's ambassador did not tell them to quit the military service. His charge was: "Do violence to no man, neither accuse any falsely; and be content with your wages" (Luke 3:14).

St. Paul calls attention to another duty which at times may prove quite irksome, yet is a service to be willingly rendered by every Christian. "Render therefore to all their dues: tribute to whom tribute is due; custom to whom custom" (Rom. 13:7). It is not only unworthy of a Christian as a citizen of the state to evade the payment of taxes, customs, and other dues, it is sinful, a violation of God's clearly expressed will.

An officer of the state to whom honor, obedience, and service is due may, of course, at the same time be subject to higher officials. Then he naturally owes him the honor, obedience, and service due to the superior officer. In a constitutional government all officials are subject to the will of the people as expressed in the constitution or charter of the commonwealth. When the governmental persons refuse to conform to the stipulations under which they hold office, they become violators of the law, and the proper steps, impeachment, etc., as prescribed by the law, may be taken to depose such violators of the law. "Where the form of government is such as to constitute the people a superior power, that power, too, is ordained of God, and to the magistrates and rulers also the word of the Apostle applies, "Wilt thou, then, not be afraid of the power? Do that which is good" (Rom. 13:3). In no instance, however, is it legitimate for the private citizen to take the law into his own hand, while a lawful government may be called upon to afford protection and administer justice. Lynching a criminal is itself a crime and a sin, a medicine more dangerous than the disease. . . . And even when the officers of the law transgress their proper bounds or even commit injustice, it is not lawful for the private citizen to offer violent resistance. When Peter had taken the sword in resentment of an injury committed against his Master by the officials of those in power, Jesus rebuked him, saying: 'All they that take the sword shall perish with the sword' (Matt. 26:52)." (*Theol. Quart.*, III, p. 437.)

BE SUBJECT FOR CONSCIENCE' SAKE

Such honor, obedience, and service is to be rendered to government for conscience' sake. The Christian knows from Scripture that civil government is an institution of God and that God demands that the Christian be subject to his government. This commandment he regards as binding upon himself, and the honor, obedience, and service required from him is to him a matter of conscience. And since it is his Redeemer God, the Author and Finisher of his faith and salvation, who tells him to be subject to the higher powers, he will gladly and willingly to the best of his ability obey, serve, and honor his government. By his cheerful and conscientious fulfillment of all his civic duties and by his manifest respect and honor shown to the authorities he will be a shining light in the midst of a wicked and perverse world, and do his share in elevating the moral standards of his community also with regard to the proper relation of citizens to their government.

Let each his lesson learn with care,
Then all the nation well shall fare.

XXV

The Doctrine of Election, or Predestination

According to Holy Scripture all that God does in time for our conversion, justification, and final glorification is based on and flows from an eternal decree of election or predestination, according to which God before the foundation of the world chose us in His Son Jesus Christ out of the mass of sinful mankind unto faith, the adoption of sons, and everlasting life.

WRITING to the Christians at Ephesus, the Apostle had invoked upon them grace and peace from God our Father and from the Lord Jesus Christ, and then he bursts forth in a magnificent hymn of praise to the Triune God of Grace. "Blessed be the God and Father of our Lord Jesus Christ, who hath blessed us with all spiritual blessings in heavenly places in Christ, according as He hath chosen us in Him before the foundation of the world that we should be holy and without blame before Him in love; having predestinated us unto the adoption of children by Jesus Christ to Himself according to the good pleasure of His will" (Eph. 1:3-5). The Christians at Ephesus knew what the spiritual blessings were with which their heavenly Father had blessed them, the very blessings enumerated by the Apostle: holiness and blamelessness (v. 4); the adoption of children (v. 5); the acceptance in the Beloved, the redemption through His blood, the forgiveness of sins (vv. 6-7); eternal salvation and the sealing with the Holy Spirit of promise (v. 13). They knew very well that they had in time past been Gentiles, without Christ, without hope, without God in the world. They knew that when Paul had come with the message of Christ crucified, they had been brought to faith, that they were now fellow citizens with the saints and of the household of God. They knew that this was not due to blind chance, or a whim of fate, nor to any effort of their own to gain God's favor, but was the work of God and the unmerited grace of God that had wrought this marvelous change and had blessed them with all spiritual blessings in heavenly places. But now the Apostle tells them that God did not become interested in them when Paul came to Ephesus, that His concern for their salvation did not begin with the moment of their birth or conception. Long before their coming into the world, yes, before the world was created, God was deeply concerned about their eternal salvation, so deeply concerned that in Christ He chose them before the foundation of the world; that He predestinated, foreordained them to their present blessed state in the timeless aeons of eternity.

This election is an election of persons. God predetermined not only the blessings He would give to the Christians, nor only the manner in which these gifts were to be procured, nor only the manner in which these blessings were to be bestowed. The Apostle very clearly and definitely speaks of an election, a choosing, a predestination of *persons*. "According as He hath chosen *us*," we are told v. 4, and in the verse immediately following we read that God predestinated *us* unto the adoption of sons. God's election is an election of persons.

Again, this election is not a universal election, not a predestination of all mankind, as He had decreed to redeem all mankind, to send His Son as the Savior of all the world. St. Paul addresses the Christians at Ephesus, who no longer were strangers and foreigners, but fellow citizens with the saints and of the household of God (ch. 2:19) and tells them that they were chosen unto such sainthood and adoption. From out of the mass of men lost in sin, dead in trespasses, they had been chosen, elected, to become God's own. In like manner Christ speaks of a particular election of His disciples out of the unbelieving world when He tells them, "If ye were of the world, the world would love his own; but because ye are not of the world, but I have chosen you out of the world, therefore the world hateth you" (John 15:19). Our fathers, and we with them, are in full keeping with God's Word when they confess, "The predestination or eternal election of God, however, extends only over the godly, beloved children of God, being a cause of their salvation, which He also provides, as well as disposes what belongs thereto. Upon this (predestination of God) our salvation is founded so firmly that the gates of hell cannot overcome it" (John 10:28; Matt. 16:18). (Formula of Concord, Epitome XI, § 4, *Triglot*, p. 833.) What marvelous grace, what undeserved honor for us to have been the objects of God's loving care already in eternity to such a degree that He has chosen us who had deserved a thousandfold to be damned eternally, predestinated us to so wonderful an adoption, to so wonderful a heritage. All praises in time and in eternity to the glory of His grace!

This passage from the Letter to the Ephesians is only one of a number of passages which speak in unmistakable terms of that everlasting love wherewith the Lord of eternity has loved His own before time began and which caused Him to draw us in His own time unto Himself with loving-kindness (Jer. 31:3). We shall briefly look at some of these statements. In his Letter to the Romans Paul writes: "We know that all things work together for good to them that love God, to them who are the called according to His purpose. For whom He did foreknow, He also did predestinate to be conformed to the image of His Son, that He might be the firstborn among many brethren. Moreover, whom He did predestinate, them He also called; and whom He called, them He also justified; and whom He justified, them He also glorified" (Rom. 8:28-30). Note the golden chain extending from God's eternal purpose and foreknowledge and predestination through time, in which we are called and justified, to eternity, our glorification above. The fact that we have been called, that God has brought us to faith, should make us sure of our election before the world began as well as of our salvation after this time and this world has ceased to be. That golden chain was forged in the fires of God's everlasting love, eternal and unchanging as God Himself, and on the anvil of Calvary, erected in eternity by God's decree of redemption, on which the Lamb slain from eternity (Rev. 13:8), having been delivered by the determinate counsel and foreknowledge of God (Acts 2:23), was made unto us wisdom, and righteousness, and sanctification, and redemption (I Cor. 1:30). That chain—and every link thereof is unbreakable—that chain guarantees to us who believe our past election and our future glorification.

Writing to his beloved associate Timothy, the Apostle praises

God, "who hath saved us and called us with an holy calling, not according to our works, but according to His own purpose and grace, which was given us in Christ Jesus before the world began" (II Tim. 1:9).

The same truth is set forth in the Second Letter to the Thessalonians: "We are bound to give thanks alway to God for you, brethren, beloved of the Lord, because God hath from the beginning chosen you to salvation through sanctification of the Spirit and belief of the truth; whereunto He called you by our Gospel to the obtaining of the glory of our Lord Jesus Christ" (II Thess. 2:13-14).

Luke, the Evangelist, tells us that when Paul preached the Gospel to the Gentiles in Antioch in Pisidia, "as many as were ordained to eternal life believed" (Acts 13:48).

Peter addressing his First Letter to the Christians in Asia Minor designates them as the "elect according to the foreknowledge of God the Father, through sanctification of the Spirit, unto obedience and sprinkling of the blood of Jesus Christ" (I Pet. 1:2).

We note that when Scripture refers to the doctrine of election, it speaks as a rule from the viewpoint of time in which the believer lives and in which God's eternal purpose is being carried out, or, in other words, in which the believer experiences in his own life the results of that decree which God conceived in the timeless ages before the world was fashioned. Scripture uses this method of referring to our election in order that we do not commit the folly of trying to peer into eternity and in this manner endeavor to ascertain whether we are included in God's degree of predestination. The Christian is to consider what God has done for him, and from these facts which he has experienced he is to draw the conclusion: Because I also am called and converted, because I am a child of God through faith in Christ Jesus, I, too, am one of the elect, for God tells me that all these spiritual blessings have come to me according to His gracious election in eternity (Eph. 1:3-6), and He also tells me that those whom He has predestinated, them He will glorify (Rom. 8:30). I can read my election in the spiritual gifts God has been and is still showering down upon me. I am His own!

It is not strange therefore that that powerful undercurrent of joy and gratitude which runs through the Apostle's life and through the life of every believer breaks forth so frequently into a jubilant hymn of praise and adoration when the Apostle speaks of this doctrine. Dr. A. L. Graebner, commenting on Eph. 1:3-6, makes the apt remark: "What Paul is about to teach is not an appalling doctrine to be viewed with fear and trembling, as exhibiting a *tremendum mysterium.* He begins, Blessed be the God and Father of our Lord Jesus Christ. . . . The words of St. Paul are part of a doxology expressing what is in the Apostle's heart and what he would elicit in the hearts of his readers, that they with him should voice forth the praises of God" (*Theological Quarterly,* V, p. 26).

Now, however, the question arises, Does not the doctrine that our salvation is based on God's election contradict the plain teaching of Scripture that our salvation rests only on the merits of our Lord Jesus? The answer is an emphatic No! God's eternal election is not an arbitrary one. His decree of predestination is not an absolute one. No, God's decree of election is founded on His decree of redemption through Christ. We are, as Scripture time and again tells us, elected in Christ. Writing to the Ephesians, Paul very definitely states that God "hath blessed us with all spiritual blessings in heavenly places in Christ according as He hath chosen us in Him" (Eph. 1:3-4). The same Apostle tells Timothy, God "hath saved us and called us with an holy calling, not according to our works, but according to his own purpose and grace, which was given us in Christ Jesus before the world began" (II Tim. 1:9). The election of grace does not eliminate or overlook or belittle the merit of Christ and its necessity, but includes it and is based on it as its indispensable and never-failing foundation.

But what about faith? Does not Scripture say that only he that believes in the Son of God as his Savior shall be saved? If God has chosen us from eternity, if He has determined even before we were born to bring us unfailingly to eternal life, does not that deny the necessity of faith? Again the answer is an emphatic No! As little as the decree of predestination excludes Christ as our Redeemer, so little does it make faith in this Christ unnecessary. That faith is not overlooked in God's decree of election is clearly stated in a number of Scripture passages. Christians are named "the called according to His purpose" (Rom. 8:28). Far from denying or setting aside the necessity of faith for our salvation, Paul tells us that the very purpose of God's eternal election was to call those whom He foreknew, to call them effectively, as Paul invariably uses this term, to bring them to faith in their Savior by the preaching of His Gospel.

Again, Paul writes, "According as God hath chosen us in Christ that we should be holy and without blame before Him." Such holiness and blamelessness is possible only through faith, and an election to holiness involves election to faith.

The Scriptural doctrine of election therefore eliminates neither the necessity of Christ's atonement nor that of faith, but gives to each of these important doctrines its proper emphasis.

THESIS II

Holy Scripture teaches that this election is not based on any good quality or act of the elect, nor on "faith unto the end which God foresaw in the elect" (intuitu fidei finalis), but solely on God's grace, the good pleasure of His will in Christ Jesus.

The doctrine of the election of grace or of predestination, as set forth in our first thesis, arouses a flood of questions in the human mind, also in the mind of the Christian. One of the questions which clamor for an answer is the question as to the cause why one person is elected, while another is not elected.

The human mind loves to find the cause of election or predestination in man himself. The "something in man" which is supposed to have moved God to elect some has been variously described as "lesser guilt," "the faculty for applying oneself to grace," a right attitude over against God's grace," "the omission of willful resistance," and, in its subtlest form, as "faith unto the end which God foresaw in the elect" (intuitu fidei finalis).

All these explanations, however, are figments of the human imagination. The Bible knows nothing of lesser guilt, of man's faculty for applying himself to grace, of a right attitude on man's part over against God's grace, or of omission of willful resistance. All that it knows and teaches concerning man as he is by nature is that he is spiritually blind, dead, and an enemy of God and that he is utterly unable either to save himself or to contribute in any way to his conversion and salvation. All he can do by nature is to resist and to hinder the work of God's Spirit.

The proponents of the "intuitu fidei" quote Scripture to prove their view. They point to such passages as Rom. 8:29: "Whom He did foreknow, He also did predestinate to be conformed to the image of His Son," and I Pet. 1:2, "Elect according to the foreknowledge of God." "Here," they say, "it is clearly stated that God predestinated those whom He foreknew, that is, of whom He foresaw that they would believe unto the end. They are elect according to the foreknowledge of God, namely, the foreknowledge that they would believe, and believe unto the end."

The careful Bible reader at once notices that here something is read into the text which is simply not there. Rom. 8:29 makes not the faith of the elect, but the elect themselves objects of the foreknowledge of God. The proponents of the intuitu fidei theory of the election change the object of God's foreknowledge. That is a most arbitrary and dangerous thing to do. If we could do that, we could read many an idea which originated in our own brain into the Scripture.

To understand what is meant by "foreknow" and "foreknowledge" when predicated of God, we must study the usage of these words in the New Testament. The verb occurs five times, twice to denote the foreknowledge of man, which does not come into consideration here (Acts 26:5; II Pet. 3:17); three times of God's foreknowledge (Rom. 8:29; 11:2; I Pet. 1:20). The noun occure twice, both times used of God's foreknowledge (Acts 2:23; I Pet. 1:2). In Acts 2:23 Christ is said to have been "delivered" to the enemies "by the determinate counsel and foreknowledge of God." In the original text the article is not repeated before "foreknowledge." When only one article is used before two nouns, the two epithets are applied to the same object. (Robertson, *Grammar*, 1st ed., p. 785.) Acts 2:23 therefore clearly identifies the determinate counsel of God with God's foreknowledge. There can be no doubt that there is such a foreknowledge of God which is more than a mere prescience, being aware of something beforehand. Hence the A. V. correctly rendered the Greek word "foreknow" in I Pet. 1:20 "foreordained"; Luther, *"zuvor versehen,"* i. e., *"zuvor bestimmt, verordnet."* When used of God, the terms "foreknow," "foreknowledge," as in Rom. 8:29, 11:2, I Pet. 1:2, do not only express the thought that God knew beforehand that certain persons would come to faith and that on this account he chose them unto salvation. Nothing is said in any of these passages of a foreseen or foreknown faith. The object in every one of these three passages is a *personal* object: "whom," Rom. 8:29; "His people," 11:2; "the strangers," I Pet. 1:2, mentioned in v. 1. The "foreknowledge" of God in these passages, therefore, denotes an affectionate and effective foreknowledge, or, as Zahn puts it, "a knowledge appropriating its object, whereby the person is transferred out of his estrangement into the sphere of God's love." (*Roemerbrief*, 3d ed., p. 419.) Cremer, quoted by Stoeckhardt (*Roemerbrief*, p. 400), "mit welchen Gott im voraus eine Gemeinschaft eingegangen," with whom God beforehand entered into a communion."

The teaching that God elected in view of foreseen faith was introduced in order to explain why some were elected rather than others. If it explains this mystery at all, then it removes the cause of our election from God and places it in us. Then our faith becomes the cause of our election. And, if we logically follow this matter through, we must also assume, against the constant teaching of Scripture, that our faith is not, at least not altogether, a gift of God, but either wholly or in part our own work.

What, then, is the cause why some who by nature are no better than others, are equally guilty and equally unable to help themselves or to contribute to their conversion and final salvation, are elected? The Bible plainly answers this question. There is nothing in man that moved God to predestinate anyone to salvation. The motivating cause for our election is solely the grace of God in Christ Jesus.

We read, "Who hath saved us, and called us with an holy calling, not according to our works, but according to His own purpose and grace" (II Tim. 1:9). The Apostle flatly denies that God saved us and called, that is, converted, us according to our works, and just as clearly teaches that God saved us "according to His own purpose and grace."

The same truth is borne out by Paul in his Letter to the Ephesians, where we read, "Having predestinated us unto the adoption of children by Jesus Christ to Himself, according to the good pleasure of His will, to the praise of the glory of His grace, wherewith He has made us accepted in the Beloved, in whom we have redemption through His blood, the forgiveness of sins, according to the riches of His grace, wherein He hath abounded toward us . . ." (Eph. 1:5-8). Dr. A. L. Graebner writes: "What prompted God in predestinating us was entirely and exclusively within God. If we ask, 'What moved God to foreordain us?' Paul answers: 'His good pleasure.' And if we ask, 'What prompted His good pleasure?' he answers, 'His will.' Hence, what is here set forth and made known to us is later on described as *mystery of His* will (v. 9), and we are said to be predestinated according to the *purpose* of Him who worketh all things after the counsel of His own will (v. 11). Not our will, or any inclination or attitude of ourselves, or anything within us which God foresaw or in His omniscience foreknew, moved or prompted God to predestinate us, but His pleasure, and that pleasure was the pleasure of His will. What God foresaw in us that was good, He foresaw as the gift of His goodness and the work of His power, not as a cause, but as an effect of His good pleasure in the execution of His counsel. . . . Again, what God foresaw in us aside of what He would himself engender and work in us was evil, and only evil continually (Gen. 6:5), not of a nature to induce God to predestinate us to sonship and heirship in the household of faith, but to consign us to perdition and to banish us forever from His face. The disposition in God to bless regardless of the merits or demerits of the objects of his blessing is God's grace. And hence, as in time by grace we are saved through faith, so before all time by grace we were predestinated unto salvation through faith" (*Theol. Quart.*, V, p. 39f.).

This becomes particularly plain when St. Paul in Rom. 9 introduces the case of Jacob and Esau, the twin sons of Isaac and Rebecca, to illustrate the election of grace. He says (vv. 10ff.): "When Rebecca also had conceived by one, even by our father Isaac (for the children being not yet born, neither having done any good or evil, that the purpose of God according to the election might stand, not of works, but of Him that calleth), it was said unto her, The elder shall serve the younger." No act of either Jacob or of Esau, but God's gracious will caused Him to prefer Jacob to Esau. Even so it is not something that we do or have done or that God has foreseen that we would do that caused Him to elect us to salvation, but solely His grace, the good pleasure of His will. Therefore our election, or predestination, is fitly called both by the Holy Scriptures (Rom. 11:5) and by the Christian Church the *Election of Grace*.

Thesis III

Scripture does not teach that there is an election of wrath for those who are lost, but consistently declares that God earnestly desires the salvation of all men and that those who are lost are lost by their own fault.

We have heard God's own answer to the question why He chose certain people from the mass of sinful, lost humanity for His own. He did it according to the good pleasure of His will, solely by grace, for Jesus' sake. But the human mind is at once ready with another question, "If those who are elected and saved are elected and saved solely by God's grace, according to the good pleasure of His will, why are not all men elected and saved?"

Sin-blinded human reason from ancient times has sought to give its own answer to this question. It has said, "If those who are elected and saved are elected and saved purely by God's grace, according to the good pleasure of His will, then it is evident that those who are lost are lost because God did not want to save them." Some have gone so far as to set side by side with the comforting doctrine of the election of grace an election of wrath, whereby God had predetermined the rest of humanity unto everlasting damnation. This was taught in the ancient Church by no less a person than St. Augustine. And it was revived and spread widely by John Calvin, after Zwingli the most influential teacher of the Reformed wing of Protestantism.

But nowhere does the Holy Scripture teach side by side with the election of grace an election of wrath to eternal damnation. Holy Scripture does not teach that any man was ever elected by God to damnation. On the contrary, it consistently teaches that God earnestly desires the salvation of all men. God swears a sacred oath to this effect when He commands the Prophet Ezekiel, "Say unto the house of Israel, As I live, saith the Lord God, I have no pleasure in the death of the wicked; but that the wicked turn from his way and live" (Ezek. 33:11). How could God disavow in plainer words all that the human mind has ever imagined concerning an election of a large part of humanity unto eternal death?

In the New Testament we read, "God is long-suffering to usward, not willing that any should perish, but that all should come to repentance" (II Pet. 3:9). And again: "God will have all men to be saved and to come unto the knowledge of the truth. For there is one God, and one Mediator between God and men, the Man Christ Jesus, who gave Himself a ransom for all" (I Tim. 2:4-6). Mark well! Paul says, "Christ gave Himself a ransom for all." He died to redeem all. And "God will have all men to be saved." God desires that all men should be saved. And Peter assures us that God is not willing that any person be lost, but that all come to faith and life eternal. Could there be a more complete negation of all tnat smacks of an eternal predestination unto wrath? Is it not strange that in spite of these clear and unmistakable statements Calvin teaches a predestination unto eternal damnation?

Or take the simplest of all Gospel passages, which even small children readily learn and love, John 3:16: "For God so loved the world that He gave His only-begotten Son, that whosoever believeth in Him should not perish, but have everlasting life." God loved the world. That includes all men, even those who are finally lost. How could God, from eternity, have decreed their damnation, if He loved them, as the Scripture affirms He did, and loved them so that He gave His own Son for their salvation?

And Christ lends emphasis to the Scriptural teaching that God earnestly desires the salvation of all men with His plaint over Jerusalem (Matt. 23:37): "O Jerusalem, Jerusalem, thou that killest the prophets and stonest them that are sent unto thee, how often would I have gathered thy children together, even as a hen gathereth her chickens under her wings, and ye would not." As earnestly and eagerly as the hen calls her chickens to the safety of her wings when she sees the hawk coming, as she is willing to die so that her chicks might be saved, so eagerly, so earnestly had Christ called Jerusalem to repentance. He was even now on the way to the Cross that they might be saved! How can we doubt the sincerity of that Savior's love? God elected no one to damnation, but earnestly desires the salvation of all men.

And yet not all are saved. The greater part is irrevocably lost. Jesus Himself tells us, "Wide is the gate, and broad is the way, that leadeth to destruction, and many there be which go in thereat" (Matt. 7:13). But why are so many lost if God earnestly desires to save them? The Savior gives the answer in three words, "Ye would not." The Jerusalemites refused to be gathered by the Savior. They rejected Him and His gracious advances to gather them, and so they were lost by their own fault, because of their stubborn resistance and unbelief.

This, and this alone, according to the constant teaching of Holy Scripture is the cause why the greater part of humanity is damned. Man refuses to accept the salvation which Christ earned for him and which God so graciously and so earnestly offers to him in the

Gospel. It is his stubborn unbelief that damns him. The fault is man's, and man's alone.

Therefore Stephen, in the sermon which ended in his martyrdom, tells the Jews, "Ye stiff-necked and uncircumcised in hearts and ears, ye do always resist the Holy Ghost; as your fathers did, so do ye" (Acts 7:51). Their unconverted state was the result not of any lack of love on God's part, much less of an eternal election unto damnation, but of their own stubborn resistance against God's Holy Spirit, who earnestly sought to convert and to save them.

It is highly significant that every one of the texts speaking of God's predestination knows only of an election of grace in Christ unto salvation and says not a word of a predestination prompted by the punitive justice of God or determined by His righteous wrath. While, *e. g.,* Scripture says of the Gentiles who were converted, "As many as were ordained to eternal life believed" (Acts 13:48), Paul and Barnabas say to the unbelieving Jews, "It was necessary that the Word of God should first have been spoken unto you; but seeing ye put it from you and judge yourselves unworthy of everlasting life, lo, we turn to the Gentiles" (v. 46). Why were not these Jews converted, even as the Gentiles? Because of an eternal decree of wrath? No, because they put the Word from themselves and judged themselves unworthy of everlasting life.

This same truth is evident even in those passages of the Bible which are sometimes mistakenly quoted as teaching a predestination unto wrath. Let us look at Rom. 9:22-23: "What if God, willing to show His wrath and to make His power known, endured with much long-suffering the vessels of wrath fitted to destruction; and that He might make known the riches of His glory on the vessels of mercy, which He had afore prepared unto glory?" "Here," we are told, "the Bible speaks of vessels of wrath fitted to destruction." A careful reading of the passage will convince us that the Apostle does not teach an election unto destruction. The text does, indeed, teach the election of grace when it speaks of "the vessels of mercy, which He (God) had before prepared to glory." But it does *not* say that God *before* prepared the vessels of wrath unto wrath. The word translated "fitted" means to be in a state of complete equipment, of being fitted out completely, of being fully ready. They are vessels fully ready for destruction. Not a syllable indicates that God got them ready, much less that God foreordained them unto such a state. We are simply told that they are vessels thoroughly fit for destruction and that God, who is willing to show His wrath upon all that are fit and ready for such wrath, still did not at once destroy them, but bore with them in great long-suffering. What can have been the purpose of God in enduring these vessels of wrath so long but to give them time for repentance, as St. Peter teaches (II Pet. 3:9)?

Nor does the Scriptural doctrine of hardening or obduration prove a predestination unto wrath. For, according to the teaching of Scripture, when God hardens anyone, He does so in punishment of previous self-hardening against the truth, as we can plainly see from the three notable examples of hardening in the Scripture: that of Pharaoh in the days of Moses and Aaron, that of Israel in the days of the Prophets, and later in the time of the Savior Himself. To all these people God had given ample opportunity for repentance and salvation, and God finally hardened them in punishment for their willful self-hardening against the gracious operations of His Holy Spirit.

In brief, Scripture nowhere teaches an election of wrath unto damnation. On the contrary, God earnestly desires to save all men, and we repeat: Those who are lost are lost by their own fault, because of their willful and persistent rejection of God's grace. The sum of the matter has been tersely expressed Hos. 13:9: "O Israel, thou hast destroyed thyself; but in Me is thine help."

Thesis IV

Holy Scripture does not solve the discrepancy which exists for the human mind between the doctrine of universal grace and the doctrines of election and of salvation by grace alone. Therefore we confess that we are here confronted with a mystery for the solution of which we must await the light of eternity.

Man hears that there is an election from all eternity in Christ unto salvation. He hears that salvation is solely by grace. Man's works are ruled out. He hears that there is no predestination to damnation, but that God would have all men to be saved, that it is man's perverse will which brings about his damnation. And at once the human mind protests. All this is not logical. It cannot be. There is a discrepancy here. Universal grace, man reasons, and the doctrine that man is saved only by grace cannot both be true. If universal grace be true, then "only by grace" must fall; if "only by grace" be true, then universal grace must fall.

This reasoning of the human mind has for many centuries divided the Christian Church. There are those who declare themselves willing to accept the doctrine of universal grace and confess that Christ died for all men and that God desires earnestly that all men should be saved. They also accept the Scriptural teaching that those who are lost are lost by their own fault, their willful, stubborn unbelief. However, in what they may regard a justifiable effort to harmonize Christian doctrine with human reason and logic, they teach that all who are saved are saved because God saw in them something that favorably distinguished them from others, perhaps some lesser guilt or some greater willingness to accept the Gospel or the omission or oppression of willful resistance. So Melanchthon wrote: "Since the promises of the Gospel are universal and there are not contradictory wills in God, there must *necessarily* be *in us* a cause of the distinction, why Saul was rejected, David accepted, that is, there must be a difference in the behavior (conduct, *actio*) of the two" (*Loci,* ed. Detzer I, 74). Because these errorists ascribe to man a faculty to apply himself to the grace of God and thus to work together with God in their conversion, they are called synergists.

In their effort to save the day for human reason, these synergists have subverted the doctrine of salvation by grace alone, since they teach man to trust in himself, in some good quality within himself rather than in the grace of God. If this doctrine is carried out to its full consequences, Christianity ceases, for Christianity is essentially the doctrine of the free grace of God in Christ Jesus (Rom. 3:23-28).

We reject the synergistic solution of the question *Cur alii, alii non?* Why some, not others? as contrary to Scripture and subversive of the Christian faith.

Another solution of this difficulty has been proposed. It is the solution of Calvinism already referred to. Calvinists reason, "Man is saved purely by God's grace. Yet many people are lost. The reason why they are lost must therefore be that God did not want them to be saved, that His grace did not include them because He had decreed from eternity to surrender them to eternal damnation. Even if the Gospel is preached to them, God has not the purpose of converting them, since He has predestinated them to eternal death."

This Calvinistic teaching, indeed, also presents a solution for the human mind, even as does the teaching of the synergists on this point. But it is a solution which is diametrically opposed to God's Word, which, as we saw, teaches that God has elected no one unto damnation, but that He earnestly desires the salvation of all men.

Where, then, is the solution of the difficulty if neither the solution offered by the synergists, who deny the "only by grace," nor that offered by the Calvinists, who deny universal grace, is the correct one?

Our answer is: "Holy Scripture does not solve the discrepancy which exists for the human mind between the doctrine of universal grace and the doctrines of election and of salvation only by grace." This claim is literally true. Holy Scripture makes no attempt to remove this difficulty for the human mind. It constantly teaches side by side both universal grace and salvation only by grace.

And lest we grow too insistent in demanding a solution of the difficulty, Holy Scripture warns us against that very effort. In the last verses of Rom. 11, at the end of a long dissertation on the doctrine of the election of grace, Paul exclaims: "Oh, the depth of the riches both of the wisdom and knowledge of God! How unsearchable are His judgments, and His ways past finding out! For who hath known the mind of the Lord? Or who hath been His counselor? Or who hath first given to Him, and it shall be recompensed to Him again? For of Him and through Him and to Him are all things, to whom be glory forever. Amen."

The true Lutheran Church in obedience to this warning of Holy Scripture refuses to try to harmonize the doctrine of universal grace and of election and salvation by grace alone. The true Lutheran Church lets both these doctrines stand side by side and teaches them both with equal emphasis, fully conscious of the fact that according to the judgment of our corrupt reason these doctrines cannot both be true. We believe them both, and we teach them both because God's Word teaches them both.

And we believe and teach them all the more gladly because we know from experience that sinful human beings need both these doctrines to set their troubled consciences at rest. Were we to sacrifice the doctrine of universal grace, as Calvinists have done, we could never for one moment be sure that we are among God's elect. Then we would always be haunted by that dreadful fear that we might be predestined to damnation, or, as milder Calvinists have put it, among those whom God's mercy passed by. No, our hope of salvation rests upon the rock of universal grace. I know that God wants me saved, because He wants all men saved.

Again, were we in the interest of human reason to sacrifice the doctrines of election and of salvation by grace alone, we could never be sure of our salvation. We would always be looking for something in ourselves on account of which God might have elected and saved us. We would be looking into our own sinful hearts and lives and would find there, not assurance, but doubt and despair. The aroused conscience needs both these seemingly contradictory doctrines, *universal grace* and *by grace alone.*

Therefore, as Scripture so constantly and so clearly teaches both these doctrines, so do we joyfully accept and teach them both, fully conscious of the fact that to our reason they may seem inharmonious and contradictory, but conscious also of the fact that they fill our souls' deepest need for the comfort of God's universal, all-sufficient grace.

And the harmonizing of these two doctrines? We are not worried about that. Though we cannot now see how they harmonize with each other, we leave that to God. We are sure that we shall behold their perfect harmony, which now escapes us, in the light of eternity, when we, who now see and know in part, shall know as also we are known, because we shall see our gracious God and Savior face to face.

"In these and similar questions Paul (Rom. 11:22ff.) fixes a certain limit to us how far we should go, namely, that in the one part we should recognize God's judgment (for He commands us to consider in those who perish the just judgment of God and the penalties of sins). For they are well-deserved penalties of sins when God so punishes a land or nation for despising His Word that the punishment extends also to their posterity, as is to be seen in the Jews. And thereby (by the punishments) God in some lands and persons exhibits His severity to those that are His (in order to indicate) what we all would have deserved and would be worthy and worth, since we act wickedly in opposition to God's Word (are ungrateful for the revealed Word and live unworthily of the Gospel) and often grieve the Holy Ghost sorely, in order that we may live in the fear of God and acknowledge and praise God's goodness, to the exclusion of, and contrary to, our merit in and with us, to whom He gives His Word, and with whom He leaves it, and whom He does not harden and reject.

"For inasmuch as our nature has been corrupted by sin and is worthy of, and subject to, God's wrath and condemnation, God owes to us neither the Word, the Spirit, nor grace; and when He bestows these gifts out of grace, we often thrust them from us and make ourselves unworthy of everlasting life (Acts 13:46). And this His righteous, well-deserved judgment He displays in some countries, nations, and persons in order that when we are placed alongside of them and compared with them (and found to be most similar to them), we may learn the more diligently to recognize and praise God's pure (immense), unmerited grace in the vessels of mercy." (*Triglot*, pp. 1081-1083.)

THESIS V

The doctrine of the election of grace properly used will not foster carnal security, but will make the believer conscious of the matchless glory of the grace of God, will serve as a constant incentive to sanctification, will comfort him in the ills and tribulations of this life, and will give him the blessed assurance of his final salvation.

Human reason will continue to insist that our doctrine of election by grace must inevitably lead to a fatalistic attitude toward life and to carnal security. They argue that if God has from eternity predetermined any person to salvation, and if this purpose of election is unfailingly carried out by the Lord, then that person will be saved no matter what he does and how he lives. On the contrary, if anyone is not elected from eternity, there is no possible hope of salvation for him, no matter what manner of life he may lead. You will be damned if you do; and you will be damned, if you don't. Therefore to tell anyone that he may be sure of his election to eternal life is tantamount to telling him that he need not worry about his salvation, that irrespective of what he does he will finally be saved. That, however, is actually a flagrant perversion of the Scriptural doctrine of God's eternal election to salvation. The Scriptural doctrine of predestination does not foster or encourage fatalism. The doctrine of eternal election does not invalidate such warnings as, "Wherefore, my beloved, work out your own salvation with fear and trembling" (Phil. 2:12). Nor does it invalidate Peter's admonition addressed to such as had been called the "elect according to the foreknowledge of God the Father" (I Pet. 1:2): "As He which hath called you is holy, so be ye holy in all manner of conversation, because it is written, Be ye holy, for I am holy" (I Pet. 1:15). Paul, who treats the doctrine of the election more frequently and more fully than any other holy writer, never thought of becoming a fatalist because he was so sure of his election; nor did he allow this assurance to make him torpid and sluggish in doing good works. On the contrary, he writes: "I therefore so run, not as uncertainly; so fight I, not as one that beateth the air; but I keep under my body and bring it into subjection, lest that by any means, when I have preached to others, I myself should be a castaway" (I Cor. 9:26-27). And again, "Brethren, I count not myself to have apprehended; but this one thing I do, forgetting those things which are behind and reaching forth unto those things which are before, I press toward the mark for the prize of the high calling of God in Christ Jesus" (Phil. 3:13). No fatalist and no careless, negligent Christian could speak like that!

The Scriptural doctrine of eternal election by grace has a purpose altogether contrary to lulling the Christian into false security and an effect upon the Christian's life altogether opposite to fatalism. The very magnitude of God's grace as evinced so gloriously in the Scriptural doctrine of election will imbue the Christian with an ever-deeper sense of gratitude to the heavenly Father, who has not only called him by the Gospel, not only redeemed him centuries ago by the sacrifice of His own Son, but who already in eternity thought of him in loving consideration and before time began chose him to be one of God's beloved children, an heir of everlasting salvation. He will join in Paul's jubilant hymn of praise: "Blessed be the God and Father of our Lord Jesus Christ, who hath blessed us with all spiritual blessings in heavenly places in Christ, according as He hath chosen us in Him before the foundation of the world that we should be holy and without blame before Him in love, having predestinated us unto the adoption of children by Jesus Christ to Himself, according to the good pleasure of His will, to the praise of the glory of His grace" (Eph. 1:3ff.).

This joyful gratitude towards God, his Savior, the Christian will manifest in an ever-increasing zeal in the work of sanctification, in ever-greater willingness to do the will of his loving God, in ever-firmer determination to fight the enemies of his salvation that attack him from within and without.

That, indeed, is one of the express purposes of the election of grace, as Scripture abundantly evidences. St. Paul says that God has chosen us in Christ before the foundation of the world "that we should be holy and without blame before Him in love" (Eph. 1:4). That means that we were chosen unto sanctification, for the purpose of being sanctified. How, then, can the doctrine of election make anyone sluggish in sanctification? Again, the same Apostle says, "God has from the beginning chosen you to salvation through sanctification of the Spirit" (II Thess. 2:13). "Through" designates the way on which their election unto salvation was to be realized—in connection with sanctification. The election of grace does not make sanctification superfluous. It includes, demands, and causes it.

That garment of sanctification and good works, which according to Col. 3:12—4:6 is to characterize the Christian in every station of life and wherever he happens to be, is to be put on by Christians because they are the elect of God (Col. 3:12). This blessed knowledge should and will urge the believers and at the same time enable them to prove by their conduct that they are indeed the elect of God, chosen by the grace of the Lord from out of the corrupt world to be God's own, a holy nation, a peculiar people.

Peter had told his readers that a lack of good works would prove that they were blind and had forgotten their purging from their old sins (II Pet. 1:5-9). He adds, as another reason why they should strive for sanctification, that by such diligence they would make their calling and election sure (v. 10). So inconsistent with the election of grace is sluggishness in sanctification that such sluggishness will deprive the Christian of the certainty of his election. In order to be sure of his election, the Christian must be diligent in good works. God tells him that he has been chosen to be holy and blameless (Eph. 1:4); elect through sanctification of the Spirit (I Pet. 1:2); and when he walks in sanctification and good works, he can be sure of his election because he walks as the elect of God walk.

No, the doctrine of the election of grace does not lead to fatalism and to neglect of sanctification. Rightly used, it becomes for the believer a powerful urge toward greater sanctification and fruitfulness in good works.

The doctrine of the election of grace also serves to comfort the believer amid the ills and tribulations of this life in that it assures him of his final salvation.

At the close of the story of the importunate widow, the Savior asks, "And shall not God avenge His own elect, which cry day and night unto Him, though He bear long with them?" (Luke 18:7.) God's elect may, indeed, suffer many afflictions here on earth, and God may bear long with them, that is, He may delay His help for reasons of His own, so that it seems to the believer as though God did not hear. But they are His elect, and therefore they need not fear that He will forget them in their sufferings. God shall speedily avenge them of their adversaries and turn their sorrows into joy.

When Paul was a prisoner, awaiting his execution, he comforted himself and his beloved Timothy with the election of grace. "Be not thou therefore ashamed of the testimony of our Lord, nor of me, His prisoner; but be thou partaker of the afflictions of the Gospel according to the power of God, who hath saved us and called us with an holy calling, not according to our works, but according to His own purpose and grace, which was given us in Christ Jesus before the world began" (II Tim. 1:8-9).

In the eighth chapter of the Letter to the Romans St. Paul assures his readers that all things must work together for good to God's elect, even the most harrowing afflictions which can befall them here on earth. Because they are God's elect, all their suffering leads heavenward. The afflictions of this life, whatever they may be, must serve our final salvation. And that salvation is sure, says the Apostle, "And whom He justified, them He also glorified." Many who are justified were not yet glorified when Paul wrote his letter. They were still living on earth and suffering afflictions. But in the eyes of God, who elected them by grace in Christ from all eternity to salvation, they are already glorified. Yes, certain is their salvation.

So determined is God not to have one of His elect perish because of the tribulations of this time that He has even promised to shorten the terrible days of the last times, when false prophets and false Christians will arise and show great signs and wonders, to deceive, if possible, even the elect (Mark 13:20ff.). He will shorten those days lest one of His elect perish. Not one of them shall perish! When the last trumpet sounds and the Son of Man comes in the clouds of heaven, "then shall He send His angels, and they shall gather together His elect from the four winds, from the uttermost part of the earth to the uttermost part of heaven" (Mark 13:27). So will God's purpose and counsel of the election of grace be carried out to the salvation of all the elect. None will be lost. That is our comfort and assurance even in the deepest tribulations which befall us here on earth. We are God's elect. Our salvation is sure.

Thank God, we also may join the Apostle in the noblest and boldest confession of the certainty of the believer's salvation in Christ—that nothing can sever us from the love of God, which is in Christ Jesus, our Lord (Rom. 8:31-39).

THESIS VI

Since the doctrine of election by grace is so clearly revealed in Holy Writ, it is written for the learning of all Christians. Therefore all Christians should diligently study this doctrine for their edification, strengthening, and consolation, and all pastors should teach this doctrine to the souls entrusted to their care.

In his exposition of Eph. 1:3-6, from which we have already quoted, Dr. A. L. Graebner writes: "What Paul is about to teach is not an esoteric *gnosis,* intended for an inner circle, but an article of the Christian faith to be propounded to the faithful in Christ Jesus. What has been revealed to him, the Apostle here commits to writing for those who have heard of the dispensation of the grace of God, in order that, when they read, they may understand his knowledge in the mystery of Christ. Thus is this doctrine made accessible, not only to theologians, but to all Christians who are able to read what is here set forth in words of human speech. But it is from this source that this doctrine must be learned. Not by human speculation and reasoning, but by reading and hearing what God has revealed by his Apostles in his Word, theologians as well as other Christians may and should learn the mystery of God's will, and a true, spiritual knowledge of these mysteries is obtained from this source only by those to whom God has given the Spirit of wisdom and revelation in the knowledge of Him, the eyes of their understanding being enlightened. Hence this doctrine was not set forth by St. Paul when he was brought unto Areopagus and when he spoke to the philosophers of the university and other superstitious men of Athens who had raised an altar 'to the unknown god.' It was a doctrine for Christians in the days of Paul, and it is a doctrine for Christians today." (*Theol. Quart.*, V, p. 25ff.)

Even if this doctrine presents mysteries unfathomable for the human mind, it has that in common with all Scriptural doctrines, and therefore the mysteries met with in this Bible truth ought not to keep the pastor from preaching and teaching also this part of the whole counsel of God. He need not be afraid to proclaim this doctrine on the basis of the clear passages of Scripture. And all Christians should be glad to learn and study what Scripture says concerning this mysterious but comforting and faith-strengthening doctrine. As we learn to understand this doctrine, we shall realize that it serves, indeed, to glorify the marvelous grace of God, that it will help us to grow in grace and sanctification, that it will comfort us in the ills and tribulations of this life. We will thank God for this doctrine which assures us that as God has called and converted us in time, so He has chosen us from eternity in Christ to be His own, and therefore will keep us in faith unto the end and will surely glorify us in His heavenly home. To Him be glory for ever and ever!

XXVI

The Doctrine of the Last Things

In the last days before His crucifixion, our Lord Jesus Christ taught his disciples, "And if I go and prepare a place for you, I will come again and receive you unto Myself, that where I am, there ye may be also. And whither I go ye know, and the way ye know."

Accordingly the Christian Church all through the ages has awaited the Lord's return. Since that time the Church and its members have expressed their faith in the Lord's certain return in various ways. In the Apostles' Creed the Church, built on the foundation of the Apostles and Prophets, has confessed concerning her Lord: "From thence He shall come to judge the quick and the dead." In the Nicene Creed the same Church expressed the same faith in the words: "And He shall come again with glory to judge both the quick and the dead; whose kingdom shall have no end." In the creed named for that great hero and contender for the faith, Athanasius of Alexandria, the Church has also confessed concerning the ascended Lord who sits at the right hand of the Father, God Almighty: "From thence He shall come to judge the quick and the dead. At whose coming all men shall rise again with their bodies and shall give account of their own works. And they that have done good shall go into life everlasting; and they that have done evil, into everlasting fire. This is the catholic faith; which except a man believe faithfully and firmly, he cannot be saved." Let us hear the last words of this creed again, for it gives direction to our consideration of these Last Things: "This is the catholic faith; which except a man believe faithfully and firmly, he cannot be saved."

About a thousand years after these creeds had been generally in use in the Christian Church, the Church of the Reformation, our

544

own beloved Church, expressed its faith in the same doctrines in the Augsburg Confession, Article 17, under the heading "Of Christ's Return to Judgment," thus: "Also they teach that at the consummation of the world, Christ will appear for judgment and will raise up all the dead; He will give to the godly and elect eternal life and everlasting joys, but ungodly men and the devils He will condemn to be tormented without end.

"They condemn the Anabaptists, who think that there will be an end to the punishments of condemned men and devils.

"They condemn also others who are now spreading certain Jewish opinions, that before the resurrection of the dead the godly shall take possession of the kingdom of the world, the ungodly being everywhere suppressed."

Still more recently, in the Doctrinal Affirmation, issued by the committees of the American Lutheran Church and our own Synod, this expression of our faith also finds a place under the now familiar heading "Of the Last Things."

Is it not remarkable and noteworthy that all these confessions of faith, arising out of Scripture, express the same truths?

We ask God to guide our hearts and minds by His Holy Spirit as on the basis of Scripture we consider the doctrine of the Last Things.

Theologians call the subject of this essay *Eschatology,* or the doctrine of the *Last Things.* The following subtopics are usually included in the consideration of Eschatology: the doctrine of the Antichrist, of Temporal Death, of the End of the World and Christ's Return to Judgment, of the Resurrection of All Flesh, of Eternal Death, and of Eternal Life. A number of these topics are treated in separate papers and will therefore be touched upon only briefly in our presentation. Nevertheless, it will be the purpose of this paper to give an overview of the entire subject of Eschatology, from its positive and negative aspects, in the hope that the Spirit of our risen Lord, the Spirit of Truth and Love, will fill our hearts anew with an understanding of His great works in our behalf now and in the future, and will strengthen us with the sure hope of salvation, final and complete, in Him who lives and reigns as Head of His Church.

I

"We believe that He shall come again."

The firm and abiding faith of the Church that her Lord shall return to take her home is not mere wishful thinking or the result of uncontrolled imagination. Rather, in addition to his many direct promises to return (Matt. 25:31-32; Mark 13:26; Luke 21:27, 36) the Lord Christ has placed a description of many signs into His Word by which believers are to recognize and be reminded that He shall come again.

These signs are revealed and indicated in both the Old and New Testaments, in the entire Bible. No doctrine of Scripture is revealed in one part of the Scriptures only; this is true also of the doctrine of the Last Things, in all its parts.

These signs are numerous, clear, and forceful, and their cumulative effect, according to God's plan, is to be unmistakable to the Church and to the individual Christian. In fact, some of these signs are so striking and so easily recognizable that the unbelievers should be able to note from many of them that the end of the world and the return of the Lord of all are impending.

Now, the question is, What are these unmistakable signs of the last times? Let us extract them from the Scriptures, as the fathers and teachers in all ages of the Church have done, to see what they are. They have usually been divided into two general groups: those that are general, repeated, and sometimes already remote, and those that are specific, explicit, and near.

To help us overcome our own inherent weakness and our regrettable forgetfulness, even as Christians, our gracious God has set up these various signposts on the highway of time in the sky and the universe, in what we call human history, and in the life and work of the Church Militant, the Kingdom of God on earth.

Signs of the last times in the physical world are those which are in the universe itself, signs in the sun, the moon, and the stars, in the planets and the constellations. So each earthquake and each flood, each eclipse and each heavenly catastrophe, each epidemic and each famine, each new plague and disease, is a warning and a sign of the last days.

At this point skeptics and cynics have interposed to say, Why, eclipses, earthquakes, floods, famines, epidemics, and the like have existed from the beginning of time, and they are nothing new. They don't mean anything more now than they used to mean.

We counter their argument with the question: why should the

frequent recurrence and their natural cause prevent God from using any or all of these phenomena as signs and tokens that the world shall come to an end? He, the Creator of the heavenly luminaries, tells us that He created them for the purpose of serving also as signs, Gen 1:14. And He told the Old Testament people, "The sun shall be turned into darkness and the moon into blood before the great and the terrible Day of the Lord come," Joel 2:31. Many centuries later our Lord of Truth repeated this warning, Matt. 24:29, 30, and added other signs, Matt. 24: 4-28; Luke 21:5-32. And Him we believe, though all the world mocks and scoffs. His words shall not pass away, and therefore we are sure that each catastrophe in nature, all decline and alteration in the manner in which the universe is made and runs, is an indication from the almighty Maker that heaven and earth shall pass away. "Now that which decayeth and waxeth old is ready to vanish away," Heb. 8:13.

We have maintained and renewed many old customs in our Church, but some of real worth we have recently neglected. For many long years it was the custom to read the account of the destruction of Jerusalem on the Tenth Sunday after Trinity. Many of you will remember that this account was even printed in our old hymn books. What made this a proper and worthy custom? It was a realization of the fact that the destruction and overthrow of even man-made things, such as glorious cities like Jerusalem of old, the decline and the fall of the great empires of the past and the present, the decay and rotting finally coming upon our human endeavors, the transitoriness and insignificance of all human glory and greatness, are a sign of the approaching end, constant reminders of the impending destruction of all things.

The first of the remote signs in human history, as has frequently been pointed out, is the gross and also the fine materialism which rules the inhabitants of the world and often even intrudes into the work of the Church and sometimes obscures its vision. In Luke 17:26-30 Christ, our Lord, already indicates, "As it was in the days of Noah, so shall it be also in the days of the Son of Man. They did eat, they drank, they married wives, they were given in marriage, until the day that Noah entered into the ark, and the Flood came and destroyed them all. Likewise also as it was in the days of Lot; they did eat, they drank, they bought, they sold, they planted, they builded . . . even thus shall it be in the day when the Son of Man is revealed." It is striking to read in one of our synodical essays, written in 1889, long before the two great world wars which most of us have personally experienced, long before the world-wide spread of the virus of atheistic Communism and its watchword of dialectical materialism, that even then already puny men held that might alone was right, that man was God, and that even then men began to write the name of God with a small *g*. It is strikingly instructive to line up for an occasion like this some of the slogans so current and so palatable, particularly in the world of Western man in the last one hundred years, the hundred years since the founding of our Church. Our Church was organized in 1847. 1848 was a year of revolution, the convulsions of which disturb the world even now. Those were the days of the humanists whose end is not yet, who maintained that man's only salvation rests in himself. Those were also the days of neopagans, who insisted that morals are relative and faith is irrelevant, the escape of weak minds, an opiate for the masses, a sugar-coated instrument of control for those who act on the principle that might is always right, who by fair means or foul would seek to manipulate and outmaneuver their fellow men. But were these former prophets of materialism in all its forms as loudly vocal and persuasive as their disciples today?

In our day we have seen the development of a philosophy of this-worldly security. Men call it social security. It is to be security from the "cradle to the grave," and of itself it is not an evil thing. But as far as most men hold, no other security is necessary. The question no longer is, "What must I do to be saved?" but rather, "What shall we eat, what shall we drink, wherewithal shall we be clothed? How can we insure for each one a chicken in every pot and a car in every garage?" As the Church of Christ always has done, so let us again raise the question "What shall a man be profited, though he gain the whole world and lose his own soul?"

Another sign of the last times which God so graciously identified and labeled is the persistent and frequent appearance within the confines of the Church itself, of spiritual fifth columnists, traitors to the truth of God, antichrists almost without number. Modern means of communication serve but to enhance their number and to increase their vehemence. Since the days of the Reformation, when God through his servant Luther restored the truths of Scripture, our Church has insisted and still insists that the great Antichrist, the man of sin, with whom it has in accordance with II Thess. 2 and other Scripture passages, identified the Pope of Rome in his dominion, and his exposing is one of the great special signs of the last times. Here it is well to repeat the words of Calov, who comments on I John 2:18: "What else is the papistic Antichrist than the collective scum of all the various heresies which assert themselves in attacks against Christ from within?" It is the task of another convention to examine the basis for the identification which our Church has made and makes in saying that the great Antichrist is the Papacy. At all events, we here are concerned with the Scriptural doctrine that the great Antichrist, his rise to power, and his revelation, though it does not bring about his complete destruction, is a sign of the last times, as St. Paul wrote in II Thess. 2:8, "Then shall that Wicked be revealed, whom the Lord shall consume with the spirit of His mouth and shall destroy with the brightness of His coming."

Another sign of the last times, according to Matt. 24:14, is the preaching of the Gospel of the Kingdom of God in all the world for a witness unto all nations. A great church historian of our day, looking back on the last one hundred years and more, has called the last century the greatest century because missionaries as never before have gone into the corners of the earth to bring this Gospel of the Kingdom into the hearts and lives of men. But let us heed again the Savior's appended notice: "And then shall the end come."

Still another sign of the impending end of all things is the coming of what St. Paul in II Tim. 3:1 calls "perilous times" in and for the Church. Our fathers and we call attention to such shifts and broadenings in the meaning of the word Christianity, as are exemplified in the temperance movement, in that substituting of life by the Law for life by faith which is included in that religious vagary which we collectively term "Sabbatarianism." We view, and properly view with alarm, the persistent attempts, even in our great land, to shove the teaching of nondescript religion into the schools maintained by the state, to develop a syncretistic hash of man-made faiths and to call this product the finest fruit of our culture. Man-centered religion and *Allerweltsreligion* are but additional instances of this sort of thing. We note men's affection for obscurantism and superstitions, for spiritualism and spiritism, for vain attempts to bridge time and eternity, to limit the boundless universe, to say nothing of limiting Him whom even the universe cannot hold.

Our Fathers also called attention to Luke 21:32 and called attention to the Jews and their tragic lot in the history of the world since the Crucifixion as a persistent warning to all men of the approaching end of the world. But their separation from the Christian Church, the people of God in New Testament times, is as nothing as a portent and sign compared with the schisms which rend the visible Church, in spite of all attempts at unification.

The last unmistakable sign of the last things, recognizable by all, but recognized by all too few, is the sad fact that men living in these very last times will not read the signs or, having read them, refuse to heed them. Of this horrifying sign St. Peter wrote (II Pet. 3): "Knowing this first, that there shall come in the last days scoffers, walking after their own lusts and saying, Where is the promise of His coming? For since the fathers fell asleep, all things continue as they were from the beginning of the creation."

Since all these signs, without known exception, have happened or are happening, there remains only one possible conclusion for us Christians: we today are living in the very last times of this world and are closer than we sometimes think to our Judge and His Day.

II

"We believe that He shall come again with glory to judge both the quick and the dead."

We believe, teach, and confess that it is the clear doctrine of Holy Scripture that our Lord's return will coincide with the end of the world (II Pet. 3:7; II Tim. 4:1). None of the many passages in Scripture permit a separation in time of these two major events. In fact, the two terms may be used interchangeably.

This end of the world will be definite; it will take place at a time set in eternity by the all-knowing God, but known to no creature (Matt. 24:36; Mark 13:32; Luke 12:40; Acts 1:7). Of the exact time of the end of the world and His return, our Lord said more than once: "Of that time and that hour knoweth no man." But that is by no means the same thing as saying that the end of the world is indefinite, a matter of chance or accident, or that no one knows. On the contrary, as Scripture clearly and repeatedly tells us, the all-knowing God knows also this. Your attention is called to the use of time designations: "that day," "that hour," and others which imply a set time. Occasionally, as in Daniel 7:25ff., there are even more precise indications of time, using human words, but defying all attempts to unriddle them. Of such Johann Gerhard said: "They are indications that a definite time has been set, but that it is known and knowable only to God."

Our spiritual ancestors have compared this uncertainty joined with certainty in the prospect of the end of the world to the similar facts concerning the day and hour of death of each individual. All the children of men know that they must die. Try as they may, they cannot escape death. But who knows with certainty the exact time of each man's death? No man; God alone knows it! Jerome of old was right when he said: "The *one* day is hid from us in order that we may pay heed to every day."

God will make an end to the world through catastrophic fire. It is necessary to stress this, since men persist in perverting this truth. A few have even held that the world and all that is therein is subject to a constant development and progressive climb—but children of wrath and war, as we are, need not seriously consider this possibility. However, the opposite is also true: the world will not come to a slow end after a gradual decline, a 'running down of the universe," as though it were a gigantic watch whose mainspring needed a rewinding which none can give. Nor will the end of the world be a chemically or physically describable disintegration. Nor will "all things continue as they were from the beginning." The end of the world and its destruction will be an act of God, an act of divine judgment and justice. All three persons of the Holy Trinity—Father, Son, and Spirit—will participate. Again, the means which God will use is fire, a horrible end for all cosmic things. This fire is not otherwise explained, and we will not quibble about it. It suffices that it is a real fire and a destructive fire. We who have seen at least pictures of the wholesale destruction of modern warfare must shudder to think of what it shall be like when heaven and earth and all that therein is shall pass away. Some in our Church have thought that this destruction means annihilation, because of the words "pass away"; others in the Church have held that the present external universe will be transformed; all must agree that according to its present form and fashion this world and all that is therein will be ended.

The purpose of God in bringing the world to an end is His own glory. Thereby His unchangeable Word and promise are vindicated; His omnipotence is once again revealed; His righteousness is impressed anew upon all mankind; and His grace, whereby He takes all His believers from this vale of tears to eternal life and light in His presence, is confirmed.

More precisely, it has been believed, taught, and confessed, that our Lord's return at the end of the world serves these purposes: (1) to bring to life again all those who are in their graves (John 5:28-29); (2) to transform suddenly the bodies of the believers; (3) to hold open and public judgment over the whole human race; and (4) to carry out the verdict of the judgment.

When our Lord returns, He does so not in order to take over the rule of this world or heaven or hell, for that He already has. But when Christ our Lord at the very end of the world comes again, He comes as Judge of all mankind. In the words of the Te Deum: "We believe that Thou shalt come to be our judge." Then not only all time is past, but also all things done in time, whether good or evil, are past, and the present and the future merge into eternity. Since the Last Day is the time of Christ's second coming, this day more frequently is called properly "Judgment Day." In other languages, it is sometimes called the "Youngest Day"; for after that day none follows, after it there is no time.

The Judgment itself extends over all peoples of all past time. For the believers God's promises are sure: there is no double entry in God's bookkeeping, no listing of their sins and shortcomings, of their trespasses and transgressions; for through their faith in their perfect Redeemer their names, and their names only, are written in the Book of Life. But for the unbelievers there is nothing but shame and disgrace, a verdict of condemnation. The very believers whom they in the days of their earthly life so often ignored, or even ridiculed and persecuted, shall be their judges. And the entire Judgment shall be accomplished with the service and the assistance of the angels of heaven.

When our Lord returns as Judge, His return will be sudden, visible, and in all His glory. He who returns is the same Lord that ascended, and He comes in like manner (Acts 1:11). Though now

He is present in His Church and in His world invisibly, though with power, when He then comes, He will be visible, for both friend and foe shall see Him (Matt. 24:30; 26:64; Mark 13:26). But His return will be sudden and, despite all the signs pointing to His coming, almost completely unexpected (Luke 21:35; 17:24; I Thess. 5:2-4; I Thess. 5:3). The suddenness and the visibility of His coming will but enhance His glory. His glory then will be manifested as the full glory of the Only-begotten of the Father, full of grace and truth, and as the glory fully equal with that of His Father (Luke 9:26; Matt. 25, 31), with whom He is One (John 10:30). The presence of the holy angels, the legions of heaven, will then be but the fringe of His glory.

Men have shed much ink in battles of words concerning the sequence of events at the time of our Lord's return. Far more to the point has been the advice often given in our Church in the past: Remember these things: (1) When Judgment Day suddenly breaks and dawns, then time ends, and there is no before and after. (2) Hold fast what Scripture teaches when it says that the end of the world and the second coming of Christ to Judgment coincide. (3) Remember that all that God promises and shows will and must happen, and be ready always to live each day as though it were your or the world's last.

III

"We believe in the resurrection of the body."

"The resurrection of the body," says the pagan, "what is that? What do you mean?" Immortality of the soul has a long and respectable standing in the philosophies and religions of the world. But the concept of the resurrection of all human flesh is something for which the unbeliever can find no support in either nature or the refinements of his own reason. The doctrine and concept of the resurrection of the body of every human being who has ever lived is something which is uniquely Christian, and that is the same as saying that the teacher of this truth is the Triune God.

God has been teaching this truth for a long time, as men count time, for all of Scripture, from Moses to John, teaches that there is a resurrection of the body. But "Moses to John" may seem too short a summary. Then let us say again what often has been said: from the Tree of Life and the promise of the Savior to come in the very Garden of Eden to the last mention of the Book of Life on the very last page of the Bible, God, men, and events bear unanimous testimony that there is in truth a resurrection of the body for all mankind. From the first parents of our race, through godly Enoch and Patriarch Abraham, we come to the words of God to Moses in Ex. 3:6. But what do those words have to do with the resurrection of the body? A great deal; for now one must also note our Lord's explanation of these words for the Sadducees, who "believed not in the resurrection" (Mark 12:26-27). This interpretation of Christ covers the whole Old Testament with the light of the resurrection and of eternal life. For not in a few single passages only, but rather in hundreds of instances, God calls Himself the God of His own and of His people, the God of the living and not of the dead.

Is there, then, still need to mention the faith in the resurrection expressed by Job, by David, by Solomon, by the long line of Prophets sent by God, or the fact of the resurrection reflected in the miracles of raising from the dead? There is, so long as men pooh-pooh miracles, attempt to fence in God, and claim that the doctrine of the resurrection of all flesh is but a gradually developing idea, whose only foundation is hope and wish. For the same reason we are constrained to call attention to such signs and symbols of our own resurrection as Jonah and Isaac.

But most of all do we note the example of the resurrection from the dead set for us by our Lord Jesus Christ, who is become our Example, the beginning of the resurrection, "the Firstborn from the dead." Verily, Jesus Christ risen from the dead is the sure and only Foundation for the resurrection of the just unto life. From our atonement through Christ it follows that we shall arise and live. Our booty from His substitutionary and victorious battle over Satan is the victory also over death. He is the Second Adam, who restored righteousness and life and who makes it sure that we too shall rise.

This resurrection of all mankind is to take place immediately upon the return of our Lord Jesus Christ and the end of the world. Scripture knows of no lapse of time between His return and the resurrection. Nor is the resurrection a long process, or even one including interruptions. There is only *one* bodily resurrection.

This resurrection is not natural, but is a supernatural act of the Triune God. Just as it is impossible for the human mind to conjure up the idea of the resurrection, just so it is impossible for any human or natural force to bring about the resurrection. Scripture ascribes this resurrection miracle to all three persons of the Holy Trinity, but in particular to the Holy Spirit, whose great function it is to distribute to men all the great spiritual goods and gifts of God.

This resurrection of the body means no less than that all men, women, and children will receive again the same bodies they possessed in their temporal life, whether it was long or short. Think of what that says! Think of what God promises! Think of all those whose funerals you have attended. Regardless of how long ago a body was laid into the grave and passed into decay, regardless of where death took place: on the battlefield, in a storm at sea, in the desert, on a mountaintop, in a horrible accident, or in bed—all shall receive again the same bodies that they possessed in their temporal life. Regardless of what happened to those dead bodies—whether they received Christian or pagan burial or lay unburied, with the bones gradually bleaching in the wind and the sun, or lay unnoticed and forgotten by fellow mortals, only to become the food and prey of the scavengers of earth or the vultures of the sky or the fish of the sea—all will receive again the same bodies they possessed in their temporal life. There is no exception, for the resurrection is as general and universal as death.

Two things are part of the resurrection: (1) the almighty God will gather together again the various parts of which the bodies were made, and (2) the remade bodies will be reunited with the souls that were theirs in their temporal life. Death is separation of body and soul, while resurrection is reunion of the body and the soul.

"But," ask some, "how much the *same* will these bodies be?" Will children still be children? And the aged, aged? Yes, the restored body will be essentially the same as that body was at the moment of death; there will be no growth and no decline (Rev. 20:12).

In the resurrection the bodies of all men will be made immortal and unchangeable, and the bodies of the believers in Christ, in addition, will be glorified and glorious. After the resurrection, the bodies of all men will never again die. This is true of the bodies of unbelievers as well as of believers.

But the bodies of the believers will also be glorified. They will be free from all sinful corruption. Freakishness and defects in form and stature are not part of the nature and essence of man, but are results of sin, and hence will be eliminated in the resurrection bodies of the believers. These glorious bodies of the believers will be powerful and spiritual; they will be similar to the glorified body of the glorified Christ. To say, in the inspired words of Paul, that the resurrection bodies will be spiritual, is not to say that they will not be real, corporeal, but rather that they will be freed from limitations of space and time.

Because of the Scriptural doctrine of the resurrection of all flesh our Church has held that the treatment accorded to the bodies of Christians should be consistent with, and expressive of, the Christian faith. The method of burial in itself is an adiaphoron, a matter neither expressly prescribed nor forbidden by God. However, to avoid every appearance of evil, Christians should avoid such methods of disposal of bodies as cremation, which is so often associated with godless defiance of the resurrection. Since circumstances can alter cases, no blanket prohibition dare be made; but the spurious and alleged advantages advanced most generally in support of cremation should be recognized as such.

His unending love and mercy moves God to raise the believers, so that they who by faith have been united with their Savior in their life on earth, may continue in His fellowship in life everlasting. His holy wrath and righteousness move Him to raise also the unbelievers; because of their impenitence, He will let them proceed from the grave by way of judgment to eternal shame and punishment. Accordingly, the purpose of the resurrection for the unbelievers is eternal damnation, for the believers eternal salvation.

But what of the bodies of those who have not died at the time of the resurrection? Here the Scripture gives explicit information in two passages only: I Thess. 4:15-17 and I Cor. 15:51-53.

IV

"We believe that they that have done evil shall go into everlasting fire."

Christ's call as Redeemer can be ignored, but Christ's call as Judge cannot be ignored, not even by those who would most like to evade it. Their attempted evasion arises out of their knowledge of both their own guilt and the righteous wrath of the God whose enemies they are. Mankind races toward hell, and meanwhile Satan has so blinded many that they deny both Satan and hell. This is not a pleasant area of study for the believers whose love, like their Savior's, includes all men. Yet all Scripture expressly teaches that there is both a hell and an eternal damnation reserved for the enemies of God.

All those who are redeemed by Christ but departed in unbelief, go to hell, with their bodies and their souls. In any discussion of this subject it is necessary to repeat ever and again that "Christ died for all," that "God will have all men to be saved," that even the damned are redeemed. Just as Scripture repeatedly tells us the great truth of Christ's redemption, so it ever and again tells us that it is unbelief, unwillingness to accept what Christ so freely offers, that damns.

Unbelievers, then, are the damned, namely, all those worldly ones, and even self-styled saints within the ranks of visible Christendom, for whom Christ died and rose again in vain.

These unbelievers, after their judgment is meted out to them by their Redeemer, who is also their Judge, proceed to and remain in everlasting hell. Their deserved damnation redounds to the greater glory of the righteous God's justice (II Thess. 1:6ff.), truthfulness (Rev. 21:5-8), and omnipotence (II Thess. 1:9).

This eternal damnation includes that they are deprived of all erstwhile earthly pleasures and enjoyments; they lack all things which the blessed have and enjoy; and they suffer indescribable torture of body and soul. As such forfeited earthly pleasures we need point out merely the riches and possessions which even the ungodly get and hold, fleshly pleasures which are too well-known to need listing, gratified desires and pleasures which lead even pagan poets to speak and sing of happiness, man-made and man-esteemed honors which more often come to men of the world than to God's people, and all the forms and degrees of might and power as men define them. Of all these the damned will be deprived, and even their memories of the past and what joys they held for them will be a torture.

But it is not merely being deprived of former earthly joys and pleasures which makes up the torture of the damned; it is also their utter lack of all the things which the less numerous blessed have and enjoy in the unending and full presence of the living God. Where the blessed see God face to face, the damned see only themselves and the devils; where the blessed are free from all evil, the damned are in the midst of all evil and are evil themselves; where the blessed experience the fullness of joy in soul and body, the damned in soul and body are devoid of joy and children of wrath; where the blessed enjoy the glorious fellowship of the communion of saints, the damned themselves form the company of the accursed.

To this complete absence of earthly and spiritual joys is added indescribable torture and pain of body and soul. Let us not permit our imagination to run wild in detailed descriptions concerning these horrible events, while Scripture itself refrains. Men have debated whether the "worm that never dies" (Mark 9:44) might not be the endless accusations of guilty consciences; or they have debated as to the nature of the fires of hell, whether they be real or immaterial. Here the voice of our Church has said, "Pray God humbly and fervently, for Jesus' sake, that the nature of the worm and the kind of fire be not taught you by experience."

The punishments of the damned last without intermission or termination. From the time when the first permanent resident of hell led our first parents to question the truth of God, children of men, it would seem, at all times and all places have questioned whether the God of love would really condemn to everlasting pain any one of his creatures. Their questioning has led to a diabolical inventiveness, which has even misused or deliberately misunderstood Scripture in a quest for support. They have flooded an eager hell-bent market with their writings. There are always those who deny the very existence of hell, or even of any life after death. There are those who hold that every man's soul is inherently mortal, and that only the souls of a few are made to be immortal. There are those who hold that the souls of the wicked will be completely destroyed and annihilated, while the righteous souls only continue alive. There are those, too, who, while denying the resurrection of the body, have held that the only torture of the damned consists in gradually diminishing pangs of conscience. Finally, there are those who argue that the goodness of God and the great worth of man make a return of every soul to God not merely possible, but also inevitable by means of some kind of divine restitution and restoration. To all these vagaries and their infinite subvarieties and subspecies the Church of God has always responded, "We believe, according to the Scriptures, that they that have done evil shall go into everlasting fire." And to those who attack the Scriptural foundation of this truth, even questioning the meaning and the force of the very words "eternal" and "everlasting," we have rejoined: These attacks are so weak that they do not deserve respect on the part of serious Bible students. Other than grammatical motives are behind these attacks.

While Scripture knows nothing of a mitigation or cessation of the sufferings of the damned, it does clearly teach that there are degrees of punishment in hell. While the manner of this difference is beyond our comprehension and understanding, the passages in which Scripture speaks of these degrees indicate that the greater the measure of God's grace that is rejected by an individual, the greater will be his punishment in hell.

Just as certainly as Scripture teaches only two destinies for mankind, just so certainly Scripture knows nothing of any alleged middle place or third place, that is, either some Hades, in which the souls of men can still be converted or made perfect, or some purgatory, in which they somehow can be cleansed from their sins after their temporal death or after the Judgment.

An imaginary Hades, a neutral realm of all the dead, is a pagan idea, and it is more than startling to find so-called moderns who wish to assume somewhere beyond the grave a place for those who could not decide for God during their lives on earth. Sometimes this Hades is actually called Paradise by them!

This pagan idea of Hades, as it intrudes into the Christian Church, generally takes one of the two forms. In its first form it is a place of a second chance. Over against this the Christian Church always says with her Lord, speaking in His Word: "It is appointed unto men once to die, but after this the Judgment" (Heb. 9:27). In its other form, Hades becomes a place of development for the believers, a place of purging, a veritable purgatory, where there is redemption from eternal punishment. The Lutheran Church today just as determinedly as the Lutheran Church of the Reformation era opposes the purgatory of Rome as a devilish device of the Antichrist, which has nothing but garbled Bible passages, questionable proofs from the Apocrypha, fallacious proofs from reason, and no proofs from Scripture to back it.

But when newly invented purgatories are posited even in the Protestant churches, then our Church insists with all possible vigor that no purgatory has the slightest Scriptural foundation, that a "purgatory of grace" is a monstrous thought for those who believe that God freely, for Christ's sake, forgives all sins to all believers. Nor does Scripture teach either Gospel preaching or conversion after death in passages like I Pet. 3:19-20. Hell is hell, and no human wish or thought will make any less of everlasting damnation.

But our Savior Jesus Christ has redeemed us from hell and protects us from it forever through lasting faith in Himself. In front of the yawning gates of hell there stands the Cross of the world's Christ, the way of escape provided by Him who said of Himself, "I am the Way, the Truth, and the Life; no man cometh unto the Father but by Me" (John 14:6). You and I, as we have studied this doctrine of the Bible concerning the everlasting punishment in hell for the damned, have perhaps shaken off a chill or a shudder and sighed a prayer of thanksgiving for our own saving faith in our Savior. Is it necessary, in addition, to remind ourselves that the naked truth of the doctrine of hell should move us to make haste and to work for the spreading of the Gospel to all men everywhere lest any should die without knowledge of the truth?

Brothers in Christ, the time is short. We live in the very last times. Let us not fritter away the time that God allots to us as individual Christians and as His Church Militant, but rather let us hasten on with faith-filled hearts, with minds of clear purpose, and with busy hands thus to meet our Judge at the end of time and things. May He, the righteous Judge of all, enable us, the faithful, by His means of grace to turn many to righteousness in Him, away from the gates of everlasting hell, and into the heavenly portals of joy with Him (Rev. 22:20).

XXVII

Eternal Life

"I BELIEVE in the life everlasting." On this note of joyful confidence and certainty ends the Apostles' Creed, the chief confession of faith of all Christendom since the days of the Apostles. God's loving purpose toward the human race, the goal and aim of creation, of redemption, and of sanctification through Word and Sacrament, is the salvation of man, the attainment of life everlasting. All that God has revealed to us in His blessed Word, all that according to His eternal decree He has resolved to do and does do in time, climaxes in eternal life. The final petition, which our Savior Himself teaches us to pray in the Lord's Prayer, is, "Deliver us from evil," that is, "Lead us safely at last into life eternal." Eternal life, therefore, is the grand prospect to which our Christian hope should constantly look forward, and which in the light of Scripture we shall now study.

THESIS I

The Word of God, both of the Old and the New Testament, teaches very clearly and abundantly that there is an everlasting life.

In the religions of all people, both of ancient and modern times, we find a belief that there is in store for man an existence after death, a blissful abode in some form, whether that be the Elysian Fields of the Greeks, the sensuous Paradise of Mohammed, the Valhalla of the ancient Germans, or the happy hunting ground of the American Indian.

How can we account for this belief? St. Paul ascribes to the Gentiles a certain knowledge of God, of His eternal power and Godhead (Rom. 1:19). And in the next chapter the Apostle writes that the Gentiles do by nature the things contained in the Law, showing

561

the work of the Law written in their hearts, and that their conscience also bears witness, their thoughts the meanwhile accusing or else excusing one another (Rom. 2:14-15). The voice of conscience, while not an absolutely reliable guide in itself, because it has been blurred by sin, nevertheless serves as a monitor to do what is right and avoid what is wrong. It will tell man that he is responsible to his Creator for his conduct during this life. The conscience of natural man also convinces him of an existence after death and the coming of a day of final accounting; and it is the fear of that inescapable fact rather than an actual questioning of it that leads unbelievers to attempt to silence the protests of conscience by denying and ridiculing the idea of a life after death.

In spite of man's dread of an eternal retribution in the hereafter, there remains in man a longing for immortality, a desire for an existence in bliss and happiness after death. Since man has only a vague idea of the possibility of such an existence, his hope for future happiness is also vague, devoid of any sure foundation. Therefore natural man is not so much inclined to worry about and make provisions for an uncertain future after death as to make sure of enjoying his life on earth. He will look for his heaven in this world and leave the next to care for itself. And Satan only too easily succeeds in picturing the pleasures and riches and honors of this world in colors so alluring that man becomes so completely absorbed in the things temporal that he neglects and ultimately loses the things eternal.

In order to gain assurance which will not fail, a knowledge and hope of eternal life that will not make ashamed, we must turn to the sure word of prophecy as it is recorded in Holy Scripture, where God Himself has revealed what no man can know about the state of man after death and in eternity. The Old as well as the New Testament sets forth in clear and unmistakable language that our hope of eternal life as expressed in the Apostolic Creed is not a man-made theory or creed, but God's own teaching. "Therefore," says Luther, "we should study the Holy Scriptures, because from it we shall be made wiser than all the world. He who does not ask Holy Scripture for counsel will know absolutely nothing as to how we should die and *where we shall go.* This we learn *only* from the book of Holy Scripture" (Erl. Ed., Vol. 45, p. 172).

Since the claim is made that the ancient Jews knew nothing about eternal life, we shall first furnish proof that also in the Old Testament this doctrine is well established. Modern theology in particular is determined to remove all proof of eternal life from Old Testament Scripture. As a matter of fact, however, the thought of eternal life is fundamental to the entire Old Testament and finds expression already in the account of man's creation. Only then could it truly be said that man was created in the image of God if he was created for eternal life; for God is immortal. The words of the Lord God to man: "In the day that thou eatest thereof, thou shalt surely die" (Gen. 2:17) imply very definitely that if man did not eat, he would not die, but live forever. After the fall of our first parents, God promised them a Redeemer to deliver them from the power of Satan, and that included his power of depriving them of eternal life, of eternal separation from God. The promised Redeemer would restore to them the hope of life eternal in everlasting communion with God.

The sudden translation from earth to heaven of Enoch, the man who walked with God, the glorious ascension of Elijah, the faithful prophet of the Lord, what else did they teach than the certainty of life eternal as a gift of God to his believing children? The statement so often repeated at the death of the Old Testament believers: "He was gathered unto his people" (Gen. 25:8, 17; 35:29; 49:29; Num. 20:24; 27:13), what else does it imply than the teaching of an eternal life? For certainly they could not be gathered to their people if that people no longer existed. None less than our Savior Himself argues thus when from the words of God spoken of the departed Patriarchs: "I am the God of Abraham, the God of Isaac, and the God of Jacob" (Ex. 3:6) He makes the inference: "God is not the God of the dead, but of the living," thereby affirming that these three were already in eternal life.

To multiply the evidence, let us note a number of passages indicating how clearly the Old Testament saints understood the doctrine of eternal life. Dying Jacob exclaims with the assurance of faith: "I have waited for Thy salvation, O Lord" (Gen. 49:18). Confidently David says: "In Thy presence is fullness of joy; at Thy right hand there are pleasures forevermore" (Ps. 16:11); and again: "I will behold Thy face in righteousness; I shall be satisfied, when I awake, with Thy likeness" (Ps. 17:15). Job must have been sure of eternal life, since he could exult: "I know that my Redeemer liveth and that He shall stand at the latter day upon the earth; and though after

my skin worms destroy this body, yet in my flesh shall I see God"
(Job 19:25-26). Likewise the Prophets testify to this doctrine.
Isaiah exclaims: "He will swallow up death in victory, and the Lord
God will wipe away tears from off all faces; and the rebuke of his
people shall he take away from off all the earth; for the Lord hath
spoken it" (Is. 25:8). And again: "Thy dead men shall live, together
with my dead body shall they arise. Awake and sing, ye that dwell
in dust.—Come, my people, enter thou into thy chambers, and shut
thy doors about thee; hide thyself as it were for a little moment,
until the indignation be overpast" (Is. 26:19-20). Daniel testifies:
"Many of them that sleep in the dust of the earth shall awake, some
to everlasting life, and some to shame and everlasting contempt"
(Dan. 12:2). And how marvelously does the eleventh chapter of
Hebrews point out that the doctrine of eternal life was well known
and firmly believed in the days of the Old Covenant.

The doctrine of eternal life, so clearly revealed in the Old Testament, is the keynote of every book in the New Testament from Matthew to Revelation. In the Gospels we hear Christ assuring His
disciples of everlasting life. "And, behold, one came and said unto
Him, Good Master, what good thing shall I do, that I may have
eternal life? And He said unto him, Why callest thou Me good?
There is none good but one, that is God; but if thou wilt enter into
life, keep the Commandments" (Matt. 19:16-17). "If thy hand
offend thee, cut it off; it is better for thee to enter into life maimed
than having two hands to go into hell, into the fire that never shall
be quenched" (Mark 9:43). "Who shall not receive manifold more
in this present time, and in the world to come life everlasting" (Luke
18:30). "He that heareth My word, and believeth on Him that sent
Me, hath everlasting life, and shall not come into condemnation;
but is passed from death unto life" (John 5:24). And Paul writes:
"The wages of sin is death; but the gift of God is eternal life through
Jesus Christ our Lord" (Rom. 6:23). James calls the believers "heirs
of the Kingdom which He hath promised to them that love Him"
(James 2:5). Peter speaks of "an inheritance incorruptible, and
undefiled, and that fadeth not away, reserved in heaven for you,
who are kept by the power of God through faith unto salvation
ready to be revealed in the last time" (I Pet. 1:4, 5); and John
writes: "This is the promise that He hath promised us, even eternal
life" (I John 2:25); and Jude exhorts: "Keep yourselves in the love

of God, looking for the mercy of our Lord Jesus Christ unto eternal life" (v. 21). We shall in the course of this paper study many other passages telling us of life everlasting. To deny this doctrine is to deny the chief purpose for which these books were written: to give to sinful man, the slave of sin and Satan and death, the glorious hope of life eternal in Christ Jesus.

Our belief in life everlasting, therefore, is not merely a logical and reasonable deduction arrived at on the basis of natural knowledge and its processes. It is an irrefutable truth founded upon God's own revelation in both the Old and the New Testaments of Scripture.

THESIS II

Scripture not only teaches the reality of eternal life. It also describes this life as a state of everlasting bliss consisting in the uninterrupted beatific vision of God, in the perfect and eternal restoration of the divine image, in the final, complete, and everlasting deliverance from all evil and in the unending enjoyment of happiness, rest, and glory.

The conceptions of natural man as to the state after death cannot rise above the level of human reason, or fancy, or experience in this life. The wisest philosopher, the most renowned scientist can give us no more reliable information about life after death than the most ignorant bushman. Neither telescope nor television nor radar nor any other human invention can penetrate that veil which God has hung over eternity. Thank God, He, the Author of life eternal, has given us in His Holy Word quite a complete picture of the heavenly home prepared for us and in which we shall spend everlasting life. Not all questions proposed by human curiosity are answered in the Bible. Much that we would like to know about heaven and eternal life will be revealed to us only after we have entered there. Neither is it necessary for us to know here and now what God in His wisdom has seen fit to withhold from us. However, all that is needful for us to know, enough to stimulate our interest in, and to create a longing for, that eternal life prepared for us, is clearly revealed in the Scripture.

THE BEATIFIC VISION

In eternal life we shall, first of all, see God. This fact is attested by a number of Scripture passages both of the Old and the New Testament. David exults: "As for me, I will behold Thy face in righteousness" (Ps. 17:15). As the context shows, he is speaking of seeing God after his resurrection. Job rejoices: "In my flesh shall I see God, whom I shall see for myself and mine eyes shall behold, and not another" (Job 19:26-27). Our Savior says in His Sermon on the Mount: "Blessed are the pure in heart; for they shall see God" (Matt. 5:8). St. Paul writes: "Now we see through a glass, darkly; but then face to face" (I Cor. 13:12). St. John, describing the future revelation of the glory of God's children, says: "We shall see Him as He is" (I John 3:2). And again he affirms: They [the servants of God] shall see His face" (Rev. 22:4).

How are we to conceive this seeing of God? One thing is sure: It will be a vision of God altogether different from the manner in which we see God in this world. St. Paul tells us: "The invisible things of Him from the creation of the world are clearly seen, being understood by the things that are made, even His eternal power and Godhead; so that they are without excuse" (Rom. 1:20). We see God as He has revealed Himself in His Word and in His works. In the Old Testament, God was seen by many patriarchs and prophets. Evidently God had assumed some visible form (cp. Gen. 17:1, 22; 18:1, 2, 8, 16, 22, 33; Ex. 33:9-11; Num. 12:5-9). Yet even Moses, with whom the Lord communed more intimately than with any other prophet (Deut. 34:10), was not permitted to see the uncovered glory of God, "for there shall no man see Me and live" (Ex. 33:17-23; cp. I Tim. 6:16). Even in His Word, the clearest revelation of His person and will we have, we see God as through a glass, in a mirror, darkly (I Cor. 13:12). In a mirror we see a reflection of ourselves or of a person standing behind us, but that reflection is not the person, and while we may learn many interesting things concerning that person from his reflection in the mirror, yet this knowledge of him is an incomplete one, not to be compared with that which we receive from seeing him face to face or after we have been in his company for some time.

The knowledge of God that we obtain from His revelation in nature and history is true as far as it goes. The knowledge derived from the Bible is a saving knowledge, able to make us wise unto salvation through faith in Christ Jesus and thoroughly furnishing us unto all good works (II Tim. 3:15, 17). Yet much concerning God's nature, His will and works, His ways and judgments, remains obscure and enigmatic to us. It is the wisdom of God spoken in a mystery (I Cor. 2:7); and therefore we know only in part (I Cor. 13:12).

In the life to come we shall attain to a complete knowledge of Him and all that pertains to Him; for "then shall I know even as also I am known" (I Cor. 13:12). That does not mean, however, that in heaven we shall know God as only He can know Himself, for then we would have to be equal with God. There is and ever will be an essential difference between God's knowledge of Himself and our knowledge of Him also in eternal life, where we shall know Him as He is (I John 3:2), even as we are known by Him (I Cor. 13:12). God's knowledge of Himself is essential to His Being, is an uncreated knowledge, unlimited in its scope and in its perfection, an eternal knowledge, having no beginning and no end, a knowledge such as only the Lord God, the great I Am That I Am, can have and without which He would not be God. Our knowledge of God in life eternal will be an image of the divine self-knowledge, a knowledge created by God in our human mind.

Although our knowledge of God will not equal God's knowledge of Himself in its fullness, yet in the light of eternity we shall see light (Ps. 36:9). Whatever we as creatures are able to comprehend and understand concerning the nature and works and ways of God, we shall fully and completely understand. Says Luther: "The way in this life (of seeing God) is that we do not see, but believe Him. Now, faith is an imperfect, obscure seeing, which requires the Word; . . . for without the Word, faith cannot exist. But the way in yonder life is that we do not believe but see Him; which is a perfect knowledge that does not require the Word" (St. Louis, XII, p. 432).

In life eternal we shall see God not only with the eyes of our mind. Scripture teaches that we shall see God "face to face" (I Cor. 13:12), in the manner expressed by Job in those memorable words: "In my flesh shall I see God; whom I shall see for myself and mine eyes shall behold, and not another" (Job 19:26-27). How this is possible we shall leave to Him who can see the holy angels, spirits as invisible to us as God is now invisible to us; who enables these spirits always to behold the face of God (Matt. 18); who made it possible for Elisha's servant to see what he could not see before (II Kings 6:17); who shall change our vile body that it may be like unto Christ's glorious body. He tells us, Ye shall see God. We take Him at His word.

Whether this vision of God shall be transmitted to us by seeing the glory of Christ given to Him by His Father (John 17:24) or by being permitted to see the fullness of the glory of God, who now dwells in the light which no man can approach unto, whom no man hath seen, nor can see (I Tim. 6:16), is a question that cannot be answered definitely in this life. Even if we see the glory of God in the face of Christ Jesus, we see God's full glory, for Christ is the brightness of God's glory, the express image of God's person (Heb. 1:3), one with the Father (John 10:30). If Philip saw the Father when he saw Christ in the days of His humiliation (John 14:9, 10), then seeing Christ in the fullness of His divine glory (John 17:24), would be a vision of the fullness of the glory of the Triune God.

THE RESTORATION OF THE DIVINE IMAGE

Furthermore, in eternal life the divine image will be fully and completely restored. St. John tells us: "Beloved, now are we the sons of God, and it doth not yet appear what we shall be; but we know that when He shall appear, we shall be like Him" (I John 3:2). We are even now the children of God and daily put on the new man, which is renewed in knowledge after the image of Him that created him (Col. 3:10), but it remains a continuous putting on, it is only the beginning of the renewal of the divine image. Only in eternal life will there be a complete restoration of the divine image. Therefore David says: "I will behold Thy face in righteousness; I shall be satisfied, when I awake, with Thy likeness" (Ps. 17:15). Here the Holy Spirit clearly testifies that when on that great day of resurrestion God's children awake, they will be adorned with the image of God. That image, once lost in the Fall, will then be fully restored. This does not mean that we shall become God, or gods. No, we are, and shall remain, creatures. A piece of iron plunged into fire does not become fire, but it soon becomes like unto it: it loses its dark color and becomes red and hot like fire, yet it retains the nature of iron. Even so we shall bear God's image in soul and body; nevertheless we shall remain creatures.

Properly to understand what the restoration of the divine image in eternal life implies, we must realize what is meant by the

divine image. May we permit Dr. Walther to define it for us in his
Epistelpostille (p. 418): "According to the Word of God the divine
image was a reflection of divine glory. The intellect of man was
illumined and permeated by a heavenly light granting to man a clear
and errorless knowledge of his Creator and His will, of the nature
of all creatures, and of himself. . . . And that was the image of divine
wisdom. In the will of man there was reflected God's holiness and
righteousness; in his sentiments, God's goodness, long-suffering, and
patience; in his inclinations and desires, God's love and compassion;
in his actions and words, God's truth, affability, gentleness, and
kindness. There was nothing in man to resist God's will, neither in
his soul nor in his body was there any evil tendency, any sinful lust
or desire. This marvelous knowledge and perfect righteousness
were the principal features of the divine image. Yet it included
many other wonderful gifts. God is almighty, the Lord of heaven
and earth; this was reflected in the complete control which at that
time man exercised over all visible creatures. God is eternal; this
was reflected in man's immortality of body and soul. God dwells in
bliss; before Him is fullness of joy and pleasures at His right hand
forevermore; this was reflected in the blissfulness enjoyed by man
already in this life. In his conscience he experienced serenity and
peace. No anxiety or care marred the ineffable joy of his heart; no
pain or disease could touch him; neither heat nor cold could hurt or
harm him; and Paradise, the abode of man, was an adumbration of
the heavenly mansions of God, where He reveals His divine majesty
and in which there is found nothing but light, nothing but love,
nothing but joy, nothing but holiness and righteousness." Such is
the glory that again awaits us.

We have already called attention to the marvelous knowledge
which shall be a precious gift of the heavenly Father to His children
in heaven, and which is part of the restored image of God according
to Col. 3:10. In this connection let us answer a question frequently
asked: Shall we recognize and know one another in heaven? Shall
we know all who dwell in bliss? We have every reason to believe
this, and we may base our belief upon the fact that we are to be
renewed in the image of God. Did not the disciples on the Mount
of Transfiguration at once recognize Moses and Elijah, whom they
had never seen (Matt. 17:4)? Is it likely, then, that in eternal life

our eyes, our memory, our mind, should be capable of less? We may be sure that we shall know our fellow saints in heaven.

In eternal life the image of God will be restored also in our will. This implies that our will then will be perfectly free, that it will reflect the holiness and righteousness of God, and that it will be imbued with perfect love toward God and all saints. The Formula of Concord states: "As they [the saints] see God face to face, so in the power of the Spirit of God dwelling in them will they do the will of God voluntarily, without coercion, unhindered, altogether sincerely and completely with unfeigned joy, and will eternally rejoice therein." Originally man's will was free, that is, he decided to obey God and His will, not under duress, but because he so desired. But this freedom of the will to choose what is good ceased completely when he became the slave of sin. It is true that in conversion the will undergoes a great change. "When man is born anew by the Spirit of God . . . he lives according to the immutable will of God comprised in the Law, and so far as he is born anew, does everything from a free, cheerful spirit. . . . But since believers are not completely renewed in this world . . . there also remains in them the struggle between the spirit and the flesh" (*Triglot*, p. 967; 17, 18). In eternal life, however, the freedom of the will is no longer weak and imperfect, but perfect and Godlike. For the very reason that our will shall then be perfect and in conformity with the image of God, we shall will all, and only that, which God wills. Hence the will of man in eternal life will again reflect the holiness and righteousness of God. Says the Formula of Concord: "In the article of the resurrection, Scripture testifies that precisely the substance of this our flesh, but without sin, will rise again, and that in eternal life we shall have and retain precisely this soul, but without sin" (*Triglot*, 873, 46). Our human nature will be divested of sin itself, and also of every inclination to sin and of every possibility ever again even to desire anything that is sinful. Nothing less makes for perfect bliss. Only thus will the image of God be found as perfect in a creature as this is possible, without the creature itself becoming God. Hence the theological axiom: "In the state of creation man was able to sin and not to sin; in the state of the fall he cannot but sin; in the state of perfection he cannot sin."

In yonder life our love toward God and all fellow saints shall be as perfect as God desires it. God, the prototype, is love; hence this love is part of the fully restored divine image. Then the whole heart, the whole mind, the whole soul, and all powers will perfectly love God and the heavenly neighbors. There will be complete fulfillment of the Law, for there is complete love, and love, according to the Word of God, is the fulfillment of the Law.

DELIVERANCE FROM ALL EVIL

In eternal life we shall at last enjoy full freedom and deliverance from all evil, the complete and everlasting realization of the daily petition of every child of God, "Deliver us from evil." In that heavenly abode there will be no evil of any kind, neither spiritual nor bodily, neither inward nor outward, neither great nor small. For St. Paul writes: "The Lord shall deliver me from every evil work, and will preserve me unto His heavenly kingdom" (II Tim. 4:18). And the great voice from the throne says: "God shall wipe away all tears from their eyes; and there shall be no more death, neither sorrow, nor crying, neither shall there be any more pain; for the former things are passed away" (Rev. 21:4). Once and for all everything that made this world a vale of tears will be done away with, for these things of the first earth have no place in the new heaven. Says Luther: "There we shall suffer no more affliction, but be delivered from all evil. Sorrow, crying, grief, pain, death, will be no more, nor will any sin dwell in our flesh, but it will be altogether pure without filth, evil lust, and desire. In brief, we shall receive in richer and better measure what we would have had in Paradise, but what we lost in Adam. We shall love God with our whole heart, etc., thank, laud, and praise Him to all eternity. Amen." (St. Louis, XII, 2070.)

First of all, the soul will be free of the greatest of evils, of sin. It will be free from original sin, that deadly poison of the soul and the root of all misery. It will be free from all actual sin, so that there will be no more occasion to cry: "The good that I would, I do not; but the evil which I would not, that I do. . . . O wretched man that I am! Who shall deliver me from the body of this death?" (Rom. 7:20, 24.) Even temptation to sin will cease there. No evil will affect any of the faculties of the soul. No unsatisfied wish, no unsolved problem, no trace of longing, no anxiety or perplexity, will remain to mar our perfect bliss.

In eternal life also the body will de delivered from all evil. In that Paradise, where He dwells, who is the Fountain of life (Ps. 36:9), "there shall be no more death" (Rev. 21:4). "The last enemy that shall be destroyed is death" (I Cor. 15:26). "This mortal must put on immortality" (I Cor. 15:53). Banished forever will be the countless host of diseases, ailments, and infirmities in children and adults. "They shall see His face; and His name shall be in their foreheads" (Rev. 22:4). "They shall hunger no more, neither thirst any more" (Rev. 7:16). Naturally not, for "it is sown a natural body, it is raised a spiritual body" (I Cor. 15:44). All reference of Scripture to the eating and drinking of the elect in heaven (Rev. 2:7; Luke 22:30; Matt. 26:29; Rev. 7:17) can therefore not be understood in a physical sense. Luther gives this interpretation: "It is not called a spiritual body in the sense that it shall have no bodily life, no more flesh and blood; for then it could not be termed a true body. But now it is called a spiritual body in the sense that it is to have its own life and yet not be an eating, sleeping, digesting body, but be spiritually nourished and sustained of God. It will nevermore think of eating and drinking" (St. Louis, VIII, 1539).

In the life eternal there will be joy and pleasure. On the basis of Scripture we confidently confess: "Jesus Christ will give unto the believers and elect eternal life and everlasting joy" (Augsb. Conf., Art. XVII). David says: "In Thy presence is fullness of joy; at Thy right hand there are pleasures forevermore" (Ps. 16:11). "They that sow in tears shall reap in joy. He that goeth forth and weepeth, bearing precious seed, shall doubtless come again with rejoicing, bringing his sheaves with him" (Ps. 126:5-6). Our Lord and Master assures us: "Blessed are ye that weep now; for ye shall laugh" (Luke 6:21). In the ecstasy of that heavenly joy "our mouth will be filled with laughter and our tongue with singing" (Ps. 126:2). "The ransomed of the Lord shall return and come to Zion with songs and everlasting joy upon their heads; they shall obtain joy and gladness, and sorrow and sighing shall flee away" (Is. 35:10).

What an essential part of eternal life this joy will be we may learn from the words spoken to the good and faithful servant: "Enter thou into the joy of thy Lord" (Matt. 25:23). Our Savior here identifies eternal life with joy. He does not call it the "joy of heaven," but the "joy of the Lord," to indicate that it is a joy so great as only the Lord God Himself can give to us, a joy as pure and everlasting as the Giver Himself. Nor does He say, May this joy of the Lord come into, or upon you, or to you, but you, you according to body and soul, shall enter into the joy of your Lord; like the waters of the sea it shall overwhelm you completely. You are not to enfold the joy, but it shall enfold you. Hence the Psalmist exclaims: "Thou shalt make them drink of the river of Thy pleasures" (Ps. 36:8).

Peter's description of the heavenly "inheritance" as "incorruptible, undefiled, and that fadeth not away" characterizes also the nature of the joy prevailing there. It is "incorruptible." While all things earthly have in themselves the seed of decay and death, our heavenly inheritance is one which neither moth nor rust nor any other destructive force can corrupt. It is "undefiled," without the least stain of imperfection or defilement by sin, and for that very reason it "fadeth not away," that is, it never terminates, we never tire or weary of it, but it is as endless and ever new as eternity itself. He that has once entered upon this joy "shall go no more out" (Rev. 3:12).

The Holy Spirit has designated eternal life by various names, every one of which is to characterize it and its joy from a particular angle.

We read: "To him that overcometh will I give to eat of the Tree of Life, which is in the midst of the *Paradise* of God" (Rev. 2:7). That first abode which God had provided for Adam and Eve afforded all that could possibly serve their pleasure, joy, and refreshment. Infinitely richer joys and pleasures will be provided for us in that heavenly Paradise, of which Eden was but the vestibule. If anyone asks, "Where is this place, and what is it like?" we would answer with Gerhard: "The nature, condition, and situation of yonder "Where" has not been revealed to us in Scripture; hence it is better to be concerned in this life about its possession rather than about its exact condition."

Our Savior says: "In My Father's house are many mansions" (John 14:2). Here Christ emphasizes the joy which flows from the unending communion of the blessed with their heavenly Father in His eternal home. As our earthly father's house attracts us not so much by its beautiful architecture, its wonderful location and surroundings, as by the intimate and affectionate communion with the loved ones dwelling there, so the everlasting fellowship with the Triune

God will constitute our principal joy in the heavenly Father's house. Sin disrupted the blessed communion of God with man in the earthly Paradise and prompted man's ejection from his Father's house. But God's own Son became man, dwelt with sinners to bring them back to their Father's house, to reunite them with God even here by faith, in order that at last they might eternally rest in the Father-arms of God, see Him face to face and forever rejoice in communion with Him. Thus it has become true: "We shall be His people, and God Himself shall be with us and be our God" (Rev. 21:3). "So shall we ever be with the Lord" (I Thess. 4:17).

Song and music will constitute a large part of the heavenly joy, as may be gathered from such passages as the following: "When He had taken the book, the four beasts and four and twenty elders fell down before the Lamb, having every one of them harps and golden vials full of odors, which are the prayers of saints. And they sung a new song" (Rev. 5:8, 9). "I saw as it were . . . them that had gotten the victory . . . stand on the sea of glass, having the harps of God. And they sing the song of Moses, the servant of God, and the song of the Lamb" (Rev. 15:2-3). Then will the Gloria in Excelsis Deo reverberate in millions of voices through the vault of heaven.

> Unnumbered choirs before the shining throne
> Their joyful anthems raise
> Till heaven's glad halls are echoing with the tone
> Of that great hymn of praise,
> And all its host rejoices,
> And all its blessed throng
> Unite their myriad voices
> In one eternal song.

Eternal life will also bring a blissful rest. Here on earth we complain with Job: "Is there not an appointed time to man upon earth? Are not his days also like the days of a hireling? As a servant earnestly desireth the shadow and as a hireling looketh for the reward of his work, so am I made to possess months of vanity, and wearisome nights are appointed to me" (Job 7:1-3). Our sighings for rest are not in vain! Our desires for peace and quiet shall be fulfilled! "Blessed are the dead which die in the Lord from henceforth; yea, saith the Spirit, that they may rest from their labors; and their works do follow them" (Rev. 14:13). Upon the battle and strife, the unrest, the distress and sweat of this life there will follow "the times of refreshing from the presence of the Lord" (Acts 3:19), for "there remaineth a rest to the people of God" (Heb. 4:9). Lazarus in Abraham's bosom not only rested from all misery, but he was also "comforted," refreshed. The blessed in eternal life will no longer bear the burden and heat of the day, but then the heavenly holiday, the heavenly eve of rest, will have begun. Says Isaiah: "And My people shall dwell in a peaceable habitation, and in sure dwellings, and in quiet resting places" (32:18).

This rest, however, is not an absolute cessation from all activity, a complete idleness. "He that is entered into his rest, he hath also ceased from his own works, as God did from His," we read Heb. 4:10. The rest of God is not idleness, inertia. When God rested from His work which He had made (Gen. 2:2), He did not cease to work. The activity of Him who needs no rest (Is. 40:28) and does not rest (Ps. 121:4; John 5:17), merely assumed a different sphere, that of enjoying and rejoicing in His work (Gen. 1:31), and of preserving and governing all creatures (Is. 40:26ff.; 44:24-28; Heb. 1:4; Ps. 121). So the rest of the people of God consists in ceasing from the works allotted to them in this time and world (Eph. 2:10) and doing those works suitable for the heavenly realms, praising God (Rev. 5:12-13); standing before His throne and serving Him day and night in ceaseless, untiring, joyful service (Rev. 7:15; 22:3); and worshiping Him who sits upon the throne, their God and the Lamb (Rev. 7:9-12). A blessed activity which is not labor, but rest, everlasting rest from all work and weariness.

Finally, eternal life will be a life of glory. St. Paul says: "I reckon that the sufferings of this present time are not worthy to be compared with the glory which shall be revealed in us" (Rom. 8:18). The Apostle would say, "When I compare the sufferings of this present time with the future glory, the eternal glory will be so infinitely great, manifold, and precious that the sufferings of this present time, be they ever so many, ever so bitter, and ever so continuous, are not worthy of mention. Balancing the one against the other, the finite can endure no comparison with the infinite."

The future glory is presented to us by Scripture under the figure of a crown. St. Paul, having fought a good fight and having finished his course in faith, triumphs: "Henceforth there is laid up for me a crown of righteousness" (II Tim. 4:8). Our Savior exhorts us: "Be thou faithful unto death, and I will give thee a crown of life" (Rev. 2:10). St. James writes: "Blessed is the man that endureth temptation; for when he is tried, he shall receive the crown of life, which the Lord hath promised to them that love Him." A crown, or wreath, in ancient times was regarded as a token of highest honor and distinction, as the coveted prize of contests. So also when eternal life is termed a crown, this is symbolic of the unspeakable glory to be revealed in those who shall endure unto the end.

In eternal life a glorious change will take place in our body also. The body which suffered with the suffering soul, which battled with the battling soul, which has been redeemed together with the redeemed soul, shall also be glorified together with the glorified soul, will be in bliss with the soul in bliss. St. Paul asserts: "Who [Jesus Christ] shall change our vile body, that it may be fashioned like unto His glorious body, according to the working whereby He is able even to subdue all things unto Himself" (Phil. 3:21). Our "vile" body, literally, the body of our humiliation, will be changed by Christ, so that it will lose its weakness, miserableness, infirmities, vanity, and mortality. The original term for this changing signifies a transformation in which a thing retains its essence but acquires other attributes. So Christ will endow our bodies with new and glorious properties after the fashion of His own glorious body. We read: "It is sown in corruption, it is raised in incorruption" (I Cor. 15:42). This corruptible body of ours will rise incorruptible, that is, clothed with immortality; for thus says our Lord of those accounted worthy to obtain that world: "Neither can they die any more" (Luke 20:36). Our bodies will be fashioned like unto the glorious body of Christ. We are told: "Christ, being raised from the dead, dieth no more; death hath no more dominion over Him" (Rom. 6:9). "I am He that liveth, and was dead; and, behold, I am alive for evermore" (Rev. 1:18). Therefore we confess on the basis of Scripture: Since my body will be fashioned like unto the body of Jesus Christ, my body, raised from the dead, can henceforth die no more; my body will live to all eternity.

Our bodies will reflect beauty, splendor, radiance, glory. "It is sown in dishonor, it is raised in glory" (I Cor. 15:43). Beautiful and glorious was man's body as it came forth from the hand of his Maker; but sin has disfigured it and made it ugly. This selfsame body will shine in heavenly glory. "They that be wise shall shine as the brightness of the firmament; and they that turn many to righteousness, as the stars forever and ever" (Dan. 12:3). Again, our Savior says: "Then shall the righteous shine forth as the sun in the kingdom of their Father" (Matt. 13:43). When Moses had been with the Lord on the mount for forty days and nights, the skin of his countenance shone, so that Aaron and the children of Israel were afraid to approach him and Moses had to veil his face when speaking to them. Thus will our glorified bodies reflect the glory of God Himself, when we shall see Him face to face eternally. Rays of this future glory were seen when on Tabor's heights the Son of Man was transfigured and His body, like unto which our bodies are to be fashioned, began to shine, His raiment became white as a light, even as snow, and His countenance became dazzling like the sun. Moses and Elijah appeared "in glory." This glory amazed and overwhelmed the disciples so that Peter exclaimed: "Lord, it is good for us to be here; here let us make tabernacles; here let us remain." What happened on Tabor will find a more wonderful repetition in heaven. There all saints will shine as the stars, as the very sun.

Scripture very clearly indicates that while all saints in heaven will enjoy the same heavenly joy and bliss, there will be degrees of glory. "Behold, I come quickly," says Christ, "and My reward is with Me, to give every man according as his works shall be" (Rev. 22:12). Not one of the good works will be forgotten; for every one Christ has a gracious reward which will be paid out in heaven. Here we sow; there we shall reap as we have sown. "He which soweth sparingly shall reap also sparingly; and he which soweth bountifully shall reap also bountifully" (II Cor. 9:6). And God told Daniel: "They that be wise shall shine as the brightness of the firmament; and they that turn many to righteousness, as the stars forever and ever" (Dan. 12:3). Thus there shall be degrees of glory in the Kingdom of Glory. Yet the greater glory of one shall not be a cause of envy, but a source of joy to the other. Being in the image of God, their will conforms to that of God, and their formerly wicked and jealous heart has been completely cleansed of all evil passions. Hence they will rejoice in the greater glory of their fellow saints.

After all that has been said it must be admitted that much of the nature and condition of eternal life is inexplicable. When St. Paul was caught up in Paradise, he heard unspeakable words (II Cor.

12:4). He did not communicate them to us. Why? He tells us that "it is not lawful for a man to utter" these words. The glory of Paradise is so great that it simply cannot be clothed in human words. For the present we must be content with the rather incomplete descriptions gathered from the Scriptures, but correct as they are, they give us but a faint idea. Yonder, however, what here remained inexpressible will resolve itself into one grand eternal Hallelujah. Someone has aptly said, "As little as any sounding lead can measure the depths of Christ's meriting blood, so little can that which has been merited be measured with the sounding lead of human tongue and thought."

This inexplicable bliss will never be interrupted or come to an end. "So shall we ever"—without a moment's interruption—"be with the Lord" (I Thess. 4:17), with whom there is "fullness of joy, and pleasures at His right hand forevermore" (Ps. 16:11). Of this also St. Peter assures us when he speaks of our inheritance as "incorruptible, undefiled, and that fadeth not away" (I Pet. 1:4).

It will also be as endless as eternity itself. All earthly joy and glory is transient; not so that of heaven. How could heaven's bliss be perfect if it were not enjoyed without end? Just this makes for its incomparable rest. Of our earthly home we say: "Home, Sweet Home"; yet there is always the uncertainty of our stay, the fear of having to leave it at some time or other; but having once reached our heavenly Father's house, we shall forever be at home. Our Savior says of the righteous: "They shall go away into life eternal" (Matt. 25:46). "God so loved the world, that He gave His only-begotten Son, that whosoever believeth in Him should not perish, but have everlasting life" (John 3:16). St. Peter calls it "the everlasting kingdom of our Lord and Savior Jesus Christ" (II Pet. 1:11). Again Jesus said: "If a man keep My saying, he shall never see death"—literally, he shall in no wise see death forever" (John 8:51). "There will be no more death" (Rev. 21:4). But where there is no more death, there is endless life, there is eternal bliss. Ah, therefore,

> My heart for joy is springing
> And can no more be sad,
> 'Tis full of mirth and singing,
> Sees naught but sunshine glad.
> The Sun that cheers my spirit

Is Jesus Christ, my King;
The heaven I shall inherit
Makes me rejoice and sing.

In order that already in this life the children of God may in a measure visualize the glorious beauty of our heavenly home, the Lord told His Apostle to describe, as well as that could be done in human language, that marvelous vision which was granted to him on the lonely isle of Patmos. John saw the Holy City coming down from God out of heaven, prepared as a bride adorned for her husband. Reading the twenty-first and twenty-second chapters of Revelation, we see the walls of New Jerusalem with its foundations of precious, multicolored stones, its gates of pearl, its streets of pure gold as transparent glass. God Himself and the Lamb is the Temple and the Light of this city. We behold the multitudes of them that are saved, drinking from the pure river of water of life proceeding out of the throne of God and the Lamb, and eating from the Tree of Life, yielding perpetual fruit. We see the vast host of those whose every tear has been wiped from their eyes standing before the throne of God and the Lamb, seeing His face and serving Him and reigning with Him forever and ever. And our heart longs, and our soul thirsts for the final consummation, and cries with the prophet of old, When shall I come and appear before God? Come, Lord Jesus! And He tells us, Behold, I come quickly, Amen. Even so, come, Lord Jesus!

Thesis III

Scripture bases the hope of eternal life exclusively on the grace of God in Christ Jesus. This grace alone has moved God to prepare a home in heaven for man by the sacrificing of His own Son. The same grace moves Him to freely offer eternal life to man in His holy Gospel, to work acceptance of this offer, faith in Christ Jesus, by means of His Gospel, to keep man in faith through the Gospel and finally to receive him into life eternal. Assurance of eternal life can be engendered and kept alive only by use of the means of grace.

Natural man knows nothing about an everlasting life prepared by the Creator of heaven and earth. He is ignorant of God's revelation concerning life eternal, and even if he reads or hears what the Spirit of God has revealed in the Bible on this subject, he will not receive it. Like all things of the Spirit of God, this doctrine also is foolishness to him (I Cor. 2:14). Neither does man by nature know the way to heaven. He hopes, if he hopes at all, for some kind of better existence after death and bases this hope on himself, on his character, his own merits. God's Word shatters this hope completely and forever. "For as many as are of the works of the Law are under the curse; for it is written, Cursed is every one that continueth not in all things which are written in the book of the Law to do them" (Gal. 3:10).

Neither can the good works of a Christian open heaven to him. While the Law promises eternal life to those who keep it, yet this promise is conditioned on perfect fulfillment of all the requirements of the Law. Such perfect fulfillment is impossible even to the most sincere Christian who earnestly strives to do the will of His God. Still he must confess with Paul: "For I know that in me (that is, in my flesh,) dwelleth no good thing; for to will is present with me; but how to perform that which is good I find not. For the good that I would I do not; but the evil which I would not, that I do" (Rom. 7:18-19). The Christian's hope of eternal life is based not on the Law, but on God's revelation in the Gospel. That same revelation which pictures to us in such vivid and attractive colors the glories of eternal life, teaches us the way to life, sets our feet on the way, and enables us to walk in this way.

The Gospel tells us the amazing news that eternal life is a free gift of God's grace to sinful man.

It is God, and God alone, who prepared eternal salvation for us. As little as man could create this world, so little can man create the world to come and the bliss in store there for all who shall enter into eternal life. The very thought of preparing a place of everlasting bliss for human beings originated with God long before any human being was created (Eph. 1:3-14). Christ tells us that the Kingdom into which the blessed of His Father shall enter on the Last Day was prepared from the foundation of the world, before the creation of man (Matt. 25:34), before there was a possibility that man should earn or merit this glory.

The Gospel tells us that it is not even necessary for man to earn or merit eternal life. God Himself has done all that was needed to procure life for sinful man. "God was in Christ, reconciling the world unto Himself" (II Cor. 5:19-21). "God so loved the world that He gave His only-begotten Son, that whosoever believeth in Him should not perish, but have everlasting life" (John 3:16). In the Gospel, therefore, God offers to all men not only His grace, not merely forgiveness of sin, but everlasting life as a free gift and invites all men: "Ho, every one that thirsteth, come ye to the waters, and he that hath no money, come ye, buy, and eat; yea, come, buy wine and milk without money and without price. Wherefore do ye spend money for that which is not bread? and your labor for that which satisfieth not? Hearken diligently unto Me, and eat ye that which is good, and let your soul delight itself in fatness. Incline your ear, and come unto Me; hear, and your soul shall live; and I will make an everlasting covenant with you, even the sure mercies of David" (Is. 55:1-3).

God's grace is not satisfied with offering eternal life to mankind. The very Gospel which invites man to come is a power unto salvation to every one that believeth (Rom. 1:16). And since this Gospel is foolishness to natural man, since man is dead in trespasses and sin and cannot by his own reason or strength believe on Jesus Christ or come to Him, the grace of God regenerates him, brings him to faith, makes him, the former enemy, a child of God and an heir of eternal life. Having created faith in us, God's grace will keep us in this faith until our end, as Paul confidently exclaims: "I know whom I have believed and am persuaded that He is able to keep that which I have committed unto Him against that day" (II Tim. 1:12), and as He assures all believers, Our Lord Jesus Christ will "also confirm you unto the end, that ye may be blameless in the day of our Lord Jesus Christ. God is faithful, by whom ye were called unto the fellowship of His Son Jesus Christ our Lord" (I Cor. 1:8, 9). And in the Last Day, Christ, our Savior, will appear unto salvation unto them that look for Him (Heb. 9:28).

Eternal life is, from beginning to end, from its conception in God's mind in the eternities before the world began to its glorious consummation in the endless eternities to come, a work of the grace and loving-kindness of our great Lord and God. For that very reason we can be so sure of our salvation that every Christian can make the words of the Apostle his own: "I am persuaded that neither death, nor life, nor angels, nor principalities, nor powers, nor things present, nor things to come, nor height, nor depth, nor any other creature shall be able to separate us from the love of God, which is in Christ Jesus our Lord" (Rom. 8:38-39).

We must never forget, however, that such assurance of eternal life, as voiced by St. Paul, is an assurance of faith, and faith cannot exist without the means of grace, through which alone the Holy Ghost has chosen to operate. Saving faith, the joyous assurance of eternal life through the atoning sacrifice of Christ Jesus, cannot be created in us without the Word of God's promises, nor can it continue to exist independent of this Gospel. A Christian who wants to be assured of life eternal must feed and nourish his faith by means of the Gospel and the Sacraments. He will make the Bible his daily companion, read it, study it, attentively, devotedly. He will frequently think of his Baptism and be a regular attendant at the Lord's Table. Therefore the Apostle exhorts us: "Let the Word of Christ dwell in you richly in all wisdom, teaching and admonishing one another in psalms and hymns and spiritual songs, singing with grace in your hearts to the Lord" (Col. 3:16).

God speed the day when "the Lord shall descend from heaven with a shout, with the voice of the archangel, and with the trump of God; and the dead in Christ shall rise first. Then we which are alive and remain shall be caught up together with them in the clouds, to meet the Lord in the air; and so shall we ever be with the Lord" (I Thess. 4:16-17).

Bibliography

1. CREATION (Southern Nebraska), G. Viehweg.
   Atlantic, 1909, Chr. Merkel.
   Canada, 1898, F. Bente; 1901, H. Wente; 1903, Wm. Moll.
   Central, 1876, E. W. Kaehler; 1885, C. Gross.
   Illinois, 1885, A. Brauer.
   Michigan, 1901, Th. Engelder.
   Nebraska, 1894, A. Graebner.
   South Dakota, 1910, 1912, R. Pieper.
   Lehre und Wehre, 22: 97, 240; 23: 273, 335, 362; 46: 8, 39, 135, 164, 217;
   F. Bente. 55: 289, 351, 454, 499, 546; J. Hoeness.
   Theological Quarterly, 9: 271, A. Graebner; 14: 78, 155, Th. Graebner.

2. CHRIST, PERSON OF (Atlantic), Louis J. Roehm.
   California, 1898, J. M. Buehler.
   Canada, 1886, F. Bente; 1891, A. Krafft.
   Central, 1883, C. M. Zorn; 1918, 1919, P. Schulz; 1921, W. Georgi.
   Eastern, 1903, A. E. Frey.
   Michigan, 1886, 1888, J. Fackler; 1904, H. Wente.
   Nebraska, 1901, R. Pieper.
   Oregon, 1915, 1916, W. J. Janssen.

3. HOLY GHOST (Southeastern), G. E. Hageman.
   California, 1900, J. W. Theiss.
   Michigan, 1916, J. Hoeness; 1918, H. Grueber.
   Southern, 1898, H. T. Kilian.

4. BIBLE, CLEARNESS AND SUFFICIENCY OF (Minnesota), Paul T. Schumm.
   Central, 1916, C. Zorn.
   Minnesota, 1882, F. Pieper.
   Texas, 1910, L. Dorn.
   Western, 1892, G. Stoeckhardt; 1897, F. Bente.
   Synodical Conference, 1868.
   Theological Quarterly, 12: 94, C. F. Drewes.

5. BIBLE, PROPER USE OF (Southern), H. B. Roepe.
   California, 1889, J. M. Buehler.
   Eastern, 1855, E. M. Buerger; 1858.
   Illinois, 1888, 1889, E. A. W. Krauss.
   Kansas, 1903, "Hearing the Word."
   Northern, 1867, 1874.
   Southern, 1919, Theo. Graebner.

6. BIBLE, IN THE HOME (Alberta and British Columbia), A. F. Miller.
   California, 1900, G. Denninger; 1915, E. Rudnick.
   Eastern, 1921, 1922, J. Sohn.
   Illinois, 1887, 1888, E. A. W. Krauss.
   Oregon, 1903, H. C. Ebeling.

7. LAW AND GOSPEL (Colorado), Walter Geihsler.
   Eastern, 1877.

583

Iowa, 1880, F. Pieper.
Kansas, 1892, F. Pieper.
Nebraska, 1915, 1916, W. Mahler.
Lehre und Wehre, 33: 154, 191, 241, 273, G. Stoeckhardt.
Pieper, F., *Christliche Dogmatik,* 1917.
Popular Symbolics, Engelder, Arndt, Graebner, Mayer, 1934.
Theological Quarterly, 10: 106, C. F. W. Walther (W. H. T. Dau).
Walther, *Gesetz und Evangelium,* 1897.

8. DECALOG, THE (Iowa West), R. Herrmann.
California, 1894, J. Buehler.
Canada, 1900, pp. 16-22.
Eastern, 1877, pp. 23-24.
Minnesota, 1883, 1885, 1886, F. Sievers; 1888, C. Ross; 1889, G. P. A.
Schaaf; 1891, G. Bernthal; 1892, 1894, A. Graebner; 1895, H. Schulz; 1898,
E. Albrecht; 1900, 1901, E. L. Arndt; 1903, H. Schulz.
Western, 1861, 1886, C. F. W. Walther.
Lehre und Wehre, 28: 416-420.
Theological Quarterly, 3: 257-270, A. Graebner.

9. FORGIVENESS OF SIN (Michigan), R. C. Rein.
Minnesota, 1915, J. C. Meyer.
Southern, 1904, E. Pardieck.

10. CONVERSION (Oklahoma), W. H. Wente.
Canada, 1882, J. Frosch.
Central, 1906, C. M. Zorn.
Eastern, 1882, H. Hanser.
Nebraska, 1883, R. H. Biedermann.
Northern, 12, C. F. W. Walther.
Oregon, 1901, H. Paul.
Southern, 1882, F. Pieper; 1894, A. Graebner.
Texas, 1919, W. Bewie.
Lehre und Wehre, 45: 313; 48: 289, F. Pieper.
Theological Quarterly, 5: 134, A. Graebner.

11. FAITH (English), E. L. Wilson.
California, 1891, 1897, J. M. Buehler.
Iowa, 1898, 1900, E. A. W. Krauss.
Minnesota, 1907, F. Pieper.
Southern, 1885, F. Pieper.
Western, 1901, C. C. Schmidt.
Synodical Conference, 1892, O. Hoyer.
Lehre und Wehre, 50: 385, 456; 51: 289, 337; 52: 241, 303, 345, F. Bente.
Theological Quarterly, 5: 6, 193, A. Graebner; 10: 1, 65; 11: 219, W. H. T
Dau.

12. SALVATION, CERTAINTY OF (Northern Illinois), A. E. Wagner.
Illinois, 1879, C. F. W. Walther.
Iowa, 1885, F. Pieper.
Oregon, 1904, 1906, 1907, 1908, W. Luessenhop.
Lehre und Wehre, 27: 37, F. Pieper; 1931, G. Stoeckhardt.

13. PRAYER (Eastern), C. A. Behnke.
California, 1912, J. W. Theiss.

Central, 1873.
Illinois, 1894, G. Mezger.
Minnesota, 1886, Fr. Sievers.
Southern, 1886, G. Birkmann; 1895, G. Wegener.
Western, 1882, C. F. W. Walther.

14. CHURCH, THE HOLY CHRISTIAN (Southern Illinois), L. W. Spitz.
Brazil, 1905, H. A. Klein.
California, 1904, J. W. Theiss.
Central, 1875, F. W. Stellhorn; 1892, E. W. Kaehler; 1912, 1913, 1915, Wm. Moll.
Central Illinois, 1921, E. Berthold.
Michigan, 1894, J. J. Bernthal; 1919, 1921, E. Berner.
Nebraska, 1909, W. H. T. Dau; 1919, W. Mahler.
Lehre und Wehre, 1928, 1929, G. Stoeckhardt.
Southern, 1888, P. Roesener; 1889, 1891, F. Pieper.

15. LUTHERAN CHURCH, THE TRUE VISIBLE CHURCH (South Wisconsin), P. F. Koehneke.
Atlantic, 1919, F. Pieper.
Canada, 1894, Chr. Hochstetter.
Central, 1867, 1868, 1871, C. F. W. Walther; 1892, E. W. Kaehler; 1894, 1895, G. Stoeckhardt.
Eastern, 1867, 1868, C. F. W. Walther; 1871, P. Brand.
General, 1866.
Illinois, 1897, F. Lindemann.
Southern, 1897, G. P. Schaaf.
Western, 1865, 1867, 1868, 1873, C. F. W. Walther.
Wisconsin, 1915, 1916, F. Eggers; 1918, J. F. Boerger.
Theological Quarterly, 14: 95.

16. PRIESTHOOD OF BELIEVERS, UNIVERSAL (Western), L. W. Spitz.
Eastern, 1862, 18-35.
Illinois, 1898, E. Pardieck.
Iowa, 1883, G. Stoeckhardt.
South Wisconsin, 1919, R. Schroth.

17. OFFICE OF THE KEYS (Central) Curtis C. Stephan.
Canada, 1889.
Central, 1858.
Eastern, 1858; 1880, F. Lindemann.
General, 1860.
Kansas, 1912, J. Herzer.
Nebraska, 1885, F. Pieper.
Northern, 1856.
Northwestern, 1875.
Western, 1858, 1919, 1921, J. A. Friedrich.
Lehre und Wehre, 20: 138; 24: 76; 26: 79.
Theological Quarterly, 9: 56, F. Kuegele.

18. CALL INTO THE HOLY MINISTRY (North Wisconsin), P. F. Koehneke.
Canada, 1879, 1880, W. Linsenmann.
Central, 1865, 1897, C. M. Zorn.
Eastern, 1889, J. P. Beyer; 1900, P. Brand.

Minnesota, 1906, 1907, H. Buegel.
Northern, 1858, M. Guenther; 1870.
Texas, 1915, R. Osthoff.
Western, 1858, 1865, 1891, F. Pieper.

19. The Lutheran Pastor (Iowa East), Mark J. Steege.
Michigan, 1907, P. Andres.
Lehre und Wehre, 5: 12, Preger; 5: 79, 181, Klinckenberg; 5: 108, Th. J. Brohm; 6: 97, W. Sihler; 20: 106, Kolbe; 24: 121, W. Sihler; 41: 22, 272, 328, 364.
Theological Quarterly, 6: 177, 206, W. H. T. Dau; 8: 47, 175, 229; 9: 47, 117, F. Kuegele.
Hartmann, L., *Pastorale Evangelicum,* Nuernberg, 1697.

20. Church, Authority in (Texas), H. Studtmann.
Canada, 1900, L. W. Dorn.
Central, 1859, F. A. Craemer, H. C. Schwan.
Northern, 1859, M. Guenther.
Western, 1883, 1885, C. F. W. Walther.
Wisconsin, 1892, 1894, C. Seuel.
Lehre und Wehre, 1936, F. Bente (Walther).

21. Missions (Ontario), Louis H. J. Henze.
Central, 1903, R. Biedermann.
Kansas, 1910, F. Streckfuss.
North Dakota, 1910, C. H. Lueker.
Oregon, 1899, J. Buehler.
Wisconsin, 1906, B. Sievers.

22. Stewardship, Christian (Northern Nebraska), W. C. Birkner.
Central, 1900, 1901, H. Katt; 1936, G. Chr. Barth.
English, 1915, M. Walker.
Texas, 1913, H. Studtmann.
Western, 1898, 1900, 1913, G. Mezger.
Kretzschmar, K., *The Stewardship Life.*
Lindemann, Paul, *Christian Stewardship and Its Modern Implications.*
Manual of Practical Church Work.

23. Dangers to Christians in These Last Days (Southern California), Carl S. Mundinger.
Eastern, 1900, P. Brand.
Michigan, 1897, 1898, C. F. Hagen.
Western, 1903, F. Brust.

24. Civil Government (South Dakota), P. F. Siegel.
Illinois, 1901, W. Heyne.
Michigan, 1909, R. Truelzsch.
Western, 1861, F. Lochner; 1885, C. F. W. Walther.
Wisconsin, 1891, 1892, F. Lochner.
Synodical Conference, 1871, A. F. W. Ernst.

25. Predestination (Kansas), Fred. Kramer.
Western, 1879, 1880, 1881, C. F. W. Walther.
Synodical Conference, 9, Walther's *Theses.*

26. Eschatology (North Dakota and Montana), W. F. Wolbrecht.

California, 1907, A. E. Michel; 1913, W. H. T. Dau.
Canada, 1915, P. Graupner.
Central, 1886, C. M. Zorn.
Eastern, 1870, 1901, A. Biewend.
English, 1918, F. Kroencke.
General, 1857, G. Schaller.
Illinois, 1886, H. Ramelow.
Nebraska, 1904, L. W. Dorn.
North Dakota, 1918, J. Cloeter.
Southern, 1918, A. O. Friedrich.
Southern Illinois, 1912, W. H. T. Dau.
Texas, 1907, W. H. T. Dau.
Western, 1856, 19; 1868; 1888, 1889, A. Graebner; 1903, F. Brust.
Lehre und Wehre, 23, A. Graebner.

27. ETERNAL LIFE (Central Illinois), E. C. Pautsch.
California, 1909, 1910, H. Haserodt.
Canada, 1883, P. Andres.
Eastern, 1876, F. W. Schmitt.
Illinois, 1885, A. Brauer.
Nebraska, 1918, G. Mezger.
Theological Quarterly, 6: 143, A. Graebner.

Topical Index

A

AUTHORITY IN THE CHURCH, 410ff.
  a divine grant, 411
  given to all believers, 412
  the right to forgive sins and
  preach the Gospel, 411f.
  to call and supervise pastors and
  teachers, 412f.; 434ff.
  based on Christ's atonement, 414
  an authority of the Word, 415f.;
  not over the Word, 416f.
  not in conflict with Christian liberty, 420f.
  no permission to lord it over congregation, 425; 427
  its administration, 431

B

BIBLE, its proper use: 67; must be regarded as God's Word, 68; to find
the Savior, 75; proper interpretation, 78ff.; for discovery and correction of false doctrine, 82; its
use in the home, 80, 85; reasons:
serving God, 92; God's command,
94; its blessing, 83, 97; Biblical
examples, 86
  in public worship, 81
  in supervised study, 82
  its mode, 101
  books to be used, 103
  improper use: failure to recognize
  its purpose, 76; used as a mere
  textbook or merely to enrich one's
  knowledge, 76; used to attack its
  contents, 76f.; used to spread false
  doctrine, 77
  neglect: of Bible study, 86; in
  Roman Catholic Church, 86ff.; in
  Lutheran homes, 90ff.; excuses,
  90ff.

C

CALL INTO HOLY MINISTRY, definition,
366
  differs from spiritual priesthood,
  333, 390

congregation has the right to call,
369, 375f., 434
auxiliary offices, 371ff.
Rome deprives the Church of this
right, 375
call into mission work, 368, 377
permanent call, 379
temporary call, 380f.
temporary assistance, 380f.
termination of, 382
reasons for, 383
attitude of congregation calling to
be avoided, 385f.; 435f.; of the
congregation whose pastor is
called, 387; 437f.
final decision rests with the pastor,
440

Capital and Labor, proper relation, 504

Certainty of Salvation, the touchstone
of Christian truth, 221ff.
  with regard to justifying faith,
  222f.
  to saving grace, 224f.
  to the means of grace, 227f.
  a treasure to be safeguarded,
  230ff.
  by faithful regard for promises of
  grace, 230
  careful distinction between Law
  and Gospel, 233
  diligent striving after godliness,
  236
  dynamic for Christian living, 238
  of Christian worship, 238
  of Christian service, 240
  of Christian separation, 242
  Christian steadfastness, 244

Christ's Person, His *deity*, 19
  in the Old Testament, 20f.
  in the New Testament, 21
  the eternal sonship, 21
  His *humanity*, 23
  sinless conception, 24
  virgin birth, 24
  personal union, 26
  the communication of attributes,
  30